PARIS

©Mark Soskolne/iStockphoto.com

Editorial Director   Cynthia Clayton Ochterbeck

THE GREEN GUIDE PARIS

Editor   Alison Coupe
Principal Writer   Paul Shawcross
Production Manager   Natasha G. George
Cartography   Alain Baldet, Michéle Cana, Peter Wrenn
Photo Editor   Yoshimi Kanazawa
Proofreader   Jonathan Gilbert
Layout & Design   Alison Rayner, John Higginbottom
Cover Design   Ute Weber

Contact Us: The Green Guide
                                   Michelin Maps and Guides
                                   One Parkway South
                                   Greenville, SC 29615
                                   USA
                                   www.michelintravel.com
                                   michelin.guides@us.michelin.com

                                   Michelin Maps and Guides
                                   Hannay House
                                   39 Clarendon Road
                                   Watford, Herts WD17 1JA
                                   UK
                                   ☎ (01923) 205 240
                                   www.ViaMichelin.com
                                   travelpubsales@uk.michelin.com

Special Sales: For information regarding bulk sales,
                                   customized editions and premium sales,
                                   please contact our Customer Service
                                   Departments:
                                   USA   1-800-432-6277
                                   UK   (01923) 205 240
                                   Canada 1-800-361-8236

Note to the Reader
While every effort is made to ensure that all information printed in this guide is correct and up-to-date, Michelin Apa Publications Ltd. accepts no liability for any direct, indirect or consequential losses howsoever caused so far as such can be excluded by law.

One Team…
A Commitment to Quality

There's just one reason our team is dedicated to producing quality travel publications—you, our reader.

Throughout our guides we offer **practical information**, **touring tips** and **suggestions** for finding the best places for a break.

Michelin driving tours help you hit the highlights and quickly absorb the best of the region. Our descriptive **walking tours** make you your own guide, armed with directions, maps and expert information.

We scout out the attractions, classify them with **star ratings**, and describe in detail what you will find when you visit them.

Michelin maps featured throughout the guide offer vibrant, detailed and easy-to-follow outlines of everything from close-up museum plans to international maps.

Places to stay and eat are always a big part of travel, so we research **hotels and restaurants** that we think convey the essence of the destination and arrange them by geographic area and price. We walk you through the best shopping districts and point you towards the host of entertainment and recreation possibilities available.

We **test**, **retest**, **check and recheck** to make sure that our guidebooks are truly just that: a personalized guide to help you make the most of your visit. And if you still want a speaking guide, we list local tour guides who will lead you on all the boat, bus, guided, historical, culinary, and other tours you shouldn't miss.

In short, we remove the guesswork involved with travel. After all, we want you to enjoy exploring with Michelin as much as we do.

The Michelin Green Guide Team

PLANNING YOUR TRIP

WELCOME TO THE CITY

S. Sauvignier/MICHELIN

CONTENTS

EXPLORING THE CITY

EXCURSIONS

YOUR STAY IN THE CITY

HOW TO USE THIS GUIDE

PLANNING YOUR TRIP

The blue-tabbed PLANNING YOUR TRIP section at the front of the guide gives you **ideas for your trip** and **practical information** to help you organize it. You'll find tours, a host of breaks in the great outdoors, a calendar of events, information on shopping, sightseeing, kids' activities and more.

WELCOME TO THE CITY

The orange-tabbed WELCOME TO THE CITY section explores **History** spanning the Gallo-Roman period through Paris today. The **Art and Culture** section covers architecture, art, film, literature, music, and language, while the **City Today** delves into the culture and geography of modern Paris.

DISCOVERING

The green-tabbed DISCOVERING section features Paris's Principal Sights, arranged alphabetically and by region, featuring

the most interesting local **Sights**, **Walking Tours**, nearby **Excursions**, and detailed **Driving Tours**.

🔲 Contact information, 🖙 admission charges, ⏱ hours of operation, and a host of other **visitor information** is given wherever possible. Admission prices shown are normally for a single adult.

STAR RATINGS★★★

Michelin has given star ratings for more than 100 years. If you're pressed for time, we recommend you visit the ★★★, or ★★ sights first:

★★★	Highly recommended
★★	Recommended
★	Interesting

Address Books - Where to Stay, Eat and more...

WHERE TO STAY

We've made a selection of hotels and arranged them within the cities by price category to fit all budgets (*see the Legend on the cover flap for an explanation of the price categories*). For the most part, we've selected accommodations based on their unique regional quality, their regional feel, as it were. So, unless the individual hotel embodies local ambience, it's rare that we include chain properties, which typically have their own imprint.
See the back of the guide for an index of where restaurants featured throughout the guide can be found.

WHERE TO EAT

We thought you'd like to know the popular eating spots in Paris. So, we selected restaurants that capture the regional experience—those that have a unique regional flavor (*see the Legend on the cover flap for an explanation of the price categories*). We're not rating the quality of the food per se; as we did with the hotels, we selected restaurants for many towns and villages, categorized by price to appeal to all wallets.
See the back of the guide for an index of where restaurants featured throughout the guide can be found.

MAPS

- 🅐 Regional **Walking Tours** map
- 🅐 **Metro** map.
- 🅐 Paris map with the **Principal Sights** highlighted.
- 🅐 Maps for Paris' **neighborhoods**.
- 🅐 **Local walking tour** maps.

All maps in this guide are oriented north, unless otherwise indicated by a directional arrow. The term "Local Map" refers to a map within the chapter or Tourism area. A complete list of the

maps found in the guide appears at the back of this book, as well as a comprehensive index and list of restaurants and accommodations.

🅐See the map Legend at the back of the guide for an explanation of map symbols.

ORIENT PANELS

Vital statistics are given for each principal sight in the DISCOVERING section:

- 🄸 **Information:** Tourist Office/Sight contact details.
- ▶ **Orient Yourself:** Geographic location of the sight with reference to surrounding boroughs, towns, and roads.
- 🅿 **Parking:** Where to park.
- 🅐 **Don't Miss:** Unmissable things to do.
- 🕓 **Organizing Your Time:** Tips on organizing your stay; what to see first, how long to spend, crowd avoidance, market days and more.
- Kids **Especially for Kids:** Sights of particular interest to children.
- 🅒 **Also See:** Nearby PRINCIPAL SIGHTS featured elsewhere in the guide.

SYMBOLS

Spa	**Spa Facilities**	📷	**Tours**
Kids	**Interesting for Children**	🅿	**On-site Parking**
🅒	**Also See**	▶	**Directions**
🄸	**Tourist Information**	✕	**On-site eating Facilities**
🕓	**Hours of Operation**	⅃	**Swimming Pool**
🕓	**Periods of Closure**	△	**Camping Facilities**
🔒	**Closed to the Public**	⚖	**Beaches**
🔗	**Entry Fees**	☕	**Breakfast Included**
⊄	**Credit Cards not Accepted**	🅐	**A Bit of Advice**
♿	**Wheelchair Accessible**	🅐	**Warning**

Contact - Addresses, phone numbers, opening hours and prices published in this guide are accurate at the time of press. We welcome corrections and suggestions that may assist us in preparing the next edition. Please send your comments to:

UK
Michelin Maps and Guides
Hannay House
39 Clarendon Road
Watford, Herts WD17 1JA
travelpubsales@uk.michelin.com
www.michelin.co.uk

USA
Michelin Maps and Guides
Editorial Department
P.O. Box 19001
Greenville, SC 29602-9001
michelin.guides@us.michelin.com
www.michelintravel.com

*View of Basilique du Sacré-Cœur
over the roofs of Paris*
Jacques Loic/Photononstop/Tips Images

WHEN AND WHERE TO GO

When to Go

SEASONS

Paris is a wonderful city to visit at any time of year. The city enjoys a typical temperate climate: cold winters and hot summers, while spring and autumn both have their unpredictable share of glorious sunny days and gloomy wet ones.

In **summer**, you can sit beneath the trees with a cold drink, idle away an evening on a café terrace, or go on an open boat tour of the Seine. The heat can be stifling at times: this is the time when Parisians converge towards the seasonal beach of Paris Plage, the open-air cafés along the Seine, and outdoor swimming pools.

Autumn weather is generally crisp and sunny with intermittent grey periods; Parisians are back from their own holidays and there is an air of energy and bustle.

Winter can be severe although there is rarely any snow and when the sun lights up the sky, Paris is most attractive. In December the streets and shop windows are bright with Christmas illuminations.

As for Paris in the **spring**, it tends to be cold and wet, but the buds on the trees and the blooming gardens mark a happy ending to the chilly winter.

WEATHER FORECAST

National forecast: ☎3250 (followed by "1" for the seven-day national forecast, or "2" for forecast by city).

Local forecast: ☎08 36 68 02 followed by the number of the *département* (☎08 36 68 02 75 for Paris). This information is also available at www.meteofrance.fr.

Where to Go

There is so much to see in Paris that it is a good idea to plan your visit very carefully. An excellent starting point is the absolute centre – the Place du Parvis in front of the magnificent Cathedral of Nôtre Dame. *See NOTRE DAME.* From here cross the Pont St Michel (bridge), walk along the Left Bank and visit the fascinating Latin Quarter (*see LATIN QUARTER*). Although there is much to keep you here, go to Montmartre (*see MONTMARTRE*) where the amazing Sacre-Couer Basilica is reason enough to come to Paris at all. Further iconic sights which should not be missed are the Eiffel Tower (*see EIFFEL TOWER*), the Arc de Triomphe (*see ARC DE TRIOMPHE*), La Madeleine (*see LA MADELEINE*) and the ornate Pont Alexander III.

No trip to the city would be complete however without strolling along the Champs Elysées (*see CHAMPS ELYSÉES*) and taking some refreshment at one of the many pavement cafés.

Walking Tours

These tours are mapped out the Walking Tours map.

Mean Temperatures					
	Jan	**Feb**	**Mar**	**Apr**	**May**	**Jun**
Min/max °F	21/59	23/59	30/70	34/75	41/81	46/88
Min/max °C	-6/15	-5/15	-1/21	1/24	5/27	8/31
	Jul	**Aug**	**Sep**	**Oct**	**Nov**	**Dec**
Min/max °F	52/91	50/88	45/84	34/75	28/63	25/55
Min/max °C	11/33	10/31	7/29	1/24	-2/17	-4/13

1 ROYAL PARIS Start from the Étoile (place Charles-de-Gaulle)

Begin by admiring the view from atop the Arc de Triomphe, down the Champs-Élysées and into the Tuileries Gardens. Beyond the palace, the Île de la Cité is the oldest part of Paris and the site of some of its most beautiful monuments: the Conciergerie, Notre-Dame, La Sainte-Chapelle.

2 LE MARAIS
Start from place de la Bastille

This walk takes you through the centuries from the Middle Ages to the golden age of the monarchy and into modern Paris. From beautiful Renaissance town houses to the stunning contemporary architecture of the Pompidou Centre, from the sublime symmetry of place des Vosges to the adventurous art of Pablo Picasso, this neighbourhood is always lively and entertaining.

3 CLASSICISM AND WORLD FAIRS Start from Les Invalides

Monumental inspiration is the order of the day as you stroll by the sumptuously restored Musée d'Orsay and the Palais Bourbon on the riverside, or cross the elaborate Pont Alexandre III to the Grand and Petit Palais. Continue to Trocadéro, where the view reveals curving flights of stone steps and a cascade of fountains and pools leading to the river. Directly in front of you rises Paris' most unmissable tower, a long swathe of green park stretching out behind it.

4 MONTMARTRE
Start from place Pigalle

Little streets twist upwards past the local vineyard, leading you from the noise and neon of naughty Pigalle to the village-like quiet of old Montmartre. Although there is always a crowd of tourists around the Sacré-Coeur and place du Tertre, the view from the steps in front of the church is memorable.

5 ST-GERMAIN-DES-PRÉS
Start from St-Germain-des-Prés

The church, the Café des Deux Magots and the Café de Flore make a cosy corner of town where the literary are wont to gather. The pedestrian Pont des Arts is a favourite bridge for painting and picnics; you can also watch the world go by from a chair in the beautiful Luxembourg Gardens. Once restored, you are ready to face the hubbub of the Montparnasse district, its shops, restaurants and cinemas.

6 LATIN QUARTER
Start from Luxembourg Gardens

This neighbourhood has long been the favoured haunt of students, and the atmosphere is appropriately animated. All kinds of shops and restaurants attract visitors, and there are plenty of historic places to discover too, such as the Cluny Museum, the Panthéon, the Jardin des Plantes and its natural history collections.

7 THE RIVER BANKS
Start from Sully-Morland

Wander from one bank of the Seine to the other, discover the islands at the heart of the city's history and complete your tour at the modern marina by the Bastille.

8 PASSY/BOIS DE BOULOGNE
Start from the Bois de Boulogne

For a change of pace from the busy city centre, head for the woods and soothe your spirit with a visit to the Marmottan-Monet Museum, where Claude Monet's inspired paintings of the flowers in his garden are like myriad rays of sunshine. On your way home stop to see Balzac's house and the Musée du Vin.

9 FASHIONABLE PARIS
Start from place Vendôme

If your money is burning a hole in your pocket, or if you like to dream in front of elegant shop window displays, don your finery and play millionaire on avenue Montaigne and Faubourg St-Honoré… before heading for the big department stores around the Opéra to pick up something special to take home.

⑩ PARIS AT PLAY Start from St-Germain-l'Auxerrois

Walk along the Grands Boulevards to see what Parisians are up to, the films they're watching, the singers they prefer. Some of the covered passages in this neighbourhood seem to be lost in the 19C, with their charming shops and tearooms. But you'll have no doubts about the date when you reach the Forum des Halles: young people gather here to scour the shops and enjoy the street theatre.

⑪ THE RIVER SEINE Start from the Eiffel Tower or the Pont Neuf

And why not make this tour aboard a boat? It is delightful to cruise below the distinctive bridges of Paris and to admire the many prestigious buildings on the waterfront. Rain or shine, day or night, this is a trip that everyone can enjoy.

Suggested Itineraries

If, alas, you only have a few days to spend in Paris, here are our suggestions for discovering the best of the city in a minimum of time.

THE MUSTS

Eiffel Tower – One of the most famous monuments in the world, affording superb views of the city.

Triumphal Way – Vista extending from the Arche de la Défense to the Arc de Triomphe then on to the Concorde along the Champs-Élysées, right through to the Louvre.

Louvre Museum – One of the largest and most prestigious European art collections in the world, from Antiquity to 1850.

Orsay Museum and Faubourg St-Germain – 19C and 20C national art collections (including Impressionist painting) housed in a former 19C railway station surrounded by elegant 18C mansions.

Île de la Cité and banks of the Seine – Notre-Dame and Sainte-Chapelle, two jewels of Gothic architecture in the historic centre of Paris.

J.-P. Clapham/MICHELIN

Jardin du Luxembourg

Montmartre Hill – Crowned by the Sacré-Coeur Basilica, it symbolises the 19C artistic world and bohemian life.

Latin Quarter – Lively student district.

Le Marais and its museums – One of the oldest districts of Paris, tastefully restored: Musée Picasso, Musée Carnavalet, Musée d'Art et d'Histoire du Judaïsme and others.

Invalides and Army Museum – Masterpiece of 17C architecture housing Napoléon's tomb.

Centre Georges Pompidou and Beaubourg district – The futuristic National Museum of Modern Art in the heart of one of the capital's oldest districts.

Rue du Faubourg-St-Honoré, Madeleine, Opéra Garnier – Luxury boutiques and imposing buildings.

La Villette, Cité des Sciences et de l'Industrie – Fascinating interactive museum complex.

Trocadéro and Alma district – Wide avenues lined with elegant mansions and a wealth of museums (Musée des Arts Asiatiques-Guimet, Musée d'Art Moderne de la Ville de Paris, Musée de la Marine, Musée Baccarat).

Make up your own itinerary from the list above or follow one of the itineraries suggested below.

IN FOUR DAYS

1. **Morning:** Notre-Dame, the banks of the Seine, Sainte-Chapelle.

   Afternoon: Louvre (*closed Tue*), Tuileries (*lunch in the museum or in the gardens*); a stroll around place Vendôme, La Madeleine, Concorde and to the Opéra Garnier.

2. **Morning:** Quartier Latin/ St-Germain-des-Prés, Musée d'Orsay (*closed Mon*).

Afternoon: La Villette (*closed Mon*), lunch at the Café de la Musique, Montmartre in the evening.

3. **Morning:** Versailles Château (*closed Mon*), park and gardens (*bring a picnic or eat at the restaurant by the Grand Canal*). Return to town in the **afternoon** via the RER, get off at Alma station, and enjoy a river tour aboard a bateau-mouche.

4. **Morning:** Place des Vosges and the Marais, Centre Pompidou (*closed Tue – lunch in the museum or in the neighbourhood*).

   Afternoon: Invalides, Eiffel Tower, Trocadéro, Champs-Élysées.

IN TWO DAYS

1. **Morning:** Notre-Dame, Les Quais, Sainte-Chapelle.

   Afternoon: Louvre (*closed Tue*) or the Orsay Museum (*closed Mon*), walk through the Tuileries Gardens and on to Place de la Concorde, Champs-Élysées, Eiffel Tower.

2. **Morning:** Le Marais, place des Vosges, Centre Pompidou (*closed Tue*).

   Afternoon: Boat tour starting from Pont Neuf, Latin Quarter, Luxembourg Gardens. Take the metro at Notre-Dame-des-Champs (line 12) to Montmartre to finish the evening.

FOR A VIRTUAL TOUR

If you would like to dream ahead, or to plan your own walk around Paris, there are some Websites to help you: **www.parisbalades.com** covers a lot of ground, and has especially good information about architecture from all periods with links to the museums of Paris and other useful sites;

www.metropoleparis.com is a quirky peek into the city life, with reviews of the latest events and entertainment by longtime Canadian expat Ric Erickson;

www.contexttravel.com offers a selection of private guided tours through different neighbourhoods and museums with well-qualified group leaders.

Themed Tours

HISTORIC PARIS

Ancient Paris – The oldest part of Paris, historically speaking, includes the **Île de la Cité** (place Dauphine, Palais de Justice, Sainte-Chapelle, Conciergerie) and the **Marais** (place des Vosges, rue des Francs-Bourgeois lined with fine mansions and a wealth of museums).

Monumental Paris – This itinerary includes two magnificent vistas: one encompasses the Trocadéro, the Eiffel Tower, the Champ de Mars and the École Militaire next to the Invalides, the other extends from Tuileries Gardens and place de la Concorde along the Champs-Élysées to the Arc de Triomphe; the River Seine provides an inspiring link between the two.

Right Bank Paris – The right bank is dominated by the extensive buildings of the Louvre. Just north across rue de Rivoli is the Palais-Royal and its peaceful gardens. To the west is avenue de l'Opéra heading towards the Opéra Garnier, rue de la Paix and place Vendôme, home to prestigious jewellery shops, rue St-Honoré and rue Royale, lined with leading fashion houses, and the Madeleine. From there, metro line 12 will take you directly to Lamarck-Caulaincourt station at the foot of Montmartre hill. As a reward for climbing to the top, you will enjoy a superb view from the Sacré Coeur Basilica.

Left Bank Paris – Strolling through the Odéon, St-Germain-des-Prés and St-Sulpice districts then across Luxembourg Gardens to the south, you will get the feel of the left-bank atmosphere. Further east stand the Panthéon and the Sorbonne overlooking the Latin Quarter. At the heart of this lively university district, the Musée de Cluny takes visitors on a delightful journey back to medieval times. Heading west along the embankment, you will walk past the *bouquinistes'* stalls displaying second-hand books and old prints. Walk as far as the Musée d'Orsay for fine views of the right-bank monuments including the Louvre.

RIVERSIDE PARIS

Along the Seine – The river banks are the favourite haunt of Parisians in summer and winter alike. They like to stroll along past lovers oblivious to the world around them, musicians who practise their instruments, unperturbed by onlookers, and anglers convinced that the Seine abounds with fish. Many strollers browse through the old books and prints displayed on the *bouquinistes'* stalls, hoping to find a rare copy or manuscript, although they know it is most unlikely nowadays.

Around Île Saint-Louis – Quai de Bourbon and quai d'Anjou, running along the northern edge of the island, offer a peaceful stroll past elegant 17C mansions full of old-world charm. Anyone venturing along rue Saint-Louis-en-l'Île finds it hard to resist Berthillon's delicious ice cream! From quai de Béthune and quai d'Orléans, the east end of Notre-Dame looks breathtakingly lovely and Pont Louis-Philippe affords a beautiful view of the Panthéon.

Along the Canal St-Martin – Dainty metallic footbridges spanning the canal at regular intervals, barges negotiating the locks and anglers lost in their thoughts form the peaceful setting of the Canal St-Martin linking the Bassin de la Villette and the Paris-Arsenal marina.

Pont Alexandre III

FASHION AND LUXURY

Paris is generally acknowledged as the capital of fashion. Couture houses and luxury boutiques are located in well-defined areas.

On the right bank: south of the Champs-Élysées, along avenue Montaigne, avenue George-V, avenue Marceau and rue François-I (fashion houses); along rue du Faubourg St-Honoré leading to place Vendôme and rue de la Paix (fashion, jewellery); place des Victoires, rue des Francs-Bourgeois and rue des Rosiers (fashion boutiques); department stores along boulevard Haussmann, around the Madeleine; rue de Rivoli (department stores and boutiques).

On the left bank: Le Bon Marché (department store) along rue de Sèvres and boutiques along rue du Bac, rue du Dragon, rue des Saints-Pères, rue du Vieux Colombier, rue du Cherche-Midi, rue du Four, rue de Rennes and rue Bonaparte leading to boulevard Saint-Germain.

UNUSUAL PARIS

Some districts have retained their old-world charm and atmosphere: Montmartre hill with its vineyard and windmill, Canal St-Martin and its metallic footbridges, the Butte aux Cailles hilltop near Gobelins, the St-Séverin Quarter near place St-Michel. Other districts, on the contrary, look so modern that they stand out against the traditional Parisian townscape: the Blibliothèque district along the Seine (13th *arrondissement*), place de Catalogne (14th *arrondissement*) and La Défense.
Some museums and monuments can also be termed unusual: Musée de la Curiosité et de la Magie (Marais district), Musée Cernuschi (Parc Monceau), Cathédrale St-Alexandre-Nevski (Monceau), Musée du Vin (Passy), Les Catacombes (Denfert-Rochereau), the Paris sewers (Alma).

GREEN PARIS

Parks and gardens

Paris has evolved into a city of trees and flowers, boasting almost 400 parks, public and private gardens, little squares, and, of course, its two vast stretches of woodland (Bois de Boulogne and Bois de Vincennes – 846ha/2 090 acres and 995ha/234.7 acres respectively) where lakes and waterfalls complement fountains and ponds.

Thanks to its varied landscape of woods, parks and gardens, Paris allows a surprising diversity of flora and fauna to thrive in the very heart of this urban metropolis. Some of the gardens provide a setting for a range of temporary or year-round exhibitions: flower shows, classical and avant-garde artwork. Here is a list, with metro stations, of some of the nicest parks in town:

Bagatelle (Ⓜ Sablons) for its irises and rose garden; the botanical gardens and greenhouses of the **Jardin des Plantes** (Ⓜ Jussieu); **Parc Mont-souris** (Ⓜ Cité Universitaire) with its English-style gardens; the most picturesque of the landscaped parks, the **Buttes-Chaumont** (Ⓜ Buttes-Chaumont); the calm, elegant **Palais-Royal Gardens** (Ⓜ Palais-Royal); the cherry trees in the gardens of the university residence (Ⓜ Cité Universitaire). The **Luxembourg Gardens** (Ⓜ Luxembourg, Port Royal, Rennes) where courting couples and students from the Latin Quarter come to relax in the sunshine; Parc **Monceau** whose wrought-iron gates open on to a collection of statues of Musset, Maupassant and Chopin (Ⓜ Monceau); the sophisticated Parc André-Citroën gardens complete with hi-tech glasshouses (Ⓜ Javel). As if this wealth of greenery were not enough, several new parks have sprung up on the cityscape in recent years: the magnificent **Parc de Bercy** (12th arr.); the **Jardin de l'Atlantique** (15th arr.) laid out on a huge concrete slab over the Gare Montparnasse; the **Promenade plantée** from Bastille to the Vincennes woods; meanwhile the **Tuileries Gardens** (1st arr.) have been restored to their former glory.

Vineyards – The area occupied by vineyards in the Île de France region as a whole remained considerable until the 18C and, even today, Paris boasts nine vineyards producing red and white wines. The most interesting are **Montmartre** (rue des Saules, 75018; Ⓜ Lamarck-Caulaincourt) with 1 762 vines; **Parc de Belleville** (rue des Couronnes, rue Piat, rue Julien-Lacroix or rue Jouye-Rouve 75020; Ⓜ Couronnes), with 140 vines tucked away inside the Parc de Belleville; **Parc Georges-Brassens** (rue des Morillons, rue des Périchaux or rue Brancion 75015; Ⓜ Porte-de-Vanves) with 700 vines; and **Parc de Bercy** (41 rue Paul-Belmondo, 75012; Ⓜ Cour Saint-Émilion) with 350 vines.

The **Musée du Vin** is situated in a quiet street of the 16th *arrondissement* (Ⓒ *see PASSY*).

PARIS BY NIGHT

The city is floodlit throughout the year from nightfall (between 5.15pm and 9.20pm according to the season)

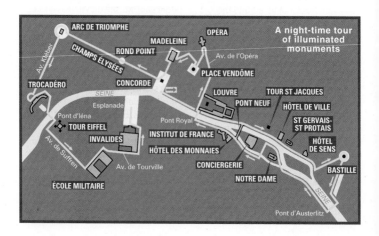

to midnight, (1am on Saturdays, the eve of bank holidays and during the summer months). The fountains are turned off during the cold weather from 1 January to 1 April.

At Christmas, the Champs-Élysées, avenue Montaigne, rue Royale or boulevard Haussmann take on a magical quality with trees and shop windows decked in seasonal lights. On foot or by car, the main sights line the **banks of the Seine: place de la Concorde** with its two fountains; the **Champs-Élysées** climbing up to the **Arc de Triomphe; Cour Napoléon** and **Pei's Pyramid**, which, together with the majestic walls of the Louvre, are reflected in the rippling waters of the flat fountains; place André-Malraux and the arcades fronting the **Comédie-Française;** the area around the abbey of **Saint-Germain-des-Prés** although not as white as the limestone of the **Sacré-Cœur**, takes on a paler hue beneath the lights; the **Invalides** with its striking gilded dome; **Notre-Dame**, which is even more impressive when the floodlights of the river boats pick out the exquisite detail of its sculpted façade, and the **Esplanade du Palais de Chaillot** from which there is a wonderful view of the Champ-de-Mars and the École Militaire, while fountains play below in the **Trocadéro** Gardens. On the other bank of the Seine, stop directly underneath the **Eiffel Tower** to gaze upwards at the latticed ironwork: monumental and yet delicate.

PARIS FOR PEDESTRIANS

See Walking Tours map.
Paris' neighbourhoods *(quartiers)* are perhaps best explored on foot. In addition to the tours mapped earlier in this book and in certain neighbourhoods, you may want to try the two signposted walks that cross Paris: one from east to west, from the Bois de Boulogne to the Bois de Vincennes; the other from north to south, from Porte de la Villette to Parc Montsouris. Each of these routes totals about 20km/12.4mi. Detailed information about walks in Paris is provided in

Paris A Pied, a guide published by the **Fédération française de randonnée pédestre**, 14 rue Riquet 75019, ☎01 44 89 93 93, www.ffrp.asso.fr.

Moveable Feast offers themed guided walks in English such as Paris is a Woman, Hemingway's Paris and The Belly of Paris. For more information: ☎06 15 19 31 64, www.lisapasold.com.

PARIS BY BUS

The bus is another excellent means of exploring Paris. There are several different tourist buses and coaches (with or without commentary) and, alternatively, Parisian **RATP** buses. Riding the regular transport system is a good way to see historic Paris in the company of the locals, for only a modest sum of money.

Balabus crosses Paris from east to west, from Gare de Lyon to La Défense. (*Balabus* or *Bb* is indicated on bus stops). The buses only run on Sundays and public holidays, from the last Sunday in April to the last Sunday in September, between 1.30pm and 8pm.

Montmartobus takes you on a tour around Montmartre between the town hall of the 18th *arrondissement* and place Pigalle. Standard bus fare.

Les cars rouges (Parisbus) – ☎01 53 95 39 53, www.carsrouges.com.
- **Stops:** Eiffel Tower, Champ-de-Mars, the Louvre, Notre-Dame, Musée d'Orsay, Opéra, Champs-Elysées-Etoile, Grand Palais, Trocadéro. Bus tour with running commentary.
- **Duration:** 2hr 15min for the complete circuit, although it is possible to get on or off at any stop on the route.
- **Prices:** 24€/adult, 12€/child. Tickets can be bought on the bus (or online) and are valid for two consecutive days.
- **Departure:** every 20min from the Eiffel Tower, starting at 9.45am.

Cityrama – 2 rue des Pyramides, 75001, ⓂPyramides. ☏01 44 55 60 00. www.cityrama.fr. Tour of the city aboard panoramic buses.

L'OpenTour – 13 rue Auber, 75009, ⓂOpéra or Havre-Caumartin. ☏01 42 66 56 56. www.cityrama.fr. Double-decker, open-top, hop-on-hop off bus tours. Designated stops are marked "L'OpenTour" (every 10 to 20min). Four routes (Grand Tour, Montmartre-Grands Boulevards, Bastille-Bercy, Montparnasse-St-Germain) with 50 stops, commentary on personal earphones. 1-day pass ☜29€ (☜15€ ages 4–11), 2-day pass ☜32€ (☜15€ ages 4–11).

RATP Buses

Like all forms of public transport, Parisian buses – depending to some extent on the line – can be slightly unpredictable in terms of punctuality and comfort: they can get extremely crowded, so it is best to avoid rush hours if possible. Nonetheless, the bus remains a great way to see Paris. All bus trips in Paris and the immediate suburbs require one ticket (no transfers). These are the same as the tickets used in the metro, and you can save money by buying a pass (ⓒsee *Reduced Rayes*) or a book of ten tickets ahead of time. On board the bus, you can buy tickets individually from the driver, at a higher price.

Line 21 (Gare St-Lazare – Porte-de-Gentilly) – Opéra, Palais-Royal, the Louvre, then along the Seine, before crossing the river towards the Latin Quarter and Luxembourg Gardens.

Line 72 (Parc-de-St-Cloud – Hôtel-de-Ville) – the right bank of the Seine: Alma-Marceau, the Grand Palais, place de la Concorde, Palais-Royal, the Louvre, Place du Châtelet and the Hôtel de Ville.

Line 73 (La Défense – Musée d'Orsay) – Place de l'Etoile, the Champs-Elysées, place de la Concorde and the Musée d'Orsay.

Line 96 (Gare Montparnasse – Porte-des-Lilas) – The St-Sulpice area, Odéon, the Latin Quarter, Île de la Cité, Châtelet-Hôtel de Ville, the Marais and finally Belleville.

THE PASSAGES OF PARIS

Here is one more suggestion for a thematic tour of the town: seek out the **Passages of Paris**. These covered alleyways, mostly built in the 19C, were once popular shopping and meeting places, where Parisians could stroll peacefully and at a safe distance from the many horses in the streets. As times changed, streets became cleaner, and pavements more prevalent, these lovely arcades slowly fell out of favour. But fortunately, many have been restored and new shops have opened in them, alongside the quaint older ones.

Galerie Vivienne – *4 rue des Petits-Champs;* ⓂBourse. Built in 1823, this is one of the most beautiful arcades in Paris. The Petit Siroux bookshop was established in 1826.

"Les cars rouges" - L'Open Tour bus

S. Sauvignier/MICHELIN

Galerie Véro-Dodat – *19 rue Jean-Jacques-Rousseau;* Ⓜ*Palais-Royal.* Opened in 1826, this arcade undoubtedly boasts the finest interior decoration. High-quality shops with windows encased in brass surrounds have been rebuilt in the original style, their windows full of old-fashioned charm like the old toy shop (Robert Capia).

Passage Brady – *18 rue du Faubourg-Saint-Denis;* Ⓜ*Strasbourg-Saint-Denis.* Scents and perfumes of India waft through this arcade where you will find restaurants and food shops.

Passage Choiseul – *23 rue St-Augustin;* Ⓜ*Quatre-Septembre.* This arcade, which is less lavish than Vivienne, opened in 1827. It contains several printers, clothes and costume jewellery shops running along the rear of the Bouffes-Parisiens Theatre.

Passage du Grand-Cerf – *145 rue Saint-Denis;* Ⓜ*Étienne-Marcel.* This arcade was built between 1825 and 1835. Paved in marble, it boasts an elegant and very high glass roof, wrought-iron walkways, and wood-framed shop windows.

Passage Jouffroy – *10 boulevard Montmartre;* Ⓜ*Grands Boulevards.* The Musée Grévin is in the middle of the passage, the first arcade in the city to

Galerie Véro-Dodat

be heated. There is an interesting second-hand bookshop which has some rare editions, a good, old-fashioned toy store, some clothing shops and gift boutiques.

Passage des Panoramas – *11 boulevard Montmartre;* Ⓜ*Grands Boulevards.* Built in 1800, its name comes from the paintings created there by Fulton (destroyed in 1831). There are several shops which deal in collectors' items, an engraver's shop and a tearoom.

Passage Verdeau – *6 rue de la Grange-Batelière;* Ⓜ*Richelieu-Drouot, Rue Montmartre.* This arcade extends beyond passage Jouffroy, not far from the Hôtel Drouot and stocks antiques and old books (La France Ancienne).

KNOW BEFORE YOU GO

Useful Websites

CYBERSPACE

www.ambafrance-us.org
The French Embassy's website provides basic information (geography, demographics, history), a news digest and business-related information. It offers special pages for children, and pages devoted to culture, language study and travel, and you can reach other selected French sites (regions, cities, ministries) with a hypertext link.

www.ambafrance-ca.org
The Cultural Service of the French Embassy in Ottawa has a bright and varied site with many links to other sites for French literature, news updates and E-texts in both French and English.

www.visiteurope.com
The European Travel Commission provides useful information on travelling to and around 34 European countries, and includes links to commercial

booking services (e.g. vehicle hire), rail schedules, weather reports and more.

www.secretsofparis.com

Secrets of Paris is a useful Resource Guide for visitors to Paris with categories including practical information on getting around, sightseeing, dining, accommodations, entertainment, shopping, and a calendar of events.

Tourist Offices

FRENCH TOURIST OFFICES ABROAD

For information, brochures, maps and assistance in planning a trip to France, travellers should apply to the official French tourist office in their own country:

Australia   New Zealand
Sydney – Level 13, 25 Bligh Street, Sydney, New South Wales 2000
☏ (02) 9 231 52 44
http://.aufranceguide.com

Canada   Montreal
1981 McGill College Avenue, Suite 490, Montreal PQ H3A 2W9
☏ (514) 288-2026
www.franceguide.com

Ireland   Dublinl
10 Suffolk St,Dublin 2
☏ 1560 235 235 (0.95€/min)
http://ie.franceguide.com

United Kingdom   London
178 Piccadilly, London WI
☏ (09068) 244 123 (60p/min)
www.franceguide.com

United States
East Coast   **New York**
444 Madison Avenue, 16th Floor, NY 10022-6903
☏ (212) 838-7830
http://.us.franceguide.com

Midwest   Chicago
875 North Michigan Avenue, Suite 3214; Chicago, IL 606011

☏ (514) 288-1904
http://ambafrance-us.org.

West Coast   **Los Angeles**
9454 Wilshire Boulevard, Suite 715, Beverly Hills, CA 90212-2967
☏ (310)-271-6665
www.franceguide.com

Request further information from:
France on Call (410) 286-8310

TOURIST OFFICES IN PARIS

Office du Tourisme et des Congrès de Paris, 25 rue des Pyramides, 75001 Paris, Ⓜ Pyramides. ☏ 08 92 68 30 00 (0.34€/min); www.parisinfo.com. 🕐 Daily Jun–Oct, 9am–7pm; Nov–May, 10am–7pm, Sun and public holidays 11am–7pm. 🕐 Closed 1 May; **Gare de Lyon**, 12th arr., 8am–6pm. 🕐 Closed Sun and public holidays; **Gare du Nord**, 10th arr. 🕐 Closed 25 Dec, 1 Jan, 1 May; **Anvers**, 72 blvd Rochechouart, 9th arr. 10am–6pm. 🕐 Closed 25 Dec 1 Jan, 1 May; **Montmartre**, 21, place du Tertre, 18th arr., 10am–7pm.

Espace du tourisme d'Île-de-France, place de la Pyramide-Inversée, Carrousel du Louvre, 99 rue de Rivoli, 75001 Paris, Ⓜ Palais-Royal/ Musée du Louvre. 🕐 Daily 10am–6pm. ☏ 0 892 68 3000; www.pidf.com.

International Visitors

EMBASSIES AND CONSULATES

Australia   **Embassy**
4, rue Jean-Rey, 75015 Paris
☏ 01 40 59 33 00; Fax 01 40 59 33 10

Canada   **Embassy**
35, avenue Montaigne, 75008 Paris
☏ 01 44 43 29 00; Fax 01 44 43 29 99

Ireland   **Consulate**
4, rue Rude, 75016 Paris
☏ 01 44 17 67 00; Fax 01 44 17 67 60

New Zealand   **Embassy**
7ter, rue Léonard-de-Vinci, 75016 Paris
☏ 01 45 00 24 11; Fax 01 45 01 26 39.

UK   **Embassy**
35, rue du Faubourg-St-Honoré, 75008 Paris
☎01 44 51 31 00; Fax 01 44 51 31 27

UK   **Consulate**
16, rue d'Anjou, 75008 Paris
☎01 44 51 31 02 (visas)

USA   **Embassy**
2, avenue Gabriel, 75008 Paris
☎01 43 12 22 22; Fax 01 42 66 97 83

USA   **Consulate**
2 , rue St-Florentin, 75001 Paris
☎01 43 12 22 22.

Duty-Free Allowances	
Spirits (whisky, gin, vodka, etc.)	10l/2.6gal
Fortified wines (vermouth, port, etc.)	20l/5.3gal
Wine (not more than 60 sparkling)	90l/23.7gal
Beer	110l/29gal
Cigarettes	3 200
Cigarillos	400
Cigars	200
Smoking tobacco	3kg/6.6lb

Entry Requirements

Passport – Nationals of countries within the European Union entering France need only a national identity card. Nationals of other countries must be in possession of a valid national **passport**. In case of loss or theft report to the embassy or consulate and the local police.

Visa – An **entry visa** is required for Canadian and US citizens who intend to stay for more than three months and for Australian and New Zealand citizens. Apply to the French Consulate.

Customs Regulations

Apply to the Customs Office (UK) for a Customs guide for travellers; available from HMRC, http://customs.hmrc.gov. uk, The US Customs Service offers a publication *Know Before You Go* for US citizens: for the office nearest you, consult the phone book, Federal Government, US Treasury (www.customs. ustreas.gov).
Americans can bring home, tax-free, up to US$800 worth of goods; Canadians up to CND$300; Australians up to AUS$400 and New Zealanders up to NZ$700. Persons living in a Member State of the European Union are not restricted in regard to purchasing

goods for private use, but the recommended allowances for alcoholic beverages and tobacco are set out in the table above.

Health

It is advisable to take out comprehensive insurance cover as the recipient of medical treatment in French hospitals or clinics must pay the bill. Nationals of non-EU countries should check with their insurance companies about policy limitations. Reimbursement can then be negotiated with the insurance company according to the policy held. All prescription drugs should be clearly labelled; it is recommended that you carry a copy of the prescription.

US citizens concerned about travel and health can contact the International Association for Medical Assistance to Travelers: ☎716 754-4883, www.iamat.org.

British and Irish citizens should apply to the Department of Health *(www. dh.gov.uk)* for **European Health Insurance card**, or EHIC , which entitles the holder to free or reduced-cost urgent treatment for accident or sudden illness in EU countries, as well as a refund of part of the cost of treatment on application in person or by post to the local Social Security Offices *(Caisse Primaire d'Assurance Maladie)*.

Accessibility

The sights described in this guide which are easily accessible to people of reduced mobility are indicated in the *Discovering Paris* section by the symbol ♿.
For information on transport, holiday-making and sports associations for the disabled, see the "Tourisme & Handicap" section of the website of the **Office du tourisme et des congrès de Paris** (www.parisinfo.com).

Web-surfers can find information for slow walkers, mature travellers and others with special needs at www.access-able.com. **For information** on museum access for the disabled contact the *Direction des affaires culturelles – Bureau des Musées,* 70 rue des Archives, 75003, ☎01 42 76 83 66.
The **Michelin Guide France** and **Michelin Camping and Caravanning in France** indicate hotels and campsites with facilities suitable for physically handicapped people.

GETTING THERE AND GETTING AROUND

By Plane

Paris is served by two major international airports: **Roissy-Charles de Gaulle** 23km/14.3mi to the north of Paris on the A1, and **Orly** 11km/6.8mi to the south along the A 6. Domestic flights are handled by Orly. Public services giving access to and from the city include Air France coaches, public transport (RATP) buses, private minibuses, RER trains and taxis.
⊚Check whether the train or bus is running before buying your ticket from an automatic ticket machine – these are not refundable!

FROM ROISSY-CHARLES DE GAULLE

Les Cars Air France run every 30min from 6am–11.30pm to Porte Maillot *(blvd Gouvion St-Cyr)* and Place Charles de Gaulle-Étoile *(corner with avenue Carnot)*. Approximate journey time: 35min. Cost ⊚14€. Alternatively, buses run to Gare de Lyon *(20 bis blvd Diderot)* and Montparnasse *(rue du Commandant Mouchotte, in front of the Meridien Hotel)* every half hour, from 7am to 9pm. Approximate journey time: 50min. Cost ⊚16€. www.cars-airfrance.com. Purchase tickets at airport desks.

Bus RATP run the ROISSYBUS to rue Scribe *(corner with rue Auber, Metro Opéra)* between Roissy-CDG and Paris from 6am to 11pm, and from Paris to Roissy-CDG from 5.45am to 11pm. Departures every 15-20min. Approximate journey time: 45–60min. ☎08 36 68 77 14. Cost ⊚8.60€.

Underground trains RER line B run every 15min from Roissy-CDG to Paris from 5am to 11.30pm, and from Paris to Roissy-CDG from 5am to midnight. Average journey time to Gare du Nord: 25min. Cost ⊚8.40€.

Taxis are subject to road traffic conditions; it is best to allow 1hr journey time into Paris. Min cost around ⊚50€, plus 1€ extra per item of baggage over 5kg/11lb..

Shuttle services offer a good alternative to expensive cabs and to lugging baggage on the RER: Paris Airports Service (⊚31€ for 2 people from Roissy-CGD; ⊚30€ from Orly; reduced rates depend on the number of people in your party) ☎01 55 98 10 80; www.parisairportservice.com.

Useful numbers – Airport Information ☎01 48 62 22 80 or 08 92 68 15 15. www.adp.fr or www.taxi-paris.net.

FROM ORLY

Les Cars Air France run every 30 min from 6.15am to 11.15pm to Les Invalides and Gare Montparnasse (rue du Commandant Mouchotte), and from 5.45am to 11.15pm from Les Invalides to Orly. Approximate journey time to Montparnasse: 30min. Cost ⊜10€. www.cars-airfrance.com.

Bus RATP run the ORLYBUS to place Denfert-Rochereau *(outside RER station)* between Orly Sud and Orly Ouest terminals and Paris from 6am to 11pm and from Paris to Orly Sud and Orly Ouest from 6am to 11pm. Departures every 12min. Average journey time: 25min. Cost ⊜6.10€. ☎08 36 68 77 14, www.ratp.fr.

Underground trains RER line C run from Pont-de-Rungis. Connection with the air-terminals is by shuttle. Trains run every 20min to Paris from 5.50am to 11.30pm, and from Paris between 5.40am and 10.50pm. Average journey time to Gare d'Austerlitz: 35min. Cost ⊜6€.

Underground trains RER line B run as far as Antony and connect with ORLYVAL, automated trains to the air-terminals. Scheduled departures in both directions from Orly Sud or Antony, every 7min, between 6am and 11pm (7am and 11pm Sunday and public holidays). Average journey time between Châtelet and Orly: 35min (40min to Etoile). Cost ⊜9.30€. ☎08 36 68 77 14.

Taxis are subject to traffic conditions. Allow at least a 45min journey time into Paris. Min cost around ⊜35€, plus 1€ extra per item of baggage over 5kg/11lb.

Useful numbers – Airport information (24hr) ☎01 49 75 15 15; on-line: www.adp.fr.

AIRLINE OFFICES

Air France: 49 avenue Opéra, 75002, ☎08 20 820 820. www.airfrance.fr.

Air Canada – 10 rue de la Paix, 75002, ☎08 25 88 08 81/01 44 50 20 55. www.aircanada.com.

Aer Lingus – ☎01 70 20 00 72/08 21 23 02 67. www.flyaerlingus.com.

American Airlines – ☎08 10 87 28 72. www.aa.com.

British Midland Airways – ☎08 90 71 00 81. www.flybmi.com.

By Ship

There are numerous **cross-Channel services** (passenger and car ferries, hovercraft) from the United Kingdom and Ireland and also the rail Shuttle through the Channel Tunnel (**Eurostar**, ☎08705 18 61 86 from the UK; ☎08 10 63 03 04 from France; www.eurotunnel.co.uk or www.eurostar.com). To choose the most suitable route between your port of arrival and your destination use the Michelin Tourist and Motoring Atlas France, Michelin map 911 (which gives travel times and mileages) or Michelin maps from the 1:200 000 series (with the yellow cover). For details, apply to travel agencies or to:

- **P & O Stena Line Ferries**
  Channel House, Channel View Road, Dover CT17 9JT, ☎08705 980 333; www.poferries.com.

- **Norfolkline**
  Norfolk House
  Eastern Docks Dover CT16 1JA Kent, ☎0870 870 10 20, www.norfolkline.com

- **Irish Ferries**
  Box 19, Alexandra Road, Ferryport, Dublin 1. ☎0818 300 400 in Ireland, 08705 17 17 17 in the UK, www.irishferries.com.

Public Transport

Paris is justly renowned for its excellent and inexpensive public transport system. The **RATP** – Independent Paris Transport Authority – was created in 1949 to manage the urban metro, bus, tram and RER (Regional Express Rail) networks. Today there are 14 Metro lines, 66 stops on the regional express lines, and around 7 000 bus stops in Paris and the suburbs.

BEST FARES

A book of ten t+ tickets **(un carnet)** costs 11.40€, child 5.70€: use one for each metro or bus ride within Paris and keep it with you (inspectors may ask to see it). Children under age 4 ride for free on a lap; under-10s pay half fare *(demi-tarif)*. Passes may be purchased for different travel zones (zones 1–2, Paris; 3, near suburbs including St-Denis, La Défense, Le Bourget; 5, the airports, Disneyland, Versailles; 8, Provins). **Paris Visite** is a 1, 2, 3 or 5 day pass valid on all modes of transport. Advantages: access to first class on SNCF trains in the valid zones; half-fare for children under age 12; no photo required; discounts for tourist attractions. Cost varies from 8.50€ (adult, 1 day, 3 zones) to 47€ (adult, 5 days, 6 zones). The monthly and weekly **Carte Orange** passes are valid from the first of the month or from Monday to Sunday, at

an advantageous rate (e.g. two zones for one week, between 15.10€ and 16.80€); photograph required. **Mobilis** is a one-day pass valid for unlimited travel in the zones selected (but does not include services to airports), costing from 5.80€ (1–2 zones) to 16.40€ (6 zones).

Ticket windows in stations open at 6.30am (first train around 5.30am depending on the station) but tickets can also be purchased from machines in stations and in *tabacs* and other shops with the RATP sign outside. The last metro leaves the end of the line around 12.30am. Insert your metro ticket in the turnstile and recover it, keepng it with you until you exit the metro.

There is a map of the Metro on the inside front cover of this book. For information 24/7, 08 92 68 77 14. You can also plan ahead with the RATP itinerary service on the internet: www.ratp.fr.

RER

The Regional Express Network includes five lines: **line A** runs from St-Germain-en-Laye, Poissy and Cergy to Boissy-St-Léger and Marne-la-Vallée; **line B** from Robinson and St-Rémy-lès-Chevreuse to Roissy-Charles-de-Gaulle, and Mitry-Claye; **line C** links Versailles (left bank), St-Quentin-en-Yvelines, Argenteuil and Pontoise to Dourdan, Massy-Palaiseau and St-Martin d'Etampes; **line D** runs from Orry-la-Ville and Coye to Crobeille, Melun and Malesherbes; **line E** from St-Lazare to Villiers-sur-Marne and Chelles-Gournay.

Regular services run between approximately 5am and 1.15am. Metro tickets may be used for RER trains within the Metro system – outside these, special fares and tickets apply (including to airports, Versailles and Disneyland-Paris).

> **Construction** – Parisians first took the metro on 19 July 1900. The first Paris line was on the Right Bank, from Porte de Vincennes to Porte Maillot.
> The engineer responsible was Fulgence Bienvenüe and Guimard designed the emblematic Art Nouveau metro entrance, in the so-called noodle style.
>
> **Facts and figures** – There are over 200km/124mi of track for the 14 lines, not including the RER, and 380 stations of which 90 are interchanges. No point in the capital is more than 500m/550yd from a metro station.

BUSES

References in the main text will help you to find the stop to look for on the bus itineraries. Bus-routes are displayed in bus shelters as well as inside the buses themselves. Buses normally operate between 6.30am and 8.30pm (Mon–Sat); designated lines operate until around 12.30am and on Sundays and holidays *(service assuré les dimanches et fêtes)*; 35 night buses *(Noctilien)* operate between 1am and 5.30am. On the bus, punch a single ticket in the machine by the door, but **do not punch a pass** – simply show it to the driver.

Taxis

There are some 14 900 taxis in Paris, cruising the streets day and night and parked in the 745 ranks alongside the kerb close to road junctions and other frequented points beneath the signs labelled *Taxis*. Taxis may also be hailed in the street when the white taxi sign is fully lit. The rate varies according to the zone and time of day (higher rates between 8pm and 6.30am). The white, orange or blue lights correspond to the three different rates A, B and C and these appear on the meter inside the cab. A supplementary charge is made for taxi pick-up at train stations, air terminals and for heavy baggage or unwieldy parcels as well as for a fourth person and domestic animals.

RADIO-TAXIS

Taxis Bleus ☎08 91 70 10 10; **Artaxi** ☎01 42 06 67 10; **Taxi G7** ☎01 47 39 47 39 (credit cards); **Alpha Taxis**: for immediate use ☎01 45 85 85 85 (24 hrs)

By Train

Eurostar runs via the Channel Tunnel between **London** (St Pancras) and **Paris** (Gare du Nord) in 3hr (bookings and information ☎08705 186 186; ☎+44 1233 617 575 outside the UK); www.eurostar.com.

Eurail Global Pass, Eurail Select Pass, Eurail Global Pass Youth, Saver and Flexi travel passes for various lengths of time may be purchased in North America. Contact your travel agent or **Rail Europe**, ☎1-888-382-7245 in the US, 1-800-361-RAIL in Canada. Information on schedules can be obtained on websites for these agencies and the **SNCF**, respectively: www.raileurope.com, www.sncf.fr. Tickets bought in France must be validated *(composter)* by using the orange automatic date-stamping machines at the platform entrance (failure to do so may result in a fine).

The French railway company SNCF operates a telephone information, reservation and prepayment service in English from 7am to 10pm (French time). In France call ☎08 36 35 35 39 (when calling from outside France, start with 00 and then drop the initial 0). Accessibility facilities for rail travel in Europe ☎212 888 7800.

Paris has six mainline stations: **Gare du Nord** (for northern France, Belgium, Denmark, Germany, Holland, Scandinavia and the UK); **Gare de l'Est** (for eastern France, Austria, Germany, Luxembourg); **Gare de Lyon** (for eastern and southern France, the Alps, Greece, Italy, Switzerland); **Gare d'Austerlitz** (for southwest France, Portugal, Spain); **Gare Montparnasse** (for western France and TGV to southwest France); **Gare St-Lazare** (for regional lines to northwest France).

By Coach/Bus

Eurolines (National Express)
For travel to all over Europe by coach (bus). ☎08705 808080 (in the UK), ☎08 92 89 90 91 (in France); www.nationalexpress.com/eurolines. Helplines; for disabled visitors ☎01 21 423 8479 and for deaf or hard-of-hearing visitors ☎0121 455 0086. For information on bus travel in Paris, see 'Public Transport'.

Eurolines(Paris)
Avenue Général du General de Gaulle 93177 Bagnolet. ☎08 92 89 90 91. www.eurolines.fr.

www.eurolines.com has information about travelling by coach in Europe.

By Car

Documents – Travellers from other European Union countries and North America can drive in France with a valid national or home-state **driving licence**. An **international driving licence** is useful because the information on it appears in nine languages (keep in mind that traffic officers are empowered to fine motorists). A permit is available (US$10) from the National Automobile Club, ☎800-622-2136, www.nationalautoclub.com; or contact your local branch of the American Automobile Association. It is necessary to have the registration papers (logbook) of the vehicle and a nationality plate of the approved size.

Insurance – Certain motoring organisations (AAA, AA™, RAC™) offer accident insurance and breakdown service schemes for members. Highway Code – The minimum driving age is 18. Traffic drives on the right. All passengers must wear **seat belts**. Children under the age of ten must travel in the back seat of the vehicle. Full or dipped headlights must be switched on in poor visibility and at night; use side-lights only when the vehicle is stationary. In the case of a **breakdown**, a red warning triangle or hazard warning lights are obligatory. In the absence of stop signs at intersections, cars must **yield to the right**. Traffic on main roads outside built-up areas (priority indicated by a yellow diamond sign) and on roundabouts has right of way. The regulations on **drinking and driving** (limited to 0.5g/l) and **speeding** are strictly enforced – usually by an on-the-spot fine and/or confiscation of the vehicle.

Speed limits – Although liable to modification, these are as follows:
- toll motorways *(péage)* 130kph/80mph (110kph/68mph when raining);

> ### 😊 A Bit of Advice 😊
>
> Do not leave anything of value in unattended vehicles at any time.

- dual carriageways and motorways without tolls 110kph/68mph (100kph/62mph when raining);
- other roads 90kph/56mph (80kph/50mph when raining) and in towns 50kph/31mph;
- outside lane on motorways during daylight, on level ground and with good visibility – minimum speed limit of 80kph/50mph.

Petrol (gas) – French service stations dispense: *sans plomb* 98 (super unleaded 98), *sans plomb* 95 (super unleaded 95), *diesel/gazole* (diesel) and some have GPL (LPG). Prices are listed on signboards on the motorways; it is usually cheaper to fill up after leaving the motorway.

Tolls – In France, most motorway sections are subject to a toll *(péage)*. You can pay in cash or with a credit card (Visa, MasterCard).

Everything you have heard about driving in Paris is true. Avoid it! Parking is restricted and while parking garages are well indicated on Michelin maps and on street signs, they are expensive. The metro and bus are usually faster than driving at most times of the day. Taxis are abundant. Parking on the street, when authorised, is subject to a fee; tickets should be obtained from the ticket machines (*horodateurs* – you'll need to pay with a pre-paid *carte de stationnement*– which you can purchase at *tabacs*) and displayed inside the windscreen on the driver's side; failure to display may result in a fine, or towing and impoundment. Visitors who arrive in August will find that it is easier to drive around the city then, but the riverside motorways are closed to traffic. Beware *axes rouges,* or red routes, along main thoroughfares where parking is prohibited in order to maintain free flow of traffic (between Gare de Lyon and Gare de l'Est, via Bastille, République, quai des Célestins and quai de la Rapée). ⊘NEVER – even in congested traffic – use the lanes reserved for buses and taxis. Severe fines are enforced.

Paris is served by a six-lane outer ring-road, the **boulevard périphérique** (35km/22mi). Traffic from the motorways into Paris all merges onto the *périphérique* before filtering into the city centre via the *Portes*. As traffic can move at considerable speed during off-peak periods, it is advisable to have pin-pointed which exit you require before getting onto the ring-road system. Once on the *périphérique*, cross onto the central lanes allowing traffic to join from the right-hand side, and cross back onto the far right lane before leaving the ring road. This may be particularly hazardous for left-hand drive vehicles. Once inside Paris, a west-to-east motorway (**Georges Pompidou motorway**) runs along the Right Bank, facilitating the flow of cars through the capital.

Rental Cars

Car rental agencies can be found at airports, air terminals and railway stations. European cars usually have manual transmission but automatic cars are available on request (⊘advance reservation recommended). It is relatively expensive to hire a car in France; US citizens in particular will notice the difference and should consider booking a car from home before leaving or taking advantage of fly-drive schemes. If you rent a car in the UK, make sure to inform the car hire company that you intend to take the car to France, for insurance purposes. Most car rental firms will not hire out to those under 21 and make an extra charge for any drivers aged between 21 and 25.

Rental Cars – Central Reservation in France	
Avis:	☎ 08 20 05 05 05
Europcar:	☎ 08 25 35 23 52
Budget France:	☎ 01 44 77 88 01
Hertz France:	☎ 01 39 38 38 38
SIXT-Eurorent:	☎ 08 20 00 74 98
National-CITER:	☎ 01 42 79 06 11
Baron's Limousine and Driver:	☎ 01 45 30 21 21

Around Town

RIVE GAUCHE (Left Bank)

This is the southern bank of the Seine, which flows roughly westwards through Paris. St Germain des Prés and the St Michel area are the heart of *rive gauche* chic. However, in other circumstances, gauche is not fashionable. For example, if you call a person *gauche*, you mean the same thing as in English: *Que je suis gauche!* (How I am lacking in social experience and grace!).

RIVE DROITE (Right Bank)

The *rive droite* style is more elegant and sophisticated than the style of the bohemian south bank: think Champs Elysées, avenue Montaigne, rue de la Paix, place Vendôme.

LE QUARTIER LATIN (The Latin Quarter)

This Left Bank neighbourhood is so named because it has been the centre of Paris university life for over 700 years. Although the students no longer speak the eponymous Latin of scholars, you can hear just about every other language on earth spoken here in the restaurants, shops and cafés in the labyrinth of old streets around St Michel.

WHAT TO SEE AND DO

Outdoor Fun

CYCLING

Paris has some 230km/138mi of cycle lanes and many more are under construction.

A north-south axis links the cycle path at Canal de l'Ourcq and place de la Bataille-de-Stalingrad to Porte de Vanves. Another, running from east to west joins the Bois de Vincennes and the Bois de Boulogne, both of which have a network of cycle paths complete with signposts. There are also combination bike-bus lanes. Designated areas where cyclists can leave their bikes are dotted around the capital; the French railway SNCF facilitates the free entry of bikes on the RER lines B, C and D, although only at particular times and in particular stations.

On Sundays, certain roads are closed to traffic for the benefit of pedestrians and cyclists:

- the roads which run parallel to the Seine from 9am to 5pm (quai des Tuileries, quai Henri-IV, quai Anatole-France and quai Branly);
- Canal St-Martin from 9am to 5pm (quai de Jemmapes, quai de Valmy);
- in the Mouffetard area from 10am to 6pm (place Marcelin-Berthelot, rue de Cluny, rue de l'Ecole Polytechnique, rue de Lanneau, rue Mouffetard, rue Descartes), the only drawback is that it is uphill!
- On the Butte de Montmartre; another steep hill reserved for strong legs!

You can also look in English publications such as the *Paris Free Voice* and *FUSAC*, available in many bookshops and restaurants, for information on guided bike tours of the city.

Remember: Parisian motorists do not always take much notice of cyclists even though, theoretically, both groups share the same status on the roads. It is therefore advisable to be extremely careful, especially of parked cars as unaware drivers may open car doors without prior warning. Remember that all road-users, including cyclists, must adhere to the Highway Code of France (http://france.oe-car-hire.co.uk/information/driving-in-france.htm). Always keep an eye on your bicycle – even if it is equipped with a padlock, detachable parts such as the saddle and the front wheel are easily stolen and re-sold.

©AlexQ/Fotolia.com

Vélib' bike station

Obligatory:

- Bell and lights.
- Use of designated parking areas.
- Wearing of a cycle helmet (soon to be a requisite).
- Use of cycle paths where they exist.

Bicycle hire

Below are some useful addresses; for further information, you can consult the *Paris à vélo* map, published by the **Mairie de Paris** and available from town halls and the **Office de Tourisme de Paris**. Always carry your passport with you, as it will be essential for hiring anything in Paris. A cycle helmet, basket and bike lock – and sometimes baby seats – are included in the price.

Paris à vélo, c'est sympa! – 22 rue Alphonse-Baudin, 75011, M Richard-Lenoir. ☎01 48 87 60 01. www.parisvelosympa.com/GB/index.html. 15€/day, 12€/half day, 25€/2 days, 25€/weekend (250€ or passport as security deposit required); tandems are double the prices respectively. This company offers guided tours (French, English, Dutch, German, Italian and Spanish) from April to October (35€). Baby seats can be provided and you can hire a bike or a tandem. No reservations necessary.

Roue libre (RATP) – 1 passage Mondétour, 75001 ☎08 10 44 15 34. Daily. www.rouelibre.fr. Guided tours available. 9€/full weekday, 14€/full day weekend, 25€ full weekend. Reservation and deposit (200€) required. Baby seats available. Bike hire is also available at Bastille (37 blvd Bourdon) and on Sundays April–October in the Bois de Boulogne hippodromes, Bois de Vincennes, and on the quai de l'Archevêché in front of Notre-Dame (same prices).

Vélib' – There is a popular self-hire bike service in Paris, available 24hr a day, seven days a week. Simply go to the self-service machines and follow the instructions to choose from a range of bikes. A Vélib' Card (valid for one year) is available, too. Visit www.velib.paris.fr.

ROLLER SKATING AND ROLLERBLADING

Every Friday evening a rollerblading rally takes place in Paris, following a different itinerary on each occasion. The event is overseen by policemen, themselves on rollerblades, who prevent the traffic accessing the roads used by the rollerbladers. Several thousand people now gather every week in front of the Gare Montparnasse, the starting point. There is a relaxed, fun atmosphere, and it's a good way to meet people. Not suitable for beginners as a good breaking technique is essential. Contact **Pari Roller**, place Raoul Dautry, 75005, ☎01 43 36 89 81, www.pari-roller.com.

Roller Skating tours

Rollers et Coquillages
75001 M Bastille. ☎01 44 54 94 42, www.rollers-coquillages.org. Meeting on Sundays at 2.30pm at Place de la Bastille. Duration: 3hr. For beginners and experienced skaters; the itinerary is different on each occasion, check the website.

Rollers Squad Institut (RSI)
7 rue Jean-Giono, 75013, M Quai-de-la-Gare. ☎01 56 61 99 61. www.rsi.asso.fr. Mon–Thu 10am–1pm, 2–6pm. This association organises various roller skating tours such as a beginners' child-friendly skate Sundays at 2.45pm and a more experienced skaters' tour on Saturdays at 2.45pm. Both meet at the Esplanade des Invalides.

BOATING

Paris would not be Paris without its bateaux-mouches. These riverboats have become quite an institution. No visit is complete without taking in Notre-Dame, the Eiffel Tower, and the rest of the sights along the riverside from on board one of these legendary boats. Something of a Parisian cliché, but nonetheless an unforgettable experience.

On the Seine

Bateaux-Mouches: boarding point: Pont de l'Alma (Right Bank), 75008, Ⓜ Alma-Marceau. ☎01 42 25 96 10, www.bateaux-mouches.fr; Round trip from Pont de l'Alma to Notre-Dame.

Les Vedettes du Pont-Neuf: boarding point: place du Vert-Galant, 75001, Ⓜ Pont-Neuf. ☎01 46 33 98 38. www.vedettesdupontneuf.com. Itinerary: from Pont-Neuf to Pont d'Iéna, including a circuit around Île de la Cité and Île St-Louis. Commentary in French and English. Duration: 1hr. Price: ⊛11€/adult, ⊛6€/child (7€/4€ online).

Les Bateaux Parisiens: boarding point: Port de la Bourdonnais, 75007, RER Champs-de-Mars-Tour-Eiffel or Ⓜ Bir-Hakeim. ☎01 44 11 33 44, www.bateauxparisiens.com. Boarding point: quai de Montebello, opposite Notre-Dame (end March to early November), Metro/RER C Saint-Michel. ☎01 43 26 92 55. Duration: 1hr. Price: 11€; 6€ child. Departures every 30min from 10am–10pm Apr–Oct; every hour Nov–Mar.

Batobus: Port de la Bourdonnais, 75007, RER C Champs-de-Mars-Tour-Eif-fel or Ⓜ Bir-Hakeim, ☎08 25 05 01 01, www.batobus.com. Eight hop-on-hop-off stops, no commentary: Eiffel Tower (Port de la Bourdonnais), Musée d'Orsay (quai de Solférino), St-Germain-des-Prés (quai Malaquais), Notre-Dame (quai de Montebello), Jardin des Plantes (quai St-Bernard), Hôtel de Ville (quai de l'Hôtel de Ville), Louvre (quai du Louvre), Champs-Elysées (Port des Champs-Elysées, near Pont Alexandre-III). Times vary from 10.30am-4.30pm in winter (10.30– 5pm 19 Dec–4 Jan) and 10am–9.30pm in summer. Departures every 25min. ⊙Closed 5 Jan–8 Feb. ⊛12€/adult and ⊛6€/child for the day; ⊛14€/adult and ⊛7€/child for two days.

Canal St-Martin

Canauxrama: boarding point at Port de Plaisance-Paris-Arsenal, opposite no 50 boulevard de la Bastille, 75011, Ⓜ Bastille. Departure times: 9.45am and 2.30pm. Another boarding point at Bassin-de-la-Villette, 13 quai de la Loire, 75019, Ⓜ Jaurès. Departure times: 9.45am and 2.45pm. Reservation recommended by calling ☎01 42 39 15 00 or online: www.canauxrama.com. This 2.5hr barge trip takes you from Port de Plaisance to Parc de la Villette or vice versa, crossing four locks and two swing bridges. Commentary. ⊛15€/adult, ⊛8€/children under 12, free for children under 4 (Saturday and Sunday afternoons

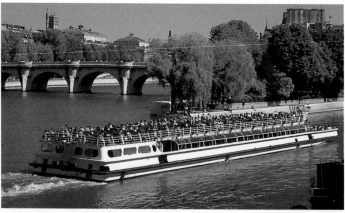

Sightseeing boat

J.-P. Clapham/MICHELIN

and public holidays: 15€/person
– reduced rates online).

Paris Canal: reservation essential,
☎01 42 40 96 97. www.pariscanal.com.
Half-day cruise along the Seine in the
centre of Paris (Louvre, Notre-Dame, Île
Saint-Louis) and along Canal St-Martin:
negotiating locks and swing bridges
and navigating through a 2km/1.2mi-
long tunnel beneath the Bastille. Two
departures daily from the end of March
to mid-November at 9.30am in front
of the Musée d'Orsay (MSolférino)
and at 2.30pm from the Parc de la
Villette (MPorte-de-Pantin). Duration:
2.5hr 45min. Price: 17€ adult; 14€
(10–25 years old); children 10€.

Marne River Cruise

Canauxrama – Reservation recommended by calling ☎01 42 39 15 00.
www.canauxrama.com. Departure
from Paris-Arsenal marina, 75012,
MBastille at 9am. All-day cruise to
Bry-sur-Marne. Price: 34€/person
without lunch. Not recommended
for children.

Great Views

The Eiffel Tower is, of course, the
place from which to view Paris, but
by no means is it the only one. Here
are some ideas of places which offer
unexpectedly stunning views over the
City of Light, by day or by night.

A few of our favourite perspectives…

Montmartre: from in front of the
Sacré-Coeur, place Émile-Goudeau.

Belleville and Ménilmontant: from
the summit of the Parc de Belleville, at
the end of rue Piat.

Passy: place du Trocadéro.

Parvis de la Défense: looking
towards Paris from the Grande Arche.

Favourite tourist views

Montparnasse Tower –
MMontparnasse-Bienvenüe
(see MONTPARNASSE).

The Eiffel Tower – MBir-Hakeim
(see Tour EIFFEL).

The Arc de Triomphe – MCharles-
de-Gaulle-Etoile (see Les CHAMPS-
ÉLYSÉES).

Notre-Dame (towers) – MCité
(see Cathédrale NOTRE-DAME).

Panthéon (upper parts) – RER
Luxembourg (see Quartier Latin).

**Georges-Pompidou Centre (5th
floor terrace)** – MRambuteau or
Hôtel-de-Ville or RER Châtelet-Les
Halles. ☎01 44 78 12 33. www.
centrepompidou.fr. Museum and
exhibitions: daily 11am–9pm
(last admission 1hr before closing).
Closed Tue. Access to the terrace
requires a ticket to the museum or to
an exhibition.

Sacré-Coeur (dome) – MAnvers or
Abesses (see MONTMARTRE).

Printemps Maison – MHavre-Cau-
martin. Mon–Sat 9.30am–7pm (10pm
on Thu). Free entry via the escalator.

**Institut du Monde arabe (9th floor
terrace)** – MJussieu. No charge
(see JUSSIEU).

*View from Altitude 95,
restaurant on the Eiffel Tower*

P. Gajic/MICHELIN

Hôtel Concorde-Lafayette (bar with panoramic view) – ⓂPorte-Maillot.

The Grande Arche at La Défense – Ⓜand RER La Défense (𝒸see La DÉFENSE).

Activities for Children

𝒸See also Entertainment in Discovering Paris.

🅺🅸🅳🆂This symbol is intended to draw attention to the sights and museums listed in this guide that are particularly suitable for children.

Some museums propose supervised educational activities such as quizzes and treasure hunts, whereas workshops give children the opportunity to try out artistic techniques for themselves. These sessions are generally held on Wednesdays and during school holidays and last between one and three hours.

Useful websites: www.takethe family.com and http://en.parisinfo. com/shows-exhibitions-paris/with-the-kids.

The Butterfly Garden – Parc Floral de Paris; 12 May–12 Oct annually. ☎01 55 94 20 20.

Georges-Ville Farm – Bois de Vincennes ;Farm animals. Jul–Aug, Tue–Sun; ☎01 43 28 47 63.

France Miniature – 258 Route du Mesnil, blvd André Malraux 78990. French microcosm; ☎08 26 30 20 40; www.franceminiature.fr.

La Cité des Sciences et de l'Industrie – Parc de Villette. Interactive exhibits cover outer space to microbiology; ☎01 40 05 80 00; www.cite-sciences.fr.

Le Musée en Herbe – Bois de Boulogne. Exhibitions and games on artistic, scientific and civic themes for families; ☎01 40 67 97 66; www.musee-en-herbe.com.

Parlez-vous anglais?

If your French is rusty or non-existent, where can you turn for current information about what's on in Paris?

The monthly magazine *The Paris Voice* features general-interest articles and reviews written from the expatriate point of view and contains listings of the month's cultural events. It is available at various English-American haunts throughout the city (bookstores, cafés, restaurants).

Calender of Events

TRADITIONAL FÊTES AND EVENTS

21 JUNE

Fête de la Musique
Venues throughout the capital and in the streets (21 June)

13 AND 14 JULY

Dancing – Firemen's Ball
In fire stations across Paris (13 July)

Military parade
Champs-Élysées (14 July)

Fireworks display
Trocadéro (14 July)

SEPTEMBER

Journées du Patrimoine
Various sites (third weekend in September)

OCTOBER

Fête des vendanges
Montmartre (second weekend of October)

DECEMBER – FEBRUARY

Outdoor skating rink
In front of Hôtel de Ville and Gare de Montparnasse.

Paris Plage

FESTIVALS

EARLY FEBRUARY

Festival mondial du Cirque de demain
Circus festival; Cirque d'hiver Bouglione; ☎01 40 55 50 06; www.circonautes.com.

MAY – JULY

Paris Jazz Festival
Parc floral de Vincennes: free concerts Sat and Sun afternoons; ☎01 55 94 20 20.

MID-JULY – MID-AUGUST

Paris quartier d'été (music, theatre)
Venues around town; ☎01 44 94 98 00; www.quartierdete.com.

Paris Plage (beach activities)
Along the banks of the Seine; free entry; www.paris.fr.

Open-Air Cinema Festival
Parc de la Villette; free entry; www.villette.com.

AUGUST – SEPTEMBER

Festival Classique au Vert
Parc floral de Vincennes: free concerts Sat and Sun afternoons; ☎01 55 94 20 20.

MID-SEPTEMBER – THIRD WEEK OF DECEMBER

Festival d'automne (theatre, cinema)
Theatres around town; ☎01 53 45 17 00; www.festival-automne.com.

EARLY OCTOBER

Nuit Blanche (art, music)
An all-night cultural festival with a different annual theme; www.paris.fr.

FAIRS, SHOWS AND EXHIBITIONS

LATE FEBRUARY

International Agricultural Show
Parc des Expositions, Porte de Versailles; www.salon-agriculture.com.

END APRIL – MID- MAY

Foire de Paris
Parc des Expositions, Porte de Versailles; www.foiredeparis.fr.

©Morane/Fotolia.com

Roland Garros

SEPTEMBER

**Biennale internationale
des Antiquaires**
Grand Palais (even years);
www.biennaledesantiquaires.com.

LATE OCTOBER

**FIAC (International
Contemporary Art Fair)**
Grand Palais & Carrousel du Louvre;
www.fiacparis.com.

EARLY DECEMBER

Salon du cheval, du poney et de l'âne
Horse, pony and donkey fair,
Parc des Expositions, Porte de
Versailles; www.salon-cheval.com.

SPORTING EVENTS

FEBRUARY – MID-MARCH

Six Nations Rugby
Stade de France, St-Denis;
www.6-nations-rugby.com.

EARLY APRIL

Paris Marathon
Through the streets of the capital;
www.parismarathon.com.

END MAY – EARLY JUNE

French Open Tennis
Roland Garros Stadium;
www.rolandgarros.com.

JUNE

Paris Grand Prix
Hippodrome de Longchamp
(last Sunday in June);
www.france-galop.com.

LATE JULY (SUNDAY)

Tour de France
Final stage on the Champs-
Élysées; www.letour.fr.

OCTOBER

Prix de l'Arc de Triomphe
Hippodrome de Longchamp (first
Sunday); www.france-galop.com.

Sightseeing

VISITING

Fees and Hours

Detailed descriptions of Paris' museums are found within the *Discovering Paris* section. There is no admission charge for museums owned by the city of Paris (the catacombs are an exception). Admission to state-owned museums and historic monuments is free for travellers with special needs, such as the handicapped – as well as those accompanying them – but the rules require that you show an identification card. Admission is free in most museums for children under 18. Admission is free for all visitors on the first Sunday in every month. In Paris, national museums and art galleries are closed on Tuesdays; municipal museums are generally closed on Mondays.

GUIDED TOURS

Guided tours of monuments, districts and exhibitions are organised by the following organisations:

Centre des monuments nationaux
– Service visites-conférences,
7 blvd Morland, 75004, ☎01 44 54
19 35. Open weekdays 9am–noon,
2pm–6pm (to 5pm on Fridays).
www.monum.fr.

Association pour la Sauvegarde et la mise en valeur du Paris historique – 44-46 rue François-Miron, 75004, ☎01 48 87 74 31. Open daily 2pm–6pm. www.paris-historique.org.

Association Fondation pour la Connaissance de Paris – 21 rue du Repos, 75020, ☎01 43 70 70 87.

Ecoute du Passé – 44 rue Maubeuge 75009, ☎01 42 65 30 47.

Communautés d'accueil dans les sites artistiques – ☎01 42 34 56 10; www.cathedraledeparis.com. Free guided tours of Notre-Dame.

⌂These guided tours, offered on a daily basis, are publicised in weekly entertainment guides (such as *Pariscope*), at the Paris Tourism Office, and posted at the sight entrances.

Looking for something specific?

⌂ *See the index for the individual sights.*

Art

Antiquities: Louvre; Musée de Cluny; Musée de l'Homme; Arènes de Lutèce.

Painting: Louvre; Musée d'Orsay; Musée National d'Art Moderne; Centre Georges Pompidou; Château de Versailles; Musée d'Art Moderne de la Ville de Paris (Palais de Tokyo); Musée Carnavalet; Musée Picasso; Musée Marmottan-Monet; Musée Maillol; Musée du Petit Palais; Musée Gustave-Moreau; Musée Eugène-Delacroix; Musée de l'Orangerie; Musée de Montmartre; Musée d'Art naïf Max-Fourny.

Sculpture: Louvre; Notre-Dame de Paris; Musée d'Orsay; Basilique St-Denis; Musée des Monuments Français; Musée Rodin; Musée Maillol; Musée Bourdelle; Musée Bouchard; Musée Zadkine; Espace Dali; Fontaine Stravinski; Jardin des Tuileries.

Literature: Maison de Balzac; Maison de Victor Hugo; Musée de la Vie Romantique; Musée Adam-Mickiewicz.

Furniture: Louvre; Musée de Cluny; Musée des Arts Décoratifs; Musée Cognacq-Jay; Musée Jacquemart-André; Musée Nissim de Camondo; Hôtel de Soubise; Faubourg St-Antoine.

Tapestries: Louvre; Musée de Cluny; Musée Nissim de Camondo; Manufacture des Gobelins.

Silver, Glass and China: Château de Vincennes; Musée Baccarat; Musée Bouilhet-Christofle.

Fashion: Musée des Arts Décoratifs; Musée de la Mode et du Costume; Faubourg St-Honoré; Musée de l'Éventail; Musée Fragonard; Musée de la Contrefaçon.

Music: Musée de l'Opéra-Garnier; Cité de la Musique.

Ethnic: Musée des Arts asiatiques-Guimet; Musée de l'Homme; Musée Cernuschi; Institut du Monde Arabe; Musée Dapper; Musée Arménien; Centre Bouddhique du Bois de Vincennes; Musée d'Art et d'Histoire du Judaïsme, Quai Branly.

Science

Natural History: Musée d'Histoire Naturelle, Jardin des Plantes.

Astronomy: Palais de la Découverte; Musée des Arts et Métiers; l'Observatoire; La Villette Planetarium.

Medicine: Hôpital Militaire du Val-de-Grâce; La Salpêtrière; Musée de l'Assistance Publique; Institut Pasteur; Musée des Moulages de l'Hôpital Saint-Louis.

Mineralogy: École Supérieure des Mines; Musée de Minéralogie; Galerie de Minéralogie.

Technology: Cité des Sciences et de l'Industrie; Palais de la Découverte; Musée des Arts et Métiers.

Books

GASTRONOMY

Paris on a Plate (2006) *by Stephen Downes.*

A gastronomic diary set in Paris during the author's youth. He recounts his experiences eating in famous restaurants and makes some observations about Paris street life. Downes also examines how the restaurant business has changed following the introduction of big money.

FICTION

The Lollipop Shoes *(2007) by Joanne Harris.*

A sequel, or in the words of the author, 'a continuation', of her best known novel *Chocolat*. Five years on, Vianne has moved to Montmartre with Anouk and now has another daughter, Rosette. Vianne is no longer the free spirit she was, due to the demands of motherhood. Into their lives steps the passionate, bohemian Zozie de l'Alba who helps Vianne regain her life but has she an ulterior motive?

HISTORY

Paris: The Secret History *(2006) by Andrew Hussey.*

The author, head of the French Department at the University of London's Paris Campus, contends that Parisians have always prized secrecy and shows that the city has for hundreds of years hosted secret societies of occultists, freemasons and many other clandestine organisations. In his view, the City of Light is also a city of darkness.

Films

Hotel du Nord *(1938) directed by Marcel Carné.*

Starring Louis Jouvet and Arletty. The relative peace of a small hôtel bar is disrupted when two lovers come seeking a room for the night. They are determined to take each other's lives but Pierre fails in his task and has to flee....

An American in Paris *(1951) directed by Vincente Minelli.*

Starring Gene Kelly and Leslie Caron. Jerry, an American expatriate living in Paris and hoping to be a successful painter, falls in love with Lise, a young French woman he meets in a restaurant. Unfortunately she is already in a relationship but after singing/dancing his way through Paris, Jerry and Lise finally get together.

Amélie *(2001) directed by Jean-Pierre Jeunet.*

Starring Audrey Tautou. The imaginative, unusual Amélie has a strong sense of justice. When she takes a job in a Montmartre bar she discovers that her main role in life is to help others and creates deceptions which allow her to intervene in the lives of those around her.

USEFUL WORDS & PHRASES

Do you speak English?	Parlez-vous anglais?
I don't understand	Je ne comprends pas
Please talk slowly	Parlez lentement s'il vous plaît
Where is…?	Où est?
Thank you	Merci
Can you help me?	Pouvez-vous m'aider?
How much/many?	C'est combien?
Hello	Bonjour
Goodbye	Au revoir
Bread	Pain
Breakfast	Petit-déjeuner
Cheese	Fromage
Fish	Poisson
Ice cream	Glace
Meat	Viande
Wine	Vin
Vegetables	Légumes
Monday	Lundi
Tuesday	Mardi
Wednesday	Mercredi
Thursday	Jeudi
Friday	Vendredi
Saturday	Samedi
Sunday	Dimanche
Open	Ouvert
Closed	Fermé

BASIC INFORMATION

Business Hours

Most of the larger shops are open Monday to Saturday from 9am to 6.30pm or 7.30pm. Smaller, individual shops may close during the lunch hour. Food shops – grocers, wine merchants and bakeries – are open from around 7am to 7.30pm; some open on Sundays. Many food shops close for an hour or two between noon and 2pm and on Mondays. Hypermarkets usually stay open until 9pm or 10pm.

Banks are usually open from 9am to 4.30pm or 5pm and are closed on Mondays or Saturdays; some branches open for limited transactions on Saturdays. Banks close early on the day before a bank holiday.

A passport is necessary as identification when cashing cheques in banks. Commission charges vary and hotels usually charge more than banks for cashing cheques for non-residents. Most banks have **cash dispensers** (ATMs) which accept international credit or debit cards and are easily recognised by the logo showing a hand holding a card. Pads are numeric and PIN numbers have four digits in France. American Express cards can be used only in dispensers operated by the CLC Bank or by American Express.

International Dialling Codes (00 + code)			
Australia	☎61	New Zealand	☎64
Canada	☎1	United Kingdom	☎44
Ireland	☎353	United States	☎1

- International operator: 00 33 12 + country code
- Local directory assistance: 12
- Special-rate numbers in France begin with 0 800 (calls from within France only).

Communications

Public phones in France use prepaid phone cards *(télécartes)*, rather than coins. Some telephone booths accept credit cards (Visa, MasterCard/Euro-card). *Télécartes* (50 or 120 units) can be bought in post offices, branches of France Télécom, *bureaux de tabac* (cafés that sell cigarettes) and newsagents and can be used to make calls in France and abroad. Calls can be received at phone boxes where the blue bell sign is shown; the phone will not ring, so keep your eye on the little message screen.

NATIONAL CALLS

French telephone numbers have ten digits. Paris and Paris region numbers begin with 01; 02 in northwest France; 03 in northeast France; 04 in southeast France and Corsica; 05 in southwest France.

INTERNATIONAL CALLS

To call France from abroad, dial the country code (33) + 9-digit number (omit the initial 0). When calling abroad from France dial 00, then dial the country code followed by the area code and number of your correspondent.

- International Information, US/Canada: 00 33 12 11

To use your personal calling card	
AT&T	☎0-800 99 00 11
Sprint	☎0-800 99 00 87
MCI	☎0-800 99 00 19
Canada Direct	☎0-800 99 00 16

MOBILE PHONES

In France these have numbers which begin with 06. The major networks are SFR, Orange, Bouygues and Virgin. Some have their own pay-as-you-go services. Phones need to be GSM 90 or GSM 1800 to work in France. Mobile phone rentals (delivery provided):

Context Paris
☎06 13 09 67 11
http://paris.contexttravel.com

World Cellular Rentals
☎1 877 626 0261 (US)
www.worldcr.com

Electricity

The electric current is 220 volts/50Hz. Circular two-pin plugs are the rule. Adapters and converters (for hairdryers, for example) should be bought before you leave home; they are on sale in most airports. If you have a rechargeable device (video camera, laptop, battery charger), read the instructions carefully or contact the manufacturer or shop. Sometimes these items only require a plug adapter, in other cases you must use a voltage converter as well or risk ruining your appliance.

Emergencies

First aid, medical advice and chemists' night service rota are available from chemists/drugstores (*pharmacie* – identified by the green cross sign).

Useful numbers – SOS Medecins,
☎01 47 07 77 77 (for emergencies).

Pharmacie Les Champs, 84 avenue des Champs-Élysées (Galerie des

Emergency numbers
Police: 17
SAMU (*Paramedics*): 15
Fire (*Pompiers*): 18

Champs-Élysées) Metro George-V.
Open 24hr a day, seven days a week.
☎01 45 62 02 41.

Pharmacie Européenne de la place de Clichy, 6 place de Clichy. Open 24hr a day, seven days a week.
☎01 48 74 65 18.

American Hospital, 63 blvd Victor-Hugo, 93 Neuilly-sur-Seine (7.5km/4.6mi from central Paris).
☎01 46 41 25 25.

British Hospital, 3 rue Barbès, 92 Levallois-Perret (7.5km/5mi).
☎01 46 39 22 22.

LOST PROPERTY

Lost property office: Préfecture de Police, Objets trouvés, 36 rue des Morillons, 75015 Paris; Metro Convention. ☎01 45 31 14 80 or 08 21 00 25 25. Open 8.30am–5pm Monday and Wednesday, Friday to 5.30pm, to 8pm Tuesday and Thursday.

Mail/Post

Post offices ⏱Open Mondays to Fridays, 8am to 7pm, Saturdays, 8am to noon. Smaller branch post offices often close at lunchtime between noon and 2pm and in the afternoon at 4pm.

Postage via air mail to:
✉ UK letter (20g) 0.60€
✉ US letter (20g) 0.85€
✉ US postcard 0.85€
✉ Australia and New Zealand letter (20g) 0.85€

Stamps are also available from newsagents and tobacconists.
Stamp collectors should ask for *timbres de collection* in any post office.

Poste Restante (General Delivery) mail should be addressed as follows: Name, Poste Restante, Poste Centrale, postal code of the *département* followed by town name, France. *Michelin Guide France* gives local postal codes.

Money

There are no restrictions on the amount of currency visitors can take into France, however, the amount of cash you may take out of France is subject to a limit, so visitors carrying a lot of cash should complete a currency declaration form on arrival.

NOTES AND COINS

Since February 2002, the **euro** has been the only currency accepted as a means of payment in France, as in the 14 member states participating in the monetary union. It is divided into 100 cents or centimes. Old notes in French francs can only be exchanged at the Banque de France (until 2012).

CREDIT CARDS

American Express, Visa (*Carte Bleue*), MasterCard/Eurocard and Diners Club are widely accepted in shops, hotels and restaurants and petrol stations.

A. ELI/MICHELIN

American Express ☎ 01 47 77 72 00
Visa ☎ 01 42 77 11 90
MasterCard/Eurocard ☎ 01 45 67 47 64
Diners Club ☎ 01 47 62 75 75

Before you leave home, learn your bank's emergency policies. Carry account numbers and emergency phone numbers separate from your wallet. Leave a copy with someone easily reachable. In the case of a lost or stolen credit card, ring one of the 24hr numbers in the box above.
These numbers are also listed at most ATM machines. Such loss or theft must also be reported to the local police who will issue a certificate to show to the credit card company.

Traveller's Cheques – Not widely accepted in France. Banks and Post Offices often give a better rate for traveller's cheques. Use Amex (dollars) or Visa (euro). You will not normally be able to pay directly with travellers cheques, as in North America.
The cheapest and most convenient way to change money is by using ATMs known in France DABs. Money will be drawn from your home account at a better rate than offered by banks and money-changers. Most ATMs will give a cash advance using Visa or MasterCard but this is a more expensive option.

Exchange Bureaux – Can be found in many places in Paris. You can exchange without commission at the following Bureau de Changes: 101 blvd Raspail, 70 blvd de Strasbourg, Le Bureau de Change 79 ave de Champs-Elysées and at the Gare de l'Est traveller's cheques.

☺ A Bit of Advice ☺

Remember to take some passport-sized photos with you if you want to purchase a public transport and museum pass on arrival. Student and teacher IDs may also help you obtain discounts.

Public Holidays

Museums and other monuments may be closed or may vary their hours of admission on public holidays.
In addition to the usual school holidays at Christmas and in the spring and summer, there are long mid-term breaks (ten days to a fortnight) in February and early November.

1 January	New Year's Day (Jour de l'An)
	Easter Day and Easter Monday (Pâques)
1 May	May Day (Fête du Travail)
8 May	VE Day (Fête de la Libération)
Thu 40 days after Easter	Ascension Day (Ascension)
7th Sun–Mon after Easter	Whit Sunday and Monday (Pentecôte)
14 July	France's National Day (Bastille Day)
15 August	Assumption (Assomption)
1 November	All Saints' Day (Toussaint)
11 November	Armistice Day (Fête de la Victoire)
25 December	Christmas Day (Noël)

Reduced Rates

Significant discounts are available for senior citizens, students, youth under age 25, teachers, and groups for public transportation, museums and monuments and for some leisure activities such as cinema (at certain times of day). Bring student or senior cards with you, and bring along some extra passport-sized photos for discount travel cards. The *Paris Museum Pass* is available from the Paris tourist office, and from participating museums and monuments.

PARIS MUSEUM PASS

This is a Museums and Monuments Pass that allows free access, in many cases without queueing (except for security check), to over 60 such sights in the capital. It may be purchased at participating museums and monuments, the Office du Tourisme de Paris, the Espace du Tourisme Île-de-France (Carrousel du Louvre). Cost: 30€, 45€ or 60€ for 2, 4 and 6 days respectively. www.parismuseumpass.fr.

Shopping

FOOD MARKETS

These take place year-round, whatever the weather, usually from 8am to 2.30pm. In Paris, there are 65 open-air markets (one, two or three times a week) and 13 covered markets (daily). Here is a list of the most interesting:

Monge, place Monge, 75005, Ⓜ Place-Monge; Wed, Fri,7am–2.30pm, Sun 7am–3pm.

Raspail, boulevard Raspail, 75006, Ⓜ Rennes; Tue, Fri, 7am2.30pm, Sun: organic produce; 9am–2pm.

Bastille, boulevard Richard-Lenoir, 75011, Ⓜ Bastille; Thu 7am–2.30pm, Sun 7am–3pm.

Belleville, boulevard de Belleville, 75011, Ⓜ Belleville; Tue, Fri 7am–2.30pm.

Aligre, place d'Aligre, 75012, Ⓜ Ledru-Rollin; Tue–Sat 8am–1pm, 4pm–7.30pm; Sun 8am–1pm.

In addition, a number of picturesque street markets take place all day on a daily basis: **rue Montorgueil** (75002), **rue Mouffetard** (75005), **rue de Buci** and **rue de Seine** (75006), rue Cler (75007), rue des Martyrs (75009), rue Daguerre (75014), rue de Passy (75016), and **rue Poncelet**, **rue de Lévis** and rue de Tocqueville (75017).

SPECIALISED MARKETS

Flea markets: Porte de Vanves (75014), Ⓜ Porte-de-Vanves, weekends from 7am to 1.30pm; Porte de Clignan-court (75018), Ⓜ Porte-de-Clignan-court, Sat–Mon from 8.30am–6.30pm and Porte de Montreuil (75020), Ⓜ Porte-de-Montreuil, Sat–Mon from 7.30am–6pm.

Plant, Flower markets: place Louis-Lépine (75004), Ⓜ Cité, Mon–Sat 8am–7pm; place de la Madeleine (75008), Ⓜ Madeleine, Tue–Fri 7am–1pm; place des Ternes (75017), Ⓜ Ternes, Mon–Sat 8am–7.30pm.

Bird market: place Louis-Lépine (75004), Ⓜ Cité, Sun 9am–7pm.

Book market: parc Georges-Brassens (75015 entrance along rue Brancion), Ⓜ Porte de Vanves, weekends.

Stamp market: Carré Marigny (75008 on the corner of avenue Marigny and avenue Gabriel), Ⓜ Champs-Élysées-lémenceau, Thu, weekends and holidays from 10am.

Art market (Marché parisien de la Création): blvd Edgar-Quinet (75014), Ⓜ Montparnasse or Edgar-Quinet, Sun 10am–sunset.

DEPARTMENT STORES

Galeries Lafayette de Paris, 40 boulevard Haussmann, 75009 Paris, Ⓜ Chaussée-d'Antin, ☏01 42 82 34 56, www.galerieslafayette.com; daily 9.30am–8pm (Thu 9pm).

Printemps, 64 boulevard Haussmann, 75008 Paris, Ⓜ Havre-Caumartin, RER Auber, ☏01 42 82 50 00, www.printemps.fr; daily 9.35am–7pm (Thu 10pm).

Le Bon Marché, 24 rue de Sèvres, 75007 Paris, Ⓜ Sèvres-Babylone, ☏01 44 39 80 00; daily 9.30am–7pm (Thu 9pm, Sat 8pm).

Le Bazar de l'Hôtel-de-Ville, 14 rue du Temple, 75004 Paris, Ⓜ Hôtel-de-Ville, ☏01 42 74 90 00, www.bhv.fr; daily 9.30am–7.30pm (Wed 9pm and Sat 8pm).

SHOPPING CENTRES

Carrousel du Louvre, 75001 Paris, Ⓜ Palais-Royal, ☎ 01 43 16 47 10; daily 9.30am–10pm (shops open 10am–8pm; more than 30 boutiques selling high-quality gift items.

Centre commercial Maine-Montparnasse, place du 18-juin-1940, 75014 Paris, Ⓜ Gare Montparnasse; multi-level complex with some 60 fashion boutiques grouped around Galeries Lafayette.

Smoking

In February 2007, France banned smoking in public places such as offices, universities and railway stations. In January 2008 this law was extended to include all enclosed public spaces (including restaurants, cafés, etc.).

Time

France is 1hr ahead of Greenwich Mean Time (GMT).

Tipping

Since a service charge is automatically included in the prices of meals and accommodation in France, it is not necessary to tip in restaurants and hotels. However, if the service in a restaurant is especially good or if you have enjoyed a fine meal, an extra tip (this is the *pourboire*, rather than the

When it is **noon in France**, it is	
3am	in Los Angeles
6am	in New York
11am	in Dublin
11am	in London
7pm	in Perth
9pm	in Sydney
11pm	in Auckland

In France "am" and "pm" are not used but the 24-hour clock is widely applied.

service) is a well-appreciated gesture. Usually 2 to 4 euros is enough, but if the bill is big (a large party or a luxury restaurant), it is not uncommon to leave 7 to 8 euros or more.

As a rule, the cost of staying in a hotel and eating in restaurants is significantly higher in Paris than in the French regions. However, by reserving a hotel room well in advance and taking advantage of the wide choice of restaurants, you can enjoy your trip without breaking the bank.

Restaurants usually charge for meals in two ways: a menu that is a fixed-price menu with 2 or 3 courses, sometimes a small pitcher of wine, all for a stated price, or à la carte, the more expensive way, with each course ordered separately.

Cafés have very different prices, depending on where they are located. The price of a drink or a coffee is cheaper if you stand at the counter (*comptoir*) than if you sit down (*salle*) and sometimes it is even more expensive if you sit outdoors (*terrasse*).

RECOVERING VAT

In France a sales tax (TVA or Value Added Tax ranging from 5.5% to 19.6%) is added to almost all retail goods – it can be worth your while to recover it. VAT refunds are available to visitors from outside the EU only if purchases exceed 175€ per store. The system works in large stores which cater to tourists, in luxury stores and other shops advertising "Duty Free". Show your passport, and the store will complete a form which is to be stamped (at the airport) by customs. The refund is paid into your credit card account. Global Refund Tax Free Shopping is a service (www.globalrefund.com) that provides customers at participating stores with a check for the amount of refund which they must have stamped at the customs office at the airport, then send to the company or cash at one of the company's offices (Orly and Roissy-Charles de Gaulle airports). The service is not free, but it does simplify the process.

CONVERSION TABLES

Weights and Measures

1 kilogram (kg) 6.35 kilograms 0.45 kilograms	**2.2 pounds (lb)** 14 pounds 16 ounces (oz)	**2.2 pounds** 1 stone (st) 16 ounces	*To convert kilograms to pounds, multiply by 2.2*
1 metric ton (tn)	**1.1 tons**	**1.1 tons**	
1 litre (l) 3.79 litres 4.55 litres	**2.11 pints (pt)** 1 gallon (gal) 1.20 gallon	**1.76 pints** 0.83 gallon 1 gallon	*To convert litres to gallons, multiply by 0.26 (US) or 0.22 (UK)*
1 hectare (ha) **1 sq. kilometre (km²)**	**2.47 acres** 0.38 sq. miles (sq.mi.)	**2.47 acres** 0.38 sq. miles	*To convert hectares to acres, multiply by 2.4*
1 centimetre (cm) **1 metre (m)**	**0.39 inches (in)** 3.28 feet (ft) or 39.37 inches or 1.09 yards (yd)	**0.39 inches**	*To convert metres to feet, multiply by 3.28; for kilometres to miles, multiply by 0.6*
1 kilometre (km)	**0.62 miles (mi)**	**0.62 miles**	

Clothing

Women					Men			
		35	4	2½			40	7½	7

Women	🇪🇺	🇺🇸	🇬🇧
	35	4	2½
	36	5	3½
	37	6	4½
Shoes	38	7	5½
	39	8	6½
	40	9	7½
	41	10	8½
	36	6	8
	38	8	10
Dresses & suits	40	10	12
	42	12	14
	44	14	16
	46	16	18
	36	06	30
	38	08	32
Blouses & sweaters	40	10	34
	42	12	36
	44	14	38
	46	16	40

Men	🇪🇺	🇺🇸	🇬🇧
	40	7½	7
	41	8½	8
	42	9½	9
Shoes	43	10½	10
	44	11½	11
	45	12½	12
	46	13½	13
	46	36	36
	48	38	38
Suits	50	40	40
	52	42	42
	54	44	44
	56	46	48
	37	14½	14½
	38	15	15
Shirts	39	15½	15½
	40	15¾	15¾
	41	16	16
	42	16½	16½

Sizes often vary depending on the designer. These equivalents are given for guidance only.

Speed

KPH	10	30	50	70	80	90	100	110	120	130
MPH	6	19	31	43	50	56	62	68	75	81

Temperature

Celsius (°C)	0°	5°	10°	15°	20°	25°	30°	40°	60°	80°	100°
Fahrenheit (°F)	32°	41°	50°	59°	68°	77°	86°	104°	140°	176°	212°

To convert Celsius into Fahrenheit, multiply °C by 9, divide by 5, and add 32.
To convert Fahrenheit into Celsius, subtract 32 from °F, multiply by 5, and divide by 9.
NB: Conversion factors on this page are approximate.

Quai de Seine and the Pont Neuf
S. Sauvignier/MICHELIN

HISTORY

Paris has been forged throughout the centuries by the changing spirit and sensibility of each era, marked by the major events and upheavals that have occurred there during its long history. For a broader perspective of the city, here is a time capsule that takes you from its origins up to the present.

Time Line

GALLO-ROMAN PERIOD

3C BC — The Parisii, a Celtic fishing tribe, settle on Lutetia, now the Île de la Cité.

52 BC — Labienus, Caesar's lieutenant, takes the city from the Gauls, who set fire to the Île de la Cité before fleeing.

1C AD — The Gallo-Romans build the city of Lutetia.

c 250 — The martyrdom of St Denis, first Bishop of the city. Christianity takes hold and the first churches are built.

360 — Julian the Apostate, prefect of the Gauls, is proclaimed Emperor of Rome by his soldiers. Lutetia is known henceforth as Paris.

Sainte Geneviève

The patron saint of Paris not only deflected the fearsome Attila the Hun's attack on Paris (he then went on to assault Orléans), she is also revered for two later exploits.

Later when the city was beseiged by Childeric, the King of the Salian Franks, she secretly crossed the siege lines and brought back grain to the city in a fleet of barges. She then went on to successfully intercede with Childeric regarding the treatment of prisoners, a feat which she was to repeat later with his successor Clovis I, who would eventually make Paris his capital.

Geneviève became Clovis' adviser and managed to convert him to Christianity. She persuaded him to build the first Christian church in Paris which was later named in her honour.

EARLY MIDDLE AGES

451 — **Ste Geneviève** deflects Attila's attack on Paris.

508 — Paris is taken over by Germanic tribes. Frankish king Clovis I makes it his capital, settling on the Cité.

8C — Paris declines in importance when Charlemagne makes Aix-la-Chapelle (Aachen) his main capital.

885 — Paris, besieged by the Normans for the fifth time, is defended by Count Eudes who is made King of France in 888.

THE CAPETIANS

Early 12C — Trade picks up on the Cité. The Watermen's Guild is at its peak. Suger, Abbot of St-Denis and minister under Louis VI and Louis VII, rebuilds the abbey.

1163 — Maurice de Sully begins construction of Notre-Dame.

1180 — During the reign of Philippe Auguste (reigned 1180-1223) a wall was erected around Paris and the Louvre was built.

1215 — The University of Paris is founded, turning the city into an important cultural centre.

1226 — Louis IX, (reigned from 1226-1270) called St Louis, commissions the building of the Sainte-Chapelle, Notre-Dame and St-Denis, and dispenses justice at Vincennes.

1253 — Foundation of a college by Sorbon, later known as the Sorbonne.

Place de Sorbonne today

1260 — The dean of the Merchants' Guild becomes Provost of Paris.

1307 — Philip the Fair dissolves the Order of the Knights Templar.

THE VALOIS

1337 — Beginning of the Hundred Years' War. Upon the death of Philip the Fair and his three sons a problem of succession arises: the French barons prefer Philip the Fair's nephew, Philip de Valois, to his grandson, Edward III, King of England. The following century is marked by battles between the French and the English, who lay claim to the French Crown, between the Armagnacs, supporters of the family of Orléans, and the Burgundians, supporters of the dukes of Burgundy.

1358 — Uprising under **Étienne Marcel**, Provost of Paris. The monarchs move to the Marais and the Louvre.

1364 — **Charles V** (reigned 1364-1380) builds the Bastille and a new wall around Paris.

1382 — During the troubled reign of Charles VI, the Parisians revolt against heavy taxes, but their loss strips them of earlier exemptions and severely weakens the Provost's power.

1407 — Duke Louis of Orleans is assassinated on the order of John the Fearless.

1408 — Fighting breaks out between the Armagnacs and the Burgundians. The English take Paris.

1429 — In vain Charles VII tries to lay siege to Paris; Joan of Arc is wounded at St-Honoré Gate.

1430 — Henry VI of England is crowned King of France at Notre-Dame.

1437 — Charles VII recaptures Paris.

1469 — The first French printing works open in the Sorbonne.

1530 — **François I** founds the Collège de France.

1534 — Ignatius Loyola founds the Society of Jesus in Montmartre.

1559 — Henri II is fatally wounded in a jousting tournament.

1572 — The struggle between Protestant and Roman Catholic factions leads to the St Bartholomew's Day Massacre.

1578 — Construction of the Pont Neuf (completed 1604).

1588 — Paris strengthens its position as the centre of political power. The Catholic League turns against Henri III, and the citizens of Paris force him to flee after the Day of the Barricades (12 May).

1589 — Returning to Paris with Henri of Navarre, Henri III is assassinated by a fanatical Dominican friar.

THE BOURBONS

1594 — Paris opens its gates to Henri IV after he converts to Catholicism.

1594 — Place des Vosges is created. La Charité and St Louis Hospitals are founded (completed 1610).

1610 — **Henri IV** is mortally wounded by Ravaillac (14 May).

1615 — Marie de Medici has Luxembourg Palace built (completed 1625).

1622 — Paris becomes an episcopal see.

1629 — The Palais-Royal is built.

1635 — **Richelieu** founds the Académie Française.

1648 — The **Fronde** (1648-1653) foments a rebellion in Paris against the Crown.

1661 — Mazarin founds the College of Four Nations, the future Institut de France.

1667 — Colbert establishes the Observatoire and restructures the Gobelins Tapestry Works.

17C — Louis XIV transfers the Court to Versailles, but increases royal control over Paris. Development of the Marais.

Late 17C — The Louvre Colonnade and the Invalides are built.

Early 18C — Construction of place Vendôme and development of the Faubourg St-Germain.

1717 — **John Law's Bank** (failed 1720).

1760 — Louis XV has the École Militaire, St-Geneviève (the future Panthéon) and place de la Concorde built (completed 1780).

1783 — First balloon flights by Pilâtre de Rozier, Jacques Charles and Aîné Roberts.

1783 — Versailles Treaty: independence of the 13 American States.

1784 — Paris has nearly 500 000 inhabitants. To the discontent of the Parisians, the Farmers-General Wall is erected, including the gateways and toll-houses by Ledoux (completed 1791).

THE REVOLUTION AND THE FIRST EMPIRE

14 Jul 1789 — Storming of the Bastille.

The taking of the Bastille on the 14 July1789 by Jean Baptiste Lallemand

©Scala, Florence/Musée Carnavalet, Paris

17 Jul
1789 — Louis XVI at the Hôtel de Ville: the tricolore flag is adopted.

14 Jul
1790 — Festival of Federation.

20 Jun
1792 — A mob invades the Tuileries.

10 Aug
1792 — Taking of the Tuileries (10 Aug) and fall of the monarchy.

2-4 Sept
1792 — September Massacres.

21 Sept
1792 — Proclamation of the Republic.

21 Jan
1793 — Execution of Louis XVI.

1793 — Opening of the Louvre Museum and institution of the Natural History Museum.

1793 — The Terror (ends 1794).

8 Jun
1794 — Festival of the Supreme Being.

5 Oct
1795 — Royalist uprising suppressed by Napoléon.

9-10 Nov
1799 — Fall of the Directory.

1800 — Bonaparte creates the offices of Prefect of the Seine and of the Police.

2 Dec
1804 — Napoléon's coronation at Notre-Dame.

1806 — Napoléon continues construction of the Louvre and commissions the Arc de Triomphe and work begins on the Vendôme Column.

1820 — Gas lamps are used to light the city's streets.

31 Mar
1814 — The Allies occupy Paris. First Treaty of Paris.

THE RESTORATION

1815 — Battle of Waterloo. Restoration of the Bourbons with Louis XVIII.

1824 — Charles X (reigned 1824-1830) mounts the throne, but his ultra-conservative policies displease the Parisians, who take to the streets to defend their freedom in the July Revolution. Fall of

The Directory

Following the discredited Convention, executive power in France passed to the Directory in August 1795.

Five 'Directors' were made jointly responsible for the conduct of the Government and assisted by a bicameral legislature consisting of the Council of the Ancients and the Council of the Five Hundred.

The first victories of the Napoléonic Wars were achieved during this period but unfortunately many of the Directors proved to be corrupt. Chaos characterised provincial administration and soon people lost faith in the system. The Directory was overthrown on 18 Brumaire (9 Nov) 1799 by Napoléon who established the Consulate with himself as First Consul.

Charles X, who flees to the Palace of Holyroodhouse in Edinburgh and is succeeded by Louis-Philippe.

1832 — A cholera epidemic kills 19 000 Parisians.

1837 — The first French railway line links Paris with St-Germain.

1840 — Return of Napoléon's ashes from St Helena.

1841 — Construction of the Thiers fortifications (completed 1845).

Feb
1848— Fall of Louis-Philippe in the February Revolution; proclamation of Second Republic.

FROM 1848 TO 1870

Jun
1848 — The suppression of the national workshops provokes socialist riots, signalling the failure of the Second Republic. Louis Napoléon is elected President of the Republic.

1852 — Louis Napoléon becomes Napoléon III, creating the Second Empire. When the Parisians once again rise up in protest, the riots are violently repressed.

1852 — Huge urban planning projects are undertaken by Baron Haussmann: Les Halles, the railway stations, the Buttes-Chaumont, Bois de Boulogne and Bois de Vincennes, the Opéra, the sewers, completion of the Louvre, and construction of the new boulevards. Paris is divided into 20 *arrondissements* (completed 1870).

1855 — **World Exhibitions** (also 1867)

1870 — Paris is besieged in winter 1870-1871 by the Prussians and capitulates. Napoléon III goes into exile in England.

THE THIRD REPUBLIC

4 Sept 1870 — The Third Republic is proclaimed at the Hôtel de Ville.

Mar–May 1871 — The Paris Commune is finally suppressed by the Men of Versailles during the Bloody Week (21-28 May); fire, destruction (Tuileries, Cour des Comptes, Hôtel de Ville, Vendôme Column) and massacres.

1879 — Executive and legislative powers are returned from Versailles to Paris.

1882 — Paris inaugurates its new Hôtel de Ville.

1889 — World Exhibition at the foot of the new Eiffel Tower.

1892 — First multi-storey building constructed of reinforced concrete.

1900 — First metro line in operation between Maillot and Vincennes. The Grand and Petit Palais are built. Cubism is born at the Bateau-Lavoir. The Sacré-Cœur Basilica is erected on the Butte Montmartre.

1914 — At the outset of the war, the government leaves Paris for Bordeaux. Paris, under the threat of German attack, is saved by the Battle of the Marne. A shell hits the church of St-Gervais.

1920 — Interment of the Unknown Soldier under the Arc de Triomphe.

Roaring Twenties — Paris is a cultural hub where new literary and artistic movements are born.

1927 — Inauguration of Monet's *Nymphéas* series at the Orangerie.

1930s — The worldwide economic crisis hits Paris.

Feb 1934 — Riots around the Chamber of Deputies end in a bloodbath.

Jun 1940 — Paris is bombed, then occupied, by the Germans. Hostages and resistance fighters detained at Mont Valérien (Suresnes).

19-25 Aug 1944 — Liberation of Paris.

27 Oct 1946 — The Fourth Republic is proclaimed at the Hôtel de Ville.

THE FIFTH REPUBLIC

1958 — Construction of the UNESCO, CNIT, and Maison de Radio-France buildings (completed 1963).

1965 — The Urban Development Plan for the greater Paris area is published.

May 1968 — Strikes and demonstrations, triggered by students at the Sorbonne, spread to the whole of France within days, leading to the largest social movement in the country's history.

1969 — Transfer of the wholesale markets from Les Halles to Rungis.

1970 — The RER (Réseau Express Régional) is launched to extend the metro system.

1973 — Completion of the boulevard Périphérique

(ring road) and Montparnasse Tower.

25 Mar 1977 — The first election of a mayor of Paris (J Chirac), 11 predecessors between 1789 and 1871 having been appointed rather than elected.

1977 — Opening of the Centre Georges-Pompidou.

1986 — Inauguration of the Orsay Museum.

1989 — The opening of the Louvre Pyramid, Grande Arche at La Défense and Opéra Bastille during bicentennial celebrations.

1995 — Jacques Chirac is elected president.

1996 — The Bibliothèque Nationale opens at Tolbiac.

1999 — Severe windstorms damage parks and monuments in Paris on 26 Dec.

2001 — Bertrand Delanoë becomes the city's first Socialist mayor in over a century.

2002 — Jacques Chirac is re-elected president.

2003 — Thousands of sick and elderly die during a brutal summer heatwave.

2006 — Opening of the Quai Branly Museum, the Simone de Beauvoir footbridge, and Josephine Baker swimming pool on the Seine.

2007 — Opening of the Cité de l'Architecture et du patrimoine (largest collection in Europe) and election of Nicolas Sarkozy as President.

2008 — Opening of the Cité de la Mode et du design (Sept) and Bertrand Delanoë is re-elected as Mayor of Paris.

Urban Growth

The capital's site was carved out of the limestone and Tertiary sands by the Seine which flowed at a level of 35m/115ft, above its present course.

The Gallo-Roman Wall: The Parisii, taking advantage of the *Pax romana*, emerged from Lutetia, built by the Gauls and defended by the river and surrounding swamps, to settle along the Left Bank of the river. The Barbarians later forced them to retreat to the Cité (c. 276). On the island, they built houses, fortifications and a rampart wall to defend themselves against future invasions.

The Philippe Auguste Wall: Between the 6C and 10C, the swamps were drained and cultivated, monasteries founded and a river harbour established near the place de Grève. Between 1180 and 1210 Philippe Auguste ordered that a massive wall be built, reinforced upstream by a chain barrage across the river and downstream by the Louvre Fortress and Nesle Tower.

The Charles V Rampart: The Town, which was on the Right Bank (as opposed to the University on the Left Bank, and the Cité), prospered as roads were built connecting it with Montmartre, St-Denis, the Knights Templar Commandery and the castle at Vincennes. By the end of the 14C, Charles V had erected new fortifications, supported in the east by the Bastille. The Paris ramparts enclosed just under 440ha/1 087 acres and protected 150 000 inhabitants.

The Louis XIII Wall: Throughout the 16C, the Wars of Religion and the siege by Henri of Navarre maintained a threat to the city, forcing Charles IX and Louis XIII to extend the 14C wall westwards to include the Louvre Palace.

The Farmers-General Wall: The monarchy moved to Versailles as Paris encroached upon the surrounding countryside, its population 500 000 strong. The Invalides, Observatory, Salpêtrière, St-Denis and St-Martin Gates were erected; new city confines were required, calling for a new wall (1784-91) complete with 57 **toll-houses** to be designed by **Ledoux**.

The Thiers Fortifications: During the Revolution many of the larger estates were broken up but little was built.

Under the Empire, Paris faced problems of overcrowding and supply. The Restoration encouraged great industrial developments and social change: gas lighting was installed in the streets, and the railway allowed for growth and economic development in outlying villages (Austerlitz, Montrouge, Vaugirard, Passy, Montmartre, Belleville). Thiers determined the capital's perimeter with another wall (1841-45), reinforced at a cannon-ball's distance by 16 bastions, the official city confines from 1859. Subsequently, 20 *arrondissements* were created in the 77.7sq km/30sq mi, as Haussmann began his transformation of the city (population in 1846: 1 050 00; in 1866: 1 800 000).

The present limits: The forts remained intact (Mont Valérien, Romainville, Ivry, Bagneux), but the walls, after serving in the city's defence in 1871, were razed by the Third Republic in 1919. Between 1925 and 1930 the confines of the city are redefined to include the Bois de Boulogne and Bois de Vincennes, but not extending elsewhere beyond a narrow circular belt to give an overall surface area of 10 540ha/26 045 acres, for a population, in 1945, of 2 700 000.

Association with the British

Many an Englishman has harboured a secret admiration for Paris, while regretting that so many Parisians live there – the French have a similar view of London!

London, England, is a mere 2hr 15min away by train. But in the realms of politics the instinct for self-preservation has maintained a certain distance, commonly known as the Entente Cordiale. This relationship has been reiterated through history with many treaties – 1763 terminating the Seven Years' War, 1814 and 1815 ending the Napoléonic era, 1856 sealing the alliance at the end of the Crimean War, 1904-10 commercial treaties which concluded in the Entente Cordiale, and 1919 the Treaty of Versailles.

Since the 17C, Paris has been a major attraction for British travellers: artists on their way to Italy (Charles Dickens, John Ruskin), gentlemen on the Grand Tour (Lord Byron), public figures fleeing from persecution at home (Oscar Wilde, Duke and Duchess of Windsor) or impoverished journalists (WM Thackeray) and students (Orwell).

By the mid-19C, Thomas Cook was organising what he called package holidays. As he stated in Cook's Excursionist and Advertiser of 15 May 1863:

"We would have every class of British subjects visit Paris, that they may emulate its excellencies, and shun the vices and errors which detract from the glory of the French capital. In matters of taste and courtesy we have much to learn from Parisians..."

Lawrence Durrell wrote: *"the national characteristics... are the restless metaphysical curiosity, the tenderness of good living and the passionate individualism. This is the invisible constant in a place with which the ordinary tourist can get in touch just by sitting quite quietly over a glass of wine in a Paris bistrot".*

Americans in Paris

The world's quintessential expatriate city, Paris has long held a special fascination for Americans. Offering an incomparable urban setting, a rich cultural legacy and a deep-rooted respect for artistic pursuits and individual freedom, the French capital has provided a stimulating environment for successive waves of celebrated American émigrés.

18C-19C: Franco-American ties developed out of shared conflict with the British and a steadfast commitment to Revolutionary ideals. Francophiles **Benjamin Franklin** and **Thomas Jefferson**, sent to France as official emissaries of the new republic, contributed to establishing early political, cultural and scientific links between the two countries.

Throughout the 19C Paris reigned as the cultural capital of the Western world and as such attracted numerous American artists including Whistler, Eakins and Impressionist Mary Cassatt. Many of

Richard Wright: A Writer in Exile

American writer and intellectual Richard Wright lived at 14 rue Monsieur-le-Prince with his wife and two daughters from 1948 to 1959. Wright's novels *Black Boy*, *Native Son* and *American Hunger* and essays forcefully exposed racism in American society. Discontented with the racial and political climate in post-World War II America, Wright was finally granted an American passport thanks to the intervention of Gertrude Stein, who arranged to have the French Government extend him an official invitation. Among the haunts frequented by Wright and other members of the black intelligentsia was the nearby Café Tournon, 20 rue de Tournon. Martin Luther King visited the writer in his rue Monsieur-le-Prince apartment in 1959. Richard Wright died in Paris in 1960. His ashes are preserved in Père Lachaise cemetery (see *CIMETIÈRE DU PÈRE-LACHAISE*).

America's leading architects – notably Richard Morris Hunt, Henry Hobson Richardson and Louis Sullivan – studied at the world-renowned **École des Beaux-Arts**, the supreme arbiter of Neoclassical 19C architectural trends.

"Where the 20C was": Referring to the city's pivotal role in the birth and development of modern literary and artistic movements, **Gertrude Stein** asserted "Paris is where the twentieth century was".

Like two other prominent life-long expatriates – Natalie Clifford Barney and **Sylvia Beach** – Gertrude Stein was lured by the city's stimulating environment, which allowed a degree of artistic and sexual freedom unthinkable in early 20C America. Beach's **Shakespeare and Company** bookshop and the celebrated literary salons of Stein and Barney became important meeting places for the city's intelligentsia.

American expatriate life in Paris reached its heyday in the 1920s. World War I was over, the exchange rate was favourable and Paris was the place to be. During that historic decade, the Left Bank was home to an astounding number of literary personalities: Ezra Pound, F Scott-Fitzgerald, Sherwood Anderson, Ford Madox-Ford and **Ernest Hemingway**, whose life and work is more intimately linked to Paris than that of any other American writer. This foremost Lost Generation novelist brilliantly captured the unbridled expatriate experience as played out in the legendary cafés, night spots and streets of Montparnasse and the Latin Quarter (*The Sun Also Rises* and

A Moveable Feast). The period's unprecedented literary production gave rise to a proliferation of avant-garde expatriate reviews *(Little Review, Transitions)* and publishers (Black Sun Press, Black Manikin Press and Hours Press founded by Nancy Cunard). The first uncensored edition of James Joyce's masterpiece *Ulysses* was published in France in 1922 by Sylvia Beach.

Simultaneously Paris played host to an international colony of prodigious artists including Picasso, Chagall, Modigliani, and Americans **Man Ray** and **Alexander Calder**. Among the expatriate performing artists were dancer **Isadora Duncan** and Revue Nègre star **Josephine Baker**, who cherished the racial equality and the international fame offered by France. The dizzying Paris scene was astutely observed by **Janet Flanner** who, under the pseudonym Genêt, authored the "Letter from Paris" column in *The New Yorker* from 1925 to 1975.

The 1930s were marked by the presence of **Henry Miller**. Like Hemingway, Miller came to Paris to become a writer and chose a Paris setting for his first novel. The quasi-autobiographical *Tropic of Cancer* (1934), banned in the US until the 1960s, explicitly depicts a seedy Paris well off the beaten expatriate trail. During his Paris years, Miller met his American protector, muse and lover, **Anaïs Nin**.

Post-World War II to the Present: Expatriate life in Paris was interrupted by the outbreak of World War II: most of the American writers of the 1920s and 30s had gone home or moved on to safer havens. Shakespeare and Company, a Left Bank institution, closed its doors in 1941 after 20 years of existence. During the late 1950s and 1960s, a new American-run bookstore and lending library opened in the Latin Quarter. This picturesque haunt (which took over the name Shakespeare and Company following Sylvia Beach's death in 1962) was frequented by Beat Generation writers Ginsberg and Burroughs, as well as by many of the newly arrived black writers. Lured by France's reputation as a nation fostering a non-racist cultural climate. The most influential member of this group was acclaimed writer and intellectual **Richard Wright** (*Native Son*), whose self-imposed Paris exile began in 1947 and lasted until his death in 1960. Fellow-expatriate black American writers included **Chester Himes**, **William Gardner Smith** and **James Baldwin** (*Another Country, Giovanni's Room*).

Although Paris' heyday as an avant-garde expatriate haven may be over, the City of Lights continues to entice Americans. For an idea of the range of activities and events organised for and by today's expatriate community, consult the monthly newspaper, *The Paris Free Voice* (available in English-language haunts throughout the city).

ART AND CULTURE

The charm of the Parisian landscape is unquestionably due to its talented artists and craftsmen over the centuries; but it is also a result of its successful blending of styles from different periods, including contemporary buildings. Paris is a dynamic city whose contrasting faces never cease to astonish visitors and inhabitants alike.

Architecture

MEDIEVAL PARIS

From the 6C to the 10C marshy areas were dried up and cultivated, while the city's port and trade activities developed around place de Grève. Walls were built around the city, and its first streets constructed – extensions of the town's few bridges. Traffic and hygienic conditions improved when Philippe-Auguste had the streets paved. Soon, fountains began to dot the Parisian landscape, and springs – such as the one in Belleville – were tapped more frequently, providing a better water service.

Romanesque architecture, known as Norman style in England, didn't blossom in Paris as it did in the rest of France. Some rare examples include the chancel columns and bell-tower porch at St-Germain-des-Prés, the apse of St-Martin-des-Champs, and a few capitals in St-Pierre-de-Montmartre and St-Aignan Chapel.

Greater Paris was the cradle of **Gothic architecture**. Vast churches were built as tall and light as possible, using ogive or pointed arches and groin vaults (St-Germain-des-Prés chancel), whose thrust and weight are contained by side aisles and external buttressing (St-Julien-le-Pauvre apse).

Early Gothic (12C) architecture is best illustrated by Notre-Dame Cathedral, where the transition of building techniques and styles from the 12C to the early 14C can be seen in the vast chancel, slightly projecting transept and the dark triforium gallery. Capitals are decorated with motifs of plants and flowers from the greater Paris area. Sources of light are limited to narrow windows in the nave, topped by small round windows, or oculi, at the transept crossing.

High or Rayonnant Gothic (13C-14C) is a style developed during the reign of Louis IX, when structural engineering reached new heights under architect Pierre de Montreuil. Walls are replaced by huge panels of glass, allowing light to flood in. Slender piers support the vault, reinforced externally by unobtrusive buttressing or flying buttresses (St-Martin-des-Champs refectory). With the new use of light, stained glass began to flourish. The *chevet* of Notre-Dame, Sainte-Chapelle and the Royal Chapel at Vincennes are Paris' masterpieces of **High Gothic** architecture. The gargoyles were another innovation, designed as spouts to drain off rainwater. It is this style, in particular, that was assimilated in England at Canterbury and London (St Stephen's, Westminster).

In the 15C a trend emerged towards more exaggerated decoration during the **Late or Flamboyant Gothic period (15C)** with an increase in purely decorative vaulting (St Merri transept, St-Germain-l'Auxerrois porch) – flame motifs flourish on window tracery; the triforium gives way to ever taller clerestory windows; piers culminating in ribs without capitals run straight to the ceiling (St-Séverin ambulatory), from which hang monumental vault bosses (St-Étienne-du-Mont).

With the outbreak of the Hundred Years' War (1337-1453), civil architecture reverted to the sombre, massive style of feudal times (the Bastille and Men at Arms Hall in the Conciergerie).

Large residences with huge gardens such as the Hôtel St-Paul were built in the Marais district, along with many small half-timbered houses, a few of which can still be seen on rue François-Miron and on Île St-Louis.

In domestic architecture, defensive features – turrets, crenellations, wicket gates – blend with richly sculpted decorative elements such as balustrades and mullioned dormer windows.

THE RENAISSANCE

In the 16C, the war with Italy kindled the interest of French artists in Antiquity and non-religious decoration. Cradle or coffered ceilings (St-Nicolas-des-Champs) replaced ogive vaults, and architectural orders – especially Ionic and Corinthian – were reintroduced. The rood screen at St-Étienne-du-Mont and the stalls at St-Gervais are the finest examples of this style. However, Paris was not entirely loyal to the Italian influence. The capital preserved its own style, at least in terms of religious architecture.

A trio of Renaissance Parisian architects – The Renaissance in France is inextricably linked with the *châteaux de la Loire*. But Paris stands out for two majestic new edifices, the Louvre and the Tuileries, built by three men: Pierre Lescot (1515-78), Baptiste Androuët Du Cerceau (1560-1602) and Philibert Delorme (1517-70). All three were influenced by Italian architecture. The former two introduced from Italy the continuous façade broken by projecting bays with semicircular pediments. The Cour Carrée in the Louvre combines the splendour of Antiquity with rich decoration: statues nestling in niches between fluted pilasters; a frieze and cornices above doorways; and inside, coffered ceilings (Henri II staircase in the Clock Pavilion of the Louvre).

Work on the first Hôtel de Ville was begun in 1533 by Le Boccador and Pierre Chambiges.

CLASSICAL ARCHITECTURE

Paris continued to expand, and new civil and religious edifices were always underway, despite the Wars of Religion and the siege of the city by Henri de Navarre. Charles IX and Louis XIII pushed the walls built by Philippe-Auguste farther west. The right bank benefited from this dynamic urban development.

Paris was transformed in the 17C with the rise of Classical art and architecture inspired by Antiquity. Rules were established by the Academy of Architecture, founded in 1671, and strengthened by an absolute monarchy, asserting the need to combine religion and Antiquity and leading Classical art to its pinnacle.

Religious architecture was modelled on Roman churches, with columns, pediments and statues competing for space.

The Jesuit style of the Counter-Reformation adopted for the design of St-Paul-St-Louis caught on and the Paris skyline was soon filled with domes. Lemercier built the Sorbonne and Val-de-Grâce (finished by Le Muet). The Sun King's architects demonstrated their progressive assimilation and mastery of the dome through the magnificent creations that beautified the city under Louis XIV: Hardouin-Mansart (Invalides, St-Roch), Libéral-Bruant (Salpêtrière), Le Vau (St-Louis-en-l'Île), Soufflot (Panthéon).

Public buildings were shaped by Classical symmetry and pure lines. Place des Vosges, place Dauphine and Hôpital St-Louis typify the Louis XIII style with the use of brick and stone; whereas Salomon de Brosse blended French and Italian features in the Luxembourg Palace built for Marie de Medici. Mansart, Androuet Du Cerceau, Delamair and Le Muet created a new design in the Marais for the Parisian town house, or *hôtel particulier*, smaller than before and featuring a garden.

Classical architecture reached its height between 1650 and 1750 with magnificent buildings by Perrault (Louvre Colonnade), Le Vau (Institut de France) and Gabriel (place de la Concorde, École Militaire). Although originality was in vogue at the end of the 17C, the Rococo style (decorations on the Hôtel de Soubise) never was very popular in Paris. Under Louis XVI, taste gravitated towards the more elegant simplicity of Antiquity (Palais de la Légion d'Honneur) as epitomised by Ledoux (Farmers General Wall toll-houses).

Urban development – Construction work was ongoing throughout the 17C in Paris. François Mansart (1598-1666) designed the Val-de-Grâce, the Hôtel de la Vrillière (Banque de France), and the façade of the Hôtel Carnavalet. His nephew, **Jules Hardouin-Mansart** (1646-1708) built the Invalides dome, place Vendôme, place des Victoires and the Hôtel Conti.

Paris was fitted out with magnificent buildings and avenues. The right and left banks tried to outdo each other. The Palais Cardinal designed by Jacques Lemercier, as well as the Cours de la Reine (Champs-Elysées), and place Royale – a model of Classical symmetry – were constructed on the Right Bank. The Hôtel Lambert was built on Île St-Louis by **Le Vau** (1612-70), who also designed St-Sulpice and the Collège des Quatre Nations (now the Institut de France) on the Left Bank. The Manufacture des Gobelins and the Observatoire were erected in the late 17C.

The building frenzy continued into the 18C, when an impressive number of new monuments appeared on the Paris skyline: the Palais-Royal arcades, the Hôtel des Monnaies, the Palais de l'Élysée, the Palais-Bourbon, the Théâtre de l'Odéon, and the Palais de Bagatelle. After the Revolution, the city was divided into chic areas and the working-class districts west of the Marais, whose winding streets add a touch of charm from the past to present-day Paris (Latin Quarter and St-Merri Quarter).

Safety and cleanliness improved with the addition of lanterns that were lit until midnight, as well as a road maintenance service and fire brigade. Traffic problems were alleviated by ring-roads built around the capital. The banks of the Seine were remodelled and new bridges constructed, allowing fresh supplies to be brought in by boat on a daily basis. Finally, Paris adopted its current system of street names and numbers with no 1 being the house closest to the Seine.

SECOND EMPIRE AND INNOVATION

The Empire and Restoration were not marked by any significant architectural achievements. Napoléon I continued construction of the Louvre and built monuments such as the Madeleine, the Arc de Triomphe and the Arc de Triomphe du Carrousel. But the real transformation of Paris took place during the Second Empire, when **Baron Haussmann**'s massive urban planning programme and the new application of cast iron in construction irrevocably altered the city. The technique of cladding metallic sub-structures was refined by Baltard (St Augustin, Pavillon Baltard at Nogent-sur-Marne), Labrouste (Bibliothèque Ste-Geneviève), and Hittorff (Gare du Nord), the most famous example of the new building method being **Gustave Eiffel**'s Tower.

Paris was enlarged to encompass some of its surrounding villages, and the current system of the 20 *arrondissements*

Opéra Garnier

was created. Haussmann's wide avenues enhance buildings such as the **Opéra Garnier**, one of the finer stone edifices of a period that was less preoccupied with monumental buildings.

Towards the end of the century, new trends developed that were different from the official style. Art Nouveau architects, the most well known being Guimard, defined a new decorative vocabulary for façades, interiors and furniture featuring stylised floral motifs, asymmetrical designs and materials such as glass and ceramics.

THE 20C

The 20C marks a turning point in urban architecture. Architects and structural engineers collaborated on ever more economical and functional designs using industrially manufactured, thus cheaper, materials (cast iron, plate-glass, artificial stone) and improved building methods. Buildings in totally different styles have gone up side-by-side. While the Grand and Petit Palais, Pont Alexandre-III and Sacré-Cœur look to the past for their inspiration, the Théâtre des Champs-Elysées (Frères Perret), Palais de Chaillot and Palais de Tokyo, fashioned in reinforced concrete, look resolutely ahead to the modern age.

Late 20C – Since 1945, under the influence of **Le Corbusier** (Fondation, Cité Universitaire), architectural design has undergone a fundamental reappraisal. A wide variety of new forms, styles and lines strive to fit into the existing urban landscape, starting with social housing in the 1970s. Ricardo Bofill's buildings use elements of Classical architecture while employing modern materials such as glass and cement.

Glass has been used to cover most new constructions (La Défense, Insti-

Some buildings from the past 30 years

The Forum des Halles, Centre Georges-Pompidou, Cité des Sciences et de l'Industrie and the nearby Cité de la Musique (*see LA VILLETTE*), Institut du Monde Arabe, Opéra Bastille, Pyramide du Louvre, the CNIT and the Grande Arche (*see La DÉFENSE*), Palais Omnisports, Ministère des Finances, and the Bibliothèque de France-site Tolbiac (BERCY), the Fondation Cartier near place Denfert-Rochereau (*see DENFERT-ROCHEREAU*), and the reflective plastic forms of the Le Ponant apartment block built on the site of the old Citroën car factory (*see VAUGIRARD*).

ABC of Architecture

Church of St-Germain-des-Prés

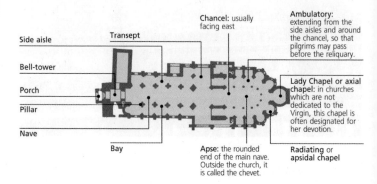

Side aisle

Transept

Bell-tower

Porch

Pillar

Nave

Bay

Chancel: usually facing east

Apse: the rounded end of the main nave. Outside the church, it is called the chevet.

Ambulatory: extending from the side aisles and around the chancel, so that pilgrims may pass before the reliquary.

Lady Chapel or axial chapel: in churches which are not dedicated to the Virgin, this chapel is often designated for her devotion.

Radiating or **apsidal chapel**

St-Séverin church: cross-section (from the east end looking towards the nave)

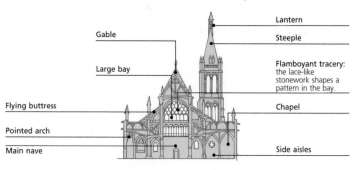

Gable

Large bay

Flying buttress

Pointed arch

Main nave

Lantern

Steeple

Flamboyant tracery: the lace-like stonework shapes a pattern in the bay.

Chapel

Side aisles

Church of St-Germain-des-Prés

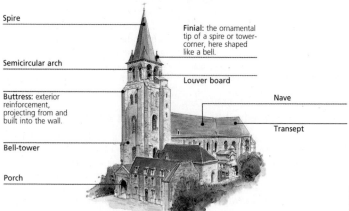

Spire

Semicircular arch

Buttress: exterior reinforcement, projecting from and built into the wall.

Bell-tower

Porch

Finial: the ornamental tip of a spire or tower-corner, here shaped like a bell.

Louver board

Nave

Transept

Chevet of Notre-Dame Cathedral

The cathedral is exquisite for its well-proportioned volumes, the purity of its lines and the craftsmanship of the decorative elements. The remarkable flying buttresses span the double ambulatory and the galleries inside.

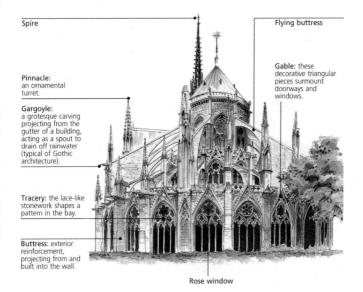

Spire

Flying buttress

Pinnacle: an ornamental turret.

Gable: these decorative triangular pieces surmount doorways and windows.

Gargoyle: a grotesque carving projecting from the gutter of a building, acting as a spout to drain off rainwater (typical of Gothic architecture).

Tracery: the lace-like stonework shapes a pattern in the bay.

Buttress: exterior reinforcement, projecting from and built into the wall.

Rose window

Church of the Sorbonne

The oldest part of the university, the church was built by Le Mercier between 1635-1642.

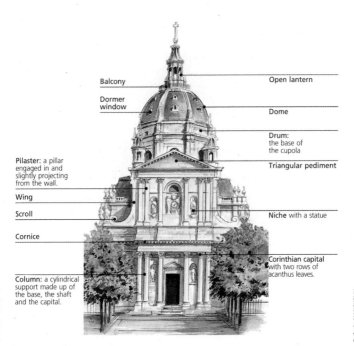

Balcony

Open lantern

Dormer window

Dome

Drum: the base of the cupola

Pilaster: a pillar engaged in and slightly projecting from the wall.

Triangular pediment

Wing

Scroll

Niche with a statue

Cornice

Corinthian capital with two rows of acanthus leaves.

Column: a cylindrical support made up of the base, the shaft and the capital.

R. Corbel/ MICHELIN

PONT-NEUF

Despite its name – "new bridge" – it is the oldest in Paris. The 12 arches are embellished with amusing mascarons.

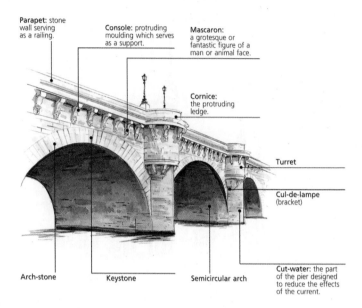

Parapet: stone wall serving as a railing.

Console: protruding moulding which serves as a support.

Mascaron: a grotesque or fantastic figure of a man or animal face.

Cornice: the protruding ledge.

Turret

Cul-de-lampe (bracket)

Arch-stone

Keystone

Semicircular arch

Cut-water: the part of the pier designed to reduce the effects of the current.

Pavillon de l'Horloge du Louvre

Also know as the Sully Pavilion, built by Le Mercier in the 17C.

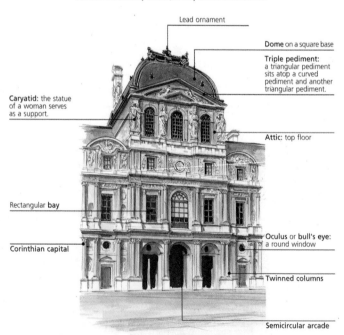

Lead ornament

Dome on a square base

Triple pediment: a triangular pediment sits atop a curved pediment and another triangular pediment.

Caryatid: the statue of a woman serves as a support.

Attic: top floor

Rectangular bay

Oculus or bull's eye: a round window

Corinthian capital

Twinned columns

Semicircular arcade

R. Corbel/ MICHELIN

INSTITUT DE FRANCE

The chapel with its dome is set between two semicircular wings which lead to two square pavilions.

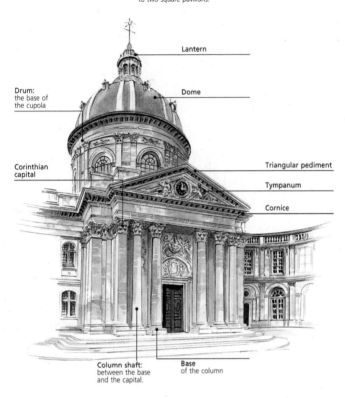

Lantern

Drum:
the base of
the cupola

Dome

Corinthian
capital

Triangular pediment

Tympanum

Cornice

Column shaft:
between the base
and the capital.

Base
of the column

PLACE VENDÔME

The magnificent architecture of this square is the work of Mansart. Arcades run along the ground level and pilasters adorn the upper floors; dormer windows are on the uppermost level.

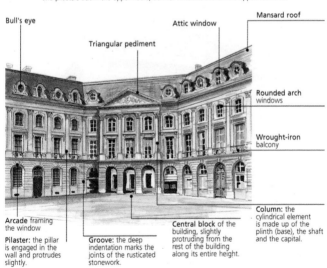

Bull's eye

Attic window

Mansard roof

Triangular pediment

Rounded arch
windows

Wrought-iron
balcony

Column: the
cylindrical element
is made up of the
plinth (base), the shaft
and the capital.

Arcade framing
the window

Pilaster: the pillar
is engaged in the
wall and protrudes
slightly.

Groove: the deep
indentation marks the
joints of the rusticated
stonework.

Central block of the
building, slightly
protruding from the
rest of the building
along its entire height.

R. Corbel/ MICHELIN

Building on rue de Seine
Louis XV façade with typical embellishments

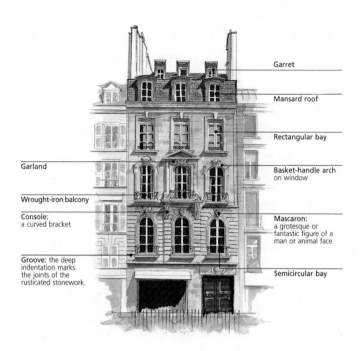

Garret

Mansard roof

Rectangular bay

Basket-handle arch on window

Mascaron: a grotesque or fantastic figure of a man or animal face.

Semicircular bay

Garland

Wrought-iron balcony

Console: a curved bracket

Groove: the deep indentation marks the joints of the rusticated stonework.

LA MADELEINE

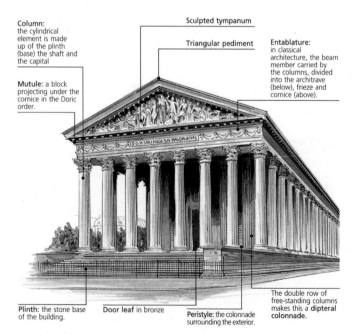

Column: the cylindrical element is made up of the plinth (base) the shaft and the capital

Sculpted tympanum

Triangular pediment

Entablature: in classical architecture, the beam member carried by the columns, divided into the architrave (below), frieze and cornice (above).

Mutule: a block projecting under the cornice in the Doric order.

Plinth: the stone base of the building.

Door leaf in bronze

Peristyle: the colonnade surrounding the exterior.

The double row of free-standing columns makes this a dipteral colonnade.

R. Corbel/ MICHELIN

GARE DU NORD
Designed by the architect Hittorff, the train station was built between 1861-1868.

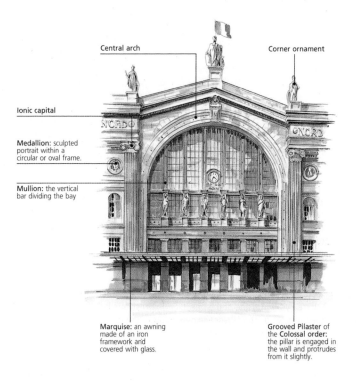

Central arch

Corner ornament

Ionic capital

Medallion: sculpted portrait within a circular or oval frame.

Mullion: the vertical bar dividing the bay

Marquise: an awning made of an iron framework and covered with glass.

Grooved Pilaster of the **Colossal order:** the pillar is engaged in the wall and protrudes from it slightly.

OPÉRA BASTILLE
Designed by Carlos Ott, 1989. The shiny, rounded surfaces seem to be pushing forward into the place de la Bastille. The main auditorium seats 2,700.

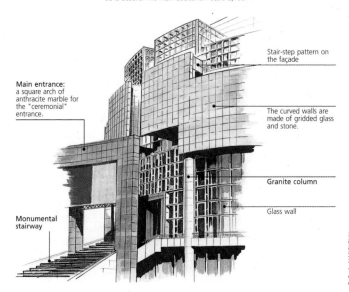

Stair-step pattern on the façade

Main entrance: a square arch of anthracite marble for the "ceremonial" entrance.

The curved walls are made of gridded glass and stone.

Granite column

Glass wall

Monumental stairway

R. Corbel/ MICHELIN

tut du Monde Arabe, Bibliothèque de France, Palais de la culture du Japon), enabling architects to achieve stunning technical effects.

Blending past and future – Architecture today falls within the wider scope of town planning, with new buildings designed as part of a larger scheme of renovations in a district (Maine-Montparnasse, Les Halles, La Villette, Bercy) or of newly created areas (La Défense, Tolbiac). Green spaces, pedestrian zones and bicycle paths have also been designed as part of the restructuring of the city.

The International Foundation for Human Rights in the Arche de La Défense, the Bibliothèque Nationale de France and the Palais Omnisports de Bercy are only a few examples of how the city's reputation as an important centre for culture and sports has been enhanced in recent years.

Paris has often chosen foreign architects to undertake its large-scale buildings. The Louvre Pyramide, one of the finest examples of a successful alliance of old and new, is the work of American architect **Ieoh Ming Pei**.

But the era of huge projects seems to be coming to an end. Today the accent is on improving and preserving existing monuments. Now, just a few years into the 21C Paris has experienced exciting contemporary developments such as Jean Nouvel's harmonius balance of glass and metal at Musée du Quai Branly.

Art

PAINTING AND SCULPTURE

Painting and sculpture have always been closely interwoven into Parisian life. After centuries of working on commission from the monarchy, 19C and 20C artists began to reach levels of freedom and creativity acclaimed throughout the world.

In the Middle Ages

Painting and sculpture appeared within a religious context during this period, as Gothic buildings were gradually decorated. Stained glass, the main medium, reached stunning heights (Sainte-Chapelle, rose windows in Notre-Dame). The palette of colours was broadened and became increasingly suffused with light. The realism of painting from the Middle Ages is striking through its expressive faces and minutely detailed clothing. Painters from this period were given the name Primitives.

Gothic sculpture also flourished. Realism and a sense of drama combined to transform what was until then mere decoration into a true art form. Churches were covered with statues: little sculptures adorn the balustrade and the sides of the chancel at Notre-Dame, whereas the Portal of the Last Judgement marks the beginning of a more sober style that developed in the 13C into French Gothic.

The Renaissance

At the beginning of the 14C the Parisian schools of painting chose a style that was still realistic but more subdued. Expressions became finer and details more important, leading to a mannerist style. Painting evolved and adopted new themes such as mythology and portraits, as well as humanist themes with Antiquity as the ideal. The influence of Italian art is omnipresent in French painting, whereas sculpture preserved its own character.

The art of stained glass was at its peak. Jean Cousin the Younger (1522-94) delved deeper into colour techniques. *The Judgement of Solomon* and the *Story of the Virgin* in St-Gervais, and the *Story of St-Joseph* in St-Merri are like paintings made of stained glass.

Jean Goujon (1510-68) – The master of 16C French statuary. While he didn't reject Italian mannerism, nature was his fundamental ideal. His works combine grace and elegance despite their complex composition. Fitting into the architectural design, they provide a preliminary idea of French Classicism. The Cariatides (Louvre) and bas-relief sculptures of the Fontaine des Innocents (1547-49) are his two greatest masterpieces.

Pilgrimage to the Island of Cythera (1717) by Jean-Antoine Watteau, Louvre

The 17C

Italian influence continued during the early 17C. Paintings were designed mainly as decoration for royal palaces such as the Louvre and Luxembourg. Sculpture also adopted the Italian style, becoming strictly decorative for the niches designated by architects.

But Classical French art asserts itself under the king's patronage in the second half of the 17C; and despite competition from Versailles, Paris was its main beneficiary. The main purpose of painting and sculpture became the glorification of the French monarchy, which enriches its 'great city' with magnificent monuments decorated by the Court's best sculptors: Girardon (Richelieu's tomb), Coysevox (Tuileries Gardens), and Coustou (The Marly Horses).

In 1648, the Academy of Painting and Sculpture was founded; it was to be the most important French art school until 1793. Quarrelling between the corporatists, represented by Vouet, and the independents, represented by Le Brun, kept things lively.

Pierre Mignard (1612-95) – Succeeding Le Brun as First Painter to the King, he was instrumental in the transition from the 17C to the 18C. His little paintings imitating Raphael are known as *mignardes*. By introducing a lighter, more elegant and realistic touch in his compositions, he started the quarrel between the Poussinist and the Rubenists similar to the literary spat between Ancients and Moderns. The modern painters gave nature the place of honour (the Le Nain brothers' landscapes), rejecting the Academy's sobriety.

Between Baroque and Classic

18C French painting was characterised by a surfeit of detail embellishing the themes of religious paintings (Boucher, *Pastoral Scene*, Louvre) as well as by the humanisation of mythology. This mannerist French style launched the "Fête Galante" genre illustrated by Watteau (1684-1721) in *Pilgrimage to the Island of Cythera* (1717, Louvre). Portraitists such as La Tour *(Portrait of the Marquise de Pompadour,* 1752-55, Louvre) preferred pastel techniques. Jean-Baptiste Siméon-Chardin (1699-1779), the great master of the French School, devoted himself to still-life paintings and portraits. Boucher's delicate landscapes heralded the pre-Romantic period.

The late 18C wavered between the pre-Romantic J-H Fragonard (1732-1806) and Neoclassicism, typified by J-L David and his *Oath of the Horatii* (1784-85, Louvre).

Monumental sculptures were as numerous as in the 17C: Robert le Lorrain *(Les*

Chevaux du soleil, Hôtel de Rohan), Bouchardon (Quatre-Saisons Fountain), and Peigalle (St-Sulpice).

The 19C and 20C

Mirroring the era's political movements, painting and sculpture reacted violently to the new trends. Bright colours and fantasy came into fashion. Géricault (1791-1824) launched Romanticism: through its bold composition, dynamism and the characters' striking expressions, *Raft of the Medusa* (1819, Louvre) is in total opposition to the Classical style. Delacroix carried on in the same spirit. The official Salons were the scenes of battles between the two major trends: one advocating the superiority of drawing, the other that of colour. Ingres (1780-1867), taking his inspiration from Antiquity, lost the battle when he exhibited *The Apotheosis of Homer* at the 1827 Salon. However, the return to Academic art was successful at the 1863 Salon.

In reaction, Manet organised the 1863 Group featuring all of the painters rejected by the Salon. Fantin-Latour (1836-1904) and Manet portray everyday pleasures on their canvases, sometimes in a provocative manner in their drawings of women (*Olympia*, 1863, Orsay). Like Courbet before them, they were the precursors of Impressionism.

From Impressionism to Expressionism – The Impressionists use the precepts of Realism (works based on nature) while adding a powerful luminosity to their paintings through the use of a chromatic palette. They also relied on the art of drawing. Edgar Degas' sketches of dancers show firm strokes. Above all, they had a strong penchant for landscapes (Claude Monet, *Argenteuil Bridge*, 1834, Orsay). Cézanne (1839-1906) and Pissarro (1830-1903) blended characters and landscapes or indoor scenes (Paul Cézanne, *The Card Players*, around 1890-95, Orsay).

The success of the genre opened up new possibilities: Seurat created scientific Impressionism in which characters are placed in a subtle balance; systematic juxtaposition of primary colours and their complementary tones gives rise to Pointillism. Nature becomes a symbol

under the brush strokes of Puvis de Chavannes (1824-98). Gauguin (1848-1903) and Van Gogh (1853-90) had a different reaction to Impressionism: while not breaking off from it, their explorations were directed towards expressive intensity through the use of bright colours. The Expressionist movement was associated with a new concern over social problems prevalent at the beginning of the 20C, as illustrated by painters such as Rouault and Soutine.

From Fauvism to Cubism – The Fauvists were a new, modernist movement in the early 20C who had nothing left in common with the Realists or Symbolists. Their palette of colours and the shapes represented are often aggressive, which created a scandal at the 1905 Autumn Salon. Vlaminck, Matisse and Derain are the masters of this movement advocating freedom. They strove to free themselves of all constraints and conventions in their daily lives, living a bohemian existence in the Bateau-Lavoir in Montmartre.

Nevertheless, Matisse reintroduced the concept of rigour and constraints, with the idea that the emphasis on colour shouldn't lead to an overshadowing of form – however primitive – or composition. Picasso brought this trend to the fore with *Les Demoiselles d'Avignon* (1907). Braque applied it to landscape painting. But some preferred more creative impulses to this spirit of discipline. Modigliani, Soutine, Chagall, Zadkine and Léger settled in the La Ruche workshop in Montparnasse, where they gave free rein to their moods, reviving Expressionism. This was the golden age of the Paris School, which came to an end with World War II, when Surrealism burst upon the scene.

Sculpture – During the Second Empire and the Third Republic, Paris was gradually transformed into an open-air museum. Works by Carpeaux (Observatory Fountain) and Rude *(Marshal Ney, the Marseillaise on the Arc de Triomphe)* precede those of the great masters of the late 19C and the period between the two World Wars, including Rodin *(Balzac, Victor Hugo, Bronze Age),* Dalou (place de la Nation), Bourdelle (Palais de Tokyo, Théâtre des Champs-Élysées), Maillol (Tuileries Gardens) and Landowski (Ste-Geneviève on the Pont de la Tournelle, *Animals* at the Porte de St-Cloud).

The Art Nouveau style is epitomised by Hector Guimard's famous wrought-iron metro entrances, created around 1900. Abstract sculpture is also given its place: Calder's mobile (*see LA DÉFENSE*), Louis Leygue, and Agam (*see LA DÉFENSE*). Renewing a 19C tradition, sculptures were erected in streets and gardens: of famous people (Georges Pompidou, Jean Moulin, Arthur Rimbaud) along with Symbolist works, and sculpture-fountains (Fontaine Stravinski, by Jean Tinguely and Niki de Saint-Phalle, next to Beaubourg).

Paris in paintings

Paris began to be the subject or background in paintings at the time of the Wars of Religion. During the reigns of Henry IV and Louis XIII, it was used as a theme by Jacques Callot (1592-1635) in his engravings and by Dutch landscape painters (De Verwer, Zeeman) fascinated by the light and atmosphere on the banks of the Seine.

The urban landscape of Paris really came into its own with the Impressionists, who preferred painting outdoors rather than in a studio.

Corot painted the Paris quaysides and Ville d'Avray a few miles away. Lépine, Monet *(St-Germain-l'Auxerrois, Gare St-Lazare)*, Renoir *(Moulin de la Galette, Moulin Rouge)*, Sisley *(Île St-Louis)* and Pissarro *(The Pont Neuf)* depict light effects in the capital at all hours and in all seasons. Paris is also an important focus in works by Seurat *(The Eiffel Tower)*, Gauguin, Cézanne and Van Gogh *(Montmartre scenes)*. Toulouse-Lautrec portrays a totally different view of Paris life in his witty, intimate sketches of cabaret artists. Among the Nabi artists, Vuillard captures the peace of Paris squares and gardens in a more poetic vein. In the early 20C, Paris figured prominently in the work of Fauve painters Marquet and Utrillo with their scenes of unfashionable neighbourhoods. Views of the capital by the naïve painters are sensitive, imaginative and highly colourful.

Moulin Rouge, Boulevard de Clichy, Paris (c. 1890) by Eugène Atget

akg-images

Among more modern artists, Balthus (Paris between the wars), Yves Brayer and Bernard Buffet have cast Paris in a new light.

PHOTOGRAPHY

In 1825, French inventor **Nicéphore Niépce** became the first to produce a permanent photograph – an image produced on a polished pewter plate. Not long after this, Niépce teamed up with **Louis Daguerre** (born near Paris) and together they refined the process. However, the breakthrough in photography came when **William Henry Fox Talbot** in England invented the negative/positive photographic process in the 1830s, which led to the modern understanding of photography.

Eugène Atget, one of the fathers of modern photography, immortalised street scenes and tradesmen in a Paris that no longer exists (cabbies, street singers, rag merchants, lace sellers).

In more recent times, **Edouard Boubat**, **izis, Brassaï** (known as the "Toulouse-Lautrec of the camera lens") and **Marcel Bovis** captured the magic of Paris at night; **Jacques-Henri Lartigue** recorded the Roaring Twenties; **Cartier-Bresson**, the archetypal globe-trotter and founding member of the Magnum agency, caught views of Paris that resemble watercolours *(Île de la Cité)*; **Willy Ronis** shot scenes of Belleville-

J. Damase/MICHELIN

Les Frères Lumière

Ménilmontant, now changed beyond all recognition.

Robert Doisneau (1912-94) – One of the great photographers of Paris, he specialised in humorous shots of ordinary people filled with depth and poetry: children playing, concierges, scenes of cafés and markets. *The Kiss,* taken in front of the Hôtel de Ville in 1950, remains his most famous work.

FILM

In the late 19C and early 20C, Paris encourages the development of the cinema by helping some of its pioneers, who were inspired by photography and theatre.

1892 – Émile Reynaud opens the Optical Theatre in the Musée Grévin, holding a total of 12 000 showings attended by 500 000 spectators.

28 December 1895 – The Lumière Brothers hold their first public showing of the cinematograph on boulevard des Capucines.

1896-1897 – Georges Meliès (1861-1938) invents double exposure and presents his first films with scripts.

1898 – Charles Pathé creates his international firm and studios. First newsreels (Pathé-Journal).

1900 – The *cinéorama* (a 100m/110yd circular screen invented by Grimoin-Sanson) was presented at the Paris Exposition.

The Lumière Brothers and the cinematograph – In February 1895, Auguste (1862-1954) and Louis (1864-1948) Lumière registered the patent for the cinematograph, a machine that projects animated scenes at a speed of 18 frames per second. Their *Sortie des usines Lumière* (shot in 1894) was a success, and showings were held in the Salon Indien at the Grand-Café, boulevard des Capucines.

Léon Gaumont (1863-1946) – Pursuing the work begun by the Lumière Brothers with his *chronophone*, he added synchronised sound to films.

Early 20C – Charles Pathé created his studios on rue Francœur and turned the cinema into an industry.

POSTERS

Paris was the major source and beneficiary of this new art between painting and photography.

The French masters – Their goal was to depict the joys and sorrows of everyday life, and to combine Parisians' social and cultural demands. **Gavarni** (1804-66) evokes the seedier side of Paris in his black-and-white posters of street-walkers and poor neighbourhoods. He created posters based on *Selected Works* by Balzac, who also inspired Grandville's *Petites misères de la vie humaine*.

Chéret revolutionised the art of poster-designing in the second half of the 19C with his inflated, or Rococo, style and lively figures in colour.

Toulouse-Lautrec (1864-1901) – As a lithographer, he adopted the principles of his teachers Chéret and Bonnat, but with a more cutting style. He portrayed the poverty in certain areas of Paris and frequented cabarets, where he created some of his greatest pieces such as *La Goulue at the Moulin Rouge*. His illustrations – verging on caricature and the grotesque – stirred up many a scandal.

Alphonse Mucha – Arriving in Paris in 1887 from his native Prague, Mucha lived in the city during a time of cultural blossoming. While Toulouse-Lautrec sought to bring out the truth of his subjects, Mucha created figures surrounded by great decorative verve and an abundance of motifs. Like Lautrec, he made poster designs for theatre openings, notably for Sarah Bernhardt.

Literature

The story of Paris as a literary capital began with the creation of its university, while the 18C saw the rise of the city's intellectual and cultural prestige.
The history of French literature is closely linked with that of Paris.
Many writers who were born in the city have celebrated it in their books, giving Paris a special place in literature.

MIDDLE AGES AND RENAISSANCE

12C-13C – The first Paris university opened its doors. It was the only university in northern France, and gave a boost to intellectual life. The Parisian dialect was adopted by the Court as its official language, putting Paris on the literary map.

15C-16C – Writers, and the heroes of their stories, "go up"' to Paris, the former in order to write, the latter to study. Low life on the streets was portrayed in epic poems and mystery plays, whereas Rutebœuf and Villon wrote poems about individuals and everyday life. Although Rabelais criticised the Parisian character, he had Gargantua and Pantagruel attend the Sorbonne; and he himself lived and died in the Marais (d. 1553).

1530 – The Collège de France was founded by François I and Guillaume Budé.
As the city grows into its role as capital, many writers choose to make it their second home, including Montaigne, Ronsard and the Pleiade poets, as well as Agrippa d'Aubigné, who witnessed the religious conflicts that overtook Paris and the rest of France in the late 16C.

THE 17C

As the city was embellished by Henri IV and Louis XIII, and agitated by the Fronde during Louis XIV's minority, writers and noted wits of the period developed the famous literary salons, first at the Hôtel de Rambouillet (17C) and later on in the homes of the Marquise de Lambert, Madame du Deffand, and Madame Geoffrin (18C).
After its role as a centre of humanism in the 16C, Paris promoted classicism in the 17C with the assertion of absolute monarchy. Writers during the reign of Louis XIV, such as Molière, went beyond prior conventions and were allowed to criticise society.

1634-1635 – The Académie Française was founded by Richelieu. Paris became the centre of French literature. Contrary to the salons, where open discussion was encouraged, the Académie sought to standardise the French language and exert a restraining influence on all branches of literature.

1680 – The Comédie Française was created under the king's patronage.

18C – REVIVAL OF THE LITERARY SALONS

In the 18C, Louis XV and Louis XVI showed little interest in literature. Society resorted to philosophy salons and cafés (Procope, La Régence), where new ideas developed and the fates of French writers were decided.

1710-1780 – Prominent authors such as Marivaux and Montesquieu attended the salons, where Voltaire and Diderot also congregated.

Marivaux and Beaumarchais *(Barber of Seville and Marriage of Figaro)* tinged their light comedies about Paris society and lifestyle with irony, whereas Jean-Jacques Rousseau (1712-78), a precursor of Romanticism who was born in the provinces, expressed disdain for the place so full of "noise, smoke and mud!" Others concerned with the dichotomy between ethics and society include the Abbé Prévost *(Manon Lescaut)*, Restif de la Bretonne *(Nights of Paris)* the Marquis de Sade and Choderlos de Laclos *(Dangerous Liaisons)*. It is Voltaire (1694-1778), master social critic, historian, novelist *(Candide)*, essayist, letter-writer, diarist, dramatist and Humanist philosopher, who perhaps epitomises the best of 18C writing in Paris: ironic and witty with a light touch and perfect turn of phrase. During the Age of Enlightenment, Paris wielded a great deal of influence in international intellectual circles with emissaries such as d'Alembert and Diderot, who secured subscriptions to their 28-volume Encyclopedia from Catherine the Great of Russia among others.

THE 19C AND 20C

After the French Revolution, literature was no longer restricted to a small section of society. Writers were active in the social and political debates of their times through its major literary trends: Realism, Romanticism, Symbolism, Naturalism and Surrealism.
Paris has a double image, portrayed at times as rich and prestigious, and at others as a more popular city full of vices. Heroes in novels head for Paris, leaving behind their native provinces. In *Les Illusions perdues,* Lucien de Rubempré dies there. In *Les Misérables* and *La Comédie humaine,* by Hugo and Balzac respectively, the city is portrayed as a character with a personality of its own subject to moods and illness. Both Julien Sorel, the hero of Stendhal's *Le Rouge et le Noir,* and Léon the notary in Flaubert's *Madame Bovary* run away from Paris society; and some of Zola's novels depict certain circles and areas of the city as a kind of prison.
Parisian writers such as Dumas the Younger, Musset, the song-writer Béranger, Eugène Sue *(Mysteries of Paris)*, Murger *(Scenes of Bohemian Life)* and Nerval vacillate between the two images of the city. Contrasts in humour and reflections on life's contradictions are explored, against the back-drop of Haussmann's upheavals, in verse by Baudelaire, the Parnassian and Symbolist poets, and in the emerging social-history, realist novel by Émile Zola *(Les Rougon-Macquart)*.
Old Montmartre lives on in the **songs** of Bruant (1851-1925), the novels of Carco (1886-1958) and Marcel Aymé (1902-67), Montparnasse in the poems of Max Jacob (1876-1944) and Léon-Paul Fargue (1876-1947); still other writers and poets such as Colette and Cocteau, Simenon, Montherlant, Louise de Vilmorin, Aragon, Prévert, Sacha Guitry, Eluard, Sartre, Simone de Beauvoir and Beckett have celebrated Paris-as-muse in their many works.

Playwrights' reputations, like novelists', are made and broken in Paris. Vaudeville, the soul of boulevard theatre, was the 19C heir to the farces featuring dialogue and songs that were performed at the St-Germain and St-Laurent fairs in earlier days, as well as the bawdy tableaux and pastiches of scenes from well-known plays. Talented playwrights also wrote serious vaudeville. Light opera and revues emerged during the Second Empire, whereas dramas were another outgrowth of boulevard theatre.

Music

Paris is rather like a grand orchestra where enchanting music is played. It has been both the theme and setting for a host of musical compositions, and its streets are often filled with the sounds of this art with its long-standing tradition in the city.

IN THE MIDDLE AGES

Late 12C – A school of polyphony was established at Notre-Dame character-ised by its refined expression of the deep religious faith of the period.

13C-14C – Musical works such as Mach-aut's Masses (c. 1300-77) and motets by contrapuntist Dufay are composed of several parts.

Under François I – A national musical printing works was created, illustrated by narrative ballads written by Janequin *(Les Cris de Paris)*. Renaissance-style mad-rigals and courtly songs accompanied on the lute become popular.

1571 – The poet Baïf founded the Acad-emy for Music and Poetry in an attempt to revive Classical verse-form and poetic rhyme.

THE RENAISSANCE

"That most noble and gallant art" devel-oped naturally at the Royal Court, first at the Louvre and later at Versailles, where sovereigns, their consorts and companions disported themselves in masques, ballets, allegorical dances, recitals, opera and comedy.
The first Parisian songs were published.

THE 17C: A MUSICAL HIGH POINT

Music, like literature, flourished under the renewed interest of the Court. Italian opera was welcomed, thanks to Mazarin, and major foreign operas such as the *Marriage of Orpheus and Eurydice* (1643) were staged in Paris.

Lully and lyric opera – Florentine com-poser **Jean-Baptiste Lully** (1632-87)

settled in Paris, and Louis XIV appointed him to direct music first at Court, then at the Académie Royale de Musique (1672). He created operas and ballets *(Ballet des Bienvenus, Ballet de la nais-sance de Vénus)*, dominating every genre. In 1661, he collaborated with Molière, developing a new genre, *ballet-comédie (Les Fâcheux, Le Sicilien, Le Bourgeois gen-tilhomme)*. Religious music was also part of his repertory *(Te Deum, 1677)*, and he attained new heights in choral music at Notre-Dame (with *Campra*) and Notre-Dame-des-Victoires.

NEW OPERATIC FORMS IN THE 18C

After the prestigious operas of the 17C, music was made more accessible to the general public in the comic operas given at the St-Germain and St-Laurent fairs. However, Jean-Philippe Rameau (1683-1764) carried on in the tradition of Lully, while accentuating the orchestra's role. His opera-ballets *(Les Indes galantes)*, lyric tragedies *(Castor et Pollux, Darda-nus)* and comedies *(Platée)* gave birth to the French style. Rameau moved away from the Italian tradition without renouncing it, prompting the so-called War of the Buffoons.

The Musical Wars – The War of the Buf-foons was a quarrel over French and Ital-ian opera in which Rameau was pitted against the Encyclopaedists. The main protagonists in the quarrel were Diderot *(Le Neveu de Rameau)* and J-J Rousseau *(Le Devin de village, Lettre sur la musique française)*, who enumerated all of the flaws in French music, which Lully still dominated.
The second war developed over the new genre, comic opera, which grew out of the Parisian fairs and was launched by Gluck and Puccini, two foreigners who had settled in Paris. Gluck stressed dra-matic intensity in his operas, reformed the opera by reducing the action to three acts and replacing the harpsi-chord by the flute. His works *(Orphée et Eurydice, Iphigénie en Aulide and Alceste)* transformed the principles of French tragic opera.

1795 – The Conservatoire de Musique de Paris was founded in 1795 and directed successively by Cherubini, Auber and Ambroise Thomas.

THE 19C

1801 – The Théâtre de Feydeau and the Théâtre de Favart joined to form the Opéra-Comique de Paris.
Music in Paris was associated with the political and military events that were taking place there: the Revolution produced many popular songs, the most famous being *La Carmagnole,* a satirical song from 1792. In the 19C the city became the international capital of music, attracting the greatest masters of the century.

1830 – Berlioz composed the *Symphonie Fantastique,* which still resounds as the manifesto-opus of the young Romantic school.

1866 – Premiere in Paris of Offenbach's *La Vie parisienne.*
From **1870**, symphonic composition and opera evolved through the work of Bizet, St-Saëns, Charpentier and Dukas, Parisians by birth or adoption. France was the leader in ballet music, which draws inspiration from history and mythology.

Debussy and **Ravel** were the two major French impressionist composers at the end of the 19C. Refusing all foreign influence (including Wagner) in symphonic music, they gave it a national character. Debussy and Ravel collaborated with Diaghilev's Ballets Russes.

1894 – The Schola Cantorum was founded by Bordes, Guilmant and d'Indy.

1885-1899 – The Chat Noir was the *chansonniers'* favourite cabaret.

1899 – Premiere of *La Prise de Troie* by Berlioz at the Opéra.

The Garde républicaine – A description of Parisian musical life wouldn't be complete without mentioning the Garde Républicaine, formed in 1871. Originat-ing with the Garde de Paris, created in 1848, it is composed of 127 musicians. Its military marches (Sambre et Meuse, Marche lorraine, La Fille du régiment) are hymns to French victories.

THE 20C

Cabarets – These popular venues were all the rage at the beginning of the century. The *chansonniers* (singers) performing in Montmartre's cabarets are portrayed by Toulouse-Lautrec in his famous posters and lithographs.

1902 – Premiere of *Pelléas et Mélisande* by Debussy at the Opéra-Comique.

1903 – The Lapin Agile opens.

The Group of Six – Founded by Auric, Durey, Honegger, Milhaud, Poulenc and Tailleferre in 1920, the group created a new musical aesthetic rejecting Romanticism and Impressionism.

1936 – Writers such as Prévert, Aragon and Apollinaire flocked to the Bœuf sur le Toit, where their works were set to music.

During World War I, Nadia Boulanger led a new Parisian movement known as the Neoclassical School, drawing inspiration from Stravinsky and Latin music. After 1920 Paris continued to nurture new forms of musical expression. From the *ondes martenot* to the Jeune-France Group and its humanist music, Schaeffer and his concrete sounds, Henry, Boulez, Xénakis and Messiaen, each one made an important individual contribution to the musical scene. As major foreign musicians continued to arrive in Paris, the Paris School was created in 1951. The piano sonatas, ballet *(Le Loup,* 1953), symphonies and orchestral pieces by composer Henri Dutilleux (b. 1916) are among the greatest works from the second half of the 20C.

National orchestras – Paris possesses some internationally renowned orchestras. The Orchestre National de France, Orchestre Philharmonique de Radio-France and its Maîtrise (Choir School created in 1981), the Ensemble Inter-contemporain, the Orchestre de Paris and Université de Paris-Sorbonne choirs and the Petits Chanteurs de la Croix de Bois interpret major works.

Parisian organists – Marie-Madeleine Duruflé-Chevalier, Olivier Latry, Philippe Lefebvre, Jean-Pierre Leguay and Riccardo Miravet; each of these organ players – many of whom are known throughout the world – is connected to a particular church. Organ music is also featured at the Festival d'Art Sacré in the autumn.

Major venues for music – While the Opéra Garnier (inaugurated in 1875) continues to be a highly prestigious opera house (home of the Paris Ballet), the Opéra Bastille (designed by Carlos Ott) has become the main venue for staging operas since it opened in 1989.

The **Théâtre des Champs-Élysées** has maintained its spirit of musical innovation since it was founded in 1913 by Gabriel Astruc. The Théâtre du Châtelet was a mecca for light opera fans from 1928 to 1970. Renamed the **Théâtre musical de Paris** in 1980, it presents prestigious concerts and opera productions.

The **Cité de la Musique** (Parc de la Villette), designed by Christian de Portzamparc, includes the Conservatoire National Supérieur de Musique, the Musée de la Musique, and the Institut National de Pédagogie Musicale, as well as a concert hall. **IRCAM** (Institute of Acoustic and Musical Research) is a department of the Centre Pompidou devoted to experimental music. Thanks to the fervour of composer Pierre Boulez and to sophisticated technology using computers, electronic laboratories and sound processors, IRCAM has won international acclaim.

THE CITY TODAY

Paris is the centre of France's political, administrative, economic and cultural life. In recent years, the city has attracted many multinational corporations and has become an important international business centre. In 1960, a century after Baron Haussmann's large-scale urban restructuring, steps were taken to resolve some of the capital's congestion problems; but much remains to be done.

Local government

Since March 1977, the **Mairie de Paris** has had an elected mayor, chosen by the 163 councillors who make up the municipal council; municipal elections are held every six years. With the exception of the police force, headed by a *préfet*, the mayor has the same status and powers of mayors of other municipalities.

The Paris municipal authority works closely with the town halls of the 20 *arrondissements*, which are the main units of local government. Paris being both a *commune* and a *département*, its Council sits as a municipal authority and a general, or departmental, council.

The city's coat of arms features the boat motif from the armorial bearings of the watermen's guild whose members were appointed by Louis IX in 1260 to administer the township. In the 16C a motto was added: *Fluctuat nec mergitur* (though buffeted by the waves, she never sinks).

The **Île-de-France** region is composed of eight *départements* (Paris, Seine-et-Marne, Yvelines, Essonne, Hauts-de-Seine, Seine-St-Denis, Val-de-Marne and Val-d'Oise), each with its own prefecture, covering a total area of 12 011sq km/ 4 637sq mi with a total population of 10 073 053 (Paris: 105sq km/40sq mi; 2 176 243).

METAMORPHOSIS

Paris' historic, architectural and archaeological treasures have been safeguarded by the enlightened policy of André Malraux and his successors, who instituted

S. Sauvignier/MICHELIN

Paris' coat-of-arms

lette, André Citroën) have been created, old parks and gardens remodelled…

Population

With over two million inhabitants, Paris is one of the most densely populated cities in the world. Although the inner-city population is declining slightly, figures show a constant influx from the provinces and abroad. Some minority groups have adopted particular neighbourhoods over the years: Russians in Montparnasse, Spaniards in Passy, North Africans in Clignancourt, La Villette, Aubervilliers, Asians in Belleville, the 13th *arrondissement* etc.

But whatever their background, true Parisians are easy to pick out among the cosmopolitan crowd: hurried, tense, protesting, frivolous, quick-witted, ever ready to poke fun or play on words.

Neighbourhoods

Each neighbourhood of Paris is a bit like a village unto itself. One of the joys of wandering around the city is that the transition from one district to the next is seamless, so that you are always in an interesting place. Here are some of the neighbourhoods *(arrondissements)* you are likely to want to visit.

PARIS NEIGHBOURHOODS

Some neighbourhoods have retained their traditional association with a medieval trade or guild, thus preserving some of the atmosphere of past centuries: seed merchants on quai de la Mégisserie; publishing and bookshops in the Odéon area; cabinet-makers in rue du Faubourg-St-Antoine; antique dealers on rue Bonaparte and rue La Boëtie; art galleries on avenue Matignon and rue du Faubourg-St-Honoré; *haute couture* houses on rue du Faubourg-St-Honoré, avenue Montaigne and rue Françoiser; luxury goods in the Opéra area; stringed instrument makers on rue de Rome; porcelain, crystal and glassware on rue de Paradis; jewellers on rue de la Paix and place Vendôme. Meanwhile

a programme of cleaning, restoration, and revitalisation of whole areas such as the Marais and preservation of archaeological finds. Meanwhile, structural engineers and planners wrestle with today's problems – traffic and transport (ring road, motorway, RER), supply (Rungis, Garonor), cultural centres (G Pompidou Centre), sports facilities (Bercy), commercial property development (La Défense, Front de Seine, Maine-Montparnasse) and urban renewal (place d'Italie, Belleville, Bercy); the emphasis being on the preservation and restoration of historic heritage.

Major cultural and architectural achievements include the Cité des Sciences et de l'Industrie and the Cité de la Musique at La Villette, the Musée d'Orsay, the Grand Louvre, the Opéra-Bastille, the Grande Arche at La Défense and the Bibliothèque Nationale at Tolbiac.

The transfer of the wholesale markets from Les Halles to Rungis, the division of the University into 13 autonomous parts, the decentralisation of the Higher Schools of learning, have all helped to relieve congestion in the city centre. Modern hospitals, both public and private, have been built. Green spaces (La Vil-

government offices line rue de Grenelle; financial institutions are located in the Bourse, Opéra, Champs-Élysées, and La Défense areas; students gather around their university buildings in the Latin Quarter. All of these blend in with the schools, workshops, warehouses and small shops which, along with the many large firms, make up Paris' infinitely varied economy.

PALAIS-ROYAL – ST-ROCH
1st arrondissement

The **Palais-Royal** gardens are among the finest in Paris. Treat yourself to an ice cream in the *Muscade* tearoom at the far end, or to window-shopping along the gallery for lead soldiers, medals or antiques. Note the old-fashioned feel. Pause by the sophisticated window display in the Salons du Palais-Royal Shiseido, the old bookshops, or the delightful little music box shop in the Beaujolais arcade on the corner with one of the passages leading onto the street of the same name. Saunter along the street from **place des Victoires**, a mecca of high fashion *(Kenzo)*, towards **avenue de l'Opéra** past the countless little restaurants, costume-jewellery or interior design shops, and a Japanese delicatessen *(Kioko)*.

BEAUBOURG – LES HALLES
1st-2nd-3rd arrondissements

Much of the erstwhile atmosphere of the "belly of Paris" went when Baltard's pavilions were removed. The Forum des Halles tunnels its way below ground like a rabbit-warren between the rotunda of the Bourse du Commerce and the brightly coloured tubes of the Centre Georges-Pompidou. Renovation of the area has opened up the space around the church of **St Eustache**, and the Stravinski Fountain brightens up the square outside St-Merri church.

The modern neighbourhood continues to bustle with people of all kinds converging upon the shops, sometimes from the provinces, drawing buskers, mime artists, and eccentrics of all kinds. During the day, the main crowds collect in the Forum, thronging **place des Innocents**, rue Pierre-Lescot and the narrow streets lying perpendicular to it (rue des Prêcheurs, rue de la Grande-Truanderie), which are lined with shops selling jewellery, postcards and posters, shoes and clothing. At night, the crowds move towards the bars and clubs of the Rue des Lombards and Rue Quincampoix.

LE MARAIS *4th arrondissement*

This old district was saved from destruction by the novelist and Arts Minister André Malraux. It accommodates both a well-established Jewish community in **rue des Rosiers** and a younger gay set around Rue Ste-Croix-de-la-Bretonnerie. Trendy bars and coffee shops have flourished and off-beat fashion designers operate from around **rue des Francs-Bourgeois**. More traditional shops survive by the rue St-Antoine. The delight-

Forum des Halles

ful **place du Marché-Ste-Catherine** is surrounded by cafés. At the end of the gardens in the Hôtel de Sully, a doorway leads to the **place des Vosges**, where arcades shelter antique shops and art galleries. The grassy square in the centre is a popular place to relax on nice days. The north end of the Marais is quieter, with a large number of museums and art galleries. Further north still is the **Temple** district, the mecca for tailored leather and wholesale jewellery shops.

ÎLE SAINT-LOUIS
4th arrondissement

Its aristocratic 17C residences provided inspiration for Baudelaire who stayed in the Hôtel Lauzun. A stroll along the river banks or quaysides on the island is one of the most romantic walks in Paris.

LATIN QUARTER
5th arrondissement

The student quarter boasts many cinemas, bars, cafés and restaurants drawing people from all walks of life. The **Boul' Mich** (boulevard St-Michel) is a colourful succession of boutiques, cafés, sandwich and kebab bars, of pizzerias and Moroccan restaurants. Crowds loiter around the Fontaine St-Michel. **Rue St-André-des-Arts**, now rather touristy, leads to the Odéon district with its many cinemas (go through the picturesque **Cour du Commerce St-André**). The statue of Danton is another traditional meeting place.

The narrow pedestrianised streets on the east side of boulevard St-Michel, around rue de la Huchette, are packed with gaudy Greek restaurants catering almost exclusively to tourists.

A quieter atmosphere pervades place Maubert and **rue Dante** where all the specialist strip-cartoon dealers have their shops. Back towards the Panthéon, rue de la Montagne-Ste-Geneviève and rue Laplace are popular student haunts. The historic **place de la Contrescarpe** leads to the **rue Mouffetard** (*la Mouffe*), one of the most charming market streets in Paris.

SAINT-GERMAIN-DES-PRÉS
6th arrondissement

The oldest bell-tower in Paris, across the square from the terrace of the *Deux Magots,* keeps watch over a district that ceaselessly hums with activity. The intellectual ferment of the golden days of the 1950s and the Existentialists may have gone, but the charm lives on. The ambience is sustained by famous cafés and brasseries on **boulevard St-Germain**, jazz clubs in rue St-Benoît and rue Jacob, pubs in rue Guisarde, rue Bernard-Palissy and rue des Canettes, and the late-opening bookshops peppered about. Upscale designer shops, antique and art galleries lend a decidedly Left Bank elegance to the old streets, picturesque crossroads and tiny squares such as **place de Fürstemberg**. The main focus of the bustle is **carrefour de Buci** with its street market, boutiques and fine traiteurs or gourmet delicatessens.

CHAMPS-ÉLYSÉES
8th arrondissement

A facelift in the late 1990s has reinstated the world-famous avenue's prestige. Stroll the high street shops (open until midnight), people-watch from a café terrace, or see a newly released film. By day as by night, tourists mingle with visitors to the capital to dine out in a neighbouring street, enjoy one of the spectacular revues at the Lido or the Crazy Horse or while away the hours until dawn at a famous club.

GRANDS BOULEVARDS AND OPÉRA *2nd-9th-10th arrondissements*

This district basked in fame from the 19C through to the 1950s, providing prestigious locations for the headquarters of major banks (CLC, BNP, Société Générale). The boulevards are busy throughout the day, drawing shoppers to **Printemps** and **Galeries Lafayette,** who might break for a drink on the terrace of the famous **Café de la Paix** before going on to one of the neighbourhood's many cinemas, including the **Grand Rex** and the **Max Linder.** At the end of the day, people meet in one of the brasseries for a bite maybe before a performance at the **Opéra**, the **Folies-Bergère** or **Olympia** to hear a favourite singer.

BASTILLE AND FAUBOURG-ST-ANTOINE *11th arrondissement*

The **Opéra Bastille** has brought lustre to a district that had become rather rundown over the years, though never lacking in character. Furniture and clothes shops abound alongside contemporary art galleries and artists' studios in the labyrinth of little streets. The Bastoche is again a lively and popular neighbourhood. With its numerous brasseries, in particular **Bofinger** which was established in 1864, place de la Bastille has become a central meeting place between the Marais on one side, and rue de Charonne, rue de la Roquette, rue de Lappe, rue St-Sabin and rue Keller on the other, where restaurants, cafés, beer cellars, wine bars and dance halls proliferate. Tequila, claret or Valdepenas may be quaffed with *tapas* in a Spanish-style bar, or look for Japanese, North African, American and Thai speciality restaurants alongside French mainstays.

GOBELINS – BUTTE-AUX-CAILLES – TOLBIAC
13th arrondissement

Like all the *buttes* or hills in Paris, Butte-aux-Cailles has its own distinctive character. The streets (rue Samson, rue des Cinq-Diamants, rue de la Butte-aux-Cailles) have the comfortable feel of a place where people still greet neighbours and shopkeepers, even though the high-rise developments at Glacière and in Chinatown beyond the place d'Italie have multiplied the population density.

MONTPARNASSE – PORT-ROYAL – ALÉSIA
14th arrondissement

At the turn of the 20C, this rural district was favoured by the artists of the Paris School; between the two World Wars its bars were frequented by the Lost Generation of American writers; today,

it is dominated by the huge **Maine-Montparnasse complex** and its skyscraper.

The streets of Montparnasse are busy day-in-day-out. Rue de Rennes is an artery for traffic and shoppers between St-Germain and Montparnasse; rue de la Gaîté is lined with theatres and peep shows; rue Montparnasse and rue d'Odessa accommodate endless *crêperies* selling pancakes to travellers coming through the Gare Montparnasse, the terminus for trains arriving from western France and Brittany. Big bins of shellfish on ice stand outside brasseries and brightly lit posters attract film-lovers to the cinemas. The quieter part of the neighbourhood is beyond the cemetery along rue Daguerre, rue Didot, rue Raymond-Losserand and avenue du Général-Leclerc.

BATIGNOLLES-TERNES
17th arrondissement

The village of Les Batignolles, which was made famous by Verlaine and Mallarmé, marks the boundary between the working-class commercial neighbourhood of the 17th *arrondissement* and its residential sector. Shops line rue des Dames and rue des Batignolles off the delightful **place du Docteur-Lobligeois** dominated by the distinctive white columns of the church of Ste-Marie-des-Batignolles. Further east, beyond avenue de Clichy is the **Cité des Fleurs** (rue Cardinet), lined with some of the finest townhouses in Paris.

West of Les Batignolles, on the other side of the railway tracks, the main attractions are the chic shops in rue Lévis and rue de Tocqueville, place and avenue des Ternes and rue Poncelet.

MONTMARTRE-PIGALLE
18th arrondissement

In the late 19C, shortly after the village was incorporated into the city of Paris, a journalist wrote: "The local bars have closed, the lilac trees have been cut, the hedges replaced by stone walls and the gardens divided into building plots. However, of all the suburbs, Montmartre has its own special brand of charm, a

P. Gajic/MICHELIN

Flea market by the Abbesses Metro station

varied and complex charm that is a combination of good and bad things". Many faces of Montmartre still exist today, glimpsed occasionally in what remains of the old provincial village.

Between **place Clichy**, one of the most crowded squares in the capital with its large number of restaurants and cinemas clustered around the unmistakable *Wepler* brasserie, and **place Pigalle**, the streets are populated with concert venues, theatres, nightclubs and sex shops. Along boulevard de Rochechouart you will find the forever-crowded Tati discount store and the noisy, cosmopolitan Barbès district.

At the foot of square Willette, the extraordinarily busy **St-Pierre Market** provides an opportunity to find fabrics and clothing at rock-bottom prices. On the other side of the boulevard, the **Goutte-d'Or** district proffers Arab and African fabrics, wholesale food shops, hardware, luggage and jewellery shops.

BELLEVILLE-MÉNILMONTANT
20th arrondissement

Like Montmartre, the Belleville and Ménilmontant neighbourhoods nestling on a hillside were annexed by Paris during the 19C. The urban redevelopment launched by Haussmann brought large numbers of working-class people to the area; these have been followed by thousands of immigrant Jews, Russians,

Poles, North Africans, Turks, Yugoslavs, Pakistanis, and lately Asians. Most of the exotic restaurants are concentrated in **rue de Belleville**.

The district is slowly being rebuilt in concrete, with new buildings standing alongside the old houses of rue Ramponneau, rue des Envierges and rue des Cascades. To the north lies the romantic, English-style **Parc des Buttes-Chaumont**, which owes its steep hills to the former gypsum quarries on which it stands.

Cultural Diversity

Paris is a cosmopolitan city with a large number of communities from outside France: Caribbean, African, Slav, Far-Eastern, Latin-American, Jewish, Indian, Pakistani... It is a pleasure to eat an exotic meal, to search for ethnic music recordings or find fabrics from the far corners of the world.

AFRO-CARIBBEAN COMMUNITY

African and West Indian communities (18th arrondissement or along the north side of the Paris ring road) have given us **zouk** music (a combination of African and West Indian musical rhythms), which evolved during the early 1980s. Radio Nova (on 101.5 FM) fashioned the concept of "world sono" which finally

Raï

This rhythmic music from the working-class districts of Oran combines *fado* with *blues*. The singer-poets are all **cheb** (i.e. young people) such as Cheb Khaled, the undisputed King of Raï, Cheb Kader, or Cheb Mami.

took off under the English name of **World Music**.

Books and Music – L'Harmattan at *16 rue des Écoles (5th arr)* and **Présence africaine** at *25 bis rue des Écoles (5th arr)*; Ⓜ*Maubert-Mutualité, Cardinal-Lemoine (5th arr)*. For tropical music, the **FNAC Forum** has a broader selection than other FNAC stores.

Art – Musée du Quai Branly at *37 Quai Branly (7th arr)*; Ⓜ*Pont Alma*. Permanent collection and contemporary exhibitions. The **Musée Dapper**, at *50 avenue Victor-Hugo (16th arr)*; Ⓜ*Victor-Hugo*, is a tiny, intimate museum that organises biannual exhibitions of exquisite African artefacts, painting, textiles, carvings… accompanied by excellent catalogues. Dealers specialising in African artefacts are grouped around Bastille (rue Keller) and St-Germain-des-Prés, including: **Argiles** *16 rue Guénégaud (6th arr)*; **Galerie de Monbrisson** *2 rue des Beaux-Arts (6th arr)*; **Mazarine** *52 rue Mazarine (6th arr)*. For printed fabrics sold by weight or by the yard, try **Chez Toto** *50 rue Polonceau (18th arr)* and other locations around town; the prices can't be beatEN.

Special shops – Izrael *30 rue François-Miron (4th arr)* is perhaps the best-known exotic grocery store in Paris and it is stacked high with goods, like Ali Baba's cave; **Marché Dejean** *rue Dejean,* between rue des Poissonniers and rue du Poulet *(18th arr).* sells fish, meat and fresh or ready-prepared African specialities sold by women from their market stalls – Saturday mornings only; **Spécialités antillaises** *14-16 boulevard de Belleville (20th arr)* has all the ingredients you need to make a fine Caribbean meal.

NORTH AFRICAN AND MIDDLE EASTERN COMMUNITY

Many writers and journalists have made Paris their home, keeping abreast of both their indigenous culture and that of their adopted land: Tahar Ben Jelloun, the comedian Smaïn, the singer Cheb Khaled, and dramatists Moussa Lebkiri or Fatima Gallaire are all an integral part of the Parisian cultural scene.

The metro line linking Nation to Porte Dauphine (no 2) crosses several important concentrations of Mediterranean culture: **Barbès** and **Goutte d'Or** *(18th arr)*, **Belleville** *(19th and 20th arr)*. The **Strasbourg-St-Denis** district between rue de Hauteville and passage Brady is predominantly Turkish, Indian and Pakistani.

La Grande Mosquée – *1-2 place du Puits-de-l'Ermite (5th arr)*; Ⓜ*Jussieu*, has been used for countless films. Mint tea is served in the Moorish café annex (©*see JUSSIEU)*; the traditional baths are open on alternate days for men and women.

Art and culture – The **Institut du Monde arabe** *(1 rue des Fossés-St-Bernard, 5th arr*; Ⓜ*Jussieu)* at the edge of the Latin Quarter, has a particularly useful library and reference section; other facilities include interesting temporary exhibitions, and an expensive roof-terrace restaurant with an excellent view.

Books and theatre – Avicenne *(25 rue de Jussieu, 5th arr)*, is the best Arabic bookshop. For contemporary theatre from North Africa and the Middle East, check the programmes of the **Théâtre du Renard** *(rue du Renard, 4th arr)*, **Théâtre de l'Arcane** *(168 rue St-Maur, 11th arr)* and **Théâtre du Lierre** *(22 rue du Chevaleret, 13th arr).*

Markets – Marché d'Aligre on *place de l'Aligre* (largest of all the Arab markets; Tuesday–Sunday); **Marché de Belleville** (Tuesday and Friday mornings); **Marché de Barbès** (Wednesday and Saturday).

JEWISH COMMUNITY

Historically, the Jewish quarter was the **Marais** *(4th arr)*, a community that was decimated during the German Occupation but whose numbers have swelled again with the arrival of North African immigrants; these have settled in the **Sentier** *(2nd arr)* and **Belleville** *(19th arr)*.

Synagogues – Liberal Synagogue, *24 rue Copernic 16th arr*, ☎01 47 04 37 27. Synagogue La Victoire, *44 rue de la Victoire 9th arr*, ☎01 42 85 71 09 or *17 rue St-Georges 9th arr*, ☎01 40 82 26 26.

History and culture – The most significant commemorative monuments are the **Shoah Mémorial** *(rue G.-L'Asnier, 4th arr)* and, in the Père-Lachaise Cemetery, the **Monument à la mémoire des déportés de Buna, Monowitz, Auschwitz III** by Tim.
The **Musée d'Art et d'Histoire du Judaïsme** *(71 rue du Temple, 3rd arr)* is in the Hôtel St-Aignan in the Marais. The collection centres around North African religious articles, models and casts and includes paintings by Chagall, Lipschitz, Mané-Katz and Benn.

Pastries – Kosher and other speciality shops and restaurants abound on rue des Rosiers, in the Marais *(4th arr)*; try the strudel at Sacha Finkelsztajn's.

CHINESE COMMUNITY

Until 1975, the predominant waves of immigrants came from Southern China; the latter-day arrivals come from postwar homelands in Indo-China, Malaysia and the Philippines. Although not as famous as the Chinatowns of New York or San Francisco, the 13th *arrondissement* (in the triangle of avenue d'Ivry, avenue de Choisy and rue de Tolbiac) boasts 150 restaurants and shops piled high with exotic produce. The district, its modern high-rises visible from afar, has succeeded in making a name for itself in tourist guidebooks. The Chinese population, the largest concentration in Europe, is particularly busy around the Chinese New Year (end of January–beginning of February).

In **Belleville**, there is a smaller group of Asian restaurants (including the huge, and hugely fun **Nioulaville** *32 rue de l'Orillon 11th arr*) and stores. A plaque on the wall of no 13 rue Maurice-Denis in this neighbourhood pays homage to the 120 000 Chinese who came to France during World War I, 3 000 of whom decided to stay in Paris at the end of the war, forming the first Chinese community near the Gare de Lyon.

Books – Le Phénix *(72 boulevard de Sébastopol 3rd arr)* has generalist books on the Far East with a specialist section on China and Japan and **You Feng** *(45 rue Monsieur-le-Prince 6th arr)* is the largest specialist bookshop on China.

Art – Paris is home to a number of pre-eminent collections of Oriental art, including the **Musée des Arts asiatiques-Guimet** *6 place d'Iéna* and its annexe **Hôtel Heidelbach- Guimet** *15 avenue d'Iéna* (Asian art from the Caucasus to Japan – *see ALMA)*; the **Musée Cernuschi** *7 avenue Velasquez* (Chinese antiques – *see PARC MONCEAU)*.

Shops – **Tang Frères** *48 avenue d'Ivry (13th arr)* and at *168 avenue de Choisy (13th arr)*; **Paris Store** *44 avenue d'Ivry*

In the Middle Ages, there were two main synagogues in rue de la Cité and rue de la Tâcherie (behind the Hôtel de Ville). By the 18C numbers of Jews had grown with settlers from Alsace and Lorraine moving to the Réamur Sébastopol area, especially around Hôtel du Chariot d'Or in rue de Turbigo. Confidence was high when all Jews were granted French nationality during the Revolution. Haussmann included two synagogues in his plans for urban development: rue de la Victoire founded in 1874 and rue des Tornelles founded in 1876. This was built with an iron substructure that was manufactured in Normandy, most probably under the auspices of Gustav Eiffel. The façade of the synagogue at 8 rue Pavée was designed by Guimard.

(13th arr) and at *12 boulevard de la Villette (19th arr)*; **Mandarin du marché** *33 rue de Torcy (18th arr)*; **Hang Seng Heng** *18 rue de l'Odéon (6th arr)*; **Odimex** *17 rue de l'Odéon* (porcelain and ceramics); **Phu-Xuan** *8 rue Monsieur-le-Prince (6th arr)* specialises in Chinese herbs and medicinal products.

JAPANESE COMMUNITY

The Japanese community (businessmen, employees of Japanese firms, students and artists) is concentrated in the area around the **Opéra** and **rue Ste-Anne** where opportunities abound to taste *sashimi, sushi* and *tempura*.

Art – The **Musée Guimet** houses a rich collection of Buddhas and Bodhisattvas brought back to France by Émile Guimet; the **Musée départemental Albert-Kahn** *14 rue du Port, 92100 Boulogne-Billancourt (see The Green Guide Northern France and the Paris Region)* is also a must, with its Japanese garden, tea house and collection of autochrome plates.

Fashion – Japanese designers have acquired an international reputation. Most of their boutiques are located around place des Victoires and in the St-Germain-des-Prés district: **Kenzo** *3 place des Victoires (1st arr)*, *16-17 boulevard Raspail (7th arr)*; **Comme des garçons** *40-42 rue Étienne-Marcel (2nd arr)*; **Yohji Yamamoto** *47 rue Étienne-Marcel (1st arr)* and at *69 rue des Saint-Pères (6th arr)*; **Issey Miyake** *201 boulevard St-Germain (6th arr)*, *17 boulevard Raspail (7th arr)*; **Irié** *8 rue du Pré-aux-Clercs (7th arr)*.

Books – Librairie Japonaise Junku *(18 rue des Pyramides, 1st arr)* for all the Japanese newspapers or a selection from thousands of *bunko* (paperbacks) and *mangas* (comic books); **L'Harmattan** *(see Afro-Caribbean)* also has books on Japan.

Food stores – Kioko *(46 rue des Petits-Champs 2nd arr)* is brimming with multi-coloured bags of cocktail snacks, sauces, sake and frozen raw fish.

Cultural encounters

The Chinese-American architect Ieoh Ming Pei is one of the most prolific contemporary architects. Pei stirred controversy with his design of a glass pyramid for the new main entrance of the Louvre Museum (completed in 1988), but it is now generally regarded with admiration for both its delightful use of light and form and for its efficient channelling of visitors to the museum.

INDIAN AND PAKISTANI SUB-CONTINENT

Most immigrants from the Indian sub-continent are not actually Indian but Pakistani, Tamils from northern Sri Lanka or recently arrived Bangladeshis. India in Paris runs along rue St-Denis (between the Gare du Nord and Porte de la Chapelle, around rue Jarry, passage Brady, and place du Caire). There are numerous food shops and restaurants in rue Gérando at the foot of the Sacré-Cœur, and beside the Lycée Jacques-Decours; Ⓜ*Anvers*.

Art and Culture – **Centre culturel Mandapa** *(6 rue Wurtz 13th arr)* stages some 100 or more Indian plays, dance shows and music concerts every year. **Maison des cultures du monde** *(101 boulevard Raspail 6th arr)* features performances of traditional Indian, Pakistani and Bangladeshi music, dance and theatre.

Books – The **Musée Guimet** bookshop has an excellent section on India, its civilizations, the arts from the Gandhâra (Greco-Buddhist art from Pakistan and Afghanistan) and from throughout the Far East.

Food shops – **Shah et Cie** *(33 rue Notre-Dame-de-Lorette 9th arr)* is the oldest Indian grocery store in Paris; **Rumi** *(71 passage Brady 10th arr)* sells Pakistani specialities.

Food and Drink

France may have a well-deserved reputation for the standard of its cuisine, but don't assume that you will be guaranteed a high standard of cooking in all the restaurants of its capital city! Having said this, it is perfectly possible to eat extremely well at reasonable prices provided you choose carefully. Much depends upon the area in which you eat as well as the type of restaurant you select. For example, if you happen to be on the Champs-Elysées, it could be very expensive – even for a modest meal in a very ordinary establishment, but select a restaurant in the quieter streets of one of the less fashionable arrondissements, choose the set menu and you can eat very well for a very modest outlay.

As with many capital cities, there are not really any such things as specialities specific to the city. There is, however, a great variety of regional cuisine to be found depending upon your tastes – Lyonnais, Norman, Basquaise and Breton are just some of the regional varieties to be found. Other areas specialise in international cuisine - for example in 13e, the area to the south east of the Place d'Italie is known as Chinatown. Cuisine from around the world – from Greek to Spanish, from Japanese to Vietnamese and from West to North Africa – can be found in many areas of the city.

Apart from the actual cuisine, there are several types of **eating place** which are common to France. The traditional restaurant usually opens twice a day, from noon–2.30pm and again from 7pm or 7.30pm until 10.30pm or 11pm. Often reservations are necessary and while children and pets are usually welcome, they are expected to behave appropriately.

Brasseries – essentially a cross between a restaurant and a café – are open every day and normally reservations are not required. However, some are very popular and it can be quite difficult to get in at peak times. Originally from Alsace – the name means brewery – they tend to serve less sophisticated fare and it is possible to eat after midnight.

Cafés and bars are numerous throughout the capital. These are normally for enjoying a coffee, a glass of wine or *pression* (draught beer), but light snacks are often available. Many offer a lunchtime *plat du jour,* or dish of the day, which is normally good value. Some cafés like Les Deux Magots and the Café de Flore are very famous and sophisticated but the great majority are inexpensive places to relax in and enjoy some refreshment while watching the world go by.

Café les Deux Magots, Saint-Germain-des-Prés

S. Sauvignier/MICHELIN

For the best little places, follow the leader.

Looking for the latest news on today's best hotels and restaurants? Pick up the Michelin Guide and look for the Bib Gourmand and Bib Hotel symbols. With 45,000 addresses in Europe, in every category and price range, the perfect place to dine or stay is never far away.

Musée du Quai Branly with the Eiffel Tower behind
©Bruno Bernier/Fotolia.com

ALMA★

For a plan of the neighbourhood with suggested walk, ⓒsee CHAMPS-ÉLYSÉES.

The area around **place de l'Alma** is one of the most luxurious quarters of Paris, with something for all tastes: a concert at the Théâtre des Champs-Élysées, an evening at the Crazy Horse, an exhibition at the Musée d'Art Moderne, or a stroll among the couturiers and perfumers at the heart of the world of fashion.

Nearby neighbourhoods: **CHAMPS-ÉLYSÉES, TROCADÉRO, PLACE DE LA CONCORDE, FAUBOURG ST-GERMAIN.**

- 🅸 **Information:** Pyramides welcome centre, 25 rue des Pyramides. ☎08 92 68 30 00 (0.34€ per min.) http://en.parisinfo.com.
- ▶ **Orient Yourself:** From the Left Bank, the Pont de l'Alma brings you right into the heart of the Alma district. From here, its main streets (the Avenues Iéna, Marceau, George V, and Montaigne) all lead to the Champs-Elysées. To the right is the embarkment for the Bateaux-Mouches.
- 🅿 **Parking:** Underground parking can be found just off the Place de l'Alma, the Avenue Montaigne, and along the Champs-Elysées.
- 😊 **Don't Miss:** The newly renovated Musée d'Art Moderne and the Buddhist Pantheon annex at the Musée Guimet.
- 🕐 **Organising Your Time:** Allow at least two hours to visit the museums.
- 🄺🄸🄳🅂 **Especially for Kids:** Tours of the Paris sewer system (Musée des Egouts) are particularly fascinating for the youngsters.
- ⓒ **Also See:** EIFFEL TOWER, TROCADÉRO, CHAMPS-ÉLYSÉES.

Asian Art in Paris

Musée national des Arts asiatiques★★★ – Guimet

6 place d'Iéna. ⓒTue–Sun 10am–6pm (5pm 24 and 31 Dec) ⓒ1 Jan, 1 May, 25 Dec. Audio-guides (1hr 30min) are available at no extra cost. ⓒ☎01 56 52 53 00. www.museeguimet.fr.

This museum, founded by Émile Guimet, a successful 19C industrialist from Lyon, contains superb Oriental works of art.

South-East Asia *(ground floor)*
A colossal statue of Nâga, a seven-head stone serpent from Angkor, sets the scene on the way to the area dedicated to **Khmer art**★★ (Cambodia). Indian divinities are displayed in the room on the left. The journey continues through Vietnam, Indonesia, Burma and Thailand with its splendid **heads of Buddha**.

The First Floor
The art of **India**, Pakistan and Afghanistan is of special interest. The collection of Ancient Chinese art includes a charming collection of Han and Tang **funerary objects**★★ from northern China, displayed in a glass case.

Second Floor
Classical Chinese arts include **Ming porcelain**★ (1368-1644) with polychrome or blue-and-white motifs. Korean arts are represented by the Celadon pottery, 18C theatre masks, and an imposing **portrait of Cho Man-Yong**, a 19C dignitary. Examples of Japanese art include the gilt-lacquer screens dating from the Edo period and the collection of etchings by Utamaro (18C), Sharaku (actors' portraits – late 18C), Hiroshige (19C) and Hokusai (**Wave off the coast of Kanagawa**★★).

The third and fourth floor exhibit **Chinese porcelain** from the Qing period and house the lacquer rotunda.

Galeries du panthéon bouddhíque de la Chine et du Japon

Hôtel Heidelbach, 19 avenue d'Iéna.
🕐*Tue–Sun 10am–6pm.* 🕐*1 Jan, 1 May, 25 Dec.* ☎*01 56 52 53 00.*
Housed in a superb Neoclassical mansion, this annex of the Guimet Museum is essentially dedicated to Chinese and Japanese Buddhism from the 5C to the 19C.

Walking Tour

2 Round tour from place de l'Alma
🚶*See map.*

Pont de l'Alma
The original bridge was replaced in 1970 by an asymmetrical steel structure with a 110m/361ft span. Only the **Zouave** (upstream by the single pile) remains of the four Second Empire soldier statues that decorated the old bridge; it serves as a high water marker and is much loved by Parisians – in January 1910, the water reached the chin of the statue.

Place de l'Alma
On the southern side of the square, at the beginning of avenue de New-York, stands a life-size gilded model of the flame held by the Statue of Liberty in New York, a gift to the city for the 100th anniversary of the *International Herald Tribune*.

Cours Albert-Iᵉʳ
The statue by **Bourdelle** (🚶*see MONT-PARNASSE)* in the gardens parallel to the river shows the Polish poet and patriot, **Mickiewicz** (1798-1855). At no 40, note the fine René Lalique façade.

Avenue Montaigne
Formerly known as allée des Veuves (Widows' Alley) this disreputable area's main attraction was the Mabille Dance Hall, which closed in 1870. Today this street exudes wealth and chic, lined with elegant buildings accommodating banks, art galleries and exclusive luxury boutiques like YSL, Prada, Céline, Versace and Dior.

Théâtre des Champs-Élysées
The theatre, designed by the Perret brothers, is one of the first major monuments built in reinforced concrete (1912). The façade sculptures are designed by Antoine Bourdelle (🚶*see MONTPAR-NASSE: Musée Bourdelle).*
The main auditorium, with its ceiling decorated by **Maurice Denis**, is one of the finest in Paris; it has a seating capacity of 2 100.
It was here that Igor Stravinski first directed his *Rite of Spring* (1913), scandalising the audience with its musical and choreographic audacity; it caused such a furore that the composer had to flee from the auditorium. Since then, the Champs-Élysées Theatre has welcomed many great stars: Richard Strauss, Paganini, **Diaghilev** with his Ballets Russes and **Jean Cocteau**; in 1925, the *Negro Review* introduced Josephine Baker dancing half-naked to a Charleston and rhythms played on the saxophone by Sidney Bechet.

▶ *Walk up avenue Montaigne then down rue François I to the square of the same name.*

At 22 **rue Bayard** is the Radio-Télé-Luxembourg (RTL) station – note the façade of the building decorated by Vasarely. Opposite is the Scottish Kirk.

S. Sauvignier/MICHELIN

The Zouave stands below the Pont de l'Alma

Address Book

SHOPPING

Noura – *27 av. Marceau,16th arr.* Ⓜ*Alma-Marceau.* ☎*01 47 23 02 20. www.noura.com. Open 9am–midnight.* Perhaps the best place to shop for Lebanese specialities in town. Taboule with parsley, hummus, mustabal, grilled meat, baklavas and other delicious specialities, all of which are presented superbly.

Avenue Montaigne – *Av. Montaigne, 8th arr.* Undoubtedly the smartest street in Paris. All the major fashion designers and luxury brands have an outlet here: Emanuel Ungaro, Loro Piana, Prada, Dior, Bonpoint, Bottega Veneta, Valentino, Vuitton, Céline, Caron, Nina Ricci, Harry Winston.

▸ *Follow rue François I and avenue Pierre-I-de-Serbie to avenue George-V.*

Avenue George-V

This street is famous for its grand **Hotel George V** at no 31; the neo-Gothic **American Cathedral in Paris**, which was consecrated at the same time as the Statue of Liberty was unveiled in New York Harbor (1886); the **Crazy-Horse** music hall at no 12, with its renowned programme of topless stage shows.

Église St-Pierre-de-Chaillot

35 avenue Marceau, on the corner of avenue Marceau. The church was rebuilt in the neo-Romanesque style in 1937. Overlooking its façade, on which the life of St Peter has been carved by Bouchard (*see AUTEUIL*), is a 65m/213ft-high belfry.

▸ *Return to place de l'Alma along avenue Marceau.*

Museums

Palais de Tokyo – Site de Création Contemporaine

13 avenue du Président-Wilson, in one of the two wings of the Palais de Tokyo. ◷*Tue–Sun noon–midnight.* ◷*Public holidays.* ◉6€. ☎*01 47 23 54 01. www.palaisdetokyo.com.*

Housed in one of the wings of the Palais de Tokyo, built for the 1937 World Exhibition, this exhibition centre opened in 2001 is exclusively devoted to contemporary culture.

Musée d'Art moderne de la Ville de Paris★★

11 avenue du Président-Wilson, in one of the two wings of the Palais de Tokyo. ◷*Tue–Sun 10am–6pm, Thu until 10pm.* ◷*Public holidays.* ☎*01 53 67 40 00. www.mam.paris.fr.*

This municipal collection illustrates the main trends of 20C art, including some of the century's major works: *France* by Bourdelle (on a terrace), *Les Disques* by Léger (1918), *L'Équipe de Cardiff* by Robert Delaunay (1912-13), *Pastorale* and **Danse de Paris**★ by Matisse (1932), *Évocation* by Picasso and *Rêve* by Chagall. Dufy's **Fée Électricité**★ *(The Good Fairy Electricity)*, the biggest picture in the world, (600sq m/6 095sq ft).

Palais Galliera (Musée de la Mode de la ville de Paris)

10 ave Pierre-Ier-de-Serbie. ◷*During exhibitions: Tue–Sun 10am–6pm.* ◷*Public holidays.* ◉7.50€. ☎*01 56 52 86 00. www.galliera.paris.fr.*

The Duchess of Galliera, wife of the Italian financier and philanthropist, had this edifice built (1878-94) in the Italian Renaissance style. The mansion houses a museum dedicated to **fashion** and costume, with thematic exhibitions drawn from a vast collection of men's, women's and children's fashion and dress from 1735 to the present day.

Musée des Égouts

On the left bank. Entrance at the corner of quai d'Orsay and pont de l'Alma. ◷*May–Sept, Sat–Wed 11am–5pm; Oct–Apr, Sun—Wed 11am–4pm.* ◷*Two weeks in Jan, 1 Jan and 25 Dec.* ◉4.20€. ☎*01 53 68 27 81. www.paris.fr.*

The Paris **sewer** system was constructed at the time of Napoléon III, and now incorporates 2 100km/1 305mi of underground tunnels.

AUTEUIL

ⓜ ÉGLISE-D'AUTEUIL, MICHEL-ANGE-D'AUTEUIL (LINE 10)
BUSES: 32, 52, 70 FOR MAISON DE RADIO-FRANCE.

It was only at the turn of the 19C that the last vineyards disappeared from Auteuil, although it became part of the City of Paris during the Second Empire. It still enjoys a village atmosphere, in contrast to the modern development and high-rise blocks across the river. Many of the houses of this desirable residential area have retained good-sized gardens, and the streets named after famous composers and writers recall the era of Salon society.

Nearby neighbourhoods: **TROCADÉRO, PASSY, BOIS DE BOULOGNE.**

ⓘ **Information:** Pyramides welcome centre, 25 rue des Pyramides. ☎08 92 68 30 00 (0.34€ per min.) http://en.parisinfo.com.

▶ **Orient Yourself:** Auteuil sits on the Right Bank just west of the Seine; two bridges give access to the Left Bank: Pont de Grenelle and Pont Mirabeau. To the northwest is the Ranelaugh quarter, and the Passy Village is to the northeast.

ⓟ **Parking:** There is plenty of parking in this residential district, and underground parking at Radio France.

☺ **Don't Miss:** The beautiful Art Nouveau villas designed by Guimard.

🕐 **Organising Your Time:** Allow at least two hours if you're on foot and don't go into any of the museums. This is an ideal district to visit on bike or by car.

Kids **Especially for Kids:** The Tenniseum at Roland-Garros includes a behind-the-scenes tour of the famous tennis stadium and its red clay courts.

⛄ **Also See:** BOIS DE BOULOGNE, PASSY, TROCADÉRO.

Walking Tour
⛄*See map.*

Place d'Auteuil
The Church of Notre-Dame (1880) is a Romano-Byzantine pastiche. The obelisk opposite the chapel of Ste-Bernadette is the last remaining tomb from the one-time cemetery.

Rue d'Auteuil

▶ *Follow rue d'Auteuil as far as place Jean-Lorrain.*

At no 11bis the 17C château is now occupied by a school. Admire at no **16** the main front of the Hôtel de Puscher; no **43-47** is an 18C mansion. The modern building at no **59** marks the site of a literary salon of Madame Helvétius, frequented by philosophers and writers from 1762 to 1800, including the Americans Thomas Jefferson, **Benjamin Franklin** and John Adams.

▶ *Continue until the Place de la Porte d'Auteuil, cross the intersection to the avenue de la Porte d'Auteuil and follow it past the Périphérique road.*

Jardin des Serres d'Auteuil
3 avenue de la Porte d'Auteuil. 🕐*Apr–Sept, daily 10am–6pm; Oct–Mar, 10am–5pm.* 🕐*Public holidays.* ☎*01 40 71 75 60.*
The formal garden, which still retains its 19C charm, is surrounded by hothouses cultivating azaleas, palm trees and ornamental plants for public buildings and official occasions. The central building contains a palm house and a tropical house with banana trees, papyrus plants and giant strelitzias. The azalea and chrysanthemum displays draw large crowds.

Beyond the garden is the **Stade Roland-Garros** (⛄*see Museums*), where the French Open Tennis Championships are held every year *(late May–early June).* When leaving the Serres d'Auteuil, take a short cut through the small **Square des Poètes** next door.

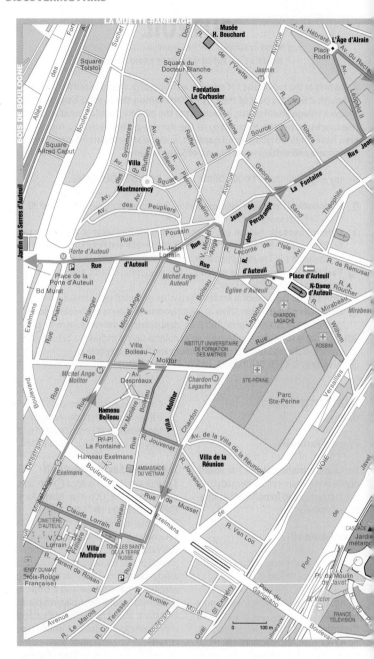

▶ *Return to the Place Jean-Lorrain and follow the rue Michel-Ange, then the rue Molitor (first left). Turn right on the rue Boileau, then a left on rue Jouvenet.*

Promenade des villas d'Auteuil★

The **villa Boileau** (no 18 rue Molitor), **hameau Boileau (**no 38 rue Boileau)**,** and **villa Molitor** (at rue Jouvenet and Chardon-Lagache) are havens of peace and greenery.

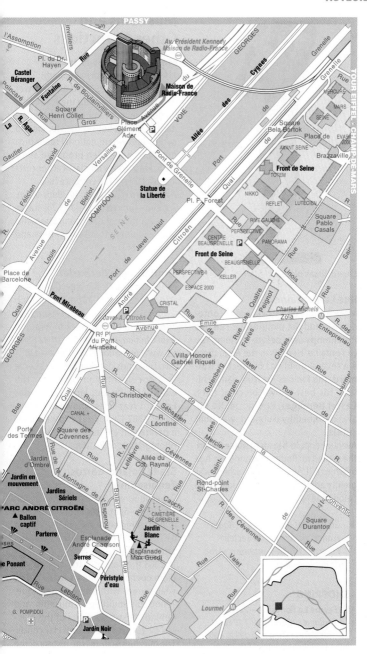

▶ *Cross boulevard Exelmans by taking rue Chardon-Lagache, then turn right along rue Charles-Marie-Widor and continue along rue Claude-Lorrain, left onto avenue G. Risler.*

The villa Mulhouse is a group of small houses reminiscent of late 19C workers' housing in the city of Mulhouse.

▶ *Head northwards back along rue Michel-Ange to place Jean-Lorrain.*

L'Âge d'Airain, place Rodin

P. Gajic/MICHELIN

Rue La-Fontaine

Make a short detour via rue Leconte-de-Lisle and the picturesque **rue des Perchamps** *(left)* before rejoining rue La Fontaine. Here, as in rue Agar, there are several buildings by **Hector Guimard,** the famous Art Nouveau architect. His best-known block of flats, **Castel Béranger,** is at no 14. No **60**, also designed by Guimard, was built in 1911.

Avenue Léopold-II leads to **place Rodin**, the setting for Rodin's allegory, The Age of Bronze (L'Âge d'Airain), which was greatly admired for its precision at the Salon of 1874.

▸ *Go towards the Maison de Radio-France, via avenue du Recteur-Poincaré, rue La-Fontaine and rue de Boulainvilliers.*

SHOPPING

La Ferme La Fontaine – *75 rue La-Fontaine - 16th arr. ☎01 42 88 07 55.* This cheese shop and deli is well known to the residents of the 16th arrondissement. Since 1890 it has been home to five generations of cheese merchants.

Museums and Other Attractions

Maison de Radio-France★

116 avenue du Président-Kennedy.
One concentric building and a tower 68m/223ft tall make up the Maison de Radio-France. Designed by Henri Bernard in 1963, it houses the studios and auditorium where national radio programmes have been produced since 1975. Free tickets for classical concerts are available in the entrance hall.

A **museum** (⏱*Mon–Fri 10.30am–11am, 2.30pm–4pm;* ☎*01 56 40 15 16*) traces the evolution of communication and the development of transmitters and receivers.

Fondation Le Corbusier

8-10 square du Dr-Blanche. ⏱*Tue–Thu 10am–12.30pm, 1.30pm–6pm, Mon 1.30pm–6pm, Fri 1.30pm–5pm, Sat 10am–5pm.* ⏱*First week in Aug and public holidays.* ☎*2.50€.* ☎*01 42 88 41 53. www.fondationlecorbusier.asso.fr*
Two buildings dating from 1923 serve as a documentation centre for the work of the famous architect Charles Édouard Jeanneret, known as Le Corbusier (1887-1965). Villa La Roche houses a permanent exhibition, a library and photographic collection.

Stade Roland-Garros/ Tenniseum★ [Kids]

2 avenue Gordon Bennett. ⏱*Wed, Fri, Sat, Sun 10am–6pm.* ⏱*Public holidays and during tournaments.* ☎*7.50€. (under-18s 4€)* ☎*01 47 43 48 48. www.fft.fr/site-tenniseum.*
In 2003 the Roland-Garros tennis stadium opened its grounds to the public year-round, with a tennis boutique, Tenniseum multimedia museum, and behind-the-scenes tours of the players' lockers and the famous clay courts. The museum features the history of the sport as well as a video library of modern matches and player interviews.

BASTILLE ★

Scene of the historic revolutions of 1789, 1830 and 1848, the Place de la Bastille remains a symbolic rallying point for demonstrations, marches and public celebrations, dominated by the commemorative July Column and the Opéra Bastille. It's also a popular student night spot, with a lively bar and club scene.

Nearby neighbourhoods: **FAUBOURG ST-ANTOINE, LE MARAIS.**

- ℹ **Information:** Pyramides welcome centre, 25 rue des Pyramides. ☎08 92 68 30 00 (0.34€ per min.) http://en.parisinfo.com.
- ▶ **Orient Yourself:** Located on the eastern edge of the Marais, the place de la Bastille sits at the crossroads of the boulevards Richard-Lenoir and Beaumarchais, the rues du Faubourg-St-Antoine and St-Antoine, and the Port de l'Arsenal.
- Ⓟ **Parking:** Underground parking can be found along the Port and the rue St-Antoine. Street parking is available along the boulevards.
- 👁 **Don't Miss:** Tours of the Opéra Bastille.
- 🕐 **Organising Your Time:** Allow an hour to visit this compact district.
- 🧒 **Especially for Kids:** The Port de l'Arsenal has a small playground in the gardens overlooking the houseboats.
- 👶 **Also See:** FAUBOURG SAINT-ANTOINE, MARAIS, RÉPUBLIQUE

A Bit of History

The Bastille prison – Charles V built this fortified residence in the 14C using forced labour recruited by press-gangs from passers-by. Besieged seven times in periods of civil strife, it surrendered six times. Political prisoners included the Man in the Iron Mask and Voltaire.

The taking of the Bastille – On 14 July 1789 a militant crowd rallied and marched first to the Invalides to capture arms, then on to the Arsenal and the Bastille. By late afternoon the Bastille was seized and the seven remaining prisoners were freed. The fortress was immediately demolished, 83 of its stones being carved into replicas and sent to the provinces. The following year there was dancing on the site.

Walking Tour

▶ *Start from the Arsenal marina.*

Port de plaisance de Paris-Arsenal

This pleasure port, a former moat of Charles V's fortifications, connects the Seine to the Canal St-Martin, which runs beneath the boulevard Richard-Lenoir and resurfaces at République.

Place de la Bastille

Paving stones mark out the ground plan of the former Bastille, best seen from the corner where the rue St-Antoine meets the Place. **Colonne de Juillet**, a bronze column (52m/171ft high) crowned by the figure of Liberty, is a memorial crypt

Le Génie de la Bastille, atop the Colonne de Juillet

P. Gajic/MICHELIN

for the Parisians killed during the uprisings of July 1830 and 1848.

Around Bastille

The area was traditionally famous for its dance halls and specialist shops selling produce from the Auvergne. The neighbourhood now hums with artists' studios, and furniture workshops. Many lively bars can be found along the narrow streets. **Rue de Lappe** is particularly trendy.

Museums and Other Attractions

L'Opéra de Paris-Bastille★

Guided tours (1hr 15min). Day and time depending on performers' and technicians' work schedules. Jul–Aug; call for information. 11€. 01 40 01 19 70. www.operadeparis.fr.

Designed by Carlos Ott, this massive glass and marble building is often likened to a ship, The curvilinear, utilitarian design accommodates a 2 700-seat auditorium with several revolving stages for quick scene changes, workshops housing 74 different trades and rehearsal rooms.

L'Arsenal

(entrance: 1 rue de Sully). Note the cannon and mortar on the roof-top balustrade, recalling the original function of the building. In 1512, the city set up a cannon foundry, which Henri II later converted to a royal arsenal producing gunpowder among other things. Destroyed in an explosion (1563), the Arsenal was rebuilt and inhabited by Sully, until Louis XIII finally closed the cannon works.

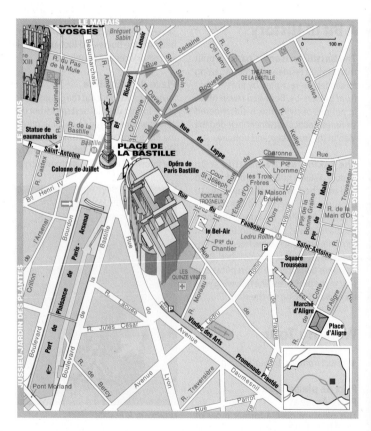

Address Book

WHERE TO STAY AND EAT

Turn to the back of the guide for selected hotels, restaurants, bistros and cafés listed by *arrondissement*. This neighbourhood is spread over the 4th, 11th and 12th arrondissements.

NIGHTLIFE

BASTILLE

Place de la Bastille, with its countless brasseries such as Bofinger (opened in 1864), has become a focal point for night-lovers on their way to and from the Marais and the restaurants, cafés, beer cellars, wine bars and nightclubs of the rue de Charonne, rue de la Roquette, rue de Lappe, rue St-Sabin, and rue Keller.

Bar sans Nom – *49 rue de Lappe, 11th arr.* ☎*01 48 05 59 36. Closed Sun.* Torch-shaped lamps and walls covered in imitation tapestries give an idea of the look of this bar which serves delicious fresh fruit juices.

Café de l'Industrie – *16 & 17 rue St-Sabin, 11th arr.* ☎*01 47 00 13 53.* The walls of this fine old café are covered in paintings and exotic bric-a-brac brought back by the owner from his extensive travels. A second location opened next door in 2003 to help accommodate its popularity.

Café des Phares – *7 pl. de la Bastille, 11th arr.* ☎*01 42 72 04 70.* It was here that the philosopher Marc Sautet (now deceased) created the first Parisian *café philo* (philosophy café). Still very popular, it is particularly crowded on Sunday mornings when budding philosophers congregate. Pleasant terrace.

La Chapelle des Lombards – *19 rue de Lappe, 11th arr.* ☎*01 43 57 24 24. Closed Sun–Mon.* Dance club with West-Indian, Latin-American and African music (zouk, salsa, etc.). All age groups.

Le Balajo – *9 rue de Lappe, 11th arr.* ☎*01 47 00 07 87. www.balajo.fr. Tue (Brazilian)–Wed (swing) 9pm–3am; Thu–Sat (fiesta) 11pm–4am; Sun 3pm–7pm (ballroom).* Founded in 1936 by Georges France (aka Jo), Balajo's is the oldest musette dance hall in Paris. Its old-fashioned atmosphere and preference for hits from the 1950s, 60s and 70s continue to attract crowds of all ages. **Pause Café** – *41 rue de Charonne, 11th arr.* ☎*01 48 06 80 33. Closed 25 Dec.* A traditional café with a fine U-shaped bar in the centre of the room. The soft lighting and subdued atmosphere make it a pleasant place for a quiet read.

SHOPPING

Caves Estève – *10 rue de la Cerisaie, 4th arr.* Ⓜ*Bastille.* ☎*01 42 72 33 05. www.cavesteve.com. Closed Sun.* Specialising in new wines, this establishment is run by young enthusiasts who publish a catalogue listing 1 300 wines and offer a selection of the best organically grown wines.

Les Caprices de l'Instant – *12 rue Jacques-Cœur, 4th arr.* Ⓜ*Bastille.* ☎*01 40 27 89 00. Closed Sun.* This wine merchant selects only vintages which uphold the spirit and traditions of their ancestry and makes it a point of honour to stock only wines which are ready for consumption. Anything suggested by the expert taste-buds of this wine enthusiast can be drunk with your eyes closed!

Art Galleries – The art galleries along rue de Charonne, rue de Lappe and rue Keller all exhibit the work of contemporary artists.

Pavillon de l'Arsenal

21 boulevard Morland. ◷*Tue–Sun 10.30am–6.30pm, Sun and public holidays 11am–7pm. Documentation centre: Tue–Fri 2pm–6pm.* ◷*1 Jan.* ☎*01 42 76 33 97. www.pavillon-arsenal.com.*

This late 19C iron and glass building accommodates an exhibition centre presenting the architecture and urban development of the capital from the earliest city walls to important contemporary projects.

BEAUBOURG★★

Acrobats, jugglers and street artists of all kinds are attracted to the hub of the Georges Pompidou Centre, where the sound of music and the movement of the crowds create a festive feel. Inside this modern art centre is a fine collection of 20C art, as well as changing contemporary exhibitions. The urban renewal project for the Beaubourg plateau mingles zany, ultra-modern elements with medieval splendour – the Stravinski fountain and St-Merri.

Nearby neighbourhoods: **CHÂTELET-HÔTEL DE VILLE, LES HALLES, LE MARAIS, RÉPUBLIQUE (Temple).**

- Ⓘ **Information:** Carrousel du Louvre Welcome Centre, Place de la Pyramide Inversée 99, rue de Rivoli. ☏08 92 68 30 00 (0.34€ per min.) http://en.parisinfo.com.
- ▶ **Orient Yourself:** Beaubourg lies between Les Halles and the Marais. The Hôtel de Ville and rue de Rivoli mark its southern border.
- Ⓟ **Parking:** There is underground parking at the Centre Pompidou. Most of Beaubourg is pedestrian-only.
- ⊙ **Don't Miss:** The panoramic city views from the top of the Centre Pompidou.
- ⊙ **Organising Your Time:** The neighbourhood can be seen in less than an hour, longer if you decide to visit the museum.
- Kids **Especially for Kids:** The colourful, twirling water sculptures of the Stravinski Fountain never fail to attract children's attention.
- ⊙ **Also See:** LE MARAIS, LES HALLES, HÔTEL DE VILLE.

Centre Georges-Pompidou★★★

Place Georges-Pompidou. ⊙Wed–Sun 11am–9pm, (last admission 1hr before closing). ⊙1 May. ⊙☏01 44 78 12 33. www.centrepompidou.fr.

Architecture

Construction was completed in 1977. The architects **Richard Rogers** (British) and **Renzo Piano** (Italian) achieved a totally futuristic building. The façade appears a tangle of pipes and tubes latticed along its glass skin, earning the establishment the nickname of "the inside-out museum".

A unique cultural centre

Beaubourg is home to the **Musée national d'Art moderne** (National Museum of Modern Art, 4th and 5th levels), the **Bibliothèque publique d'information** (the public library known as the BPI, 1st, 2nd and 3rd levels), and the **IRCAM** (Institute for Acoustic and Musical Research beneath place

Stravinski). The centre also houses several **temporary exhibition halls** on the 1st (mezzanine) and 6th levels.

In addition, the centre provides live entertainment (dance, music, theatre), cinema performances and spoken reviews. The library is especially popular with Parisians, thanks to its late hours, open access and up-to-date collection of printed and other resources.

There is a bookshop on level 0, a design shop and a nice café (view over the main entrance) on level one, and a good restaurant *(reservations required, ⊙see Address Book)* on level 6.

Musée national d'Art moderne★★★

Place Georges-Pompidou ⊙Wed–Sun 11am–9pm (last admission 1hr before closing) Atelier Brancusi 2pm–6pm. ⊙1 May. Museum and exhibitions ⊙€10; no charge for the museum 1st Sun in the month. ⊙☏01 44 78 12 33. www.centre pompidou.fr.

This certainly ranks high among the most significant collections dedicated to modern art in the world (50 000 works and objects). It traces the evolution of art from Fauvism and Cubism to the contemporary art scene. The modern collection (1905-60) is housed on the fifth floor, whereas contemporary exhibitions from the 1960s onwards are held on the fourth floor.

Outside the museum, the Parisian sculpture workshop of **Constantin Brancusi** (1876-1957) has been reconstituted in its entirety in a small building in the square, featuring the artist's tools and personal art collection.

The modern collection

Fifth floor. Forty galleries present around 900 works *(changed every 18 months)*. Throughout the exhibition, the juxtaposition of painting and sculpture with the design and architecture of the same decade enables the visitor to obtain an overview of 20C creativity.

Galleries dedicated to a single artist (Matisse, Léger, Picasso, Rouault, Delaunay) alternate with thematic rooms. All the main movements of the first half of the 20C are represented here, such as **Fauvism** (1905-10; Derain, Marquet, Dufy and Matisse); **Cubism** (**Braque** and **Picasso** in 1907), **Dada** (from 1913; **Marcel Duchamp**), the **Paris School** (1910-1930; **Soutine**, **Chagall**, **Modigliani**, Larionov, Gontcharova), the Abstract School (from 1910; **Kandinsky**, **Kupka**, **Mondrian**, **Klee**), and the **Bauhaus School**.

Surrealism is represented by De Chirico, **Salvador Dali**, Max Ernst, **Magritte**, Brauner, André Masson, Tanguy, Giacometti, Picasso and **Mirò**.

During the 1950s Abstract art appealed to many French and foreign artists (Hartung, Poliakoff, De Staël, Dubuffet). The **Cobra** movement (1948-51) advocated spontaneous expression through the free use of bold colour and energetic brush strokes (Alechinsky, Appel, Jorn). American art from the 1940s to the 1960s is represented by **Pollock**, **Rothko** and **Newman**.

Colour and purity of line are all-important to **Matisse**, in his distinctive gouache cut-outs or "drawing with scissors", as the artist put it, whereas in sculpture, **Brancusi** and Calder pursue abstraction for its own sake.

The contemporary collection

Fourth floor. These exhibitions are regularly changed, representing the main artistic trends are represented, together with major personalities, combining to create a world of colour, form and movement linking art with everyday life.

Major works include *Requiem for a dead leaf* (Tinguely), *Red Rhinoceros* (Veilhan). **Pop Art** is represented by **Warhol** and Rauschenberg, **New Realism** by **Klein**, **Arman**, César, **Niki de Saint-Phalle**, **Op** and **Kinetic Art** by **Agam** (Antechamber

Centre Georges-Pompidou, rue Beaubourg

S. Sauvignier/MICHELIN

of the *Élysée Palace private apartments)* and Vasarely, and there are installations by **Dubuffet** *(The Winter Garden)*, **Beuys** *(Plight)* and **Raynaud** *(Container Zero)*. Three rooms contain examples of design and architecture from the 1960s to the present day (Starck, Nouvel, Perrault, Toto Ito). Space is also devoted to the cinema (**Jean-Luc Godard**), multimedia installations (**Ugo Rondinone**) and Happening (**Gutaï** and **Fluxus**).

Sixth floor

A splendid **view**★★ extends over the Paris rooftops – from right to left: Montmartre dominated by the Sacré-Cœur, St-Eustache, the Eiffel Tower, Maine-Montparnasse Tower, St-Merri in the foreground with Notre-Dame behind.

Walking Tour

St Merri Quarter

Rue Quincampoix

This is the site where the South Sea Bubble of the Scots financier **John Law** was situated. Law founded a bank here in 1719, attracting all kinds of speculators and expanding into the neighbouring houses. The street became crowded with people making fortunes overnight – a hunchback was said to have been paid 150 000 livres for the use of his back as a desk. The frenzy lasted until 1720 when the bank crashed and the speculators fled. Law's house was razed when rue Rambuteau was built.
Several old houses *(nos 10, 12, 13, 14)* survive with unusual paved courtyards,

Stravinski Fountain and Église St-Merri

mascarons (stone masks), intricate wrought-iron balconies and nailed or carved doors.
Continue north on this narrow pedestrianised street to discover a clutch of art galleries, boutiques and bars typifying the stylish urban atmosphere that has permeated the quarter since the construction of the Pompidou Centre.

Église St-Merri★

Access to the church is through the main façade on rue St-Martin or through the St Merri presbytery (76 rue de la Verrerie). ⏱*Daily 11am–7pm.* ☎*01 42 71 93 93.*
St Merry or Medericus, who died here in the 7C, used to be invoked to assist in the release of captives. The former parish church of the Lombard usurers, although dating from 1520 to 1612, curiously conforms to the 15C Flamboyant Gothic style.
Outside, the west front stands directly on the narrow rue St-Martin, crowded in with small houses and shops, much as it might have been in the Middle Ages. The Flamboyant interior remodelled under Louis XV retains 16C stained-glass windows in the first three bays of the chancel and transept, and fine ribbed vaulting at the transept crossing.
Don't miss the majestic 17C organ loft – the organ at one time played by **Camille Saint-Saëns** – and beautiful wood panelling by the Slodtz brothers (pulpit, sacristy and the glory at the back of the choir). One bell dating from 1331, probably the oldest in Paris, survives from the medieval chapel that stood on the site of the present church.

▸ *As you come out of the church, take rue de la Verrerie to the left and walk round the east end via rue des Juges-Consuls.*

Note the restored 18C house on the corner of rue du Cloître-St-Merri.
Decorating place Stravinski is the **Stravinski fountain**★ with black and coloured mobile sculptures by Tinguely and Niki de Saint-Phalle, respectively, illustrating the works of the great composer *(the Rite of Spring, Firebird and other works).*

Address Book

WHERE TO STAY AND EAT

♿Turn to the back of the guide for selected hotels, restaurants, bistros and cafés listed by *arrondissement*. This neighbourhood is in the 4th arrondissement.

NIGHTLIFE

Café Beaubourg – *43 rue St-Merri – 4th arr.* ☎*01 48 87 63 96. Closed Wed.* This wonderful café, designed by Christian de Porzamparc, has a pleasant terrace overlooking the incessant toing-and-froing of visitors, buskers and fire-eaters on the esplanade in front of the Centre Georges-Pompidou. Magazines and a framed text by Philippe Sollers set the establishment's literary and artistic tone. The tables are beautifully decorated and the little alcoves upstairs are perfect for private conversations.

Le Petit Marcel – *65 rue Rambuteau – 4th arr.* ☎*01 48 87 10 20. Closed 1 Jan, 1 May and 25 Dec.* Visitors to this delightful turn-of-the-19C café may feel as if they've stepped back in time to when the nearby Halles was still the capital's fruit and vegetable market. Perfect for a coffee or a drink.

Andy Wahloo – *69 rue des Gravilliers – 3rd arr.* ☎*01 42 71 20 38. Closed Sun.* This intimate Moroccan bar decorated with Middle Eastern pop art attracts a hip, cosmopolitan crowd, many of whom drop in for cocktails and tapas before heading out to the popular Moroccan restaurant, 404, right next door.

La Boîte à perles – *194 rue St-Denis – 2nd arr.* ☎*01 42 33 71 72.* This old-fashioned boutique has an amazing selection of hundreds of beads and pearls, with all you need to make your own jewellery.

Le Comptoir des Ecritures – *35 rue Quincampoix – 3rd arr.* ☎*01 42 78 95 10. Closed Sun. www.comptoiredesecritures. com.* A boutique dedicated to the fine art of calligraphy, with plumes, inks, and hand-made papers.

ART

Rue Quincampoix – *rue Quincampoix – 3rd arr.* – Ⓜ *Rambuteau.* Among the many art galleries which are clustered along this street, are Tendance, with rare works of well-known artists, and fashion designer Agnès B.'s Galerie du Jour, specialising in street art.

Rue St Merri

On the north side of place Stravinski, this street is across from rue du Renard.
Note nos 9 and 12 with their fine front-ages, and beyond, impasse du Bœuf, perhaps the oldest cul-de-sac in Paris.

▸ *Return to rue Beaubourg and follow it around the front of the Centre Pompidou, to the Place Georges Pompidou.*

Plateau de Beaubourg – Place Georges Pompidou

The area takes its name from the old village included within the Philippe Auguste perimeter wall at the end of the 12C. Run-down and derelict, the old quarter was cleaned up in 1939 and subjected to major redevelopment in 1968. The Beaubourg plateau was to have been the site of a public library; however, in 1969, on the initiative of **Georges Pompidou** (1911-74), the then President of France, it was decided to create a multi-purpose cultural centre.

▸ *Explore the passages on the north side of the plateau.*

Quartier de l'Horloge

Le Défenseur du Temps, an unusual brass and steel electronic clock with a Jack known as the Defender of Time, was designed by Jacques Monestier. On striking the hour, this life-size figure armed with a double-edged sword and shield, confronts one of three animals symbolising the elements: a dragon (earth), a bird (air) and a crab (water).

BELLEVILLE★

Ⓜ BELLEVILLE (LINES 2 AND 11), PYRÉNÉES (LINE 11), MÉNILMONTANT (LINE 2), GAMBETTA
(LINES 3 AND 3 BIS) – BUSES: 26, 96

Built on the highest hill in Paris after Montmartre (128m/420ft), Belleville owes part of its charm to the unexpectedly steep paths and winding streets. Despite the mushrooming of modern buildings, Belleville has, on the whole, kept its traditional atmosphere, its quiet streets and their secluded life, vacant lots and little snatches of greenery. The main streets, however, are full of popular ethnic restaurants (Chinese, Vietnamese).

- 🛈 **Information:** Pyramides welcome centre, 25 rue des Pyramides. ☎08 92 68 30 00 (0.34€ per min.) http://en.parisinfo.com.
- ▶ **Orient Yourself:** Belleville straddles the north end of the 20th *arrondissement*, bordered by the wide boulevard de Belleville and the narrow rue de Belleville.
- 🅿 **Parking:** Street and underground parking along the boulevard de Belleville.
- ⊘ **Don't Miss:** The view of Paris from the Rue Piat, above the Parc de Belleville.
- 🕐 **Organising Your Time:** Allow two-three hours for this hilly neighbourhood.
- 🚸 **Especially for Kids:** The Parc de Belleville and Maison de l'Air.
- ⚲ **Also See:** PÈRE-LACHAISE, BUTTES-CHAUMONT, PARC DE LA VILLETTE.

A Bit of History

A very old village – Once the country retreat of the Merovingian kings, then the property of several abbeys and priories, the hill and particularly the ancient ham-let of **Ménilmontant** were, for a long time, inhabited only by quarry workers and a handful of wine growers. In the 18C, it became known as Belleville, probably a corruption of *belle vue* or beautiful view, becoming a commune in 1789.

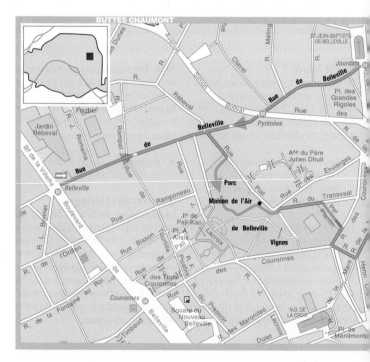

In 1860, the village, whose population had grown at an increasing pace, was annexed to Paris and allocated between the 19th and 20th *arrondissements*.
A succession of different immigrant populations has resulted in a lively, popular place to live, particularly among the young.

Walking Tour

Starting from the Belleville metro station and following rue Belleville uphill gives the walker a chance to appreciate the particularly lively character of the neighbourhood.

Rue de Belleville

This lively shopping street lined with Chinese food shops stretches from Belleville metro station to the Porte des Lilas. Edith Piaf was born at no 72.

▷ *Retrace your steps and turn left along rue Piat.*

Parc de Belleville★   Kids

Passage Julien-Lacroix, with its stone steps, is the main thoroughfare through this 4.5ha/11-acre park, converted from an quarry on Belleville Hill to a contemporary park in 1988. The differences in ground level have been used to create tiered gardens, with cascades and waterfalls. From the top of the park, above the Maison de l'Air, there is a magnificent **view**★★ of Paris.
The park has several play areas for children.

▷ *Leave the park at the top via rue Transvaal, taking the passage Plantin on the right, then turn right again onto rue des Couronnes, which overlooks the old railway line. Take rue de la Mare, then rue de Savies.*

Rue des Cascades, narrow, winding and paved, is among the quaintest in the neighbourhood, reminiscent of a small provincial town. There is a magnificent view over Paris from the corner of the steps of rue Fernand-Raynaud.
The **Regard St-Martin** at no 42, opposite rue de Savies, is one of four buildings of its kind constructed in Belleville to channel the supply of water to the capital by means of underground aqueducts. The **Regard des Messiers** is at no 17. Descend the steps. The Messiers were the guards who kept watch over the vines and fields.

▷ *At the end of rue des Cascades, take rue Ménilmontant on the left, then rue de l'Ermitage.*

Address Book

WHERE TO STAY AND EAT

♿Turn to the back of the guide for selected hotels, restaurants, bistros and cafés listed by *arrondissement*. This neighbourhood covers the 11th, 19th and 20th arrondissements.

NIGHTLIFE

Lou Pascalou – *14 rue des Panoyaux, 20th arr.* ☎*01 46 36 78 10.* This old-fashioned Belleville café is the unofficial headquarters for local characters of all ages who come in to gossip, drink coffee, read the paper, or enjoy a cool drink on the terrace in the summer.

Le Baratin – *3 rue Jouye-Rouve, 20th arr.* ☎*01 43 49 39 70. Closed Sun, Mon, 2 weeks in Aug and the first week of Jan.* Only 2min from Belleville park and its Chinese restaurants, this unsophisticated wine bar and bistro is popular with the local artists.

ARTIST ATELIERS

Les Ateliers d'Artistes de Belleville (AAB) – *32 rue de la Mare, 20th arr.* ☎*01 46 36 44 09. www.ateliers-artistes-belleville.org.* This gallery is home to the association of over 200 artists who live and work in Belleville and the surrounding neighbourhoods. They organise regular exhibits and the annual Portes Ouvertes in May.

Belleville villas and passages

Leave rue de l'Ermitage via **Villa de l'Ermitage**, a journey back in time through a picturesque village. Across rue des Pyrénées, rue de l'Est leads to **passage de la Duée,** one of the narrowest streets in Paris (1m/3.28ft).

Along rue de la Duée you will come to **villa Georgina** and rue Taclet, particularly pretty in the springtime.

A little further on, at no 40 **rue du Télégraphe**, **Claude Chappe** (1763-1805) conducted his first experiments on the telegraph in 1793.

Mur des Otages

53 rue du Borrégo. In a courtyard near the church of Notre-Dame-des-Otages, built in 1936, can be seen a fragment of the wall in front of which 52 hostages (priests, nuns, Paris civilian guards) from Grande-Roquette prison were shot by the *communards* on 26 May 1871.

Museum

Maison de l'Air   Kids

Parc de Belleville, 27 rue Piat. 🕐 *Apr–Sept, Mon–Fri 1.30pm–5.30pm, Sat–Sun 1.30pm–6.30pm (last admission 30min before closing); Oct–Mar, Tue–Fri 1.30pm–5pm.* 💶*3.35€, 7–11yrs 0.75€, 11–18yrs 1.65€.* ☎*01 43 28 47 63.*

On display is an attractive and educative permanent exhibition with games for children, explaining everything about the air which surrounds us.

Stars of Belleville

On 19 December 1915, Giovanna Gassion was born to abject poverty on the steps of 72 rue de Belleville. She later sang in the streets, before becoming a radio, gramophone and music hall success in 1935 under the name of **Édith Piaf**. Beloved for the instinctive but deeply moving inflexions of her voice, she came to embody the spirit of France *(La Vie en rose, Les Cloches).* A small private **museum** in rue Crespin-du-Gast contains souvenirs of the great singer.

Another famous figure to come from this neighbourhood was **Maurice Chevalier** (1888-1974) – film star, entertainer and *chansonnier* – he paired with Jeanne Mistinguett at the Folies-Bergère (1909) and sang at the Casino de Paris between the wars. Before attaining fame on Broadway in black-tie and boater, he was known at home for songs that were rooted in Belleville: *Ma pomme, Prosper* and *Marche de Ménilmontant.*

BERCY ★

Once the historic centre of the wine bottling industry, Bercy was transformed in the 1990s into an entertainment district, with a 13ha/32-acre riverside park, a large stadium, shops and cinemas. The massive new premises of the Ministry of Finance dominate the whole area.

- **Information:** Pyramides welcome centre, 25 rue des Pyramides. ☎08 92 68 30 00 (0.34€ per min). http://en.parisinfo.com.
- **Orient Yourself:** Bercy stretches along the Right Bank of the Seine in southeast Paris, with the Ministry of Finance at one end and Bercy Village at the other.
- **Parking:** There are several underground parking garages around the stadium, park, and Bercy Village cinemas.
- **Don't Miss:** The newly opened Cinémathèque Française within the renovated Frank Gehry building, and the historic Maison du Jardinage in the park.
- **Organising Your Time:** The main sights can be seen in about an hour or two.
- **Especially for Kids:** There are several play areas within the Parc de Bercy.
- **Also See:** BASTILLE, BOIS ET CHÂTEAU DE VINCENNES.

Sights

The Ministry of Finance

Transferred from its former home in the Rivoli wing of the Louvre, the Ministry occupies a massive modern structure straddling the embankment expressway with a foothold in the Seine.

Palais omnisports de Paris-Bercy

This new sports complex was built to stage international indoor sporting events. Outside, grass-covered walls slope down at 45 degrees. The glass roof is sheathed with a network of girders. In the square to the east of the stadium, an unusual fountain with a deep gully, the Canyoneaustrate by Gérard Singer, recalls geological formations in the North American continent.

La Cinémathèque Française

51 rue de Bercy Ⓜ Bercy *(entrance overlooking the Parc de Bercy)* ⓒ*Museum: Mon, Wed–Sat noon–7pm (until 10pm Thu) Sun 10am–8pm. Screenings: Wed–Mon, times vary.* ⊜*5€ exhibition; 6€*

Ministry of Finance

A. Eli/MICHELIN

film screenings. ☎01 71 19 32 00. www.cinematheque.fr.

The Cinémathèque houses both a cinema museum, with a permanent collection as well as many temporary exhibitions, and a theatre for regular screenings that showcase particular directors, periods, or styles from France and around the world. There's also a cinema library and research centre.

Walking Tour

▶ *Start at Parc de Bercy.*

Parc de Bercy "memory gardens"★

This public space was designed to take the place of the old wine storehouses that once stood here; a few have been left standing as historical landmarks. There are three sections to the Parc de Bercy: a vast expanse of grass lawns at the northwest end, and two gardens divided by the rue J. Kessel. The eastern one (named in honor of the assasinated Israeli president Yitzhak Rabin) includes an orchard, a vegetable garden, a vineyard and a rose garden. Water meanders and cascades through to the romantic garden to the east, with a small lake and a hilltop labyrinth.

▶ *Walk eastwards out of the park, cross rue François-Truffaut and walk beneath the arcades of the former wine warehouses to Bercy Village.*

Cour St-Émilion – Bercy Village★

Twenty years ago, the air was still filled with the smell of wine. The former stone warehouses have been converted and now house boutiques , wine bars and a cinema.

▶ *Retrace your steps to the park's grassy lawn and follow the stairs of the waterfall to the Simone de Beauvoir footbridge (opened in summer 2006). Cross to the Left Bank.*

Bibliothèque Nationale de France: site François-Mitterand★

🕐*Tue–Sat 9am-7pm, Mon 2pm–7pm, Sun 1pm–7pm.* 🗣*Guided tours by request.* 🕐*Public holidays and from 2nd–4th Mon in Sept.* ☎*3.30€.* ☎01 53 79 59 59. www.bnf.fr.

Designed by architect Dominique Perrault, the library is set atop a vast rectangular esplanade planted with trees. The tall buildings represent the shapes of four open books, framing the central area (entry ☎3.30€–10€).

Address Book

WHERE TO STAY AND EAT

♿Turn to the back of the guide for selected hotels, restaurants, bistros and cafés listed by *arrondissement*. This neighbourhood covers the 12th arrondissement.

NIGHTLIFE

Le Batofar – *Quai François-Mauriac, 13th arr.* ☎01 53 60 17 30. *Tue–Sun 8pm until at least 2am. www.batofar.org.* This former boat-lighthouse, painted red and moored opposite the François Mitterrand Library, is an invitation to travel around Europe's multiple cultures and forms of musical experimentation (electronic and avant-garde jazz). Visitors walk along the gangplanks, through cosy areas in living room-cabins to a dance floor playing house and techno music.

SPORT

Palais omnisports de Paris-Bercy (POPB) – *8 blvd de Bercy, 12th arr.* Ⓜ*Bercy.* ☎0892 390 100 (0.34€/min). www.bercy.com. It is here that many of the major sporting and musical events of the capital take place. The sports range from ice-skating (Lalique trophy), go-carting and roller skating to cycling (Open des Nations), horse jumping and gymnastics. In terms of music, many international stars of pop, rock or variety have performed here: Elton John, Bruce Springsteen, Sting, Madonna.

BOIS DE BOULOGNE★★

🚇 PORTE-MAILLOT (LINE 1), SABLONS (LINE 1), PORTE D'AUTEUIL (LINE 10) – RER: PORTE-MAILLOT (LINE C) – BUSES: 43, 52, 63, 73, 82, PC

This vast 19C park of 846ha/2 100 acres is cut by wide shaded roads, tracks for pedestrians, horses and cyclists. There are lakes and waterfalls, gardens, lawns and woodland, cafés and restaurants. Horse races take place at the Longchamp and Auteuil and music concerts take place in the Bagatelle and Pré Catalan gardens. A victim of its own popularity on the weekends, the park is a pleasant place for a stroll on weekday mornings.

Nearby neighbourhoods: **AUTEUIL, PASSY.**

- 🛈 **Information:** Pyramides welcome centre, 25 rue des Pyramides. ☎08 92 68 30 00 (0.34€ per min.) http://en.parisinfo.com.
- ▶ **Orient Yourself:** Located on the western edge of the city, the park is bordered on the west by the Seine, with the Port Maillot and the suburb of Neuilly to the north, Porte d'Auteuil and the suburb of Boulogne-Billancourt to the south.
- 🅿 **Parking:** There is parking near the Lac Inférieur and the Porte d'Auteuil.
- 👁 **Don't Miss:** The world-famous roses at the Parc de Bagatelle, the Shakespeare Garden at the Pré Catelan, and the picturesque Lac Inférieur.
- 🕐 **Organising Your Time:** Allow a half day to visit all of the sights. The best way to get around is by bike.
- 🄺🄸🄳🄸 **Especially for Kids:** The Jardin d'Acclimatation amusement park.
- 👶 **Also See:** AUTEUIL, PASSY.

A Bit of History

A royal forest – In Merovingian times the forest was hunted for bear, deer, wolves and wild boar. Later, the royal forest became a refuge for bandits, and in 1556 Henri II enclosed it with a wall pierced by eight gates. In the 17C Colbert adapted it for hunting with a crisscross of straight roads. Louis XIV opened the wood to the public as a place for country walks, but its reputation soon left a lot to be desired! According to one chronicle, 'marriages from the Bois de Boulogne do not get celebrated by the priest.

Decline – During the Revolution the forest again provided refuge to those on the run, the destitute and poachers. In 1815, the English and Russian armies set up camp in the forest, devastating a great section. In the replanting, oaks were replaced by horse chestnuts, acacias, sycamores and maples, though sadly many of these were uprooted in the great storm of 26 December 1999 and the heatwave of 2003.

The wood today – When Napoléon III gave the forest to the city in 1852, his urban planner Haussmann demolished the surrounding wall and landscaped the area, creating winding paths, ornamental lakes and ponds, the Longchamp racecourse, restaurants, kiosks and pavilions. The Auteuil racecourse was built after 1870. The 20C has seen the construction of the Paris ring road, the Jardin des Serres, the **Roland-Garros** and **Parc des Princes** stadia.

Walking Tour

In and Around The Park

Avenue Foch

This imposing avenue completed by Haussmann is 120m/394ft wide and lined on both sides by lawns and side alleys. As soon as it was inaugurated in 1854, it became the fashionable haunt of carriages on their way to the Bois de Boulogne. Private mansions and luxury

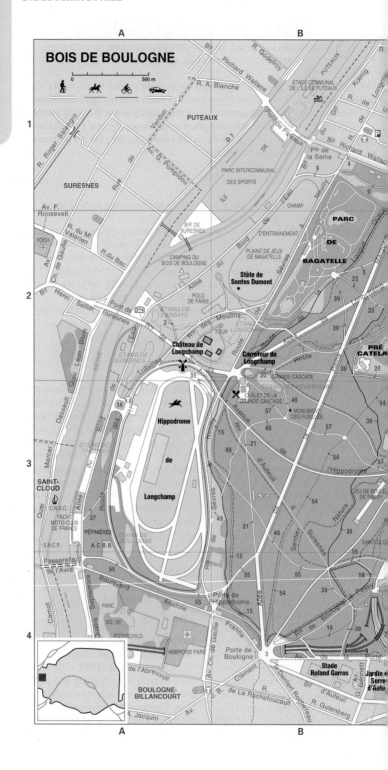

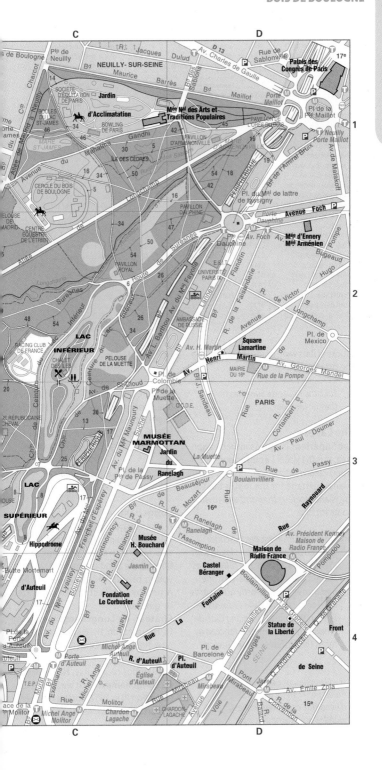

BOIS DE BOULOGNE MAP INDEX

blocks of flats were gradually built along the grass borders.

▶ *Take the Route de Suresnes to the Lac Inférieur.*

The Lakes★

Lac Supérieur is a pleasant recreation area, as is the larger **Lac Inférieur**, which is particularly popular on Sundays. It has a landing-stage for the motor boat to the islands *(café-restaurant)* and rowing boats for hire.

▶ *From the Carrefour des Cascades, situated between the two lakes, skirt the west shore of the Lac Inférieur as far as route de la Grande-Cascade and turn left then shortly afterwards right onto chemin de la Croix-Cate-lan running past the Racing Club de France's sports complex. Proceed as far as the Carrefour Croix Catelan.*

"I will not describe the Bois de Boulogne. I cannot do it. It is simply a beautiful, cultivated, endless, wonderful wilderness. It is an enchanting place." Mark Twain

Pré Catelan★

This attractive well-kept park is named after a court minstrel from Provence murdered there in the reign of Philip IV. It includes a luxurious café-restaurant, lawns and shaded areas and a copper beech nearly 200 years old with the broadest spread of branches in Paris.

▶ *Continue westwards along route de la Cascade.*

Longchamp

A picturesque although man-made waterfall (Grande Cascade) graces the crossroads **(carrefour de Longchamp)**. Beyond the pond is a monument to 35 young people shot by Nazis in 1944. A nearby oak is still visibly scarred by gunshot.

Château de Longchamp was given to Haussmann by Napoléon III and now houses the Centre International de l'Enfance.

The famous racecourse, **Hippodrome de Longchamp**, which was opened by Napoléon III in 1857, hosts a number of important racing events.

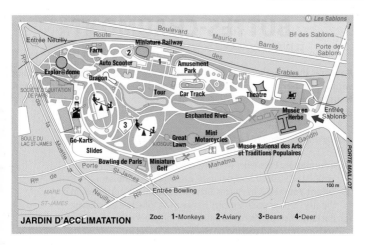

Museums and Other Attractions

Jardin d'Acclimatation   Kids

♿ 🕑 *May–Sept, 10am–7pm; Oct–Apr, 10am–6pm.* Ⓢ*2.7€.* ☏*01 40 67 90 82. www.jardindacclimatation.fr.*

This park, primarily arranged as a children's amusement park, includes a small zoo with a pets' corner, a typical Norman farm and an aviary. The **Musée en Herbe** (🕑*daily 10am–6pm;* 🕑*1 Jan and 25 Dec;* Ⓢ*4€;* ☏*01 40 67 97 66; www.musee-en-herbe.com)* is an art-museum-cum-workshop designed for youngsters.

The **Explor@dome** (🕑*daily 10am–6pm;* 🕑*public holidays and first two weeks in Aug;* Ⓢ*5€;* ☏*01 53 64 90 40; www. exploradome.com)* is a science and multimedia area.

Parc de Bagatelle★★

Route de Sèvres-à-Neuilly. 🕑*Jun–Sept, daily 9.30am–8pm; Oct–Dec & Mar–May until 6pm; Jan–Feb until 5pm.* Ⓢ*3€.* ☏*01 40 71 75 60.*

In 1775 the Count of Artois – future Charles X – waged a bet with his sister-in-law, **Marie-Antoinette**, that he would have a house designed and built, complete with its landscaped garden, within three months. He won. Bagatelle survived the Revolution and was passed to Napoléon, the Duc de Berry, the Hertford family and finally sold to the City of Paris in 1905. Bagatelle is well known for its beautiful garden.

Parc de Bagatelle

BUTTES-CHAUMONT★

Ⓜ BUTTES-CHAUMONT, BOTZARIS (LINE 7 BIS) – BUSES: 26, 60, 75

Known as the *mont chauve*, the denuded (literally *bald*) rise of Chaumont, riddled with open quarrying and full of dumped rubbish, used to be a sinister place until **Haussmann** and **Napoléon III** transformed the area by creating the very first park on the northern edge of Paris, between 1864 and 1867.

Nearby neighbourhoods: **LA VILLETTE, BELLEVILLE**.

🅸 **Information:** Pyramides welcome centre, 25 rue des Pyramides.
☎08 92 68 30 00 (0.34€ per min). http://en.parisinfo.com.

▶ **Orient Yourself:** The Buttes-Chaumont are in the northeastern corner of the city (19th *arrondissement*), between La Villette and Belleville.

🅿 **Parking:** There is plenty of parking in this predominantly residential area, and underground parking on the avenue Secretan.

☺ **Don't Miss:** The panoramic views from the park's temple.

🕐 **Organizing Your Time:** Allow an hour for the park and surrounding streets.

Visit

The park★
Built along the contours of the original quarry, the park is known for its dramatic hills and cliffs. In the centre is a man-made lake, landscaped with an island and huge rocks 50m/164ft high (half natural, half artificial). Access was provided by two bridges: one in brick, nicknamed the suicide bridge, the other a footbridge. The Corinthian style Sybille

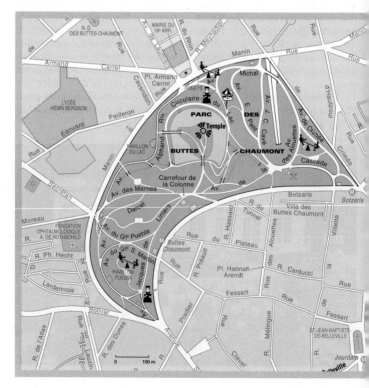

Address Book

WHERE TO STAY AND EAT

🍴 Turn to the back of the guide for selected hotels, restaurants, bistros and cafés listed by *arrondissement*. This neighbourhood covers the 16th arrondissement.

LEISURE ACTIVITIES

Bike Rental - ☎*01 47 47 76 50. Open daily mid-Apr to mid-Oct; open Wed, Sat–Sun and holidays mid-Oct–mid-Apr.* ⚹*5€/hr.* Bike rental stands are

found by the entrance of the Jardin d'Acclimatation and the north end of the Lac Inférieur.

Petit Train du Jardin d'Acclimatation – *Service between the Porte Maillot and the amusement park. May–Sept , daily 10am–7pm; Oct–Apr, 10am–6pm.* ⚹*6€.* ☎*01 40 72 16 16.*

Boat Rental – *At the north end of the Lac Inférieur.* ☎*01 45 25 44 01. Open daily May–Sept, 10am–6pm; Oct–Apr, noon–5.30pm.* ⚹*10€/hr.*

---

temple on the island, modelled on the Roman temple of the same name in Tivoli, Italy, commands a good view over Montmartre and St-Denis. Additional folly features include a waterfall and cave encrusted with stalactites. There are 5km/3mi of walks past lawns and a variety of indigenous and exotic trees such as Cedars of Lebanon, Byzantine Hazelnut, and Siberian Elm which make this one of Paris' favourite parks.

Quartier d'Amérique
To the east of the park.

Hidden behind a screen of modern buildings, this area consists of charming small houses built at the end of the 19C for the workers of eastern Paris. Today, this maze of flower-decked villas looks like a provincial enclave within Paris.

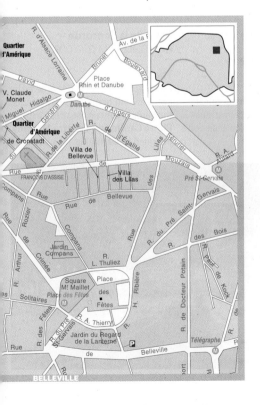

CHAMPS-ÉLYSÉES★★★

Ⓜ CONCORDE (LINES 1, 8 AND 12), CHAMPS-ÉLYSÉES-CLEMENCEAU (LINES 1 AND 13), FRANKLIN-D.-ROOSEVELT (LINES 1 AND 9), GEORGES-V (LINE 1), CHARLES-DE-GAULLE-ÉTOILE (LINES 1, 2 AND 6) – BUSES: 22, 28, 31, 42, 52, 73, 83, 84, 92, 94

The most famous thoroughfare in Paris is at once an avenue with a spectacular view, a place of entertainment and a street of smart luxury shops. The vista extending down the Champs-Élysées, with the Arc de Triomphe silhouetted against the sky, is known the world over. To Parisians it is the Voie Triomphale or **Triumphal Way**. At times of great patriotic fervour, the triumphal avenue continues to be the spontaneous rallying point for the people of Paris.

Nearby neighbourhoods: **ALMA, PLACE DE LA CONCORDE, TUILERIES, FAUBOURG ST-HONORÉ, INVALIDES, TROCADÉRO, MONCEAU.**

- 🛈 **Information:** Pyramides welcome centre, 25 rue des Pyramides. ☎082 68 300 (0.34€ per min). http://en.parisinfo.com.
- ▶ **Orient Yourself:** The Champs-Élysées stretches from the Arc de Triomphe to the Place de la Concorde on the Right Bank of the Seine.
- 🅿 **Parking:** Underground parking can be found on the avenue.
- 👁 **Don't Miss:** Views from the Arc de Triomphe platform, pastries at Ladurée.
- 🕐 **Organizing Your Time:** Allow 1–2 hours if you plan on stopping in shops, longer if you want to visit the museums.
- 🅺🅸🅳🆂 **Especially for Kids:** The marionnette theatre near the Rond-Point des Champs-Elysées and the Palais de la Decouverte.
- 👟 **Also See:** LES INVALIDES, PLACE DE LA CONCORDE, JARDIN DES TUILERIES.

Walking Tours 👟*See map*

1 Walking up the Champs-Élysées

This walk starts from the splendid place de la Concorde and continues through the gardens in the lower part of the avenue.

Place de la Concorde –
👟*see PLACE DE LA CONCORDE.*

The Gardens★
Landscaped with trees and bordered by avenues with grand horse-chestnuts, the gardens contain theatres **L'espace Pierre Cardin** and **Théâtre Marigny**, designed by **Garnier** in 1853, and used

Looking up the Champs-Élysées to the Arc de Triomphe

A. Eü/MICHELIN

Address Book

NIGHTLIFE

Bound – *49 av. George-V, 8th arr.* ☎*01 53 67 84 60. Daily.* The former BarFly now has a chic, contemporary décor, house and lounge background music and deep armchairs. Soft lighting and a young, relatively well-to-do clique of regulars set the scene for this quintessential international bar and restaurant.

Flûte Etoile Champagne Bar *19 rue de l'Etoile, 17th arr.* ☎*01 45 72 10 14. www. flutebar.com. Closed Sun, Mon.* Very discreet bar with a New York feel to it. On two levels with a bar downstairs and a cosy mezzanine level with red velour seats. Fifteen different champagnes on offer.

Charlie Birdy – *124 rue La-Boétie, 8th arr. Daily .* ☎*01 42 25 18 06. www. charliebirdy.com.* A large Anglo-American pub with Chesterfield sofas and Indian décor touches, frequented by a young, cheerful crowd. Live jazz and blues music every Sunday. Good quality hamburgers, and an Ice Bird Bar on the lower level.

Fouquet's (Barrière) – *99 av. des Champs-Élysées, 8th arr.* Ⓜ*Georges-V.* ☎*01 47 23 50 00. Daily.* Now a listed monument, Fouquet's has one of the few remaining historical terraces on the Champs-Elysées. It is equally in favour with TV and film celebrities as with the literary world. Renovated in 1999, Fouquet's now combines a brasserie-style menu with the inventive cuisine of Jean-François Lemercier, elected best craftsman of France in 1993.

Montecristo café – *68 av. des Champs-Élysées, 8th arr.* ☎*01 45 62 30 86. Daily.* One of the best places to enjoy the magic of Cuba in Paris. A smart crowd congregates here for a drink, lunch or dinner, and also to dance or smoke a cigar within the walls covered in Cuban graffiti and attractive mural frescoes. Salsa lessons available on Sunday afternoons and in the evenings from Tuesday to Friday. Very crowded at the weekends.

Sir Winston – *5 rue de Presbourg, 16th arr.* ☎*01 40 67 17 37. Daily.* This large bar-restaurant stands behind a very British-looking façade. The interior decoration has combined a whole host of influences: a Chinese room, a leopard lounge in the basement and small private booths. The place is bathed in soft lights, world music rhythms and hip-hop beats.

SHOPPING

Ladurée – *75 av. des Champs-Élysées, 8th arr.* Ⓜ*Franklin-D.-Roosevelt.* ☎*01 40 75 08 75. Daily. www.laduree.fr.* This historic pastry shop and tea room has the best macarons in Paris, in no less than 13 flavours.

Guerlain – *68 av. des Champs-Élysées, 8th arr.* Ⓜ*Franklin-D.-Roosevelt.* ☎*01 45 62 11 21. www.guerlain.fr.* Mon–Wed 9am–7pm, Thur–Sat 9am–8am. The history of this illustrious family so acclaimed in the perfume world began back in 1828. Today the marble floors and walls of this perfumery and beauty institute are listed monuments. It sells all of Jean-Paul Guerlain's creations.

Drugstore Publicis – *133 av. des Champs-Élysées, 8th arr.* Ⓜ*Charles De Gaulle Etoile.* ☎*01 44 43 79 00. www. publicisdrugstore.com. Daily.* Don't let the name fool you; more than a drugstore, Publicis is a Paris institution since the 1950s, with a café, restaurant, international press and tabac, luxury gift boutique, wine cellar, book shop and even a cinema house. A stylish place to see and be seen, the building was given a contemporary new look in 2003.

Disney® Store – Ⓚ *44 av. des Champs-Élysées, 8th arr.* Ⓜ*Franklin-D.-Roosevelt.* ☎*01 45 61 45 25. Daily. Closed 1 May and 25 Dec.* Toys, clothes, disguises, accessories, music, videos, etc. All of Disney's products are presented here in this vast children's bedroom, equipped with a giant screen which projects clips from all the latest cartoons all day long.

Stamp market – *Carré Marigny (on the corner of avenue de Marigny and avenue Gabriel), 8th arr.* Ⓜ*Champs-Élysées-Clemenceau. Thu, weekends and public holidays 9am–6pm.*

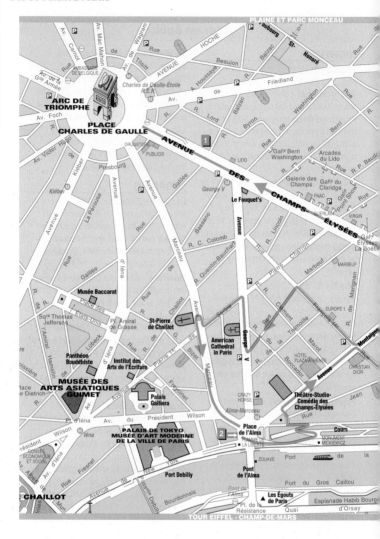

almost exclusively by Jacques Offenbach from 1855 to amuse the Parisian public with his operettas. Four monuments evoke heroes of past wars: in place Clemenceau stands a bronze statue of the statesman **Georges Clemenceau**, *The Father of Victory*, by François Cogné (1932). Across avenue Winston-Churchill stands the statue of **Général de Gaulle** by J Cardot (2000). The monument on the corner with avenue Marigny honors Resistance leader **Jean Moulin**. Near cours de la Reine is the statue of **Sir Winston Churchill**, looking resolute as ever.

Avenue Gabriel

Shaded gardens on the northern side, running parallel to the Champs-Élysées, stretch along the back of smart mansions lining the Faubourg St-Honoré: the **Elysée Palace** (fine wrought-iron gate with gilded cockerel, 1905), the British Embassy, the United States Embassy (in the former home of the gastronome Grimod de la Reynière).

Avenue des Champs-Élysées★★★

Today, the Champs-Élysées is lined with restaurants and cafés, motor-car showrooms and banks, cinemas and night

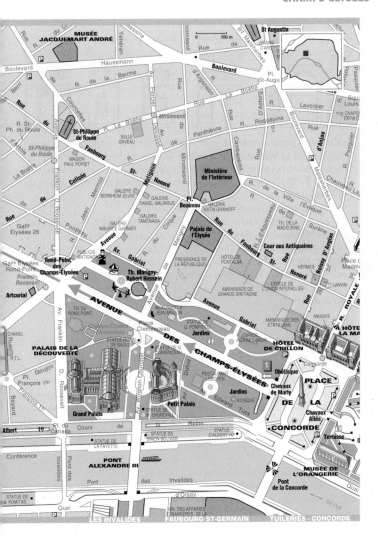

clubs. Most of the shops are international chains, with the majority of the luxury fashion boutiques found along the side streets like avenues George V and Montaigne. The Second Empire private houses and amusement halls that once lined it have vanished; the only exception is no **25**, a mansion built by La Païva, a Polish adventures, whose house was famous for dinners attended by philosophers, painters and writers, and for its unique onyx staircase. **Le Colisée**, an amphitheatre built in 1770 to hold an audience of 40 000, has left its name to a street, a café and a cinema.

Arc de Triomphe★★★

The arch and **place Charles-de-Gaulle★★★**, which surrounds it, form one of Paris' most famous landmarks. Twelve avenues radiate from the arch which explains why it is also called **place de l'Étoile** (*étoile* meaning star). The arch commemorates Napoléon's victories, evoking at the same time imperial glory and the fate of the Unknown Soldier, whose tomb lies beneath.

A Bit of History

By the end of the 18C the square was already star-shaped despite having only five roads leading from it. At the centre

115

Facing the Champs-Élysées: **1** – *The Departure of the Volunteers* in 1792, commonly called **La Marseillaise**★★, Rude's sublime masterpiece represents the Nation leading her people to defend their independence; **2** – *General Marceau's Funeral;* **3** – *The Triumph of 1810* (by Cortot) celebrating the Treaty of Vienna; **4** – *The Battle of Aboukir.*

Facing avenue de Wagram: **5** – *The Battle of Austerlitz.*

Facing avenue de la Grande-Armée: **6** – *Resistance* (by Etex); **7** – *The Passage of the Bridge of Arcola;* **8** – *Peace* (by Etex); **9** – *The Capture of Alexandria.*

Facing avenue Kléber: **10** – *The Battle of Jemmapes.*

Beneath the monument, the flame of the Unknown Soldier is rekindled each evening at 6.30pm. Lesser battles are engraved on the arch's inner walls together with the names of 558 generals – the names of those who died in the field are underlined.

was a semicircular lawn. **Napoléon** commissioned **Chalgrin** to construct a giant arch in 1806. It wouldn't be finished until 1836, under **Louis-Philippe**. In 1840 the carriage bearing the Emperor's body passed beneath the arch. **Haussmann** redesigned the square in 1854, creating a further seven radiating avenues, while Hittorff planned the uniform façades which surround it.

On 14 July 1919, victorious Allied armies, led by the marshals, marched in procession. The unknown soldier killed in the Great War was laid to rest in 1921. On 26 August 1944, Paris was liberated from

Grand Palais

S. Sauvignier/MICHELIN

German occupation, and Général de Gaulle marched through the arch.

The arch

Chalgrin's undertaking, inspired by Antiquity, is truly colossal, measuring 50m/164ft high by 45m/147.6ft wide, with massive high reliefs. The arch's proportions and the relative scale of the sculpted reliefs are best appreciated from a distance.

Rude was commissioned to carve the four main panels, but Etex and Cortot managed to steal work for three of the four groups – Rude's is the only inspired one. Pradier's Fames, four trumpet-blowing figures, abut the main arches. A frieze bustling with hundreds of figures, each 2m/6.5ft tall, encircles the arch.

The Arch platform

🕐*Apr–Sept, 10am–11pm (last admission 30min before closing); Oct–Mar, 10am–10.30pm.* 🕐*1 Jan, 1 and 8 May (morning), 14 Jul (morning), 11 Nov (morning), 25 Dec.* ⊜*8€.* ☎*01 55 37 73 77.*

From here there is an excellent **view**★★★ of the capital: in the foreground the 12 avenues radiating from the square; you are halfway between the Louvre and La Défense, at the top of the Champs-

Élysées. Assembled in a small museum are mementoes of its construction and the celebratory and funerary ceremonies it has hosted.

2 Place de l'Alma
See ALMA.

Museums and other Attractions

Musée du Petit Palais★
Avenue Winston-Churchill. ⏰Tue–Sun 10am–6pm ⏰Public holidays. ♿☎01 53 43 40 00. www.petitpalais.paris.fr.
Completely restored and reopened in May 2006, the Petit Palais, Musée des Beaux-Arts de la ville de Paris features the Dutuit (antiques, medieval and Renaissance art objects, paintings, drawings, books, enamels, porcelain) and Tuck (18C furniture and objets d'art) bequests, alongside the city of Paris' collection of 19C paintings (**Ingres, Delacroix,** Courbet, Dalou, **Barbizon School,** Impressionists). Note in particular *The Good Samaritan* (1880) by A Morot and *Ascension* (1879) by **Gustave Doré**.

Grand Palais★
This great exhibition hall is formally fronted by an Ionic colonnade running the length of the building, before a mosaic frieze. Enormous quadrigae punctuate the corners; elsewhere turn-of-the-19C modern-style decorative elements are scattered. Inside, a single glazed space is covered by a flattened dome.

With an exhibition area of nearly 5 000sq m/5 980sq yd, the **Galeries du Grand Palais** *(3 avenue du Général-Eisenhower. ⏰Wed–Sun 10am–8pm (until 10pm on Wed). ⏰1 May and 25 Dec. ☜10€; with reservation, 11.50€; www.rmn.fr)* have now become a cultural centre for temporary exhibitions from around the world.

Palais de la Découverte★★ Kids
Inside the Grand Palais; entrance on avenue Franklin-D.-Roosevelt. ⏰Tue–Sun 9.30am–6pm, Sun and public holidays 10am–7pm (last entrance 1hr before closing). ⏰1 Jan, 1 May, 14 Jul, 15 Aug and 25 Dec. ☜7€; children 4.50€). Planetarium 3.50€. ☎01 56 43 20 20. www.palais-decouverte.fr.
This museum, founded by a physicist in 1937 and dedicated to scientific discovery, is a centre both for higher scientific study and for popular enlightenment. *Allow half a day.* Many interactive attractions are specially intended for children, particularly in the field of biology. Other themes dealt with (mathematics, nuclear physics) are intended for visitors who are already competent in these fields.
The domed **planetarium**★ *(level 2)* presents a clear and fascinating introduction to the heavens including the course of the planets in the solar system.

Baron Haussmann

More than anyone else, Georges Eugène Haussmann (1809-1891) was responsible for the way the city of Paris appears today. A lawyer by training, he went on to become a professional civil servant and was appointed Prefect of the Seine by Napoléon III in 1852. He set about demolishing the filthy crowded streets of the medieval city, which were thought to have caused the cholera epidemic of 1832, in which about 20 000 Parisians perished. His vision was to create a well-ordered, airy city within a geometrical pattern and he set about widening the existing Grand Boulevards in addition to building new ones such as the Boulevard Richard Lenoir. His work can be best appreciated from the viewing platform of the Arc de Triomphe. Although not responsible for the Arc itself, which had been finished by Louis-Philippe in 1836, Haussmann completed a star of twelve magnificent avenues radiating from the Place de l'Étoile in which the world famous monument is located.

CHÂTELET-HÔTEL DE VILLE★

Ⓜ CHÂTELET (LINES 1, 4, 7, 11 AND 14), HÔTEL-DE-VILLE (LINES 1 AND 11) – RER: CHÂTELET (LINES A, B, D) – BUSES: 21, 69, 70, 72, 74, 75, 76, 81, 96

This is the heart of Paris, bounded to the south by the Seine and traversed by the busy rue de Rivoli. Despite the neighbourhood's reputation as a busy shopping district and transportation hub, its many historic buildings attest its important role in the significant events of the city throughout the centuries.

Nearby neighbourhoods: **BEAUBOURG, LES HALLES, ÎLE DE LA CITÉ, CONCIER-GERIE, NOTRE-DAME, SAINTE-CHAPELLE, QUARTIER LATIN, ÎLE ST-LOUIS, LE MARAIS.**

- 🛈 **Information:** Carrousel du Louvre Welcome Centre, Place de la Pyramide Inversée 99, rue de Rivoli. ☎08 92 68 30 00.(0.34€ per min). http://en.parisinfo.com.
- ▶ **Orient Yourself:** The Place du Châtelet is the centre of this district, between the Seine and the intersection of the two major roads, rue de Rivoli and boulevard Sébastopol.
- 🅿 **Parking:** Underground parking is found around the Hôtel de Ville.
- 🚫 **Don't Miss:** The imposing façade of the Hôtel de Ville and the Gothic architecture of St-Germain-l'Auxerrois.
- 🕐 **Organizing Your Time:** Allow an hour to visit this compact neighbourhood.
- 🧒 **Especially for Kids:** There's a carrousel on the square at the Hôtel de Ville.
- 👣 **Also See:** LE MARAIS, LE GRAND LOUVRE, ÎLE DE LA CITÉ.

A Bit of History

Maison aux Piliers – Paris was administered by a representative of the king until the 13C when municipal government was introduced, monopolised by the powerful watermen's guild, which controlled the Seine. The municipal assembly, headed by a merchant provost (Étienne Marcel) and four aldermen, was based at the Pillared House on place de Grève (👣*see below*) from 1357.

The Hôtel de Ville – Under François I, the dilapidated Pillared House was replaced by a mansion designed by Domenico Bernabei. The first stone was laid in 1533 but not finished until the early 17C. The central section of the present façade reproduces the original.

July 1789 – After the fall of the Bastille, the rioters marched on to the town hall for arms. Throughout the Revolution the town hall was controlled by the Commune. On 17 July 1789, Louis XVI appeared in the hall to kiss the newly adopted tricolour cockade. Between red and blue, the city colours since the provostship of Étienne Marcel in the 14C, La Fayette introduced the royal white.

The Second Republic – In 1848, when Louis-Philippe was dismissed, it was in the Hôtel de Ville that the provisional

Étienne Marcel

This rich draper, a merchant provost, became leader of the States General in 1357 and came out in open revolt against royal power. By holding Paris, he tried to rally the whole of France to arms, allied himself with the peasants in revolt and allowed the English into the city. But Charles V who had taken refuge in the Hôtel St-Paul resisted victoriously, leaving Marcel to die a miserable death at the hands of the Parisians in 1358, just as he was about to open the city gates to Charles the Bad, King of Navarre.

Address Book

WHERE TO STAY AND EAT

🕭 Turn to the back of the guide for selected hotels, restaurants, bistros and cafés listed by *arrondissement*. This neighbourhood is in the 1st and the 4th arrondissements.

NIGHTLIFE

Sunside/Sunset – *60 rue des Lombards 1st arr.* ☎*01 40 26 46 60. www.sunset-sunside.com. Daily.* One of the hotspots for Parisian jazz, the intimate Sunside (upstairs) and Sunset (downstairs) host nightly concerts by musicians from around the world. All types of jazz, from the 1940s up until today.

SHOPPING

Rue de Rivoli – Built during the reigns of Napoléon I and Louis-Philippe, this street witnessed two important events:

the proclamation of the Republic on 21 September 1792 and the arrest of General von Choltitz in August 1944. Today it is one of the main shopping streets in central Paris with several department stores between the Place de la Concorde and the metro St-Paul.

Le Bazar de l'Hôtel de Ville – *55 rue de la Verrerie, 4th arr.* Ⓜ*Hôtel-de-Ville.* ☎*01 42 74 90 00. www.bhv.fr. Closed Sun.* This eternally packed department store is one of the capital's landmarks. If you're looking for something in the realms of decoration or home improvement, you will be hard-pressed not to find it here.

Etam – *67 rue de Rivoli, 4th arr.* Ⓜ*Hôtel-de-Ville.* ☎*01 44 76 73 73. Closed Sun.* A trendy women's clothing and accessories store on five levels in one of the historic Samaritaine department store buildings.

---

government was set up and from there that the Second Republic was proclaimed on 24 February 1848.

The Second Empire and Commune of 1871 – Louis Napoléon proclaimed himself emperor in 1851 and charged his Prefect of the Seine, Baron Haussmann, with re-planning the area around the Hôtel de Ville. He razed the adjoining streets, enlarged the square and built the two barracks in rue de Lobau.
On 4 September 1870, after the defeat of the French Army at the Battle of Sedan, Gambetta, Jules Favre and Jules Ferry proclaimed the Third Republic from the Hôtel de Ville and instituted a National Defence Government. The capitulation of Paris on 28 January 1871, however, roused the citizens to revolt against the government, installing in its place the Paris Commune. In May during its final overthrow, the Hôtel de Ville, the Tuileries and several other buildings were set on fire by the Federalists.

25 August 1944 – It was from here that General de Gaulle made his famous speech *"Paris! Paris outragé! Paris brisé! Paris martyrisé! mais Paris libéré! libéré par lui-même! libéré par son peuple avec*

le concours des armées de la France…". Since 1977, the Hôtel de Ville is Paris' official reception and city government building.

Sights

Église St-Germain-L'Auxerrois★★

In what is now place du Louvre, the Roman Labienus pitched his camp when he crushed the Parisii in 52 BC, as did the Normans when they besieged Paris in 885. Until the Second Empire, fine mansions stood between the Louvre and the church, including the Petit Bourbon (demolished 1660).
The church, named after St Germanus, Bishop of Auxerre in the 5C, spans five centuries of architectural development from the Romanesque (belfry) via High Gothic (chancel) and Flamboyant (porch and nave) to the Renaissance (doorway). Substantial restoration in the hands of Baltard and Lassus (1838-55) emphasised its composite nature further.
When the Valois moved into the Louvre in the 14C, St-Germain became the king's parish church and thereby received embellishments and endowments. On

the night of 24 August 1572, the bells rang for matins giving the signal for the **St Bartholomew's Day Massacre** when thousands of Huguenots, invited to celebrate the marriage of Henri of Navarre to his cousin, Marguerite of Valois, were slaughtered according to a plan hatched by the Cardinal Duke of Guise, Catherine de' Medici, Charles IX and the future Henri III.

Many poets (Jodelle, Malherbe), painters (Coypel, Boucher, Nattier, Chardin, Van Loo), sculptors (Coysevox, the two Coustous), architects (Le Vau, Robert de Cotte, Gabriel the Elder, Soufflot) and others associated with the court and the Louvre are buried in the church.

Porch

The porch is the building's most original feature, dating from between 1435 and 1439. The column-statues are modern. The outermost, lowest, bays accommodate small chambers, covered with slate, in which the chapter placed the church archives and treasure. The three middle bays have multi-ribbed Flamboyant vaults, flanked by a plain Gothic bay. The most interesting, the central doorway is 13C. The figure in the right embrasure represents St Geneviève holding a candle which a small devil tries to snuff out, while an angel nearby, stands ready with a taper to rekindle it.

Interior

The restored 18C organ comes from the Sainte-Chapelle. The **churchwarden's pew**, dating from 1684, is thought to have been used by successive kings and their families. In the fourth chapel is a fine early 16C, Flemish **altarpiece**.

The **stained glass** in the transept and the two rose windows date from the 16C. The **chancel** is surrounded by an 18C grille before which stand 15C polychrome statues of St Germanus and St Vincent. The **Chapel of the Holy Sacrament** *(on the right of the entrance)* contains a 14C polychrome stone statue of the Virgin.

La Samaritaine

This department store overlooking the Pont Neuf is named after a pump (1602) under the bridge that drew water from the river to supply the Louvre and which, being decorated with a figure of the woman of Samaria giving Jesus water at the well, became known as the *Samaritaine*. ☞*The department store is closed indefinitely for structural renovations. www.lasamaritaine.com.*

Quai de la Mégisserie

This section of the embankment gets its name from the stinking public slaughterhouse (*mégisserie* meaning tawing) that lined the river until the Revolution. Now there are rows of garden and pet shops. An attractive **view**★★ extends over the law courts, Conciergerie, and the old houses across the river.

Tour St-Jacques and the Hôtel de Ville

P. Gajic/MICHELIN

Place du Châtelet

The area gets its name from the Grand Châtelet, a great fortress that guarded the northern entrance into the city, over the Pont au Change. The fort in turn accommodated the city notaries, surrounded by the halls of powerful guilds (butchers, sausage-makers, skinners and tanners). The Châtelet or **Palm Fountain** (1806-07) commemorates Napoléon's victories; the base was decorated with sphinxes in 1858.

The two theatres on either side were built by the architect Davioud in 1862. The Châtelet or Théâtre Musical de Paris (west side) staged performances by Diaghilev's Ballets Russes, Caruso, Mahler, Nijinski and others. Opposite, the Théâtre de la Ville, formerly the Sarah Bernhardt Theatre, is a centre of popular culture (east side).

S. Sauvignier/MICHELIN

Place du Châtelet

Tour St-Jacques★

The tower is the former belfry of the church of St-Jacques-la-Boucherie, built in the 16C and one of the starting points for pilgrims journeying up rue St-Jacques and on to Santiago de Compostela in Spain. The church was pulled down in 1802 and the tower converted to a weather station. ⚊*Closed for restoration.*

Place de l'Hôtel-de-Ville

Place de Grève, as it was known until 1830, shelves gently down to the Seine. In the Middle Ages, the foreshore or *grève,* became a meeting place for those out of work, hence the expression *faire la grève* meaning not working or on strike.

During the Ancien Régime, it was where *bourgeois* and commoners were hanged and where gentlemen were beheaded by the axe or the sword; witches and heretics were burnt at the stake; murderers were condemned to the wheel and punishment for treason consisted of being drawn and quartered.

Hôtel de Ville★

The Hôtel de Ville was entirely rebuilt between 1874 and 1882, following the fire during the fall of the Paris Commune in 1871. It was built in the neo-Renais-sance style by Ballu and Deperthes, its façades adorned with 146 statues of illustrious people and French towns.

Bazar de l'Hôtel de Ville

This store was founded in 1856 by Xavier Ruel, a street pedlar who had realised the commercial value of the site. A major part of its stock has always consisted of home improvement and decoration materials.

Pont Notre-Dame

(1913) This was the Great Bridge in Roman times, as opposed to the Small Bridge (Petit Pont) on the far side of the island. Burnt down by the Normans and rebuilt on piles in 1413, it was the first to be given an official name, and the houses built on it were the first to be numbered in Paris. It fell down in Louis XII's reign (1499), but was rebuilt and lined with identical houses with richly decorated façades, since it was on the royal route of solemn entries into Paris.

Pont au Change

The Money Changers' Bridge was established in the 9C by Charles the Bald. It was so tightly lined with workshops and houses all through the Middle Ages that one could cross the river without glimpsing it! These were cleared in 1788. Louis VII instituted a money exchange here in 1141, where all foreigners and visitors to Paris bartered for the best rate of exchange. The present bridge dates from 1860.

ÎLE DE LA CITÉ★★★

Ⓜ CITÉ (LINE 4) – RER: ST-MICHEL-NOTRE-DAME (LINE C) – BUSES: 21, 27, 38, 58, 70, 96

The Île de la Cité is the cradle of Paris, geographically at the very heart of the capital. Its history, architecture and remarkable setting make it one of the city's principal attractions; its most impressive monument is undoubtedly the Cathedral of Notre-Dame (Ⓒ see NOTRE-DAME), closely followed by the most exquisite Sainte-Chapelle (Ⓒ see SAINTE-CHAPELLE) and the Conciergerie (Ⓒ see CONCIERGERIE).

Nearby neighbourhoods: **ÎLE ST-LOUIS, CHÂTELET-HOTEL DE VILLE, QUARTIER LATIN, MAUBERT.**

- 🅸 **Information:** Carrousel du Louvre Welcome Centre, Place de la Pyrmide Inversée 99, rue de Rivoli. ☎08 92 68 30 00 (0.34€ per min). http://en.parisinfo.com.
- ▶ **Orient Yourself:** The Île-de-la-Cité is in the geographical centre of Paris; with the Left Bank to the south and the Right Bank to the north.
- 🅿 **Parking:** Underground parking can be found on rue de Lutèce and rue de la Cité.
- 🅓 **Don't Miss:** The flower market on the Place Lépine, the view of Notre Dame from the Square Jean XXIII, and the stained glass windows of Ste-Chapelle.
- 🕑 **Organizing Your Time:** Allow 1–2 hours to visit all of the sights on the island.
- 🅚🅘🅓🅢 **Especially for Kids:** There is a playground in the gardens of the Square Jean XXIII.
- 🅐 **Also See:** QUARTIER LATIN, CHÂTELET-HÔTEL DE VILLE, ÎLE ST-LOUIS.

A Bit of History

Lutetia – Around 200 BC Gaulish fishermen and **boatmen** of the Parisii tribe discovered and set up their huts on the largest island in the Seine – Lutetia was born. The township was conquered by Roman legions in 52 BC and prospered on shipping. The boatmen's existence has been confirmed by the discovery beneath Notre-Dame of one of their pagan altars.

In AD 360 the Roman prefect, Julian the Apostate, was here proclaimed emperor by his legions. At the same time, Lutetia was renamed after its inhabitants and shortened to Paris.

The view of the Île de la Cité with the Cathédral de Notre-Dame from the Île St-Louis

G. Targat/Michelin

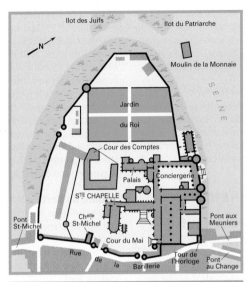

ILE DE LA CITÉ : DOWNSTREAM END IN THE 15C

Sainte Geneviève – In AD 451 Attila crossed the Rhine with 700 000 men; as he reached Laon the Parisians began to flee. Geneviève, a young girl from Nanterre who had dedicated her life to God, calmed them with the assurance that the town would be saved by heavenly intervention; the Huns approached, hesitated and turned away to advance on Orléans. Parisians adopted the girl as their protector and patron.

Ten years later when the island was besieged by the Franks and suffered famine, Geneviève escaped the enemy watch, loaded boats with victuals in Champagne and returned undetected as if by miracle. She died in AD 512 and was buried at King Clovis' side.

The Count of Paris becomes King – In AD 885, for the fifth time in 40 years, the Normans sailed up the Seine. The Cité – the name adopted in AD 506 when **Clovis** made it his capital – was confronted by 700 ships bearing 30 000 warriors bent on pillaging Burgundy. Assault and siege proving unsuccessful. Eudes, Count of Paris and the leader of the resistance, was thereupon elected king.

Cathedral and Parliament – During the Middle Ages the population grew, spilling onto both banks of the river. The number of schools around the cathedral proliferated, many becoming famous throughout Europe. Among the teachers were Alexander of Paris, creator of the 12-footed *alexandrine* line in poetry and, at the beginning of the 12C, the philosopher **Abelard**, whose moving romance with Héloïse, the niece of the canon Fulbert, began in the cloisters of Notre-Dame. Chapels and convents multiplied on the island; by the close of the 13C, there were at least 22 bell-towers! The Cité, the seat of Parliament, the highest judiciary in the kingdom was, inevitably, involved in revolutions and uprisings such as that attempted in the 14C by **Étienne Marcel** (*see CHÂTELET-HÔTEL DE VILLE*) and the **Fronde** in the 17C. During the Terror of 1793-94 the Conciergerie prisons were crowded, while next door the Revolutionary Tribunal continued to sit in the law courts, endlessly pronouncing merciless sentences.

Transformation – Under Louis-Philippe and to an even greater extent, under Napoléon III, the entire centre of the island was demolished: 25 000 people were evacuated. Enormous administrative buildings were erected: the Hôtel-Dieu, barracks (now the police prefecture), the commercial courts; the Law Courts were doubled in size; place du Parvis before the cathedral was quadrupled in size; boulevard du Palais was built ten times wider than before.

August 1944 – The Paris police barricaded themselves in the prefecture and hoisted the tricolour. For three days they held the Germans at bay until relieved by the arrival of the French Army Division under Général Leclerc.

Walking Tours

1 From Pont Neuf to Notre-Dame

Pont Neuf★

Pont Neuf is the oldest of the Paris bridges, and was the first road in Paris to benefit from pavements separating pedestrians and traffic. The original equestrian statue

of **Henri IV** was melted down at the Revolution in 1792 and replaced during the Restoration with the present figure, made of bronze. Built in two halves between 1578 and 1604, the bridge is on a broken axis. The 12 rounded arches each have a keystone carved with humorous grotesques. In the olden days, it used to be crowded with stallholders, tooth pullers, comic characters such as Tabarin and the Italian Pantaloon, Scarlatini, the all-time charlatan and a host of gawpers and pickpockets.

Square du Vert-Galant

Down the steps behind the Henri IV statue, this serene stretch of green is at its natural ground level, before the land was built up by **Henri III**. From the tip is a fine view of Pont Neuf, the Louvre and the Mint.

The square's name derives from the nickname given to Henri IV, alluding to

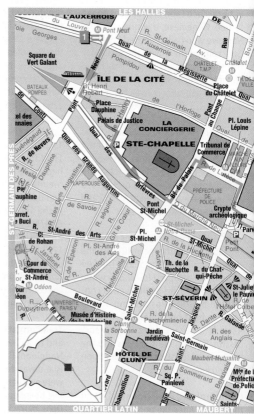

his reputation as an amorous gentleman despite his age.

Place Dauphine★

For a long time the western tip of the island gave way to a muddy marshy area broken by the river currents. In 1314, **Philip the Fair** had a stake erected on one of the mounds of ground. It was there that he ordered the execution by fire of the Grand Master of the **Order of Templars, Jacques de Molay**. The king watched him burn from his palace window. The gardens (Jardin du Roi) which extended from the Conciergerie into the river became the first botanical garden under **Marie de' Medici**.

At the end of the 16C Henri III decided to reorganise this untidy no man's land: the mud ditches were filled in, a great earth bank was amassed to support the future Pont Neuf, and the south bank was raised by some 6m/19.7ft. In 1607 a triangular square was built, surrounded by a series of houses constructed of brick, white stone and slate to a uniform design. The square was named after the Dauphin, in honour of the future Louis XIII. Only a few façades such as no **14** retain their original features.

Quai des Orfèvres

The properties along the river front were during the 17C and 18C the jewellers' quarter: Strass, inventor of the synthetic diamond, Boehmer and Bassenge who fashioned Marie-Antoinette's celebrated necklace, had their shops in place Dauphine and along the quay. No **36** is today well known as the headquarters of the CID (Police Judiciaire).

Place Louis-Lépine

A colourful **flower market** is held in front of the administrative offices of the Hôtel-Dieu, the police headquarters and the commercial court which have surrounded the square on three sides

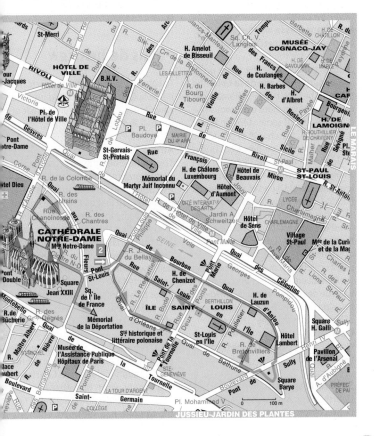

since the Second Empire. On Sundays a bird market replaces the flower stalls. The **Hôtel-Dieu** hospice, first mentioned as early as the 9C, moved into its present premises between 1864 and 1877 (the old building stood on the opposite end of the Parvis by the statue of Charlemagne.

Notre-Dame★★★ –
see NOTRE-DAME.

Ancien quartier du Chapitre
The area extending north of Notre-Dame to the Seine belonged to the cathedral chapter. Enclosed in a wall with four gates, it was populated by the cathedral canons who each lodged their own students. Although considerably restored, the quarter is the only reminder of what the Cité looked like in the 11C and 12C when **Abelard**, St Bonaventure and St Dominic built up the reputation of the cathedral school which was later to merge with the **Sorbonne** (*see QUARTIER LATIN).*

Rue Chanoinesse was the main thoroughfare of the former chapter. Numbers **24** and **22** are the last two medieval canons' houses; note the stone posts in the courtyard. In **rue de la Colombe** traces of the Lutetian Gallo-Roman wall of Lutetia remain; note the curious tavern at the top of some steps. In laying rue d'Arcole, the chapel of Ste-Marie was razed, where "de-flowered" brides could be married, sealing their vows with a ring made of straw. **Rue des Ursins** is level with the old banks of the Seine and Port St-Landry, Paris' first dock until the 12C when facilities on the Hôtel de Ville foreshore were established. At the end of the narrow street stand the last vestiges of the medieval chapel, St-Aignan, where priests celebrated mass secretly during the Revolution. At the picturesque corner with **rue des Chantres** stands a medieval mansion past which there is a fine view of Notre-Dame's skyline.

Quai aux Fleurs affords a vast panorama of St-Gervais and of the tip of the Île St-Louis.

Square Jean-XXIII
Until the beginning of the 19C, the area between Notre-Dame and the tip of the island was crowded with houses, chapels and the Archbishop's Palace. These were severely damaged in a riot and later razed to the ground (1831). The square opened as a formal garden with a neo-Gothic fountain in 1844.

Square de l'Île-de-France
Napoléon III built the Cité's municipal morgue on the upstream tip of the island, attracting until 1910 those with a morbid fascination.

Mémorial de la Déportation
Apr–Sept, 10am–noon, 1.15pm–7pm; Oct–Mar, 10am–noon, 2pm–5pm. 01 46 33 87 56.
A modern crypt accommodates a metal sculpture by Desserprit, funerary urns and the tomb of the Unknown Deportee from Struthof, to commemorate the suffering and loss of so much life in the Nazi camps.

2 Tour of St-Louis –
see ÎLE SAINT-LOUIS.

Palais de Justice★

To balance the power of the Church, the Île de la Cité also accommodated the Law Courts – the pre-eminent seat of the civil and judicial authorities.

King's Palace
The stone buildings erected by the Roman governors for their administrative and military headquarters were requisitioned first by the Merovingian kings then by the early Capetian kings who fortified the palace with a keep and built a chapel in the precincts. Clovis died here. In the 13C Louis IX built the Sainte-Chapelle; Philip the Fair constructed the Conciergerie, a sumptuous palace "more beautiful than anyone in France had ever seen". The Hall of the Men-at-Arms was the largest ever built in Europe.

On 22 February 1358, the mob under **Étienne Marcel** entered the apartments of the Dauphin, the future **Charles V**, and Regent whilst his father John the Good was being held in England. When the troubles had subsided, Charles V

Point Zero

All roads may no longer lead to Rome but do all roads in France lead to Paris? Point Zero, an eight-pointed bronze star with four stones laid around it to create a circle, appears to suggest this. This unusual symbol, located discreetly in the cobbles of the Place du Parvis in front of the west façade of Nôtre Dame Cathedral beside the main entrance, is the point from which all road distances in France are measured. Officially known as Point Zero des Routes de France, a marker was first placed here by the cartographers of the Ancien Régime in 1769, although the current star was not set into the pavement until 1924. Point Zero also marks the geographic centre of the City and many believe that visitors who stand at this spot will almost certainly return to Paris.

moved out of the palace where he had been compelled to witness the bloody slaughter of his counsellors, preferring to live at the Louvre, the Hôtel St-Paul or at Vincennes outside Paris. In the palace, he installed his Parliament.

Judicial Palace

Parliament was the kingdom's supreme court of justice. Originally its members were nominated by the king, until 1522 when **François I** sold the rights for money on condition that the position become hereditary; thus the highest dignitaries in the land (the chancellor, peers of the realm, royal princes) secured their position by right or privilege.

Fires were frequent, damaging the Grande Salle (1618), Sainte-Chapelle spire (1630), the *Cour des Comptes* (Debtors' Court – 1737), and the Gallerie Marchande (1776). In 1788 Parliament demanded the convocation of the States General – not a good idea, because the General Assembly announced its suppression and the Convention sent the members to the guillotine!

The Law Courts

The Revolution overturned the judicial system. New courts were installed in the old buildings which took the name of Palais de Justice. Restoration lasted from 1840 to 1914, interrupted only by the Commune fire; the building was given its present façade overlooking place Dauphine and its extension along quai des Orfèvres.

Tour of the buildings

Enter via the Cour du Mai. ◐*Mon–Sat 8.30am–6pm. Visitors are normally allowed to attend a civil or criminal hearing. General public not admitted to the Galerie des Bustes and Children's Court.* ◐*Public holidays.* ☎*01 44 32 52 52.*

Cour du Mai

The Louis XVI wrought-iron grille is especially fine. The name *cour du Mai* is derived from a very old custom by which the clerks of the court – an important corporation – planted in the courtyard a tree from one of the Royal forests each year on 1 May. A similar practice prevailed in England often in honour of a particular person, often festooned in (yellow) ribbons.

The Galerie Marchande was once the most animated part of the building, bustling with plaintiffs, lawyers, clerks, court officials, souvenir peddlers and hangers-on. The ornate Première Chambre Civile de la Cour d'Appel (Chamber of the Civil Court of Appeal) and the Cour de Cassation (Chamber of the Court of Cassation) are decorated with frescoes and tapestries.

Enter the **Salle des Pas-Perdus** (Lobby), formerly the Gothic Grand'Salle of Philip the Fair, twice destroyed, and reconstructed most recently after the Commune of 1871. Notice the monument to the 19C barrister, Berryer, on the right, with the tortoise – maligning the delays in the law. At the end on the left is the former apartment of Louis IX, used as **Parliamentary Grand Chamber** when Louis XII had it decorated with a fine ceiling, and then by the Revolutionary Tribunal under Fouquier-Tinville (1793-94). It is now the First Civil Court.

CONCIERGERIE★★

Ⓜ CITÉ (LINE 4) – BUSES: 21, 27, 38, 70, 85, 96

The beauty of its medieval architecture conceals the bloody history of the Conciergerie. During the Revolution noblemen and ordinary citizens alike were imprisoned here, usually on their way to the guillotine.

Nearby neighbourhoods: ÎLE ST-LOUIS, CHÂTELET-HÔTEL DE VILLE, QUARTIER LATIN.

- **Information:** Carrousel du Louvre Welcome Centre, Place de la Pyramide Inversée 99, rue de Rivoli. ☎08 92 68 30 00 (0.34€ per min). http://en.parisinfo.com.
- ▶ **Orient Yourself:** The Conciergerie is on the Île-de-la-Cité, an island in the geographical centre of Paris, overlooking the Seine next to the Palais de Justice.
- **Parking:** Underground parking can be found on the rue de la Cité.
- **Don't Miss:** The ancient clock on the Tour de l'Horloge (*blvd du Palais*).
- **Organising Your Time:** Allow a half hour for a visit of the Conciergerie.
- **Also See:** ÎLE-DE-LA-CITÉ, SAINTE-CHAPELLE, NOTRE-DAME.

A Bit of History

A noble keeper – The name *Conciergerie* was given to a section of the old palace precinct controlled by the *concierge* or keeper of the king's mansion. It served as a prison from the 14C.

The guillotine's antechamber – At the time of the Revolution as many as 1 200 men and women were held at once in the Conciergerie; during the Terror the building became the antechamber to the Tribunal, which in nine cases out of ten meant the guillotine.

Among those incarcerated here were Queen **Marie-Antoinette**; Madame Élisabeth, sister to Louis XVI; **Madame du Barry**, the favourite of Louis XV; Philippe-Égalité, father of the future King Louis-Philippe; and Revolutionaries **Danton** and **Robespierre**. In all, nearly 2 600 prisoners were guillotined between January 1793 and July 1794.

Visit

Exterior★

The best **view** is from Mégisserie Quay on the Right Bank, with its four towers reflected in the Seine which originally flowed right up to their base. This is the oldest part of the palace built by the Capetian kings. The oldest tower is the crenellated one on the right, Tour Bonbec. The square **Tour de l'Horloge** has since 1370 housed the first public clock to be installed in Paris.

Interior★

Entrance at blvd du Palais. ◷*Mar–Oct, 9.30am–6pm; Nov–Feb, 9am–5pm.* ◷*1 Jan, 1 May, 1 and 11 Nov, 25 Dec.* ◉*6.50€ (combined ticket with the Sainte-Chapelle 9.50€).* ☎*01 53 40 60 93.*

Salle des Gardes

Stout pillars with interesting capitals support the Gothic vaulting in this dark room.

Conciergerie, Salle des Gens d'Armes

B. Kaufmann/MICHELIN

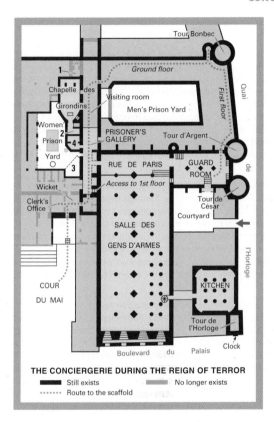

THE CONCIERGERIE DURING THE REIGN OF TERROR

■ Still exists ▧ No longer exists
•••••• Route to the scaffold

Salle des Gens d'Armes★★
(Hall of the Men-at-Arms)
This magnificent four-aisled Gothic hall covers an area of 1 800sq m/2 153sq yd, on a par with those of the Mont-St-Michel and the Palais des Papes in Avignon. Above used to be the palace's Great Hall and royal apartments. On the first pillar in the central row is marked the level reached by the Seine in 1910. The Revolutionary Tribunal sat in this hall from 1793 to 1795.

The four huge fireplaces in each corner of the old **kitchens** fulfilled a specific function: cooking enough meat, spit-roasted or boiled in cauldrons, to feed between 2 000 and 3 000 mouths, including the royal family.

Prison
The Galerie des Prisonniers served as the main axis of the prison, where penniless prisoners slept on the bare ground while the rich paid for their own cell and better food. Prisoners were ushered from the Grande Chambre du Parlement down a spiral staircase hidden in the Bonbec Tower, and onto the council room which on one side served as antechamber *(parloir)* to the men's prison yard (Préau des Hommes) and on the other opened onto a staircase (**1**) up to the Tribunal. The prisoner, hands firmly tied behind the back, had collars cut away and hair cut short. Batched up, the condemned crossed through the wicket gate *(guichet)* past the clerk of the court *(greffe* means register office) into the **May Courtyard** and out to the tumbrils.

The history of the prison and important political prisoners is presented on the first floor. These include the Scots captain of the guard Montgomery who delivered a fatal blow to Henri II's eye during a tourney; Châtel who wounded Henri IV; Ravaillac who killed him; Louvel the assassin of the Duc de Berry and Robespierre.

The Terror (1793-1794)

The Conciergerie was to come into its own during the period of 'The Terror', or more correctly the Reign of Terror, which took place during the French Revolution between September 1793 and the fall and execution of Robespierre in July 1794. Louis XVI had been executed in January but amongst the first to be guillotined during the Terror was the Queen Marie-Antionette. Subsequently many thousands of people were condemned to death after first being incarcerated in this building and, while these figures included a number of aristocrats, there were many others from both the middle and working classes who in one way or another were thought to have transgressed against the notorious Committee for Public Safety.

Leading Revolutionaries feared a counter-revolution and a full restoration of the monarchy. They felt under threat from abroad as many foreign Governments, including those of the United Kingdom and Austria, were hostile to the Revolution fearing the spread of the concept to their own realms. In France there had been many attempts to overthrow the Revolution – in March, a peasant rebellion in the Vendée was viciously suppressed and similar events occurred in other regions. Two thousand people were drowned in the River Loire at Nantes and hundreds executed by cannon fire at Lyons because it was thought that the guillotine was too slow.

The Committee for Public Safety was set up on April 6th 1793 with nine members, led unofficially by Danton. Gradually Robespierre's supporters gained control and by the summer Danton had been voted off the Committee. Robespierre was voted on during July and for the next year ruled it with an iron fist. Anyone seen to oppose the Committee's work or offend Robespierre himself would be sent to the guillotine. The redoubtable Danton himself fell victim to the paranoia which gripped the Committee and on 5 April 1794 he too was executed but not before predicting "Robespierre will follow me; I drag down Robespierre."

Although the Committee was apparently unified, this unity began to unravel as members worried that they may be the next to suffer the wrath of Robespierre. If Danton could be removed so easily then lesser men must be vulnerable. Also it was recognised that while the threat from both abroad and at home was beginning to subside, the number of executions was rising. Soon Robespierre was accused of seeking to become king as he was increasingly acting in a tyrannical way. His colleagues moved against him and took matters into their own hands. Robespierre was sentenced without trial and executed on 28 July 1794 just as Danton had forecast. The Great Terror was finally at an end.

Chapelle des Girondins

Ground floor. The chapel was transformed into a collective prison where prisoners heard mass through the grille on the upper storey. From here, one can visit the cell occupied by Marie-Antoinette (2 August to 16 October 1793) and transformed into an expiatory chapel (**2**) in 1816.

Cour des Femmes

In the centre is a patch of grass and a lonely tree where women prisoners were allowed out of their cells during the day. The corridor known as the **Côté des Douzes** (**3**) was where prisoners of both sexes could talk through the bars, and from where daily the 12 inmates selected for the guillotine embarked on their final journey.

Back in the prison corridor a door on the right leads to a reconstruction of **Marie-Antoinette's cell** (**4**). The furniture consisted of a cot, a chair and a table. A screen separated the queen from watchmen, day and night.

PLACE DE LA CONCORDE★★★

Ⓜ CONCORDE (LINES 1, 8 AND 12) – BUSES: 31, 42, 72, 73, 84, 94

Everything about this square – site, size, general elegance – is impressive, particularly the obelisk, which dominates the scene. Place de la Concorde is one of the most beautiful squares in Paris, but also one of the busiest. The point of the obelisk indicates international time, making it the largest sundial in the world.

Nearby neighbourhoods: **FAUBOURG ST-HONORÉ, CHAMPS-ÉLYSÉES, LA MADELEINE, LES TUILERIES, LE LOUVRE, FAUBOURG ST-GERMAIN, MUSÉE D'ORSAY.**

- **Information:** Pyramides welcome centre, 25 rue des Pyramides. ☎08 92 68 30 00 (0.34€ per min). http://en.parisinfo.com.
- ▶ **Orient Yourself:** The square is located on the Right Bank overlooking the Seine between the Champs-Elysées and the Jardin des Tuileries.
- P **Parking:** Underground parking is available on the Place de la Concorde.
- **Don't Miss:** Cour des Femmes.
- ⏱ **Organising Your Time:** The square can be visited in half an hour.
- **Also See:** JARDIN DES TUILERIES, AVENUE DES CHAMPS-ÉLYSÉES.

A Bit of History

Paris aldermen, wanting to find favour with Louis XV, commissioned Bouchardon to sculpt an equestrian statue of Le Bien-Aimé (the beloved) as he was known, and organised a competition to find an architect for the square. Gabriel's designs for an octagon bordered by a dry moat and balustrade won. Work began in 1755 and continued until 1775. In 1792 the royal statue was toppled and the name of the square was changed from place Louis-XV to place de la Révolution. On Sunday 21 January 1793, a guillotine was erected in the northwest corner (near where the Brest statue now stands) for the execution of **Louis XVI**. On 13 May, "the national razor", now installed near the grille to the Tuileries, began to claim a further 1 343 victims, including Marie-Antoinette. The Directory, hopeful of a better future, renamed the blood-soaked area place de la Concorde.

Under Louis-Philippe, the square's decoration was completed by the neutral symbol of an obelisk, two fountains inspired by those in St Peter's Square in Rome, and eight statues representing

View of the Place de la Concorde from the Tuileries

B. Kaufmann/MICHELIN

S. Sauvignier/MICHELIN

Fountain on the Place de la Concorde

eight French cities: Brest, Rouen, Lille, Strasbourg, Lyon, Marseille, Bordeaux and Nantes.

Visit

🔹 *See map CHAMPS-ÉLYSÉES.*

Two mansions★★

The colossal mansions on either side of the opening to rue Royale are among the finest examples of the early Louis XVI style. Their architect, Jacques-Ange

---

Gabriel succeeded his father, Jacques Gabriel, at the head of the Academy of Architecture. The right pavilion, the **Hôtel de la Marine**, was until 1792 the royal store; it then became the Admiralty Office. Today it houses the Navy Headquarters. The **Hôtel Crillon**, across the street, was at first occupied by four noblemen. It now accommodates the French Automobile Club and a famous hotel and is flanked on the left by the American Embassy. To the right of the Hôtel de la Marine is the Hôtel Talleyrand (today home to the American Consulate), where the statesman and diplomat **Talleyrand** died in 1838.

Obelisk★

In the centre of the square stands an obelisk from the ruins of the temple at Luxor, given to France in 1831 by Mohammed Ali, Viceroy of Egypt. It reached Paris via the Seine four years later and was erected on 25 October 1836. The pink granite monument is 3 300 years old and covered in hieroglyphics; it is 23m/75.5ft tall, and weighs more than 220 tonnes.

Views★★★

The obelisk provides the best point from which to get a view of the Champs-Élysées, framed by the **Marly Horses** (commissioned from **Guillaume Coustou** for Marly, Louis XIV's superb château near Versailles) looking up the avenue towards the Arc de Triomphe. Coysevox's Winged Horses frame the view across the Tuileries towards the Louvre. Replicas have replaced the two original marble groups of horses, which are in the Louvre.

Pont de la Concorde

The bridge was designed in 1787 by the civil engineer, Perronet. It was completed by 1791, with the stones from the Bastille prison used in its construction so that, it was said, "the people could forever trample the ruins of the old fortress". The bridge is classified as a UNESCO World Heritage Site, and offers a spectacular **view**★★★ of the Seine and place de la Concorde, towards La Madeleine.

LA DÉFENSE★★

CENTRAL PARKING AREA: ACCESS ROAD DÉFENSE 4 FROM THE RING ROAD
Ⓜ ESPLANADE DE LA DÉFENSE (LINE 1), É/RER: GRANDE ARCHE DE LA DÉFENSE (LINE 1/A)
– BUSES: 73, 141, 144, 161, 174, 178, 258, 262, 272

The new business district of La Défense, juxtaposing traditional office space with highly experimental developments, is a truly exceptional environment. The Grande Arche stands at the extreme west of an axis along Champs-Élysées, which starts at the Louvre and passes through the Arc de Triomphe.

🛈 **Information:** Espace Info Défense, 15 place de La Défense. ☏01 47 74 84 24. www.ladefense.fr.

▶ **Orient Yourself:** This western business district is divided into 11 zones, the 130ha/321-acre site falls in the **Puteaux**, **Nanterre** and **Courbevoie** districts.

🅿 **Parking:** Underground parking is available beneath this pedestrian district.

👁 **Don't Miss:** The views from the platform of the Grande Arche.

🕐 **Organising Your Time:** Allow for 1-2 hours to visit La Défense.

The business sector and park – The Esso building first opened in 1964 and since then 48 towers have been completed providing office space for over 900 companies.

La Grande Arche★★

🕐 *Apr–Sept, 10am–8pm, Oct–Mar, 10am–7pm.* ✎*9€.* ☏*01 49 07 27 55. www. grandearche.com.*

The Grande Arche, designed by Otto von Spreckelsen, is perhaps one of the most controversial of the *Grands Projets* instigated by President François Mitterrand. This gigantic open cube (110m/361ft wide) weighs 300 000t, carried on 12 piles sunk below ground. The cathedral of Notre-Dame could fit into the arch. The top part of the arch is occupied by galleries, a restaurant and a belvedere offering exceptional views of the **capital's historic vista**★★★ including the Arc de Triomphe and the Louvre.

Walking Tour

Esplanade de la Défense

This pedestrian area provides the opportunity for a splendid **walk**★★ to admire the modern architecture and 20C sculp-

La Grande Arche

©Michal Bednarek/Dreamstime.com

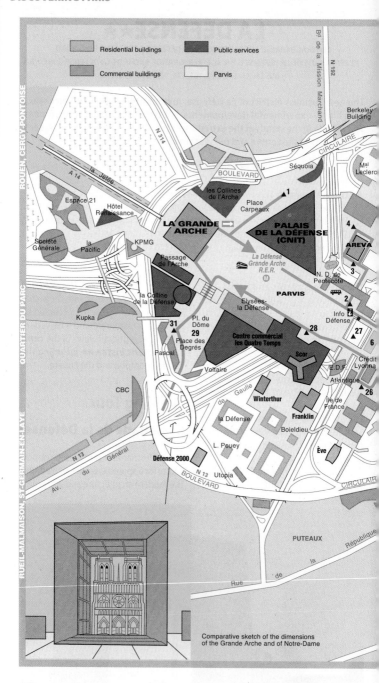

Residential buildings
Commercial buildings
Public services
Parvis

Comparative sketch of the dimensions of the Grande Arche and of Notre-Dame

tures exhibited in this open-air gallery. Starting in place Carpeaux, is César's *Thumb* (**1**), whereas to the right of the Great Arch is a metal sculpture by the Japanese artist Miyawaki.

The **Palais de la Défense (CNIT)** ★, the first construction (1958) is remarkable for the boldness of its architecture. Its record breaking concrete vault (220m/722ft span) has only three points

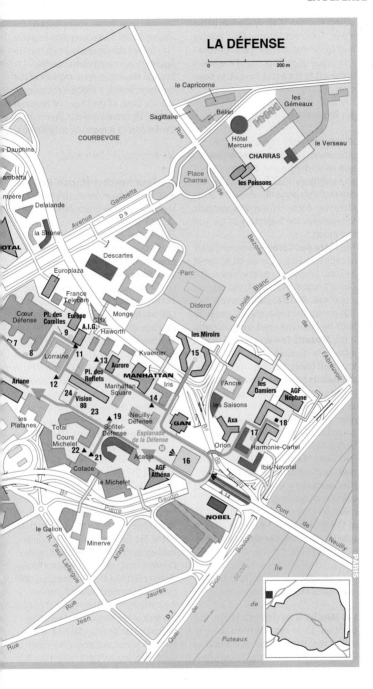

LA DÉFENSE

0 ———————— 200 m

le Capricorne

les Gémeaux

Sagittaire

Béliet

COURBEVOIE

Rue

Hôtel
Mercure

le Verseau

s Dauphins

CHARRAS

Place
Charras

les Poissons

ambetta

Delalande

Gambetta

Avenue

D 9

de

mpère

la Sirène

Bezons

TOTAL

Descartes

Europlaza

Parc

France
Telecom

Monge

R. Louis Blanc

Diderot

R.

Cœur
Défense

Pl. des
Corolles

Europe

CBX

de

9

A.I.G.

Haworth

les Miroirs

l'Abreuvoir

7

8

Lorraine

11

Kvaerner

15

Aurore

13

Ariane

12

Pl. des
Reflets

MANHATTAN

Iris

l'Ancre

les
Damiers

AGF
Neptune

24

Vision
80

Manhattan
Square

14

les Saisons

23

19

Neuilly-
Défense

Axa

18

les
Platanes

Total
Cours
Michelet

Sofitel-
Défense

GAN

Bd

17

Orion

Harmonie-Cartel

22

21

Acacia

M

16

Ibis-Novotel

Coface

AGF
Athéna

de

le Michelet

Neuilly

Pont

Pierre

Gaudin

A 14

de

NOBEL

Boulon

Neuilly

le Galion

R. Paul Lafargue

Minerve

Arago

SEINE

Île

de

PARIS

Rue

Jaurès

D 7

de

de

Rue

Jean

Quai

Dion

Puteaux

of support. Further on, to the left, on place de la Défense is **Calder**'s last work, a red stabile (**2**) 15m/49ft high.

▶ *Walk through the opening on the left to the Fiat Tower.*

The **Tour Framatome**, with the **Elf Tower**, is the tallest building rising 45 storeys to 178m/584ft. At the foot of the tower, *The Great Toscano* (**3**) a bronze bust by the Polish artist Mitoraj, evokes an antique giant. Pass round the tower to the left to see a sculpture (**4**) in polyester resin by Delfino.

▶ *Return to the esplanade.*

In the centre of the esplanade is a monumental **fountain by Agam** (**6**) and an underground **Gallery** (**7**) for art exhibitions. Pass in front of the *Midday-Midnight* pond (**8**) where the artist Clarus has decorated a ventilation shaft to represent the trajectory of the sun and moon.

The **Place des Corelles** is named after its copper fountain, *Corolla* (**9**), sculpted by Louis Leygue. A ceramic fresco, *The Cloud Sculptor* (**11**), by Attila adorns a low wall. Philolaos' *Mechanical Bird* (**12**) adorns the terrace, as he carefully folds his immense steel wings. Nearby is the **Moretti Tower**, covered in 672 differently coloured tubes. Beyond the Vision 80 Tower, built on stilts, is **place des Reflets** overlooked by and reflected in the shimmering **Aurore Tower**, in vibrant contrast to its neighbouring rose-coloured Manhattan Tower and the green GAN Tower. Note the allegory by Derbré of *The Earth* (**13**).

The **Tour Manhattan** is one of the most original structures of the complex, designed as a series of curves and counter-curves that mirror the sky. In place de l'Iris the slender silhouette of the *Sleepwalker* (**14**) balanced on a sphere poised on the ridge of a cuboid, is by H de Miller.

▶ *Turn left in front of the **Tour GAN**, shaped like a Greek cross.*

Les Miroirs is by Henri La Fonta: the fountain (**15**) in the courtyard consists of ten cylinders decorated with mosaics. East of the esplanade the **Takis pond** (**16**) consists of a stretch of water on which the reflection of 49 multicoloured flexible light-tubes seem to play. On Square Vivaldi the *Conversation Fountain* (**17**) by Busato represents two bronze figures in animated conversation.

In place Napoléon-Ier at the foot of the Neptune Tower, a monument shaped like the Cross of the Légion d'Honneur medal (**18**) commemorates the return of the Emperor's remains from St Helena.

▶ *Return to the Takis pond.*

The **Tour Hoechst-Marion-Roussel**, an attractive blue-green, steel and glass high-rise, was the first to be built (1967) at La Défense.

The bronze low relief *Ophelia* (**19**) is by the Catalan sculptor Apel les Fenosa.

Go around the Sofitel Hotel on your left. From the terrace overlooking the square cours Michelet you can see Venet's 14m/46ft-high painted steel sculpture (**21**) and further on to the right Jakober's assemblage of welded iron resembling an American footballer's mask (**22**).

Further on stands a large frog-shaped fountain (**23**) with drinking water. In the square below the esplanade, 35 flower-planters (**24**) interspersed with faces and clasped hands are the work of Selinger. A white-marble sculpture, *Lady Moon* (**26**) by Julio Silva, can be seen between the Atlantique and Crédit Lyonnais Towers. Barrias' bronze group entitled *La Défense* (**27**) is at the foot of the Agam fountain.

In front of the Quatre Temps shopping centre is a brightly coloured sculpture (**28**) of two figures by Miró. Steps to the left of the Élysées-La Défense building lead up to the **UGC CinéCité** cineplex On place des Degrès, the sculptor Kowalski has created a *mineral landscape* (**29**): parts of pyramids, wave of granite…

A bronze *Icarus* (**31**) by César stands at the foot of the elegant IBM building.

A short distance away, *Slat* (**32**) a sculpture by R Serra consisting of five sheets of steel weighing 100t and rising 11m/36ft, has been installed at a crossroads.

DENFERT-ROCHEREAU

Ⓜ DENFERT-ROCHEREAU (LINES 4 AND 6) – RER: DENFERT-ROCHEREAU (LINE B) –
BUSES: 38, 68.

Underground are the disused quarries that became the catacombs, filled with
several million skeletons… above ground is a pleasant district, with peaceful
residential and commercial avenues, refashioned by Haussmann.

Nearby neighbourhoods: **MONTPARNASSE, PORT-ROYAL, GOBELINS.**

🅘 **Information:** Carrousel du Louvre Welcome Centre, Place de la Pyramide Inversée
99, rue de Rivoli. ☎08 92 68 30 00 (0.34€ per min). http://en.parisinfo.com.

▸ **Orient Yourself:** Located in the centre of the Left Bank south of the Latin Quarter,
Denfert-Rochereau lies at the intersection of boulevards Raspail and St-Michel.

🅿 **Parking:** An underground parking garage is located beneath the square.

🌀 **Don't Miss:** The typically Parisian cafés and shops of the rue Daguerre.

🕐 **Organising Your Time:** Allow two hours to visit all of the sights.

Kids **Especially for Kids:** Older kids tend to enjoy the creepy Catacombes.

🦽 **Also See:** MONTPARNASSE, LUXEMBOURG.

Walking Tour

Place Denfert-Rochereau

The reduced bronze version of
Bartholdi's Lion in the middle of place
Denfert-Rochereau commemorates
Colonel Denfert-Rochereau, who
defended Belfort in 1870-71. The two
elegantly proportioned buildings adorned by sculpted friezes are examples
of Ledoux' city gates and toll-houses,
which punctuated the city's fortified
wall built between 1784 and 1791.

Rue Froidevaux runs along Montparnasse Cemetery. Located at nos 21-23
are artist ateliers built in the 1920s.

▸ *Take rue Victor Schoelcher to blvd
Raspail, crossing over to the rue
Campagne-Première.*

Many artists lived on this street, such as
Modigliani (no 3), Man Ray (no 31bis),
and, at the passage at no 17, Picasso,
Kandisnsky Max Ernst, and Miro.

▸ *Return to blvd Raspail to the Fondation Cartier (🦽 see Museums).*

South of Place Denfert-Rochereau, is the
rue Daguerre with its small shops.

Les Catacombes★

Entrance: 1 place Denfert-Rochereau.
🕐*Tue–Sun 10am–5pm. Long stairways.*
🕐*Public holidays.* ◉5€. ☎01 43 22 47
63. www.carnavalet.paris.fr.
These Gallo-Roman quarries were transformed into ossuaries between 1785
and 1810 with several million skeletons
from Parisian cemeteries, notably of the
Innocents.

Address Book

WHERE TO STAY AND EAT

🦽 Turn to the back of the guide for
selected hotels, restaurants, bistros
and cafés listed by *arrondissement*.
This neighbourhood is in the 14th
arrondissement.

NIGHTLIFE

Au Vin des rues – *21 rue Boulard,
14th arr.* ☎01 43 22 19 78. *Mon–Sun
noon–3pm, Mon–Sat 6.30pm–
11.30pm, Sun 7pm–11pm. Closed first
week in Aug and public holidays.*
This old-fashioned bistro continues
to serve excellent wines in a traditional setting. The warm welcome
and atmosphere make it very
popular. Live accordion music on
Thursday evenings.

EIFFEL TOWER★★★

**Ⓜ BIR-HAKEIM (LINE 6), ÉCOLE MILITAIRE (LINE 8)
RER: CHAMP-DE-MARS-TOUR-EIFFEL (LINE C) – BUSES: 82, 92**

The best-loved monument in Paris, if not in the entire world, straddles gardens once used for military parades. Nearby is a fine example of Classical French architecture, the École Militaire. The tower is the perfect place for a bird's-eye view of the city.

Nearby neighbourhoods: **INVALIDES, TROCADÉRO, ALMA, FAUBOURG ST-GERMAIN.**

- **ℹ Information:** Pyramides welcome centre, 25 rue des Pyramides. ☎08 92 68 30 00 (0.34€ per min). http://en.parisinfo.com.
- ▶ **Orient Yourself:** The Eiffel Tower is on the west end of the Left Bank, across the Seine from Trocadéro.
- 🅿 **Parking:** Street parking is possible in front of the École Militaire.
- 🚫 **Don't Miss:** The Peace Wall monument on the Champ de Mars.
- 🕐 **Organising Your Time:** Allow two hours if you plan on going up the Tower, or an hour if you just walk along the sights.
- 🧒 **Especially for Kids:** There are several play areas around the Champ de Mars.

The Eiffel Tower

A. Eli/MICHELIN

A Bit of History

The Eiffel Tower, built for the Exposition Universelle of 1889, was the tallest construction in the world when it was erected, measuring 300m/984ft. The addition of television aerials has increased its height by 20.75m/68ft.

The engineer **Gustave Eiffel** (1832-1923) began the project in 1884; between 1887 and 1889 three hundred skyjacks pieced the tower together using 2.5 million rivets. Eiffel, in his enthusiasm, exclaimed "France will be the only country with a 300m [984ft] flagpole!". Artists and writers, however, were appalled; the "Petition of the 300" was signed by artists, writers and even **Charles Garnier**, architect of the Opéra. Despite the critics, its very boldness and novelty brought it also great acclaim. By the beginning of the new century it had become a subject for celebration by a new generation of poets (Apollinaire), dramatists (**Cocteau**) and painters (Pissarro, Dufy, **Utrillo**, Seurat, Marquet, Delaunay), now recognised the world over.

In 1909, when its planning concession expired, the tower was nearly pulled down – but saved on account of its huge antennae so vital to French radio telegraphy.

Gustave Eiffel (1832-1923)

Engineer and Entrepreneur in equal measure, Eiffel was to enjoy both success and failure during his long life. Mostly remembered today for his Tower, he was also responsible for several other massively impressive structures both in France and further afield. The Garabit Viaduct, the Pest Railway Station and the internal structure of the Statue of Liberty are just three examples of his fine work still in use. Unfortunately Eiffel became embroiled in the scandal caused by the French Panama Canal Company, a scheme seriously mismanaged by Ferdinand de Lesseps which failed causing severe financial losses. Although not involved in the finances of the enterprise, Eiffel was found guilty of fraud, a decision which was later to be reversed. Forced to retire, he spent the rest of his life as a scientist using his greatest achievement, the Eiffel Tower, for wind resistance experiments, as an aerial mast and a weather station.

Eiffel Tower

Lift: mid-Jun–end Aug, 9am–12.45am; (last lift to the summit 11pm) early Sept–mid-Jun, 9.30am–11.45pm (last lift to the summit 10.30pm). ∞4.80€ (1st floor), 7.80€ (2nd floor), 12€ (3rd floor). Stairs (1st and 2nd floor only): mid-Jun–end Aug, 9am–12.45am (last access midnight); early Sept–mid-Jun, 9.30am–6.30pm (last access 6pm). ∞4€. ☎01 44 11 23 23. www.tour-eiffel.fr.

The tensile masterpiece – The tower weighs about 7 000t, and uses 50t of paint every seven years. The sway at the top in the highest winds has never been more than 12cm/4.7in – whilst its height can vary by as much as 15cm/6in – depending on the temperature. There are three platforms – the first is at 57m/187ft; the second at 115m/377ft; the third at 276m/905.5ft – and 1 652 steps in all to the top.

View★★★
From the third platform, the view of Paris and the suburbs can extend 67km/42mi in ideal conditions *(viewing tables)*, but it is more often hazy. The best light is usually 1hr before sunset. At night the illuminated tower has a jewel-like quality, sparkling for the first 10 minutes of every hour. At level 3, Eiffel's sitting room can be seen through a window. The second floor houses a restaurant, brasseries and boutiques. On the first floor is a museum, a gift shop, a post office and a restaurant. In winter there's even an ice rink.

Walking Tours

1 From Tour Eiffel to Maison de l'UNESCO

Once used for military parades, fairs and world exhibitions, the **Champ-de-Mars** is now a vast formal garden closed at one end by the École Militaire and at the other by the Trocadéro on Chaillot Hill. On your right, as you walk towards the École Militaire, is the **Village suisse** *(54 avenue de la Motte-Piquet; ⊙Thu–Mon 10.30am–7pm; ☎01 47 34 47 19)*, a conglomeration of 150 antique and bric-a-brac shops.

École militaire★
1 place Joffre. Thanks to prompting by **Mme de Pompadour**, Louis XV's favourite mistress, a Royal Military Academy was built in 1751 where young gentlemen without means might be trained to become accomplished officers. Designed by the architect **Jacques-Ange Gabriel**, the impressive building is fronted by 10 superb Corinthian columns, each two storeys high supporting a carved pediment, with displayed trophies and allegorical figures. Facing the central pavilion, is the equestrian statue of Marshal Joffre by Real del Sarte (1939). Aged 15, the young cadet Bonaparte was formally sworn-in in the Academy chapel in 1784; his final report stated that he would "go far in favourable circumstances."

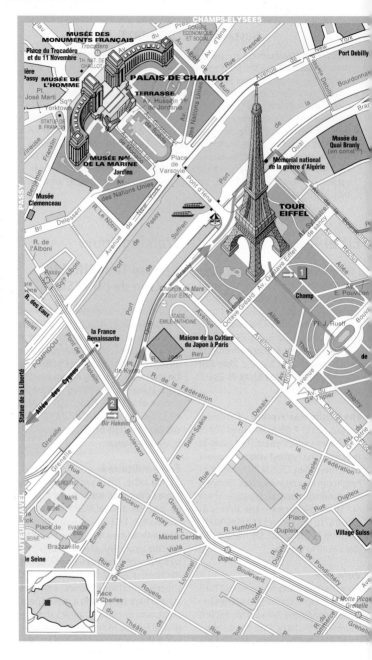

The military tradition – The institution was suppressed at the time of the Revolution, but the buildings have retained their status both as military quarters and as an training centre for French and foreign officers attending the School of Advanced War Studies, and the Higher School for National Defence.

▸ *Walk around the academy by way of avenue de Suffren and avenue de Lowendal to place de Fontenoy.*

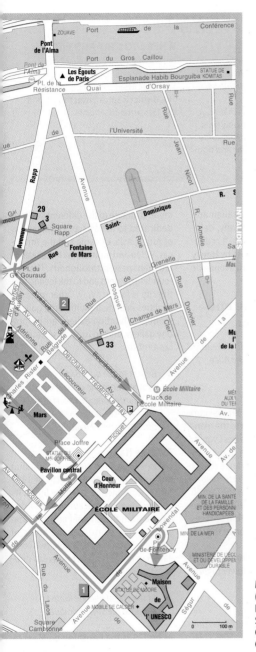

▶ *Walk across place de Fontenay to the right.*

Maison de l'UNESCO★ (United Nations Educational, Scientific and Cultural Organisation HQ)

From the semicircular square, look across the sports ground to the **main courtyard**★, lined on either side by beautiful porticoes with paired columns. At the back is the central pavilion, flanked by colonnaded buildings terminating in projecting wings.

7 place de Fontenay. ⓒ*By reservation only.* ☏*01 45 68 16 42.*

The home of UNESCO was opened in 1958 and is the most truly international undertaking in Paris: the membership by 185 states and the construction of the buildings jointly by Breuer, Nervi

Address Book

SHOPPING

La Maison de l'escargot – *79 rue Fondary, 15th arr.* Ⓜ*Émile-Zola.* ☎*01 45 75 31 09. www.maison-escargot.com. Open Tue–Sat 9.30am–7pm. Closed holidays and end Jul–mid-Aug.* Open since 1894, this shop only sells hand-prepared snails from Burgundy and Savoy for the *Bourgogne* and from Provence for the *petits gris*.

WHERE TO STAY AND EAT

Ⓒ Turn to the back of the guide for selected hotels, restaurants, bistros and cafés listed by *arrondissement*. This district is spread over the 7th and the 15th arrondissements.

---

and Zehrfuss, American, Italian and French architects respectively, demonstrate unique cooperation. A monumental statue, *Fiure in Repose* by **Henry Moore**, can be viewed from avenue de Suffren.

② Along the Seine and Around the Tower

▸ *Begin at metro station Bir Hakeim, and cross the bridge to the Allée des Cygnes.*

Allée des Cygnes

From halfway across the Bir-Hakeim Bridge there is access down to the man-made islet in the Seine. Allée des Cygnes, or Swans' Walk, provides a good view of the Maison de Radio-France (Ⓒ*see AUTEUIL*). The figure of *France Renaissante* looking upstream is by the Danish sculptor Wederkinch (1930); a bronze replica of the **Statue of Liberty** faces downstream in the direction of the US.

▸ *Backtrack to the quai Branly, and follow it past the Eiffel Tower to the Musée du Quai Branly.*

Musée du Quai Branly

37 quai Branly. Ⓒ*Tue–Sun 11am–7pm, Thu, Fri, Sat until 9pm.* ☞*8.50€ (13€ combined for the permanent and temporary exhibitions).* ♿☎*01 0 56 61 70 00. www.quaibranly.fr.*
Designed by the architect Jean Nouvel, this new primitive arts museum opened in summer 2006. The setting is remarkable: undulating leather-clad low walls lead visitors through the glass and

metal structure to the different sections dedicated to the arts and civilizations of Africa, Asia, Oceania and the Americas. Video and multimedia installations are interspersed throughout. The surrounding gardens add to the feeling that the city is far, far away. Other museum facilities include a multimedia gallery, themed exhibition gallery, anthropology gallery, and an upscale restaurant, Les Ombres.

▸ *Return to the quai Branly and turn left onto the avenue de La Bourdonnais, then left onto rue Général Camou, which leads directly to no 29 avenue Rapp.*

Avenue Rapp

At no 29 is an Art Nouveau building designed by Jules Lavirotte in 1901 for the ceramicist Alexandre Bigot. Its elaborate ceramic façade was awarded a prize from the City of Paris the same year. Nearby, at no 3, is the home of Lavirotte himself, constructed two years earlier in the famous Art Nouveau noodle style.

▸ *At the end of avenue Rapp turn left onto rue St-Dominique.*

At no 129, is the **Fontaine de Mars** by François-Jean Bralle (1750-1832), who also designed the fountain at place du Châtelet. On the way towards the Ecole-Militaire metro station, stop on the rue du Champ-de-Mars to see the elegant floral façade at no 33, designed by Raquin in 1900.

LES GOBELINS

Ⓜ GOBELINS (LINE 7) – BUSES: 27, 47, 83, 91

You may have admired Gobelins tapestries hanging in many of the great museums and great houses, but the history of their manufacture is less well known. An opportunity to see these national treasures being made in the traditional style is not to be missed.

🛈 **Information:** Carrousel du Louvre Welcome Centre, Place de la Pyramide Inversée 99, rue de Rivoli. ☎08 92 68 30 00 (0.34€ per min). http://en.parisinfo.com.

▶ **Orient Yourself:** The district sits on the south edge of the Latin Quarter.

🅿 **Parking:** Underground parking is available at the Italie 2 commercial centre.

👁 **Don't Miss:** The Bièvre river running through Square René-Le-Gall.

🕐 **Organising Your Time:** Allow two hours to visit the neighbourhood.

Kids **Especially for Kids:** A large play area can be found at the Square René-Le-Gall.

👁 **Also See:** QUARTIER LATIN, DENFERT-ROCHERAU.

A Bit of History

In about 1440 the dyer, Jean Gobelin, who specialised in scarlet, set up a workshop beside the River Bièvre. This continued through the generations until the reign of Henri IV when it was taken over by two Flemish craftsmen, summoned by the king (early 17C).

Under Louis XIV the tapestry and carpet-weaving industry around the Gobelins workshops became, in 1662, the Manufacture Royale des Tapisseries de la Couronne (Royal Factory of Tapestry and Carpet Weavers to the Crown). The artist, Charles Le Brun, was appointed as director. Five years later it became associated with the Manufacture Royale des Meubles (Royal Cabinet-Makers).

The greatest craftsmen, including gold-smiths and gilders, thus worked side by side to decorate and furnish the sumptuous palaces of the Sun King and create a Louis XIV style.

Manufacture des Gobelins ★

42 avenue des Gobelins. 🚶Guided tours (1hr) Tue–Thu at 2pm and 2.45pm. 🕐Public holidays. 🎟8€. ☎01 44 54 19 33. www.museums-of-paris.com.

Working methods have changed little since the 17C: warp threads are set by daylight, the colours being selected from a range of over 14 000 tones. Each weaver, working with mirrors, completes

---

The Four Great French Tapestry Workshops

Aubusson: producing hangings for the lesser 17C and 18C aristocracy and bourgeoisie; subject matter includes floral and organic compositions, animals and beasts, Classical mythology and landscapes. Rococo Chinoiseries and pastoral scenes (after Huet) are also common.

Beauvais: very finely woven often with vivid coloured silks which, unfortunately, have faded. Motifs include grotesques, Fables after La Fontaine (by Oudry), Boucher's figures from the Commedia dell'Arte, Classical mythology, Chinoiseries, and pastoral scenes (after Huet). The use of 18C designs continued into the 19C.

Felletin: coarser weave hangings with rustic subject matter.

Gobelins: sumptuous hangings often interwoven with gold. Renowned for the originality of design, series include The Seasons and Elements, The Life of the King, The Royal Residences, Louis XV at the Hunt, as well as paintings by Oudry and Boucher (Loves of the gods). Their most influential weaver during the late 18C was Neilson, a Scot.

Address Book

WHERE TO STAY AND EAT

🕐Turn to the back of the guide for selected hotels, restaurants, bistros and cafés listed by *arrondissement*. This district is spread over the 5th and the 13th arrondissements.

NIGHTLIFE

The Butte-aux-Cailles is a lively, Bohemian style district and abounds with little bars, cafés and restaurants.
La Folie en Tête – *33 rue de la Butte-aux-Cailles, 13th arr.* ☎*01 45 80 65 99. Closed Sun.* The musical instruments hung on the walls keep watch over this pleasant spot where visitors can play chess, draw, discuss or listen to music. Young crowd.

SHOPPING

Cave des Gobelins – *56 av. des Gobelins, 13th arr.* Ⓜ*Gobelins or Place d'Italie.* ☎*01 43 31 66 79. Closed Sun and Aug.* Following in the footsteps of his father, the equally friendly Eric Merlet has taken over the management of this exceptional wine cellar, with among others, a few very rare vintage spirits (including a cognac from 1809!) together with a selection of practically every fine wine produced over the last 40 years.

Les Abeilles – *21 rue de la Butte-aux-Cailles, 13th arr.* Ⓜ*Corvisart or Place d'Italie.* ☎*01 01 45 81 43 48. www. lesabeilles.biz. Tue–Sat 11am–7pm.* This apiculture boutique sells not only bee-keeping supplies, but every kind of honey product, including candies, royal jelly, soap, beeswax, vinegar, sweet bread, and honey by the jar.

---

from 1 to 8sq m/1 to 9.5sq yd per year depending on the design.

In 1989, the Manufacture des Gobelins accepted a commission from Denmark for 10 large tapestries illustrating the history of the country to be offered to Queen Margrethe as a birthday gift. It took the Manufacture ten years to complete the order.

Walking Tour

▶ *Starting in place d'Italie and finishing at the Gobelins workshop.*

Place d'Italie

This square stands on the edge of an area bristling with high-rise buildings. The 19C local council building (*mairie*) stands opposite the contemporary Italie 2 commercial centre.

▶ *Take boulevard A. Blanqui, then follow rue du Moulin-des-Près (first left) as far as place Paul-Verlaine.*

La Butte-aux-Cailles

On 21 November 1783, after taking off from the vicinity of La Muette, the physi-cist **Pilâtre de Rozier** landed his hot-air balloon on this mound, then occupied by several solitary windmills. This was the first free-flight in a hot-air balloon. Today the hilltop is one of surprising contrasts as old cobblestone streets and low-lying houses slowly give way to modern blocks of flats with new urban development.

▶ *Take rue de la Butte-aux-Cailles, then turn right along rue Barrault. Cross boulevard Auguste-Blanqui and take rue Corvisart.*

Square René-le-Gall

Rue de Croulebarbe and rue Berbier-du-Mets drive the River **Bièvre** (seen in the corner of the park) underground. Up to the 17C the willow-bordered stream was of sparkling clear water, and ice taken from the surrounding marshes during the winter was packed into wells and then covered with earth. It was this activity that gave the locality its name, **Glacière**, meaning ice house. Dyeing, tanning and bleaching turned the river into a murky evil-smelling stream and in 1910 it was filled in.

▶ *Exit via rue de Croulebarbe (north-west)*

The **Mobilier national** building is by Auguste Perret (1935) and the two concrete hounds are by André Abbel.

▶ *Follow the first street on the left, rue Berbier-du-Mets then continue along rue G.-Geffroy.*

The **Hôtel de la Reine-Blanche** *(no 17)* was probably named after Blanche de Bourgogne, the unfaithful wife of Charles IV. It was here in 1393 that Charles VI was almost burnt alive at one of the many festivities organised on his physicians' orders in an attempt to cure his insanity.

▶ *Rue G.-Geffroy leads to avenue des Gobelins.*

Chinatown

During the 1960s the Authorities decided to improve an underdeveloped part of the City known as the "Triangle de Choisy", made up of the area around Avenue de Choisy, Avenue d'Ivry and the Boulevard Masséna to the south of the Place d'Italie. They constructed several tower blocks and by the early 1970s large numbers of immigrants from South East Asia settled in the area. The Tang Frères shop on the corner of avenue de Choisy and avenue Edison is a good introduction this quarter, and there are many Chinese, Thai and Vietnamese restaurants nearby. The district may not quite have all the charms of Chinatown in San Francisco or London, but it is lively and entertaining.

LES GRANDS BOULEVARDS ★

Ⓜ RICHELIEU DROUOT (LINES 8 AND 9), STRASBOURG-ST DENIS (LINES 4, 8 AND 9), GRANDS BOULEVARDS (LINES 8 AND 9) – BUSES: 20, 38, 39, 47, 48

Thronged with pedestrians hurrying on business or idly window gazing, the broad tree-lined avenues full of cars, café tables spilling out onto the pavement, innumerable cinemas, theatres and a thousand shops, a profusion of signs, advertising slogans, glowing flashing neon at night: the atmosphere lives on.

Nearby neighbourhoods: **OPÉRA, FAUBOURG POISSONNIÈRE, RÉPUBLIQUE.**

- ⓘ **Information:** Pyramides welcome centre, 25 rue des Pyramides. ☎08 92 68 30 00 (0.34€ per min). http://en.parisinfo.com.
- ▶ **Orient Yourself:** The Grands Boulevards district is at the centre of the Right Bank, the heart of the boulevards that run from Madeleine to Bastille.
- Ⓟ **Parking:** There is street parking on the side streets of the boulevards.
- ⊛ **Don't Miss:** The historic covered shopping passages off the blvd Montmartre.
- ⊙ **Organising Your Time:** Allow 1.5hrs for the neighbourhood and museum.
- **Kids Especially for Kids:** The Grévin Wax Museum fascinates kids of all ages.
- ⟁ **Also See:** OPÉRA, Palais-Royal.

A Bit of History

The ramparts transformed – In 1660 **Louis XIV** had the city's obsolete fortifications – built between the Bastille and the Madeleine under Charles V, Charles IX and Louis XIII – dismantled and filled in. The land was terraced with a broad carriageway and double rows of trees, and triumphal arches replaced the fortified gates. The name boulevard was coined from the military term for a terreplein (sloping bank behind a rampart used by the artillery). At first the area surrounded by open countryside remained deserted; safe for the odd game of *boules* by day, unsafe after dark.

The fashionable stroll – Around 1750 the boulevard became a fashionable place for fancy carriages and gentry on horseback. Under the Directoire, boulevard des Italiens, then boulevard Montmartre, were frequented by members of High Society, who built themselves fine town houses and became known as *Boulevardiers* – an epithet for ephemeral, superficial creatures that flirted with fad and fashion.

Improvements – The roads were paved in 1778, and gas lamps appeared in passage des Panoramas in 1817, and along the boulevard in 1826. The first omnibus appeared on 30 January 1828 linking the Madeleine to the Bastille.

The modern boulevards – Haussmann's radical urban planning transformed the area by inserting broad avenues between place de l'Opéra and place de la République. The attributes of fashion changed ceaselessly through the years, but the colours, the noise and the bustle are constants. The area boasts a number of famous theatres and night spots.

Walking Tour

▶ *From place de l'Opéra to place de la République.*

Boulevard des Italiens

The history of this thoroughfare is inextricably linked with that of fashion. At the time of the Directoire, the area was haunted by Muscadins – bow-legged and hunched fops in exaggerated garb; *Merveilleuses* dressed in high-waisted, transparent dresses in the style of Antiquity or with huge extravagant Turkish-style hats. During the Restoration, these were followed by the *Gandins*, moustachioed with side-whiskers, in top hat, cravat and jacket with broad turned-down collar. Under **Louis-Philippe,** the *Dandys* and the *Lions* followed the fashion from across the Channel: they began to smoke in public (1835). The Second Empire was a more sober age, waxed moustaches and close-cut goatee beards appeared, ladies sported crinolines and café society flourished. The boulevard got its name from the acting troupe of the **Opéra-Comique** *(along rue Favart)*, known as the Italians. Today the area is popular for the pro-

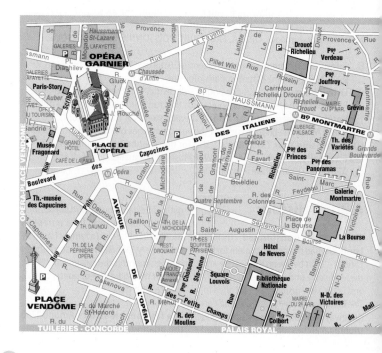

liferation of cinemas and chain restaurants, which have gradually slipped in between banking headquarters. The CLC and BNP banks in particular have attractive façades (between rue Taitbout and Laffitte). On reaching the latter, there is a good **view**★ of Sacré-Coeur.

Boulevard Montmartre

Particularly lively. On the right at no 11 is **passage des Panoramas** which was opened in 1799 and leads to the Stock Exchange (La Bourse). At no **47** in the arcade an engraver's shop retains its old-fashioned frontage. **Passage Jouffroy** at no 10 is also worth a visit, with small cafés and interesting shops.

▶ *Follow boulevard Poissonnière and boulevard de Bonne-Nouvelle.*

The **Cinéma Grand Rex** is a genuine temple to the glory of the silver screen, its baroque décor and its large screen make the building one of Europe's landmark cinemas.

Les Étoiles du Rex [Kids]

(1 blvd Poissonnière. ⏰*Wed–Sun 10am–7pm* ⮕*9.80€ (under-12s 8€).* ☎*08 92*

Porte St-Denis

B. Kaufmann/MICHELIN

68 05 96 (0.34€ per min). www.legrand rex.com) is a 50min interactive tour that reveals the backstage legends and stars of Europe's most famous film theatre. Special effects, sounds, and sets all combine to put the visitor in the heart of the action.

Just before Porte St-Denis, the **view**★ of the crossroads of rue Cléry, rue Beauregard and rue de la Lune gives an idea of what Paris must have looked like in the 19C.

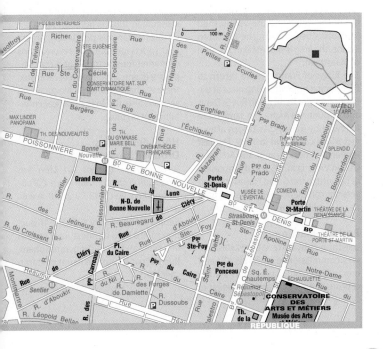

Porte St-Denis★

This impressive gate, 24m/78.7ft high, was erected at the city's expense in 1672 by the architect and military engineer Nicolas François Blondel to celebrate Louis XIV's victorious campaigns on the Rhine. Said to be the inspiration for the Arc de Triomphe, it has on its southern façade a bas relief represents the crossing of the Rhine and the vanquished territories beyond. On the northern façade, the king is shown taking control of Maastricht.

The Kings of France would return to their capital from attending mass at the Basilica at Saint Denis along Rue St Denis and through the Arch – the same route followed by Napoléon's troops after a victorious campaign in 1816. The last monarch to pass through the Arch was Queen Victoria in 1855 on the occasion of her visit to the Grand Exposition Universelle, completing a ritual dating back nearly a millennium.

Porte St-Martin★

Like the nearby Porte St Denis, this gate was commissioned by Louis XIV and erected in 1674 to commemorate the capture of Besançon and the defeat of the German, Spanish and Dutch armies. A mere 17m/55.7ft high, the arch was designed by Pierre Bullet to bear carvings by eminent artists who had worked at Versailles. On the southern façade there is an inscription in Latin which states , "To Louis the Great, for having vanquished the German, Spanish, and Dutch armies: the Dean of the Guild and the Aldermen of Paris."

Boulevard St-Martin

This leads down to place de la République. The area was built up on an old rubbish dump, hence the undulations and the need for laying the road at a different gradient and level from the pavements. The boulevard runs past place J Strauss (on the left) adorned with a bust of the famous Viennese composer.

Museums and other Attractions

Musée Grévin★ Kids

10 boulevard Montmartre. 🕒*Daily 10am–6.30pm (Sat–Sun until 7pm; last admission 1hr before closing).* ⊛*18.50€ (under-14s 11€).* ♿☎*01 47 70 85 05. www.grevin.com.*

Grévin, a caricaturist, founded the museum in 1882. In addition to waxen effigies of famous politicians, artists and sports-people and re-creations of momentous historical and contemporary events in the form of tableaux, there is a hall of mirrors. Live conjuring sessions also add to the magical entertainment on offer.

Hôtel des Ventes Drouot Richelieu

9 rue Drouot. 🕒*Sept–Jul, Mon–Sat (and 1 Sun in month) 11am–6pm.* 🚫*Public holidays.* ☎*01 48 00 20 20. www.drouot.com*

Reopened on 13 May 1980 the 16 auction rooms hold business daily at 2pm in a lively and interesting atmosphere. Rue Drouot is also the haunt of stamp collectors.

LES HALLES

Ⓜ LES HALLES (LINE 4) – RER: CHÂTELET-LES-HALLES (LINES A, B AND D)
BUSES: 29, 38, 47

The demolition and displacement of the City's main wholesale market has radically altered the area's character. Today, a busy shopping centre with a garden occupies the site of the old trade halls, once known as The Belly of Paris (the title of a novel by Émile Zola). Some of the old streets remain, as does one of Paris' most beautiful churches, St-Eustache.

Nearby neighbourhoods: **BEAUBOURG, CHÂTELET-HÔTEL DE VILLE, PALAIS-ROYAL, PLACE DES VICTOIRES, RÉPUBLIQUE (Temple).**

- 🛈 **Information:** Carrousel du Louvre Welcome Centre, Place de la Pyramide Inversée 99, rue de Rivoli. ☎08 92 68 30 00. (0.34€ per min). http://en.parisinfo.com.
- ▶ **Orient Yourself:** Les Halles is on the Right Bank between the Louvre and the Marais.
- 🅿 **Parking:** Underground parking garages are under the Forum des Halles.
- 🚫 **Don't Miss:** Organ recitals at St-Eustache and the market at rue Montorgeuil.
- 🕑 **Organising Your Time:** Allow two-three hours to visit this excellent shopping district.
- 🧒 **Especially for Kids:** The Jardin des Halles has an elaborate Jardin des Enfants.
- 👤 **Also See:** BEAUBOURG, LOUVRE, CHÂTELET-HÔTEL DE VILLE.

A Bit of History

The Old Halles – In 1135 there was already a twice-weekly market at Les Halles, where each street specialised in a particular trade. By the 16C, with a growing population of 300 000 in the capital, the trade in foodstuffs became of paramount importance, eventually replacing all other types of trade in the market. On the orders of Napoléon, the wine and leather markets were transferred to the Left Bank.

Until the Revolution, a pillory stood near St-Eustache crossroads; dishonest traders, thieves and prostitutes were publicly exposed there.

By the 19C the great market was in urgent need of reconstruction. Wide avenues through the quarter were opened (rue de Rivoli, rue du Pont-Neuf, rue du Louvre, rue Étienne-Marcel) and ten halls of iron girders and skylight roofs designed by **Baltard** and **Callet** were constructed (1854-74). The animated market scene and the rich variety of colour and smell are vividly described in Zola's novel, *The Belly of Paris*. Locals enjoyed eating onion soup, snails and pig's trotters at 5am in simple but excellent restaurants with colourful names (Le Chien qui Fume, Le Pied de Cochon). As the old buildings became inadequate, they were demolished and removed, and the market was relocated to the outskirts of the city at Rungis (1969).

Façade of St-Eustache

©Jozef Sedmak/Dreamstime.com

Walking Tour

Galerie Véro-Dodat, created in 1826 by two eponymous pork butchers just off rue Jean-Jacques-Rousseau, was one of the first streets in Paris to have gas lighting. Today the artisan boutiques have an old-fashioned air.

▷ *Turn left along rue Jean-Jacques-Rousseau, to reach place des Deux-Écus, whose buildings still retain their original façades.*

La Bourse du Commerce

2 rue de Viarmes. The circular Commodities Exchange building was built in 1889 to replace a wheat market built in Louis XVI's reign. Inside, the vast circular hall lit by a glass dome is now used by the Paris Chamber of Commerce.

Jardin des Halles

A garden (5ha/12.3 acres) includes pergolas along rue Berger, water fountains, grassy lawns, children's play areas and a tree-lined mall linking the semicircular area by St-Eustache, where a massive 70t stone head *(Écoute)* by H de Miller stands.

Ëglise St-Eustache★★

Place du Jour. Gothic in plan and structure, but Renaissance in decoration, this is one of Paris' most beautiful churches.

In 1214 a chapel dedicated to St Agnes was built on this spot. A few years later, the chapel was re-dedicated to St Eustache, a converted Roman general. But the Halles parish, which had become the biggest in Paris, dreamed of a church worthy of its new status. Grandiose plans were made and the foundation stone was laid in 1532. Construction was

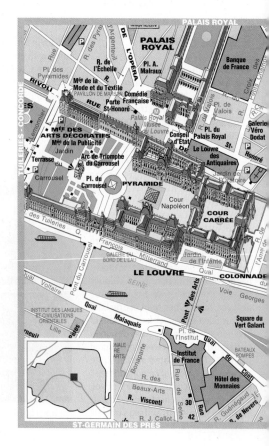

slow, however, in spite of liberal gifts and the church was not consecrated until a century later, in 1640. The **west front** was never completed but later rebuilt in the Classical style (1754). In 1844 the edifice was badly damaged by fire and subsequently restored by **Baltard**.

North transept façade★

This fine Renaissance composition is flanked by twin staircase turrets ending in pinnacles. Beneath the gable point is a stag's head with a Cross between the antlers recalling St Eustache's conversion. The statues on the door shafts are modern. The pilasters, niches, mouldings, grotesques and roses are delicately fashioned.

Interior

St-Eustache measures 100x44x34m/ 328x144x111.5ft. The plan resembles Notre-Dame, with nave and chancel encircled by double aisles and flat tran-

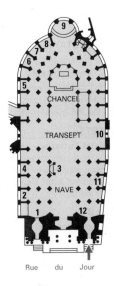

septs. The vaulting above the nave, transept and chancel is Flamboyant,

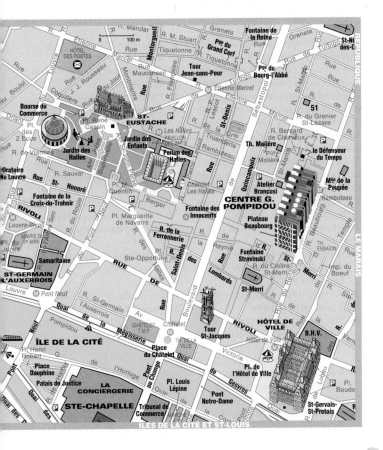

Address Book

WHERE TO STAY AND EAT

♿Turn to the back of the guide for selected hotels, restaurants, bistros and cafés listed by *arrondissement*. This neighbourhood is spread over the 1st and the 2nd arrondissements.

CONCERTS

Église Saint-Eustache – Regular concerts *(see the posters outside)* of organ music played by today's masters Jean Guillou and André Fleury, directed by Father Martin.

NIGHTLIFE

Duc des Lombards – *42 rue des Lombards, 1st arr.* ☎*01 42 33 22 88. www.ducdeslombards.com. Open daily 6.30pm, concert 9pm.* Modern jazz has pride of place in this small room on boulevard Sébastopol. Some of its regulars include the pianist Martial Solal, bass player Henri Texier, saxophonist Steve Lacy and drummer Aldo Romano.

SHOPPING

Agnès B. – *6 rue du Jour, 1st arr.* Ⓜ*Les Halles.* ☎*01 45 08 56 56. www.agnesb. com. Closed Sun and public holidays.* Clothes for men, women and children, accessories and jewellery. All of Agnès B's collections can be found behind one of the elegant windows of the five shops which line this little street.

La Droguerie – *9–11 rue du Jour ,1st arr* Ⓜ*Les Halles.* ☎*01 45 08 93 27. Closed Sun.* This shop stocks absolutely everything necessary for the budding dress or jewellery maker.

Strohrer – *51 rue Montorgueil, 2nd arr.* Ⓜ*Etienne-Marcel.* ☎*01 42 33 38 20. www.stohrer.fr. Closed 1–15 Aug.* Nicolas Stohrer started his career in Louis XVs court at Versailles, and opened this pastry shop and delicatessen at its current location in 1730. The décor is a classified historical monument, and the baba is the house speciality.

---

adorned with numerous ribs and richly carved hanging keystones.

The elevation, however, is entirely different from the cathedral's. The aisles, devoid of galleries, rise very high, the arches being so tall that between them and the clerestory windows there is space only for a small Renaissance-style gallery.

The stained-glass windows in the chancel are after drawings by Philippe de Champaigne (1631). St Eustace appears at the centre, surrounded by the Fathers of the Church and the Apostles.

The chapels are decorated with frescoes.

1) On the door tympanum: the *Martyrdom of St Eustace* by Simon Vouet (17C).
2) *Adoration of the Magi*, a copy of a painting by **Rubens**.
3) Churchwarden's pew presented by the Regent, Philippe of Orleans in 1720.
4) Colourful naïve sculpture by R Mason commemorating the fruit and vegetable market's move out of Paris on 28 February 1969.
5) *Tobias and the Angel,* by Santi di Tito (16C).
6) *The Ecstasy of Mary Magdalen,* a painting by Manetti (17C).
7) *The Pilgrims at Emmaüs,* an early Rubens.
8) Colbert's tomb designed by **Le Brun**; **Coysevox** carved the statues of the minister and of Abundance; Tuby that of Fidelity (left).
9) Statue of the Virgin by **Pigalle**. Chapel frescoes by Thomas Couture (19C).
10) 16C statue of St John the Evangelist.
11) Bust of the composer **Jean-Philippe Rameau** who died in 1764.
12) Epitaph to 17C Lieutenant-General Chevert.

Walk down the narrow rue du Jour (no 4 once belonged to Montmorency-Bouteville who was beheaded in 1628 for contravening Richelieu's ban on duelling) then turn right onto rue Montmartre.

From no 3 and 4 rue Montmartre there are fine views of the church.

▶ *At the end of rue Montmartre, turn left to rue Montorgueil.*

S. Sauvignier/MICHELIN

Forum des Halles and St-Eustache Church

Rue Montorgueil

This pedestrianised shopping neigh-bourhood, renovated in the 1990s, still has some of its old-fashioned bou-tiques such as l'Escargot, Stroher, and Le Rocher de Cancale. The rue Mon-torgueil is crossed by some interesting side streets such as the **rue Maucon-seil**, once home to theatre troupes, the **rue Tiquetonne**, with its historic facades, and the **rue Marie Stuart**, which leads to the shopping passage du Grand-Cerf.

▶ *Go through the passage du Grand-Cerf (built in 1825 and restored in the 1980s) and turn right onto the rue St-Denis to rejoin the rue Etienne-Marcel.*

Tour de Jean-sans-Peur

20 rue Etienne Marcel. ⏲ *4 Apr–11 Nov, Wed–Sun 1.30pm–6pm; 12 Nov–end Mar, Wed, Sat–Sun 1.30pm–6pm.* ◉5€. ☎ *01 40 26 20 28. www.tourjeansans peur.com.*

This square machicolated tower *was* built by John the Fearless for his own protection in 1409 following the assas-sination, on his orders, of the Duke of Orléans. The tower formed part of the **Hôtel de Bourgogne**. The interior reconstructs scenes from a typical medi-eval chateau, including the oldest toilets in Paris – from 1411!

▶ *Double-back to the rue de Turbigo (cross Etiienne Marcel), which leads to the Forum des Halles.*

Forum des Halles

This underground commercial centre and cineplex, with direct access to the metro and RER stations, extends over 7ha/17 acres to the east of the Commo-doties Exchange.

▶ *Leave by the Porte du Louvre and cross to rue Sauval.*

Opposite, on the corner of rue St-Honoré and rue de l'Arbre-Sec is the **Fontaine de la Croix-du-Trahoir** created by Souf-flot (1775).

▶ *Return along rue St-Honoré to place Marguerite-de-Navarre.*

Fontaine des Innocents★

The 19C square stands on the site of the cemetery and church of the Holy Inno-cents which dated back to the 12C.
The cemetery was once encircled by a charnel house where bones from the communal graves were collected. In 1786, the cemetery was closed and nearly two million skeletons were trans-ferred by night over a period of many months to the former quarries of La Tombe-Issoire, which became known as the Catacombes.

INSTITUT DE FRANCE★★

Ⓜ PONT-NEUF (LINE 7), ODÉON (LINES 4 AND 10)

BUSES: 24, 27, 58, 70

The Institut is one of the gems of the Left Bank; among the five academies housed within its walls is the renowned Académie Française. Only open to visitors with a guide, getting into this seat of learning is not easy. The building is best admired from the Pont des Arts, and the surrounding streets contain souvenirs of Molière, Racine and Balzac.

Nearby neighbourhoods: ODÉON, QUARTIER LATIN, ST-GERMAIN-DES-PRÉS, MUSÉE D'ORSAY, LE LOUVRE.

- **Information:** Carrousel du Louvre welcome centre, Place de la Pyramide Inversée 99, rue de Rivoli. ☎0892 68 3000 (0.34€ per min). http://en.parisinfo.com.
- ▶ **Orient Yourself:** The institute sits on the Left Bank in the St-Germain-des-Prés district. It's connected to the Louvre by the pedestrian Pont des Arts.
- Ⓟ **Parking:** Underground parking on rue Bonaparte and blvd St-Germain.
- **Don't Miss:** The view of the Institut de France from the Pont des Arts.
- 🕐 **Organizing Your Time:** One–two hours depending upon whether you visit both the museum and the Institut.
- **Also See:** ST-GERMAIN-DES PRÉS

A Bit of History

A prestigious legacy – The building we admire today came into being as a result of a bequest by the Cardinal Mazarin, three days before he died in 1661, for a college of scholars from France's newly acquired provinces. The Institute was founded in 1795 and consists of five ,academies: the Académies des Inscriptions et Belles Lettres, Sciences, Beaux-Arts, Sciences morales et Politiques, and the famous Académie Française, best known by linguists for safeguarding the French language *from* franglais. The main activity of the 40 *immortels* is the constant revision of the definitive Dictionary of the French Language (see The Academy).

Address Book

WHERE TO STAY AND EAT

Turn to the back of the guide for selected hotels, restaurants, bistros and cafés listed by *arrondissement*. This neighbourhood is in the 6th arrondissement.

NIGHTLIFE

Hôtel d'Aubusson (Café Laurent) – *33 rue Dauphine, 6th arr.* ☎*01 43 29 43 43. www.hoteldaubusson.com. Daily.* Located in the former Grands Augustins convent, this café was very popular among 18C philosophers. Renamed the Café Tabou in 1946, it became one of the favourite haunts of Sartre and Camus. Today a modern room opens onto one of the former period rooms with original beams (1606) and hearthplace. For tea and a quiet read. Live music at weekends.

ART

Rue de Seine – *rue de Seine, 6th arr.* Ⓜ*Mabillon.* A large number of art galleries line rue de Seine and neighbouring streets (rue des Beaux-Arts, rue Visconti, rue Jacob, rue Jacques-Callot, etc.). Maps can be obtained in each gallery.

The Academy

Founded by Cardinal Richelieu in 1635, the job of the Academie Française is to regulate French grammar, spelling and literature. Suppressed during the Revolution, the Académie was fully restored by Napoléon Bonaparte in 1816 and has been in operation ever since. The Académie has 40 members called Les Immortels; its motto is À l'immortalité or "To immortality". While there is not a bar on non-French members, there have been very few, and the Académie appears not to be an equal opportunity organisation since only four women have ever been members – the first being Marguerite Yourcenar in 1980.

Strangely, the recommendations of the Académie carry no legal power but they do produce a dictionary of acceptable French usage, entitled 'Le Dictionnaire de l'Académie Française', which is looked upon as official in France even though it is often ignored even by government departments and strangely not on sale to the general public!

Increasingly the problem for the Académie is that French culture and language has come under pressure from the widespread use of English as the main international language and also the parallel growth of the internet. Words borrowed from English, whilst widely understood by the French, are discouraged by the Académie. Email should be referred to as 'courriel' while computer software should be 'logiciel' and the computer has to be l'ordinateur.

Much more controversial, however, is the issue of what to call a female in an occupation which has a masculine noun as the job title. Lionel Jospin's government, for example, used the form 'la ministre' to refer to a female colleague following the example set by the Swiss, Canadian and Belgian governments. Greatly frowned upon by Les Immortels, this matter remains unresolved.

Whilst the concept of protecting the Culture and Language of La Belle France is admirable, there is perhaps an echo of King Canute. Even the most ardent supporters of the French language may eventually have to concede the inevitable!

Visit

23 quai de Conti.
The Centre des Monuments Nationaux (National Monuments Centre) organises guided tours of the Institut de France one weekend a month. 8€ *(under-25s, 6€). The tour includes the interior courtyards, the dome and Mazarin's tomb. Reservations:* 01 44 54 19 30/35) A magnificent dome distinguishes the building from afar. The central chapel is flanked by two pavilions by **Le Vau**, architect of the Louvre. In the courtyard, to the left of the dome, is the **Mazarin Library**★. Inside, the former chapel is now the formal audience chamber where members are sworn in, with a Mazarin commemorative monument by **Coysevox**.
A second courtyard is surrounded by the buildings where the scholars once lived.

Walking Tour

② Around the Institut de France

See map SAINT-GERMAIN-DES-PRÉS.

Quai des Grands-Augustins
The oldest quay in Paris dates from 1313, and derives its name from the Great Augustine monastery established by St Louis in the 13C on a nearby site. Note, as you pass, two 17C mansions: no **51**, now the famous Lapérouse Restaurant, and no **35**, the former Hôtel Feydeau-Montholon.

▶ *At the beginning of quai de Conti, turn left onto rue de Nevers.*

Rue de Nevers
This curious, picturesque alley created in the 13C which maintains its medieval character. It abuts a fragment of the old

Pont des Arts leading to Institut de France

Olivier Nicolas/Photononstop/Tips Images

wall built by Philippe Auguste around the city.

▶ *Take rue de Nesle to rue Dauphine, then passage Dauphine onto rue Mazarine.*

Rue Mazarine

A narrow street containing small art galleries. As you leave the passage, look at the building opposite: it is decorated with statues perched on stilts. No **42**, formerly an indoor tennis court converted into the **Guénégaud Theatre**, was where opera was presented for the first time in France in 1671. At no **30**, the first Paris **fire station** was home to the capital's first fire brigade in 1722. At no **12**, beyond Place Gabriel Pierné, stood a theatre where **Molière** made his first appearance as an actor.

▶ *Take rue J Callot to reach rue Visconti.*

Rue Visconti

This narrow alleyway was known in the 16C as Little Geneva because of its Protestant community. 17C cabaret at no **26**. The playwright **Racine** died at no **24** in 1699. Two hundred years later, Balzac founded a printing house at **no 17** (1826) which soon went bankrupt. Later still, **Delacroix** had his studio here from 1836 to 1844.

▶ *Take rue Jacob to rue des Saints-Pères; turn right on the quai Malaquais.*

Quai Malaquais

The École nationale supérieure des Beaux-Arts *(on your right)* has stood here since 1816. On the corner with rue Bonaparte at no **9** stands a 17C stone and brick house, visited by Manon Lescaut in the story by Abbé Prévost.
The writer Anatole France (1844-1924) was born at no **19** (plaque on no **15**), which also served George Sand between 1832 and 1836, when she wrote *Lélia*.

Pont des Arts

The bridge dating from 1803 was the first in Paris to be built of iron and the first pedestrian bridge. Access was subject to a toll, as it was for most of the bridges, levied until 1849. Its success was immediate: 65 000 Parisians paid to cross it the day it opened. The present construction is steel and has seven arches instead of the original eight.
The **view**★★★ is outstanding, encompassing the full length of Pont Neuf and the Île de la Cité including Notre-Dame; downstream the Louvre, the Grand Palais and the Carrousel Bridge.

Hôtel des Monnaies et Médailles★

11 quai Conti. ⏱*Tue–Sun 11am–5.30pm, Sat–Sun noon–5.30pm.* ⊜*5€.* ☎*01 40 46 56 56. www.monnaiedeparis.fr.*
In the 18C Louis XV installed the Mint here, selecting the architect, **Antoine**, to design the workshops which were built between 1768 and 1775. The simplicity of line, sober rustication and restrained decoration was praised by the contemporary public, tired of excessive Classical orders and colonnades. Before being transferred to Pessac, all of France's currency was minted here. Collection pieces, medals and decorations are still produced here.
The **Coin Museum** *(back of the main courtyard)* occupies the refurbished minting and milling halls. Exhibits retrace the history of French coin making and minting from 300 BC. A fine collection of coins, medals, banking documentation, paintings, engravings and drawings illustrate various political, social and financial developments.

LES INVALIDES★★★

This fine neighbourhood elbowing the Faubourg St-Germain is endowed with elegant buildings that include the most outstanding single monumental group in Paris: the noble Dôme church that houses the tomb of **Napoléon** and the adjacent Army Museum endowed with its rich and spectacular collections.

Nearby neighbourhoods: **FAUBOURG ST-GERMAIN, MUSÉE D'ORSAY, SÈVRES-BABYLONE, CHAMPS-ÉLYSÉES, TOUR EIFFEL.**

- 🄸 **Information:** Pyramides welcome centre, 25 rue des Pyramides. ☎08 92 68 30 00 (0.34€ per min). http://en.parisinfo.com.
- ▶ **Orient Yourself:** Les Invalides overlooks the Seine from the Left Bank, between the Eiffel Tower and St-Germain-des-Prés.
- 🅿 **Parking:** There is above and below ground parking along the esplanade.
- 👁 **Don't Miss:** The intricate suits of armour belonging to King François I and Henri II in the Army Museum.
- 🕐 **Organizing Your Time:** Allow at least three hours to visit the entire museum.
- 🄺ⁱᵈˢ **Especially for Kids:** There's a playground in the Square Santiago du Chili.
- 👁 **Also See:** MUSÉE D'ORSAY, FAUBOURG-ST-GERMAIN.

A Bit of History

Barracks for 4 000 men – Before Louis XIV's reign, old or invalid soldiers were, in theory, looked after in convent hospitals. In reality, most were reduced to beggary. In 1670 the Sun King founded the Invalides on the edge of what was then the Grenelle Plain. The dome was added in 1706, lifting the overall effect from the strictly utilitarian to the monumental.

Pillage – On the morning of 14 July 1789, rebels on the way to the Bastille advanced on the Invalides in search of arms. They crossed the moat, disarmed the sentries and entered the underground rifle stores, making off with 28 000 rifles.

Napoléon's return – In 1793, the Revolution transformed the two churches, which were still adjoined, into a Temple to Mars, and had the captured enemy standards transferred there from Nôtre-

Aerial view of the Hôtel des Invalides

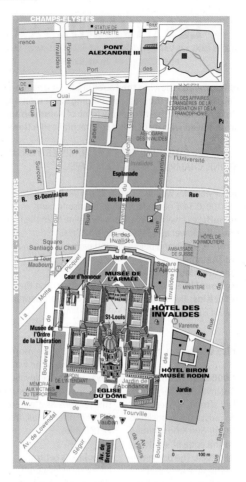

Dame. When Napoléon had Marshal Turenne (d. 1675) interred in the church in 1800, it became a military mausoleum, receiving further countless trophies from the imperial campaigns. In 1840 Napoléon's remains were brought back to Paris and finally placed beneath the Dôme on 3 April 1861.

The institution's revival – After the two World Wars the institution reverted to its original purpose in providing shelter and care to the war wounded with modernised hospital facilities. The buildings today are occupied by military administration and the Army Museum. To celebrate the bicentenary of the French Revolution in 1989 the Dôme was re-gilded, using 12.65kg/27.8lb of gold leaf.

Within the Hotel des Invalides

&Apr–Sept, 10am–6pm (last admission 30min before closing); Oct–Mar, 10am–5pm. 1st Mon in the month, 1 Jan, 1 May, 1 Nov, 25 Dec. 8€; under-18 no charge (one ticket for admission to all museums and Dôme). 01 44 42 38 77. www.invalides.org.

Musée de l'Armée★★★

The galleries of one of the world's richest army museums, containing over 500 000 exhibits, lie on either side of the main courtyard, on several floors. Five main themes are illustrated.

Arms and armour (west side) illustrate the evolution of methods of defence

ÉGLISE SAINT-LOUIS
DES INVALIDES

3   2

1

Lyautey   Foch

NAPOLEON'S

Turenne   Vauban

TOMB

Jérôme   Joseph
Bonaparte   Bonaparte

and attack with real weapons and suits of armour from prehistoric times to the 16C. The Ancien Régime and 19C *(east side)* section presents the collection of weapons and uniforms from the 17C to the Second Empire, including many uniforms and souvenirs relating to Napoléon. Banners and artillery are displayed around the courtyard, on different floors, including 200 cannons in the **Salle Gribeauval** *(west side)* and French banners dating from 1619 to 1953 in the **ground-floor galleries**.

World Wars I and **II** *(west side)* sections feature animated maps showing troop movements show the development of World War I and three floors are devoted to World War II, the Free French forces, and the Resistance movement. The displays follow a chronological order from the 1940 defeat and General de Gaulle's radio appeal to the French people on 18 June 1940 to the concentration camps and the capitulation of Japan in 1945. Personal objects, weapons, models, video films, photos and documents illustrate the role each party played in this worldwide conflict.

Musée des Plans reliefs★★
4th floor, west side. A collection of scale models of towns, harbours and fortresses (1:600) from the time of Vauban (17C) to the present illustrates the evolution of fortifications in France over the last 300 years.

Église du Dôme★★★
The church is one of the major masterpieces of the age of Louis XIV, reaching new heights in the French Classical style. Louis XIV commissioned **Hardouin-Mansart** to design a church that would complement the Invalides buildings of Libéral Bruant. In 1677, work began on the royal church, joined to the Soldiers' Church by a common sanctuary. It was completed by Robert de Cotte in 1735. Decorated with trophies, garlands and other ornaments, the dome is capped by an elegant gold lantern. The dome roof consists of lead sheeting, attached by copper nails to a wood frame. It was first given its golden splendour in 1715.

Interior
The decoration is sumptuous: painted cupolas, walls adorned with columns

Address Book

WHERE TO STAY AND EAT

Turn to the back of the guide for selected hotels, restaurants, bistros and cafés listed by *arrondissement*. This neighbourhood is in the 7th arrondissement. The Hôtel des Invalides has its own cafeteria with free access independent of the museum.

TICKETS FOR THE MUSEUMS

The Invalides are comprised of three museums: Army, Relief maps and the Order of Liberation. The ticket provides access to all three, together with the Dôme Church and Napoléon's tomb. The ticket is valid all day and it is possible to come and go at will.

SHOPPING

Pétrossian – *18 blvd de Latour-Maubourg, 7th arr.* ⓜ *Latour-Maubourg.* ☎ *01 44 11 32 22. www.petrossian.fr. Closed Mon in Aug and Sun.* In this magnificent 1920s shop, Paris' caviar and smoked fish specialists introduce their customers to real Scottish and Norwegian salmon, smoked for five days over a fire of different wood essences, as well as wild white salmon from the Baltic. Their foie gras is also delicious.

and pilasters framing low-relief sculptures by the greatest contemporary artists. In 1842, two years after the return of Napoléon's body, Visconti enlarged the high altar (**1**), replaced the original baldaquin and had the crypt dug to receive the 'Eagle's' sarcophagus. By the entrance to the crypt are the tombs of Generals Duroc (**2**) and Bertrand (**3**).

Napoléon's tomb

The majesty of the setting perfectly befits the Emperor's image. In order to preserve the design of the church and a view of the altar, **Visconti** dug a circular crypt for the red porphyry sarcophagus on its base of green granite from the Vosges. Two massive bronze statues stand guard at the crypt entrance, one bearing an orb, the other the Imperial sceptre and crown; 12 statues by Pradier surround the crypt. The Emperor's body is placed in six coffins, one contained inside the other: the innermost is of tinplate; the second of mahogany; the third and fourth of lead; the fifth of ebony; the last of oak.

Musée de l'Ordre de la Libération★

www.ordredelaliberation.fr. The Order of Liberation, created by Général de Gaulle at Brazzaville in 1940, honoured as companions those who made an outstanding contribution to the final victory. The list includes service personnel and civilians, and a few overseas leaders including King George VI, Winston Churchill and General Eisenhower. The museum also perpetuates the memory of French heroes from the African campaigns, major operations of the Resistance and the concentration camps. Displays include documents, trophies and relics.

Walking Tour

Pont Alexandre III★★

This bridge was built for the 1900 World Exhibition and is an example of the popular steel architecture and ornate style of the period. The armorial bearings of Russia and France evoke the memory of Alexander III, father of Nicholas II of Russia who laid the foundation stone. It has a splendid single-span, surbased arch.

Hôtel des Invalides★★★

Access from esplanade des Invalides.

Garden

Fronting the Invalides is a series of gardens, bordered by a wide dry moat, ramparts lined with 17C and 18C bronze cannon and an 18-piece triumphal battery used to fire salutes on such occasions as the Armistice (11 November 1918) and the Victory March (14 July 1919).

Façade★★

The façade is majestic in style and line, and in proportion and size – 196m/643ft long. The central block is dominated by a magnificent doorway, flanked by twin pavilions. An equestrian statue shows Louis XIV supported by Prudence and Justice in the rounded arch above the entrance.

Cour d'honneur★

Access through the gate.

Napoléon took great pleasure in reviewing his veterans here, before the perfect proportions of the Classical building. At the centre is his statue by Seurre, which stood for some years at the top of the column in place Vendôme.

An impressive series of cannon are laid around the courtyard: note the *Catherina* (1487) and the *Württemberg* culverin (16C); near the stairs is a Renault tank and one of the Marne taxis used to carry soldiers to the front in World War I.

▶ *From the main courtyard, walk up one of the corner staircases to see the small enclosed courtyards which can also be seen from the Musée de l'Armée.*

Église de St-Louis-des-Invalides★

The church, also known as the Soldiers' Church, was designed by Libéral Bruant and built by Mansart. Its design seems cold and functional, the only relief being the captured enemy banners overhanging the upper galleries. A window behind the high altar provides a glimpse of the baldaquin in the Dôme Church.

The magnificent 17C organ is enclosed in a loft designed by Hardouin-Mansart. It was here that **Berlioz**'s *Requiem* was first heard in 1837.

▶ *On your way out of the church, follow either the right-hand or left-hand corridor leading to the Église du Dôme.*

Napoléon – Artillery Officer to First Consul

Arguably the most famous Frenchman of all time, Napoléon Bonaparte was not actually French but Corsican with Italian antecedents. He became a professional soldier at the age of 16, and after the Revolution of 1789 he returned to Corsica where he sided with the Jacobins against the Royalists and Corsican Nationalists.

Napoléon's exploits during various battles led to his becoming friendly with Robespierre's brother. This proved to be a bit of a setback when Robespierre was guillotined and Napoléon spent a short period in jail.

As commander of the revolutionary forces in Paris, Bonaparte impressed Barras, leader of the new Directory, and was soon appointed commander of the Army of Italy. He led a successful campaign against the Austrians and his feats in Italy made him popular in France, where he sought unsuccessfully to become a member of the Directory.

There followed the campaign in Egypt against the Ottomans which was very successful on land but much less so at sea. The British, not keen to see the expansion of French power in the Mediterranean, deployed the Royal Navy led by Nelson, which destroyed the French Fleet during the battle of the Nile.

With political instability at home Napoléon was recalled by the Directory which was rapidly losing popularity. He seized his chance, and on 9th November he dispersed the Legislative Council in the Coup de Brumaire and emerged as joint First Consul. In 1802 he became First Consul in his own right, becoming first Consul for Life. The stage was now set for him to later become Emperor of France – the young artillery officer was now reaching the pinnacle of his career.

JARDIN DES PLANTES★★

Ⓜ/RER: GARE D'AUSTERLITZ (LINES 5 AND 10/C) – BUSES: 24, 57, 61, 63, 65, 91

The Jardin des Plantes is an Ali Baba's cave that manages to combine culture and pleasure, thus making science accessible to all. Together, the complex encompasses the Botanical Gardens and its menagerie of 1 200 animals, the Natural History Museum, and various other study collections of minerals and fossils.

Nearby neighbourhoods: **JUSSIEU, MOUFFETARD, QUARTIER LATIN, MAUBERT, GOBELINS.**

- **Information:** Pyramides welcome centre, 25 rue des Pyramides. ☎08 92 68 30 00 (0.34€ per min). http://en.parisinfo.com.
- ▶ **Orient Yourself:** The gardens are on the eastern Left Bank overlooking the Seine.
- Ⓟ **Parking:** At the Gare d'Austerlitz.
- **Don't Miss:** The quiet Jardin Alpin.
- ◔ **Organizing Your Time:** Allow a half day to visit the museum and gardens.
- **Kids Especially for Kids:** The Menagerie and carrousel.
- **Also See:** QUARTIER LATIN.

Sight

A royal garden

In 1626 Hérouard and Guy de la Brosse, physicians to Louis XIII, were granted permission to move the Royal Medicinal Herb Garden from the tip of the Île de la Cité to the St-Victor district. The garden evolved to encompass a school for botany, natural history and pharmacy. In 1640 the garden was opened to the public.

The gardens were at their greatest during the curatorship of Buffon (1739-88), who published his 36 volume *Natural History*, extended the gardens to the banks of the Seine, planted avenues of lime trees and the maze, and built the amphitheatre and galleries.

Muséum National d'Histoire Naturelle★★

Grande Galerie de l'Évolution★★★   Kids

36 rue Geoffroy-Saint-Hilaire. ◔*Wed–Mon 10am–6pm.* ◔*1 May.* ☞ *8€ (children 6€).* ☎*01 40 79 54 79.* www.mnhn.fr.

This is one of the world's greatest conservatories in the field of natural science. At the Revolution **Bernardin de Saint-Pierre** was nominated curator of the Royal Botanic Gardens, renamed by the Convention (10 June 1793) the National Museum for Natural History. The same year a menagerie was instituted with animals from zoos, often privately owned by princes and circus performers that astounded Parisians had never seen: elephants, bears, giraffes, etc. In 1870, however, when Paris was under siege, the citizens' hunger exceeded their curiosity and most of the animals

Jardin des Plantes

were killed for food. With **Géoffroy-Saint-Hilaire**, **Lamarck**, **Lacépède**, **Cuvier**, **Becquerel** and many other great names, the institute won through its teaching and research in the 19C the international recognition which it maintains today.

The great story of evolution

The theory of evolution is one of the most important in scientific development. It draws together a large number of disciplines which, without it, would have remained isolated. Here, it serves as a constant theme throughout the Gallery presentations.

The ground and first levels feature **the diversity of living species** according to their environment. The polar regions are illustrated by polar bears, walruses and an enormous sea elephant; the African savannah by its famous caravan of zebras, giraffes, buffalo, lions and antelopes; the rain forest by magnificent display cases of gorgeous insects, and a steel ladder as a perch for monkeys and birds. *On the first level there is a children's discovery room.*

Level two shows the effects of human action on evolution, illustrated by the magnificent **Galerie des Espèces menacées ou disparues**★★ (Gallery of Endangered or Extinct Species).

On the third floor is the museum's oldest stuffed animal, a rhinoceros from Asia which belonged to Louis XV and Louis XVI. A historical display introducing the scientists who questioned the origin of the diversity of living beings and whose ideas paved the way for the **theory of evolution**, in particular Charles Darwin (1809-82).

Ménagerie

Mon–Sat 9am–6pm, Sun and holidays 9am–6.30pm. 7€ (children 5€). ☎01 40 79 37 94. www.mnhn.fr.
Large reptiles, birds and wild animals are presented in a somewhat old-fashioned but serene setting. The rotunda, the oldest building in this section, houses a **Micro Zoo**, with microscopes to help visitors to discover the world of minute creatures.

Galerie de Minéralogie et de Géologie★

Apr–Oct, Wed–Mon 10am–5pm, 1 May. 7€. ☎01 40 79 56 01. www.mnhn.fr.
This gallery possesses exceptional examples of **minerals**, meteorites and **precious stones** and a collection of **giant crystals**, many of which come from Brazil. In the basement are shown the most precious stones, objets d'art and jewels from Louis XIV's collection.

Galerie de Paléontologie et Anatomie comparée

Wed–Mon 10am–5pm, 1 May. 6€. ☎01 40 79 56 01. www.mnhn.fr.
The ground-floor gallery presents the **comparative anatomy** of vertebrates with 36 000 specimens. **Fossils** are displayed on the first and second floors among reproductions of large prehistoric animals and extinct species.

Jardin des Plantes★★

Entrance on place Valhubert. ○*Daily 7.30am–7.30pm.* ○*Public holidays.* ♿☎*01 40 79 56 01.*

Botanic gardens

In the 17C a large accumulation of public waste occupied the site, over which Buffon laid a **maze**; at the heart a small gazebo overlooks the gardens from the highest point. The famous cedar of Lebanon is one of two planted by Bernard de Jussieu in 1734. Legend has it that he carried the plants in his hat after dropping and breaking the pots on his way back from Kew Gardens in England! One of the oldest trees in Paris is a Robinia or false acacia planted here in 1636, near allée des Becquerel.

Les Grandes Serres (hothouses)

○*Oct–Mar, daily 9am–4.30pm; Apr–Sept, Mon–Sat 9am–5.30pm, Sun until 5pm.* ○*11.30am–1.30pm except Serre Madagascar.*

The winter garden glasshouse contains an important collection of tropical plants. Opposite, the Australian hothouse contains Mediterranean and Australian species. The Mexican hothouse displays a collection of cacti.

School of Botany

○*Daily 8am–7.30pm.* ○*Public holidays.* ♿☎*01 40 79 56 01.*

Over 10 000 species of flora, edible and/or medicinal herbs, are classified by family in the botanical study beds. The **Jardin Alpin** (○*Mon–Fri 8am–4.50pm; Sat–Sun 1.30pm–6pm;* ✎*1€*) groups its high-altitude plants by soil type and orientation of the sun: Corsica, Morocco (south face), the Alps and the Himalayas (north face).

There is also a garden with 180 varieties of antique and hybrid **roses**, a walled **iris garden** combined with perennial and climbing plants, and beds of annuals on the **central alley** that change every season.

JAVEL

Ⓜ/RER: JAVEL (LINE 10/C) – BUS: 42

This former industrial quarter was famous for manufacturing Citroën cars and bleach (*eau de javel* means bleach). Today a magnificent contemporary garden named after André Citroën has replaced the factories.

Nearby neighbourhoods: **PASSY, AUTEUIL, VAUGIRARD.**

▶ **Orient Yourself:** Located on the western end of the Left Bank, overlooking the Seine.
Ⓟ **Parking:** Along rue Leblanc.
🚲 **Don't Miss:** Views from anchored Eutelsat hot-air balloon.
○ **Organizing Your Time:** Allow half an hour to visit the park.
Kids **Especially for Kids:** Aquaboulevard.
�}︎ **Also See:** EIFFEL TOWER.

Parc André-Citroën★★

As you come out of the Javel metro station (facing the river), turn left along the Port de Javel Bas. Kids
André Citroën (1878-1935) went into manufacturing during World War I when he built a factory here for producing shells. It was converted into a Citroën

manufacturing plant in 1919; it operated here until the mid-1970s.
The vast 14ha/35-acre site left by the closure of the Citroën factory has been transformed into a modern park with open lawns where vegetation merges with stone, glass and above all water, which is omnipresent.

The orangery houses exhibitions during the summer; another contains native shrubs from the Australian subcontinent. Between the two extends a water peristyle where 100 water fountains enact their synchronised dance.

The white garden

On the other side of rue Balard,
at the entrance to the park.
High walls enclose a small square planted with white-flowering perennials. To the north, water tumbles over a series of striated granite blocks.

The black garden★

Here, connoisseurs will recognise spirea, reeds, bear's breech, rhododendrons, poppies, irises, amid the bushy, dark-leafed vegetation. Magnificent clipped conifers recall bonsai. A circuitous path leads into an open space with 64 fountains.

The serial gardens★

A series of six beds is bisected by stretches of cascading water. Ramps and walkways provide a bird's-eye view over the whole area including its most secret nooks. Each garden is a concept: yellow is associated with gold and the sixth sense, silver with sight, red with bauxite and taste, orange with rust and

touch, green with oxidised copper and hearing, blue with mercury and smell. Paths paved in stone or over wooden ramps thread their way through open space or dense foliage, under a pergola or through the air.

The restless garden

Clumps of rustling bamboo and random trees punctuate this man-made wilderness where apparently wind-sown plants are left to grow in the uncut grass, ever changing with the seasons.

Additional Sight

Aquaboulevard Kids

4–6 rue Louis-Armand (Porte de Sèvres)
– Ⓜ Balard. Ⓞ*Mon–Thu 9am–11pm, Fri 9am–midnight, Sat 8am–midnight, Sun 8am–11pm (last entry 9pm).* Ⓞ*Two weeks in Jan.* ☞*18.50€.* ☎*01 40 60 10 00. www. forest-hill.com.*
This indoor water-world complex, set among trees and greenery, includes a swimming pool with jacuzzi, wave machine and giant slide. Additional fun is provided by mini-golf, bowling lanes, tennis and squash courts, exercise and body-building rooms, restaurants and shops.

JUSSIEU ★

Ⓜ JUSSIEU (LINES 7 AND 10), CARDINAL LEMOINE (LINE 10), PLACE MONGE (LINE 7)
BUSES: 24, 63, 67, 86, 87, 89

Dominated by the University of Paris buildings, this neighbourhood hosts a rich cultural diversity of Gallo-Roman ruins, science and natural history colleges, the Institute of the Arab World and the Paris Mosque.

Nearby neighbourhoods: **MAUBERT, QUARTIER LATIN, JARDIN DES PLANTES.**

- **Information:** Pyramides welcome centre, 25 rue des Pyramides. ☎08 92 68 30 00 (0.34€ per min). http://en.parisinfo.com.
- ▸ **Orient Yourself:** This area is bordered by the banks of the Seine, the Latin Quarter and the Gare d'Austerlitz.
- **Parking:** Street parking is possible on some of the smaller residential roads.
- **Don't Miss:** Notre-Dame seen from the 9th-floor of the Arab World Institute.
- Ⓞ **Organizing Your Time:** Allow two hours for the walk and museum visits.
- Kids **Especially for Kids:** The open-air sculpture garden along the Square Tino Rossi is particularly child friendly.
- **Also See:** QUARTIER LATIN, JARDIN DES PLANTES.

Walking Tour

La Mosquée★ (The Mosque)

Place du Puits-de-l'Ermite. ⏱*Sun–Thu 9am–noon, 2pm–6pm.* ⏱*Muslim feast days.* 🚶*Guided visits* 🎫*3€.* ☎*01 45 35 97 33. www.mosquee-de-paris.net.*

This exotic walled compound of white Hispano-Moorish buildings overlooked by a minaret was erected between 1922 and 1926. Most of the interior decoration and courtyard design was entrusted to craftsmen from Muslim countries.

▶ *Follow rue Quatrefages to reach rue de Navarre.*

Arènes de Lutèce

This, and the Cluny public bath house (👁*see QUARTIER LATIN: Hôtel de Cluny*) are the only two Parisian monuments to survive from the Gallo-Roman period. The arena, the exact date of whose construction remains unknown, was destroyed in 280 by the Barbarians and lay buried for 1 500 years before being rediscovered by accident when rue Monge was laid in 1869.

The arena seems to have been designed for circus and theatrical presentations; although many of its stone tiers have now vanished, the stage and layout of the dressing rooms survive.

La Mosquée

S. Sauvignier/MICHELIN

Pierre and Marie Curie University

Place Jussieu.

The former wine market is now lined with the modern high-tech buildings of the university, although these are in need of a facelift *(work in progress)*. During term-time, this precinct in France's biggest university campus contrasts sharply with the quiet streets in the immediate vicinity.

Collections des Minéraux★

Pierre and Marie Curie University, 34 rue Jussieu. ⏱*Wed–Mon 1pm–6pm.* ⏱*1 Jan, Easter, 1 May, 14 Jul, All Saints Day, 25 Dec.* 🎫*4.50€.* ☎*01 44 27 52 88. www.lmcp. jussieu.fr.*

This geology museum presents its superb study collections of stones, rocks and dazzling crystals – ranking perhaps among the best collections in the world.

▶ *Before taking rue des Fossés-St-Bernard towards the river, turn left up rue du Cardinal-Lemoine.*

Hôtel Charles Le Brun

49 rue Cardinal-Lemoine.

Now used as offices, this fine building was built by Boffrand in 1700 for Charles II Le Brun, nephew of the famous painter at the court of Louis XIV. Watteau lived here in 1718, as did **Buffon** in 1766; it was here that he completed his treatise on Natural History in several volumes. Fine Classical façade with large carved triangular pediment.

▶ *Take rue des Fossés-St-Bernard.*

Institut du Monde arabe★

(👁*see Museums and Other Attractions*)

▶ *Walk along quai St-Bernard.*

Musée de la Sculpture en plein air

Quai Saint-Bernard.
♿⏱*Year-round, 24hr a day.*

Square Tino-Rossi. The riverside garden was initiated by Gilioli César in 1980 and contains contemporary sculpture by Brancusi, Stahly, Zadkine, César, Rougemont, etc.

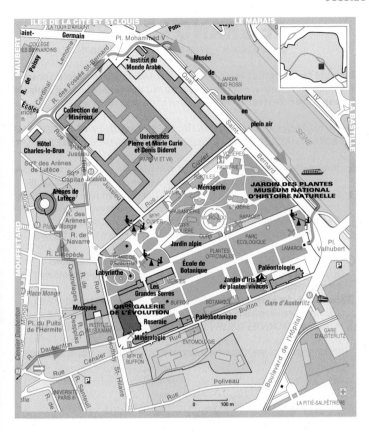

Museums and other Attractions

Institut du Monde arabe★

1 rue des Fossés-Saint-Bernard. ○*Tue–Sun 10am–6pm.* ○*1 May. Free entry to the building; museum* ○*5€.* &○*01 40 51 38 38. www.imarabe.org.*

The aim of the Institute set up by France in conjunction with 20 Arab countries is to promote Islamic culture, cultural exchanges and cooperation. The building enclosed in a mantle of glass and aluminium and covered by a sheath of translucent alabaster, was conceived by the architect **Jean Nouvel** and the Architecture Studio.

Museum

On display are works of art from the 9C to the 19C from countries ranging from Spain to India illustrating Arab history: cut and over-painted glass, lustre ware, chased bronze, wood and ivory sculpture, geometric or floral carpets. Palace and mosque architecture and scientific achievements in the fields of medicine, astronomy and mathematics are also featured. There is a fine collection of astrolabes: these instruments were used to observe and calculate the position of heavenly bodies before the invention of the sextant.

On the lower level, exhibitions of art from the Arab world since 1950 are held comprising painting, sculpture, calligraphy and the graphic arts, and photography.

From the **9th-floor terrace** there is a fine view of the east end of Notre-Dame, Île St-Louis and the Bastille neighbourhood.

LE GRAND LOUVRE★★★

Ⓜ PALAIS-ROYAL – MUSÉE DU LOUVRE (LINES 1 AND 7)

For eight centuries the Louvre was the seat of kings and emperors. Constant alterations by successive rulers made it into a vast royal palace. Today it is famous for one of the richest collections of art and antiquities in the world.

Nearby neighbourhoods: **JARDIN DES TUILERIES, PLACE DE LA CONCORDE, PALAIS-ROYAL, CHÂTELET-HÔTEL DE VILLE, INSTITUT DE FRANCE, MUSÉE D'ORSAY.**

- **Information:** Carrousel du Louvre welcome centre, Place de la Pyramide Inversée 99, rue de Rivoli. ☎08 92 68 30 00 (0.34€ per min). http://en.parisinfo.com.
- **Orient Yourself:** The Louvre stretches out along the centre of the Right Bank between the Seine and the rue de Rivoli. *For access,* Ⅼ *see Address Book.*
- **Parking:** Underground parking along the rue de l'Amiral de Coligny.
- **Don't Miss:** The Napoléon III Apartments and the French School 19C large format paintings.
- **Organizing Your Time:** Allow a minimum of a half day. If time allows, it is best to visit a selection of galleries at one time and return for others another time.
- **Especially for kids** There's a children's bookstore and gift boutique with Louvre-related items and guidebook in the Carrousel du Louvre.
- **Also See:** JARDIN DES TUILERIES, LES HALLES, CHÂTELET-HÔTEL-DE-VILLE.

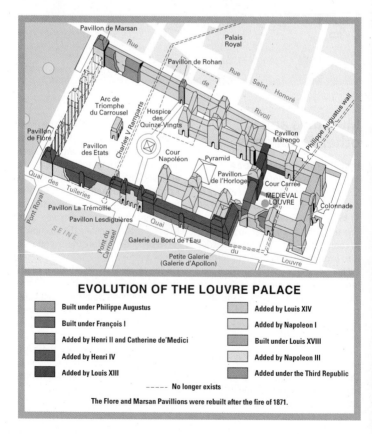

EVOLUTION OF THE LOUVRE PALACE

- Built under Philippe Augustus
- Built under François I
- Added by Henri II and Catherine de'Medici
- Added by Henri IV
- Added by Louis XIII
- Added by Louis XIV
- Added by Napoleon I
- Built under Louis XVIII
- Added by Napoleon III
- Added under the Third Republic
- - - - - No longer exists

The Flore and Marsan Pavillions were rebuilt after the fire of 1871.

A Bit of History

Philippe Auguste (1180-1223) lived in the Palais de la Cité. In 1190 he had the Louvre fortress built on the north bank of the Seine, at the weakest point in his capital's defences against its English neighbours. This fortress was located on the southwest quarter of the present Cour Carrée. **Philip the Fair** (1285-1314) installed his arsenal and the royal treasury in the Louvre, where they were to remain for the next four centuries.

Charles V (1364-80) transformed the old fortress into a comfortable residence, without changing its dimensions. In it, he installed his famous **library** of 973 books, the largest in the kingdom. A miniature in the *Very Rich Hours* of the Duke of Berry depicts this attractive Louvre, surrounded by new ramparts, which put an end to its military career. After Charles V, the Louvre was not to be inhabited by royalty for the next century and a half.

François I (1515-47) lived mainly in the Loire Valley or the Marais. In 1528, in desperate need of money, he prepared to demand contributions from the Parisian population. To soften them up, he announced his intention to take up residence in the Louvre. Rebuilding began: the keep, a bulky form, which

cast a shadow over the courtyard, was razed, and the advance defences were demolished; however, orders for a new palace for the King of France to be built on the foundations of the old fortress were not given to **Pierre Lescot** until 1546. Lescot's designs in keeping with the style of the Italian Renaissance which had found such favour on the banks of the Loire, were new to Paris. By 1547, at the death of the king, construction was barely visible above ground level.

Henri II (1547-59) took up residence in the Louvre and retained Lescot as chief architect. The old great hall was transformed into the **Salle des Caryatides**; on the first floor, the Salle des Cent-Suisses reserved for the Palace Guard, preceded the royal suite in the south wing (that of the Queen was on the ground floor). The coffered vaulting over the Henri-II-style staircase leading to the two rooms was carved by Jean Goujon.

Catherine de' Medici (1519-89) withdrew to the Hôtel des Tournelles, her residence in the Marais, after the accidental death of her husband Henri II. Once declared Regent, she decided to take up residence in the Louvre, on the floor since known as the Logis des Reines (Queens' Lodging), but was not at all happy living in the middle of Les-

The Louvre, Centre for the Arts

The city of Paris gradually engulfed the area around the Louvre site. The abandoned palace apartments were let to a wide variety of people. A Bohemian colony of artists set up camp in the galleries, organising living quarters on the mezzanine level, the floor above was used as a passageway (in which the King touched those afflicted with scrofula on five occasions a year). Resident artists included **Coustou**, **Bouchardon**, **Coypel** and **Boucher**; the palace lanterns were tended by **Hubert Robert**'s wife. The space along the Colonnade was divided into apartments; rows of stove chimneys pierced the wonderful façade; shacks were erected in the courtyard; cabarets and taverns accommodated lean-tos along the outside façade. The royal apartments became occupied by the *Académies* – the Académie Française, having been installed there before Louis XIV moved out of the Tuileries, attracted other academic bodies dedicated to writing and literature, architecture, science, painting and sculpture. The fine arts academy began organising exhibitions of members' work in 1699, an event held around the feast of St Louis (25 August) which was to become a regular feature in the Salon Carré from 1725, and which lasted until the 1848 Revolution. Diderot, followed by Baudelaire, became critics of these salons, at which taste in art during the 18C and early 19C was formulated.

Address Book

LE GRAND LOUVRE

Opening times – ♿ *Wed–Mon 9am–6pm. Some sections open Wed and Fri until 9.45pm. Temporary exhibits under the Pyramid: 9am–6pm (9.45pm Wed). Closed 1 Jan, 1 May, Aug 15 and 25 Dec.*

Admission charges – Permanent collection and temporary exhibits (single ticket, except for temporary exhibits in the hall Napoléon): *9€, 6€ after 6pm on Wed, Fri (under-18s no charge; no charge the 1st Sun of the month).* Tickets valid all day long, even if you leave the museum. *Ticket sales until 5.15pm (9.15pm Wed and Fri).* Advance ticket purchase from the FNAC store *08 92 68 46 94 (0.34€/min). (1.50€ commission fee added to price),* from Ticketnet *08 92 39 01 00 (0.34€/min) (1.10€ fee); tickets remain valid for an unlimited time.*

Passes and discounts – The Paris Museum Pass (valid 2, 4 or 6 days for 70 museums and monuments) is for sale in the shopping gallery of the Carrousel du Louvre and allows you to enter the permanent collections immediately, without waiting. The "carte Louvre jeunes" pass (valid 1 year for those under age 26, for sale under the Pyramid or by mail) and "Carte des Amis du Louvre" (valid 1 year, purchase from the Amis du Louvre booth between the Pyramid and the inverse Pyramid in the entrance area) allow entrance to permanent collections and temporary exhibits as well as cultural activities reserved for museum members, discounts on events held in the auditorium and for guided tours, *01 40 20 51 04.*

Temporary exhibits – In the Hall Napoléon (under the Pyramid): *9am–6pm (9.45pm Wed and Fri),* or in the Richelieu and Sully wings (during opening hours).

Guided tours– Guided tours are available in English, and there are also activities in workshops. Tours are conducted Wed–Mon and last 1hr 30min. Individual visitors should buy their tickets at the window marked "Accueil des groupes" under the Pyramid, *01 40 20 51 77.*

In many rooms, there are explanatory texts for consultation in several languages, placed at visitors' disposal in racks near the door.

---

cot's building site. In 1564, she ordered **Philibert Delorme** to build her a residence of her own on the site known as Les Tuileries, in which she would have greater freedom of movement.

Between the two palaces, the Queen Mother planned to have a covered passage built to enable people to walk the 500m/547yd unnoticed, under shelter from inclement weather. The connecting galleries – the **Petite Galerie** and the **Galerie du Bord de l'Eau** (or Grande Galerie), along the banks of the Seine were duly begun, but work was brought to a halt by the Wars of Religion. The old Louvre was to keep its two Gothic and two Renaissance wings until the reign of Louis XIV.

Henri IV (1589-1610) continued work on the Louvre on his arrival in Paris in 1594. **Louis Métezeau** added an upper floor to the Galerie du Bord de l'Eau; **Jacques II Androuet Du Cerceau** completed the Petite Galerie and built the **Pavillon de Flore,** with another gallery leading off at right angles to link it with the Tuileries Palace, while seeing to the interior decoration of the Tuileries. The scale of construction on the Louvre site reflected the high status that the monarchy was once again enjoying at this time.

Louis XIII (1610-43) enjoyed living at the Louvre, but the Court endured severely cramped conditions. Urged by Richelieu, Louis undertook to enlarge the Louvre fourfold. Lemercier built the Clock Pavilion, and the north-west corner of the courtyard, a Classical statement in response to Lescot's design. The Royal Mint and the Royal Press were accommodated in the Grande Galerie.

Louis XIV (1643-1715). After the death of Louis XIII, Anne of Austria moved to the

The Louvre and the pyramid

S. Sauvignier/MICHELIN

Palais-Royal with the under-age Louis. Nine years later, they moved to the Louvre having found the Palais-Royal less than secure, intimidated by the Fronde uprisings. Louis XIV turned to **Le Vau** to resume work on the extension of the Louvre; he had him build the **Galerie d'Apollon** and requested a worthy façade be designed to close off the Cour Carrée (the **Colonnade**). In 1682, the king moved his court away from the capital to Versailles. Construction was brought to a halt; Le Vau's and Perrault's buildings were left without roofs.

18C-19C By now, the Louvre was so run down as to prompt talk of pulling it down altogether. After the brief interval of the Regency (1715-22), Louis XV lived at Versailles, whence Louis XVI was brought to Paris on 6 October 1789, briefly occupying the Tuileries until his incarceration at the Temple prison.

The Convention used the theatre and the Committee of Public Safety installed itself in the royal apartments of the Tuileries, until appropriated by Bonaparte, the Premier Consul.

Napoléon I (1799-1814) while living in the Tuileries, took great interest in the Louvre; his first undertaking was to expel its lodgers. The emperor commissioned the architects **Percier** and **Fontaine** to complete the Cour Carrée, to enlarge place du Carrousel so that he might review his troops there, and to

build the Arc de Triomphe du Carrousel. The fall of the emperor stopped work in 1814.

Napoléon III (1852-70), also resident in the Tuileries, oversaw the completion of the Louvre. He entrusted first **Visconti**, then **Lefuel** with the task of closing off the Grande Cour to the north. The latter compensated for the difference in levels of the two arms of the Louvre by rebuilding the **Pavillon de Flore**★ in an exaggeratedly grandiose style (high relief by **Carpeaux**, **The Triumph of Flora**★) and by modifying the western section of the Galerie du Bord de l'Eau. It was at this time that the Carrousel entrance gates *(guichets)* were inserted.

The Republic – The uprising of the Paris Commune (a week of bloodshed from 21 to 28 May 1871) resulted in the Tuileries Palace being burned down; its collections, however, were saved at the last minute. In 1875, **Lefuel** undertook the restoration of the Louvre, proposing along with others that the Tuileries be rebuilt. In 1882 the Assembly after due deliberation, had the ruins removed, thereby obliterating any political significance or association with the past regime.

The **Grand Louvre** project was implemented by **François Mitterrand** from 1981 onwards. Most of the work was finished by 1993, with the opening of the

Richelieu wing. A fashion museum has been created in the Rohan wing.

Brief history of the collections –
François I was the first eminent patron of Italian artists of his day. Twelve paintings from his original collection, including the *Mona Lisa* by Leonardo da Vinci, *La Belle Jardinière* by Raphael and a *Portrait of François I* by Titian, are among the most important works presently in State hands. By the time Louis XIV died, over 2 500 paintings hung in the palaces of the Louvre and Versailles.

The idea of making the collection accessible to the public, as envisaged by Marigny under Louis XVI, was finally realised by the Convention on 10 August 1793 when the doors of the Grande Galerie were opened to visitors.

Napoléon subsequently made the museum's collection the richest in the world by exacting a tribute in works of art from every country he conquered; many of these were reclaimed by the Allies in 1815.

In turn, Louis XVIII, Charles X and Louis-Philippe all further endowed the collections: scarcely had the *Venus of Milo* been rediscovered when she was brought to France by Dumont d'Urville. Departments for Egyptian and Assyrian art were opened.

Gifts, legacies and acquisitions continue to enrich the collections of the Louvre, with over 350 000 works now catalogued.

Colonnade

J.-P. Clapham/MICHELIN

Walking Tour

The Louvre Palace Exterior

As well as being a museum, the Louvre is a palace steeped in history. A stroll around the outside helps one appreciate the scale of the buildings. Visiting the exhibition on the History of the Louvre and the excavations discovered below ground also provides an understanding of how the construction has evolved. *For this you need an entrance ticket.*

▸ *Start from the church of St-Germain l'Auxerrois, near the Louvre-Rivoli metro station. Coming from rue de Rivoli, head towards the Seine. Opposite is the immense colonnade of the Louvre Palace.*

Colonnade★★

In 1662, Louis XIV decided that the palace exterior on the side facing Paris was still not quite grand enough for a royal residence. Three French architects – **Perrault**, **Le Vau** and **D'Orbay** – were commissioned. The true height and Classical harmony of the structure can be admired fully now that moats have been cleared to a depth of 7m/23ft around the rusticated base, in accordance with the original 17C plans.

▸ *Head towards the river and turn right. Opposite the Pont des Arts, cross the Jardin de l'Infante to gain access to Cour Carrée.*

Cour Carrée★★★

The fine elegant Renaissance façade between the Clock Pavilion and the south wing is the work of **Pierre Lescot**. The graceful, expressive sculpture of the

Cour Carrée

Daniel Thierry/Photononstop/Tips Images

three avant-corps (projecting bay) and the upper storey are by the master **Jean Goujon**, depicting allegorical scenes in high relief, animated figures in niches, friezes of children and garlands. At night a new system of illumination sets off the most impressive remnant of the old Louvre to full effect.

▶ *Leave the courtyard by passing under the Clock Pavilion.*

The **pavillon de l'Horloge** was built in 1640 during the reign of Louis XIII by **Lemercier**, who was also responsible for the northwest wing, a replica of Lescot's façade.

▶ *Enter Cour Napoléon and head for the Pyramid.*

Pyramid★★

The pyramid, 21m/69ft high and 33m/108ft wide at the base, was designed by the architect **Ieoh Ming Pei**; it is built of sheet glass supported on a framework of stainless-steel tubes. It is from directly below the pyramid, in the museum reception area over which it forms a huge vault, that one can fully appreciate the originality of design and materials used.

An **equestrian statue of Louis XIV,** a copy of a marble statue by Bernini, stands on the axis leading to the Champs-Élysées, slightly at an angle with the old Louvre.

▶ *Cross the road that traverses place du Carrousel, in the direction of the Tuileries Gardens.*

Arc de Triomphe du Carrousel★

This delightful pastiche, inspired by the Roman triumphal arch of Septimus Severus, was built from 1806 to 1808. The six bas-relief sculptures commemorate the Napoléonic victories of 1805. On the platform, where Napoléon placed the four horses removed from the basilica of San Marco in Venice (until they were returned there in 1815), **Bosio** sculpted an allegorical goddess, representing the Restoration of the Bourbons, accompanied by Victories and driving a quadriga.

The square takes its name from the lavish equestrian and theatrical tournament held there in honour of the birth of the Dauphin in 1662.

From directly beneath the arch there is a magnificent **view**★★★ along the axis that runs from the Louvre through the Tuileries, place de la Concorde, the Champs-Élysées, and the Arc de Triomphe, as far as the Grande Arche at La Défense.

▶ *Descend one of the flights of stairs near the Carrousel, or go through the Pyramid and the main entrance.*

La Galerie Carrousel du Louvre

The inverted crystalline pyramid provides a well of light in the central area

Arc de Triomphe du Carrousel

A. Simpson/MICHELIN

Address Book

LE LOUVRE

Access – The main entrance is via the **Pyramid**. Direct access to the **Carrousel du Louvre** shopping centre is possible via the **Palais-Royal Musée du Louvre** metro station, on either side of the **Arc du Carrousel** or at no 99 rue de Rivoli.

The Carrousel-Louvre car park *Daily 7am–11pm.* It has space for 80 coaches and 620 cars. Access via the underground passage avenue du Général-Lemonnier, then enter the shopping centre through the old Charles V fortifications.

HALL NAPOLÉON

Under the Pyramid, this hall is the nerve centre of the visitor network designed by the architect Pei. Visitors are immediately orientated towards one of three wings of the museum: Denon, Richelieu or Sully. This vast reception hall also houses a certain number of other services: bookshop, Le Grand Louvre restaurant, group facilities and an auditorium.

INFORMATION

General information can be obtained by calling or consulting the following:
☎*01 40 20 51 51 (answering machine);*
☎*01 40 20 53 17 to speak to someone at the desk (six languages);*
internet: www.louvre.fr
Some galleries are closed on certain days (or even for restoration); check the schedule of open rooms online or call in advance to avoid disappointment. Fourteen video screens in the hall provide information about events on a daily basis in the museum. There is also a general activity programme (six languages) available at the main information desk which comes out every three months.
Audio-guides can be hired (six languages) on the mezzanine level in the various wings.

SHOPPING

Carrousel du Louvre – *rue de Rivoli, 1st arr.* ☎*01 43 16 47 10.* The combination of a museum with a shopping gallery of some 16 000sq m/19 135sq yd,

including a performing arts centre (Studio-Théâtre), many brand name shops and a variety of multi-purpose halls (congresses, exhibitions, etc.) is one of the more original ideas invented by the Grand Louvre.

Boutique des Musées Nationaux – Reproductions, books, games, etc.

Boutiques du Musée du Louvre – Chalcographie (prints and engravings), **postcards** (hundreds of postcards of the museum's main works of art, reproductions of paintings), **posters** and a **bookshop** (including an extensive art history section). Upstairs is a wide choice of **reproductions, plaster casts, jewellery** and **children's books**.

Other shops – Virgin (music shop and bookshop focused on 20C arts – cinema, photography, architecture), Nature et Découvertes (nature-oriented objects and activities), Lalique (crystal), l'Occitane, Résonances and Esprit (fashion), a bank and currency exchange bureau, Les Minéraux (minerals) together with shops devoted to home decoration and a post office.

HOW THE MUSEUM IS ORGANISED

The collections have been divided into three main sections: **Denon**, **Richelieu** and **Sully**, which make up two wings and Cour Carrée.

SULLY

- History of the Louvre: *Entresol.*
- Medieval Louvre: *Entresol.*
- Egyptian Antiquities: *Ground and 1st floors.*
- Greek Antiquities (Cariatides room, Hellenic period): *Ground floor.*
- Oriental Antiquities (Iran and art of the Levant): *Ground floor.*
- Greek Antiquities (Bronze room, Campana gallery): *1st floor.*
- 17C-18C objets d'art: *1st floor.*
- 17C-19C French painting, including Graphic arts: *2nd floor.*
- Beistegui collection (room A): *2nd floor.*

DENON

- Italian sculpture: *Entresol and Ground floor.*
- Scandinavian sculpture: *Entresol.*
- Roman and Coptic Egypt: *Entresol (rooms A, B and C).*
- Greek Antiquities: *Ground and 1st floors.*
- Etruscan and Roman Antiquities: *Ground floor.*
- Italian painting: *1st floor.*
- Spanish painting: *1st floor.*
- 19C French painting (large sizes): *1st floor.*
- Objets d'art (Apollon gallery): *1st floor.*

RICHELIEU

- Exhibitions-documents: *Entresol.*
- Islamic art: *Entresol (closed until 2010; will reopen in Denon).*
- French sculpture (Marly and Puget rooms): *Ground floor.*
- Oriental Antiquities (Mesopotamia): *Ground floor.*
- Objets d'art (including Napoléon III's apartments): *1st floor.*
- 14C-17C French painting: *2nd floor.*
- Scandinavian schools: *2nd floor.*

NIGHTLIFE

Angelina – *226 rue de Rivoli, 1st arr. ☎01 42 60 82 00. Daily.* This charming, very genteel tearoom just opposite the Tuileries, is known throughout Paris for its mouth-watering cakes and pastries and its unctuous (and very filling) hot chocolate called l'Africain.

Café Marly – *93 rue de Rivoli, 1st arr. ☎01 49 26 06 60. Daily.* Located in the Richelieu wing of the Louvre Museum, this haven of peace and good taste has a worldly, cosmopolitan, arty aura. Ideal to take tea or to meet special friends or customers. From the terrace under the arcades, it provides a view over the pyramid.

Le Fumoir – *6 rue de l'Amiral-de-Coligny, 1st arr. ☎01 42 92 00 24. www.lefumoir.com. Daily. Closed late Dec.* A library, a bar which achieved its fame during the Prohibition years, an excellent cocktail menu, a few sofas and wide bay windows overlooking the Louvre and the Église Saint-Germain l'Auxerrois: the stage is set for a quiet afternoon. In the evening a more trendy crowd arrives for Happy Hour martinis.

WHERE TO STAY AND EAT

Turn to the back of the guide for selected hotels, restaurants, bistros and cafés listed by *arrondissement*. This neighbourhood is in the 1st arrondissement. The Louvre's shopping complex (*see above*) also has a wide range of cafés and restaurants.

of the arcade; concrete masonry, rows of windows and subdued lighting combine to give the main arcade the appearance of a large entrance hall.

▶ *Go back towards the main entrance via the underground passage.*

The Museum

History of the Louvre★

The two galleries on each side of the rotunda, decorated with stone reliefs by Jean Goujon, present the architectural and decorative evolution of the Louvre building during its transformation from fortress to royal residence and finally to museum.

▶ *Carry on from the rotunda into the Sully crypt.*

Medieval Louvre★★★

Here, a dark line on the floor indicates the location of one of the ten towers which made up part of the old Louvre. Further on, the visitor encounters the impressive surroundings of the **fortress** built by Philippe Auguste in the early 13C.

The wooden walkway follows the line of the north and the east moats. On the east side, a trapezoidal construction indicates the location of the foundations of the residence added by Charles V in 1360. In the middle of the ditch, the supporting pier of the drawbridge is framed by the twin towers of the **east gate** of Philippe Auguste's castle. Its rectangular stones are evenly placed and feature putlog holes and heart-shaped engravings carved by the stonemasons.

A modern gallery leads to the moat around the circular keep or **Grosse Tour** built for Philippe Auguste between 1190 and 1202. The moat, with an average width of 7.5m/24.6ft, was once paved with enormous stones.

The tour of the Medieval Louvre ends with two galleries. The first contains the earthenware items discovered during the excavation of Cour Carrée. The second, the **Salle Saint-Louis** with mid-13C vaulting, has a display of royal items found at the bottom of the well in the keep. These include a replica of Charles VI's parade helmet, the **chapel doré**.

Egyptian Antiquities★★★

There are two ways to visit the Egyptian Antiquities: either via the Oriental galleries in the Richelieu wing, turning right at the end of the Sackler wing, or by the Sully entrance on the ground floor, through the Medieval Louvre section, which brings you to the Crypte du Sphinx and follows a themed circuit. Take the staircase up on the left. The descriptions given follow the second route.

The department of Egyptian Antiquities is the legacy of **Jean-François Champollion**, who drew on the work of the English physicist Thomas Young (1773-1829) for help in unravelling the mysteries of hieroglyphics in 1822, thus founding Egyptology. A consistent policy of purchasing, collecting and acquiring excavated material continued until World War II, endowing the Louvre with thousands of artefacts.

Sphinx
In the crypt, Sully wing, gallery 1.
This colossal monolith in pink granite, 4.8m/15.7ft long, was found at Tanis in the Nile delta, the capital of Egypt during its decline.

Themed circuit
Through works of art and ordinary objects, 19 galleries illustrate the everyday life and culture of ancient Egyptian society. Wall panels and

laminated information boards help to enhance the presentation of this fascinating collection.

Agriculture, hunting and fishing
Galleries 2 to 5. The small statues in gallery 2 represent the fauna found in the Nile. Agricultural practices and food are evoked by means of statues and models destined for furnishing tombs, along with stelae and samples of food (bread dating from 3 500 years ago), and bas-relief sculptures, particularly those in the **Mastaba of Akhout-Hetep**★★.

Art and Crafts
Galleries 6 and 7. The principles of hieroglyphic writing are exhibited along with the materials used and the gods who protected the scribes. Note the rare bronze of Horus on a pedestal.

Domestic life
Galleries 8 to 10. Furniture, pottery, jewels, toiletry articles clothes, musical instruments and toys evoke the décor of wealthy homes.

Temples
Galleries 11 and 12. Egyptian temples were reached via avenues of sphinxes, and this idea is evoked in the corridor leading to the Henri IV gallery: statues of gods and goddesses, portraits of dignitaries, engraved historical records.

Funerary rites
Galleries 13 to 17. Much has been learned of everyday life in ancient Egypt from the reconstitution of the living world in tombs. Starting from the Crypt of Osiris and the **royal tomb of Ramses III**, is an impressive series of shaped mummy cases.

Divinities
Galleries 18 and 19. The gods and goddesses of ancient Egypt are displayed in alphabetical order, listing the appearance, role, and attributes of each one next to a collection of metal, pottery and stone statues. The role of magic and the animal kingdom in religion is also shown with mummified cats and sarcophagi for animals.

Chronological circuit

First floor. Go up the stairs at the end of the themed circuit. In this display, information panels give the main dates of Egyptian civilization. Most of the major pieces of the Louvre's collection are on this floor. The galleries date from the time of Charles X, when they first received the antiquities collection, and the ceilings of some rooms (27 to 30) have preserved their original decoration.

Knife of Gebel-el-Arak★★

Gallery 20. This is one of the earliest known knives to feature low-relief carving (Prehistoric Era c. 3200 BC).

Stele of the Serpent King

Gallery 21. This primitive work (Thinite Period) depicts King Djet, one of the first Pharaohs, identified by his symbol the serpent, beneath his protector, a falcon, against the backdrop of the façade of his palace.

Old Kingdom (2700-2200 BC)

Gallery 22. Some of the earliest examples of Egyptian statuary, including the couple **Sepa and Nesa** (Third Dynasty) and the **Head of King Didoufri** (Fourth Dynasty, 2570 BC). This work is a contemporary of the Great Pyramids and one of the first to be adapted to fit a sphinx. It is crowned with the royal headdress.

Seated Scribe★★★

This famous statue in painted limestone from the Fifth Dynasty (c. 2500 BC) was excavated at Sakkara. Strikingly realistic, the facial expression is alert, the hands poised as if ready to commit to papyrus what he hears, the eyes, inlaid with coloured rock crystal and the eyelids outlined in copper seem to engage the viewer.

Galleries 23 to 27 display works from the **Middle Kingdom (2000-1700BC)** and the **New Kingdom** (1550-1200BC), including the exquisite royal **Jewels of Rameses II**, the son and heir of Sethi I.

Seated Scribe

Zatac/Tips Images

Akhenaton and Amarnian art (c. 1370-1350 BC)

Room 25. Amenophis IV changed his name to Akhenaton in deference to the sun god Aton and, together with his queen, Nefertiti, introduced monotheism. Among the Royal portraits from their reign note in particular the bust of a princess, a teenage dignitary with the hint of a sulky pout, and the extraordinarily sophisticated features of the **bust of Akhenaton**★★ with its highly developed realism.

The last pharaohs (1000-30 BC)

Galleries 29 and 30. The end of pharaonic Egypt was interspersed with a number of intermediate periods when the kingdom was subject to exterior rule (Persians, Greeks). Some refined works of art date from this period, such as the statue of **Queen Karomama** in bronze inlaid with gold and silver, and the precious **Osorkon Triad**, in gold and laps-lazuli, regrouping Osiris, seated on an altar, his wife and sister Isis and their son Horus, protector of the monarchy.

▶ *The Egyptian department's collection continues in the Denon entresol (lower ground floor), with the late antiquities of the Roman period (gallery A) and Coptic Christians (galleries B and C).*

LE LOUVRE: DEPARTMENTS

- Oriental Antiquities
- Egyptian Antiquities
- Greek, Etruscan and Roman Antiquities
- Sculptures
- Medieval Louvre
- Services
- Closed to the public

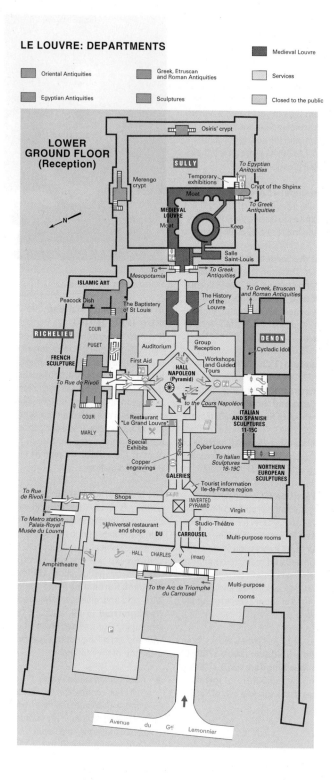

LOWER GROUND FLOOR (Reception)

Osiris' crypt

SULLY

To Egyptian Anitquities

Merengo crypt

Temporary exhibitions

Crypt of the Shpinx

Moat

MEDIEVAL LOUVRE

To Greek Antiquities

Moat

Keep

Salle Saint-Louis

To Mesopotamia

To Greek Antiquities

ISLAMIC ART

To Greek, Etruscan and Roman Antiquities

Peacock Dish

The Baptistery of St Louis

The History of the Louvre

RICHELIEU

COUR PUGET

Auditorium

Group Reception

DENON

Cycladic Idol

FRENCH SCULPTURE

First Aid

Workshops and Guided Tours

To Rue de Rivoli

HALL NAPOLEON (Pyramid)

to the Cours Napoléon

COUR MARLY

Restaurant "Le Grand Louvre"

ITALIAN AND SPANISH SCULPTURES 11-15C

Special Exhibits

Cyber Louvre

To Italian Sculptures 16-19C

NORTHERN EUROPEAN SCULPTURES

Copper engravings

Shops

GALERIES

Tourist information Ile-de-France region

To Rue de Rivoli

Shops

INVERTED PYRAMID

Virgin

To Metro station Palais-Royal - Musée du Louvre

Universal restaurant and shops

DU

CARROUSEL

Studio-Théâtre

Multi-purpose rooms

Amphitheatre

HALL CHARLES V (moat)

To the Arc de Triomphe du Carrousel

Multi-purpose rooms

P

N

Avenue du Gal Lemonnier

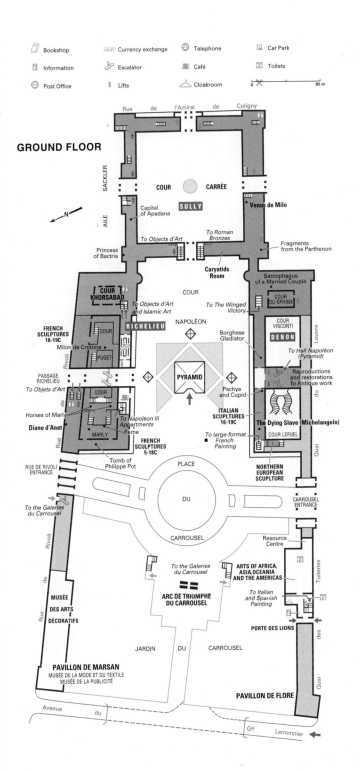

GROUND FLOOR

Bookshop
Information
Post Office
Currency exchange
Escalator
Lifts
Telephone
Café
Cloakroom
Car Park
Toilets

0 ———— 80 m

Rue de l'Amiral de Coligny

SACKLER
AILE

COUR CARRÉE
SULLY

Capital of Apadana
Venus de Milo

To Objects d'Art
To Roman Bronzes

Princess of Bactria
Fragments from the Parthenon

Caryatids Room

COUR
Sarcophagus of a Married Couple

COUR KHORSABAD
To Objects d'Art and Islamic Art
COUR DU SPHINX

FRENCH SCULPTURES 18-19C
COUR
RICHELIEU
To The Winged Victory
NAPOLÉON
COUR VISCONTI
DENON

Milon de Crotone
PUGET
Rivoli
Borghese Gladiator
To Hall Napoléon (Pyramid)
Louvre

PASSAGE RICHELIEU
To Objets d'Art
COUR
PYRAMID
Reproductions and restorations fo Antique work

Horses of Marly
de
Pschye and Cupid
The Dying Slave (Michelangelo)

Diane d'Anet
Rue
MARLY
To Napoleon III Appartments
Fame
ITALIAN SCULPTURES 16-19C
COUR LEFUEL

RUE DE RIVOLI ENTRANCE
FRENCH SCULPTURES 5-18C
To large-format French Painting
NORTHERN EUROPEAN SCULPTURE

Tomb of Philippe Pot
PLACE
DU
Quai

To the Galeries du Carrousel
Rivoli
CARROUSEL
CARROUSEL ENTRANCE

Resource Centre

de
To the Galeries du Carrousel
ARTS OF AFRICA, ASIA, OCEANIA AND THE AMERICAS
Tuileries

MUSÉE
Rue
DES ARTS
DÉCORATIFS
ARC DE TRIOMPHE DU CARROUSEL
To Italian and Spanish Painting

PORTE DES LIONS

JARDIN DU CARROUSEL
des

PAVILLON DE MARSAN
MUSÉE DE LA MODE ET DU TEXTILE
MUSÉE DE LA PUBLICITÉ
PAVILLON DE FLORE
Quai

Avenue du
Gal Lemonnier

LE LOUVRE: DEPARTMENTS

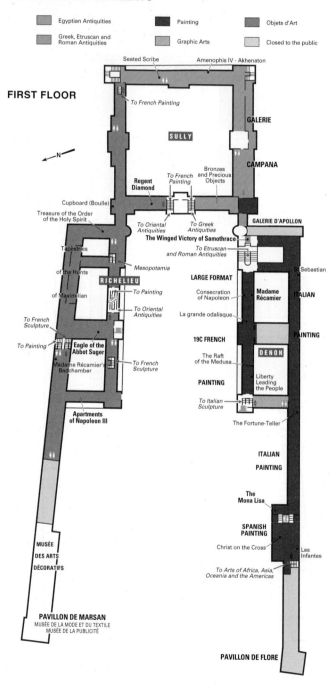

- Egyptian Antiquities
- Greek, Etruscan and Roman Antiquities
- Painting
- Graphic Arts
- Objets d'Art
- Closed to the public

FIRST FLOOR

Seated Scribe

Amenophis IV - Akhenaton

To French Painting

GALERIE

SULLY

CAMPANA

N

Regent Diamond

To French Painting

Bronzes and Precious Objects

Cupboard (Boulle)

Treasure of the Order of the Holy Spirit

To Oriental Antiquities

To Greek Antiquities

GALERIE D'APOLLON

The Winged Victory of Samothrace

Tapestries

To Etruscan and Roman Antiquities

of the Hunts

Mesopotamia

St Sebastian

LARGE FORMAT

RICHELIEU

To Painting

of Maximilian

To Oriental Antiquities

Consecration of Napoleon

Madame Récamier

ITALIAN

La grande odalisque

PAINTING

To French Sculpture

To Painting

Eagle of the Abbot Suger

19C FRENCH

DENON

The Raft of the Medusa

Madame Récamier's Bedchamber

To French Sculpture

Liberty Leading the People

PAINTING

To Italian Sculpture

Apartments of Napoleon III

The Fortune-Teller

ITALIAN

PAINTING

The Mona Lisa

MUSÉE

DES ARTS

DÉCORATIFS

SPANISH PAINTING

Christ on the Cross

Les Infantes

To Arts of Africa, Asia, Oceania and the Americas

PAVILLON DE MARSAN
MUSÉE DE LA MODE ET DU TEXTILE
MUSÉE DE LA PUBLICITÉ

PAVILLON DE FLORE

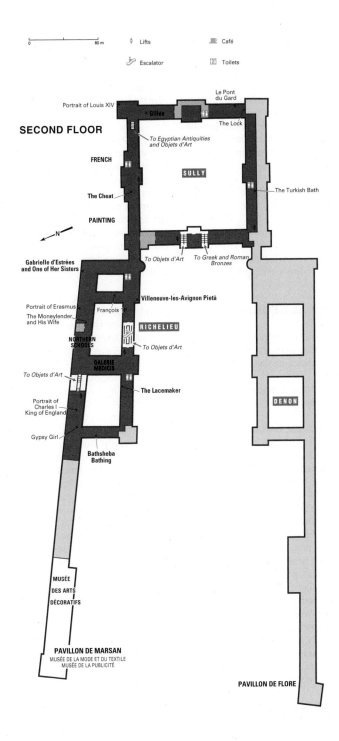

0   80 m

⇕ Lifts   ⏃ Escalator

▮ Café   🚽 Toilets

Le Pont du Gard

Portrait of Louis XIV

Gilles

The Lock

SECOND FLOOR

To Egyptian Antiquities and Objets d'Art

FRENCH

SULLY

The Cheat

The Turkish Bath

PAINTING

→ N

To Objets d'Art

To Greek and Roman Bronzes

Gabrielle d'Estrées and One of Her Sisters

Villeneuve-les-Avignon Pietà

Portrait of Erasmus

François 1er

The Moneylender and His Wife

RICHELIEU

NORTHERN SCHOOLS

To Objets d'Art

GALERIE MEDICIS

To Objets d'Art

The Lacemaker

Portrait of Charles I King of England

DENON

Gypsy Girl

Bathsheba Bathing

MUSÉE DES ARTS DÉCORATIFS

PAVILLON DE MARSAN
MUSÉE DE LA MODE ET DU TEXTILE
MUSÉE DE LA PUBLICITÉ

PAVILLON DE FLORE

Roman Egypt

Room A. Attractively displayed in a vaulted gallery, this collection illustrates a new influence from the Roman and Hellenist world of the Mediterranean, as expressed in funerary customs. There are a number of painted plaster death masks for men, women and children, shrouds decorated with portraits of the defunct, and votive stelae. Note the **mummy** dating from the Roman Period with its painted portrait inserted in the swaddling over the face.

▶ *Walk through the gallery devoted to pre-Classical Greece.*

Coptic Egypt is displayed in Gallery B, and fragments of the monastery of St Apollo (6C-7C AD), originally from the village of Bawit in Middle Egypt, are in Gallery C.

Greek Antiquities★★★

The Greek Antiquities section is one of the jewels in the Louvre's collection.
To visit the collection in chronological order, start with gallery 1 in the entresol (lower ground floor) of the Denon wing.

Pre-classical Greece

This gallery presents Cycladic (Idol's Head, c 2500 BC), Minoan and Mycenaean art before coming to the pre-Classical age. The limestone statue of the **Lady of Auxerre** is one of the earliest examples of Greek sculpture (c. 630 BC), a gauge for the austere Dorian style, with its rigid, full-frontal pose (the face in line with the body). Although dating from only two generations later, the **Kore of Samos** from the Temple of Hera, is more Ionian in style; it is more sophisticated with its stylised draperies. The **Rampin Horseman** (named after its donor) exemplifies the refined detail of mid-6C BC Attic style. This severe style is also evident in the **stele depicting the Exaltation of the Flower** which is from Pharsalus.

▶ *Take the stairs up to the ground floor.*

Classical Greece

The **metopes** from the Temple of Zeus (c. 460 BC) are shown off to advantage in gallery 4.

Cross galleries 5 and 6. During this time the **Venus of Milo** *can be seen in Gallery 74 of the Sully wing, 1st floor.*

Gallery 7 contains sculptural fragments from the **Parthenon**, a Doric temple built in honour of Athena on the initiative of Pericles c 445 BC on the Athens Acropolis at the height of the great period of Hellenistic Classicism. The **fragment of the frieze**★★★ (a large part of which is in the British Museum, London) depicts the young girls who embroidered the veil offered to the city's patron goddess during the Panathenaic procession (every four years).

Replicas of statues, 5C-4C BC

Galleries 14 to 16. Very few great Greek original bronze statues survive, since this material has been melted down and put to other uses over the centuries. However, many marble copies were made to satisfy the eclectic tastes of the Romans. Several statues recall the severe style, notably the *Apollo Citharoedus* and the torso of a discus thrower.

The most important works exhibited here are by **Polyclitus** (*Diadumenus and the Wounded Amazon, badly restored in the 17C*) and **Phidias** (*Apollo of the Kassel type – of which the best copy is the head of Athena Parthenos*).

Apart from the muse Melpomene from the Theatre of Pompeii (1C BC), gallery 16 is devoted to replicas of works by the great sculptor **Praxiteles** (active 370-330 BC), who breathed life into the marble he sculpted, his figures having a fluid and careless grace yet charged with spirituality. *Apollo the Lizard-Slayer* poses informally, a youth poised on one leg, his weight carelessly swung on one hip; **Diana of Gabies**★ embodies all the femininity and modesty of Artemis, the huntress, goddess of the moon, as she fastens her cloak, qualities shared by *Venus of Arles* and the **Cnidian Aphrodite**★★ (*during renovations, located in Gallery 74, 1st floor of Sully wing*), the most prized female statue of Antiquity.

Among the original works from the Classical period is the Piombino Apollo, which came from the workshops of the Greek empire in Sicily and southern Italy, and was found in the sea off Tuscany.

▶ *At gallery 16, turn left and walk back to gallery 12.*

Original statues, 2C BC

Gallery 12. The natural, serene beauty of the **Venus of Milo**★★★ (or more properly, the Aphrodite of Milo), twisted in a graceful spiral of movement echoed in the draperies around her body, make this statue one of the masterpieces of Antique statuary.

Salle des Caryatides★★

Gallery 17. This gallery was once the great hall of the old Louvre Palace modified by Pierre Lescot. It is named after the four monumental draped female **statues** by Jean Goujon, which support the minstrels' balcony. The *Nymph of Fontainebleau* above the minstrels' balcony is a copy of the work by the Florentine, **Benvenuto Cellini** (16C), the original of which is found in the sculpture department.

The sculptures displayed are copies dating from the Hellenistic Period (4C BC), harmonising well with the Renaissance décor. Figures with elongated proportions attributed to be after **Lysippus** are almost Mannerist in style, caught at the point of action: *Hermes tying his sandal,* *Crouching Aphrodite* of Vienna, *Artemis* known as **Diana of Versailles**, *The Three Graces,* and **Sleeping Hermaphrodite** (on a mattress by Bernini).

▶ *The collection continues on the 1st floor, up the Escalier Daru.*

Winged Victory of Samothrace★★★

Early 2C BC. From its pedestal at the top of the Escalier Daru, designed especially for it, this statue seems on the point of taking flight. This masterpiece of Hellenistic art, the figurehead on a stone ship's prow, commemorates a naval victory at Rhodes.

▶ *Pass to the left of the Winged Victory.*

Roman and Greek glassware

Galleries 34 to 38. In Louis XIV's former Grand Cabinet, designed by Le Vau, a hundred pieces of 6C BC glassware are exhibited for the first time. Following the Salle Clara (gallery 35) three rooms show Ancient and Classical Greek **terracotta** pieces.

Galerie Campana★★

This occupies the wing facing the Seine, galleries 39 to 47.

The collection of the **Marquis Campana**, an enthusiastic antiquarian who excavated the Etruscan necropolises of northern Latium (👆 *see below – Etruscan Antiquities*) was bought almost in its entirety in 1861 by Napoléon III. The different forms and functions of Greek vases are presented firstly, with a panorama of the different subjects found in their decoration, from everyday life to legends and from religion to love *(gallery 39).*

The conventions of standard black-figure vase painting seem to have been contradicted first by the potter of Andokides (c. 530 BC), who painted-in the background and details of his figures in black, leaving the main profiles in red biscuit. The technique was perfected c. 500 BC by **Euphronios** and Douris *(gallery 40).* The final gallery displays the delicate

Winged Victory of Samothrace

Photononstop/Tips Images

and graceful Myrina and **Tanagra figurines** so full of movement.

Salle des Bronzes et objets précieux★★

Gallery 32. Antique bronzes and jewellery are displayed alongside examples of Archaic pitcher handles with Gorgon head masks. A fascination for apparently unidealised human features, at times even bizarre ones, are most characteristic of this period; portrayals of infancy or old age, stunted growth and deformity are most remarkable: note in particular *Eros and Psyche* with the faces of young children; a black adolescent with his hands tied behind his back; a giant. The handsome **bust of a young man from Beneventum** draws inspiration from the works of Polyclitus.

Boscoreale Treasure★★

Salle Henri II (gallery 33). Its blue and black ceiling was painted by Braque in 1953 *(The Birds)*. This splendid collection was found at the heart of a vine growing area, in a place called Boscoreale, in the ruins of a Roman villa destroyed by the eruption of Mount Vesuvius in AD 79. The treasure trove consisted of coins, jewellery and **silver tableware**, all of which had been put into a wine tank for safe keeping.

▶ *Take the Daru staircase down to the ground floor.*

Original statues, 2C-1C BC

Gallery B. The Greek collection finishes with the Gallerie Daru, on the ground floor, among the statues and sarcophagi of the Roman empire, with the c. 100 BC **Borghese Gladiator★★** – a statue of the fighting warrior – exemplifies the standardisation of attitude and expression typical of this period.

Salle du Manège

Gallery A. This former imperial riding room now displays the antiquity statues, both imitations and originals, collected by François I and Napoléon I.

Etruscan antiquities★★

This collection is found on the ground floor of the Denon wing, beginning with gallery 4 (Olympie) and continuing through galleries 18 to 20.

The origins of the Etruscan people remain uncertain: some claim them to be descended from tribes indigenous to central Italy west of the Apennines, some from Aeneas' men from Troy... What is undisputed is their civilization, drawn in part from Ancient Greece and absorbed completely by Ancient Rome. In 265 BC Etruria ceded its independence becoming a part of the Roman Empire. Many of the finest artefacts have been recovered from tombs; these include domestic utensils in bronze and terracotta, jewels in gold and precious stones, frescoes, sculpted sarcophagi and funerary urns, bronze toys and devotional objects.

Villanovian articles *(gallery 18)* made of iron or bronze are inscribed with geometric patterns (throne in laminated bronze); Etruscan terracotta includes the three Campana painted plaques, impasto pottery and antefixes (decorative tiles for the ends of roof joints) in the shape of women's heads. The main exhibit, however, is the famous painted terracotta **Sarcophagus of the Married Couple★★★** (6C BC), found at Cerveteri along with its pair, now at the Villa Giulia in Rome.

Bucchero black earthenware *(gallery 19)* fashioned to imitate metal is typical of the Orientalising Period (mid-7C). Simple forms with engraved textures gradually ceded in the 6C BC to more complicated designs (deeply grooved lines, details in relief). Much of this pottery was copied from Greek prototypes, first the black-figure painting (early 6C) and later the red (5C-4C).

Roman and Palaeo-Christian Antiquities★★

Appartement d'été d'Anne d'Autriche★★

Galleries 21 to 27. Anne of Austria's summer suite with ceilings painted by **Romanelli** displays two of the most original genres in Roman art: the por-

Sarcophagus of the Married Couple (6C BC)

trait (a cold and idealised *Marcellus*, posed in the nude, by Cleomenes the Athenian; four effigies of *Augustus* at different stages of his life; bust in basalt of *Livia Drusilla,* wife of Augustus); and the relief carving, whether historical (fragment of the *Ara Pacis,* the Altar of Peace consecrated by Augustus) or mythological (sarcophagus of the *Nine Muses,* sarcophagi from Saint-Médard-d'Eyrans in the Galerie Daru).

Galleries 28 to 31

3C-4C AD portraits *(Gordian III; Auriga)* surround the *Pillars of the Incantada* (enchanted palace), the remains of a portico from Thessalonika *(gallery 27).* The opulent residences were adorned with magnificent **mosaics**★ *(The Phoenix, The Judgement of Paris, Preparations for a banquet),* as were the floors of churches in north Africa and the Middle East (Kabr Hiram, near Tyre in the Lebanon). Note also the fragments of frescoes from Pompeii *(Winged Spirit).* The old Cour du Sphinx contains the great frieze from the Temple of Artemis at Magnesia on the River Maeander. The marvellous **mosaic floor** depicting the seasons comes from a villa in Antioch.

Near-Eastern Antiquities★★★ (Antiquités Orientales)

Ground floor of the Richelieu wing.

In 1843, **Paul-Émile Botta**, the French Consul in Mosul (Iraq), excavated the remains of the city built by Sargon II of Assyria – now the site of Khorsabad – thereby discovering a lost civilization. The first Assyrian museum opened at the Louvre in 1847. Further digging was actively undertaken by *Victor Place* until the 1930s, when the Oriental Institute of Chicago took charge. The new Louvre galleries house the oldest treaties, laws and representations of historical scenes known to man.

Mesopotamia

Galleries 1 to 6. The Sumerian site of **Telloh** (ancient Girsu) was home to the famous **vultures stele** (c. 2450 BC – *fragments displayed straight ahead of entrance*), immortalising the victory of the King Eannatum of Lagash over the rival city of Umma.

On display by the entrance to gallery 1b, note the votive relief of Ur-Nanshe *(to the left),* the founder of the Lagash dynasty, and the silver and copper vase dedicated by King Entemena of Lagash to the god Ningirsu *(to the right).*

The Sumerian culture spread northwards to what is now Syria (site of **Mari**); one custom was to offer small statues of worshippers intended to perpetuate the prayers of the faithful. The Louvre has an impressive collection of these statuettes dedicated to Ishtar; the most memorable of these being that of the **Intendant of the palace of Ebih-II**★ (middle of

ImageState/Tips Images

the 3rd millennium BC), with beautiful blue (lapis lazuli) eyes, and clothed in a voluminous, fluffy sheepskin skirt.

The Semitic dynasty of Akkad (2340-2200 BC) succeeded in uniting Mesopotamia around the ancient Babylonian city of Agade. Wonderful artefacts dating from this dynasty include the marvellous **stele of Naram-Sin** (2250 BC) in pink sandstone, which depicts the victorious king climbing a mountain over the dead bodies of enemy soldiers. Towards 2130 BC, the striking group of about a dozen fairly large **statues of Prince Gudea** and those of his son Ur-Ningirsu were produced in Lagash. The sovereign, wearing a robe on which there is a long prayer of dedication to the gods, is sometimes represented with an architect's materials.

At the beginning of the 2nd millennium BC, **Babylon** made its first impact on history: the Babylonian king destroyed Mari and conquered Mesopotamia. In the centre of the gallery stands the famous **Code of Hammurabi**★ (c. 1790 BC-1750 BC), a black basalt stele 2.5m/8ft high; at the top, the king is depicted receiving from the sun god Shamash (who carries measuring instruments – ruler, surveyor's cord – symbolising justice) 282 laws which are engraved below in the Akkad language *(gallery 3)*.

After the 6C BC, when Babylon reached the height of its power under King Nebuchadnezzar *(Passing Lion*, a relief in green and gold coloured glazed bricks adorned the triumphal route of the palace of Nebuchadnezzar II), the Eastern world, from the Mediterranean to India, was united under the rule of the Persian Empire.

Cour Khorsabad★★

The large Assyrian reliefs from the palace of Sargon II at Dur-Sharrukin (Iraq's modern Khorsabad) greet visitors at the same height as they would have been during the Assyrian era. Two **winged bulls** with five legs, so that two legs are visible when viewed from the front and four when in profile, reconstitute part of the decoration of the third doorway of the Khorsabad palace complex. The wall opposite is a reconstruction of the façade of the throne room (the bull on the left, with its head turned to look at the viewer, is a cast of the original now in the Oriental Institute, Chicago).

The Hittites, who brought the Hammurabi dynasty of Babylon to ruin, settled on the Anatolian plateau (at the heart of modern Turkey) in the middle of the 2nd millennium BC. Their hieroglyphic script can be seen on the **stele of the god of the storm**, Tahunda *(gallery 5)*. The palace of the provincial capital **Til Barsip** was decorated with frescoes, rather than carving. Here, the fragments have been complemented by reconstructions of the original works *(gallery 6)*.

Cour Khorsabad

Daniel Thierry/Photononstop/Tips Images

Arslan-Tash was another provincial capital with sites that yielded spoils of war from Phoenician or Armenian cities including some wonderful **ivories** *(Cow suckling calf).*

The central display case contains fragments of the bronze door from the palace of King Salmanasar III at Balawat (9C BC).

Reliefs from the palace of Ashurnasirpal II depict winged spirits, some with the heads of birds, giving blessing in front of the sacred tree. Further on, King Ashurnasirpal II (883-859 BC) is shown with his armour bearer.

The **reliefs**★★ from the palace of Ashurbanipal at **Nineveh** are numbered among the masterpieces of world sculpture.

Iran

Galleries 7 to 16. Transhumance between the Fars mountains (to the east, on the mountainous plateau where Persepolis was later to be built) and the Susa plain perpetuated the Mesopotamian influence, and gave rise to the first Iranian state: **Elam**. From the end of the 5th millennium, Elamite potters (the capital of Elam was Susa) were becoming renowned for their beautiful, highly stylised animal (large vase with ibex) or geometric decoration.

Among the furniture from tombs and temples in the 3rd millennium is the statue of the goddess Narundi (c. 2100 BC), and the painted terracotta **secret-compartment vase** (labelled *vase à la cachette)* found containing various objects including alabaster vases, weapons and copper tools *(gallery 8).*

The unusual open-work circular *standard* (with little linked human figures) supported by two bulls *(display case to the left, rue de Rivoli side)* belongs to

Luristan culture, a region in the north-west of Elam widely reputed for its metalwork. Within the bounds of central Asia, a great civilization was flourishing in **Bactria** (Afghanistan). The figurine known as the **Princess of Bactria**★★ wears a marvellous blue robe with full sleeves and a crinoline-like skirt, in a fleecy textile reminiscent of that on the statue of the *Intendant Ebih-II (see gallery 1b above).* Immediately to her right, **Le Balafré** (Scarface – he has also lost an eye) is the nickname given to the statuette of a mountain spirit.

The art of bronze reached its apogee during this period: see the **Statue of Queen Napirasu** in the centre of the gallery (note in particular the embroidery on her robe). Panels of cast bricks *(along the wall to the right)* depict alternately half-bull-half-man figures protecting a palm tree and Lama goddesses. These would once have adorned a temple *(gallery 10).*

From the 6C to the 4C BC Susa reached its apogee under the Achaemenid kings. Gold- and silversmiths produced outstandingly delicate works of art (bracelets and goblets, winged ibex). The enormous **Apdana capital**★★ from the palace of Darius at Susa gives some indication of the gigantic scale of the palaces of Persian rulers, which were decorated with enamel brick friezes. The **mosaics** from the palace of Bichapur (3C AD) date from the Sasanian period and mark the transition to Muslim art.

Levantine art

This collection is divided between the west wing of Cour Carrée, for the part representing the earliest evidence up to IC BC (starting from gallery 10) and the final galleries in the Sackler wing.

Islam in the West (10C-15C)

The contribution made by the civilizations of Islam to Western philosophy, art and science is considerable *(gallery 3).* The kingdom of Granada in Spain flourished until 1492. Note the *Peacock aquamanile* (Spain, 13C), the work of a Muslim craftsman in the service of a Christian prince; marvellous caskets and ivory pyxes (sculpted cylindrical boxes) from Spain and Sicily, in particular the **pyx called after Al-Mughira** (10C, with a domed lid); the *Lion with an articulated tail* (Spain, 12C-13C) with a very large, wide-open mouth, possibly once part of a fountain.

Palestine and Transjordania

West wing, galleries D to A. On the **stele of Mesha,** King of Moab (9C BC) commemorates his victory over the kings of Israel and the Omri dynasty. Its reference to the Hebrew state is the earliest known.

Central Syria

Terracottas (vase bases, models of houses with storeys) and statuette of a seated god.

Excavation of Ugarit (modern Ras Shamra) has uncovered Phoenicia, the crossroads of the Ancient world: Egyptian-influenced **breast-plate** decorated with the royal falcon (2000-1600 BC); **stele of Baal with a Thunderbolt** (god of the storm), a beautiful **patera** depicting a royal hunting scene in repoussé gold (14C-13C BC). For the first time, c 1300 BC, the cuneiform alphabet is used in place of syllabic script.

Sackler wing

Galleries 17 to 21. Among the Phoenician tombs, the **sarcophagus in the form of the mummy of Eshmunazar II**★★, King of Sidon (5C BC) betrays Egyptian influence in Syria. It is engraved with the text of a curse. Marble sculptures from Sidon evoke the cult of Mithra, and bronzes that of Jupiter from Heliopolis (modern Baalbek) in Syria, during the Roman era.

Stele of Baal

©Scala, Florence/Musée du Louvre

There are astonishingly intense funeral portraits from Palmyra, as well as a lovely **Aphrodite with a Tortoise**★.

The colossal Basin of Amathus in limestone was made in the 5C BC, probably to collect the water supply necessary for the ceremonies of the city's temple *(gallery 21).*

Cult statues from the island of Cyprus (7C-3C BC) and funerary strips in gold leaf.

The Art of Islam★★

⚲*Closed temporarily.*
New exhibition spaces dedicated to Arts of Islam will open in a new building in the Denon Wing during 2010.

Galerie d'Apollon

Denon wing; first floor, Gallery 66.

This gilded masterpiece, created by Le Vau under Louis XIV, has 28 tapestries, 118 sculpted figures and 41 paintings by Charles Le Brun and, later, Eugene Delacroix, make this one of the most elaborately decorated rooms in the Louvre. The French crown jewels are on display, including the **Regent diamond**★★★ weighing 140 carats. Purchased in 1717, its exceptional clarity and perfect shape make it one of the most famous precious stones in the world, having adorned among other things the coronation crown of Louis XV, the parade sword of Premier Consul Bonaparte and the diadem of the Empress Eugénie. Other display cases contain Louis XIV's impressive collection of **semi-precious stone vases**★.

Italian School: painting★★★

Denon wing; first floor, to the right of the Winged Victory of Samothrace.

The collection of Italian paintings, one of the glories of the Louvre, was carefully acquired as a result of a passion harboured by the kings of France for the art of that peninsula. Renaissance masterpieces include such key works as the *Mona Lisa, The Wedding at Cana* and *The Man with the Glove,* but it is the Baroque pieces, favoured by Louis XIV, that are most especially unique. The collection is presented in chronological order.

Primitives and Quattrocento (15C)

In the *Salle Percier* and *Salle Fontaine,* by way of introduction to Italian painting, are the frescoes from the *Villa Lemmi* by **Botticelli** commemorating the marriage of Lorenzo Tornabuoni (surrounded by allegories of the Liberal Arts) with Giovanna degli Albizzi (offering her bridal veil to Venus and her attendants the three Graces). Fra Angelico's *Crucifixion* is found in the Salle Duchâtel.

Salon Carré

Thirty of the large-format Florentine **Primitives** hang where the former salons of the Académie des Beaux-Arts were held. During the early part of the 14C, it is **Giotto** who maintains the momentum to greater realism. Narrative scenes are reduced to the essentials: in the large portrait of **Saint Francis of Assisi receiving the stigmata**★★, the saint is depicted in a rugged landscape of monumental proportions.

A Dominican monk, **Fra Angelico** the Blessed, the painter of the convent of San Marco in Florence, evoked life in Paradise as serenely mystical. Saints and angels crowd round in the *Coronation of the Virgin,* painted in 1435 for the church of San Domenico at Fiesole outside Florence.

Intrigued by the problems of portraying perspective, *Paolo Uccello* painted the *Battle of San Romano,* in which the forces of Florence beat those of Siena in 1432 (the other panels, painted for the Medicis, are in Florence – Uffizi – and London – National Gallery): lances articulate the background space into regular stripes; the captain Michelotto Attendoli's black charger suggests depth; the surging crowd of armed warriors in magnificent plumed helmets are depicted ready to advance or retreat, accentuating the theatrical effect of movement and action.

Salle des Sept-Mètres

Gallery 4. In Siena, the jewel-like art of **Simone Martini** (small panel of the *Way to Calvary*) recalls the art of illumination.

The Quattrocento was a period of quest and rationalisation: how should space and volume be represented on a two-dimensional plane? Portraiture provided an opportunity for detailed observation and sensitive analysis: the medallion portrait in profile of *A Princess of the House of Este* by **Pisanello**; the authoritarian and enigmatic *Sigismondo Malatesta* by **Piero della Francesca**.

Grande Galerie

The immense cyma displays 13C to 15C works in its first part, as far as the famous Salle des États, and in the second part 16C and 17C works.

Subject matter, physiognomy and pose evolve. *Saint Sebastian* by *Mantegna* is so precisely observed as to be almost sculptural; the sorrowful *Resurrected Christ giving Blessing* by **Giovanni Bellini**. The *Portrait of an Old Man and a Young Boy* by **Ghirlandaio** combines Florentine elegance with Flemish realism, featured also in the strong, proud features of *Il Condottiere* and the face of the suffering *Christ at the column* by **Antonello da Messina**.

The High Renaissance

Grande Galerie (second part devoted to the 16C and 17C). The fulfilment of objectives and the successful application of ideal principles marked a new phase of the Renaissance, this time concentrated in Rome and nurtured by a reformed Papacy. When the city was sacked in 1527, Venice became the power-base and ultimate patron of the Arts, a possession guarded until the end of the 16C.

▶ *From the Grande Galerie, turn right into the Salle des Etats (galleries 6-7).*

Leonardo da Vinci (1452-1519), acclaimed as a universal genius, ranks in pride of place among the artists of this period. *The Virgin of the Rocks,* a mature work in which the play of the hands is particularly remarkable, strengthening the harmonious pyramidal arrangement of the figures against the rather menacing rocky crags of the background landscape; *The Virgin and Child with St*

©Scala, Florence/Musée du Louvre

Wedding at Cana (1563) by Veronese

Anne, analysed by Sigmund Freud as suggesting Leonardo's childhood inhibitions: brought up by his grandmother and then his mother, he suffered recurrent nightmares about being attacked by a ravening vulture (seen in the folds of the Virgin's robes).

The portrait of **Mona Lisa**★★★, wife of the Florentine Del Giocondo, was finally moved here in 2006 after 55 years at the end of the Grand Galerie, with special lighting, protective glass and acoustics to absorb crowd noise.

Across from *La Joconde* is the **Wedding at Cana**★★★ by **Veronese**, executed in 1563 for the refectory of a convent in Venice, which covers one entire wall. The painter uses the scene from the Gospel as a pretext for painting the Golden Age of Venice, *La Serenissima* with its majestic architecture and sumptuous lifestyle in a composition of consummate skill. The 130 figures in this enormous painting (66sq m/79sq ft), recently restored, are mainly portraits of contemporary figures (Emperor Charles V, Suleiman the Magnificent, Titian, Bassano, Tintoretto and the artist himself, playing the viola).

▶ *Return to the Grande Galerie (gallery 8).*

Raphael (1483-1520), the pupil of Perugino, imbues his paintings with gentleness, his landscapes reflect the soft undulating countryside around his native Urbino. **La Belle Jardinière**★★ portrays a gentle Virgin watching over the Infants Jesus and John the Baptist, combining humanity and harmony with religious faith. In the *Portrait of Balthazar Castiglione,* the temperament of the gentleman who was a close friend of Raphael is economically portrayed.

Correggio, who was a keen observer of women's sensibilities, developed in Parma a style combining a delicate and slightly self-conscious sensuality with a romantic elegance that was to influence painting into the 18C: *The Mystical Marriage of St Catherine, Antiope Sleeping.*

Counter-Reformation (late 16C) and Seicento (17C)

▶ *Beyond the passage that leads to the Mollien wing, housing graphic works (drawings for tapestries by Lodi di Cremona, gouaches by Correggio).*

This period is dominated by the Bolognese School, following the founding of the Accademia degli Incamminati (Academy of the Progressives) by the Carracci brothers. A *Circumcision* is on display by the revivalist **Barocci**.

The canvases of the Aemilian School (from the Emilia Romana region) are eclectic, fusing a tendency towards the academic, a legacy from the study of the masters of the Renaissance (Domenichino's *Saints*), with forward-looking realism. The school's main exponents were **Annibale Carracci** (who often drew in the country; *Fishing* and *Hunting* might be said to be among the best landscapes in the Louvre), **Guido Reni** (who tended more to an aristocratic, decorative style: *Deianeira and the Centaur Nessus; David holding the head of Goliath*) and **Il Guercino** (painter of marvellously accurate human figures: *The Resurrection of Lazarus*).

This realism was adopted even more forcefully by **Caravaggio**, who modelled his figures upon people drawn from the poorer walks of life (**The Fortune-Teller**★★). *The Death of the Virgin,* one of his most powerful works, was rejected by the chapter of the Roman church which had commissioned it because of its unorthodox use of an ordinary woman as the model for the Virgin.

At the end of the Grande Galerie, in the Pavillon des États, 17C works are exhibited in the Salle Salvatore Rossa: **Pietro da Cortona**, who practised in Rome (*Romulus and Remus discovered by Faustulus*); **Domenico Fetti** of Venice (*Melancholy*); and **Luca Giordano** of Naples (*Portraits of Philosophers* dressed in the clothes of ordinary people).

Settecento (18C)

Painting from this period is housed in the Piazzetta gallery and the small adjacent rooms. The opulent lifestyle of the noble classes during the Age of Enlightenment is reflected in the works of Pannini (*Concert given in Rome on the occasion of the marriage of the Dauphin, son of Louis XV*). **Guardi** captured the atmosphere of the lagoon of Venice in the dazzling series **Ascension Day Ceremonies**★, during which the Doge, in a sumptuous state barge, celebrated the marriage of Venice with the Adriatic by throwing a ring into the sea.

The luminous religious and mythological compositions of **Giambattista Tiepolo** contrast strongly with the scenes of street life painted by his son, **Giandomenico Tiepolo** (*The Charlatan, Carnival*). The life of the common man is also portrayed in the work of **Pietro Longhi**, often with a humorous touch (*Presenta-tion*). *The Flea,* by **Crespi** of Bologna, is reminiscent of Dutch painting.

Spanish School: Painting★★

Galleries 26-32. Spanish painting is characterised by realism and mysticism. The collection of 15C **Spanish Primitives** including *The Flagellation of Saint George* by Martorell of Catalonia, *The Flagellation of Christ* by Jaime Huguet and *Man with a Glass of Wine* by a Portuguese master precede the Mannerist Domenikos Theotokopoulos, an icon painter of Cretan origin, pupil of Tintoretto in Venice, better known as **El Greco**. His **Christ on the Cross**★★, with its stretched figure outlined against a dark, stormy, almost abstract background, appears almost expressionist.

José de Riberac took subjects which were the social antithesis of the Spanish Golden Age, for example the **Club-footed Boy**, depicting the unfortunate cripple armed with his crutch and a note begging for charity (to indicate he was dumb as well), nonetheless with an open smile. Note also **The Young Beggar**★★ by **Murillo**, unusually lit transversely. The humane realism of such paintings contrasts with the spirituality of **Zurbarán** (*Funeral Ceremonies of Saint Bonaventura*), the baroque exuberance of Carreño de Miranda (*Mass for the founding of the Trinitarian Order*) and the stiff court Infanta portraits by **Velasquez**. The delightful Madonnas painted by Murillo in muted colours have the quality of pastels. The **Beistegui Collection** (*Sully wing, 2nd floor, take the Escalier Henri II*) includes the portrait of the Marquesa de la Solana, one of **Goya's** best, along with that of the *La Comtessa de Santa Cruz*.

French School: 19C Monumental Painting★★★

Through the ground floor of the Denon wing (Salle du Manège and Galerie Daru), go up the Escalier Daru, before reaching the Winged Victory of Samoth-

race, take the ramp opposite. The monumental works of the French Revolution, Empire and the early 19C are displayed in the Daru and Mollien galleries (75-77), parallel with the Grande Galerie. The rest of the French School (14C-19C) is in the Richelieu wing, 2nd floor.

The Oath of the Horatii, commissioned by Louis XVI, which **David** despatched from Rome for the Salon of 1785, embodies the main elements of Neoclassicism in painting. As a History painting it tells a story drawn from Classical literature in an uncompromising way, bold in its statement of virtue; masculine strength is contrasted with female sensibility. It was immensely well received.

A preliminary sketch for the **Coronation of Napoléon I**★ shows the new Emperor crowning himself; in the final composition, however, Napoléon is shown in the act of crowning Josephine. The unfinished Portrait of Madame Récamier, opposite, depicts Bonaparte's opponent at the age of 23, reclining in the style of Classical Antiquity on a day bed (see also Objets d'art).

Ingres' overwhelming concern with the expressive and sensual use of line can be clearly seen in La Grande Odalisque and his Portrait of Mademoiselle Rivière, where the aesthetic prevails over anatomical Realism.

Théodore Géricault gave artistic expression to current political issues; **The Raft of the Medusa**★★ (1819) drew its subject matter from a recent disastrous shipwreck thought largely to be the result of governmental incompetence. The effects of back-lighting and the positions of the unfortunate victims of the shipwreck of the Medusa – only one of whom is facing the viewer – evoke the wild fluctuations between hope and despair among the ragged survivors, who have just caught sight of the flag of the Argus (the ship which was eventually to rescue them) on the horizon.

Eugène Delacroix, the leading exponent of Romanticism, expressed his support for the cause of Greek independence in The Massacres at Chios, inspired by the brutal repression imposed on the inhabitants of that island. His reaction to the days of violence in the 1830 Revolution was **Liberty leading the People**★★, which he exhibited at the Salon. The Women of Algiers was painted in the wake of his trip to Morocco and Algeria, and demonstrates Delacroix' use of contrasting colour (red for foreground, green for depth). In **The Death of Sardanapalus**★, the East is portrayed in a mixture of magnificence and barbaric decadence, as the Sultan had ordered that everything and every-

The Raft of the Medusa (1819) by Théodore Géricault

©Scala, Florence/Musée du Louvre

one he held dear should be destroyed in front of him, before he himself committed suicide.

Northern Schools: Painting★★★

▶ *In the Richelieu wing, take the main escalator to the 2nd floor. Turn left off gallery 3 (French Painting).*

This section includes the painting of the German, Flemish and Dutch Schools from the 14C to the 17C. Light in these galleries filters through an overhead structure of cruciform beams, designed by Pei.

Flemish Primitives

The Flemish Primitives paint delicate, oval faces, carefully drawn folds of clothing and exquisite textures while paying close attention to domestic detail.

The most famous work on display is the **Madonna with Chancellor Rolin**★★ by **Jan van Eyck**, the artist who, with his brother, pioneered the technique of painting with oils. The **Braque Family Triptych** is an intensely spiritual work painted by **Roger van der Weyden** in his mature period. The *Annunciation* is depicted against the background of a luxuriously furnished interior.

Hans Memling lived in the peaceful surroundings of Bruges with its beguine convents. He formulated a type of woman in his works, serene and beautiful; in the magnificent **Triptych of the Resurrection** and the *Portrait of an Old Woman,* Realism is compromised by a mood of gentle meditation. **Hieronymous Bosch**'s sharp sense of ridicule is well portrayed in *The Ship of Fools.*

German School

The chronological presentation of panels enables a comparison of the Flemish Primitives with those of the German School. The general self-contained harmony of the former is succeeded by the more self-consciously disturbed style of the latter: the colours are harsh; magnificent draperies are as minutely described as are the textures of jewellery and weapons; facial expression is often hard and tormented.

In the centre of the gallery, an original **painted table top** by Hans Sebald Beham depicts scenes from the life of David. The small room adjoining the gallery houses the prize exhibits of the collection: *Portrait of the Humanist Erasmus* by **Hans Holbein the Younger;** *Venus standing in the centre of a landscape* by **Lucas Cranach the Elder; Albrecht Dürer's** *Self-Portrait* with a thistle, the symbol of fidelity, intended for his fiancée.

16C and 17C Flanders

Flemish Renaissance art retained many medieval features from the International Gothic painting style for some time: *Altarpiece of the Lamentation of Christ* by **Joos van Cleve** (note the predella); interesting portraits by Jan Gossaert, known as **Mabuse** (*Carondelet Diptych*).

The Moneylender and his Wife★★ is one of the most famous works by **Quentin Metsys**. It depicts the couple absorbed in weighing and counting money – note the exquisite rendering of the hands complete with their shadowy veins; a profusion of minutely observed detail characterises the attributes of their household, a veritable still-life study on the shelves behind including a manuscript and pearls. In the centre of the picture, a convex mirror testifies to the presence of a third character or witness to the scene; a window provides a landscape view of the world outside.

Rubens, master of the Baroque, seems to exalt life itself with fleshy bodies and sumptuous attire. All these elements abound in the 24-panel cycle celebrating the Life of Queen Marie de' Medici, now housed in the **Galerie Médicis**★★ (gallery 18) designed by Pei. **Jordaens**, a pupil of Rubens, cultivated a highly coloured realism which verged on earthiness (*gallery 19, on the cour Napoléon side*): *The King Drinks!, Jesus chasing the Merchants from the Temple, The Four Evangelists.* **Van Dyck** was the portraitist to the Genoese and English aristocracy par excellence (*gallery 24*), catching the refined elegance of both courts: *Charles I, King of Eng-*

land, *The Marquessa Spinola-Doria, The Palatine Princes*.

17C Dutch School

The Netherlands, a maritime republic, fashioned its art to bourgeois taste depicting domestic scenes, portraiture and landscape *(galleries 28 to 39)*.

Frans Hals pioneered the character portrait with pictures such as the *Gypsy Girl* and the *Lute-player*. His robust style was to influence Fragonard (*see French Painting*) and Manet. Wonderful landscapes are portrayed by **Jacob van Ruisdael** *(Ray of Sunlight)* and **Van Goyen**, his silvery river scenes stretching into far distances *(gallery 38)*.

Rembrandt gradually forsook *chiaroscuro* in favour of a more limited, but more subtle, palette ranging through warm, rich, earthy tones of gold and brown; highlighted detail projects out of the darkness, giving a somewhat unreal but nonetheless highly emotive effect *(The Philosopher in Meditation)*. Note the rendering of the nude in *Bathsheba bathing*, a portrait of his second wife, and of the problems and loneliness that beset the artist in his old age, painfully etched on the face in his poignant *Self-Portrait before an Easel (gallery 31)*.

Other masters of this period include **Ter Borch**, **Pieter de Hooch**, **Gerrit Dou** and **Adriaen van Ostade**, who were principally genre painters. **Vermeer van Delft** imbues his contemplative scenes of domestic activity with poetic peace (**The Lacemaker★★**, **The Astronomer★★**) a quality achieved by his use of indirect light and oblique shadows.

French School: Painting★★★

Richelieu wing: take the main escalator to the 2nd floor. Large-format 19C French Painting is exhibited in the Denon wing.

It is difficult to define the particular characteristics of the French School of painting, despite the extensive collection of the Louvre spanning the 14C to the 19C. Categorised retrospectively into move-ments, stylistic development is punctuated by strong individual characters who often sought inspiration from abroad: Italy, Flanders, the Netherlands. The collection is arranged chronologically by genre, each serving very well as the focus of a visit in itself (the Primitives, the Fontainebleau School, the Caravaggisti, 17C religious painting, etc.). Certain groups of works by particular artists are outstanding: Claude Lorrain, Poussin, Fragonard, Chardin and Corot.

14C

Galleries 1 and 2. **Jean le Bon**, soon to be King of France, posed for a **Portrait★** (1350) at a time when the subjects of painting were almost exclusively religious.

15C

Galleries 3 to 6. The International Gothic tradition of portraying narrative subjects on a gold background was maintained by the Court of Burgundy *(Altarpiece of Saint Denis* by Henri Bellechose, *gallery 3)*. Provençal art, with its severe style and strong contrasts in light, is represented by the *Pietà of Villeneuve-lès-Avignon* by **Enguerrand Quarton**. In central France, Jean Hey, known as the **Master of Moulins**, trained in Flanders, adds a French predilection for elegance to his meticulous drawings.

16C

Galleries 7 to 10. Renaissance artists were passionately interested in Humanism. Consequently, many works of art of this period focus on the individual, hence the profusion of portraits, such as those by **Jean Clouet (François I★)** and his son **François Clouet**. The Italian artists summoned by François I during the construction of the Château de Fontainebleau introduced Mannerism into French decorative and applied arts. The First and Second Schools of Fontainebleau are represented respectively by *Diana the Huntress*, which has been thought to be the portrait of Diane de Poitiers, Henri II's mistress, and **Gabrielle d'Estrées with one of her sisters★**, probably painted to celebrate the birth of one of Henri IV's illegitimate children.

The Cheat by George de la Tour

17C

Galleries 11 to 34. This century opened with the Caravaggisti, known for their distinctive use of *chiaroscuro* and the direct realism of his figures (👂 *see Italian Painting, Denon*) such as **Valentin de Boulogne** (*The Concert* bas-relief) and **Claude Vignon**, *Young Singer*. During the reign of Louis XIII, the somewhat academic allegories of **Simon Vouet** (*Wealth*) contrast with the austere, controlled style of **Philippe de Champaigne**, who emphasises in his **Portrait of Cardinal de Richelieu**★ the dignity and unbending will of the statesman.

Georges de la Tour (1593-1652) is a famous master of the illuminated figure on a black background, as exemplified in **The Cheat**★, where the card players exchange intriguing glances. **Nicolas Poussin** (1594-1665), the artist-philosopher who settled in Rome, is regarded as the most Classical of French academic painters, drawing from the formal canons of Beauty and yet remaining sensitive to the sensuality of colour inspired by Titian. Platonic ideas of Nature as a nourishing force and of the cyclical progression of life and time are expressed in **The Four Seasons**★★. **Claude Gellée** (1600-82), otherwise known as **Le Lorrain**, provides another high point.

He was perhaps the first painter to attempt to paint the sun as a direct light source, hence his influence upon the English painter Turner and later the Impressionists.

Galleries 25 to 29

Numerous genre scenes and small-format still-life works were executed by painters inspired by Flemish artists working in Paris, such as **Lubin Baugin**. Painting becomes a vehicle for portraying social reality in the works of **Le Nain brothers** where sober realism hints at the moderate wealth of a middle-class patron: **Peasant Family at home**★. **Eustache Le Sueur** (1616-55) was both a painter of religious subjects (*Life of Saint Bruno, gallery 24*) and a sophisticated decorative artist influenced by Raphael.

Gallery 31-32

Chancellor Séguier on horseback is a solemn, official portrait by **Le Brun** of his first patron, shown surrounded by his pages, exuding an awareness of the responsibility conferred on him by Louis XIII. A huge composition by Le Brun depicts scenes from the life of Alexander. In the same gallery, **Philippe de Champaigne** displays his talent for creating penetrating portraits of his contemporaries (*Portrait of Robert*

Arnault d'Andilly). He also painted the famous **ex-voto of 1662**, a reflection of the Jansenist spiritual ideal, in thanksgiving for the miraculous cure of his daughter, a nun at the convent of Port-Royal-des-Champs.

18C

Galleries 34 to 54. The Portrait of Louis XIV by **Rigaud** (1701) was so well received by the monarch that he kept the original for himself, despite its having been commissioned as a present for his grandson, Philip V of Spain, who had to be content with a copy. Only a few years separate this image of the Grand Siècle from the dreamy, elegant canvases of **Watteau** (d. 1721), heralding the spirit of the Age of Enlightenment. In the marvellous **Pilgrimage to Cythera**★★.

Theatre was another source of inspiration for painters as demonstrated in works by Watteau's teacher, **Claude Gillot** (Quarrel of the Cabmen, inspired by the Commedia dell'Arte), and in those of Watteau himself, such as the strange and famous figure of **Gilles**.

The hunting scenes by **Jean-François de Troy** and **Carle van Loo** were painted for the dining room in the Royal Suite at Fontainebleau. **Boucher** often drew his subject matter from mythology, allowing him free licence to treat them with a delicacy not untinged with eroticism: **Diana resting after her bath** and **Odalisque** (gallery 38), both painted in fresh, shimmering tones.

A more modest realism fashions the works of **Chardin** in both his still-life paintings (**The Ray**★, The Buffet, The Copper Cistern) and his genre paintings (The Purveyor, Child saying Grace).

Galleries 41 to 45

The collection of delicate pastels and miniatures in the Couloir des Poules and adjacent galleries by **Quentin de la Tour (Portrait of the Marquise de Pompadour**★), Chardin and others surround the great religious and mythological paintings contained in gallery 43: Pentecost by **Restout**; Meal at Simon's House by **Subleyras**.

Galleries 48 and 49

Fragonard's light touch and happy sense of movement are combined in The Bathers and his **fantasy figures** (Portrait of Abbé de Saint-Non). **The Lock**★, while still light-hearted in spirit, is more formal in composition, succumbing to the Neoclassical influence of Jacques-Louis David.

Shortly before the Revolution, Hubert Robert undertook to paint a series of canvases for the apartment of Louis XVI at Fontainebleau, thereby initiating a taste for Romanticised Roman ruins, idealised and juxtaposed irrespective of topographical accuracy (The Pont du Gard).

Gallery 51

Note also, by the same painter, two canvases depicting the **Grande Galerie du Louvre**, one as a construction project, the other as a ruin.

Following Diderot's advice, **Greuze** began painting scenes with moral subjects, thus formulating a new genre. Gallery 52 is devoted to the delicate portraits of **Elisabeth Vigée-Lebrun**.

Neoclassicism

Gallery 54. Devoted to **David** (Portrait of Madame Trudaine) and his pupils (Bonaparte at Arcole, by Gros), who mark the transition from the 18C to the 19C.

19C

Galleries 55 to 73. Works by **Prudhon**: Marie-Marguerite Lagnier; Venus Bathing or Innocence.

Ingres, pupil of David, best epitomises the softer Neoclassical taste of the Empire. Clarity of line and form are the main concerns of this artist who vigorously opposed those of the colourists Delacroix and Géricault, imposing a different interpretation of exotic subjects beloved to both factions of the Romantic School: **The Turkish Bath**★, painted 54 years after **The Valpinçon Bather**★, uses the same nude subject seen from behind. The Portrait of Monsieur Bertin draws inspiration from Flemish Realism. Ingres was Director of the Académie de France in Rome (Villa Medici) when his pupil **Hippolyte Flandrin** painted his

Elisabeth Louise Vigée-Lebrun (1755-1842)

Vigée-Lebrun was, in her time, one of Europe's most famous portraitists. As a woman, she was not allowed formal training, but through skill and drive she achieved admission to the Royal Academy. When her patrons were exiled or executed during the French Revolution, she began 12 years of travel in Europe with her young daughter and her paintbrushes (but without her husband). It is curious that she was both an ardent monarchist and defender of the social order, and a freedom-loving, single working mother. Her uncritical, flattering style of portraiture has been criticised, but recently art historians have taken a second look at this prolific artist (by her own account, 877 pictures), who now has her own room at the Louvre (Gallery 52).

study *Young Nude Man by the Sea* (1837 – gallery 63).

Géricault regularly painted horses racing (**Epsom Derby**★), thrilled by the latent power of the horse, just as his excellent portraits *(The Madwoman obsessed with Gambling – La Monomane du jeu)* show his fascination with personality through physiognomy.

Delacroix's Romantic passion is apparent through his free and speedy brushwork notably in his **Self-Portrait**★; his *Landscape* prefigures the Impressionists (gallery 62). Other notable works include his *Young orphan girl at the cemetery* (gallery 71); the reworked study of the head of a young man in the *Massacres at Chios* (see Large-Format 19C French Painting, Denon wing).

The final galleries are devoted to **Corot**, who is recognised by his landscapes, often bathed in nostalgia, vibrant with scintillating light in the fresh, clear air *(Souvenir of Mortefontaine, Marissel Church, Bridge at Mantes)*. *Douai Belfry* was painted during his stay in northern France.

Beistegui Collection★

Take the Escalier d'Henri II to the 2nd floor and turn left (the end of the tour of the galleries of French painting is to the right).

The entire **collection of Carlos Beistegui** (1863, Mexico-1953, Biarritz) consisting above all of portraits, is displayed in a special gallery.

Note the *Portrait of a Young Artist* and a scene of dissolute living *(Le Feu aux poudres)* by **Fragonard; David's** famous *Unfinished Portrait of Napoléon; The Duchess of Chaulnes as Hebe* by Jean-Marc Nattier; *Dido's Suicide* by **Rubens**; and **The Marquesa de la Solana**★ (1794), one of **Goya's** best-known works.

Italian School: Sculpture★★

Denon wing: at entresol level.
The collection continues on the ground floor.

Donatello Gallery

13C Italian sculpture is stylised and static (*Virgin* from Ravenna), produced at a time of instability often coined as the Dark Ages. A century later, artists and sculptors learnt to review Roman reliefs, re-interpreting their subject matter as Christian narrative. From Pisa (graceful *Virgin* by Nino Pisano) to 15C Siena (Jacopo della Quercia *seated Madonna*) and Florence, sculpture evolved to conform with Renaissance aesthetics, towards idealised form and calculated proportion (**Donatello** bas-relief of **The Virgin and Child**★, **Verrocchio** two delightful little angels).

Michelangelo Gallery

The two marble **Slaves**★★★ (1513-20) sculpted by **Michelangelo** for the tomb of Pope Julius II, although uncompleted are famous masterpieces as expressions of strength apparently breaking out of the rough stone. The Neoclassical **Psyche Revived by the Kiss of Cupid**★★ (1793) is quite exquisite, contrived by

The Dying Slave (1513-15) by Michelangelo

Cour Marly and Cour Puget. The Renaissance collection is very comprehensive; any gaps in medieval sculpture may be filled by a visit to the Cluny Museum (✆ *see QUARTIER LATIN*).

High Middle Ages and Romanesque

Galleries 1 to 3. The 12C **Courajod Christ**, once part of a Deposition, exemplifies the degree of skill attained in this art form at this time. Other particularly remarkable exhibits include: *Saint Michael vanquishing the dragon,* a marvellous triangular composition from Nevers; a *Virgin in majesty* from Auvergne; **capitals** from Burgundy and Poitiers *(David fights Goliath, Harvest scene)*; and finally, the **Carrières-sur-Seine altarpiece** *(gallery 3 on the side of Cour Marly)*, which marks the transition from Romanesque to Gothic art.

Gothic

Galleries 4 to 9. The Gothic Middle Ages, the age of cathedrals, produced figurative sculpture imbued with such grace, poise, sophistication and serene beauty on the one hand and such expressive realism on the other as to bear comparison with the best creations from Antiquity. The rigid, linear style of the **statue columns** from the old church of Corbeil, Solomon and the Queen of Sheba, reflect the spirituality of nascent Gothic art. Subsequent galleries accommodate fragments of funerary monuments.

Late Gothic

Galleries 10 to 12. Funerary monuments become much larger in the 15C: the **tomb of Philippe Pot**★★, Seneschal of Burgundy, is particularly impressive with its famous hooded mourners. In gallery 11, the *Saint George fighting the dragon,* a famous bas-relief by **Michel Colombe**, heralds the Renaissance.

Renaissance

Galleries 13 to 19. The *Mort-Saint-Innocent* gallery is named after the macabre effigy of death which once stood at the centre of the Parisian cemetery of this name (✆ *see les HALLES*). To the right of the entrance, note the **altarpiece of**

Canova to blend the Antique with a Rococo lightness of touch.

Northern Schools: Sculpture★★

Denon wing: at entresol level, beyond the Italian sculptures, and continued on the ground floor above in the west wing of Cour Lefuel.
The brittle, deeply folded drapery of the *Virgin of Isenheim,* near Colmar, is typical of sculpture of the German School of the late Middle Ages, often executed in polychrome lime wood. Swabian sculptors imbue their figures with greater serenity (*Mary Magdalen* by Gregor Erhart), whereas the great Franconian master Tilman Riemenschneider produced more delicate pieces such as the marble **Virgin of the Annunciation**★.

French School: Sculpture★★★

The collection dominates the ground floor of the Richelieu wing: Cour Marly, Crypte Girardon and Cour Puget together with surrounding galleries.
Sheltered by wonderful glass roofs, the sculptural groups which adorned 17C and 18C Royal parks may be surveyed in

the **Resurrection of Christ**, a delicately executed work in stone combining Flamboyant Gothic motifs with Renaissance ornamentation.

The influence of Italian art is tempered by ideals of grace and detail. The distant sensuality of **Diana of Anet** echoes the tendencies of the School of Fontainebleau (👁️*see French School: Painting-16C*). The *Longueville pyramid* in the final gallery is decorated with beautiful reliefs in bronze gilt. Architectural form dominates over sculpture in the funerary monument of Jacques-Auguste de Thou.

The staircase, **Escalier Lefuel**, features an impressive array of arcades and banisters *(leading to the Objets d'art Department: medieval treasure, and 17C Flemish Paintings)*.

The 17C

French sculpture evolved little during the reigns of Henri IV and Louis XIII before enjoying a great vogue through the reign of Louis XIV. The **Cour Marly** ★★ (the famous rearing **Marly horses**★★), **Crypte Girardon**★ (*The Grand Condé*, bronze by **Antoine Coysevox**), and the **Cour Puget**★★ (**Milo of Croton**★★ by **Pierre Puget**) display the best of French sculptures that once adorned the parks of royal residences at Marly, Versailles, Sceaux and the Tuileries.

The 18C

Galleries along rue de Rivoli. The exquisite **Cupid putting a finger to his lips**★ by **Falconet** *(gallery 22)* was commissioned by Madame de Pompadour to adorn the garden of her mansion, the Hôtel d'Évreux, now the Palais de l'Élysée. **Cupid whittling a bow from Hercules' club**★ by **Bouchardon** *(gallery 23)* was ill-received when presented to the Court in 1750, as Cupid was felt to be too realistic.

Gallery 25 contains fragments of sculpture received by the Académie Royale de Peinture et de Sculpture: the version of **Pigalle**'s masterpiece *Mercury (display case on the right)* is more sophisticated than that in bronze in the courtyard. *Psyche Abandoned* (because she had just looked on the face of her lover, Cupid, thereby disobeying his request that she

should not see him) caused an uproar because of its complete nudity and stark realism *(gallery 27)*.

The **gallery of great men** *(in the centre of gallery 29)* regroups a series of marble effigies between *Diana the Huntress* by Houdon, and *Peace*.

Mythological figures by **Jean-Jacques Pradier**, the official sculptor, adopt Mannerist poses *(Three Graces)*.

The final gallery *(33)* is devoted to the work of **François Rude**, author of the *Marseillaise* on the Arc de Triomphe *(a model of the face in a display case)* and **Antoine-Louis Barrye**, who is famed for his observation of animals, sculpted in minute detail.

Objets d'Art★★★

These are exhibited on the 1st floor of the Richelieu wing, and of the west wing of Sully. For a chronological visit, take the corridor on the right, then the escalator designed by Pei.

The galleries of the Richelieu wing were redesigned in 1993. The department, however, already had a long history dating back to the Revolution when part of the treasure of St-Denis was deposited here in 1793.

The beautiful presentation cases are designed by **Jean-Michel Wilmotte**.

Medieval treasure of the Louvre★★★

This is one of the high points of a visit to the Louvre. The most famous exhibits come from the Royal Abbey of St-Denis (👁️*see EXCURSIONS*), which served the French monarchy as a mausoleum. The gold and silver plate and above all the ivories, some of which are over 1 000 years old, are quite astounding.

The entrance to gallery Λ is flanked by two pink porphyry columns with the bust of an emperor projecting from each just above head level. These columns are supposed to have been part of the atrium of the basilica of St Peter in Rome, built by Constantine in the 4C AD.

Byzantium

Gallery 1 displays the spoils of Constantinople, pillaged by the Crusaders (1204). **Ivories**, luxurious possessions, date mainly from the 10C and 11C, a period when the empire had reached the apogee of its splendour under the Macedonian dynasty.

Charlemagne and the High Middle Ages

Opposite the entrance is displayed a 9C **equestrian statue of Charlemagne** or possibly of **Charles the Bald**, modelled on Antique equestrian statues *(the horse has been restored)*. Also displayed are objects discovered in 1959 in the tomb of Queen Arnegonde, wife of Clovis' son Clothair I (511-561), at St-Denis.

Romanesque and early Gothic art

Suger, the Abbot of St-Denis (1122-51), hoped to make his abbey one of the leading churches in Christendom. He experimented with a new type of construction, based on ogive vaulting, and enriched his treasury with liturgical vases. The most famous of these, the **Eagle of Abbot Suger★★**, incorporates an Antique porphyry vase (display case opposite the entrance).

The central display case contains a **coronation sword** known as **Charlemagne**'s or the **Joyeuse**. Next to it are the coronation spurs.

Gothic art

Gallery 3. Opposite the entrance stands the exquisite ivory statue of the **Virgin and Child** made for the chapel of the palace of Saint Louis (now the Sainte-Chapelle). It follows the Rayonnant Gothic style for large statuary. The striking silver gilt Virgin and Child group known as the **Virgin of Jeanne d'Evreux★** after its royal donor, Philip the Fair's widow, was given to the abbey of St-Denis in 1339.

At the far side of gallery 4, against the magnificent backdrop of the monumental Italian **Embriachi altarpiece★★** made of wood and ivory, note the **sceptre of Charles V**, made for the coronation of his son; the statuette on top represents Charlemagne.

The display cases to the right of the sceptre of Charles V contain the most famous exhibits from the treasure of St-Denis: the large, diamond-shaped **ornamental clasp** decorated with a

fleur-de-lis, and the beautiful **bookbinding** enclosing a 14C Parisian ivory. Gallery 6 displays masterpieces of the art of gold or silversmithing.

Renaissance

Galleries 7 to 17. This series of galleries encircle the gallery hung with the 15C tapestries of **The Hunts of Maximilian★★** *(Gallery 19).* Works include painted enamels dating from the reign of Louis XII and the **Sauvageot Collection** illustrating the art of glassmaking in Europe.

Galerie de Scipion★

Gallery 20. This series of tapestries, commissioned from the Gobelins workshops by Louis XIV, depict scenes from the life of Scipio Africanus; they are copied from one of the most famous series of tapestries from Renaissance Brussels known as **The Great Scipio** commissioned by François I.

Jean Boulogne Rotunda★

Gallery 26. This houses a number of bronzes by this master and his pupils. The walls are hung with beautiful tapestries from Ferrara depicting scenes of metamorphosis.

Treasure of the Order of the Holy Spirit★★

Galleries 27 and 28. This, the most prestigious order of the Ancien Régime, was founded by Henri III while the Wars of Religion were raging, to secure the loyalty of the nobility to the crown. The honour's insignia is the blue sash.

Salle d'Effiat★

Gallery 32. Louis XIII furniture from the Château d'Effiat in the Puy-de-Dôme (Auvergne) appears somewhat severe in style.

The 17C, Louis XIV's reign

Galleries 33 and 34. Return to the Jean Boulogne rotunda and turn left. The very fine tapestry illustrating *Moses in the Bulrushes* is one of a series on themes from the Old Testament, designed by **Simon Vouet,** and made for the Louvre. In the centre of gallery 33 is the ornate **gold Anne of Austria casket**.

The 18C

Galleries 35 to 45 and 47 to 61 (⚷ closed for renovations until 2011). Note in the entrance *(display case on the right)* the sober lines and decoration of Marie-Antoinette's **travelling case**, in sharp contrast to the queen's infamous extravagant taste for ribbons and nosegay ornamentation. Seats by **Jacob**, one of the pioneers of the Empire style *(⚷ see Madame Récamier's Bedchamber below),* are displayed alongside lacquer furniture by **Carlin**. The cylindrical writing desk by **Riesener**, a new type of furniture in 1770, stands in front of the splendid desk by **Benneman**, at which Napoléon worked when he was at the Tuileries. The Gobelins **tapestries** with pink backgrounds *(Loves of the Gods),* woven to designs by **Boucher**, the candelabra, and cabinets all reflect the degree of artistic imagination of the times, testifying to the delicate tastes of one of the most sophisticated periods in French history.

The Restoration and Louis-Philippe periods (1815-48)

Galleries 75-81 display what remains of the exquisite treasure of the last kings of France: Louis XVIII, Charles X, and Louis-Phlippe.

Empire style (1798-1815)

Richelieu wing, first floor, access via the Lefuel staircase. The sophisticated furniture from **Madame Récamier's Bedchamber**★ *(gallery 69),* designed by the **Jacob** brothers (1798), epitomises Empire-style design, distinguished by elegant line. The young lady's salon was the hub of opposition to Napoléon *(⚷ see Large-Format 19C French Painting, Denon).*

Napoléon III Apartments★★★

These are also accessible via Cour Marly, up the Escalier du Ministre (towards the Pyramid).

This majestic carpeted staircase, decorated with a very fine wrought-iron bannister, leads the visitor into a stunning world of gold, crimson velvet and crystal. These apartments provide one of the few examples of great Second Empire

décors to have survived complete with their original furnishings.

They consist of an antechamber, a presentation hall, a *salon-théâtre* (used for musical entertainment), a great hall (with a capacity for 265 spectators), a boudoir or *salon de terrasse* (with a view of the gardens) and a small and a large dining hall. The halls were inaugurated in 1861; some ten years later, they were appropriated by the Ministry of Finance.

African, Asian, Pacific Island and American art

If the Louvre has long been regarded as a museum of Western art and antiquities, its collection now includes ethnic art, or so-called primary art, with the creation in 2 000 of these new galleries, next to quai des Tuileries. *Access is via the Porte de Lions.*

Africa, Asia, Pacific Islands and the Americas

Four galleries present 120 sculptures and other masterpieces chosen for their artistic value and historic context. Among the pieces on display are a statue of a man from the Nagada II period of pre-dynastic Egypt (5-4 millennia BC) and a superb Sokoto terracotta head from Nigeria; a stone sculpture which once belonged to André Breton, from the Indonesian island of Nias and a sculpture over 2 000 years old from Chupicuaro in Mexico.

Dining Room, Napoléon III Apartments

LE LUXEMBOURG★★

Ⓜ ODÉON (LINES 4 AND 10), CLUNY-LA-SORBONNE (LINE 10)
RER: LUXEMBOURG (LINE B) – BUSES: 21, 27, 38, 82, 84, 85, 89

The historic gardens of Luxembourg Palace, seat of the French Senate, are a magnificent oasis of greenery in the heart of the Latin Quarter, making it a popular place where locals and visitors alike can sit and absorb the atmosphere of Paris.

Nearby neighbourhoods: **QUARTIER LATIN, ODÉON, ST-GERMAIN-DES-PRÉS, PORT-ROYAL, MONTPARNASSE.**

- **Information:** Carrousel du Louvre welcome centre, Place de la Pyramide Inversée 99, rue de Rivoli. ☎082 68 300 (0.34€ per min). http://en.parisinfo.com.
- ▶ **Orient Yourself:** The gardens are in the centre of the Left Bank, straddling the 5th and 6th arrondissements.
- Ⓟ **Parking:** There's underground parking at the south end of the gardens.
- **Don't Miss:** The espaliered fruit trees in the orchard and the Medici Fountain.
- Ⓞ **Organising Your Time:** The gardens can be visited in under an hour, but children may prefer to stay and play longer.
- **Especially for Kids:** Playgrounds, a marionnette show, and pony rides.
- **Also See:** LE PANTHÉON, CATACOMBES.

A Bit of History

Religious beginnings – In 1257 a community of Carthusians, with the help of St Louis, laid claim to the area and built a vast monastery with extensive grounds.

Marie de' Medici's palace – After the death of Henri IV, Queen Marie de' Medici, who disliked living at the Louvre, built her own palace on lands purchased from the Duke de Luxembourg. It was modelled on the Palazzo Pitti in Florence, where she had spent her childhood. Construction started in 1615, with a commission in 1621 for **Rubens** to paint 24 large allegorical pictures representing the queen's life (these are now in the Louvre).

The palace as parliament – In 1790 when the monastery was suppressed, the palace gardens were extended to the avenue de l'Observatoire. After serving as a prison during the Terror, the palace successively became home to a parliamentary assembly for the Directory, the Consulate, the Senate and its successor the Peers' Chamber. The Germans occupied the building during World War II. Today the palace is the seat of the **Sénat** (the French Upper House), composed of 319 members.

Luxembourg Palace★★

Exterior

To give a Florentine quality to his design for the palace, architect Salomon de Brosse used bosses, ringed columns and Tuscan capitals, while keeping the typically French ground plan of a central block built around an arcaded courtyard, with a central domed gateway-pavilion. The **Petit Luxembourg**, now the residence of the president of the Senate, comprises the original Hôtel de Luxembourg given to Richelieu by Marie de' Medici and also the cloister and chapel of a convent founded by the queen. The **Musée du Luxembourg** *(enter at 19 rue de Vaugirard;* Ⓞ*during exhibitions Mon–Fri 11am–7pm, until 10pm Fri, Sat–Sun 9am–7pm;* ✎*10€;* ☎*01 42 34 25 95; www.museeduluxembourg. fr)* houses temporary exhibitions in the former orangerie.

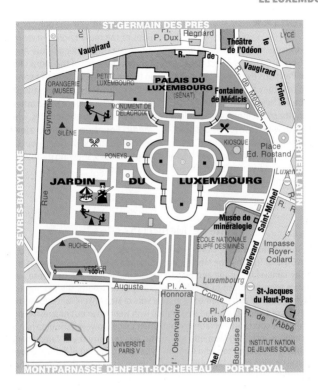

Address Book

WHERE TO STAY AND EAT

☙Turn to the back of the guide for selected hotels, restaurants, bistros and cafés listed by *arrondissement*. This district is in the 5th and 6th arrondissements.

OUTDOOR ACTIVITIES

In the summer, open-air concerts take place in the **Luxembourg Gardens** (boulevard St-Michel side). The **Gardens** also have a shady café-terrace.

OUTDOOR ACTIVITIES FOR CHILDREN

Kids On rue de Guynemer side, the **garden** is very well supplied with swings, merry-go-rounds and even puppet shows. There is a fenced area where young children can play safely and sand pits for all ages. Most of the paying activities are on the expensive side.

NIGHTLIFE

Le Rostand – *6 pl. Edmond-Rostand, 6th arr.* ☎*01 43 54 61 58. Daily.* This elegant café has been popular with generations of students and professors from the Sorbonne for years. Wicker furniture and walls hung with paintings await the cinema-goer or walker who has strayed from the nearby Luxembourg Gardens.

SHOPPING

Christian-Constant – *37 rue d'Assas, 6th arr.* Ⓜ*Notre-Dame-des-Champs. Daily.* ☎*01 53 63 15 15. www.christian constant.com.* Inventor of the Appellation d'Origine Pur Cru, this chocolate, pastry and ice-cream maker is not only one of Paris' best craftsmen, he is also an adventurer of the palate. He creates the most amazing sweets and desserts which both astound and delight the taste buds.

Gardens★★ Kids

🕐*The park is open during daylight hours.* Luxembourg Gardens exert a great draw on Parisians ever since Napoléon decreed that they should be dedicated to children. They attract students and young mothers or nannies with children who stop to watch the tennis or *boules*, to see the *marionnette* puppet shows or listen to the free concerts, to sail boats on the *grand bassin*, or ride miniature ponies. Overall the gardens conform to a formal layout, with the only serpentine lines of the more English-style garden along rue Guynemer and rue Auguste-Comte. The spirit of the monks lives on in the serious tending of trees and bees in the southern end of the park. Statues of the queens of France and other illustrious women line the terraces, while the **Medici Fountain** (1624) has a leafy setting at the far end of a long pool shaded by plane trees, showing its obvious Italian influence.

Marie de' Medici (1573-1642)

Born in Florence in 1573, Marie was the daughter of Francesco de' Medici the Grand Duke of Tuscany. The Medicis were for a time one of the most powerful and wealthy families in Europe and helped to launch the Italian Renaissance which was very soon to spread to France. Very pretty in her youth, she did not marry until the age of 27 and became the second wife of Henri IV of France. It was not a successful marriage as she had to compete with Henri's various mistresses, often shocking the court with her rather colourful language. However, she bore him several children, including Henrietta Maria who was to marry the ill-fated Charles I of England. Her eldest son who went on to become Louis XIII of France following the assassination of his father in 1610 was, however to have the biggest impact on her life.

Although Marie had hitherto shown little interest in politics, she become regent to the infant Louis and during this time the Palace and Gardens of Luxembourg were created for her. Marie referred to her new home as the Palais Médecis but, unfortunately for her, she was unable to enjoy this beautiful 25 hectare estate for very long because when the Regency came to an end in 1617, she was exiled by her son to Blois before the palace and garden was actually finished.

The period of her regency had not been a success. Thought by many to have been aware of the plot to kill her husband, she was considered to be not very bright and was certainly very stubborn. She had been too easily influenced by her maid's husband, the pro Habsburg and pro-Spanish Concini, who was eventually assassinated on the orders of Louis. She had, however, introduced to court the very able Cardinal Richelieu, who was soon to become the king's Chief Minister, and it was he who was instrumental in bringing her back from exile in 1622. By 1625 Marie had installed herself in the recently completed Palace but was only to spend six years in her magnificent new home and garden because she made the fatal mistake of trying to persuade her son to get rid of Richelieu. Louis promised to do this but secretly had no intention of losing such an able minister. The day this happened, November 12th 1630, was to become known as the Day of Deceit or as the French call it, the Journée des Dupes. The result was that the by now obese Marie was exiled again in 1631, spending her last years scheming against Richelieu in Brussels, Amsterdam and Cologne where she died penniless in 1642 and, one would imagine, more than a little peeved by the turn of events.

A reminder of Marie today is the Baroque Fontaine de Médicis created in 1624 and set at the end of an oblong pool in a shady corner of the garden leading towards the Boulevard St-Michel. It acts as a reminder of the woman who was once Queen of France and ended her life as a pauper but nevertheless bequeathed to Paris a wonderful garden to be enjoyed by all.

LA MADELEINE★★

Ⓜ MADELEINE (LINES 8, 12 AND 14) – BUSES: 24, 42, 52, 84, 94

La Madeleine, the church dedicated to St Mary Magdalen, is a distinctive land-mark for its striking Greek temple appearance and its convenient position at the junction of the boulevards connected to Place de la Concorde.

Nearby neighbourhoods: **PLACE DE LA CONCORDE, FAUBOURG ST-HONORÉ, OPÉRA, ST-LAZARE.**

- **Information:** Pyramides welcome centre, 25 rue des Pyramides. ☏08 92 68 30 00 (0.34€ per min). http://en.parisinfo.com.
- ▶ **Orient Yourself:** The Madeleine is at the crossroads of the 1st, 2nd and 8th arrondissements, between the Place de la Concorde and the Gare St-Lazare.
- **Parking:** Underground and street parking surround the church.
- **Don't Miss:** The famous epicure *épiceries,* or food stores, Fauchon and Hédiard in the square behind the church.
- **Organising Your Time:** Allow 45 minutes to visit the church.
- **Also See:** PLACE DE LA CONCORDE, OPÉRA GARNIER, PLACE VENDÔME.

A Bit of History

A Rough Start – Few churches have had such a stormy history as La Madeleine. It was started in 1764 based on the church of St-Louis-des-Invalides, then razed and restarted as a model of the Panthéon. Under Napoléon it was going to be a temple to the glory of the Great Army, but then was restarted again as a Greek temple. In 1814 Louis XVIII decided the Madeleine should be a church, although in 1837 the building was nearly selected for use as Paris' first railway terminal. The church's vicissitudes ended with its

consecration in 1842, although its priest was shot by the Commune in 1871.

Sights

Rue Royale★

The street runs from the Madeleine with its immense pediment raised high on its line of columns, to place de la Concorde. The famous restaurant Maxim's, at no **3**, was formerly the Hôtel de Richelieu. At the end of the 18C the writer Mme de Staël lived at no **6**, and Gabriel at no **8**.

La Madeleine

Address Book

WHERE TO STAY AND EAT

🛏 Turn to the back of the guide for selected hotels, restaurants, bistros and cafés listed by *arrondissement*. This district corresponds to the 1st and the 8th arrondissements.

SHOPPING

Chanel – *31 rue Cambon, 1st arr.* Ⓜ *Madeleine. ☎01 42 86 28 00. www.chanel.com. Closed Sun.* Such is its fame, this legendary house needs no introduction, because it is now synonymous with France's reputation for elegance and luxury throughout the world. Leather sofas and an attentive staff continue to uphold Chanel's tradition of high-quality service and products.

Baccarat – *11 pl. de la Madeleine, 8th arr.* Ⓜ*Madeleine. Other shop: Hôtel Concorde La Fayette 3 Place du Général Koenig, 17th arr. ☎01 42 65 36 26. www.baccarat.fr. Closed Sun and public holidays.* The flagship shop of this prestigious house is a veritable museum of crystal. The simple design and discreetly luxurious surroundings enhance the shapes and forms of the objects on display: vases, jewellery, accessories, artists' creations.

Betjeman and Barton – *23 blvd Malesherbes, 8th arr.* Ⓜ*Madeleine. ☎01 42 65 86 17. www.betjemanandbarton.com. Closed Sun, public holidays and 2 weeks in Aug.* This English-inspired brand of high-quality French teas will delight all tea-enthusiasts by the quality of its products and the elegance of their presentation.

Fauchon – *24–30 pl. de la Madeleine, 8th arr.* Ⓜ*Madeleine. ☎01 70 39 38 00. www.fauchon.fr. Closed Sun.* Delicatessen, pastry maker, high-class grocery and tearoom all rolled into one.

Fauchon sells luxury goods from France and abroad. Very popular with the Parisian bourgeoisie and foreign visitors who come to admire the shop's sumptuous decorations at Christmas time.

Hédiard – *21 pl. de la Madeleine, 8th arr.* Ⓜ*Madeleine. ☎01 43 12 88 88. www.hediard.fr. Closed Sun and public holidays.* At the entrance, a delicious array of exotic fruits and spices invites gourmets to venture into this house of mouth-watering delicacies. The wine cellar, managed by a competent, young wine expert, is also worth a look.

Lalique – *11 rue Royale, 8th arr.* Ⓜ*Concorde or Madeleine. Other address: Carrousel du Louvre, 1st arr. ☎01 53 05 12 12. Closed Sun and public holidays except 8 May, Ascension and 11 Nov.* Lalique's first creations are now owned by collectors from all over the world. Renowned for its specialised work in transparent-satin finishes, this prestigious house manufactures crystal in all shapes and sizes from the famous Bachantes vase to watches and perfume bottles.

Les Trois Quartiers – *23 blvd de la Madeleine, 8th arr. ☎01 42 97 80 06.* Ⓜ*Madeleine. Closed Sun.* This shopping complex right in the centre of the Madeleine quarter is of course devoted to luxury: fashion, beauty, jewellery, gifts, home decoration, sport, etc.

Rue Royale – *rue Royale, 8th arr.* Ⓜ*Concorde or Madeleine.* Fashion (Adolfo Dominguez, Gucci), jewellery (Poiray, Fred), crystal (Christofle, Cristallerie Saint-Louis) or chinaware (Bernardeau), this wide avenue has the flagship shops of many of Paris' most prestigious and most luxurious brand names.

▶ *As you walk up rue Royale towards the Madeleine, make a short detour along rue Saint-Honoré (🛏see Palais-Royal) as far as place Maurice-Barrès.*

Église Notre-Dame-de-l'Assomption

Place Maurice-Barrès. This was the former chapel of the Convent of the Sisters of the Assumption (now a Polish Church). The circular building capped by a dispro-

Camille Saint Saëns (1835-1921)

The great composer Camille Saint Saëns is strongly associated with La Madeleine, as he was the organist there from 1857-1876 during which time he composed many of his most well-known pieces.

An infant prodigy, Saint Saëns was taught music by his mother Clémance and a great-aunt, having lost his father at the age of two. His first public piano performance was given at the tender age of five and by seven he was receiving tuition from established teachers of the day. Around this time he had already begun to compose his own music.

Admitted to the Paris Conservatoire by the age of thirteen, he studied organ and composition. Very soon his work was being admired by such musical talents as Schumann, Berlioz, Gounod and, most importantly, Liszt with whom he enjoyed a close working and personal relationship.

In 1853 he was appointed as organist at Saint Merry and then in 1857 he moved to the same post at La Madeleine where he stayed till 1876. These were significant and well paid posts, which ensured that he was financially secure thus enabling him to contemplate marriage. In 1875 he married Marie-Laure Truffot, a young lady of 19 who bore him two sons – both boys died in unfortunate circumstances and Saint-Saëns left the matrimonial home, blaming her for the deaths.

One of Saint-Saëns best known pieces is 'The Carnival of the Animals' written whilst on holiday with friends in 1886 in which he satirised his fellow musicians portraying them as animals. He would not allow the composition to be performed in public during his lifetime and it was premiered only in 1922. This piece is still greatly enjoyed by children who enjoy the pictures it paints whilst learning a great deal about music. He also wrote poetry, scientific papers and essays about music in which he was not afraid to criticise his contemporaries.

After the death of his mother in 1888 he withdrew from life in Paris and travelled the world occasionally performing and composing. He visited Asia, South America and North Africa and it was in Algiers in 1921 that he died of pneumonia. His body was brought back to Paris to be buried at Montparnasse Cemetery where his tomb can be seen today.

portionately large dome dates from the 17C. Above the main altar is an Annunciation by Vien (18C) and to its right an Adoration of the Magi by Van Loo. In the dome is a fresco of the Assumption by Charles de la Fosse (17C).

La Madeleine★★

A majestic colonnade of Corinthian **columns** – 52 in all, each 20m/65.6ft tall – encloses the church on all sides and supports a sculptured frieze. A monumental flight of steps (28) leads to the imposing peristyle giving on to place de la Madeleine and a splendid **view**★ down rue Royale, the obelisk at the heart of place de la Concorde and beyond to the Palais-Bourbon and the Invalides dome. Reliefs on the bronze doors represent the Ten Commandments. The single nave church has a dark vestibule, decorated with works by Pradier and Rude. The nave is crowned by three domes. Chopin's funeral took place here in 1849. In 1858, Camille Saint-Saëns was hired to play the organ, where he composed some of his most remarkable pieces.

Place de la Madeleine

Next to the church is a flower-market and surrounding it famous epicure *épiceries* or food stores, upscale fashion houses and gourmet restaurants.

LE MARAIS★★★

🇲 CHEMIN-VERT (LINE 8), ST-PAUL (LINE 1) – BUSES: 20, 29, 69, 76, 96

The Marais district is unusual for its fine pre-Revolution residential architecture, including many illustrious mansions restored and converted into museums, and the place des Vosges, the city's oldest square. A popular district ever since its revival in the late 20th century, today the Marais is home to the Jewish quarter, hip and avant-garde fashion boutiques, contemporary art galleries and a lively gay community.

Nearby neighbourhoods: **BEAUBOURG, CHÂTELET-HÔTEL DE VILLE, BASTILLE, ÎLE SAINT-LOUIS.**

- 🛈 **Information:** Carrousel du Louvre welcome centre, Place de la Pyramide Inversée 99, rue de Rivoli. ☎08 92 68 30 00 (0.34€ per min). http://en.parisinfo.com.
- ▶ **Orient Yourself:** The Marais is on the Right Bank, bordered by the place de la Bastille and the Hôtel de Ville, the Seine and the **quartier du Temple**.
- 🅿 **Parking:** Underground parking only, at Hôtel de Ville, Place de la Bastille.
- ⊛ **Don't Miss:** The free permanent collection of the Musée Carnavalet, the architecture of the Place des Vosges, and the antique shops of the Village St-Paul.
- 🕐 **Organising Your Time:** At least a half day, ideally a full day to visit the sights.
- 🄺 **Especially for Kids:** Musée de la Curiosité et de la Magie
- ☾ **Also See:** BEAUBOURG, BASTILLE, HÔTEL DE VILLE.

A Bit of History

In the 13C marshland (*marais*, in French) surrounding the raised rue St-Antoine, a highway since Roman times, was drained and converted into arable land. Philippe Auguste's defensive wall, which also served as a dike, and the Charles V wall ending in the powerful Bastille fortress in the east, brought the Marais within the city limits. Royal patronage began after the flight of **Charles V** from the royal palace to the **Hôtel St-Paul**. Charles VI also took up residence there and by the beginning of the 17C the then place Royale, now place des Vosges, built by Henri IV, had become the focal point of the Marais.

Splendid mansions were erected and decorated by the best contemporary artists. The *hôtel particulier*, a discreet Classically designed private residence, standing between entrance court and garden, developed as a distinctive fea-

Église St-Gervais-St-Protais viewed from rue des Barres

G. Targat/Michelin

Address Book

WHERE TO STAY AND EAT

♿Turn to the back of the guide for selected hotels, restaurants, bistros and cafés listed by *arrondissement*. This district corresponds to the 3rd and 4th arrondissements.

CHARACTER OF LE MARAIS

This old district of Paris, saved by Malraux, is the centre of Paris' Jewish community and the HQ of its gay population. Hip, cool bars have sprung up everywhere (crossroads of rue Vieille-du-Temple and rue Sainte-Croix-de-la-Bretonnerie) and fashion shops line the pavements of rue des Francs-Bourgeois. Rue des Rosiers and the Rue de Ecouffes form the heart of the traditional Jewish neighbourhood, although its scruffy old charm is slowly making way to upscale fashion boutiques. The delightful place du Marché-Sainte-Catherine is surrounded by restaurants, while the arcades of place des Vosges shelter restaurants, fashion shops, antique dealers and art galleries. The northern part of the Marais is quieter and home to many museums. Even further north is the old district of the Temple, traditional home of leather goods dealers and also, more recently, the contemporary art scene.

LATE-NIGHT CAFÉS AND BISTROS

Le Petit Fer à Cheval – *30 rue Vieille-du-Temple, 4th arr.* ☎*01 42 72 47 47. www.cafeine.com. Daily.*
This delightful little bistro, now a very fashionable meeting place, owes its name to its old bar in the shape of a horse shoe. A few tables on the pavement. Often packed in the evening. The restaurant is behind the bar.

L'Ébouillanté – *6 rue des Barres, 4th arr.* ☎*01 42 71 09 69. www.restaurant-ebouillante.com. Closed Mon.*
This little tearoom – possibly the smallest in Paris – has a pleasant terrace on a pedestrian street with a view of the church of Saint-Gervais-Saint-Protais. Pastries, salads and bricks (North African stuffed pancakes). Completely packed on sunny Sunday afternoons.

La Belle Hortense – *31 rue Vieille-du-Temple, 4th arr.* ☎*01 48 04 74 60. www.cafeine.com. Daily.* Named after a novel by Jacques Roubaud, this establishment's shelves are devoted to the marriage between wine and literature. Lively literary discussions liberally washed down with regional produce. At the rear, art exhibitions in the green room. Smart and popular with artists and writers.

La Tartine – *24 rue de Rivoli, 4th arr.* ☎*01 42 72 76 85. Closed two weeks in Aug, 1 Jan and 1 May.* This genuine Parisian bistro will appeal to those who appreciate the old-fashioned, worn smoky look. Taste one of the 100 gold prize winner wines awarded at the Paris Agricultural Show. Ideal meeting place or for a short break.

Le Loir dans la Théière – *3 rue des Rosiers, 4th arr.* Ⓜ*St-Paul.* ☎*01 42 72 90 61. Daily.* This cosy light-green tearoom, equipped with well-worn armchairs, has been serving good home-made snacks, cakes and pastries for over 20 years. The rich hot chocolate is among the best in Paris.

Les Étages – *35 rue Vieille-du-Temple, 4th arr.* ☎*01 42 78 72 00. Daily.* One almost wants to tiptoe into this four-storeyed bar, such is the intimate, almost private atmosphere inside. The succession of amusingly decorated little rooms provides a wide choice for a quiet rest in one of the well-worn sofas.

Les Marronniers – *18 rue des Archives, 4th arr.* ☎*01 40 27 87 72. Daily.* Many visitors to this café never get further than the pleasant terrace outdoors on rue des Archives, overlooking the reformed Billettes Church and the BHV department store. The colourful upstairs room is however well worth a visit. A quiet spot for an afternoon pause. Brunch on Sundays.

Lizard Lounge – *18 rue Bourg-Tibourg, 4th arr.* ☎*01 42 72 81 34. www.cheapblonde.com. Daily. Closed one week in Aug.* Warm, relaxed and intimate, this establishment clearly favours the American bar style. Food is served upstairs and a DJ mixes tunes for dancers in the cellar bar (no cover charge).

Mariage Frères sign

Sacha Finkelsztajn – *27 rue des Rosiers, 4th arr.* ⓜ*St-Paul or Hôtel-de-Ville.* ☎*01 42 72 78 91. www.finkelsztajn.com. Closed Tue and mid-July–mid-Aug.* Following in his father's footsteps, Sacha Finkelsztjan upholds the tradition of Yiddish gastronomy and pastries from Central Europe and Russia in his friendly yellow shop. Strange, foreign spices and flavours, delicious, mouth-watering pastries, cheeses, tarama and olive caviar await visitors.

ART

Galerie Vidal Saint-Phalle – *10 rue du Trésor, 4th arr.* ⓜ*St-Paul.* ☎*01 42 76 06 05. Closed Sun, Mon, public holidays and Aug.* This modern art gallery exhibits the work of well-known artists, little seen in France, such as Rafols-Casamada, Max Neuman, Christopher Le Brun, Pierre Tal-Coat or Martin Assig.

Rue Vieille-du-Temple – *rue Vieille-du-Temple, 3rd arr* ⓜ*Filles-du-Calvaire.* At the top of rue Vieille-du-Temple (from rue du Perche on) and in the surrounding streets (rue Charlot, rue de Poitou), there are a large number of art galleries. Each gallery has a brochure with a map of the neighbourhood.

sells biscuits, jams and chocolate, all tea-flavoured, together with teapots and crockery, without of course forgetting a selection of over 500 teas from some 20 countries.

SHOPPING

Antik Batik – *18 rue de Turenne, 4th arr.* ⓜ*Bastille. St-Paul or Chemin-Vert.* ☎*01 44 78 02 00. Daily. Closed ten days in Aug.* This ethnic style fashion shop sells the creations of designers influenced by Latin America, India and Indonesia. Always colourful, their originality has long found followers among Paris' youth.

Izrael Épicerie du Monde – *30 rue François-Miron,4th arr.* ☎*01 42 72 66 23. Closed Sun, Mon and Aug.* This grocery shop-cum-delicatessen, reminiscent of Ali Baba's cave, is one of the best known in Paris.

ture in French architecture. Women of the world attracted free-thinkers and philosophers through their *salons* – the brilliant conversational groups who frequented their houses. Two churches, St-Paul and St-Gervais, attracted famous preachers and musicians. Gradually, the nobility began to move west to Île St-Louis, then Faubourg St-Germain and Faubourg St-Honoré. After the taking of the Bastille, the quarter was virtually abandoned. In the 20C, the derelict quarter was essentially saved from complete destruction by **André Malraux**, Charles de Gaulle's Culture Minister.

Walking Tours
⚙*See map.*

The Marais can be visited by following two walking tours: the **St-Paul circuit** and the **Marais circuit**.
The descriptions of museums and the collections housed in the most attractive of the hotels are found at the end of the chapter, under the heading *Museums and Other Attractions.*

1 St-Paul Circuit
This walk takes you through the southern part of the Marais.

▶ *Start from the St-Paul metro station.*

La Reine Margot

Marguerite de Valois known affectionately as 'La Reine Margot' was divorced from King Henri IV in 1599 but part of the agreement was for her to keep the title of Queen. Henri quickly married Marie de' Médici who persuaded her new husband to allow Queen Margot, with whom he remained on good terms, back to Court following her exile in the Auvergne. From 1605 she lived in the Hôtel des Sens in the Marais district and was able to continue her lavish lifestyle whilst conducting her many love affairs.

Église St-Paul-St-Louis

99 rue Saint-Antoine. In 1580 the Jesuits were given land by Louis XIII to build a new church (1627-41) modelled on the Gesù Church in Rome. After the demolition of an old church dedicated to St Paul, St-Louis absorbed the parish and became known as the church of St-Paul-St-Louis (1802).

Façade

The tall, Classical orders of superimposed columns screen the dome, a feature favoured by the Jesuits but which was subsequently abandoned when the Sorbonne, Val-de-Grâce and Invalides churches were built.

Interior

It has a single aisle and inter-communicating barrel-vaulted chapels; a cupola with a lantern hovers above the transept crossing and tall Corinthian pilasters line the walls.

This well-lit, spacious church with its ornate decoration and sculptures, drew an elegant congregation attracted by musical excellence (directed by **Marc-Antoine Charpentier**) and eloquent preaching. Many of its rich furnishings were lost at the Revolution. The twin shell-shaped stoups at the entrance were given by **Victor Hugo** who lived nearby in place des Vosges. In the transept three 17C paintings illustrate scenes from the life of St Louis. A fourth painting disappeared, and has been replaced by a painting of *Christ on the Mount of Olives* by Delacroix (1827).

▶ *Leave the church by the left-hand door, as you look towards the altar. A passageway leads to rue St-Paul.*

Village St-Paul

The maze of courtyards bordered by rue des Jardins-St-Paul, rue Charlemagne, rue St-Paul and rue Ave-Maria has been restored and now houses antique shops.

Rue des Jardins St-Paul

The largest surviving fragment of the **Philippe Auguste City Wall** (Enceinte de Philippe Auguste), intersected by two towers, can still be seen in this street, bordered by a high school sports field. To the north is a view of the dome of the St-Paul-St-Louis church.

▶ *Turn right onto rue de l'Avé Maria and continue into rue de l'Hôtel de Ville; go on for c. 80yd/87.5yd.*

Hôtel de Sens★

1 rue du Figuier. The Hôtel de Sens, Hôtel de Cluny and Jacques Cœur's house are the only great surviving private medieval residences in Paris. Constructed between 1475 and 1507 as a residence for the archbishops of Sens, it was used by Cardinal of Guise during the period of the **Catholic League** in the 16C. In 1594 Monsignor de Pellevé died of apoplexy within its walls while a *Te Deum* was being sung in Notre-Dame to celebrate Henri IV's entry into Paris. In 1605, **Queen Margot, Henri IV**'s first wife, came to live here after her long exile in Auvergne. At the age of 53, the former queen had a busy social life and many gallant callers. The house was subsequently occupied by several businesses including the Lyons Stage Coach Company and a candy manufacturer before being purchased by the city and renovated in the early 20th century.

The Flamboyant Gothic porch leads into the courtyard with a square battlemented tower enclosing a spiral staircase. Turrets and beautiful dormer windows adorn the external walls. The **Forney Library** (○*Tue–Fri 1.30pm–8pm,* *Sat 10am–8pm;* ○*public holidays and two weeks in Jul; temporary exhibitions* ○*4€;* ○*01 42 78 14 60.)* is devoted to the Decorative and Fine Arts, and industrial techniques.

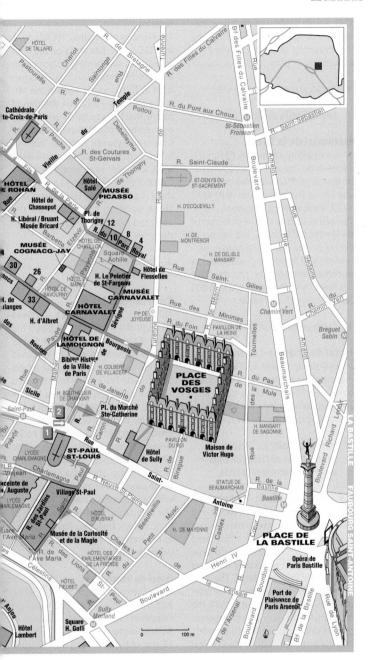

▶ *Return to rue de l'Hôtel de Ville; take first right up rue de Fourcy, then first left.*

Hôtel d'Aumont

7 rue de Jouy. Built in the early 17C by Le Vau, it was later remodelled and enlarged by Mansart, and decorated by **Le Brun** and Simon Vouet. Four successive dukes of Aumont lived there until

1742. A large garden has since been created between the house and the river. It is presently occupied by the Paris administrative court.

▶ *Return to rue de l'Hôtel de Ville; turn right just after Cité Internationale des Arts.*

Mémorial de la Shoah

17 rue Geoffroy-l'Asnier. ♿ ⏱ *Sun–Fri 10am–6pm (Thu until 10pm).* ⊘*On Jewish feast days.* ☞*Guided tour in English, 2nd Sun each month at 3pm.* ☎*01 42 77 44 72. www.memorialdelashoah.org.* Opened in 2005 on the site of Mémorial du Martyr Juif Inconnu, this memorial centre on the Holocaust houses permanent and temporary exhibitions, a documentation library, and the "Mur des Noms" with the names of the 76 000 Jews deported from France.

▶ *Continue on rue Geoffroy-l'Asnier.*

Hôtel de Châlons-Luxembourg

26 rue Geoffroy-l'Asnier. Built in 1610, this mansion once owned by a merchant named Châlons and Madame de Luxembourg has a carved main gate and an interesting stone and brick façade.

▶ *Walk back down rue Geoffroy-l'Asnier to rue de l'Hôtel de Ville; turn right onto rue des Barres.*

Église St-Gervais-St-Protais★

Place St-Gervais. The church stands on a low mound emphasised by steps leading up to the façade. A basilica dedicated to the brothers Gervase and Protase, Roman officers martyred by Nero, has stood on the site since the 6C. The main part of the present building, in Flamboyant Gothic, was completed in 1657. The imposing façade (1616-21) with superimposed Doric, Ionic and Corinthian orders was the first expression of the Classical style in Paris.

The elm in the square was, according to medieval custom, a place where justice was dispensed as well as a place for gambling, employment and rendezvous.

Interior

The Flamboyant vaulting, 16C windows and 16C to 17C fine stalls carved with misericords representing various trades are from the original building. The organ built in 1601 and enlarged in the 18C is the oldest in Paris. The position of organ-master was held successively by members of eight generations of Couperins between 1656 and 1826.

In the third chapel of the north aisle, a 13C low relief altar-front depicts the Death of the Virgin. In the Lady Chapel there is a remarkable Flamboyant keystone, hanging 1.5m/5ft below the vault and forming a circlet 2.5m/8ft in diameter.

▶ *Exit the church onto rue François Miron*

Rue François Miron

This road, once a Roman highway through the marshes, still bears the name of a local magistrate of the time of Henri IV. In the Middle Ages it was lined with the town houses of several abbots of the Île-de-France. The half-timbered and much restored nos **13** and **11** date back to the reign of Louis XI (15C). The beautiful Marie Touchet, mistress of Charles IX, is said to have lived at no **30**. Behind the front building *(access via no 22 rue du Pont-Louis-Philippe, at the end of the corridor)*, there is a tiny Renaissance courtyard remarkably decorated with carved wood panels.

The association for the preservation of Paris' historic buildings has uncovered in the basements of nos **44–46** fine Gothic **cellars**★.

Hôtel de Beauvais★

68 rue François Miron. In 1654 Catherine Bellier, known as One-Eyed Kate, first woman of the bedchamber to Anne of Austria, bestowed her favours on the 16-year-old Louis XIV and was rewarded with a fortune. In addition, for her services, she and her husband Pierre Beauvais and were ennobled and acquired the site of the former (13C) town house of the abbots of Chaalis. They commissioned the architect Lepautre, to build them a splendid mansion from the balcony of which Anne of Austria, the

1785: The Affair of the Diamond Necklace

Cardinal de Rohan had lost favour with Queen Marie-Antoinette. An unscrupulous adventuress, the Comtesse de la Motte, devised an elaborate ruse to persuade Rohan to act as the purchaser of a diamond necklace worth 1 600 000 livres. She convinced him that the Queen wanted to acquire the piece surreptitiously, even arranging a brief meeting in the gardens of Versailles one night, with a prostitute playing the role of the Queen! The plot came to light when the Cardinal was unable to make the payments, and it was discovered that the necklace had been broken up and sold in London. Rohan was tried and acquitted, but deprived of his offices. The Comtesse was sentenced to flogging, branding and life in prison, but instead fled to England and published her kiss-and-tell *Memoires*, vilifying the Queen.

Queen of England, Cardinal Mazarin and dignitaries watched the triumphal entry of Louis XIV and Marie-Thérèse into Paris in 1660. In 1763 seven-year-old Mozart stayed here with his father and sister, courtesy of the Bavarian ambassador.

▶ *Continue along rue François Miron to rue de Fourcy.*

Maison européenne de la Photographie

5–7 rue de Fourcy. ♿ 🕑*Tue–Sun 11am–8pm.* 🕰*Public holidays.* ☑*6€.* ☎*01 44 78 75 00. www.mep-fr.org.*
This centre for contemporary photographic art houses an exhibition area, a large library, a video viewing facility and an auditorium. The mansion between rue François Miron and rue de Fourcy was built in 1704 for Hénault de Contobre, the royal tax collector. Selected as the site for the photography museum, the building was restored and completed by an additional wing on rue de Fourcy. The façade overlooking the street, the period ironwork and the central staircase are fine examples of Classical architecture. The centre exhibits in rotation works representing the cutting edge of photographic art (12 000 in all dating from 1958 onwards).
The Hénault-de-Cantobre hall is devoted to temporary exhibitions on historic and scientific themes. The basement houses a library, video library and an auditorium.

[2] Marais Circuit

▶ *Starting from the St-Paul metro station, follow rue de Sévigné,* then turn first right along rue d'Ormesson.

Place du Marché-Sainte-Catherine★

In the 13C a priory dedicated to St Catherine was built here. In the 18C the square was surrounded by large houses, harmonious in style, with mulberry trees planted in the middle. Today it's a pedestrian zone with outdoor cafés and restaurants.

▶ *Follow rue d'Ormesson to the end, turn right onto rue de Turenne, which leads to rue St-Antoine.*

Rue St-Antoine

From the 14C this unusually wide street became a popular setting for gatherings and celebrations. The area in front of the church was turned into a tilt-yard after the cobbles had been removed and the ground covered with sand.
It was here that in 1559 **Henri II** received a fatal blow to his eye in a tourney with his Scots captain of the guard, Montgomery. The king died in the Hôtel des Tournelles. Montgomery fled but was executed in 1574. In the 17C rue St-Antoine was the city's most elegant thoroughfare.

Hôtel de Sully★

62 rue St-Antoine. 🕰*Public access to the courtyard and gardens only: Tue–Sun 10am–6pm.* ☎*01 44 61 20 00.*
This fine mansion was built in 1625 by Du Cerceau and bought 10 years later by the ageing Sully, former minister of Henri IV. Part of the building is used by the Caisse Nationale des Monuments Historiques

Place des Vosges

et des Sites (Ancient Monuments and Historic Buildings Commission).

The main gate, between massive pavilions, has been restored and opens into the inner **courtyard**★★, an outstanding Louis XIII architectural composition with ordered decoration, carved pediments and dormer windows; allegorical figures represent the Elements and the Seasons. The main building retains its original painted ceilings (1661, restored), which can be seen in the bookstore. Temporary photography exhibitions *(see Jeu de Paume)* are held in the garden wing.

▸ *At the far end of the garden, the Orangery (1625) opens onto place des Vosges.*

Place des Vosges★★★

This is Paris' oldest square. Once the site of the **Hôtel des Tournelles**, acquired by the Crown in 1407 on the assassination of the **Duke of Orléans**, the residence was pulled down by **Catherine de' Medici** after the death of Henri II. Subsequently named **Place Royale**, in 1605, Henri IV transformed it into a vast square surrounded by houses built to a like symmetry. On its completion in 1612,

the Royal Square became the centre of elegance, courtly parades and festivities. Duels were also fought there in spite of **Cardinal Richelieu's** ban. From 1800 it took the name of place des Vosges after the Vosges *département*, the first to pay its taxes.

The 36 houses retain their original symmetrical appearance: two storeys with alternate stone and brick facings are built over the ground-level arcade rising to steeply pitched slate roofs pierced by dormer windows. The soberly decorated King's Pavilion on the south side and the largest house in the square, is balanced by the Queen's Pavilion (Pavillon de la Reine) to the north. Also of interest around the square are no **1 bis** where Madame de Sévigné was born, no **21** where Richelieu lived (1615-27), and no **6** where Victor Hugo spent 16 years *(see Museums)*.

Today the square is a peaceful place to sit, either near the fountains in the central garden or under the cool arcades, where small orchestras play on Sundays.

▸ *Walk through Place des Vosges; turn left onto rue des Francs-Bourgeois*

Rue des Francs-Bourgeois★

This old street was originally known as rue des Poulies after the pulleys *(poulies)* on the looms of the local weavers' shops. It took its present name in 1334 when almshouses were built in it for the poor who were known as the men who pay no tax or *francs bourgeois.*

Hôtel d'Albret

Nos 29 bis and *31.* Built in the 16C for the Duke of Montmorency, Constable of France, this mansion was remodelled in the 17C. It was in this house that the widow of the playwright Scarron, the future **Marquise de Maintenon**, became governess to the children of **Mme de Montespan**, mistress of Louis XIV. The unusual façade was altered in the 18C. The restored mansion houses the city's Cultural Affairs Department.

Noteworthy Hôtels Particuliers

Hôtel Barbes *(no 33)*, with its fine courtyard, was built around 1635. The **Hôtel de Savourny** *(4 rue Elzevir)* has an attractive courtyard. **Hôtel de Coulanges** *(nos 35–37)* now Europe House, is 17C. **Hôtel de Sandreville** *(no 26)* dating from 1586, has been converted into flats. **Hôtel d'Alméras** *(no 30)* has a brick and stone façade hidden behind a gateway featuring curious rams' heads. **Hôtel Poussepin** *(no 34)* now serves as the Swiss Cultural Centre. The **Maison de Jean Hérouet**★ *(54 rue Vieille-du-Temple)*, built around 1510, belonged to the treasurer to Louis XII; it still has its mullioned windows and an elegant corbelled turret. Nearby stood, in the 15C, the **Hôtel Barbette**, the discreet residence of Queen Isabella of Bavaria who began the fashion for masked balls, while the king, Charles VI, resided at the Hôtel St-Paul.

Église de Notre-Dame-des-Blancs-Manteaux

The interior has remarkable woodwork – an inner door, organ loft, communion table and a magnificent Flemish **pulpit**★ with marquetry panels inlaid with ivory and pewter, framed in gilded and fretted woodwork, typical of the period's Rococo style (1749).

The Detail of the low relief depicting Horses of Apollo, Hôtel de Rohan

Rue des Archives

A peaceful street which houses the national archives behind the façades of its fine mansions.

Hôtel de Soubise★★

No 58. This is the oldest of the mansions, dating from the 14C. The **gateway**★, known as the **porte Clisson**, is flanked by a pair of corbelled turrets *(58 rue des Archives)*.

From 1705 to 1709 the mansion was remodelled into an elegant palace with a majestic horseshoe-shaped **courtyard**★★. The Musée de l'Histoire de France is housed in the building (*see Museums and Other Attractions*).

Hôtel de Guénégaud★★

No 60. This mansion, built c 1650 by **Mansart**, was lightly remodelled in the 18C and beautifully restored in the 20C. With its plain harmonious lines, its majestic staircase and its small formal garden, it is one of the finest houses of the Marais, now home to the Musée de la Chasse (*see Museums and Other Attractions*).

▶ *Exit the Hôtel; turn left onto rue des Quatre-Fils.*

Note the garden and rear façade of the mansion.

Cathédrale Ste-Croix-de-Paris★

Rue Charlot. ⏰*Sun 10am–1pm; weekdays by appointment with the parish priest.* ☎*01 44 59 23 50.*

This much-restored church was erected in 1624 as a Capuchin monastery chapel and was attended by Mme de Sévigné. It is now the Armenian church. The chancel is adorned with 18C gilded panelling from the former **Billettes Church**. To the left stands a remarkable **statue**★ of St Francis of Assisi by Germain Pilon (16C).

▶ *Go back to rue de Quatre-Fils; continue until it meets rue Vielle-du-Temple.*

Hôtel de Rohan★★

87 rue Vieille-du-Temple. ◷*Wed–Mon 10am–12.30pm, 2pm–5.30pm, Sat–Sun 2.30pm–5.30pm.* ◷*Public holidays.* ◷*3€; free 1st Sun in month.* ☎*01 40 27 60 96.*
In 1705 Delamair started work on the mansion simultaneously with the Hôtel de Soubise, for the Soubise's son, the Bishop of Strasbourg, who later became Cardinal de Rohan. It was successively the residence of four cardinals of the Rohan family, all of whom were bishops of Strasbourg. The last one lived there in grand style until his disgrace in the affair of the queen's necklace (1785). It was occupied by the state press (Imprimerie Nationale) under Napoléon and later in 1927 by the national archives. The main façade gives onto the garden which serves both properties.
The interior decoration dates from 1750, with Gobelin tapestries in the entrance hall. A staircase leads to the Cardinals' **apartments**★. The first salons are adorned with Beauvais tapestries after drawings attributed to Boucher. Also of interest are the Gold Salon and the amusing small Monkey Room with animal decorations by Christophe Huet, and the delicate panelling and wall hangings of the smaller rooms.

▶ *Follow rue de la Perle.*

Place de Thorigny

This crossroads is a good place to sit down and admire the façades of the **Hôtel de Chassepot** at 3–5 rue de la Perle, and at no 1 in the same street, of the **Hôtel Libéral Bruant**. This elegant mansion has been restored to its original appearance. In rue Thorigny, at no 5, is the **Hôtel Salé**, which contains the Picasso Museum (◐*see Museums and Other Attractions*).

Rue du Parc-Royal

The 17C mansions lining the street opposite Léopold-Achille Square form a remarkable architectural group notwithstanding remodelling: **Canillac** (no **4**), **Duret-de-Chevry** (no **8**, extensively restored), **Vigny** (no **10**, a National Documentation Centre) and **Croisilles** (no **12**) which houses the library and archives of France's historic buildings commission.

▶ *Return to rue des Francs-Bourgeois via rue Payenne or rue de Sévigné.*

Rue Payenne

Square Georges-Cain, lined by the orangery and the façade of the Hôtel St-Fargeau, is laid as a lapidary garden for the adjoining Musée Carnavalet. The neighbouring **Hôtel de Marle** or **de Polastron-Polignac** *(no* **11***)* has a fine mask above the entrance and a keel-shaped roof attributed to Philibert Delorme; once owned by the Countess of Polignac, the governess of Marie-Antoinette's children, this house now accommodates a Swedish Cultural Centre. The architect François Mansart died at no **5**. The old gateway was uncovered during restoration.

Rue de Sévigné

Beyond the Hôtel Carnavalet is the **Hôtel Le-Peletier-de-Saint-Fargeau** *(no* **29***)* built by Pierre Bullet (1686-90) and named after its owner who voted for Louis XVI's death sentence. Number **52**, the much-restored **Hôtel de Flesselles**, bears the name of Paris' last provost.

Hôtel Carnavalet★★

23 rue de Sévigné. Constructed in 1548 for Jacques des Ligneris, president of Parliament, the mansion was given its present appearance by **François Mansart** in 1655. Marie de Rabutin, the **Marquise de Sévigné**, author of the famous *Letters* which give a lucid picture of day-to-day events, lived in the house from 1677 to 1696.
In 1866, the city of Paris acquired the mansion as a home for its historic collections, adding the buildings surrounding the garden courts.

Exterior
Jean Goujon carved the lions at the main entrance which is 16C, and the

keystone cornucopia. The supporting globe was later recarved into a carnival mask in allusion to the mansion's name. The **statue** of Louis XIV in the courtyard by **Coysevox**, the only surviving pre-Revolution royal statue, was originally at the Hôtel de Ville.

> ▶ *Follow rue des Francs-Bourgeois to the right, and turn left onto rue Pavée.*

Hôtel de Lamoignon★
24 rue Pavée. The Hôtel d'Angoulême, which was built around 1585 for Diane of France, the legitimised daughter of Henri II, was bought in 1658 by Lamoignon, president of the first Parliament in Paris. There he entertained Racine, Mme de Sévigné, and Bourdaloue. in 1763 it became the **Bibliothèque historique de la ville de Paris**, a library rich in French Revolution documents; the painted ceiling of its **reading room** is one of the finest in Paris.

> ▶ *Follow rue Pavée south until it turns right into rue des Rosiers.*

Rue des Rosiers
This street, together with the adjoining rue des Écouffes, which derives its name from a pawnbroker's shop sign, is the main axis of the **Jewish quarter** which has grown up in Paris' 4th arrondissement.

Rue Vieille-du-Temple and **rue du Roi-de-Sicile** are full of small shops selling the latest fashions, jewellery and decorative items. Rue du Roi-de-Sicile ends in a small, café-lined square, **place du Bourg-Tibourg**.

Museums and Other Attractions

Maison de Victor Hugo★
6 place des Vosges. ◷*Tue–Sun 10am–6pm.* ◷*Public holidays.* ⊛*Charge for temporary exhibitions.* ☎*01 42 72 10 16.* Home to the writer from 1832 to 1848 and turned into a museum in 1903, this residence overlooking the Place des Vosges features drawings by Hugo himself as well as furniture and objects from his various residences in France and in

MUSÉE CARNAVALET

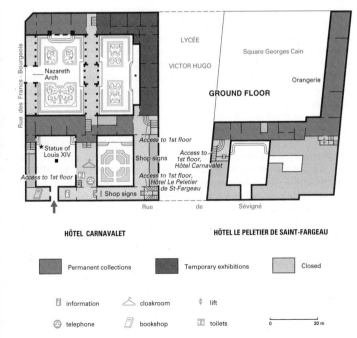

Rue des Francs - Bourgeois

LYCÉE

Square Georges Cain

Nazareth Arch

VICTOR HUGO

Orangerie

GROUND FLOOR

★Statue of Louis XIV

Access to 1st floor

Access to 1st floor, Hôtel Carnavalet

Shop signs

Access to 1st floor

Access to 1st floor, Hôtel Le Peletier de St-Fargeau

Shop signs

Rue   de   Sévigné

HÔTEL CARNAVALET

HÔTEL LE PELETIER DE SAINT-FARGEAU

Permanent collections	Temporary exhibitions	Closed

ℹ information   △ cloakroom   ↕ lift

⊚ telephone   📖 bookshop   🚻 toilets   0   20 m

exile abroad which show his talent as a decorator.

Musée de la Curiosité et de la Magie★ [Kids]

11 rue Saint-Paul. ⏱Wed and Sat–Sun 2pm–7pm. Call for information during school holiday periods. ☜9€ (children 7€). ☎01 42 72 13 26. www.museedela magie.com.

The collection of ingenious accessories dispels some of the mystery from the art of magic, conjuring, legerdemain, prestidigitation and sleight-of-hand. Midway through the museum, a stage, a few seats and a number of tiers provide the setting for regular magic shows *(about 30min; included in the entry fee).*

Musée d'Art et d'Histoire du Judaïsme★★

Hôtel de Saint-Aignan, 71 rue du Temple. ♿⏱Mon–Fri 11am–6pm, Sun and public holidays 10am–6pm. ⏱1 Jan, 1 May, 25 Dec, Jewish holidays. ☜6.80€. ☎01 53 01 86 60. www.mahj.org.

An ultra-modern museum in an historical setting, presenting both ancient and contemporary exhibits. Accompanying explicative notes provide the visitor with an in-depth view of Jewish culture.

The Jewish religion and diaspora

The most important and unifying elements of the faith throughout the centuries are the Law (the Torah), religious teaching and cultural festivals. The history of the Jewish diaspora is one of journeys and exiles. Galleries illustrate the settlement of the Jews in France in the Middle Ages, and in Italy from the Renaissance to the 18C, showing the integration of the Jewish community, the problem of discrimination and their everyday life. There are also rooms dedicated to the two separately evolved communities, the Sephardic Jews from Muslim Spain and the Ashkenazic Jews from Eastern Europe.

Contemporary Judaism

Under the First Empire, the Age of Enlightenment in the early 19C favoured the emancipation of the Jews in France, but by the end of the century modern anti-Semitism was all too present, with the Dreyfus affair and the Deportation leading to the creation of Zionism. This exhibition finishes in galleries 11 and 13 with an illustration of Jewish influence on 20C art and the contemporary Jewish world (temporary exhibitions).

Musée de l'Histoire de France★

Hôtel de Soubise, 60 rue des Francs-Bourgeois. ⏱Mon, Wed–Fri 10am–12.30pm, 2pm–5.30pm, Sat–Sun 2pm–5.30pm. ☎01 40 27 60 96. www.archivesnation ales.culture.gouv.fr/chan.

The building is a museum in its own right and has retained its original décor.

The apartments★★

Delamair's Classical architectural style, typical of Louis XIV's reign (simple façade, vast courtyard and suite of rooms), contrasts with Boffrand's extravagant Rococo decoration under Louis XV, when formal décor gave way to more intimate interiors. Between 1735 and 1740 the most gifted painters (Boucher, Natoire, Van Loo) and sculptors of the period worked under Boffrand, a pupil of Mansart, to decorate with all the delicacy and flourish of the Rococo style as was fashionable at Versailles.

On the first floor, beside the Guise Chapel is the Salle des Gardes (guardroom) which served as the League headquarters during the Wars of Religion. The Assembly rooms, decorated with painted panels by Carl Van Loo and Boucher, contain a model of the Bastille made with stones from the fortress .

Chambre de la Princesse

This spectacular, dazzling interior has survived intact. A large bed with baldaquin furnishes this splendid room fitted with white and gold panelling. Two superb paintings by Boucher hang on either side of the bed. In the **Salon ovale de la Princesse** the masterful display of Rococo is at its most refined, with the sky-blue ceiling contrasting well with Nattier's feminine hues in his depiction of the *Story of Psyche*. In the **Petite chambre de la Princesse** fine roundels illustrate the Elements, and panels by Van Loo, Restout, Trémolières and Boucher are set over the doors.

Musée de la Chasse et de la Nature

Hôtel Guénégaud, 60 rue des Archives. *Tue–Sun 11am–6pm.* *Public holidays.* 6€. 01 53 01 92 40. www.chasse nature.org.

Housed in a magnificent 17C mansion designed by François Mansart, the collection includes arms from prehistory to the 19C and trophies and souvenirs from big game expeditions. Tapestries, ceramics and sculptures on the theme of the hunt are also on view.

Musée Picasso★★

Hôtel Salé, 5 rue de Thorigny. *Apr–Sept, Wed–Mon 9.30am–6pm; Oct–Mar, Wed–Mon 9.30am–5.30pm.* *1 Jan and 25 Dec.* 6.50€ (under-18s no charge; no charge 1st Sun of month). 01 42 71 25 21. www.musee-picasso.fr.

The house was originally built from 1656 to 1659 for a salt tax collector, hence its name. Restored in the 70s by the architect Simounet, the mansion became the Picasso Museum in 1985. Inside, the main **staircase**★ with its spacious stairwell and splendid wrought-iron-work rises majestically to the first floor and a profusely carved ceiling.

The museum's origins

One of the dominant figures of 20C art, Pablo Ruiz Picasso (1881-1973) was born in Malaga. After studying art in Barcelona and Madrid, young Picasso settled in France at the age of 23, where he pursued his long and active career. Between 1936 and 1955, Picasso lived at 7 rue des Grands Augustins (6th), where he painted Guernica (1937). Following his death at Mougins in 1973, Picasso's heirs donated an outstanding collection of the artist's works in lieu of estate duties, comprising over 250 paintings, sculptures, collages, 3 000 drawings and engravings, and 88 ceramics.

Tour

To follow the chronological order of Picasso's prodigiously productive and long painting career, start on the first floor with his *Self Portrait* from the Blue Period. All the artist's styles and techniques are represented in his sketches for *Les Demoiselles d'Avignon, Still Life with Cane Chair* and *Pipes of Pan* and other favourite subjects such as female nudes, travelling acrobats and portraits of couples and of his own family. Also exhibited is Picasso's private collection of works by his friends and contemporaries such as Braque, **Cézanne** and **Rousseau**. There is an unusual fountain by Simounet in the formal public garden beyond the museum's garden.

Cognacq-Jay Museum★★

Hôtel Donon, 8 rue Elzévir. *Tue–Sun 10am–6 pm.* *Public holidays.* 01 40 27 07 21. www.cognacq-jay.paris.fr.

This collection of 18C European art was bequeathed to the city of Paris by Ernest Cognacq (1839-1928), founder of the **Samaritaine department store**. The **Hôtel Donon** provides a worthy setting for the collection. The late 16C main part of the building with its tall roof is typical of Philibert Delorme's syle. In the panelled ground-floor rooms is a selection of drawings by Watteau and paintings by Rembrandt, Ruisdael, Largillière and Chardin. Portraits bring to life some of the personalities of Louis XV's court: his queen, Marie Leczinska (1703-68), their daughter Madame Adélaïde, and Alexandrine, the daughter of **Madame de Pompadour**, Louis XV's mistress.

On the second floor, watercolours by Mallet illustrate the austere but elegant life of the Bourgeoisie under **Louis XVI** (1774-92). In the Oval Room Fragonard's portrayals of children and Rococo pastoral pictures contrast with terracottas by Lemoyen and paintings by Greuze. The sculpture gallery groups together works showing a strong Italian influence (Falconet, Houdon and Clodion) alongside paintings by Hubert Robert and Boucher.

The third floor is dedicated to Mme Vigée-Lebrun and her period, pastels including a self-portrait by La Tour, and British School paintings. In the carved oak-panelled salon are an oval table and *commode* signed RVLC by Roger Vandercruse, better known as Lacroix, and a pair of *commodes* by Martin Carlin. The study is hung with Venetian paintings, including Guardi's *St Mark's*

Square. Showcases display Meissen and Sèvres porcelain, snuffboxes and *bonbonnières.*

Musée Carnavalet-Histoire de Paris★★

Hôtel Carnavalet, 23 rue de Sévigné. ◔*Tue–Sun 10am–6pm.* ◕*Some public holidays.* ◌*Varying prices for temporary exhibitions.* ☎*01 44 59 58 58. www.carnavalet.paris.fr.*

The museum illustrating the history of Paris is housed in two separate mansions, the Hôtel Carnavalet and the Hôtel Le-Peletier-St-Fargeau: the variety of its exhibits make it one of the capital's most attractive museums.

Paris from its tribal origins to the end of the Middle Ages is vividly depicted by means of archaeological finds such as the wooden **Neolithic canoes** found in Bercy in 1999; the oldest dates from 4 400 BC.

The museum also brings back to life some of the main events of the capital's history, such as the French Revolution or the Commune.

The museum is particularly rich in decorative arts: painted and carved wood panelling and ceilings from other Parisian mansions have been reconstructed here (drawing rooms from the Hôtel de la Rivière painted by Lebrun, Belle-Époque décor of the Fouquet jewellery shop).

Literary history is illustrated by many portraits, pieces of furniture and souvenirs evoking famous writers (Marcel Proust's bedroom).

MARCHÉ AUX PUCES★

Ⓜ PORTE-DE-CLIGNANCOURT (LINE 4) – BUS: 85

Looking for old furniture, medals, uniforms, dolls or a hat that was once fashionable? The Saint-Ouen flea markets are a source of never-ending interest. They are open at weekends and on Mondays all year round, but beware pickpockets and fake Rolexes from street vendors. Organised guided group or individual visits are available: ☎01 40 11 77 36; www.st-ouen-tourisme.com.

- ⓘ **Information:** Espace Accueil et Information du Marché aux Puces, 7 impasse Simon – 93400 Saint-Ouen. ☎01 58 61 22 90. www.marchesauxpuces.fr.
- ▶ **Orient Yourself:** The fleamarket is actually just outside Paris, in the suburb of St-Ouen, a five-min walk from the metro Clignancourt (go north under the boulevard Périphérique to reach the markets).
- Ⓟ **Parking:** There is underground parking at the markets along rue des Rosiers.
- ☺ **Don't Miss:** The lively atmosphere at the flea market bistros.
- Ⓞ **Organising Your Time:** Allow at least three hours to wander the market stalls and soak up the atmosphere.
- ☞ **Also See:** MONTMARTRE, SACRÉ-COEUR.

Visit

This is the most famous flea market in Paris and is located on the northern edge of the city on the Av. de la Porte de Clignancourt. and held every Sat, Sun and Mon from 10am–6pm. Flea markets are starting to look more like shops these days, although the neighbourhood retains the atmosphere of an unusual and picturesque village. There are between 2 500 and 3 000 stalls in total and **twelve** particular markets. If you search long enough bargain carefully, you may find something to treasure among the assorted bric-a-brac – a real collector's paradise.

Marché Vernaison

One of the oldest markets in the *Puces*, which goes by the name of its original proprietor. In about 1885 he rented a part of his property to dealers, known as *chiff-tir* or *biffins* (rag-pickers), who resold the objects they collected. This is

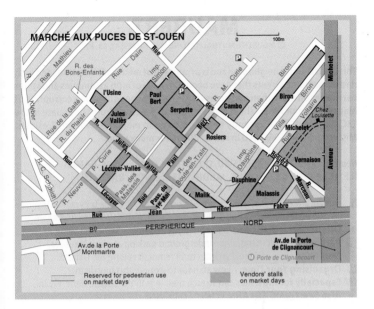

MARCHÉ AUX PUCES DE ST-OUEN

Reserved for pedestrian use on market days

Vendors' stalls on market days

still true today: knick-knacks, furniture, vintage fabrics.

Marché Antica
Antique furniture collections.

Marché Biron★
Founded in 1925 by 70 antique dealers. Don't be put off by appearances on seeing the first street, as the second is a treasure-trove of period furniture, reminiscent of grand châteaux. This is the smartest of the flea markets, with a warm, friendly atmosphere.

Marché Cambo
Antique furniture, paintings.

Marché Jules Vallès
Bric-a-brac. Has a reputation as the market with the most affordable prices.

Marché Lécuyer-Vallès
Bottom-of-the-pile goods, but worth a look for special, unexpected finds.

Marché Malik
Second-hand clothes, ethnic arts and crafts, glasses, records.

Marché Paul-Bert
Open-air market of retro and rustic furniture, garden accessories, and oversized architectural remnants. The tourism office for the market is located here.

Marché des Rosiers
Furniture, knick-knacks, paintings. Nearly all antique dealers are specialists in glass paste jewellery and Art Nouveau furniture.

Marché Serpette
One of the most recent markets. Old and country furniture, knick-knacks, old weapons.

Marché Dauphine★
Specialised in old books, prints, and paintings. There's also furniture and bric-a-brac to suit every taste and from all periods. This is the most up-to-date market, not only the setting (metal-framed architecture on two floors with a glass roof), but also in the way it trades: a certificate is provided for buyers who request it (there is an independent valuation office in rue des Rosiers).

Mallassis
Antique furniture. Inside there is a terrace restaurant.
The adjoining streets are full of temporary markets selling clothes of all descriptions.

MAUBERT

Ⓜ MAUBERT-MUTUALITÉ (LINE 10) – BUSES: 47, 63, 87

This Latin Quarter neighbourhood is a fragment of medieval Paris, threaded with narrow, winding streets that have been the scene of mob assemblies and street barricades on more than one occasion. Its name is thought to be a corruption of Maître Albert or Albert the Great who taught theology from the square in the 13C. "La Maube" has recently been subjected to major restoration. President Mitterrand (1916-96) lived in rue de Bièvre for many years.

Nearby neighbourhoods: **JUSSIEU, QUARTIER LATIN, NOTRE-DAME, ÎLE DE LA CITÉ, ÎLE ST-LOUIS, JARDIN DES PLANTES, BASTILLE.**

🛈 **Information:** Carrousel du Louvre welcome centre, Place de la Pyramide Inversée 99, rue de Rivoli. ☎0892 68 3000 (0.34€ per min). http://en.parisinfo.com.
▶ **Orient Yourself:** Located in the 5th arrondissement along the Seine.
🅿 **Parking:** Difficult in this area; underground parking at place Maubert.
👁 **Don't Miss:** The medieval architectural remnants along rue Galand.
🕐 **Organising Your Time:** Allow an hour to explore this tiny district.
Kids **Especially for Kids:** Kids can stretch their legs in the Square René-Vivani.
👣 **Also See:** QUARTIER LATIN, CLUNY, SORBONNE.

Walking Tour
👣*See map.*

▶ *Start by walking along the river.*

Quai de la Tournelle
Just before the Pont de l'Archevêché (1828) are a line of old houses with a splendid **view**★★★ of Notre-Dame from the bridge. Opposite Île St-Louis, the **Pont de la Tournelle** boasts a striking statue of St Geneviève by Landowski. Number 15, opposite the bridge, is the very old Tour d'Argent restaurant where Henri IV is said to have discovered the fork.

Quai de Montebello
In the Middle Ages, wood for building and heating was floated on rafts down to Paris and stored at the Port-aux-Bûches between the Petit Pont and the **Pont au Double.**

▶ *Just after the square, turn left.*

Square René-Viviani
The small church garden contains one of the oldest trees in Paris, a Robinia or false acacia planted in 1601. The **view**★★★ is remarkable: the church of St-Julien itself stands out behind a curtain of trees; **rue St-Julien-le-Pauvre** bustles with life beneath a picturesque jumble of roofs; the Île de la Cité; and finally, above all, Notre-Dame is seen from its best angle.

Église St-Julien-le-Pauvre★
1 rue St-Julien-le-Pauvre. The present building was constructed at the same time as Notre-Dame. It is named after Saint Julian the Confessor, the medieval Bishop of Le Mans, also known as the Poor because he gave so much away.

Rue St-Julien le Pauvre
Number 14 dates from the 17C and used to be the house of the governor of the Petit Châtelet. The **view**★★ of St-Séverin across the entrance to rue Galande is one of the most picturesque of old Paris, and still a popular subject for painters.

Rue Galande
At nos **54-46** cellars and pointed medieval arches have been unearthed; a carved stone above the door of no **42** shows St Julian the Hospitaller in his boat. Note the 15C gable of no **31**. **Rue du Fouarre** was one of the places where, in the Middle Ages, public lectures were given by the university in the open air attended by students seated

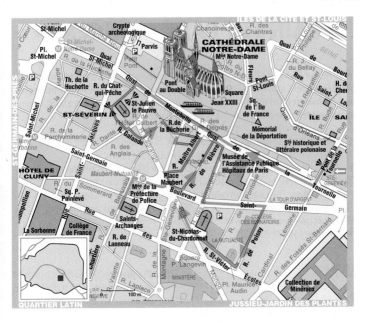

on bundles of straw *(fouarre)*. Dante is said to have attended lectures in this street in 1304.

▶ *Cross rue Lagrange, follow rue de l'Hôtel-Colbert to rue de la Bûcherie.*

Winding Streets

The École d'Administration on the **rue de la Bûcherie** now occupies the premises of the first Medical School founded in the 15C. **Impasse Maubert** was home to a Greek College founded in the in 1206 and the house where the infamous Marquise de Brinvilliers concocted her poisons in the 17C. The old houses of the **rue Maître-Albert** rise above a network of underground passages down to the banks of the Seine that sheltered rogues and conspirators up until the 20C. Since the early Middle Ages, the **Place Maubert** has been a traditional rallying point for students, with barricades at times. The **rue de Bièvre** is a paved-over tributary of the Seine, once used by tanners and boatmen.

▶ *Coming out onto quai de la Tournelle, turn right and then right again along rue des Bernardins until it joins boulevard St-Germain. Turn left, then right onto rue de Poissy.*

Rue de Poissy

This street was laid through the gardens of the former **Bernardins College**, founded in 1246 to educate monks and taken over by the Cistercians in the 14C. Since 1845 the buildings have served as a fire station (nos 18–24 rue de Poissy). From the road, one catches a glimpse of the refectory with its three ogive-vaulted aisles. ⊶ *Closed to the public.*

▶ *Turn right.*

Église St-Nicolas-du-Chardonnet

23 rue Bernadins. A chapel was constructed in what was a field of thistles (chardons) in the 13C. In 1656 it was replaced by the present building; the façade was completed only in 1934.

▶ *Return to place Maubert via rue Monge. Turn left along rue Jean-de-Beauvais.*

Église des Sts-Archanges

9 bis rue Jean-de-Beauvais. Purchased by the Romanian Orthodox Church in 1882, this much restored chapel is dedicated to the archangels Michael, Gabriel and Raphael.

PLAINE ET PARC MONCEAU★★

Ⓜ MONCEAU (LINE 2) – BUSES: 30, 84, 94

In 1778 the Duke of Chartres, the future Philippe-Égalité, commissioned the painter-writer Carmontelle to design a garden inspired by the romantic English and German style of the day. A century later elegant mansions were built around its perimeter, several of which are now museums.

- **ℹ Information:** Pyramides welcome centre, 25 rue des Pyramides. ☎08 92 68 30 00 (0.34 per min). http://en.parisinfo.com.
- ▶ **Orient Yourself:** Located to the north of the Champs-Elysées district.
- 🅿 **Parking:** This residential district has plenty of street parking.
- 👁 **Don't Miss:** The beautiful café of the Jacqumart-André Museum.
- 🕐 **Organizing Your Time:** Allow a half day to visit the park and museums.
- **Kids Especially for Kids:** The Parc Monceau has large play areas for children.
- ♿ **Also See:** CHAMPS-ELYSÉES.

Visit

Parc Monceau★

Entrance via the rotunda (north, next to the metro station). The rotunda, with its fine wrought-iron gates at the entrance, known as the Chartres Pavilion, part of Ledoux's 18C toll-houses built in the **Farmers-General perimeter wall**.

▶ *Leaving the park, follow avenue Van-Dyck, then turn right onto rue de Courcelles and left onto rue Daru.*

Cathédrale St-Alexandre-Nevsky

12 rue Daru. 🕐*Tue, Fri, Sun 3pm–5pm.* ☎*01 42 27 37 34.*

Elaborate entrance gate of Parc Monceau

H. Le Gac/MICHELIN

This, the Russian Orthodox Church of Paris, was erected in 1860 in the Russian neo-Byzantine style.

Museums

Musée Cernuschi★

7 avenue Vélasquez. ♿🕐*Tue–Sun 10am–6pm.* 🕐*Public holidays.* ☎*01 53 96 21 50. Free entry. www.cernuschi.paris.fr.*
The banker Henri Cernuschi bequeathed his house and extensive collection of Oriental art to the City of Paris in 1896.

Musée Nissim de Camondo★★

63 rue de Monceau. 🕐*Wed–Sun 10am–5.30pm (last admission 30min before closing).* 🕐*1 Jan, 1 May, 15 Aug and 25 Dec.* ⊙*6€ (inc. audio guide).* ☎*01 53 89 06 .50. www.lesartsdecoratifs.fr.*
In 1936 Count de Camondo presented his house and art collection to the nation.

Musée Jacquemart-André★★

158 boulevard Haussmann. ♿🕐*Daily 10am–6pm (last admission 30min before closing).* ⊙*9.50€.* ☎*01 42 89 04 91. www.musee-jacquemart-andre.com.*
This elegant late 19C house formerly owned by the avid art collectors Edouard André and Nélie Jacquemart contains outstanding 18C European and Italian Renaissance art.

Address Book

LEISURE ACTIVITIES

Park Monceau – 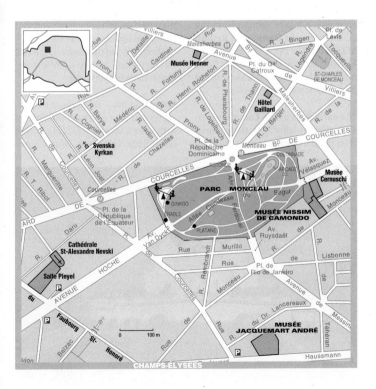There are children's play areas scattered throughout the park, such as roller skating, sandpits and merry-go-rounds.

Salle Cortot – *78 rue Cardinet, 17th arr. ☎01 47 63 80 16. www.ecolenormalecortot.com. All year 8.30am–1.30pm.* This handsome room with seating for 400, now a listed monument, was designed by Auguste and Gustave Perret in 1929. It is part of the Paris School of Music and puts on concerts of classical music, but also masterclasses with artists such as Rostropovitch, François-René Duchâble, Felicity Lott. Some of the best acoustics in Paris.

ART AND CHOCOLATE

Galerie Lelong – *13 rue Téhéran, 8th arr. ⓂMiromesnil. ☎01 45 63 13 19. www.galerie-lelong.com. Closed Aug.* One of Paris' most famous galleries. It displays work by several international artists: Alechinsky, Appel, James Brown, Chillida, Dibbets, Judd, Kounellis, Michaux, Miro, Pignon-Ernest, Rebeyrolle, Saura, Scully, Tàpies…

Maison du Chocolat – *225 rue du Faubourg St-Honoré, 8th arr. ⓂTernes. ☎01 42 27 39 44. www.lamaisonduchocolat.com. Closed Sun and public holidays.* This house of chocolate is a Parisian favourite. Try the delectable *ganaches* elegantly displayed pastries, and miss their famously thick hot chocolate.

WHERE TO STAY AND EAT

Turn to the back of the guide for selected hotels, restaurants, bistros and cafés listed by *arrondissement*. This district lies in the 17th arrondissement.

MONTMARTRE★★★

Ⓜ ANVERS (LINE 2), ABBESSES (LINE 12), LAMARCK-CAULAINCOURT (LINE 12) –
BUSES: 30, 54, 67, MONTMARTROBUS

The Butte (or hillock) as it is known locally, is the part of Paris most full of contrasts – anonymous boulevards run close to delightful village streets and courts, steep stone steps lead to open terraces, pilgrims tread the streets beside nightclub revellers. On the southern side, a funicular provides access to one of Paris' most famous landmarks: Sacré-Cœur.

Nearby neighbourhoods: **PIGALLE.**

- 🅸 **Information:** 21 Place du Tertre ☎08 92 68 30 00. http://en.parisinfo.com.
- ▶ **Orient Yourself:** Montmartre is at the far north edge of the city, in the 18th arr.
- 🅿 **Parking:** Best along the boulevards from Anvers to Blanche metro stations.
- 🕙 **Don't Miss:** The adorable houses around the Clos du Montmartre vineyard.
- 🕒 **Organizing Your Time:** Allow at least a half day to explore the Butte.
- 🄺🄸🄳🅂 **Especially for Kids:** The carrousel and playground in the Square Willette.
- 🕯**Also See:** PIGALLE, MARCHÉ AUX PUCES.

A Bit of History

Martyrs' Mound – In Roman times, Montmartre had two hill-top temples dedicated to Mercury and Mars. It was known as martyrs' mound from the 8C after after **St Denis**, first **Bishop of Lutetia**, was beheaded here by the Romans. According to legend, St Denis picked up his head and walked to the place now known as St-Denis.

The early days of the Commune – In 1871, after the fall of Paris, the working-class people of Montmartre collected 171 cannons on the hill to prevent their capture by the Prussians. The new royalist government – that had officially capitulated – tried to seize the cannons from the "rebels" on 18 March but the crowd seized the generals and shot them. This bloody episode was to mark the beginning of the Commune: a civil war that lasted until the Communards' defeat three months later.

Bohemian life – Throughout the 19C, artists and men of letters were drawn to the free-and-easy way of life as lived on the Butte. Composers, writers, paint-

S. Sauvignier/MICHELIN

Basilique du Sacré-Cœur atop Montmartre

ers and poets made up the great 1871-1914 generation of young artists seeking inspiration on place Pigalle, where artists' models and seamstresses led a Bohemian existence. In the early days, poets congregated at Le Chat Noir, enlivened with songs by **Aristide Bruant**, poems by Charles Cros and Jehan Rictus, drawings by André Gill and **Toulouse-Lautrec**. The Moulin Rouge opened in 1889 with Cancan star Louise Weber, nicknamed *La Goulue*. The Butte, thanks to the **Lapin Agile** café and **Bateau-Lavoir** studios, remained until the outbreak of the Great War the capital's literary and artistic centre. As the next generation of artists and émigrés congregated in Montparnasse, Montmartre abandoned itself to its nocturnal entertainments. Today Montmartre draws tourists from far afield in search of the spirit of the Belle Epoque, or more simply to enjoy the view over the city.

Walking Tours
&See map.

From boulevard de Rochechouart to Sacré-Coeur

▷ *Take rue de Steinkerque to rue d'Orsel for a fine view of Sacré-Coeur; turn left.*

Place Charles-Dullin
An attractive shady little square. The small theatre nestling among the trees was founded in the early 19C as the Théâtre de Montmartre; it grew to fame between the wars when Charles Dullin founded the **Théâtre de l'Atelier** in 1922.

▷ *Take rue des Trois-Frères; turn left onto rue Yvonne-Le-Tac.*

Martyrium
11 rue Yvonne-Le-Tac. A chapel has replaced the medieval sanctuary built to mark the site where St Denis is presumed to have been decapitated. It was here in the former crypt on 15 August

1534, that **Ignatius Loyola** founded the Jesuit Order.

Place des Abbesses★
This animated little square is the very heart of the community, with its distinctive **Hector Guimard** Art Nouveau entrance to the metro station (the only other is at Porte Dauphine).

Église St-Jean-de-Montmartre
South side of the square. This unusual church designed by Baudot was the first to be built of reinforced concrete (1904); it continues to impress structural engineers on account of its audacious use of the material.

▷ *Leave square Jean-Rictus by rue des Abbesses and turn right onto rue Ravignan.*

Place Émile-Goudeau★
This high point in artistic and literary realms was frequented from 1900 by the pioneers of modern painting and poetry; **Picasso**, Van Dongen, Braque, and Juan Gris, evolved Cubism – with Picasso's famous *Demoiselles d'Avignon*, whereas Max Jacob, **Apollinaire** and Mac Orlan broke away from traditional poetic form and expression. They met at no 13, Le **Bateau-Lavoir**, a rickety wooden building which was rebuilt after burning down in 1970; it still houses artists' studios and apartments.

▷ *Continue up rue Ravignan to place Jean-Baptiste-Clément and along rue Norvins past a former water tower.*

Carrefour de l'Auberge de la Bonne-Franquette
The **crossroads** with rue Norvins, rue des Saules and rue St-Rustique was often painted by **Utrillo**, who successfully evoked the spirit of Old Montmartre. During the latter half of the 19C, this haunt was frequented by Pissarro, Sisley, Cézanne, Toulouse-Lautrec, **Renoir**, **Monet** and **Émile Zola**.

▷ *Take rue Poulbot on the right, leading to the minute place du Calvaire which commands an exceptional view over Paris.*

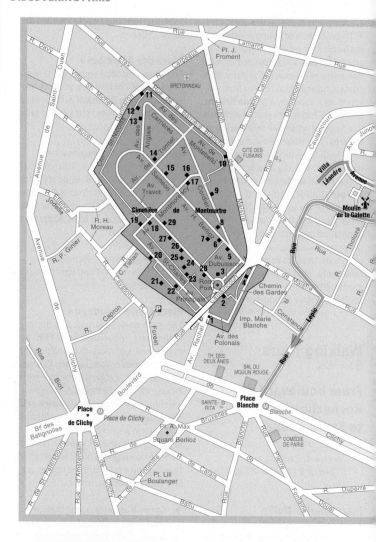

MONTMARTRE CEMETERY

1) Lucien and Sacha Guitry (playwrights and actors).
2) Émile Zola (novelist).
3) E Labiche (playwright).
4) Dalida (singer).
5) Hector Berlioz (composer).
6) Greuze (painter).
7) Heinrich Heine (poet and writer).
8) François Truffaut (film producer).
9) Théophile Gautier (poet and critic).
10) Edgar Degas (painter).
11) Leo Delibes (composer).
12) Poulbot (illustrator).
13) Jacques Offenbach (composer).
14) Charles Fourier.

15) Nijinsky (dancer).
16) Ernest Renan and Ary Scheffer (philosopher; painter).
17) Alexandre Dumas the Younger (novelist).
18) Henri-Georges Clouzot.
19) Edmond and Jules de Goncourt (novelists).
20) Alfred de Vigny (poet).
21) Louis Jouvet (actor).
22) Alphonsine Plessis, the Lady of the Camelias.
23) Georges Feydeau.
24) Marcel Jouhandeau.
25) André Ampère.
26) Madame Récamier.
27) Stendhal (H Beyle) (novelist).
28) La "Goulue" (cabaret dancer).

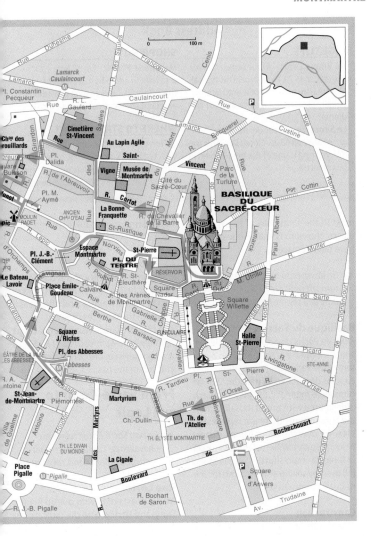

Place du Tertre★★

This simple, shaded square fronted with small houses is a peaceful village in the early morning hours; later, invaded by sightseers, it becomes a busy tourist attraction animated by cafés, restaurants, art galleries, the bustle of street artists offering their canvases, a personalised charcoal portrait or paper cut-outs. Number **21** is the seat of the Free Commune, founded in 1920 to preserve the traditions of the Butte; it now houses the Tourist Information Centre. Number **3**, once the local town hall, is now Poulbot House to commemorate local children (P'tits Poulbots), popularised in the artist's delightful line drawings and illustrations from the early 20C.

Église St Pierre-de-Montmartre★

2 rue du Mont-Cenis. The church of Saint Peter is the last surviving vestige of the great abbey of Montmartre and one of the oldest churches in the capital, dating back to 1134. The nave was revaulted in the 15C; the west front dates from the 18C. The three bronze doors showing St Denis, St Peter and the Virgin, are by the Italian sculptor, **Gismondi** (1980). The oldest pointed arches in Paris (1147) meet in the single bay of the apse. In places, the worn Romanesque capitals have been replaced.

▶ *Go down onto rue St-Eleuthère; turn left onto rue Azais; follow it until you see the basilica.*

Basilique du Sacré-Cœur★★

Place du Parvis-du-Sacré-Cœur. The tall, white silhouette of the basilica is a feature of the Paris skyline, with its pointed cupolas dominated by the 80m/262.4ft campanile. Internally, this pilgrim church is decorated with bright mosaics. From the church steps there is a remarkable **view**★★ over the capital. Immediately below is square Willette laid out in 1929 (a funicular train shuttles up the steep hill thereby saving a steep climb for the price of a metro ticket).

Construction

After the disastrous Franco-Prussian War of 1870, a group of Catholics vowed to raise money by public subscription to erect a church to the Sacred Heart on Montmartre hill. Construction on the neo-Roman-Byzantine basilica began in 1876 and concluded in 1914. The church was consecrated in 1919 and has attracted countless pilgrims ever since.

The dome

🕑*Daily 9am–7pm (9am–6pm winter).* ☞*5€.* ☎*01 53 41 89 00. www.sacre-coeur-montmartre.com.*
From inside there is a bird's-eye view down into the church and from the external gallery a **panorama**★★★

extending for over 30km/18.6mi on a clear day.

La Savoyarde

Hanging in the belfry, this is one of the heaviest bells in the world (19t). It was cast in 1895 at Annecy, and offered as a gift from the dioceses of Savoy.
The church plate is visible in the **crypt** (🕑*daily 9am–6pm;* ☎*01 53 41 89 00),* as is an audiovisual display on the history and cult of the basilica.

From Sacré-Cœur to rue Lepic

▶ *Go pasr Sacré-Coeur; follow rue Chevalier-de-La-Barre; turn right onto rue du Mont-Cenis; take first left.*

Rue Cortot

No **12** boasts of having put up Renoir, Dufy, and **Utrillo**, and the radical poet Pierre Reverdy over the years. It is now the entrance to the Montmartre Museum.

▶ *Continue on rue Cortot until rue des Saules on the right.*

The vineyard

On the first Saturday in October, the grapes are harvested for the *Clos du Montmartre* wine.

Rue St-Vincent

The junction with rue des Saules is one of the most delightful corners of the Butte: flights of steps drop away mysteriously straight ahead while another road rises steeply beside the **ceme-**

tery... the picturesque charm is further enhanced by the famous **Lapin Agile**, a traditional cabaret that attracted a host of often penniless writers and artists between 1900 and 1914; it still draws a crowd (○*Tue–Sun 9pm–2am*). **Hector Berlioz** once lived in the house on the corner with rue du Mont-Cenis, where he composed *Harold in Italy* and *Benvenuto Cellini*.

Cimetière St-Vincent

This modest cemetery is the resting place of the musician Honegger, the painter Utrillo, the writer Marcel Aymé, and Émile Goudeau, the founder of the Club des Hydropathes. Nearby (*52 rue Lamarck*), the most fashionable restaurant in Montmartre, the Beauvilliers, was named after Antoine **Beauvilliers**, a famous chef at the court of Louis XVIII; note the exuberant late 19C décor (sculptures, paintings).

▶ *Walk up the steps on the left then turn right onto a narrow lane.*

Château des Brouillards

This was built in the 18C as a folly; it was later used as a dance hall. Its grounds have become square Suzanne-Buisson (a statue of St Denis stands on the spot where he is said to have washed his decapitated head).

▶ *Go through Square S. Buisson and down onto avenue Junot.*

Avenue Junot

This peaceful thoroughfare is home to artists' studios and private houses: the **Hameau des Artistes** (no 11) and the **Villa Léandre**★ (no 25). There is a view of the windmill from no 10.

▶ *Stay on ave Junot; take a sharp left at rue Lepic.*

Moulin de la Galette

The dance hall, which enjoyed such a rage at the turn of the 20C, inspired many painters including **Renoir** (*see ORSAY*), **Van Gogh** and Willette. The windmill, which has topped the hill for more than six centuries, is the old

Blute-fin, which was defended against the Cossacks in 1814 by the heroic mill-owner Debray, whose corpse was finally crucified upon the sails.

Rue Lepic

The old quarry road that winds gently down the steep hill is the scene each autumn of a veteran car rally. Van Gogh lived with his brother at no **54**.

▶ *Go down rue Lepic, which joins boulevard de Clichy at place Blanche.*

Additional Sights

Musée de Montmartre

12 rue Cortot. ○*Tue–Sun 11am–6pm.* ○*1 Jan, 1 May, 25 Dec.* ⊕*7€.* ☎*01 49 25 89 37. www.museedemontmartre.fr.*
The museum houses a rich collection of mementoes evoking the quarter's Bohemian life, its nightclubs and personalities.

Halle St-Pierre

2 rue Ronsard.
At the foot of Montmartre stands a fine 19C cast-iron textile market transformed into an exhibit hall. The ground floor hosts temporary year-long exhibitions. On the first floor, the **Musée d'Art naïf Max Fourny** (&○*Sept–Jul, daily 10am–6pm; Aug, Mon–Fri noon–6pm.* ○*1 Jan, 1 May, 14 Jul, 15 Aug, 25 Dec;* ⊕*7.50€;* ☎*01 42 58 72 89; www.hallesaintpierre.org*) displays naive paintings and sculpture by contemporary artists.

Cimetière de Montmartre

Avenue Rachel. ○*Sun–Fri 8am–6pm, Sat 8.30am–6pm; (closes 5.30pm in winter).* ⚍*Guided tours by appointment.* ☎*01 40 71 75 60.*
Many famous people, among them artists and writers, are buried here, including the dramatist Labiche, painter Edgar Degas, the great dancer Nijinsky, actor Louis Jouvet, composer Jacques Offenbach, and film director François Truffaut. & *See Montmartre Cemetery map key for a fuller list.*

MONTPARNASSE★★

Ⓜ MONTPARNASSE-BIENVENUE (LINES 4, 6, 12 AND 13), EDGAR-QUINET (LINE 6), VAVIN
(LINE 4), GAÎTÉ (LINE 13) AND RASPAIL (LINES 4 AND 6)
BUSES: 28, 48, 58, 82, 89, 91, 92, 94, 95, 96

Although this neighbourhood has changed since the days when artists and
philosophers made it their own in the early 1900s, and although chain restaurants now vie for space with the famous cafés, Montparnasse is still a great
place to spend an evening, have a drink, see a film, enjoy a meal and tune in to
the energy of the crowd.

🛈 **Information:** Carrousel du Louvre Welcome Centre, Place de la Pyramide Inversée
99, rue de Rivoli. ☎08 92 68 30 00 (0.34€ per min). http://en.parisinfo.com.
▶ **Orient Yourself:** Montparnasse is in the centre of the Left Bank.
🅿 **Parking:** Street and underground parking on the boulevards and at the Tour.
☺ **Don't Miss:** The charming Musée Bourdelle, views from Tour Montparnasse.
🕐 **Organizing Your Time:** Allow two hours, or a half day to visit the museums.
Kids **Especially for Kids:** The Jardin Atlantique is popular with kids of all ages.
👁 **Also See:** LUXEMBOURG, QUARTIER LATIN, ST-GERMAIN-DES-PRÉS.

A bit of History

Mount Parnassus – The debris from
age-old quarries formed a deserted
rough-grass-covered mound. Students
came to freely declaim poetry, naming
this wild place Mount Parnassus after
the sacred mountain where Apollo
entertained his Muses.

A pleasure ground – At the time of the
Revolution, cafés and cabarets mush-
roomed on the city's outskirts, and the
polka and the cancan were first introduced to Paris. As the sprawl continued,
Haussmann intervened, organizing
the area into neighbourhoods around
the villages Plaisance, **Vaugirard** and
Montrouge, accessed by rue de Rennes,
boulevard Arago and boulevard d'Enfer
(now boulevard Raspail).

Bohemian Montparnasse – At the turn
of the 19C, avant-garde artists, poets
and writers, moved to Montparnasse
following a lead set by **Henri Murger**
who had already described the lifestyle
in his *Scenes of Bohemian Life*. Newcom-
ers included **Apollinaire**, Max Jacob
and Jean Moréas. The former Wine
Pavilion from the 1900 Exhibition was
reconstructed at no 52 **rue de Dantzig**.
The main pavilion, circular in shape,
with a cubist roof, accommodated 24

painters in narrow cells or "coffins" on
two floors thereby earning its name **La
Ruche**, meaning Beehive. This replaced
the **Bateau-Lavoir** (👁*see MONTMAR-
TRE*) by providing lodging and studios
to impoverished, often foreign, artists,
notably Modigliani, **Soutine**, Chagall,
Zadkine and Léger. It was from such
cramped quarters that the Expressionist movement emerged.

Discussion and debate were animated
by the Russian political exiles (Lenin,
Trotsky), composers (Stravinsky, Satie
and the Six), foreign artists and writers
(Hemingway, Foujita, Picasso, Eisenstein,
Blasco Ibañez, **Man Ray**, Cendrars, Far-
gué, André Breton, **Cocteau**). This was
the golden age of the **Paris School**
lasting into the mid-1930s, and ending
with the outbreak of war in Spain and
Western Europe.

This former international Bohemian
quarter became entirely Parisian in the
post-war materialistic age, frequented
by the trendy set and sporty 'stylish'
hatchback cars. Cocktail bars began to
replace the old-time cafés, late-night
opening stretched ever further into the
morning – such was the American influence of the 1950s.

During the 1960s, the pace became too
much; Aragon, Cocteau, **Braque**, **Sartre**,
De Beauvoir continued to be glimpsed,
but already the likes of Foujita, Picasso,

Chagall had moved on. Today there are still quiet patches of traditional Parisian streets, but the busy Maine-Montparnasse complex has become the nucleus of a neon-lit business area where locals and out-of-towners are drawn to the shops, cafés, cinemas and nightclubs.

Sights

Montparnasse has two faces: the modern tower, train station and place de Catalogne, and the traditional cafés and theatres reminiscent of the area's bohemian past.

Place du 18-Juin-1940

Until 1967 this site was occupied by a railway station, remembered as Général Leclerc's headquarters during the liberation of Paris, and where, on 25 August 1944, the German military governor surrendered. Today the square is lined with cinemas and cafés. The Centre Commercial houses department stores and luxury boutiques.

Tour Montparnasse★★

⏰*Oct–Mar, Sun–Thu 9.30am–10.30pm, Fri, Sat and day before public holidays 9.30am–11pm (last admission 30min before closing); Apr–Sept, 9.30am–11.30pm.* ✆*10€.* ☎*01 45 38 52 56. www.tourmontparnasse56.com.*
Completed in 1973, this 209m/685.7ft-high tower dominates the whole quarter, adding a modern landmark to the Paris skyline. The foundations are sunk to a depth of 70m/230ft, bearing 120 000t of masonry and shafts. It takes 40 seconds to reach the 56th floor observatory, which affords a magnificent **panorama★★★** of Paris and its suburbs. There is also a bar and panoramic restaurant at this level. From the open roof terrace (59th floor) the view can extend as far as 50km/31mi.

Gare Montparnasse

This immense 18-storey glass, steel and concrete block train station on five levels connects with the metro and supplies every amenity, even a small chapel to St Bernard (entrance at no 34) – the lectern was carved from a railway sleeper.

A massive concrete slab suspended over the tracks has been laid with a large expanse of garden, the **Jardin Atlantique**★. Typical of Paris' modern green oases, it appeals to all the senses, with textured walkways, fountains, and colourful flowers.

Place de Catalogne

The two six-storey, strikingly modern yet Neoclassical buildings were designed by Ricardo Bofill around oval squares. The continuous semicircular façades of the stone Amphithéâtre surround a vast sunken disc-shaped fountain in the centre. Walk beneath the arch formed by the façade and past the park to the **Église Notre-Dame-du-Travail**, an unusual church (1900) with an audacious metal interior structures of bare iron girders meant to honour the combined ideals of work and worship.

▸ *Continue down rue Vercingétorix, turning left on rue Desprez, following rue Francis-de-Pressensé; turn left onto rue Raymond-Losserand.*

Rue Raymond-Losserand

Once the main road from the village of Vanves into Paris, this market street was renamed in 1945 after a local municipal representative executed by the Germans in 1942. Be sure to note the charming cobblestone passage, rue Thermopyles (at no 91).

▸ *Turn left at rue Lebouis, then take a right at the passage Lebouis.*

Fondation Henri Cartier-Bresson

2 impasse Lebouis. ⏰*During exhibitions, Tue–Sun 1pm–6.30pm, Wed 1pm–8.30pm, Sat 11am–6.45pm.* ⏰*Public holidays, between exhibitions, Aug.* ✆*6€.* ☎*01 56 80 27 00. www.henricartierbresson.org.*
Installed on several levels in a bright atelier, the foundation houses the works of the famous and prolific photographer Cartier-Bresson (1908-2004). There are also regularly scheduled projections, videos, debates and conferences on photography.

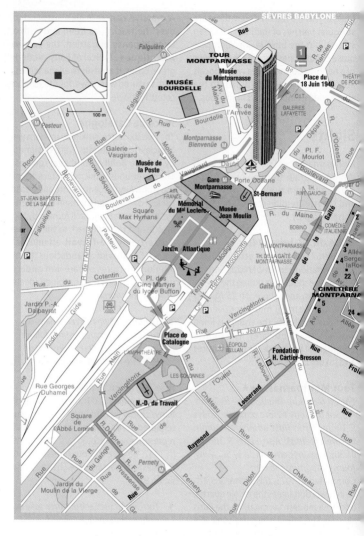

▶ *Walk across avenue de Maine to the rue de la Gaîté, on the left.*

Rue de la Gaîté

This road has been synonymous with pleasure since the 18C, lined with cabarets, dance halls, restaurants and other places of entertainment. Its reputation is maintained today by the **Montparnasse** Theatre (no **31**), the **Gaîté-Montparnasse** Theatre (no **26**), the famous **Bobino** Music Hall (no **20**), the **Comédie Italienne** (no **17**) and the **Rive-Gauche** Theatre (no **6**).

▶ *Walk along boulevard Edgar-Quinet, away from the Tour, to the cemetery.*

Cimetière Montparnasse

Free map at the entrance. ◷ *Mon–Sat 8am –5.45pm (5.15pm Nov–Mar).* ☞ *Guided tours possible by appointment.* ☎ *01 44 10 86 50.*

Opened in 1824, this tranquil spot traversed by shaded avenues of linden trees. is the permanent resting place for Baudelaire, Serge Gainsbourg, Sartre and Simone de Beauvoir, Jean Seberg, Samuel Becket, and the unfortunate Captain Dreyfus.

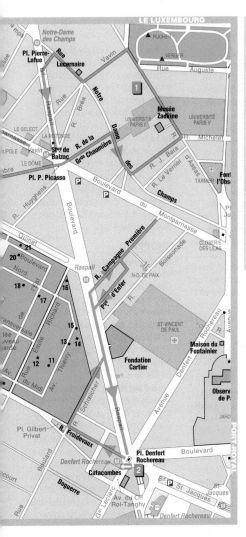

Cimetière du Montparnasse

1 - J.-P. Sartre
2 - Soutine
3 - Baudelaire (tombe Aupick)
4 - H. Laurens
5 - Tristan Tzara
6 - Zadkine
7 - Jussieu
8 - Rude
9 - Serge Gainsbourg
10 - Henri Poincaré
11 - César Franck
12 - Guy de Maupassant
13 - Bartholdi
14 - Kessel
15 - André Citroën
16 - Le Baiser, par Brancusi
17 - Sainte-Beuve
18 - Saint-Saëns
19 - H. Langlois
20 - Léon-Paul Fargue
21 - Marguerite Duras
22 - Man Ray
23 - Julio Cortazar
24 - Jean Carmet

▶ *Walk back along boulevard Edgar-Quinet towards the Tour as far as place Edgar-Quinet, then turn onto the charming rue Delambre leading to carrefour Vavin.*

Carrefour Vavin (Place Pablo Picasso)

This crossroads, originally the summit of the Parnassus Mound, continues to bustle with life at the heart of the old quarter. The famous brasseries Le Dôme, La Rotonde, Le Sélect, and La Coupole serve oysters and other specialities late into the night.

Rue de la Grande-Chaumière – At no 10 is the Académie Charpentier, where Gauguin, Manet and Whistler worked; no 14 is the Académie de la Grande-Chaumière, open since 1904, where the Russian and Polish artists of the Paris School worked. A bit further, the Sennelier boutique sells its art supplies, including the oil pastels that Henri Sennelier developed especially for Picasso.

Rue Notre-Dame-des-Champs

Note the interesting sculptures on the façade of no 82. Fernand Léger lived in the atelier at no 86 at the end of his life.

Address Book

NIGHTLIFE

L'Utopia – *79 rue de l'Ouest,14th arr.* Ⓜ*Pernety.* ☎*01 43 22 79 66. www.utopia-cafeconcert.fr. Closed Sun, Aug and 25 Dec.* Rock and blues concerts set this somewhat abandoned district swinging. A cosmopolitan crowd.

La Coupole – *102 blvd du Montparnasse, 14th arr.* ☎*01 43 20 14 20. www. lacoupoleparis.com. Daily.* Originally a wood and coal depot, this café, opened in 1927, owes its name to the glass dome that formerly hung over the restaurant. Its 33 pillars and pilasters were decorated by a large number of artists, many of whom were students of masters such as Matisse and Léger. It played a key role in the capital's literary world in the 1930s and was frequented by Faulkner, Giacommetti, Sartre and Beckett. Revamped in 1988, it is as busy and popular with Parisian night-owls as ever it was. The downstairs dance floor is famous for its salsa evenings: there is a thé-dansant on Sundays and an old-fashioned ball at the weekend.

La Rotonde – *7 pl. du 25-Août, 14th arr.* ☎*01 45 40 48 26. www.rotondemont parnasse.com. Daily.* Lenin was a waiter here and Trotsky was a regular. Picasso, Derain, Modigliani, Matisse and Vlaminck would meet here for heated discussions. Open since 1903, it is a symbol of modern 20C history. It's still popular with some of Paris' foreign communities (Russia and South America).

Le Dôme – *108 blvd du Montparnasse, 14th arr.* ☎*01 43 35 25 81. Closed Sun and Mon in Aug.* Opened in 1906, this grande dame was a haven for writers and painters, and much in vogue with bohemian Americans in the 1920s and post-war. Today it is frequented by the neighbourhood locals, often from the fashionable worlds of show-biz or politics.

Le Rosebud – *11 bis rue Delambre, 14th arr.* ☎*01 43 35 38 54. Daily. Closed Aug, Christmas and New Year.* Located in a smart street. The corporate business look is not at all out of place in this chic bar, with a literary and cinema flavour to it.

Le Sélect – *99 blvd du Montparnasse, 14th arr.* ☎*01 45 48 65 27. Daily. Closed Christmas.* An Art Deco institution, it was *the* place for artists and intellectuals when it first opened in 1924. Next door to other flashier brasseries, the Select has retained a quiet, intimate feel.

SHOPPING

Roi de Bretagne – *10 rue du Maine.* Ⓜ*Montparnasse.* ☎*01 43 20 84 60. Closed Sun.* The best products from Brittany, including cider, crepes, traditional artwork and the famous *kouign amann* buttercake. **Marché parisien de la Création** – *Boulevard Quinet.* ☎*08 72 57 89 91. www.marchecreation.com.* Around 100 artists exhibit their works on Sundays.

Jean-Paul Hévin – *3 rue Vavin, 6th arr.* Ⓜ*Vavin or Notre-Dame-des-Champs.* ☎*01 43 54 09 85. www.jphevin.com. Closed Sun, Mon, 3 weeks in Aug and public holidays.* One of the capital's four best chocolate makers. For over 10 years, this master craftsman has been delighting patrons with his bitter *ganaches* made from a variety of cocoa beans. Don't miss his delicious macaroons or his legendary chocolate *millefeuille*.

WHERE TO STAY AND EAT

⌖Turn to the back of the guide for selected hotels, restaurants, bistros and cafés listed by *arrondissement*. This district lies in the 6th, 14th and 15th arrondissements.

▶ *Turn left at rue Joseph Bara and left onto rue d'Assas to the Musée Zadkine (in the passage at no 100 bis). Continue along rue d'Assas, turn left on rue Vavin, then right back onto rue N.-D.-des-Champs.*

At no 53 is the **Lucernaire**, an experimental theatre with two cinemas, a restaurant and the popular *Avant-Scène* café.

Cimetière Montparnasse with a view of the tower

Place Pierre-Lafue

On this tiny island between boulevard Raspail and rue N.-D.-des-Champs is the statue by Louis Mitelberg (aka "Tim", 1919-2002) called "Hommage au Capitaine Dreyfus".

▶ *Continue up the boulevard Raspail to the famous statue of* **Balzac** *by* **Rodin**, *and back into the heart of Montparnasse's lively café scene.*

Museums

Musée Bourdelle★★

18 rue Antoine-Bourdelle. ◷*Tue–Sun 10am–6pm (last admission 30min before closing).* ◷*Public holidays.* ⊚*4.50€.* ☎*01 49 54 73 73. www.bourdelle.paris.fr.*
Antoine Bourdelle's (1861-1929) house, garden and studio have been converted to display the artist's sculptures, paintings and drawings. Having studied under Rodin, his work evolved from an animated naturalistic figurative style to a more stylised and archaic one modelled on Romanesque, Byzantine and Gothic examples. In the great hall are the original plaster prototypes for his huge sculptures cast in bronze including **Heracles the Archer★★**. Outstanding items among his immense output include the huge bronzes now in the garden and his portrait busts of his contemporaries (**Rodin**, Anatole

France). The bronze **Head of Apollo★**, *Rodin Working* and the 21 **portraits of Beethoven★** are in the second series of studios. The 1992 extension to the museum, designed by Christian de Portzamparc, presents all the studies and fragments relating to the *Monument to Adam Mickiewicz,* erected near place de l'Alma, and the 1870 *War Monument* in Montauban.

Musée de la Poste★

34 boulevard de Vaugirard. ◷*Mon–Sat 10am–6pm.* ◷*Public holidays.* ⊚*5€.* ☎*0142 79 24 24. www.museedelaposte.fr.*
The museum presents an attractive account of the postal services through the ages, from incised clay tablets from 2500 BC, medieval manuscripts on parchment, carrier pigeons, to the 18 000 French post offices of today. Of particular note are the stamp printing and franking machines displayed, a complete collection of French stamps since the first issue in 1849 and displays of other national collections.

Musée du Montparnasse

21 avenue du Maine. ◷*Tue–Sun 12.30pm–7pm.* ◷*1 May, 14 July.* ⊚*5€.* ☎*01 42 22 91 96. www.museedumontparnasse.net.*
The ivy covered artists' studios, former studio of the Russian painter Maria Vassilieff, exude a charm from another era. Exhibits recounting the history of the

district and its artists are changed every four months.

Mémorial du Maréchal Leclerc de Hautecloque et de la Libération de Paris – Musée Jean Moulin

Jardin Atlantique. &⏰*Tue–Sun 10am–6pm.* ⊘*Public holidays.*☎*01 40 64 39 44. www.ml-leclerc-moulin.paris.fr.*

Exhibitions are dedicated to documents, photographs and artefacts commemorating two French heroes of World War II, one a symbolic figure for the Free French, the other a hero of the Resistance.

Musée Zadkine

100 bis, rue d'Assas. &⏰*Tue–Sun 10am–6pm.* ⊘*Public holidays.*☎*01 55 42 77 20. www.zadkine.paris.fr.*

This tiny cottage atelier tucked between the large surrounding buildings features 300 sculptures in stone and wood by the Russian-born French artist Ossip Zadkine (1890-1967), spanning Cubism to abstraction. Zadkine was a very talented artist, to the extent that he has been likened to Picasso.

The small museum is not generally very crowded, so it makes a pleasant stop on a walk around the Montparnasse area.

PARC MONTSOURIS★

Ⓜ PORTE D'ORLÉANS (LINE 4) – RER: CITÉ UNIVERSITAIRE (LINE B)
BUSES: 21, 67, 88, PC

The Montsouris Park forms a large green open space to the south of the city, a real haven of peace with a lake, open lawns, century-old trees and colourful flower beds. The surrounding streets are lined with quaint small houses, while the Cité Universitaire explores the many styles of international architecture.

Nearby neighbourhoods: **DENFERT-ROCHEREAU**.

- **Information:** Pyramides welcome centre, 25 rue des Pyramides. ☎0892 68 3000 (0.34€ per min). http://en.parisinfo.com.
- **Orient Yourself:** Montsouris is in southeastern Paris, on the Left Bank.
- **Parking:** Street parking is possible on the side streets around the park.
- **Don't Miss:** The scenic waterfall in the Parc Montsouris.
- **Organizing Your Time:** Allow an hour or two to visit the area.
- **Especially for Kids:** There are several playgrounds within the park.
- **Also See:** DENFERT-ROCHERAU.

Visit

Parc Montsouris★

Following **Haussmann**'s instructions, Adolphe Alphand began work on this area undermined by quarries and capped by dozens of windmills in 1868. By 1878 he had turned it into a 16ha/50-acre English-style park with paths snaking up the mounds and circling the cascades, and a large artificial lake (the engineer specifically involved in the construction committed suicide, when the lake suddenly dried out on opening day). The park is decorated with sculptures, including the **South bearing** *(mire du Sud)* of the Paris **meridian**. The city's meteorological observatory is housed in a building in the park, with weather predictions posted on the door.

Beyond the park – At the turn of the 19C, painters attracted by the park's peace and its proximity to Montparnasse came to live here, notably **Douanier Rousseau** and Georges Braque. Explore **rue du Parc Montsouris**, **rue Braque** and **square de Monsouris** before heading north along rue Saint-Yves to **Villa Seurat**. During the inter-war period, famous residents of the **Villa Seurat** included the artist Gromaire,

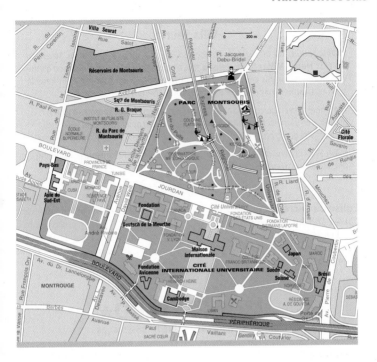

Lurçat, Orloff the sculptor, Henry Miller (installed in Artaud's studio at no 18 by Anaïs Nin), Dalì and **Soutine**. No **2** avenue Reille was designed by Auguste Perret and no **53** by Le Corbusier.

The avenues Reille and René-Coty are overlooked by the grass-covered **Montsouris reservoirs**, where half the city's water supply is collected in the 100-year-old reservoirs from the Vanne, Loing and Lunain rivers.

Cité internationale universitaire★

Main entrance: 19–21 boulevard Jourdan. 🕓 *8am–9pm.* 👁 *Guided visits the 1st Sun of the month, 3pm at the Collège Néenderlais, 57 boulevard Jourdan.* 👁 *8€.* ☎ *01 44 88 18 70. www.ciup.fr.*
The city on the edge of Montsouris Park spreads over an area of 40ha/100 acres, housing over 5 500 students from 120 different countries in its 37 halls of residence. Each hall forms an independent community, its architecture and individual character inspired by the country which founded it. The very first hall to be built was the **E-and-L-Deutsch-de-la-**

Meurthe Foundation, inaugurated in 1925. The Maison Internationale (1936) with a swimming pool, theatre and vast rooms was sponsored by John D Rockefeller Jr. The Fondation Suisse and Fondation Franco-Brézilienne were designed by **Le Corbusier**.

Address Book

SHOPPING

Fil'O Fromage – *4 r. Poirier-de-Narçay, 14th arr.* Ⓜ *Porte-d'Orléans.* ☎ *01 40 44 86 75. Closed Sun, public holidays and Aug.* People come from afar to shop here, such is the reputation of this magnificent cheese shop and its legendary façade. For over ten years, Mrs Boubrit, a perfectionist, has been providing impeccable cheeses.

WHERE TO STAY AND EAT

👁 Turn to the back of the guide for selected hotels, restaurants, bistros and cafés listed by *arrondissement*. This district is in the 14th arrondissement.

Villa Seurat

18 Villa Sourat, just off rue de la Tombe-Issoire (see map). In the 1930s American novelist **Henry Miller** immortalised this tranquil cul-de-sac (fictionalised as the Villa Borghese) in his controversial novel *Tropic of Cancer* (published in Paris in 1934 and banned in the USA and England until the 1960s).

The whole street is given up to quiet, joyous work. Every house contains a writer, painter, musician, sculptor, dancer or actor. It is such a quiet street and yet there is such activity going on, silently…

Miller Walks (www.millerwalks.com) offers walks around Montsouris, including one which incorporates 18 Villa Seurat.

Église du Sacré-Cœur

Wed and Sat 2pm–7pm, Sun 9am– 12.30pm. ☎01 46 57 70 18.
Built between 1931 and 1936 on the edge of the city parish boundary, it now stands on the far side of the boulevard Périphérique in Gentilly, and is reached by a footbridge. Its façade has a relief by Saupique, dominated by a great bell-tower.

MOUFFETARD ★

CENSIER-DAUBENTON (LINE 7) – BUSES: 47, 89

This area on the fringe of the Latin Quarter is dotted with small cafés and boutiques catering for the many students that permanently throng the neighbourhood.

Nearby neighbourhoods: **QUARTIER LATIN, JUSSIEU, JARDIN DES PLANTES, GOBELINS, PORT-ROYAL.**

- **Information:** Pyramides welcome centre, 25 rue des Pyramides. ☎08 92 68 30 00 (0.34€ per min). http://en.parisinfo.com.
- **Orient Yourself:** Mouffetard lies at the southeastern end of the Latin Quarter.
- **Parking:** Underground parking is available near the Passage des Patriarches.
- **Don't Miss:** The interesting façades of the buildings along rue Mouffetard.
- **Organizing Your Time:** Allow an hour to explore this market street.
- **Especially for Kids:** A small playground in the St-Médard church yard.
- **Also See:** QUARTIER LATIN, PANTHÉON, GOBELINS, JARDIN DES PLANTES.

Walking Tour

- *Start from the Censier-Daubenton metro station and follow rue Daubenton. A gate and passage lead from no 41 rue Daubenton to a small side entrance to the church.*

Église St-Médard

141 rue Mouffetard. *Tue–Sun.* *1 and 8 May, Pentecost, and 11 Nov.*
The church, started in the mid-15C, was completed in 1655. The Flamboyant Gothic nave has modern stained glass. In 1784 the pillars were transformed into fluted Doric columns. There are paintings of the French School, a remarkable 16C triptych *(behind the pulpit)* and, in the second chapel to the right of the chancel, a *Dead Christ* attributed to Philippe de Champaigne.

- *Continue along rue Mouffetard.*

Rue Mouffetard ★

The *Mouffe*, as it is known, winds downhill to St-Médard, lined with old houses and crowded most mornings with market shoppers in search of a bargain; on Sundays, street musicians add further

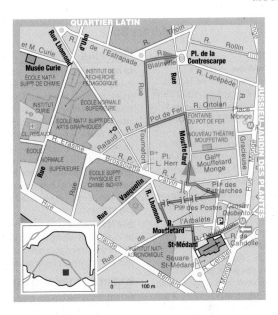

touches of colour to the area. Picturesque painted signs are a reminder of past times, like that at no 69 where a carved oak tree once topped the sign for *Le Vieux Chêne* and At the Clear Spring at no **122**. Nos **104** and **101** mark the entrances to passage des Postes and passage des Patriarches. The **Pot-de-Fer Fountain** like others in the district, runs with surplus water from the Arcueil Aqueduct which **Marie de' Medici** had constructed to bring water to the Luxembourg Palace.

Other streets in the vicinity

Denis Diderot (1713-84) lived at **3 rue de l'Estrapade** between 1747 and 1754 while overseeing the publication of his famous Encyclopaedia. There is a striking view to be caught over the dome of the Panthéon.

Rue Lhomond is lined with flights of steps – an indication of the former height of the hill. At no **30** stands the chapel serving the Séminaire du Saint-Esprit built in 1780 by **Chalgrin**. **Passage des Postes** starts level with no 55.

At **10 rue Vauquelin**, **Pierre and Marie Curie** isolated radium in October 1898 and discovered the principles of radioactivity.

▶ *Continue further along rue Mouffetard; take the first left onto rue du Pot de Fer; follow thia and take the first right onto rue Tournefort, then the first right onto Blainville.*

Place de la Contrescarpe★

An inscription at no 1 recalls the Pinecone cabaret, La Pomme-de-Pin, described by Rabelais. René Descartes lived at **14** rue Rollin during his stay in Paris (1644-48).

The Convulsionnaries

In 1727 a Jansenist deacon with a saintly reputation died at the age of 36 of mortification of the flesh and was buried in St-Médard churchyard beneath a raised black marble stone. Sick Jansenists came to pray before the tomb, to lie upon and underneath it giving rise to a belief in miraculous cures that led to massive scenes of collective hysteria.

In 1732, Louis XV decreed an end to the demonstrations; the cemetery was closed. The inscription nailed to the gate translates as:

*By order of the King, let God
No miracle perform in this place!*

Address Book

NIGHTLIFE

Finnegans Wake – *9 rue des Boulangers, 5th arr.* ☎*01 46 34 23 65. Daily.* One of the capital's oldest Irish pubs with a quiet atmosphere and excellent Guinness®. Concerts on Fri evenings and live sports on TV.

The Fifth – *62 rue Mouffetard, 5th arr.* ☎*01 43 37 09 09. Daily.* A friendly bar on two levels with a predominantly English-speaking staff and young clientele. Regularly scheduled theme nights, billards table, live sports and a large cocktail menu make for a lively atmosphere.

Place de la Contrescarpe – *Pl. de la Contrescarpe, 5th arr.* This square is lined with cafés and is always full of rue Mouffetard's colourful, motley crowd who invade the pretty terraces of the numerous cafés. The Café Contrescarpe and La Chope have the largest terraces, but the nearby Irlandais, Café des Arts, Teddy's Bar and the Mayflower are also very pleasant.

SHOPPING

La Maison des trois thés – *5 rue du Pot-de-Fer, 5th arr.* ☎*01 43 36 93 84. www.maisondestroisthes.fr. Closed Sun, Mon.* This establishment can boast international renown thanks to the master of tea, Tseng Yu Hui, who has set up shop here. It sells close to 450 teas, and some of the finest and rarest China teas, which can reach several hundred euros a kg. Tastings cost between 10€ and 686€! Can be closed due to expeditions to Asia.

Rue Mouffetard – These colourful market stands (along the St-Médard end of the street) are open Tue–Sat and Sun morning (closed at lunch).

WHERE TO STAY AND EAT

⏱Turn to the back of the guide for selected hotels, restaurants, bistros and cafés listed by *arrondissement*. This district is in the 5th arrondissement.

Denis Diderot (1713-1784)

Perhaps the most well-known inhabitant of Mouffetard was Denis Diderot, one of the leading thinkers of the French Enlightenment, an eighteenth century philosophical movement which sought to encourage the freedom of thought and promote a reliance on reason.

Diderot was concerned that Church and State conspired to discourage attempts to break away from tradition and prejudice. For a thousand years the Church had burned and suppressed books and had also routinely tortured and threatened scientists like Galileo who held unorthodox views. Diderot produced the *Encyclopedie*, a complete history of everything that was known and which contained a thousand of his own articles as well as some from other thinkers such as Benjamin Franklyn and Thomas Jefferson. This Encyclopaedia was distributed far and wide in an effort to prevent the destruction of knowledge by those who had much to gain by its suppression.

The Pope placed the *Encyclopedie* on the Vatican's 'Index of Forbidden Books' but by this time the Old Order was increasingly being challenged. Although Diderot did not live to see the French Revolution, there is no doubt that he helped set in motion an inevitable train of events which were to change the face of Europe.

LA MUETTE-RANELAGH ★

LA MUETTE (LINE 9) – RER: BOULAINVILLIERS (LINE C) – BUSES: 22, 32, 52

The original Muette Estate was developed as an elegant quarter, and today enjoys the green open space of the Ranelagh Gardens and the attraction of the Marmottan Museum with its rich collection of art.

- **Information:** Pyramides welcome centre, 25 rue des Pyramides. ☎08 92 68 30 00 (0.34€ per min). http://en.parisinfo.com.
- **Orient Yourself:** Located on the western edge of Paris' 16th arrondissement.
- **Parking:** Street parking and underground parking along the Rue de Passy.
- **Don't Miss:** Monet's paintings at the Musée Marmottan.
- **Organizing Your Time:** Allow two hours if you want to visit the museum.
- **Especially for Kids:** The Jardin du Ranelagh has several play areas.
- **Also See:** PASSY, BOIS DE BOULOGNE.

A Bit of History

Charles IX (1550-74) had a hunting lodge here where he kept his falcons when in moult (French *en mue,* hence Muette). The name was preserved when Philibert Delorme built a château set in a park extending to the Bois de Boulogne.
The château had many royal residents: Marguerite de Valois, first wife of Henri of Navarre (**Queen Margot**); Louis XIII; Duchesse de Berry; Louis XV used the château as a clandestine meeting place during his affair with the **Marquise de Pompadour**; the future Louis XVI and Marie-Antoinette spent the first years of their married life here. At the Revolution the estate was divided up, and eventually torn down in 1920.

Walking Tour

Square Lamartine

This peaceful district grew up around the Passy artesian wells dug in 1855. Residents collected their supply of sulphur-rich water at a temperature of 28°C/82°F from a depth of 600m/1 968.5ft. Rodin's monumental bronze sculpture *Victor Hugo et les Muses* stands at the point where the elegant **avenue Henri-Martin** meets avenue Victor-Hugo, a street lined with prestigious jewellery and fashion houses.

- *Avenue Henri-Martin leads to place de Colombie; bear left along avenue Raphaël.*

Jardin du Ranelagh

Originally, Parisians came to the area to dance in the open air. In 1774 a café was built, named the Petit Ranelagh after Lord Ranelagh's very fashionable pleasure gardens outside London, and extended to accommodate a dance-hall-cum-stage. The present gardens were laid out by **Haussmann** in 1860.

Allée Pilâtre-de-Rozier

On 21 November 1783, the famous aeronaut accomplished the first free flight in a hot-air balloon, witnessed by the royal family. The marble relief at the end of the avenue honouring Victor Hugo is entitled *The Poet's Vision*.

Rue André-Pascal

André Pascal was the pen-name used by Baron Henri de Rothschild to publish his writings; it was for this same banker that the adjacent sumptuous mansion was built. Since 1948 the mansion has been classified as international territory and houses the seat of the Organisation for European Cooperation and Development (☛ *closed to the public).*

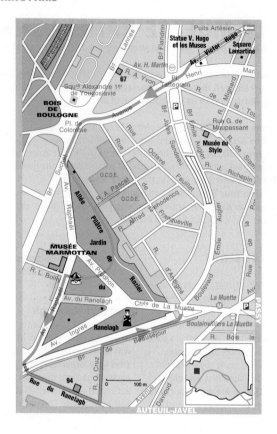

Museums

Musée Marmottan-Monet★★

2 rue Louis-Boilly. ⏰*Tue–Sun 11am–6pm, Tue 11am–9pm.* ⏰*1 Jan, 1 May, 25 Dec.* ♿*9€.* ☎*01 44 96 50 33. www.marmottan.com.*

In 1932 the art historian **Paul Marmottan** bequeathed his private house and collections of Renaissance tapestries and sculpture, Consular and First Empire portraits (26 of Boilly), medallions, paintings (Vernet) and furniture (Desmalter) to the Académie des Beaux-Arts. In 1950 Mme Donop de Monchy donated a part of her father's collection, including works by the Impressionists befriended and treated by Dr de Bellio *(Impression – Sunrise,* which gave the Impressionist movement its name). In 1971, Michel Monet left 65 of his father's painted canvases to the museum which has been further endowed by the Wildenstein legacy of

228 13C-16C illuminated manuscripts from various European schools.

The collection of **Claude Monet** paintings, probably the most important known body of work by the Master of Impressionism, is accommodated by a special purpose-built underground gallery; many of the works were painted at the artist's Normandy home at Giverny, depicting his beloved water-lilies, wisteria, iris, rose-garden, weeping willows and Japanese bridge. Other panels show the painter's preoccupation with light *(The Houses of Parliament – London, The Europe Bridge, Rouen Cathedral).*

The Duhem Bequest of about 60 paintings, drawings and watercolours includes **Gauguin**'s splendid *Bouquet of Flowers* painted in Tahiti and an interesting pastel by **Renoir**: *Seated Girl in a White Hat.* Exceptional pictures by Albrecht Bonts, Fragonard and Renoir provide interesting points of comparison.

Address Book

SHOPPING

Pascal Le Glacier – *17 rue Bois-le-Vent, 16th arr.* Ⓜ *La Muette.* ☎*01 45 27 61 84. Tue-Sat 10.30am–7pm. Closed public holidays and Aug.* Pascal and his wife are quite obsessed – with quality.
Each sorbet is prepared in small quantities with fruits of the season, distilled water and a great deal of love and care. Their current success has not altered the attention to quality or high standards of this remarkable duo.

Réciproque – *95 rue de la Pompe, 16th arr.* Ⓜ*Rue-de-la-Pompe.* ☎*01 47 04 30 28. Closed Sun, Mon and public holidays.* The 800 sq m/8 611sq ft of this second-hand fashion, accessories, and jewellery shop are more than worth a glance. Only luxury goods in excellent condition are sold, displayed by designer. From an Hermès scarf to a Vuitton bag, it's all there.

WHERE TO STAY AND EAT

Turn to the back of the guide for selected hotels, restaurants, bistros and cafés listed by *arrondissement*. This district is in the 16th arrondissement.

L'Institut des Arts de l'Écriture: Musée du Stylo et Écriture

3 rue Guy-de-Maupassant, Ⓜ*Rue-de-la-Pompe.* Ⓢ *Sun and public holidays 10am–noon, 2pm–6pm. Mon–Sat by request.* ⊚*2€.* ☎*06 07 94 13 21.*
A collection of some 1 500 examples of pens, from the 19C on, is exhibited in the institute.

The museum reveals the history and development of writing implements from Roman times to today, while at the same time implying the relationship between pen and paper. Exhibits include calligraphy writing equipment, Chinese brush pens, ink wells, quills and modern pens. Most of the collection was stolen during a robbery in 2001.

Madame de Pompadour (1721-1764)

Arguably one of the most well-known royal mistresses in history, Jeanne-Antoinette Poisson, later to be known as the Marquise (and later still, Duchesse) de Pompadour was to become the mistress of King Louis XV. Married to the nephew of her guardian at 19 and wealthy due to receiving a wedding gift comprising the estate at Étoilles, she became known for her Salon to which the eminent writer Voltaire was a regular visitor.

Étoiles happened to be on the edge of the royal hunting ground at Sénart and she engineered an encounter with the King one day in the Royal forest. Impressed by her beauty, the King invited her to a masked ball at Versailles and within two months she was installed as a Royal Mistress. Now legally separated from her husband, Louis gave her the estate of Pompadour and the title of Marquise. During this period the Château at La Muette was used as a secret meeting place between the two.

Although not as politically influential as many believed, she was undoubtedly very powerful behind the scenes and was certainly approached by foreign dignitaries who believed she had the ear of the King. Later, she was blamed by her enemies for the disastrous Seven Year's War but was probably guilty of nothing more than comforting the King with the phrase 'Après nous, le déluge' meaning 'I don't care what happens when we're dead and gone'. Although there were other royal mistresses, Louis remained devoted to her till her death in 1764 and mourned her passing. Voltaire himself wrote: "I am very sad at the death of Madame de Pompadour. I was indebted to her and I mourn her out of gratitude. It seems absurd that while an ancient penpusher, hardly able to walk, should still be alive, a beautiful woman, in the midst of a splendid career, should die at the age of forty-three".

CATHÉDRALE NOTRE-DAME★★★

Ⓜ CITÉ (LINE 4), ST MICHEL (LINE 4) – RER: ST-MICHEL NOTRE-DAME (LINE B)
BUSES: 21, 38, 47, 85

At the heart of Paris and in the heart of the Parisians, the cathedral of Notre-Dame has witnessed some of the greatest moments of the capital's history. This magnificent religious edifice is one of the supreme masterpieces of French art, and has been a source of visual and literary inspiration over the centuries.

Nearby neighbourhoods: **ÎLE ST-LOUIS, QUARTIER LATIN, MAUBERT.**

- **Information:** Carrousel du Louvre Welcome Centre, Place de la Pyramide Inversée 99, rue de Rivoli. ☎0892 68 3000 (0.34€ per min). http://en.parisinfo.com.
- ▶ **Orient Yourself:** The cathedral is on the Île-de-la-Cité in the centre of Paris.
- 🅿 **Parking:** There's underground parking right in front of the Cathedral.
- **Don't Miss:** The stained glass Rose windows, the view from the tower.
- 🕐 **Organizing Your Time:** An hour for the tower, half-an-hour for the interior.
- **Especially for Kids:** There's a playground in the garden behind the cathedral.
- **Also See:** ÎLE DE LA CITÉ, SAINTE-CHAPELLE, LA CONCIERGERIE.

A Bit of History

Construction – For 2 000 years prayers have been offered from this spot. A Gallo-Roman temple, a Christian basilica, and a Romanesque church preceded the present cathedral founded by Bishop **Maurice de Sully** to rival the St-Denis basilica by Abbot Suger. Construction began in 1163, during the reign of Louis VII, under **Jean de Chelles** and **Pierre de Montreuil**, architect of the Sainte-Chapelle. By about 1300 the building was complete. Notre-Dame is the last large galleried church and one of the first to be supported by flying buttresses.

Ceremonial Occasions – Long before it was completed, Notre-Dame had become the setting for major religious and political ceremonies. **St Louis** entrusted it with the Crown of Thorns in 1239 pending the completion of the

The east end (chevet) of Notre-Dame

J.-P. Clapham/MICHELIN

Return Policy

<u>With a sales receipt</u>, a full refund in the original form of payment will be issued from any Barnes & Noble store for returns of new and unread books (except textbooks) and unopened music/DVDs/audio made within (i) 14 days of purchase from a Barnes & Noble retail store (except for purchases made by check less than 7 days prior to the date of return) or (ii) 14 days of delivery date for Barnes & Noble.com purchases (except for purchases made via PayPal). A store credit for the purchase price will be issued for (i) purchases made by check less than 7 days prior to the date of return, (ii) when a gift receipt is presented within 60 days of purchase, (iii) textbooks returned with a receipt within 14 days of purchase, or (iv) original purchase was made through Barnes & Noble.com via PayPal. Opened music/DVDs/audio may not be returned, but can be exchanged only for the same title if defective.

<u>After 14 days or without a sales receipt</u>, returns or exchanges will not be permitted.

Magazines, newspapers, and used books are not returnable. *Product not carried by Barnes & Noble or Barnes & Noble.com will not be accepted for return.*

Policy on receipt may appear in two sections.

Return Policy

<u>With a sales receipt</u>, a full refund in the original form of payment will be issued from any Barnes & Noble store for returns of new and unread books (except textbooks) and unopened music/DVDs/audio made within (i) 14 days of purchase from a Barnes & Noble retail store (except for purchases made by check less than 7 days prior to the date of return) or (ii) 14 days of delivery date for Barnes & Noble.com purchases (except for purchases made via PayPal). A store credit for the purchase price will be issued for (i) purchases made by check less than 7 days prior to the date of return, (ii) when a gift receipt is presented

Barnes & Noble Booksellers #2511
15 Backus Ave
Danbury, CT 06810
203-730-2733

STR:2511 REG:003 TRN:7421 CSHR:Leah G

Michelin Travel Guide: P
  9781906261375
    (1 @ 19.99)   19.99

Subtotal   19.99
Sales Tax (6.000%)   1.20
TOTAL   21.19
CASH   100.20
CASH CHANGE   79.01-

A MEMBER WOULD HAVE SAVED   2.00

            Thanks for shopping at
               Barnes & Noble

101.21E   07/19/2010 01:37PM

                 CUSTOMER COPY

Sainte-Chapelle. In 1302 **Philip the Fair** formally opened the kingdom's first Parliament. Celebrations, thanksgivings and state funerals have followed each other down the centuries: high points in French history include the coronation of young Henry VI of England (1430); the re-trial of Joan of Arc (1455); the crowning of **Mary Stuart** as Queen of France following her marriage to François II; the unusual marriage ceremony of Marguerite of Valois to the Huguenot, Henri of Navarre (1572), when she stood alone in the chancel and he by the door, although he came later to agree that "Paris is well worth a mass" and attended subsequent ceremonies inside the cathedral; and the marriage of Henrietta Maria by proxy to Charles I of England (1625).

It has also been subjected to radical maltreatment: the destruction of the rood screen by **Mansart** and **Robert de Cotte** (1699), the replacement of the medieval stained glass by plain glass (18C), the vandalism of the main doorway by Soufflot to make way for an ever more grandiose processional dais (1771). During the Revolution, the statues of the kings of Judea and Israel were decapitated, the building became a Temple of Reason and then of the Supreme Being. All but the great bell were melted down and the church interior was used to store forage and food.

On 2 December 1804 the church, decked with hangings and ornaments to mask its dilapidation, received Pope Pius VII for the coronation of the Emperor (*see the painting by David in the Louvre*).

Restoration – As a result of **Victor Hugo's** novel *The Hunchback of Notre-Dame* (1831) and a general popular feeling roused by the Romantic Movement, the July Monarchy ordered in 1841 that the cathedral be restored. Entrusted to **Viollet-le-Duc** and Lassus, the restoration program lasted 23 years: statuary and glass checked, extensions and appendages removed, the roof and upper sections repaired, doors and chancel restored, a spire added and a sacristy erected.

Today as before – Notre-Dame emerged virtually unscathed from the Commune of 1871 and the Liberation of 1944, and continues to participate in major historical events, happy or sad: the magnificent Te Deum of 26 August 1944 during which an assassination attempt was made on **General de Gaulle**, the moving Requiem Mass in his honour on 12 November 1970 and the magnificat followed by a solemn mass celebrated on the parvis by Pope John-Paul II on 31 May 1980.

Visit

🕐*Daily 8am–6.45pm, Sat–Sun 8am–7.15pm.* 👓*Guided tours in English, Wed and Thu 2pm, Sat 2.30pm.* ☎*01 42 34 56 10. www.cathedraledeparis.com.*

Exterior

Place du Parvis

In the Middle Ages, when religious plays were enacted before churches and cathedrals, the porch was used to represent the door to paradise *(paradis)* – hence the evolution of the name parvis. The square was quadrupled in size as cramped surrounding buildings were cleared away by Haussmann in the 19C, so today the cathedral can be seen in all its radiant glory. A bronze plaque in the centre of the square marks the zero point from which all road distances in France are measured.

The **Crypte archéologique**★ (🕐*Tue–Sun 10am–6pm;* ₰*3.30€;* ☎*01 55 42 50 10; www.cathedraledeparis.com*) beneath the parvis displays traces of excavated buildings and monuments dating back to 3C, including two Gallo-Roman rooms heated by hypocaust, fragments of the Late Roman Empire rampart, medieval cellars, and foundations of an orphanage.

The **Cathedral Museum** (*10 rue du Cloître-Notre-Dame;* 🕐*Wed, Sat 2.30pm–5pm;* ₰*3€;* ☎*01 43 25 42 92.*) catalogues the long sequence of restoration work and the major moments in the cathedral's history since the 17C. Pottery uncovered from under the parvis is also displayed.

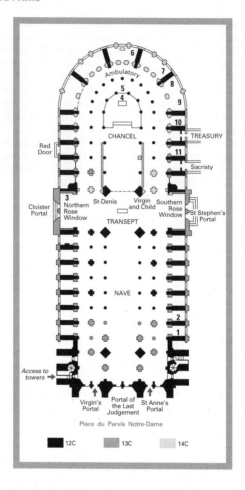

Red Door

CHANCEL

TREASURY

Sacristy

Cloister Portal

Northern Rose Window

St-Denis

Virgin and Child

Southern Rose Window

St Stephen's Portal

TRANSEPT

NAVE

Access to towers →

Virgin's Portal

Portal of the Last Judgement

St Anne's Portal

Place du Parvis Notre-Dame

12C   13C   14C

The West Front

The overall design is majestic and perfectly balanced despite being asymmetrical; the central doorway is the largest of the three, the left gabled. This medieval concept was to avoid monotony in design and symbolise the lack of perfect order on earth.

In the Middle Ages **the portals** would have looked completely different: brightly coloured statues stood out against a gold background. Designed to be read like a Bible in stone, the scriptures and the legends of the saints are graphically retold for an illiterate congregation. Legend has it that the locksmith who created the magnificent wooden door panels with the wrought-iron strap-hinges sold his soul to Satan. The central doors are 19C replacements.

Portal of the Virgin (left) – The fine tympanum has served as prototype to stonemasons throughout the Middle Ages. It shows the *Ark of the Covenant* flanked by three prophets speaking of Mary's destiny and three Kings from whom she is descended; above, a depiction of the *Death of the Virgin* with Christ and the Apostles; at the apex, the *Coronation of the Virgin* with Christ handing a sceptre to his mother, crowned by an angel. Small low-relief carving representing the labours of the months and the signs of the Zodiac fill the sections on either side of the doorway. The statues in the embrasures were added by Viollet-le-Duc and include St Denis attended by two angels, John the Baptist and St Stephen.

Portal of the Last Judgement (central) – This sculptural composition of the struggle of Good over Evil is far removed from its original condition: the tympanum was breached by Soufflot in 1771 and Viollet-le-Duc has substantially restored the two lower lintels. Above a depiction of the *Resurrection* is the *Weighing of the Souls,* in which the Good are led up to Heaven by angels, the Damned by demons to Hell; at the apex, a seated *Christ in Majesty* is flanked by the kneeling Virgin and St John, interceding for the lost souls. The six archivolts represent the celestial court. At the lowest level, Abraham receives the righteous *(left)* and condemned *(right)* symbolising Heaven and Hell. The figures of the Wise and Foolish Virgins, differentiated by open *(left)* and closed *(right)* doors to paradise, are modern. In the embrasures, Viollet-le-Duc's Apostles stand over medallions representing the Virtues *(upper tier)* and Vices *(lower tier).*

Portal to St Anne (south) – The cathedral's oldest statues fill the two upper levels of the tympanum. Created c 1165, they pre-date the building by some 60 years and were evidently intended for a narrower door. A rather formal *Virgin in Majesty with the Infant Christ* draws on Romanesque prototypes; she is attended by two angels and the cathedral patrons: Bishop Maurice of Sully *(standing, left)* and Louis VII *(kneeling, right)*. The 12C lintel shows scenes from the Life of the Virgin. The central pier carries a 19C figure of St Marcellus, the 5C Bishop of Paris who is meant to have delivered the capital from a dragon. Abutting the piers between portals are additional 19C statues *(from left to right)* of St Stephen, the Church, the Synagogue (blindfolded) and St Denis.

Gallery of Kings (above the portals) – The 28 kings of Judea and Israel represent the Tree of Jesse, Christ's forebears. The original figures were destroyed in 1793 by the revolutionaries who took them for the kings of France.

Rose window – The central great rose, nearly 10m/32.8ft across, is so perfectly designed that its elements have not moved in over seven centuries. From outside it provides the standing statue of the Virgin and Child. At the same level stand the figures of Adam *(left)* and Eve *(right)*, against stone masonry separating the window lights. Together, the group (restored by Viollet-le-Duc) portrays Redemption after the Fall from Grace.

Towers – The twin towers soar to a height of 69m/226.4ft, pierced by slender 16m/52.5ft lancets. Emmanuel, the great bell in the south tower, weighs 13t, its clapper nearly 500kg/1 102lb. The perfect pitch of its toll (F-sharp) is said to be due to the gold and silver jewellery cast into the molten bronze by *Parisiennes* when the bell was re-struck in the 17C.

Steep steps climb to a platform (varying hours – phone for details; access at the foot of the north tower (402 steps); 1 Jan, 1 May, 25 Dec. 7€ (under-18s free); 01 53 10 07 00) in the south tower provide a splendid **view**★★★ of the spire and flying buttresses; the Cité and Paris beyond. Note the famous chimeras (carved wild beasts) and great bell above the great gallery. In the chapel, a museum-video retells the story of Notre-Dame (15min).

North Side

The street is named after the cloister formerly flanked the north side. The magnificent **Cloister Portal** was built by Jean of Chelles (c. 1250), who applied experience gained from building the Sainte-Chapelle (completed 1248) to maximise the amount of light permeating the interior. The large intricate rose perfectly integrates with the clerestory to form an unexpectedly tall opening (18m/59ft high), slightly larger in diameter (13m/42.6ft). Below, the many gabled, carved doorway is markedly more ornate than the doors of the west front, installed 30 years before. The three-tiered tympanum illustrates events from the *Life of the Virgin* and from the story of Théophile selling his soul to the Devil. The **Red Door**, built by Pierre of Montreuil was reserved for members of the cathedral chapter. Its tympanum illustrates the Coronation of the Virgin attended by King Louis IX and his Queen; the archivolts illustrate the Life of St Marcel. Seven 14C **bas-relief sculptures** inlaid into the foundations of the chancel chapels depict the Death and Assumption of the Virgin.

East End

At the beginning of the 14C, the cathedral's east end was reinforced by a series of flying buttresses to counteract the thrust of the vaulting. Splendid vistas of the east end and the Seine can be enjoyed from the small John XXIII Square. From here can be seen a 13C section of roof which retains the original timberwork, and the 90m/295ft-high spire reconstructed by Viollet-le-Duc who included himself among the decorative copper figures of Evangelists and Apostles!

South Side

Beyond the 19C sacristy is the magnificent **St Stephen's** doorway, similar to the cloister door but richer in sculpture. Initiated by Jean of Chelles (1258), and completed by Pierre of Montreuil, it has a remarkable tympanum illustrating the life and stoning of St Stephen, to whom the former church that pre-dated the cathedral had been dedicated. At the base of the buttresses, eight small 13C low-relief sculptures depict street and university scenes.

The transept

G. Boullay/MICHELIN

Interior

Transitional Gothic – The sheer size (130m/426.5ft long x 48m/157.4ft wide) and soaring height (35m/114.8ft) mark a turning point in the development of Gothic architecture and building techniques on a grand scale. Besides the elevation, the floor plan also breaks new ground: the nave is given double aisles and the chancel a double ambulatory, separated in the middle by transepts that project only slightly from the outer aisles, thereby producing a unified space.

The Windows – In the 13C and 14C, the clerestory windows were enlarged to allow extra light into the chapels. Not only was the wall mass reduced and lightened, the gallery was lowered; the weight and thrust of the vault therefore had to be diffused across the aisles and down to solid masonry at gallery level: the problem was ingeniously resolved with the invention of the flying buttress. A section of the 12C elevation can still be seen at the transept crossing. The medieval stained glass was replaced by clear glass inscribed with fleur-de-lis in the 18C and by *grisaille* glass in the 19C. The modern glass by Le Chevalier, installed in 1965, returned to medieval manufacturing processes and colours.

Note the massive piers measuring 5m/16.4ft across, supporting the towers, and the organ (restored in 1992) which boasts the largest number of pipes of any organ in France *(concerts on Sundays at 5.45pm)*.

Chapels – Notre-Dame is edged with a continuous ring of chapels built between the buttresses in the 13C in response to demand from an increasing number of guilds and noble families. In keeping with a tradition renewed in 1949, the Goldsmith's Guild of Paris endowed the cathedral with a work of art annually in *May*. Among the most beautiful are Mays by Le Brun (**1, 2**) and Le Sueur (**3**).

Transept – The **windows**, remarkable for their sheer size and weight, are testimony to the technical skill of the medieval masons. The north rose,

Mary Stuart (1542-1547)

The magnificent Cathedral of Notre-Dame was the setting for the crowning of Mary Stuart as Queen of France in 1559, following her marriage the previous year to the Dauphin. A spectacular event, the coronation should have been the next step for Mary in fulfilling her destiny as Queen of four realms, Scotland, France, England and Ireland. However, it was not long before events were to take an unfortunate turn and she was to lose everything.

Crowned Queen of Scotland at less than a year old, her regents were, before long, keen for her to become betrothed to Henry VIII's son, Edward. However, as Henry became more and more difficult to deal with in his later years, the Scots abandoned the idea, preferring instead an allegiance with France. This was achieved by securing an agreement for her to marry the heir to the French throne, Francis, the son of the French King Henri II.

Five-year-old Mary was sent to France in 1548 quickly becoming a favourite of the French king who thought she was a perfect child even giving her precedence over his own daughters, since she was already a Queen in her own right. She soon met the Dauphin and they quickly became friends, travelling everywhere together. An intelligent girl, Mary already spoke French and quickly learned Latin, Italian and some Greek. In addition she could sing, dance, play the lute and converse well – all important and necessary accomplishments for a future Queen of France.

She quickly adopted the French spelling of her name and signed documents as 'Marie R' also using the French 'Stuart' rather than the Scottish 'Stewart'. Every inch a Queen, Mary was tall, beautiful and regal, but unfortunately her reign as Queen of France lasted only till the end of 1560 when Francis died. Mary was obliged to leave, returning to a troubled Scotland.

After two disastrous marriages she became very unpopular and was dominated by Scottish nobles who eventually forced her to abdicate. She fled to England where she hoped to seek refuge from her cousin Elizabeth I, but was considered too great a threat. As the granddaughter of Henry VIII's older sister, Margaret, her claims on the English throne were considerable and so she was imprisoned and executed in 1587 aged only 44. Few attending her splendid coronation in Notre-Dame so long ago could have imagined that her seemingly illustrious career would end up in such tragic failure.

which has survived almost intact since the 13C, depicts Old Testament figures around the Virgin; in the restored south rose Christ is surrounded by saints and angels.

At the entrance to the chancel, a statue of St Denis by Nicolas Coustou complements the beautiful 14C **Virgin and Child**. On the southwest pier is a plaque commemorating the deaths of the British citizens lost in World War I, many of whom are buried in French soil.

Chancel – In front of the high altar lies Geoffrey Plantagenet, son of Henry II of England (d. 1186). The chancel was redecorated by Robert de Cotte (1708-25). Seventy-eight original stalls remain from the embellishment, as do a Pietà

by Guillaume Coustou (**4**), Louis XIII by Coustou and Louis XIV by Coysevox. The only remarkable 14C **low-relief** scenes to survive pertain to the Life of Christ and His Apparitions, restored by Viollet-le-Duc. Tombstones for the bishops of Paris who are buried in the crypt, line the ambulatory (**5-11**).

Treasury

🕐 *Mon–Fri 9.30am–6pm, Sat 9.30am–6.30pm, Sun 1.30pm–5.30pm.* ✆ *3€.* ♿ ☏ *01 42 34 56 10.*

The sacristy, built by Viollet-le-Duc, contains manuscripts, ornaments and 19C church plate. The Crown of Thorns, the Holy Nail and a fragment of the True Cross are displayed on Fridays during Lent and on Good Friday.

ODÉON★

Bordering the Latin Quarter and the St Germain-des-Prés neighbourhood, this area brims with cafés, bookstores and cinemas permanently animated by young students, university staff, publishers, and night revellers.

Nearby neighbourhoods: **QUARTIER LATIN, ST-GERMAIN-DES-PRÉS, INSTITUT DE FRANCE, MAUBERT, LUXEMBOURG.**

- 🛈 **Information:** Carrousel du Louvre Welcome Centre, Place de la Pyramide Inversée 99, rue de Rivoli. ☎0892 68 3000 (0.34€ per min). http://en.parisinfo.com.
- ▶ **Orient Yourself:** Odéon is at the northeast end of the 6th arrondissement.
- 🅿 **Parking:** Underground parking at place St-André-des-Arts, near St-Michel.
- 🕭 **Don't Miss:** The charming boutiques of the Cour du Commerce-St-André.
- 🕘 **Organizing Your Time:** Allow 90 minutes to stroll this neighbourhood.
- 👓 **Also See:** ST-GERMAIN-DES-PRÉS, QUARTIER LATIN.

Walking Tour

③ Quartier de l'Odéon
👓*See map ST-GERMAIN-DES-PRÉS.*

Carrefour de l'Odéon (place Henri-Mondor)
This great junction is dominated by a bronze statue of Danton (1759-94), erected at the end of the 19C on the site of the famous Revolutionary leader's house.

Cour du Commerce-St-André★
Entrance via 130 boulevard St-Germain, opposite Danton's statue. This courtyard was opened in 1776 on the site of a **real tennis court** *(jeu de paume)* used for an archaic form of the game. It was here in a loft in 1790 that Dr Guillotin demonstrated his humane decapitating machine using sheep. At no **8, Marat** printed his revolutionary paper *L'Ami du Peuple (The People's Friend)*. In the first alleyway (gated) to the right, one of the towers of the Philippe Auguste city wall can be seen on the corner.

Cour de Rohan
A series of three courtyards once (15C) formed part of a mansion owned by the archbishops of Rouen (Rohan is a corruption of Rouen). The middle one is overlooked by a fine Renaissance house where Diane de Poitiers lived. The peaceful rue du Jardinet, built on the site of former gardens, runs onto rue de l'Éperon, home to Paris' first girls' school (1893), the Lycée Fénelon.

Rue de l'Ancienne-Comédie
Formerly rue des Fossés-St-Germain, this street was renamed in 1770, the date the Comédie-Française moved out. On the brink of financial ruin the company went to the Tuileries Palace Theatre before finally moving to the Odéon.

Carrefour de Buci
In the 18C the Buci crossroads was the focal point of the Left Bank. It boasted a sedan chair rank, a corps of 20 sentries, a gibbet and a pillar with an iron collar for miscreants.

The area around the Buci crossroads is particularly lively on Saturdays *(rue Grégoire-de-Tours, rue de Bourbon-le-Château)*; there are many fashion boutiques and restaurants as well as antique shops along rue Mazarine and rue Dauphine leading to the river.

▶ *Follow rue de l'Ancienne-Comédie to carrefour de l'Odéon.*

Rue de l'École-de-Médecine
At no **5** the long-gowned Brotherhood of Surgeons, founded by St Louis in the 13C, performed anatomical operations of every kind until the 17C. At no **15** stood the **Couvent des Cordeliers** – a Franciscan monastery of high reputation

Address Book

NIGHTLIFE

Bob Cool – *15 rue des Grands-Augustins – 6th arr* – ⓂOdéon and Saint-Michel. ☎01 46 33 33 77. A camouflage net hangs over the central room, adding an original flavour to the lively evenings organised here once a month. Regular painting and photography exhibitions. Ideal for a cocktail after having been to see one of the classics shown at the nearby Studio Christine.

La Palette – *43 rue de Seine – 6th arr* – ☎01 43 26 68 15. *Closed 3 weeks in Aug, 1 week in Feb and all public holidays.* This is one of St-Germain's best-known bistros: its pleasant provincial Parisian terrace has somewhat invaded the pavement. Decorated with paintings and palettes, the influence of the nearby art school is obvious. One of the waiters, whose painting hangs on the wall of the large room, has become a celebrity of sorts over the years.

Le Dix Bar – *10 rue de l'Odéon – 6th arr* – ☎01 43 26 66 83. The meeting place of the district's students, decorated with Belle Epoque theatre posters. In the basement, mirrors have replaced the tubes of the splendid 1901 organ from Northern France.

Le Procope – *13 rue de l'Ancienne-Comédie – 6th arr* – ☎01 40 46 79 00 – www.procope.com. Founded in 1686, it is the oldest existing café in Paris and renowned for its former popularity with literary giants such as La Fontaine, Voltaire, or later on, Daudet, Oscar Wilde and Verlaine. Now it is a restaurant, more popular with tourists than writers, but it is still possible to stop by for tea or coffee in the afternoon.

Les Étages Saint-Germain – *5 rue de Buci – 6th arr* – ☎01 46 34 26 26. This popular establishment fills out the two floors of an old house, leading visitors through a maze of tiny rooms, all decorated differently. From the second floor, there is a good view of rue de Buci and rue Grégoire-de-Tours. Young clientele, but more conventional than its sister establishment in Le Marais.

SHOPPING

Le Coupe Papier – *19 rue de l'Odéon – 6th arr* – Ⓜ Odéon – ☎01 43 54 65 95. *Closed Aug, Mon in Jul, public holidays.* A bookshop devoted to theatre, cinema, opera and dance, it publishes a full reference catalogue and specialises in contemporary arts. It also has a selection of English and Italian language works.

Le Moniteur – *7 pl. de l'Odéon – 6th arr* – Ⓜ Odéon. ☎01 44 41 15 75. www.editionsdumoniteur.com. *Closed public holidays.* Designed by Wilmotte, this bookshop, specialising in architecture and urban planning, and is always packed with students and tourists. Some books about Paris in English and a large number of international magazines and reviews.

WHERE TO STAY AND EAT

👌Turn to the back of the guide for selected hotels, restaurants, bistros and cafés listed by *arrondissement*. This district is in the 6th arrondissement.

---

in the Middle Ages for its teaching. In 1791, the revolutionary group formed by Danton, Marat, Camille Desmoulins and Hébert, known as the Cordeliers, took over both the monastery and its name; opposite, lived Jean-Paul **Marat** (1743-93) the pamphleteer who was stabbed in his bath by Charlotte Corday on 13 July 1793. The present buildings, now part of the university (Paris VI), were built between 1877 and 1900 to house the School of Practical Medicine. The central part of the former Medical School (no 12), now known as the **René Descartes University** (Paris V), dates back to 1775.

Musée d'Histoire de la Médecine
Université René-Descartes, 12 rue École-de-Médecine. 🕐*Mid–Jul–Sept, Mon–Fri 2pm–5.30pm; Oct–mid-Jul, Mon–Wed and Fri–Sat 2pm–5.30pm.* 🚫*22 Dec–3 Jan, public holidays.* ⊷*3.50€.* ☎01 40 46 16 93. www.bium.univ-paris5.fr/musee. The College of Surgeons' collections of surgical instruments from Ancient Egypt to modern times.

▶ *Take rue Dupuytren.*

Danton

Dominating the Carrefour de l'Odeon is the impressive bronze statue of Georges-Jacques Danton on the site of his former house. One of the leading figures in the drama of the French Revolution, Danton is often thought of as a more normal human being than his cold dispassionate colleague Robespierre, his eventual nemesis. Unlike many revolutionaries, he was pragmatic rather than idealistic, well educated (he could speak five languages) and liked 'the good life'. Born in 1759 at Arcis-sur-Aube, Danton was a robust child. He studied law at Reims and qualified as a lawyer, seeming destined for an ordinary middle-class existence until he became involved in revolutionary politics.

Often referred to as the man of 'August 10th' for his part in the Tuileries uprising of 1792, he became Minister of Justice and later, the first president of the Committee of Public Safety. Unlike Robespierre, he regretted many of the excesses which took place during this period and eventually became disillusioned with politics. Accused of venality and leniency towards the enemies of the Revolution by Robespierre, the result was inevitable and he was executed on 5 April, 1794.

Rue Monsieur-Le-Prince

The door at no 4, formerly of the Hôtel de Bacq, is typical of the 18C style. At no 10 is the apartment where the philosopher **Auguste Comte** lived from 1841 until his death in 1857. Now open to the public, the Maison Auguste Comte (☎01 43 26 08 56; www.augustecomte.org; ○Wed 2pm–5pm; ○public holidays and Aug) presents the residence as it looked when the philosopher died.

Place de l'Odéon

This semicircular square has remained essentially unchanged since its creation in 1779. At no **1**, the Café Voltaire was frequented by the Encyclopaedists and, at the turn of the 19C, by famous writers and poets: Barrès, Bourget, Mallarmé, **Verlaine**, **Gide**, **Hemingway** and others.

Théâtre de l'Odéon

In 1782 a theatre was built in the gardens of the former Condé mansion to accommodate the French Comedians who had been confined to the Tuileries Palace Theatre. The new theatre, built in the popular Antique style of the day, was given the name Théâtre Français. **Beaumarchais**' Le Mariage de Figaro was particularly well received in 1784. With the advent of the Revolution, the actors split between Royalists and Republicans disbanded in 1792. In 1797 the theatre was taken over and renamed

the Odéon, after the building used by the Greeks to hold musical competitions. In 1807 the building was rebuilt to its original plans after a fire. In spite of the great success of Alphonse Daudet's play, L'Arlésienne, set to music by **Bizet**, the theatre's audience dwindled, migrating to theatres on the Right Bank. Between 1946 and 1959, known first as the Salle Luxembourg and then as the Théâtre de France, it began to specialise in 20C plays, achieving pre-eminence in 1968 under Jean-Louis Barrault and Madeleine Renaud. Inside, the ceiling is painted by André Masson (1963). In 1983, the theatre became the Théâtre de l'Europe (Place de l'Odéon; ☎01 44 85 40 40. www.theatre-odeon.fr) first on a part-time basis, then completely assuming this identity in 1990.

Rue de l'Odéon

Sylvia Beach opened the original Shakespeare & Co. bookstore at no 12, where she published James Joyce's Ulysses in 1922. At no 9 the Arts et Autographes gallery sells letters signed by de Gaulle, Monet, Freud, and Matisse.

▶ Follow the rue Regnard to rue Condé, towards Luxembourg gardens (○see LUXEMBOURG), then take the rue de Tournon, lined with luxury boutiques, back to the Carrefour de l'Odéon.

OPÉRA★★

This district, encompassing the distinctive Palais Garnier Opera House with its long avenue stretching down to the Palais-Royal and the splendid place Vendôme, is at the hub of theatre land. Home to many contemporary fashion designers, the streets are thronged with elegantly attired people day and night.

Nearby neighbourhoods: **GRANDS BOULEVARDS, MADELEINE, ST-LAZARE, PALAIS-ROYAL.**

- 🅸 **Information:** Pyramides welcome centre, 25 rue des Pyramides. ☎0892 68 3000 (0.34€ per min). http://en.parisinfo.com.
- ▶ **Orient Yourself:** This district straddles the 1st and 9th arrondissements.
- 🅿 **Parking:** Underground parking available at the place Vendôme.
- 🅐 **Don't Miss:** The grand marble staircase of the Opéra Garnier.
- 🕐 **Organizing Your Time:** Allow two hours to visit this neighbourhood.
- 🅐 **Also See:** La Madeleine, Palais-Royal, Tuilleries, Louvre, Concorde.

Walking Tour
🅐*See map.*

▶ *Start from the intersection of rue de Rivoli and rue de Castiglione, Ⓜ Tuileries.*

Rue de Castiglione

Formerly known as passage des Feuillants after the Benedictine monastery which it skirted, the rue de Castiglione affords a view of the place and Colonne Vendôme.

Place Vendôme★★

Place Vendôme epitomises the full majesty of 17C French design. It is named after the Duke of Vendôme, the illegitimate son of Henri IV. In 1680, the Superintendent of Buildings conceived the idea of designing a square lined with splendid buildings around a monumental statue of Louis XIV, and commissioned **Jules Hardouin-Mansart** to design it.

Place Vendôme

B. Kaufmann/MICHELIN

Address Book

NIGHTLIFE

Bar Hemingway, Hôtel Ritz – 15 pl. Vendôme, 1st arr. ☎01 43 16 33 65. www. ritzparis.com. Daily. Hemingway, introduced by F Scott Fitzgerald, was a client of this cosy, little bar, now decorated with photographs of the writer and complete with a library. Cigar evenings with cocktails specially designed for the event (Wednesdays). Smart dress.

Harry's New York Bar – 5 rue Daunou, 2nd arr. ☎01 42 61 71 14. www. harrys-bar.fr. Daily. Closed 24–25 Dec. Forever popular with Parisian expatriate Americans and all those keen on Bloody Mary's and Blue Lagoons.

Café de la Paix – 12 blvd des Capucines, 9th arr. ☎01 40 07 36 36. www.cafe delapaix.fr. Daily. Opened in 1862, this elegant café overlooks one of the capital's busiest crossroads. Many artists ate here: Maurice Chevalier, Josephine Baker, Mistinguett, Serge Lifar to name but a few.

SHOPPING

Goyard – 233 rue St-Honoré, 1st arr. ⓂTuileries. ☎01 42 60 57 04. www. goyard.fr. . Closed Sun and public holidays. This reputable luggage-maker has recently changed hands but has retained its former spirit. At the back of the shop, an impressive early 20C mahogany staircase leads up to a room where the establishment's first creations are displayed, including a trunk-desk designed for Conan Doyle.

WHERE TO STAY AND EAT

Turn to the back of the guide for selected hotels, restaurants, bistros and cafés listed by arrondissement. This district is in the 9th arrondissement.

The column

During the Revolution the royal statue was destroyed and in 1810 **Napoléon** erected the column at its centre. The original statue mounted on the column was of Napoléon as Caesar; in 1814 it was replaced by one of Henri IV, removed for the 100 Days (1815) when Napoléon attempted to regain power. Louis XVIII then had a colossal fleur-de-lis hoisted there; Louis-Philippe re-established Napoléon, this time in military uniform, and Napoléon III substituted a replica of the original. The Commune tore down the column in 1871 – an incident for which the painter Gustave Courbet was blamed and exiled.

The Residents

No **15** now houses the **Ritz Hotel**; nos **13** and **11**, occupied by the Ministry of Justice, were formerly the Royal Chancellery – the official measure for the metre was inlaid in the façade in 1848; no **9** was the house of the military governor of Paris at the end of the 19C; **Chopin** died at no **12** in 1849; no **16** was the home of the German, Dr Mesmer, founder of the theory of Mesmerism.

The square and its surrounding area collect together all the great names in jewellery design: Van Cleef & Arpels, Boucheron, Mauboussin and others. At a stone's throw, in rue Cambon, is the house from which **Coco Chanel** reigned over the fashion world for half a century, while living at the Ritz.

Rue de la Paix

In the French version of Monopoly, this is the most expensive street in Paris. Jewellers and goldsmiths, **Cartier** (no **11**) among others, have brought it international fame making its name synonymous with elegance and luxury.

Place de l'Opéra★★

Haussmann envisaged place de l'Opéra not simply as a setting for the National Music Academy but also as a circus from which a number of roads should radiate. This vision was criticised for being too grandiose: the square seemed enormous at that time, whereas today, choked with traffic, it barely seems big enough! The square is presently lined with luxurious shop-windows proffering elegant leather goods (Lancel) and jewellery (Clerc) whereas the Café de la Paix terraces provide an enticing break to the foot-weary.

▶ *Turn left onto boulevard des Capucines.*

Boulevard des Capucines

This street takes its name from a Capuchin monastery that once stood here. No 27 has a splendid façade embellished with brass and copper panels by Frantz Jourdain, maestro of the Art Nouveau decorative style.

▶ *Turn right onto rue Scribe.*

Rue Scribe

Named after Eugène Scribe (1791-1861), who directed the Théâtre Comique Français for 30 years. At no 4, **Le Grand-Hôtel** is a grand vestige from the era of Napoléon III (1862); the Opéra salon has been converted into a restaurant.

▶ *Take rue Auber to return to boulevard des Capucines, and turn right onto rue de la Michodière.*

Place Gaillon

Erected in 1707, this fountain was re-modelled by Visconti in 1827.

▶ *Rue Gaillon leads to avenue de l'Opéra.*

Avenue de l'Opéra★

One of the main arteries of the city, this luxurious thoroughfare was begun simultaneously at either end by Haussmann in 1854 and completed in 1878. For the tourist the avenue is the ideal shopping centre for perfumes, scarves, gifts and *articles de Paris* (fancy souvenirs).

Museums and Other Attractions

L'Opéra-Garnier/Paris Opéra★★

Place de l'Opéra. ◷*Mid-Jul–Sept, daily 10am–5pm (except during matinée or special event); Sept–mid-Jul, 10am–6pm.* ◖*Guided tours of the public foyers and museum Wed, Sat, Sun 11.30am and 2.30pm (daily Jul–Aug).* ◉*8€ (12€ with*

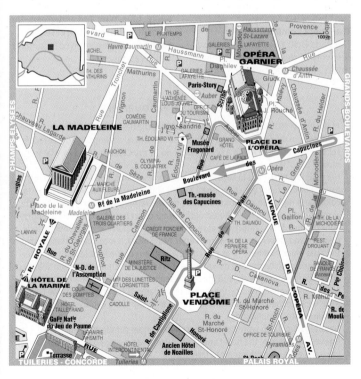

Opéra Garnier

S. Sauvignier/MICHELIN

tour). ⊘*1 Jan and 1 May.* ☎*08 92 89 90 90. www.operadeparis.fr.*
The celebrity of France's first home of opera, the prestige of its ballet company, the architectural magnificence of the great staircase and foyer, the sumptuous decoration of the auditorium, make attending a performance a gala event. It is well worth taking the tour of the Opéra, which has recently been completely restored, inside and out.

The Opéra Company

The Paris Opéra has been based successively at the Palais-Royal Theatre (1673), at the Salle des Machines in the Tuileries Palace (1764), then back at the Palais-Royal for great performances of Rameau and Gluck, the Salle Favart (1820), the Salle Le Peletier (1821) and the Palais Garnier (1875) before being partly transferred to the Opéra-Bastille in 1990. Since 1994 the Palais Garnier and the Opéra Bastille have been collectively known as the Opéra National de Paris (ONP).

The Opera House

Under Napoléon III the idea for a purpose-built opera house was born and **Charles Garnier**, a 35-year-old unknown architect was awarded the contract. The large theatre has a vast stage that holds up to 450 performers.

The building

Considered the most brilliant monument of the Second Empire, the main façade overlooking the place de l'Opéra features a series of sculpted figures.

Interior★★★

A feature of the building's originality is Garnier's use of multicoloured marbles quarried in different parts of France: white, blue, pink, red and green. The magnificent **Great Staircase** and the **Grand Foyer** are conceived for sumptuous occasions.

Coco Chanel's Headquarters

At the end of 1910, Gabrielle Chanel (1883-1971), the descendant of a family of stall holders from the Cévennes, and well versed in financial dealings and horse racing, set up shop as a milliner in a basement at no 21 rue Cambon. Ten years later she moved to no 31.

Her essential talent was in fabric cutting and dressmaking, applied with skill in the use of humble fabrics such as jersey, tweed and plaid. She had an expert eye for colour and designed clothes that relied on line rather than ornament for effect, austere but graceful. Her tailored outfits were often based on the British Sporty Look designed for comfort and ease of movement, popular among modern, independent and career-minded women after World War I. It is to Chanel that we owe the little black number – that prerequisite element of the female wardrobe, versatile enough to be dressed down if worn with flat court shoes or up with stilettos and large imitation jewels, and the tailored suit. Survival of Chanel's business during the war was ensured by the launch of the famous Number 5 perfume (1920), a stable, indefinable scent blending animal and vegetable extracts with artificial stabilisers still popular today.

Naturally slim, Coco wore her hair short, often under simple hats. Impressed and forever interested in the ballet and the theatre, Chanel shaped the trends in fashion – she even made the sun-tan fashionable!

MUSÉE D'ORSAY ★★★

Ⓜ SOLFÉRINO (LINE 12) – RER: MUSÉE-D'ORSAY (LINE C) – BUSES: 24, 73

Since 1986, the immense space of the former Gare d'Orsay has served as a fine arts museum, whose collection covers the years 1848 to 1914. It's an impressive place, both for the setting and the masterpieces it contains. A footbridge across the Seine links the museum with the Tuileries Gardens opposite.

- 🛈 **Information:** Pyramides welcome centre, 25 rue des Pyramides.
  ☎08 92 68 30 00 (0.34€ per min). http://en.parisinfo.com.
- ▶ **Orient Yourself:** The museum overlooks the Seine from the Left Bank.
- Ⓟ **Parking:** Underground parking just outside the museum.
- 👁 **Don't Miss:** The scale model of a cross-section of the Opéra Garnier.
- 🕐 **Organizing Your Time:** The museum can be visited in two hours.
- ♿ **Also See:** INVALIDES, ST-GERMAIN-DES-PRÉS, JARDINS DES TUILERIES.

A Bit of History

From railway station to museum
– At the end of the 19C, the Orléans rail company acquired the site of the ruined Orsay Palace, which had been set ablaze in 1871 during the Commune. Designed to harmonise with the buildings of this elegant quarter, the iron and glass structure is screened on the outside by a monumental façade modelled on the Louvre across the Seine and on the inside by a coffered ceiling with stucco decoration. The building was inaugurated two years later on 14 July 1900.
For nearly 40 years Orsay station handled about 200 trains daily on the Paris-Orléans route. As electrification spread to the rest of the network, longer trains came into service, outgrowing the platforms at Orsay station. In 1939 progress out-paced the building's capabilities; the main-line station functioned briefly for suburban traffic before succumbing to closure. It was put to a number of uses: as reception centre for prisoners at the Liberation, a film-set for Kafka's *The Trial* filmed by Orson Welles in 1962, and temporary **auction-rooms** during the refurbishment of the Hôtel Drouot in 1974.

In 1977 President V Giscard d'Estaing entrusted the architect Gae Aulenti, to transform the station into a museum of 19C art, and the Musée d'Orsay was inaugurated nine years later by President F Mitterrand.

Musée d'Orsay seen across the Seine

Camille Moirenc/Photononstop/Tips Images

Visit

62 rue de Lille. ⏱️🕐*Tue–Sun 9.30am–6pm, Thu 9.30am–9.45pm.* 🕐*1 Jan, 1 May, 25 Dec.* 🎫*8€ for the permanent collection, 9€ for access to the permanent and temporary collections; no charge 1st Sun in the month.* ☎*01 40 49 48 14. www. musee-orsay.fr.*

Permanent exhibitions

The collections are presented in chronological order and by theme. Each major artistic movement from the period 1848 to 1914 is represented, and the collection is divided into four major categories: painting, sculpture, architecture and decorative arts.

The permanent collection begins on the ground floor, continues on the uppermost level, and finishes on the middle floor. A free plan of the museum is available at the reception desk, showing the exact content of the galleries. This will help the visitor to relate to the main artistic movements mentioned here.

Painting and Sculpture

Neoclassicism

This movement, which was inspired by the works of Antiquity, dates from the end of the 18C and reached its height

Girl in Pink Dress (1860-65) by Camille Corot

©Scala, Florence/Musée d'Orsay

in the early to mid-19C. Artists include the sculptors Cavelier, Guillaume and **Pradier**, and the painter **Jean-Auguste-Dominique Ingres** (1780-1867).

Romanticism

Running parallel with Neoclassicism, Romanticism developed first in England and Germany and concentrated on colour and movement. Still popular in 1860, artists included the sculptors Barye, Rude and Préault, and the painters Chassériau and **Eugène Delacroix** (1798-1863).

Realism

From 1830 until the end of the 19C, these artists started painting from their observations of everyday life and of nature, abandoning contemporary academic practice. **Artists** include the sculptor Meissonnier, the painters Rosa Bonheur, Antigna, Fantin-Latour, **Honoré Daumier** (1808-79), Jean-François Millet (1814-75) and Gustave Courbet (1819-77), whose paintings caused a scandal, especially *The Origin of Life*. *The Burial at Ornans* (1849) is perhaps the first real expression of Realism. Likened to his contemporary Émile Zola who developed the Realist novel, Courbet here depicts the real life of ordinary people from his home village, full of dignity and reverence while attending the funeral of a working man.

The Barbizon School

The development of industrial towns prompted some artists to rediscover the countryside. **Camille Corot** (1796-1875) moved to Barbizon in 1830, favouring dark, earthy hues of colour, muted tones of twilight, inspired by the wooded landscapes around Fontainebleau. Théodore Rousseau (1812-67) is considered as the leader of the Barbizon School of painters, skilfully catching the effect of fleeting light.

Eclecticism

This broad movement, covering the second half of the 19C, and corresponding to the Second Empire in France, was followed by official painters. It no longer favoured only Antiquity, but a mixture of all previous styles. Note the harmonious marble sculpture *Sleeping Hebe* (1869) by Carrier-Belleuse, in the central alley, as well as Carpeaux's *Ugolin* (1862) and *The Dance* (1869), created for the façade of the Opéra Garnier. Other eclecticism works by the sculptors Debois, Clésinger, Cordier and Jean-Baptiste Carpeaux (1827-75); the painters Winterhalter, Fromentin and Guillaumet.

Academism

This label re-groups all the artists who continued to work in the established academic tradition throughout the second half of the 19C, including the sculptors Fremiet, Mercié and Albert Carrier-Belleuse (1824-87), and the painters Blanche, Cabanel, Duran and Gérôme.

Symbolism

Between 1855 and 1900 there was a reaction towards expressionism and against naturalism and impressionism. These artists rejected reality and sought to explore hidden worlds by graphic means. Sculptors include Bartholomé, Camille Claudel and **Auguste Rodin** (1840-1917), who felt that *Balzac* (1897) was a true expression of his own art, representing the great novelist in an abstracted pose that contrasts with the brilliance of his creative genius. Symbolist painters included Burne Jones, Hodler, Homer, Mucha, Doré, Detaille, Levy-Dhurmer, Munch, Klimt, Carrière, Puvis de Chavannes, and Gustave Moreau (1826-98), whose poetic mysterious vision is suffused with languid sensuality (*Orpheus*, 1865).

The origins of Impressionism

The new generation of artists, in reacting against the sombre shades used by their predecessors, set out to render the vibrations of light and to capture impressions of colour; hence their choice of subjects: sunlit gardens, snow, mist and flesh tones.

The early **Impressionists** include Boudin, Bazille, Cézanne, Renoir, Monet, Edgar Degas (1834-1917) and Edouard Manet (1832-83), who broke with studio convention by the boldness of their colours and compositions. *Le Déjeuner sur l'herbe* was shown at the 1863 Salon des Refusés. Manet's naked Bourgeois figures depicted in a harsh uncompromising light scandalised contemporary audiences. Two years later, Manet was further to affront his public with *Olympia* who unlike her idealised nude Renaissance counterparts is depicted with realism, unashamedly naked.

Impressionism

The 1870 war prompted artists to disperse and to regroup in the Île-de-France region: Pontoise, Auvers-sur-Oise. As the official Salons repeatedly rejected their paintings, they decided to show their work independently: the first exhibition was held in 1874 at the studio of the photographer **Nadar** where the contemptuous term impressionists was first coined after Monet's *Impression-Sunrise* (&see LAMUETTE-RANELAGH: *Musée Marmottan-Monet*). **Artists** include the sculptors Degas and Rosso, the painters **Degas, Sisley, Cézanne, Manet, Berthe Morisot, Pissarro,** Gustave Caillebotte (1848-94; also renowned as a patron of the arts), **Pierre-Auguste Renoir** (1841-1919), and **Claude Monet** (1840-1926), whose work epitomised this new relationship between the artist and nature. Among the best-known works from this group of artists are *Planing the floor* (1875) by Caillebotte (gallery 30), Renoir's *Le Moulin de la Galette* (1876), and the bronze *Little 14-Year-Old Dancer* (1881) by Degas.

Naturalism

This movement lasted from 1870 to 1920 and continued the tradition of Realism, this time as expressed by official or academic artists such as the sculptors Aubé, Dalou and Constantin

Meunier (1831-1905), and the painters Breitner, Bashkirtseff, Bastien-Lepage and Cormon.

The Pont-Aven School

The charming Breton village of Pont-Aven attracted artists from 1885 to 1895, who together formulated a new style by eliminating detail, simplifying forms and using flat, bright colours. **Paul Gauguin** (1848-1903), who later moved to Tahiti in search of a mythical Eden, painted his *Self-portrait with the yellow Christ* (1889) at Pouldu, in Brittany.

Neo-Impressionism

1886 marks the official end of Impressionism, but research into the nature of light continued with Divisionism or Pointillism, suggesting light by means of dabs of pigment. Here small dots of pure colour are painstakingly juxtaposed to evoke shimmering light. Artists of this style include **Matisse**, Renoir, Cross, Paul Signac (1863-1935), Paul Cézanne (1839-1906), Georges Seurat (1859-91), **Henri de Toulouse-Lautrec** (1864-1901), and **Vincent Van Gogh** (1853-90), whose tormented temperament was reflected in the anguished movement of his work (*Self-portrait*, 1889; *The church at Auvers-sur-Oise*, 1890).

The Nabis

This group of painters whose name is derived from the Hebrew for prophet, devised the Nabis pictorial manifesto under the direction of Gauguin in October 1888 at Pont-Aven. The movement continued until 1910. All the artists involved were concerned as much with easel paintings as with large decorative panels, book illustration, prints and stage sets, including the painters Roussel, Vallotton, Édouard Vuillard (1868-1940), Pierre Bonnard (1867-1947), who was strongly influenced by Japanese prints, and Maurice Denis (1870-1943), who published pamphlets outlining the group's aspirations. Note Bonnard's *Game of Croquet* (1892), *The Muses* (1893) by Denis and Vuillard's *Public Garden* (1894).

The Crib (1872) by Berthe Morisot

©Scala, Florence/Musée d'Orsay

La table de cuisine (1888-90) by Paul Cézanne (detail)

©Scala, Florence/Musée d'Orsay

Architecture

This section is limited to the architecture of the Second Empire period (1852-70). Among the architectural models is a fascinating study of the Opéra district, with a cross-section through the Opéra Garnier showing the stage and its machinery.

Decorative and Applied Arts

1850-80

The key quality inherent in the exhibits of this period is versatility, as fashion and taste succumbed to the influence of colonisation, foreign travel, the universal exhibitions, in particular that of 1867, which revealed Japanese art. New industrial businesses employed artists who combined good design with practicality, able to produce one-off pieces as well as the mass-produced. **Christofle** radically changed their orientation as electro-plating processes enabled mass production of silver-plate without losing the fine art of crafting quality. The **medal cabinet**, regarded as one of the most original pieces of the 1867 exhibition, is decorated with scenes from Merovingian history (low relief in silver-plated bronze by Frémiet).

French Art Nouveau

A desire for change and for a new form of expression away from the past swept through Europe in around 1890. Art Nouveau, or the Modern Style, is characterised by serpentine lines and organic decoration. Art in everything, a fundamental concept to the style, broke down distinctions between artist and craftsman, painter and decorator, to achieve the most complete design. In France Art Nouveau was launched by the Nancy School. After studying sculpture and painted wallpapers, Lalique (1860-1945) turned his hand to moulded glass and jewellery, inspired by the natural shapes of plants. Other artists include Majorelle, Gruber, Carabin and Charpentier.

International Art Nouveau

From 1880 the first examples of Art Nouveau appeared in England and soon spread to other parts of Europe (Glasgow, Vienna) and to the United States. Artists included the Belgians Van de Velde and Victor Horta (1861-1947), the Austrians Loos and Thonet, known for his curved wooden furniture, the American Frank Lloyd Wright and the Scot, Charles Rennie Mackintosh, pioneer of Functionalism.

Photography

The most recent addition to the museum, the photography galleries on the ground floor are consecrated to about 50,000 images of every type: slides, negatives, albums. Anonymous photos as well as works by Stieglitz, Nadar, Le Gray, and others make up the collection, which showcases the evolution of the medium from 1839 to 1920.

PALAIS-ROYAL★★

In this part of Paris, the grandiose setting of the Palais-Royal and the church of St-Roch remind one vividly of the city's past, in contrast to rue de Rivoli and rue St-Honoré which seem to epitomize the present with their bustling shops.

Nearby neighbourhoods: **LES HALLES, FAUBOURG ST-HONORÉ, LE LOUVRE, LES TUILERIES, PLACE DES VICTOIRES.**

- **Information:** Pyramides welcome centre, 25 rue des Pyramides. ☎0892 68 3000 (0.34€ per min). http://en.parisinfo.com.
- **Orient Yourself:** The Palais-Royal is on the north side of the Louvre Museum.
- **Parking:** Underground parking on the rue des Pyramides.
- **Don't Miss:** The charming boutiques of the Passage Vivienne.
- **Organizing Your Time:** Allow an hour for the walk, three to visit the museums.
- **Especially for Kids:** The Palais-Royal gardens have a sandbox playground.
- **Also See:** LE GRAND LOUVRE, JARDINS TUILERIES, OPÉRA.

A Bit of History

The Cardinal's Palace – In 1624, **Richelieu**, having just become Prime Minister, acquired a mansion near the Louvre and commissioned the architect **Jacques Lemercier** to build the huge edifice, known as the Cardinal's Palace.

The Royal Palace – On his deathbed in 1642 the Cardinal left his mansion to Louis XIII who soon followed him to the grave. The king's widow, Anne of Austria, left the Louvre for the beautiful mansion, which was smaller and more com-

fortable, with her young son, the future Louis XIV. It was henceforth known as the Royal Palace. The Fronde in 1648 forced their hasty departure. When Louis XIV returned to Paris he settled back in the Louvre, lodging various royal family members in the Palais-Royal, including **Queen Henrietta** Maria of France, widow of Charles I of England.

The Orléans – In 1780 the palace passed to Louis-Philippe of Orléans who, being forever short of money, undertook to redevelop the site: around three sides of the garden he commissioned the architect **Victor Louis** to build uniformly fronted blocks of apartments over arcades of shops at ground level. Three new streets were called after the younger Orléans brothers: Valois, Montpensier and Beaujolais. The Théâtre Français (now the **Comédie-Française**) and the Palais-Royal Theatre at the corner of rue de Montpensier and rue Beaujolais (also still in operation) were added in 1786 and 1790. After the Revolution, the palace became a gambling house until, in 1801, Napoléon converted it into offices, and in 1807 into the Exchange and Commercial Court. Louis XVIII returned the mansion to the Orléans family and it was from there that Louis-Philippe set out for the Hôtel de Ville, in 1830, to be proclaimed king.

Palais-Royal

S. Sauvignier/MICHELIN

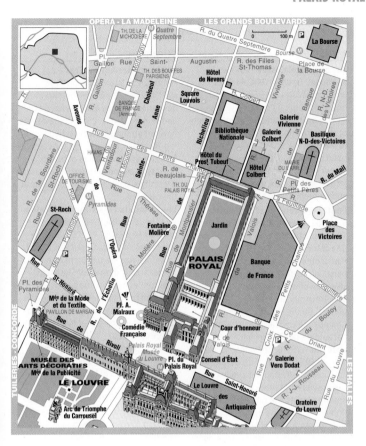

Sights

Place des Pyramides

The equestrian statue of **Joan of Arc** is by the 19C sculptor, Frémiet. It was here that she was wounded on 8 September 1429 when leading her attack on the capital.

Rue de Rivoli★

It was Napoléon who, in 1811, had the part of the avenue between rue de Castiglione and place des Pyramides constructed, although it was not to be completed until nearly the middle of the century. The houses facing the Tuileries are of uniform design above arcades lined with both luxury and souvenir shops.

Place du Palais-Royal

The façade of the Palais-Royal overlooking the square consists of a central block (occupied by the Conseil d'État) with two recessed lateral wings, the whole decorated with restrained, 18C carvings of military trophies and allegorical figures by Pajou. The square is also flanked by the **Louvre des Antiquaires**, consisting of 250 antique shops.

Place André-Malraux★

From this crossroads there is a splendid view up avenue de l'Opéra. Created in the time of Napoléon III and ornamented with modern fountains, it was formerly known as place du Théâtre-Français, taking its present name from the writer and Minister of Culture under De Gaulle.

Address Book

NIGHTLIFE

Bar de l'Hôtel Costes – *239 rue St-Honoré, 1st arr.* ☎*01 42 44 50 25. www.hotelcostes.com. Daily.* In what is one of the capital's smartest addresses, a maze of little rooms provides a variety of styles, ranging from Second Empire to Mediterranean. The Italian-style patio is popular in the fine weather. In favour with the capital's cosmopolitan jet-set, who flock here to listen to see and be seen.

Fontainebleau Bar at Le Meurice – *228 rue de Rivoli, 1st arr.* ☎*01 44 58 10 10. www.lemeurice.com. Daily.* This is one of the nicest palace hotel bars in Paris: sober and luxurious, with wood panelling, leather armchairs and a fine selection of whiskies, malts, Cognac and Armagnac all served in crystal glasses. Try the Meurice Millénium Champagne cocktail or the Italian bartender's perfect Bellini.

Café Ruc – *159 rue St-Honoré, 1st arr.* ☎*01 42 60 97 54 Daily.* This purple-coloured café/restaurant overlooking the busy place Malraux is a favourite among tourists and members of the Comédie Française's troupe, who meet here for tea, a glass of wine or a late supper. Served in a tasteful, but unpretentious décor. It owes its name to one of its early owners.

La Scala – *188 bis rue de Rivoli, 1st arr.* ☎*01 42 61 64 00. www.lascalaparis.com. Closed Mon and Tue.* This ultra-modern dance complex has three floors, with bars, laser beams and a giant screen. The clientele are in their 20s and 30s.

SHOPPING

Le Louvre des Antiquaires – *2 pl. du Palais-Royal, 1st arr.* Ⓜ*Palais-Royal.* ☎*01 42 97 27 27. www.louvre-anti-quaires.com. Closed Mon all year, Sun and Mon in Jul–Aug.* 250 antique dealers have set up shop in this vast building. Paintings, archaeology, jewellery, furniture etc. This gallery of beautiful objects displayed in superb show cases is worthy of a museum. Ask for a map at the entrance.

Les Salons du Palais-Royal Shiseido – *142 gal. de Valois, 1st arr.* Ⓜ*Bourse or Palais-Royal.* ☎*01 49 27 09 09. www.salons-shiseido.com. Closed Sun. Closed public holidays.* Serge Lutens, the former artistic director of Shisheido, now creates his own fine perfumes. Based on the night and day theme, this fan of Morocco has designed a setting full of mystery to present his fragrances of rare essences.

Verlet – *256 rue St-Honoré, 1st arr.* Ⓜ*Palais-Royal.* ☎*01 42 60 67 39. Closed Sun, Sat–Sun May–Oct and 3 weeks in Aug.* The pleasant smell of freshly ground coffee seeps out of the establishment of this coffee shop-cum-tearoom. Since 1880, the house has stocked a variety of coffees and teas and in the winter, preserved fruits, to the delight of the faithful regulars of this genuine craftsman.

WHERE TO STAY AND EAT

Turn to the back of the guide for selected hotels, restaurants, bistros and cafés listed by *arrondissement*. This district is in the 1st arrondissement.

Comédie-Française

2 rue de Richelieu. The best way to appreciate the interior of one of the finest theatres in Paris is to attend a performance. The repertoire is mainly classical, although the works of more modern authors are now included. In the foyer are Houdon's famous bust of **Voltaire**★★ and the chair in which **Molière** was sitting when taken fatally ill on stage in 1673 in a performance of *Le Malade imaginaire.*

Walking Tour

Around Palais-Royal★

Richelieu's palace now accommodates the Ministry of Culture, Constitutional Council, and the Council of State (⊶ *closed to the public).*

Main courtyard

Pass through the covered passage into the courtyard enclosed within a continuous arcaded gallery. An impressive central façade surmounted by allegorical statues overlooks the controversial modern composition (280 black and white columns of unequal height) by **Daniel Buren**. Separating the courtyard from the garden is a double colonnade, the Orléans Gallery, built at the time of the Restoration (1814-30) and formerly covered by an iron and glass roof. The Valois side gallery is known as the Prow Gallery because of its nautical decoration (Richelieu was Minister for the Navy).

▸ *Take a detour through the passage leading out of the arcades to the place de Valois, following the rue Montesquieu to the Galerie Véro-Dodat.*

Galerie Véro-Dodat

Created in 1826 by two butchers Véro and Dodat, it was one of the first Parisian streets with gas lamps. The interior décor of the covered passage is Neoclassic in style, housing many charming arts and antiques boutiques.

▸ *Return to the Palais-Royal.*

Jardin du Palais-Royal★★

The quiet garden has retained its 18C atmosphere, surrounded by the elegant façades designed by the architect Victor Louis. The shops along the gallery are a mix of upscale couture and art as well as dusty stamp and medal collectors. The writer Sidonie **Colette** (1873-1954) died at the age of 81, at 94 Galerie de Beau-

jolais. **Jean Cocteau** (1889-1963), poet, playwright and film-maker, lived for 20 years in an apartment overlooking the gardens at 36 rue de Montpensier.

Rue de Richelieu

The 19C **Molière** fountain by Visconti with statues by Pradier stands just before no **40**, the site of Molière's house, to which he was taken after collapsing on stage on 17 February 1673 at the age of 51. No **61** served as home to Henri Beyle (1783-1842), more commonly known as **Stendhal**, where he wrote his novels *Le Rouge et le Noir* and *Promenades dans Rome*.

Rue Ste-Anne

No **47** is the house the composer **Lully** had built in 1671, borrowing 11 000 *livres* from Molière to do so. Note the music masks and motifs ornamenting the façade.

Rue de l'Échelle

So called after the ladder or flight of steps leading to a scaffold which stood on the site during the Ancien Régime, used to publicly humiliate polygamists, perjurers and blasphemers.

Rue St-Honoré★

The windows of the section of rue St-Honoré between rue Royale and rue de Castiglione are a window-shopper's paradise. Under the Ancien Régime, before rue de Rivoli was laid, this road

Jardin du Palais-Royal

S. Sauvignier/MICHELIN

A Turbulent History

In 1680 Louis XIV combined Molière's company with the troupe at the **Hôtel de Bourgogne** and granted it the sole right of performance in the capital. The new company took the name Comédie-Française.

The company, caught up in endless quarrels with the authorities at the Sorbonne, was constantly on the move. During the Revolution a dispute broke out in the company between players who supported the Republicans and those favouring the Royalists. In 1792 the former, led by Talma, took over the present theatre. Napoléon showed a great interest in the Comédie-Française, and also in the leading lady, Mlle Mars. In 1812 he decreed that the company should consist of an association of actors, active associates, apprentice players and retired players on pension. Today the theatre continues to be managed by a director nominated by the State.

was the main route out of Paris towards the west where members of the royal court, nobility and financiers, all came to do their shopping.

Église St-Roch★

Some idea of the scale of Baron Haussmann's earth-moving undertakings can be gained from the fact that to enter the church nowadays you have to walk up 13 steps, whereas before the construction of Avenue de l'Opéra you had to go down just seven steps.

On 5 October 1795 St-Roch was the scene of bloody fighting. A column of Royalists leading an attack on the Convention, then in the Tuileries, aimed to march through rue St-Roch. A young General Bonaparte, who was in charge of the defence, mowed down the men massed on the church steps and perched on its façade with gunfire. The bullet holes can still be seen.

The foundation stone of the church was laid by Louis XIV in 1653. Funds quickly ran dry, but work was able to continue as a result of a lottery organised in 1705. Instead of completing the nave, however, a series of chapels was constructed beyond the apse, so that the church's original length (80m/262.4ft) was extended to 125m/410ft. This effectively destroyed the unity of design. The **Lady Chapel**★ by Jules Hardouin-Mansart, with its tall, richly decorated dome, leads into a Communion Chapel with a flat dome and finally a Calvary Chapel, rebuilt in the 19C. In 1719 a gift of 100 000 *livres* from **John Law**, who

had recently converted to Catholicism, enabled the nave to be completed. Robert de Cotte's Jesuit-style façade dates from 1736.

Among those buried in St-Roch in the Lady Chapel and side chapels are the playwright Corneille, the garden designer **Le Nôtre**, the philosophers **Diderot** and d'Holbach, and **Mme Geoffrin**, hostess of a famous 18C salon.

Works of Art:

1) Tomb of Henri of Lorraine, Count d'Harcourt by Renard (17C) and bust of the 17C Marshal de Créqui by **Coysevox** (17C).
2) Tomb of Duke Charles de Créqui.
3) **The Triumph of the Virgin**★ painted by J B Pierre on the dome. *The Nativity* at the altar by the Anguier brothers, was brought from the Val-de-Grâce.
4) *Resurrection of the Son of the Widow of Naïm* by Le Sueur (17C).
5) Le Nôtre bust by Coysevox and funerary inscription.
6) *Baptism of Christ* by Lemoyne.
7) Baptismal Chapel: frescoes by Chassériau (19C).

Museums and Other Attractions

Musée de la Mode et du Textile★

107 rue de Rivoli. ♿ ◷ *Tue–Fri 11am–6pm, Sat–Sun 10am–6pm.* ◷ *1 Jan, 1 May, 15 Aug and 25 Dec.* ◉ *8€ (ticket combined*

with the Museum of Decorative Arts). ☎01 44 55 57 50. www.lesartsdecoratifs.fr.
The collection at this museum of fashion and textiles encompasses over 20 000 outfits, 35 000 accessories and 21 000 fabric samples dating from the 18C to the present day, displayed in changing exhibitions. Famous names include Poiret, Lanvin, Schiaparelli, Dior and Paco Rabanne.

Musée des Arts décoratifs★★

111 rue de Rivoli. ♿🕐*Same opening hours and fees as for the Musée de la Mode et du Textile (♿ see above). www.lesarts decoratifs.fr.*
Reopened after extensive renovations in September 2006, the numerous period rooms provide a broad cross-section of the evolution of design and taste in the decorative and applied arts in France from the Middle Ages to the 20C: sculpture, painting, ceramics, furniture, jewellery, glass and tableware. Most of the paintings and sculptures come from churches and monasteries.

Musée de la Publicité

107 rue de Rivoli. ♿🕐*Same as for the Musée de la Mode et du Textile.* ☎*01 44 55 57 50. www.museedelapub.org.*
Permanent and frequently changing temporary exhibitions. A **database**★ composed of thousands of posters and advertising films is available for consultation.

Oratoire du Louvre

4 rue St-Honoré. ☎*01 42 60 21 64.* 🕐*Fri noon–3.30pm.* The Oratorian Congregation founded by Cardinal Pierre de Berulle, a secular priesthood dedicated to teaching and preaching later to rival the Jesuits, had a church built by Lemercier (1621-30). This became the royal chapel in the reigns of Louis XIII, Louis XIV and Louis XV. At the Revolution the chapel became an arms depot. Napoléon ceded the church to the Protestants in 1811 before the seminary was re-established in 1852.

Cardinal Richelieu (1585–1642)

Cardinal Richelieu is often called the first 'Prime Minister' in the modern sense of the term, because he was referred to by King Louis XIII as his 'Chief' or 'First' Minister. Richelieu was a formidable politician who controlled the power of the nobility by suppressing internal opposition to the monarchy and he succeeded in turning France into a strong centralised state.

A leading character in Dumas senior's novel *The Three Musketeers*, Richelieu is often portrayed, especially in the film adaptations of the book, as being more powerful than the King himself. He had begun his rise to power when appointed Bishop of Luçon in 1606 at the age of 19, after securing a special dispensation from the Pope and by 1614 had been elected as a representative of Poitou at the States-General in Paris. He soon became known as an advocate for the clergy in their efforts to become more involved in politics and be exempt from taxation.

As a result he came to the notice of Anne of Austria, the wife of King Louis, being appointed as her Almoner. Soon the influential Concini, then the most powerful minister in France, recognised his talents and appointed him Secretary of State for War and Foreign Affairs.

Richelieu's burgeoning career received a setback in 1617, however, when Concini was murdered. He accompanied the King's mother, Marie de' Medici when she was exiled to Blois for apparently siding with her son's enemies – a very wise move as it turned out. During this period Richelieu acted as a go-between for mother and son, leading finally to her re-instatement at Court in 1622. In return, Marie persuaded her son to appoint Richelieu as an adviser, and by the year 1622 he had been made a Cardinal. The path was now clear for Richelieu's almost inevitable rise to power and he was appointed 'First Minister' in 1624 – a position he held till his death in 1642.

PASSY

Ⓜ PASSY (LINE 6) – RER: KENNEDY-RADIO FRANCE (LINE C) – BUSES: 22, 32, 52, PC

In the 18C the hillside village of Passy, known for its ferruginous waters, was covered in vineyards. Large blocks of flats replaced the gardens and cottages when Passy became part of Paris in 1859, but a few vestiges of the old village still survive in this peaceful residential quarter.

Nearby neighbourhoods: **TROCADÉRO, AUTEUIL, JAVEL, BOIS DE BOULOGNE.**

- 🅸 **Information:** Pyramides welcome centre, 25 rue des Pyramides. ☎08 92 68 30 00 (0.34€ per min). http://en.parisinfo.com.
- ▶ **Orient Yourself:** Passy is a southwestern district of the Right Bank.
- 🅿 **Parking:** Underground on rue de Passy, street parking on the side streets.
- 👓 **Don't Miss:** Balzac's charming cottage house, the caves of the Musée du Vin.
- 🕐 **Organizing Your Time:** Allow three hours to visit the district and museums.
- 🅺🅸🅳🅨 **Especially for Kids:** The Parc de Passy (off rue Raynouard) has a playgroud.
- 👁 **Also See:** LA MUETTE-RANELAGH, TROCADÉRO, AUTEUIL.

Walking Tour

- ▶ *At Passy station, go down the stairs to square d'Alboni, turn right on rue des Eaux.*

Rue des Eaux

Named for the natural spring discovered here in 1650, this street now leads to the Musée du Vin (👓 *see Museums and Other Attractions*).

- ▶ *Turn right when leaving the museum, and go up the staircase Passage des Eaux.*

Rue Raynouard

Many famous people have lived in this street, including the Enlightenment philosopher **Jean-Jacques Rousseau**. The little cottage on the left, at no 47, belonged to the prolific writer **Honoré de Balzac** (👓 *see Museums and Other Attractions*). The modern residences in reinforced concrete at nos 51 to 55 show a confident application of the new material by architect Auguste Perret who lived here from 1932 until his death in 1954. **Benjamin Franklin** resided at no 66 while negotiating the alliance between Louis XVI and the new Republic of the United States; he erected France's first lightning rod over his house.

- ▶ *Take a detour on the left and down the stairs.*

Rue Berton★ is one of the most unusual in Paris, its ivy clad walls and gaslight brackets giving it an old country atmosphere. Number 24 was the back entrance to Balzac's house, where he would escape from creditors.

- ▶ *Double-back to the rue Raynouard and turn left onto rue de l'Annonciation.*

Rue de l'Annonciation

Overlooking this quaint commercial street at the place du Père Marcelin-Champagnat is the 17C **Eglise Notre-Dame-de-Grace-de-Passy**. *Exit by the door on the left behind the chancel, and turn left to get back to rue de l'Annonciation.* The street becomes pedestrianised after rue Lekain, with shops and cafés lining the lively **place de Passy**. The **rue de Passy** is lined with fashionable boutiques.

- ▶ *Follow rue de Passy to place de Costa Rica and turn left onto rue Benjamin Franklin, to the place du Trocadéro (👓 see TROCADÉRO); turn left onto avenue Paul-Doumer.*

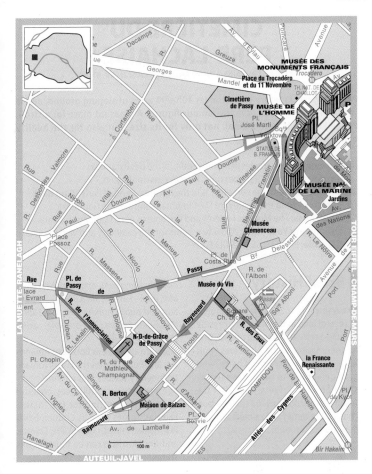

Cimetière de Passy

2 rue du Commandant-Schloesing. ◯*Mid-Mar–early Nov, 8am–6pm, Sat 8.30am–6pm, Sun and public holidays 9am–6pm; early Nov–mid-Mar, 8am–5.30pm, Sat 8.30am–5.30pm, Sun and public holidays 9am–5.30pm.* ↝*Guided tours (2hr) at* ✆*6€.* ☎*01 43 28 47 63.*

Passy Cemetery contains the somewhat extravagant graves of the local residents as well as famous writers and artists.

Museums

Maison de Balzac

47 rue Raynouard. ◯*Tue–Sun 10am–6pm.* ◯*Public holidays.* ☎*01 55 74 41 80. www. balzac.paris.fr.*

Down its original metal stairway, half-hidden in a garden, is the house occupied illicitly by Honoré de Balzac between 1840 and 1847; often on the run from his creditors, he was able to make use of the back route out of the house. Manuscripts, caricatures and engravings pertaining to the author of *La Comédie Humaine* described in his novels complement an adjoining library.

Musée du Vin – Caveau des Échansons

5–7 square Charles-Dickens. ♿◯*Tue–Sun 10am–6pm; until 5pm 24 Dec and 31 Dec.* ◯*25 Dec, 1 Jan.* ✆*8.90€.* ☎*01 45 25 63 26. www.museeduvinparis.com.*

No 5 rue des Eaux marks the original entrance to the former quarries. The underground galleries now house a wine museum with waxwork figures and implements recalling the days when monks produced wine there.

CIMETIÈRE DU PÈRE-LACHAISE★

PÈRE-LACHAISE (LINES 2 AND 3) – BUSES: 26, 60, 61, 69

Paris' largest cemetery spreads over 40ha/99 acres of sloping ground, and is the final resting place of many famous figures. A pleasant place for a stroll, Père-Lachaise is exceptional, not only for its size, but also for the quality of its statuary.

- **Information:** Pyramides welcome centre, 25 rue des Pyramides. 08 92 68 30 00 (0.34€ per min). http://en.parisinfo.com.
- **Orient Yourself:** The cemetery is in the northeast end of Paris' Right Bank.
- **Parking:** Along the boulevard Ménilmontant and avenue Gambetta.
- **Don't Miss:** The Mur des Fédérés and the houses of La Campagne à Paris.
- **Organizing Your Time:** Allow two hours for the cemetery and walking tour.
- **Also See:** BELLEVILLE, BASTILLE.

A Bit of History

The name – In 1626 the Jesuits bought a piece of land in the open countryside to build a retreat for retired priests. One frequent visitor to the place was Louis XIV's confessor, Father La Chaise, who gave generously to the house's reconstruction in 1682. Forty years after the Jesuits' expulsion in 1763 the city purchased the land for a cemetery to be designed by Brongniart.

Visit

Cemetery – *Mid–Mar–early Nov, 8am–6pm, Sat 8.30am–6pm, Sun and public holidays 9am–6pm; early Nov–mid-Mar, 8am–5.30pm, Sat 8.30am–5.30pm, Sun and public holidays 9am–5.30pm. Guided tours (2hr) possible, 6€. 01 55 25 82 10.*

Maps are available at Porte des Amandiers and Porte Gambetta. Full of romantic funerary statues, this national heritage site has over 3 000 trees, creating an attractive setting for the tombs. Famous figures such as Chopin, Edith Piaf, Balzac, Proust, Oscar Wilde, Colette, and Jim Morrison can be found in this stunning setting.

Le Mur des Fédérés (Federalists' Wall) – On the evening of 27 May 1871 the last insurgents of the Paris **Commune**,

Cimetière du Père-Lachaise

S. Sauvignier/MICHELIN

An Américaine in Paris

"Paris was where the twentieth century was."

American expatriates **Gertrude Stein** and **Alice B Toklas** lived just minutes from the Luxembourg Gardens at no 27 rue de Fleurus.

From 1903 to 1937, their courtyard apartment and atelier, with its famed collection of paintings by contemporary masters, hosted Paris' most avant-garde expatriate *salon*; their guest list reads like a Who's Who of the early 20C art and literary world: Picasso, Juan Gris, Matisse, Erik Satie, Hemingway, Pound, Sherwood Anderson... Although Gertrude Stein significantly influenced numerous expatriate writers (the term Lost Generation is attributed to her), international recognition for her own experimental works came only in 1933 with the publication of *The Autobiography of Alice B Toklas*.

In 1938 the two women moved nearby to no 5 rue Christine (in the Odéon quarter). Stein died in 1946 and was buried in Père Lachaise Cemetery. Toklas joined her in 1967 (her name is on the back of the tombstone).

having shot their hostages in Belleville, rallied in the cemetery, fighting the Versailles troops among the tombstones. At dawn the 147 survivors were shot against the wall in the south-east corner and buried where they fell in a communal grave – a place of pilgrimage for many ever since. Perhaps the most moving monument is the one next to the wall, dedicated to the resistance movement and deportees of World War II.

Walking Tour

The Village of Charonne

▶ *From the cemetery, go to place Gambetta, then to Porte de Bagnolet via rue Belgrand. From the metro (Porte-de-Bagnolet), head for the northeast corner of the square with the same name, then take the steps in rue Géo-Chavez.*

Address Book

NIGHTLIFE

La Flèche d'or – *102 bis rue de Bagnolet, 20th arr. ☎01 44 64 01 02. www.flechedor.fr. Open concert nights.* Paris' underground culture reigns over this former train station. Free indie-rock and electronic concerts are held here for a varied public, but which is predominantly young and cool. Restaurant overlooking the old rail tracks.

La Maroquinerie – *23 rue Boyer, 20th arr. ☎01 40 33 35 05. www.lamaroquinerie.fr. Closed Sun, public holidays and Aug.* Located in a former leather workshop, this alternative café operates primarily as concert venue (world music, jazz, rock), but there are also literary readings and club nights. Restaurant.

La Mère Lachaise – *78 blvd de Ménilmontant, 20th arr. ☎01 47 97 61 60. Daily.* This popular locals' café has opted for a vintage flea-market décor in a jungle of plants. Fine terrace close to Père-Lachaise. Chess and newspapers available; traditional cuisine, brunch on Sundays.

SHOPPING

La Campagne à Paris – *1210 rue des Pyrénées, 20th arr. ☎01 46 36 88 57. Closed Sun afternoon.* A charming retro-style boutique selling sweets, chocolates, foie gras, wines and teas.

WHERE TO STAY AND EAT

Turn to the back of the guide for selected hotels restaurants, bistros and cafés, listed by *arrondisement*. This district is in the 20th arrondissement.

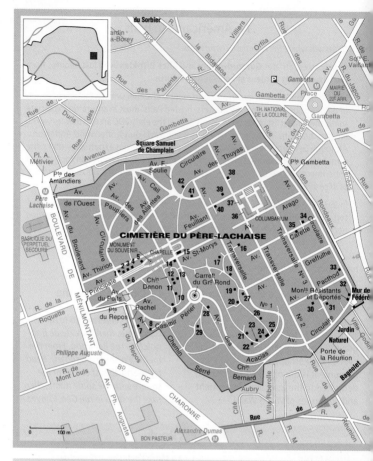

Cimetière du Père Lachaise

1 - Colette

2 - Rossini (cenotaph)

3 - Alfred de Musset (under a willow, at his request)

4 - Baron Haussmann

5 - Generals Lecomte and Thomas

6 - Arago

7 - James de Rothschild

8 - Abelard and Heloise

9 - Miguel Angel Asturias

10 - Chopin

11 - Cherubini

12 - Boieldieu (cenotaph)

13 - Bellini

14 - Thiers

15 - Sarah Bernhardt

16 - Corot

17 - Molière and La Fontaine

18 - Alphonse Daudet

19 - Hugo Family

20 - Bibesco Family (Anna de Noailles)

21 - Maréchal Ney

22 - Beaumarchais

23 - Maréchaux Davout, Masséna, Lefebvre

24 - Murat and Caroline Bonaparte

25 - David d'Angers

26 - Auguste Comte

27 - Jim Morrison

28 - Modigliani

The village of Charonne kept its country atmosphere until recently, and still provides a haven of peace and quiet, not far from the busy Paris ring-road. The charming garden houses of **La Campagne à Paris**★ were built for working-class families at the end of the 19C atop a former quarry dump. A pleasant stroll can be enjoyed around the more working-class area, along rue du Père-Prosper-Enfantin, rue Irénée-Blanc, rue Mondonville and rue Jules-Seigfried.

▶ *Take rue de Bagnolet.*

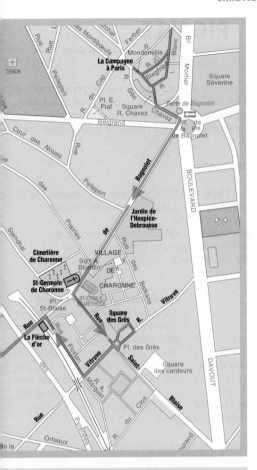

Église St-Germain-de-Charonne★

4 place St-Blaise. The church and square were the focal point of the village of Charonne. The stunted bell-tower dates from the 13C and has interesting carved capitals.

Rue St-Blaise★

Formerly the main thoroughfare of the village, this is now a pretty little street, partly pedestrianised. The carefully restored 19C houses at **square des Grès**★ and **rue Vitruve** mingle with more modern buildings.

PIGALLE

Ⓜ PLACE DE CLICHY (LINES 2 AND 13), PIGALLE (LINES 2 AND 12), BLANCHE (LINE 2)
BUSES: 30, 54, 67

A century ago, Pigalle was home to painters' studios and literary cafés such as the influential Nouvelle Athènes Café. Today, the cosmopolitan crowd which throngs its pavements is attracted by the neon lights of cabarets, nightclubs, bars and sex shops. Its name comes from the renowned local sculptor **Jean-Baptiste Pigalle** (1714-85).

Nearby neighbourhood: **MONTMARTRE.**

- ☒ **Information:** 21 place du Tertre. ☎08 92 68 30 00. http://en.parisinfo.com.
- ▶ **Orient Yourself:** Pigalle is at the foot of Montmartre's southern hillside.
- ☒ **Parking:** Along the boulevard de Clichy.
- ☺ **Don't Miss:** The garden tearoom at the Musée de la Vie Romantique.
- ☒ **Organizing Your Time:** Allow 90 minutes for this neighbourhood.
- ☒ **Also See:** MONTMARTRE, OPÉRA, GRANDS BOULEVARDS.

Visit

Boulevard de Clichy

Restaurants, cinemas, theatres and nightclubs make it a centre of Paris nightlife. The bustling **Place de Clichy** was the site of one of Ledoux's toll-houses, where in March 1814 Marshal Moncey's troops put up a spirited defence against the Allied army.

Boulevard de Rochechouart

The dance halls and cabarets of years gone by (La Boule Noire, 1822, Le Chat Noir, 1881) have disappeared, although the original façade of the Élysée-Montmartre is still visible (no 72). La Cigale (no 120) and other modern clubs have recently brought new life to the district with rock and techno music.

Address Book

NIGHTLIFE

Chao-Ba Café – *22 blvd de Clichy, 18th arr.* ☎*01-46 06 72 90 . Closed 24, 25 Dec.* Fans, bamboo, parasols, cane furniture; the stage is set for this Asian-style bar. The two floors provide a great escape from the neighbourhood bustle.

La Locomotive – *90 blvd de Clichy, 18th arr.* ☎*01 53 41 88 89. www.laloco.com. Daily.* Just next door to the Moulin-Rouge, the Loco as it is known, is always packed with tourists and night-owls. Several dance floors provide a variety of musical styles (disco, funk, rock).

SHOPPING

À l'Étoile d'Or – *30 rue Fontaine* – Ⓜ *Blanche.* ☎*01 48 74 59 55. Closed Sun, Aug and public holidays.* The finest confectionery in France can be found in this elegant 1900-style boutique run by the eternally young-at-heart Denise Acabo.

Arnold Delmontel 39 Rue des Martyrs, 9th arr. ☎01 48 78 29 33. www.arnaud-delmontel.com. Daily. This Boulangerie-Pâtisserie not only produces the best baguettes in Paris (official!), but also superb Renaissance bread and perfect pastries, biscuits and almond croissants.

WHERE TO STAY AND EAT

☒Turn to the back of the guide for selected hotels restaurants, bistros and cafés, listed by *arrondisement.* This district is in the 9th arrondissement.

FAUBOURG POISSONNIÈRE★

Ⓜ GARE DE L'EST, POISSONNIÈRE, CADET
BUSES: 30, 31, 32, 38, 39, 46, 47, 56, 65

Up until 1750 the street was called rue Ste-Anne, after a chapel that stood at no 77. It became rue du Faubourg Poissonnière as it was the last leg of the fish-traders' journey from the coast to the wholesale markets at Les Halles.

- **Information:** Pyramides welcome centre, 25 rue des Pyramides. ☎08 92 68 30 00 (0.34 per min€). http://en.parisinfo.com.
- ▶ **Orient Yourself:** This district straddles the 9th and 10th arrondissements.
- 🅿 **Parking:** Undergroung parking garages on the rue du Faubourg Poissonnière.
- **Don't Miss:** The excellent food shops along the rue du Faubourg St-Denis.
- 🕐 **Organizing Your Time:** Allow an hour to visit this area.
- **Also See:** GRANDS-BOULEVARDS, LE SENTIER.

Walking Tour

Église St-Laurent
68 boulevard de Magenta. The belfry is all that remains of the 12C sanctuary. The nave was rebuilt in the 15C and the church altered in the 17C (chancel sculpture and woodwork).

▶ *Walk north along boulevard de Magenta to square A.-Satragne (on the left).*

Ancienne maison St-Lazare
107 rue du Faubourg St-Denis. In the Middle Ages this was the capital's leper house. St Vincent de Paul, died here in 1660. It's been a hospital since 1935.

▶ *Follow rue du Faubourg St-Denis to rue de Paradis and turn right, then right again at rue d'Hauteville to place Franz-liszt.*

Église St-Vincent-de-Paul
Pl. Franz-Liszt. The church was built by the architect **Hittorff** (1824-44) who was also responsible for the final decoration of place de la Concorde.

Museums and other Attractions

Hôtel Bourrienne
58 rue d'Hauteville (at the back of the courtyard). ♿🕐*Beginning to mid-Jul and Sept, noon–6pm; otherwise by appoint-ment. Guided tours (45min).* ☜*6€–7€.* ☎*01 47 70 51 14.*

This 18C house was owned by Fortunée Hamelin, a famed *Merveilleuse* who, crippled by debt, ceded her house to Louis-Antoine Fauvelet de Bourrienne, secretary of the First Consul. There, between 1813 and 1824, the witty Mme de Bourrienne established one of Paris' most brilliant salons.

Musée de la Franc-Maçonnerie★
16 rue Cadet. ♿🕐*Tue–Fri 2pm–6pm, Sat 1pm–5pm* 🕐*Public holidays and first 3 weeks in Aug.* ☜*2€.* ☎*01 45 23 74 78. www.godf.org.*

A large room in this modern building accommodates a collection of documents (Constitution of Anderson from 1723), badges, and portraits that encapsulate the history of the main Masonic lodge of France.

SHOPPING
Furet – *63 rue de Chabrol,10th arr.* Ⓜ*Poissonnière.* ☎*01 47 70 48 34. Mon–Sat 8am–8pm. Closed Aug and public holidays.* This 1947 sweet shop sells legendary *Tanrade* jams, still prepared using cottage-industry techniques and fruits of the season.

WHERE TO STAY AND EAT
Turn to the back of the guide for selected hotels restaurants, bistros and cafés, listed by arrondisement. This district is in the 9th and 10th arrondissements.

PORT-ROYAL

RER: PORT-ROYAL (LINE B) – BUSES: 38, 83, 91

The Port-Royal neighbourhood is centred on the crossroads of Boulevard de Port Royal and Avenue de l'Observatoire, where traffic lanes are separated by a pretty garden.

Nearby neighbourhoods: **MONTPARNASSE, LUXEMBOURG, GOBELINS.**

- **Information:** Carrousel du Louvre welcome centre, Place de la Pyramide Inversée, 99 rue de Rivoli. ☎08 92 68 30 00 (0.34€ per min). http://en.parisinfo.com.
- **Orient Yourself:** Port Royal is below Luxembourg Gardens on the Left Bank.
- **Parking:** Underground on the boulevard Montparnasse.
- **Don't Miss:** The impressive architecture of Val-de-Grâce.
- **Organizing Your Time:** Allow an hour to visit this area.
- **Also See:** LUXEMBOURG, DENFERT-ROCHEREAU, MONTPARNASSE.

Sights

Avenue de l'Observatoire

The wide avenue with its central flower borders is lined with university buildings. The **Observatory Fountain**★ (1873) by Davioud is known for its famous four quarters of the globe by Carpeaux.

▶ *Take rue du Val-de-Grâce, to the right off the boulevard St-Michel.*

Val-de-Grâce★★

1 place Alphonse-Laveran.

In the early 17C Mother Angélique Arnauld ordered the construction of Port-Royal, the dependency of the Jansenist Port-Royal-des-Champs. Anne of Austria visited the community frequently to pray and discreetly to plot against Richelieu. At 37, Anne, who had been married 23 years, was still childless; she promised the gift of a magnificent church if her prayers were answered, and kept her vow on the birth of Louis XIV in 1638. The plans for the church of Val-de-Grâce were drawn by **François Mansart**, and the foundation stone laid by the young king himself in 1645. Val-de-Grâce became a military hospital in 1793. On site there is the **Musée de Service de Santé des Armées**.

Church★★

Free access Sun 11am (mass).

The church, probably the most Roman-looking in France, was erected in the Jesuit style after the Sorbonne and before the Invalides. The **dome**★★ is frescoed by Mignard with 200 figures three times life-size.

Address Book

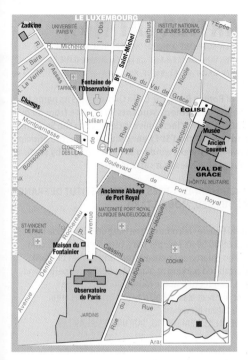

Former convent

Beyond the porch *(right of the church)* is the Classical cloister, with two superimposed tiers of bay and a mansard roof. The pavilion used by Anne of Austria is distinguished by its porch with ringed columns.

Ancienne abbaye de Port-Royal

123 boulevard de Port-Royal. ◷*Apr– 8 Nov, Wed–Mon 10.30am–12.30pm, 2pm–6pm, Sat–Sun 10.30am–6.30pm; Nov–Mar, Wed–Mon 10am–noon, 2pm–5.30pm, Sat–Sun 10.30am–6pm.* ◷*1 May, 22 Dec–4 Jan.* ✆*4.60€.* ☎*01 39 30 72 72.*

The convent became in turn a prison, a home for abandoned children, and finally the Baudelocque maternity hospital in 1818. All that remains of the former abbey are the Hôtel d'Atry, the cloisters, the chapel and the chapter-house which has retained its period woodwork.

▸ *Walk down the avenue de l'Observatoire.*

Observatoire de Paris★

61 avenue de l'Observatoire. ☎*01 40 51 22 21. www.obspm.fr.*

The construction, on orders from **Colbert** and to plans by **Claude Perrault**, was begun at the summer solstice, on 21 June 1667, and completed in 1672. Important discoveries at the Observatory include the calculation of the true dimensions of the solar system (1672), the exact determination of longitudinal meridians (Louis XIV remarked that the Academician's calculations had considerably reduced the extent of his kingdom), a calculation of the speed of light, the production of a large map of the moon (1679) and the discovery by mathematical deduction of the planet Neptune by **Le Verrier** (1846).

The building

The four walls face the cardinal points of the compass, the south side of the building determines the capital's latitude, and its median plan is bisected by the **Paris Meridian**, calculated in 1667. This determined 0° longitude until 1884 when Greenwich Mean Time was adopted.

QUARTIER LATIN★★

Ⓜ ST-MICHEL (LINE 4), CLUNY-LA-SORBONE (LINE 10) OR CARDINAL-LEMOINE (LINE 10)
RER: ST-MICHEL-NOTRE-DAME (LINES B AND C), LUXEMBOURG (LINE B)
BUSES: 21, 27, 38, 82, 83, 84, 85, 86, 87, 89

Built on the Left Bank ruins of Roman Paris, the Latin Quarter gets its name from the common language spoken by theology students who came from all over Europe beginning in the 13C to study at local universities such as the Sorbonne. Although the Panthéon and the church of St-Étienne-du-Mont are the principal landmarks, the area is known for its lively, winding streets thronged by students and the bookstores and budget eateries that cater to them.

Nearby neighbourhoods: **ST-GERMAIN-DES-PRÉS, ODÉON, INSTITUT DE FRANCE, LUXEMBOURG, MAUBERT, JUSSIEU, MOUFFETARD.**

- 🛈 **Information:** Carrousel du Louvre welcome centre, Place de la Pyramide Inversée, 99 rue de Rivoli. ☎08 92 68 30 00 (0.34€ per min). http://en.parisinfo.com.
- ▶ **Orient Yourself:** The Latin Quarter is on the eastern end of the Left Bank.
- 🅿 **Parking:** Look for underground parking at place Maubert or place Rostand.
- 👁 **Don't Miss:** The ancient architecture at the Musée du Moyen Age.
- 🕐 **Organizing Your Time:** Allow at least a half day to explore this area.
- 🧒 **Especially for Kids:** The Jardin Medieval.
- 👶 **Also See:** MAUBERT, ODÉON, LUXEMBOURG, JARDIN DES PLANTES.

A Bit of History

Gallo-Roman Lutetia – In the 3C Lutetia was a small town of some 6 000 inhabitants: Gauls occupied the Île de la Cité, while Romans settled around what is now known as Montagne Ste-Geneviève, provided their community with an aqueduct stretching 15km/9.3mi, and a network of paved roads through the Latin Quarter.

The medieval Alma Mater – In the 12C teachers, clerks and scholars migrated to the monastic communities of Ste-Geneviève and St-Victor on the Left Bank. With authority from Pope Innocent III (1215) the group founded the University of Paris, the first in France. Latin, as the language of educated men and lingua franca among the different nationalities, continued to be spoken in the area until the Revolution in 1789.

From tutelage to autonomy – In 1806 Napoléon founded the Imperial University of France, with academies being made responsible for education by the State. Gradually, the enormous influx of students made the system unworkable, and new buildings were erected in order to decentralise the faculties, but this did not prevent unrest.

In **May 1968** the tension came to a head, provoked by the forced evacuation of the Sorbonne on 3 May (due to a scheduled student protest against the Vietnam war) and the closure of the main faculties on 6 May. Demonstrations and street violence left 945 injured as the area was barricaded and the students declared the Sorbonne to be a *commune libre*. Trade unions followed with large-scale strikes, bringing chaos to the nation. On 30 May President de Gaulle was forced to dissolve his government.

Walking Tour

Quai St-Michel

No stroll along the Seine would be complete without a quick scan of the *bouquiniste* stalls – an integral part of the Paris scene. The **view** of Notre-Dame across the river is particularly fine from here, while the narrow **rue du Chat Qui Pêche** on the left demonstrates the neighbourhood's medieval dimensions.

Place St-Michel, a favourite meeting point for students

Place St-Michel

This is a popular meeting point for students and night revellers. The present square and fountain by Davioud date from the reign of Napoléon III.

Around St-Séverin

This is perhaps one of the oldest quarters of Paris. **Rue de la Harpe** was the main north-south Gallo-Roman road; **rue de la Parcheminerie** (Parchment Street) was once lined with public scribes, letter-writers and copyists. Today, the bustle continues with local residents, students and tourists attracted by experimental cinemas and theatres such as the **Théâtre de la Huchette** (23 rue de la Huchette), where **Ionesco's** absurdist plays, the Bald Soprano and The Lesson have been performed nightly since 1957.

Église St-Séverin★★

1 rue des Prêtres-St-Séverin. Building of the present church began in the first half of the 13C. The west door dates from this era, whereas above, windows, balustrades and rose window are all 15C Flamboyant Gothic, as are the tower superstructure and spire. The width of the building compared to its length is immediately striking. The extra breadth dates from the 14C and 15C when expansion was possible only laterally.

The first three bays of the nave are far superior to the rest with tracery typical of the Late Gothic Rayonnant style. In the later bays, columns are reduced to

shafts devoid of capitals. In the chancel, the five arches around the apse stand taller than those of the nave, reaching up to the well-articulated Flamboyant vaulting. The double **ambulatory**★★ encircling the chancel is a spectacular further expression of Flamboyant architecture with its bouquets of ribs rising from elegant shafts, faceted with straight or spiralling surfaces. Piers in the chancel are faced with marble and wood.

The beautiful **stained glass**★ in the upper windows is late 15C; modern glass in the chevet is by Bazaine. Outside are the restored ruins of the **St-Séverin cloister** (accessible Sun mornings only).

▶ *Take the rue de la Parchiminerie to rue de La Harpe; turn left to the blvd St-Germain.*

Jardin medieval

This garden presents medieval plants and their symbolic meaning. A clearing has been specifically designed for children. A path on the left side of the garden leads around to the entrance of the **Musée national du Moyen Âge – Thermes et Hôtel de Cluny** (see Museums and Other Attractions).

Boulevard St-Michel

The Boul' Mich, as it is known, is the heart of the area with its café terraces, publishing houses and bookshops. It leads past the ruins of the Cluny's Roman baths.

Rue des Écoles

Dating from the 19C, this street takes its name from the Quartier des Écoles. The main entrances of the **Collège de France** and the **Sorbonne** are found here.

Place de la Sorbonne

Lined with cafés, bookstores and other shops, this square serves as the courtyard for the Sorbonne, watched over by the statue of philosopher Auguste Comte.

La Sorbonne

47 rue des Écoles. In 1257 a college for 16 poor students who wished to study theology was founded by King Louis IX, at the instigation of his confessor, Robert de Sorbon (named after his native village of Sorbon in the Ardennes). From such a simple beginning was to develop the Sorbonne, the centre of theological study in pre-Revolutionary France and the seat of the University of Paris.

Under pressure from Philip the Fair, the theological faculty condemned the Knights of the Templar, who were burned at the stake in 1314. During the Hundred Years War, the Sorbonne sided with the Burgundians and the English, sending their most eminent bishop to Rouen as prosecutor in the trial of Joan of Arc. The Sorbonne steadfastly opposed all Protestants in the 16C and all philosophers in the 18C.

The buildings

Originally restored under Richelieu in the 17C, the Sorbonne was rebuilt and expanded to become the most important university in France between 1885 and 1901. The complex accommodates 22 lecture halls, two museums, 16 examination halls, 22 seminar rooms, 37 tutorial rooms for teaching staff, 240 laboratories, a library, a physics tower, an astronomy tower, administration offices, and the chancellor's lodge.

Église de la Sorbonne★

○━ *Closed for renovations.*
☎*1 40 46 20 25*

The church was designed by **Lemercier** between 1635 and 1642 in the Jesuit style. In the chancel is the white-marble **tomb**★ of Cardinal Richelieu, designed by Le Brun, and magnificently carved by **Girardon** (1694). The cupola pendentives painted with Richelieu's coat of arms and Church Fathers are by Philippe de Champaigne.

▶ *Return to boulevard St-Michel and follow it uphill to the rue Soufflot.*

Rue St-Jacques

This street got its name from the pilgrims on their way to Compostela in Spain, who were lodged in a hostel on this site in the 14C. To the left, the street is bordered by the austere façades of

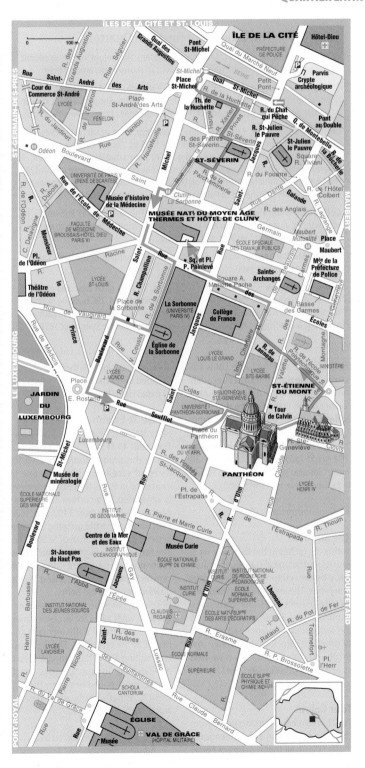

ÎLES DE LA CITÉ ET ST-LOUIS

ÎLE DE LA CITÉ

Hôtel-Dieu

PRÉFECTURE DE POLICE

Quai des Grands Augustins

Pont St-Michel

Quai du Marché Neuf

Parvis
Crypte archéologique

R. des Grands Augustins

R. Séguier

Rue Saint- André

des Arts

St-Michel

Place St-Michel

Quai St-Michel

SEINE

Petit Pont

Cour du Commerce St-André

R. de l'Éperon

R. du Jardinet

Place St-André/des Arts

Th. de la Huchette

R. Xavier Privas

R. du Chat qui Pêche

Pont au Double

Q. de Montebello

LYCÉE

FÉNELON

Rue Danton

Rue Hautefeuille

R. de la Huchette

R. St-Julien le Pauvre

St-Julien le Pauvre

R. de la Bûcherie

Odéon Boulevard

Rue Michel

R. des Prêtres St-Séverin

R. St-Séverin

ST-SÉVERIN

Jacques

Square R. Viviani

R. de l'Hôtel Colbert

UNIVERSITÉ DE PARIS V (RENÉ DESCARTES)

Rue Saint

R. de la Parcheminerie

R. du Fouarre

Galande

R. Dante

Rue de l'École de

Médecine

Musée d'histoire de la Médecine

Cluny La Sorbonne

MUSÉE NAT¹ DU MOYEN ÂGE THERMES ET HÔTEL DE CLUNY

R. des Anglais

R. Lagrange

MAUBERT

FACULTÉ DE MÉDECINE BROUSSAIS-HÔTEL DIEU PARIS VI

Rue Racine

Saint-

Rue

Germain

Maubert Mutualité

Place Maubert

R. des Carmes

C. Delavigne

R. Monsieur le Prince

Rue de l'Odéon

R. A. Dubois

R. Champollion

ÉCOLE SPÉCIALE DES TRAVAUX PUBLICS

Mée de la Préfecture de Police

Pl. de l'Odéon

LYCÉE ST-LOUIS

Sq. et Pl. P. Painlevé

Square A. Mariette Pacha

Saints-Archanges

des

R. Basse des Carmes

Théâtre de l'Odéon

Place de la Sorbonne

La Sorbonne (UNIVERSITÉ PARIS IV)

Collège de France

Écoles

Rue de Vaugirard

Jacques

Rue de Médicis

LE LUXEMBOURG

Rue de Prince

Boulevard

Rue V. Cousin

Église de la Sorbonne

LYCÉE LOUIS LE GRAND

R. de Lanneau

R. de l'école Polytechnique

Montagne

MINISTÈRE

LYCÉE J. MONOD

Place E. Rostand

Rue Saint

Cujas

R. Valette

LYCÉE STE-BARBE

ST-ÉTIENNE DU MONT

JARDIN DU LUXEMBOURG

St-Michel

Rue Soufflot

BIBLIOTHÈQUE STE-GENEVIÈVE

UNIVERSITÉ PANTHÉON-SORBONNE

Tour de Calvin

Rue Clovis

Luxembourg

Musée de minéralogie

Place du Panthéon

MAIRIE DU V ARR.

R. des Fossés

R. Clotaire

Ste-Geneviève

ÉCOLE NATIONALE SUPÉRIEURE DES MINES

Rue St-Jacques

PANTHÉON

LYCÉE HENRI IV

Boulevard

Rue

INSTITUT DE GÉOGRAPHIE

Pl. de l'Estrapade

Rue R.

de

R. de l'Estrapade

R. Thouin

Centre de la Mer et des Eaux

INSTITUT OCÉANOGRAPHIQUE

R. Pierre et Marie Curie

Musée Curie

INSTITUT CURIE

INSTITUT NATIONAL DE RECHERCHE PÉDAGOGIQUE

St-Jacques du Haut Pas

R. de l'Abbé de l'Épée

Jacques

Gay

ÉCOLE NATIONALE SUPÉ DE CHIMIE

INSTITUT CURIE

ÉCOLE NORMALE SUPÉRIEURE

Rue d'Ulm

Lhomond

R. du Pot de Fer

Barbusse

Boulevard

INSTITUT NATIONAL DES JEUNES SOURDS

CLAUDIUS REGAUD

ÉCOLE NATLE SUPRE DES ARTS DÉCORATIFS

Rataud

Tournefort

Henri

LYCÉE LAVOISIER

Saint-

R. des Ursulines

Rue Erasme

ÉCOLE NORMALE SUPÉRIEURE

R. P. Brossolette

Pl. l'Herr

R. Nicole

des Feuillantines

Lussac

Rue Claude Bernard

ÉCOLE SUPRE PHYSIQUE ET CHIMIE INDUEES

MOUFFETARD

R. Pierre

SCHOLA CANTORUM

ÉGLISE

Rue

Rue du Val de Grâce

Musée

VAL DE GRÂCE (HÔPITAL MILITAIRE)

PORT-ROYAL

0   100 m

The Colleges of the Latin Quarter

Whether ancient or more recent, these represent the height of the academic humanist tradition in France. A certain amount of rivalry exists among them.

Collège des Écossais – *65 rue du Cardinal-Lemoine*. The **Scottish College**, a building with a noble façade, which has belonged to the Roman Catholic Church of Scotland since the 14C. It is one of the oldest colleges of the University of Paris.

Collège de Navarre – *1 rue Descartes*. Several important academic bodies have been based at this address. First founded in 1304 by Jeanne of Navarre, wife of Philip the Fair, it was originally intended for 70 poor scholars, among whom, at different times, Henri III, Henri IV, Richelieu and Bossuet were numbered. In 1794 the Convention initiated the École Polytechnique to replace a deficit in engineers. The college was transferred to Palaiseau on the outskirts of Paris, in 1977.

Collège de Montaigu – *10 place du Panthéon*. This college was known for its teaching, its austere discipline and its squalor – its scholars were said to sleep on the ground amid lice, fleas and cockroaches.

College Ste Barbe – *rue Valette*. The last surviving building of the Latin Quarter colleges, dating from 1460.

Collège de France – *11 place Marcelin-Berthelot*. With its great past and an equal present-day reputation, this college offers free public lectures. 19C building reorganisations have been replaced in the 20C by vast additions. The college retains complete academic autonomy but has been dependent financially on the State since 1852.

the Sorbonne and the Lycée Louis-Le-Grand. To the right the street becomes more narrow, with older buildings. Further down is the **Centre de la Mer et des Eaux** (*see Museums and Other Attractions*) and, past rue Gay-Lussac, the **Église St-Jacques-du-Haut-Pas** (*252 rue St-Jacques*). The church, built in the Classical style between 1630 and 1685, became a Jansenist centre.

▶ *Continue up the rue Soufflot.*

Rue Soufflot

Notice the niches in the façade at no 3, with its mythological statues. The pharmacy below retains its ancient apothecary style. The imposing **Panthéon**★★ (*see Museums and Other Attractions*) dominates the street, surrounded by the semicircular square lined with the symmetrical block of the former Law Faculty (by Soufflot 1772) – now used as university offices – and the City Hall for the 5th arrondissement.

Tour Calvin

19–21 rue Valette. Looking north from the square you can see a hexagonal tower (1560), all that remains of Fortet College where, in 1585, the Duke of Guise founded the Catholic League which was to expel Henri III from Paris.

Église St-Étienne-du-Mont★★

Place Ste-Geneviève. ◷*Tue–Sun 10am–7pm.* ☎*01 43 54 11 79.*

It is in this unique church, known for its **rood screen**★★, the only one in existence in Paris, that Ste Geneviève is venerated. The current church was constructed bewteen 1492 and 1626 to accommodate the growing abbey of St Geneviève and parish of St Stephen. The **façade**★★ is highly original. Three superimposed pediments stand at the centre, their lines emphasised by the upward sweep of the belfry.

Despite its date, the structure is Gothic. Tall aisle walls allow for large windows; an elegant line of balusters cuts the height of the tall pillars. The Flamboyant vaulting above the transept is most eye-catching. The stained glass, which for the most part dates from the 16C and 17C, is particularly unusual in the ambulatory and chancel.

1) 1650 **pulpit**★ supported by a figure of Samson.

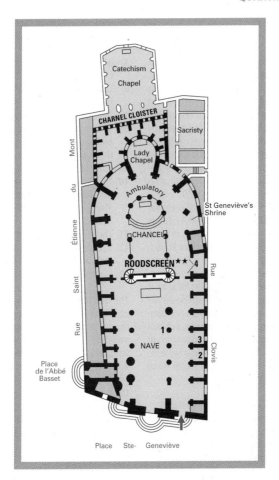

2) **Stained-glass window**★
of 1586 illustrating the parable
of those invited to the feast.
3) 17C Entombment.
4) The epitaphs of Racine
(by Boileau) and Pascal.

Cloisters

Also known as the Charnel Cloisters. At
one time the church was bordered to
the north and east by two small burial
grounds. The cloisters are built off the
right side of the ambulatory at the
church's east end, and may at one time
have been used as a charnel house. The
stained glass windows★ date back to
the 17C. A small Catechism Chapel was
added by Baltard in 1859.

▶ *From rue de la Montaigne
St-Geneviève, turn left on the rue
Ecole Polytechnique, following the
charming rue Lanneau to rue des
Ecoles and the square P. Painlevé.*

Museums and Other Attractions

Le Panthéon★★

Place du Panthéon. ○*Apr–Sept, Tue–Sun
10am–6.30pm; Oct–Mar, Tue–Sun 10am–
6pm.* ▰*Guided tours in French Apr–Oct.*
○*Public holidays.* ▰*7.50€.* ☏*01 44 32 18
00. www.monuments-nationaux.fr.*
The Panthéon's distinctive silhouette on
the hilltop and its role as the necropolis
of France's greatest citizens makes it a
popular national monument.

A royal vow

Louis XV vowed, when desperately ill in 1744, that should he recover he would replace the semi-ruined church of the abbey of Ste-Geneviève with a magnificent edifice. The project was given to the architect Jacques **Soufflot** (1713-80), whose plans for a vast church 110m/361ft long by 84m/275.6ft wide by 83m/272.3ft high won him contempt from all sides. A lack of funds and cracks in the structure caused by ground movements delayed completion until after Soufflot's death (1780), in 1789.

In April 1791 its function as a church was suspended by the Constituent Assembly in order to "receive the bodies of great men who died in the period of French liberty" – thus it became a Pantheon. Voltaire and Rousseau are buried here, as were Mirabeau and Marat for a short while. Successively the Panthéon served as a church under the Empire, a necropolis in the reign of Louis-Philippe, a church under Napoléon III, the headquarters of the Commune and finally as a lay temple to receive the ashes of Victor Hugo in 1885.

1) Saint Denis' prediction (Galand).
2) Scenes from the life of St Geneviève (Puvis de Chavannes).
3) Charlemagne crowned Emperor, and protector of the Humanities (H Lévy).
4) Miraculous Cure of Quiblinf and procession of the reliquary of St Geneviève (Maillot).
5) Battle of Tolbiac and Baptism of Clovis (J Blanc).
6) Death and funeral of St Geneviève (J-P Laurens).
7) Towards Glory (Ed. Detaille).
8) St Geneviève watching over Paris and St Geneviève bringing food to the town (Puvis de Chavannes).
9) Story of Joan of Arc (J-E Lenepveu).
10) The Concept of Fatherland, Plenty, Home and Plague (Humbert). Monument to the Unknown Heroes (Landowski).
11) The life of St Louis (Cabanel).
12) St Geneviève encourages and reassures the Parisians (Delaunay).
13) Martyrdom of St Denis (Bonnat).

The **dome★★**, strengthened with an iron framework, can be best surveyed from a distance. Eleven steps rise to the peristyle composed of fluted columns supporting a triangular pediment, the first of its kind in Paris. This is inscribed with its dedication 'To the great men, the nation is grateful' in gold letters. Above, sculptured figures (1831) by David d'Angers represent Liberty handing crowns of laurel to the Nation.

Panthéon

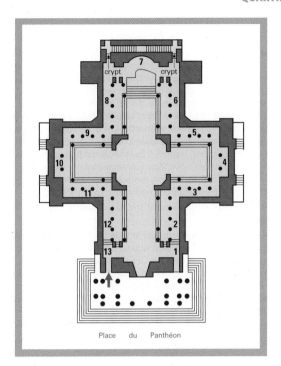

Place du Panthéon

Interior

Greek-cross in plan, the nave is divided from the aisles by a line of columns supporting a frieze, cornice and balustrade, roofed with flattened domes. Soufflot designed the great central dome as supported on free-standing columns but these have been substituted with heavy piers. The upper section has a fresco by Baron Antoine Jean Gros (1771-1835) depicting *St Geneviève's Apotheosis*.

The walls are decorated with **paintings**★ dating from 1877 onwards. Stairs lead up to the dome from where there is a fine **view**★★ over Paris.

Crypt

Access from the east end. The crypt extends under the full length of the building. Although strangely eerie and empty, it contains the tombs of great men in all walks of life throughout France's history: La Tour d'Auvergne, Voltaire, Rousseau, Victor Hugo, Émile Zola, Marcelin Berthelot, Louis Braille, Jean Jaurès, the explorer Bougainville. More recent heroes to be so honoured are the Nobel Prize winners Pierre and Marie Curie (who was also the first female Nobel Prize winner), the Resistance leader Jean Moulin.

Foucault's Pendulum

In 1851 **Léon Foucault** took advantage of the dome's height to repeat publicly his experiment that proved the rotation of the earth – a discovery he had made in 1849 using a brass pendulum (28kg/62lb) hung from a steel cable (67m/220ft), which deviated from its axis during oscillation in a circular movement. The pendulum can now be seen at the Musée des Arts-et-Métiers (*see RÉPUBLIQUE*).

Musée national du Moyen Âge★★ – Thermes et Hôtel de Cluny

6 place Paul-Painlevé. Wed–Mon 9.15am–5.45pm (last admission 30min before closing). 1 Jan, 1 May, 25 Dec. 7.70€, no charge 1st Sun in the month. 01 53 73 78 00. www.musee-moyenage.fr. This museum encompasses the old residence of the abbots of Cluny, the ruins of the Roman baths and a collection of medieval arts and treasures.

From Abbots' Residence to Museum

About 1330, Pierre of Châlus, Abbot of Cluny-en-Bourgogne, the influential Burgundian Abbey, bought the ruins and the surrounding land to build a residence for abbots visiting Paris. Jacques of Amboise, Bishop of Clermont and Abbot of Jumièges in Normandy, rebuilt the house to its present design between 1485 and 1500. Hospitality was offered to many guests, including in 1515 Henry VIII's sister, Mary, widowed at 16 by the death of Louis XII of France, a man in his fifties who survived the marriage only three months. The white queen – as royal widows endured their period of mourning dressed in white – was closely watched over by Louis' cousin and successor, François I, lest she should bear a child which might cost him his throne. Indeed, when Mary was discovered one night in the company of the young Duke of Suffolk, the king compelled her to marry the Englishman in the chapel there and then before despatching her to England.

In the 17C the house accommodated the papal nuncios, the most illustrious being Mazarin.

At the Revolution the residence classed as State property was sold, passing to a variety of owners including a surgeon who used the chapel as a dissecting room, a cooper, a printer and a laundress. The City of Paris acquired the baths in 1819 and agreed to cede their rights to the land on condition that the whole be opened as a museum. In 1833 Alexandre Du Sommerard came to live in the house, installing his substantial collection of artefacts from the Middle Ages and the Renaissance. At his death in 1842 the mansion and its contents were purchased by the State; Edmond du Sommerard, son of the former owner was appointed as curator in 1844.

Hôtel de Cluny

This mansion, together with the Hôtel de Sens, is one of only two 15C private houses in Paris. Despite much restoration, original medieval details survive in features such as the wall crenellations and turrets. In the main courtyard is a fine 15C well kerb. The left wing is articulated with arches; the central building has mullioned windows; a frieze and Flamboyant balustrade, from which gargoyles spurt, line the base of the roof, ornamented with picturesque dormer windows swagged with coats of arms. A pentagonal tower juts out from the central building. Concerts of medieval and baroque music are often held here.

Les Thermes★

Excavations have determined the plan of these **Gallo-Roman public baths** dating from AD 200. The present ruins cover about one third of the vast complex ransacked and more or less destroyed at the end of the 3C by the barbarians.

The best-preserved area is the frigidarium. Vault ribs rest on consoles carved as ships' prows – an unusual motif suggesting the idea that the building was con-structed by the Paris guild of boatmen. It was this same guild that, in the reign of Tiberius (AD 14-37), dedicated a pillar to Jupiter, discovered beneath the chancel of Notre-Dame: known as **le pilier des Nautes**★ (Boatmen's Pillar), it is Paris' oldest existing sculpture.

Chapel★

The chapel, on the first floor, was designed as the abbots' oratory. It has an elegant Flamboyant vault supported by a central column.

Museum★★

The museum's 24 galleries are devoted to the Middle Ages, displaying the richness and skill of the applied arts of the period. Most of the art treasures collected evoke aspects of everyday life, notably in religious communities. These include illuminated manuscripts, furniture, arms and armour, church plate, ironwork, and stained glass.

Room 8 contains fragments of figurative sculpture from the façade of Notre-Dame: notably 21 heads of the kings of Judah from the Gallery of Kings, vandalised during the Revolution. Some of the finest masterpieces of the late Middle

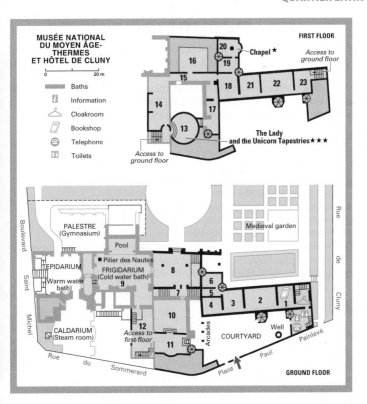

MUSÉE NATIONAL
DU MOYEN ÂGE-
THERMES
ET HÔTEL DE CLUNY

0   20 m

Baths
Information
Cloakroom
Bookshop
Telephone
Toilets

FIRST FLOOR

Chapel ★

Access to
ground floor

The Lady
and the Unicorn Tapestries ★★★

Access to
ground floor

PALESTRE
(Gymnasium)

Pool

Medieval garden

TEPIDARIUM
(Warm water
bath)

Pilier des Nautes

FRIGIDARIUM
(Cold water bath)

CALDARIUM
(Steam room)

Access to
first floor

Arcades

COURTYARD

Well

Rue   du   Sommerard

Place   Paul   Painlevé

Boulevard   Saint   Michel

Rue   de   Cluny

GROUND FLOOR

Ages are grouped in Room 14: the Taras-con *Pietà*, a tapestry depicting the story of the Prodigal Son; and sculptures in stone, marble and wood including two Flemish altarpieces.

La Dame à la Licorne★★★ (The Lady and the Unicorn *Room 13, 1st floor*) panels are the most exquisite examples of 15C and early 16C tapestries of the *mille-fleurs* or thousand flower design, woven in the south of the Netherlands. The six tapestries, armorial bearings of the Le Viste family from Lyon, portray the lion (chivalric nobility) and the unicorn (bourgeois nobility) on either side of a richly attired lady. Five are thought to be allegories of the senses with the sixth, to my heart's desire, showing the young woman depositing a necklace in a casket, symbolising a renouncement of such earthly, sensual pleasures.

Musée de Minéralogie★★

60 boulevard St-Michel. ⓘ*Tue–Fri 1.30pm–6pm, Sat 10am–12.30pm, 2pm–5pm.* ⓘ*Public holidays, Sat from mid-Jul–mid-Aug.* ⓘ*5€.* ⓘ*01 40 51 91 39. www.musee.ensmp.fr.*

The museum is in the École Supérieure des Mines, founded in 1783, which moved to its present site, the former Hôtel de Vendôme, in 1815. The **min-eralogical collection** is among the world's richest: precious stones, minerals, crystals and meteorites.

RÉPUBLIQUE

Ⓜ TEMPLE (LINE 3), RÉAUMUR-SÉBASTOPOL (LINES 3 AND 4), ARTS-ET-MÉTIERS (LINES 3 AND 11), RÉPUBLIQUE (LINES 3, 5, 8, 9 AND 11) – BUSES: 20, 54, 56, 65, 74

This neighbourhood encompasses the bustling place de la République, on the periphery of the Marais and Beaubourg, the Temple, and the Oberkampf district which, with its many bars, is a popular place for an evening out.

Nearby neighbourhoods: **CANAL ST-MARTIN, FAUBOURG POISSONNIÈRE, LE MARAIS, GRANDS BOULEVARDS.**

- 🛈 **Information:** Pyramides welcome centre, 25 rue des Pyramides. ☎08 92 68 30 00 (0.34€ per min). http://en.parisinfo.com.
- ▸ **Orient Yourself:** On the Right Bank between the Marais and Canal St-Martin.
- 🅿 **Parking:** Underground parking on the avenue de la République.
- 🚷 **Don't Miss:** The recently renovated Musée des Arts et métiers.
- 🕒 **Organizing Your Time:** Allow two hours if visiting the museum and area.
- 🧒 **Especially for Kids:** There's a playground in the square du Temple.
- 🔍 **Also See:** LE MARAIS, GRANDS BOULEVARDS, CANAL ST-MARTIN.

A Bit of History

Place de la République – In 1854 Haussmann incorporated this small square into his grand urban scheme and it was named in honour of the First, Second and Third Republics. It is situated roughly on the site of the bastion and gateway to the Temple, once the stronghold of the Knights Templar in Paris. In 1879 the City Authorities held a competition to design a monument to commemorate the proclamation of the new Republic and this was won by

Sculpture on the monument at the Place de la République

the Morice brothers: Léonard who completed the Sculpture and Charles who produced the base. The Statue to the Republic was erected and inaugurated on 14 July 1883, with bronze low-relief sculptures around the base representing the great events in the history of the Republic from its inception to the first 14 July national celebration in 1880.

Quartier du Temple – This quarter was once the domain of the Knights Templar and the Benedictines from St Martin-des-Champs. Their original impressive stronghold no longer exists today having been demolished by Napoléon and Napoléon III during the nineteenth century. Constructed by the Templars in 1240 during the reign of King Louis IX, it was confiscated from them by King Philip the Fair after they fell from grace in 1307. There were a number of buildings on the site which included a church, a huge Keep called the Grosse Tour (the Great Tower) and the smaller Tour de César (Caesars Tower). Today it is a busy district of jewellery and garment wholesalers, restaurants, and a renowned technical training school.

The Temple Prison – On 13 August 1792, the royal family were all imprisoned in the Temple Tower. On 20 Janu-

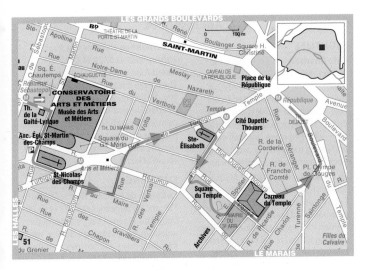

ary 1793, Louis XVI was condemned by the Convention and sent to the guillotine. On 2 August, the queen was transferred to the Conciergerie; she left only to go to the guillotine on 16 October. Other royal prisoners held here were: Madame Élisabeth, sister of the King, who was guillotined in 1794: Princess Marie Thérèse, the daughter of the King who was later exiled and the young King Louis XVII, who died in the prison aged 10 years.

Following the Terror, the prison became a place of pilgrimage for Royalists and so it was demolished on the orders of Napoléon in 1808.

Walking Tour

▶ Start from Réaumur-Sébastopol metro station.

Théâtre de la Gaîté Lyrique

⌒ *Closed for renovations until end of 2010.* Inaugurated in 1862, this was once one of the most beautiful Haussmann-era theatres. It became a circus and mime school in the 1970s, and lost most of its original interior architecture in 1986 when it was transformed into a children's amusement centre. Closed since 1990, it is currently being renovated to house a centre for digital arts.

Conservatoire national des Arts et Métiers★★

This former Benedictine priory became a Conservatoire for technical studies under the Convention in 1794. Today it also houses a technology museum (⌒ *see Museums and Other Attractions*). In rue du Vertbois, a **watchtower** (*échauguette*) and fragments of the medieval (1273) priory wall can be seen. In the courtyard, on the right, the former monastery **refectory**★★ was designed by **Pierre de Montreuil** (13C).

▶ *Turn left in rue de Turbigo to approach the **Ancienne Église St-Martin-des-Champs**★ with its Romanesque east end (1130 – restored), fine capitals, belfry and Gothic nave.*

OBERKAMPF: ONE OF THE TRENDIEST PARTS OF PARIS

From place de la République, go up avenue de la République to rue Oberkampf (7th road on the left). Rue Oberkampf and the surrounding streets (rue Saint-Maur, rue Jean-Pierre-Timbaud) are a long string of bars, some styled to re-create the atmosphere of Ménilmontant at the turn of the 19C, others with more modern décor. Greatly in favour with young Parisians.

Address Book

NIGHTLIFE

Café Charbon – *109 rue Oberkampf, 11th arr.* ☎*01 43 57 55 13. Closed Fri–Sun. DJ from 10pm.* This former early 20C theatre café (which also used to sell coal – hence the name) is one of the district's most popular venues. In a high-ceilinged room, with tall mirrors and a long bar, a young, arty crowd flocks here for a drink and brunch.

Le Blue Billard – *111 rue St-Maur, 11th arr.* ☎*01 43 55 87 21. Daily.* Even before the Oberkampf neighbourhood had reached its current fashionable status, the Blue Billard was catering to the capital's snooker and billiards fans. Today it still provides some 20 or so French and American billiard tables, delicious cocktails and pleasant relaxed atmosphere.

Le Cithéa – *114 rue Oberkampf, 11th arr* ☎*01 40 21 70 95. Closed Sun, 1 Jan and 25 Dec.* This former cinema-theatre is one of the trendiest places in town. A predominantly young and cool clique meets here to drink, dance and listen to live music every night: acid jazz, house, funk, soul or world music starting from midnight.

Le Gibus – *18 rue du Fg-du-Temple, 11th arr.* ☎*01 47 00 78 88. www.gibus. fr. Closed Sun, Mon.* This former rock temple is now devoted to techno and house music and every week a succession of the best DJs around ensure that a half-gay, half-straight clientele spend their nights in feverish dancing. Trendy but not exclusively 'clubby', it is focused first and foremost on dance in a low-ceilinged, concrete setting (for some it is a suffocating garage atmosphere, for others, pure heaven).

Le Scherkhan – *144 rue Oberkampf, 11th arr.* ☎*01 43 57 29 34. Daily. Closed 1 Jan and 25 Dec.* In homage to The Jungle Book film, a stuffed tiger stands threateningly at the entrance of this bar. The low-lit space is nonetheless calm and peaceful and decorated in a pleasant pseudo-exotic style. Perfect to meet friends for a quiet drink, to the sound of jazz.

SHOPPING

La Bague de Kenza – *106 rue St-Maur, 11th arr .* Ⓜ*Parmentier.* ☎*01 43 14 93 15. Daily.* This Algerian pastry shop, quite unique in Paris, sells high-quality, subtly flavoured cakes and pastries, together with a wide range of breads, some of which are exclusive to the house. Particularly in vogue with the press and fine gourmets, famous and otherwise.

Rougier and Plé – *13 blvd des Filles-du-Calvaire, 3rd arr.* Ⓜ*Filles-du-Calvaire.* ☎*01 44 54 81 00. www.crea.tm.fr. Mon–Sat 9.30am–7pm.* Arts and crafts galore! Three floors with everything you could need for bookbinding, printing, drawing, graphics, modelling, etc. If you are looking for a bag of colourful feathers to adorn your hat, or a glass-paste gem to repair your favourite brooch, this is the place.

WHERE TO STAY AND EAT

♿Turn to the back of the guide for selected hotels restaurants, bistros and cafés, listed by *arrondisement*. This district is in the 3rd and 11th arrondissements.

Église St-Nicolas-des-Champs★

The church was built in the 12C, rebuilt in the 15C, and enlarged in the 16C and 17C. The façade and belfry are Flamboyant Gothic, the south door is Renaissance (1581). Inside hang a number of 17C, 18C and 19C paintings; on the double-sided altar is a retable by Simon Vouet (16C) and four angels by the 17C sculptor, Sarrazin.

▶ *Walk along rue au Maire, then turn left onto rue Volta and right onto rue de Turbigo which leads to the back of Ste-Élisabeth, walk around the church.*

Église Ste-Élisabeth

This former monastic chapel (1628-46) dedicated to St Elisabeth of Hungary is now the church of the Knights of

The Knights Templar

In 1140 the religious and military order, known as the Order of Knights Templar, founded during 1118 in the Holy Land by nine knights to protect pilgrims, established a house in Paris. Independent of any ruling monarch, they were soon entrusted with great wealth which enabled them to create a substantial and unrivalled international banking system. By 13C their property investments amounted to almost one quarter of the land area of Paris – including all the Marais neighbourhood (⌖ see LE MARAIS).

King Philip IV, or as he was better known Philip the Fair, decided to suppress this state within a state. He was becoming more and more concerned about the increasing power of the Templars – who, as a religious order, were answerable only to the Pope – as well as being jealous of their great wealth. He persuaded Pope Clement V, the Frenchman Bernard de Got to support his intentions. On 13 October 1307, all the Templars in France were arrested, including the leader, Jacques de Molay, and 140 knights were imprisoned in Paris.

Having been granted the authority he needed by Clement V, the king dissolved the order and had de Molay together with 54 knights tortured and burned at the stake. Two-thirds of the estates were confiscated by the Crown, the rest was given to the Knights of St John of Jerusalem, later known as the Knights of Malta. According to legend, de Molay cursed both Philip and Clement as he was consumed by the flames, prophesying that they would both appear before God's Tribunal within the next year. As it transpired, both were dead within months of the execution – Clement in just over a month and Philip by the end of the year!

Malta. Of particular interest are the 100 early 16C Flemish low-relief sculptures depicting biblical scenes around the ambulatory.

Square and Carreau du Temple

&♿ ⏰Tue–Sat 9am–12.30pm, Sat 9am–1pm, Sun and holidays 8am–1pm.
Next to the town hall and garden square is the Carreau, a clothing market. It was converted into an open air market after the Temple was pulled down during the Napoléonic era and it specialised in second-hand clothing. It became known as the Carreau du Temple because the clothes were displayed on the carreaux or paving stones. In 1957 a covered market was built by Haussmann and in 1904 the inaugural Foire de Paris or Paris Fair took place here. The Carreau du Temple is now designated as a historic monument.

Museums and other Attractions

Musée des Arts et métiers★★

⏰Tue–Sun 10am–6pm (until 9.30pm Thu). ⏰Public holidays. ⊚6.50€. ☎01 53 01 82 00. www.arts-et-metiers.net.

The museum illustrates technical progress in industry and science. The visit begins with instruments used to explore the **infinitesimal** and **infinitely remote**. Next come **machines** and models showing **building techniques**. **Communication** is illustrated through printing, television, photography, computing etc. The theme of **energy** is represented by a model of the Marly machine (1678-85), turbines, boilers and various engines, whereas **locomotion** explores all means of transport: cycles, cars, aircraft (including Blériot's with which he crossed the channel) and 19C railways. The magnificent chapel is used to display the first steam buses, a model of the Statue of Liberty, of the engine of the European rocket Ariane and of Foucault's pendulum that proved the rotation of the earth. The finest exhibits include **Pascal's arithmetic machine** (1642), **Edison's phonograph** (1878), the **magic lantern** used by the **Lumière brothers** in 1895, Volta's battery (1800), an **automata theatre** which brings back to life Marie-Antoinette's dulcimer-playing puppet of 1784.

FAUBOURG SAINT-ANTOINE

Ⓜ BASTILLE (LINES 1, 5 AND 8), LEDRU-ROLLIN (LINE 8), FAIDHERBE-CHALIGNY (LINE 8) OR
NATION (LINES 1, 2, 6 AND 9) – RER: NATION (LINE A) – BUSES: 20, 65, 69, 76, 86, 87, 91

The old, densely populated streets around the Faubourg St-Antoine have been
the centre of the cabinet-making industry for centuries, and today they retain the
charm of their former days despite the influx of high street shops and bars.

Nearby neighbourhood: **BASTILLE.**

- 🛈 **Information:** Pyramides welcome centre, 25 rue des Pyramides. ☎08 92 68 30 00
  (0.34€ per min). http://en.parisinfo.com.
- ▶ **Orient Yourself:** This district is east of place de la Bastille on the Right Bank.
- Ⓟ **Parking:** Underground parking on ave Daumesnil and ave Ledru-Rollin.
- ⊛ **Don't Miss:** The colourful open-air and covered markets at the place d'Aligre.
- 🕓 **Organizing Your Time:** Allow two hours for this neighbourhood visit.

A Bit of History

In the 12C Louis XI allowed the fortified Royal Abbey of St Antoine to dispense justice locally and exempted the
craftsmen from the rules of the powerful and restrictive guilds. From 1657,
the cabinet-makers of St-Antoine were
licensed by Colbert to replicate pieces
from the royal workshops, to use exotic

woods instead of being bound to oak,
and to develop the decorative use of
bronze and marquetry. These freedoms
helped create the independent spirit of
the faubourg. At 31 rue de Montreuil,
Réveillon pioneered the production of
painted wallpapers, but the crowded
conditions in his workshops provoked
social unrest that erupted into violence
on 28 April 1789, forcing the industrialist

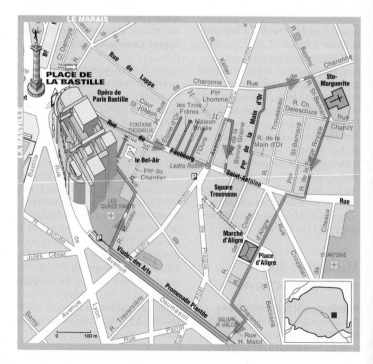

Address Book

NIGHTLIFE

Barrio Latino – *46/48, rue du Fg-St-Antoine, 12th arr.* ☎*01 55 78 84 75. www.buddhabar.com.* A little piece of Havana in the heart of Paris well known by Salsa fans. Spread over four levels and connected by a magnificent staircase, this listed building was designed during the nineteenth century by Gustav Eiffel. A tapas bar on the ground floor is open all day and in the evening the place is taken over by a DJ with his exciting Bossa Nova and Salsa rhythms. South American dishes such as Brazilian feijoada are offered on the mezzanine while a Cuban bar on the third and a nightclub with a VIP bar on the fourth, should cater for everyone's tastes.

Sanz Sans – *49 rue du Fg-St-Antoine, 11th arr.* ☎*01 44 75 78 78. www.sanzsans. com. Daily. Closed Sun lunch and 25 Dec.* If you were planning on slipping in unnoticed here, forget it! A camera films all those who pass the threshold and projects them up on a giant screen in the handsome rear room. Kitsch décor, drapes, armchairs, loud music

(hip hop, soul and dance) and DJs: it is fashionable, often noisy, but nonetheless worth a visit and good fun.

MARKET

Marché d'Aligre – *Pl. d'Aligre, 12th arr.* Ⓜ*Ledru-Rollin. Closed Mon.* Large, noisy, colourful food and flea market.

SHOPPING

La Maison du Cerf-Volant – *7 rue de Prague, 12th arr.* Ⓜ*Ledru-Rollin.* ☎*01 44 68 00 75. www.lamaisonducerfvolant. com. Closed Sun, Mon.* For beginners or experienced flyers, this whimsical kite shop has something for everyone, with both ready-to-fly and kits to build your own.

WHERE TO STAY AND EAT

🕯Turn to the back of the guide for selected hotels, restaurants, bistros and cafés listed by *arrondissement*. This district is in the 11th and 12th arrondissements.

---

to flee. The Revolution soon followed, and incorporated guilds were abolished. In the face of mechanisation and labour-saving industrial processes, traditional multi-skilled craftsmen had to evolve specialised trades to survive. Small workshops abounded, but still in June 1848 when the national workshops were disbanded, the unemployed rallied to build numerous barricades in protest, leading to further revolutionary violence in the Faubourg.

Walking Tour

▸ *Start from place de la Bastille.*

Rue du Faubourg-St-Antoine

The street is lined with furniture shops and the surrounding area honeycombed with courtyards and arcades, often with picturesque names, such as Le Bel-Air★ (no 56), l'Étoile d'Or (no 75), les Trois-Frères (no 83), l'Ours, la Bonne-Graine.

Fontaine Trogneux, on the corner with rue de Charonne, is an attractive fountain from 1710.

Passage de la Main-d'Or

133 rue du Faubourg-St-Antoine. Typical of the old quarter, this arcade comes out onto rue de Charonne.

Église Ste-Marguerite

36 rue St-Bernard. ☎ *01 43 71 34 24.* 🕘*Mon–Sat on request at the Acceuil.* The interior of this church, built in the 17C and enlarged in the 18C has a marble *Pietà* (1705) behind the high altar by Girardon, a fragment of a tomb intended for his wife; to the left of the chancel, the chapel dedicated to the Damned Souls has unusual *trompe-l'œil* frescoes (1765) by Brunetti.

▸ *Follow rue de la Forge-Royale, across rue du Faubourg-St-Antoine, to rue d'Aligre.*

Some of the Great Ébénistes (Cabinet-Makers)

Associated with the Louis XV and Louis XVI style are the following:

André Boulle (1642-1732): furniture supplier to the court, the most distinctive feature is the exquisite quality of brass and tortoiseshell inlay. His style enjoyed a revival during the Second Empire.

Charles Cressent (1685-1768): his bureaux and commodes are perhaps the most elegant of the Regency style, embellished with curvilinear ornamental ormolu (gilded bronze) mounts.

Jean-François Oeben (1720-63): the master of Riesener and Leleu, marks the transition between the Louis XV and Louis XVI styles. His intricate geometric marquetry and furniture with hidden mechanisms are particularly famous.

Jean-François Leleu (1729-1807): the master of the Louis XVI style at its most grandiose, rich in ormolu *appliqués* to complement overall design.

Jean Riesener (1734-1806): 30 workshops and retail outlets on rue St-Honoré. He was one of the innovators of the Louis XVI style and highly successful. His mahogany chests of drawers and *bureaux* with bronze mounts are distinctively sober in form and line.

Georges Jacob (1739-1814): established near Porte St-Martin, he dominates furniture design between Louis XVI and the First Empire. Renowned for his armchairs, he is credited with the invention of the *fauteuil à la reine*.

Place d'Aligre

An open-air food and flea market (*morning only*) is held here Tuesday–Sunday outside the covered marché Beauveau (*open morning and late afternoon*).

▸ *Continue along rue d'Aligre, cross rue de Charenton and walk along rue Malot which leads to the Viaduc des Arts and Promenade plantée.*

Viaduc des Arts★

This stone and pink-brick viaduct used to carry the old suburban railway from the Bastille. The 60 restored vaulted archways house a variety of businesses – silver and **goldsmiths**, cabinet-makers, fine art and sculpture restorers, and craft boutiques. Above, the railway has been transformed into a pedestrian **Promenade Plantée**★ with trees, gardens and shaded arbours.

Nearby

Place de la Nation

This was originally named the Throne Square in honour of the throne erected for the official entry into Paris by Louis XIV and his bride, the Infanta Maria-Theresa, on 26 August 1660. It was renamed place du Trône-Renversé (the Overturned Throne) by the Convention in 1794, and a guillotine was erected. It was given its present name on 14 July 1880, the first anniversary celebrations of the Revolution.

Dalou (1838-1902) took 20 years to perfect the composition of his monumental bronze group, **Le Triomphe de la République**★ (11m/36ft high and 38t in weight). The two columns on either side of avenue du Trône were subsequently topped with statues of Philippe Auguste and St Louis.

Cimetière de Picpus

🕑*Tue–Sun, Easter–Sept 2pm–6pm, Oct Easter 2pm–4pm.* ✆*2.50€.* ☏*01 43 44 18 54.*

In 1794, the guillotine installed in place de la Nation claimed 1 306 lives. The bodies were placed in two communal graves located in a sand quarry nearby. Later on, the families of the victims bought the surrounding ground and turned it into a cemetery. The *champ des martyrs* (martyrs' field), planted with cypress trees, can be seen through a railing.

FAUBOURG SAINT-GERMAIN★★

Ⓜ ASSEMBLÉE-NATIONALE (LINE 12), SOLFÉRINO (LINE 12), VARENNE (LINE 13) –
RER: MUSÉE D'ORSAY (LINE C) – BUSES: 73, 83, 84, 94

The Faubourg Saint-Germain was originally the aristocratic suburb *(faubourg)* of the abbey of Saint-Germain-des-Prés. The Revolution closed its sumptuous town houses and today the district is known more for its government ministries. Only through a half-open door will you catch glimpses of the 18C atmosphere.

Nearby neighbourhoods: **ST-GERMAIN-DES-PRÉS, MUSÉE D'ORSAY, INVALIDES, SÈVRES-BABYLONE.**

- **Information:** Pyramides welcome centre, 25 rue des Pyramides. ☎08 92 68 30 00 (0.34€ per min). http://en.parisinfo.com.
- **Orient Yourself:** This Right Bank quarter overlooking the Seine sits between the Hôtel des Invalides and the Musée d'Orsay.
- **Parking:** Underground off the boulevard St-Germain, or on the side streets.
- **Don't Miss:** The Musée Rodin gardens, the views from the Musée d'Orsay.
- **Organizing Your Time:** Allow a half day for the walk and museum visits.
- **Especially For Kids:** Playground in the Musée Rodin gardens.
- **Also See:** ST-GERMAIN-DES-PRÉS, INVALIDES, LOUVRE.

A Bit of History

At the end of the 16C the university acquired a strip of meadow at the river's edge from the abbey of St-Germain-des-Prés, known as the Pré aux Clercs (Scholars' Meadow). Marguerite of Valois, first wife of Henri IV, took the east end of the meadow in the 17C from the university and build a vast mansion with a garden running down to the Seine.

On the death of Marguerite in 1615 the university tried to reclaim the land but succeeded only in having the main street of the new quarter named rue de l'Université. The district was at its most fashionable in the 18C. Noble lords and rich financiers built houses which gave the streets an individual character: one monumental entrance followed another, each opening onto a courtyard closed at the far end by the façade of an elegant mansion, beyond which lay a large garden.

The Revolution closed many of the mansions, and more were pulled down when boulevard St-Germain and boulevard Raspail were opened in the late 19C. The finest houses remaining now belong to the State or serve as ambassadorial residences.

The most famous house, of course, is the **Hôtel Matignon** at no 57, built by Courtonne in 1721 but since considerably remodelled. Talleyrand, diplomat and statesman to successive regimes, owned it from 1808 to 1811, then Madame Adelaïde, sister to Louis-Philippe. Between 1884 and 1914 it housed the Austro-Hungarian Embassy, in 1935 it became the office of the President of the Council of Ministers (as the prime minister was known at the time) and in 1958 the Paris residence of the prime minister.

Edith Wharton (1862-1937), author of **The Age of Innocence**, lived at both no 53 and no 58 rue de Varenne for 13 years (1907-20) before moving north to the Pavillon Colombe near the Montmorency Forest. At the heart of literary circles that included Morton Fullerton, Henry James, André Gide, she entertained the upper-class Faubourg society in the manner of a Belle Epoque salon hostess. She is buried in the city of Versailles.

Address Book

NIGHTLIFE

Café des Lettres – *53 rue de Verneuil, 7th arr.*☎*01 42 22 52 17. Daily. Closed 1 May and 1 week at Christmas.* Located in the 18C Hôtel d'Avejan, headquarters of the House of Writers and of the National Book Centre, this little café has a terrace in the inner courtyard where you can stop for a drink in the summer outside the normal restaurant hours. Scandinavian cuisine.

SHOPPING

Barthélémy – *51 rue de Grenelle, 7th arr.* Ⓜ*Rue-du-Bac.* ☎*01 45 48 56 75. Closed Sun, Aug and public holidays.* Barthélémy is not only one of the best cheese merchants in town, he is also a man who adores sharing his love of cheese. This magnificent shop has retained its original 1900 décor.

Le Cabinet de Porcelaine – *37 rue de Verneuil, 7th arr.*☎*01 42 60 25 40. Closed Sun, Mon, Aug and public holidays.* This quaint boutique on a street of antique shops specializes in antique porcelain, from delicate tulips and orchids to amazingly life-like fruits and vegetables.

WHERE TO STAY AND EAT

👜Turn to the back of the guide for selected hotels, restaurants, bistros and cafés listed by *arrondissement*. This district is in the 6th and 7th arrondissements.

Walking Tour

This area includes the buildings that house the French Government headquarters, the Assemblée Nationale and several sumptuous 18C residential houses, now mainly serving official functions.

Rue de Varenne

There are several attractive old houses in this street: at no 73 the great Hôtel de Broglie (1735); nos 78-80, the Hôtel de Villeroy (1724), now the Ministry of Agriculture; no 72, the large Hôtel de Castries (1700). No 56, the Hôtel de Gouffier de Thoix, has a magnificent doorway ornamented with a shell carving. No 47, the Hôtel de Boisgelin is now the Italian Embassy.

Hôtel Biron★★

77 rue de Varenne. This 18C mansion belonged to the poet Rainer Maria Rilke, before being converted into a convent for the education of wealthy girls. After convents were disbanded in 1904, part of the property became the Lycée Victor-Duruy. The State loaned the house to Auguste Rodin, who lived there rent-free until his death in 1917 in exchange for his art works (👜*see Museums and Other Attractions*).

Hôtel Matignon

Built in 1721, this is considered one of the most beautiful mansions of the *faubourg*. It belonged to the statesman Tallyrand (1808-1811), the Austro-Hungarian embassy (1884-1914), and finally became the Prime Minister's official residence in 1958.

▶ *Double-back to rue de Bellechasse, then turn left onto the rue de Grenelle.*

Rue de Grenelle

Many old mansions survive on this street: at no 79 stands the **Hôtel d'Estrées** (1713); no 85 is the **Hôtel d'Avaray** (1728); no 110, the **Hôtel de Courteilles** (1778), dominating the street with its massive façade, is now the Ministry of Education; no 118 is the Hôtel de Villars, built in 1712 and extremely elegant with twin garlanded, oval windows; no 136, the **Hôtel de Noirmoutiers** (1722), at one time the army staff headquarters was the house in which Marshal Foch died on 20 March 1929. It is now the official residence of the préfet of the Île-de-France region.

▶ *Turn right onto rue de Bourgogne and follow it to the Palais de Bourbon.*

Palais Bourbon★

33 quai d'Orsay. ☞ *Visits suspended indefinitely. www.assemblee-nationale. fr.* In 1722 the Duchess of Bourbon, daughter of **Louis XIV** and **Mme de Montespan**, acquired land on which to build a house fronting onto rue de l'Université. Louis XV later bought the property, and in 1764 Louis XVI sold it to the Prince of Condé who enlarged and embellished it. Finally, the adjoining **Hôtel de Lassay** was added and renamed Le Petit Bourbon.

The palace was confiscated during the Revolution for the Council of the Five Hundred. Next it was used to house archives, before serving as accommodation for the École Polytechnique. In 1807 Napoléon commissioned Poyet to design the present façade overlooking place de la Concorde in harmony with the Greek plan of the Madeleine Church. At the Restoration the palace was returned to the Condé family, only to be bought back in 1827 and converted for use by the Legislative Assembly.

Exterior

The Antique-style façade with a portico is decorated with an allegorical pediment by Cortot (1842), statues *(copies)*, on high, of Minerva by Houdon and Themis by Roland. The allegorical low-relief sculptures on the wings are by Rude *(right)* and Pradier *(left)*.

Interior

Among the most impressive of the many rooms decorated with paintings and sculpture, are the lobby, with its ceiling by Horace Vernet, and the semi-circular Council Chamber (**Salle des Séances**) where the President of the **National Assembly** presides over 577 deputies, arranged left to right according to party. The **Library**★★ is a fine room in itself, magnificently decorated with a History of Civilization, painted by **Delacroix** between 1838 and 1845.

Rue de Lille

This street, named after the town of Lille, is typical of the old noble *faubourg*. Nos 80 and 78 were designed by the architect Boffrand in 1714. The first, the **Hôtel**

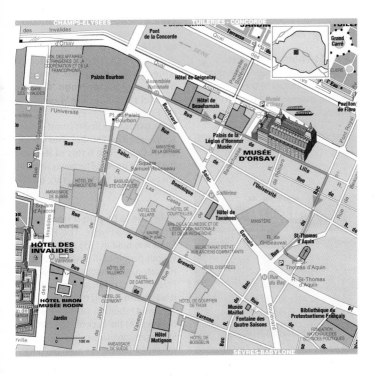

de Seignelay, was owned originally by Colbert's grandson, then by the Duke of Charost, tutor to the young Louis XV and aristocrat philanthropist who was saved from the guillotine by his own peasants. The **Hôtel de Beauharnais**, next door, was purchased and lavishly redecorated by Napoléon's daughter Hortense and son-in-law Eugène in 1803. Since 1818 the house has been the seat of first the Prussian, and later, the German diplomatic missions to France. Now restored, it is the residence of the German ambassador. Other buildings of interest include no **71** the Hôtel de Mouchy (1775), and no **67** the Hôtel du Président Duret (1706). The **Hôtel de Salm** at no 64 houses the Palace and Museum of the Legion of Honour, facing the **Musée d'Orsay**★★★ (&see Museums and Other Attractions).

▶ Turn right onto rue du Bac.

Rue du Bac
At no 44 lived **André Malraux**, who in 1933 wrote *La Condition humaine*, the novel for which he received a Nobel Prize for Literature.

▶ Turn left onto the rue Gribauval.

Église St-Thomas d'Aquin
Place St-Thomas-d'Aquin. The church, formerly the chapel of the Dominican noviciate monastery, was begun in 1682 in the Jesuit style to plans by Pierre Bul-

let. Inside are 17C and 18C paintings and a ceiling painted by Lemoyne in 1723 of the Transfiguration.

Museums and Other Attractions

Musée d'Orsay★★★ –
&See MUSÉE D'ORSAY.

Musée Rodin★★
🕐Apr–Sept, Tue–Sun 9.30am–5.45pm; Oct–Mar, Tue–Sun 9.30am–4.45pm. 🕐1 Jan, 1 May, 25 Dec. ◉6€ (1€ for garden only), no charge 1st Sun of the month. ☎01 44 18 61 10. www.musee-rodin.fr.
The house and garden enable one to see Rodin's sculptures in a peaceful residential setting. Creation, in the guise of restless figures emerging from the roughly hewn rock, was a favourite theme (**Hand of God**) although it was his renderings of the nude that demonstrated his true technical genius (**St John the Baptist**) and won him public acclaim in 1879. His most expressive works include **The Cathedral**, **The Kiss**, **The Walking Man**, **The Man with a Broken Nose**, **Eve** and the **Age of Bronze**. One room is devoted to drawings by the artist which are exhibited in rotation.
Upstairs are plaster *maquettes* for the large groups and for the statues of **Balzac** and **Victor Hugo**. **Camille Claudel**'s sculpture **The Wave** is also on display.
In the **garden** are Rodin's most famous sculptures: **The Thinker**, **The Burghers of Calais**, **The Gates of Hell** and the **Ugolin group**. The newly restored chapel is used for temporary exhibitions.

Palais de la Légion d'honneur
2 rue de Bellechasse. The **Hôtel de Salm** was built in 1786 and owned by various people until it was acquired by Napoléon, who made the mansion the Palace of the Legion of Honour in 1804. It was burnt during the Commune of 1871 and rebuilt in 1878 to the original plans. At the back of the palace is a lovely semicircular pavilion contrasting the severe lines of the main building.

©Bruno Bernier/Fotolia.com

Musée Rodin

SAINT-GERMAIN-DES-PRÉS★★

Ⓜ ST-GERMAIN-DES-PRÉS (LINE 4) – BUSES: 39, 63, 70, 86, 87, 95, 96

This old quarter on the Left Bank is known for its beautiful church, its famous cafés, its narrow streets, and antique shops. Post-war jazz clubs and intellectual spirit have mostly made way for upscale fashion and home décor boutiques.

Nearby neighbourhoods: **ODÉON, QUARTIER LATIN, INSTITUT DE FRANCE, FAUBOURG ST-GERMAIN, SÈVRES-BABYLONE, ST-SULPICE, MUSÉE D'ORSAY.**

- **Information:** Carrousel du Louvre welcome centre, Place de la Pyramide Inversée, 99 rue de Rivoli. ☎08 68 300 (0.34€ per min). http://en.parisinfo.com.
- **Orient Yourself:** The quarter is in the centre of the Left Bank along the Seine.
- **Parking:** Underground parking possible throughout the district.
- **Don't Miss:** The charming square in the rue de Furstemberg.
- **Organizing Your Time:** Allow an hour to visit this neighbourhood.
- **Also See:** INSTITUT DE FRANCE, ODÉON, FAUBOURG ST-GERMAIN.

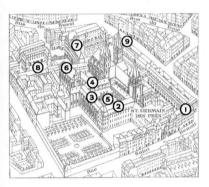

ABBEY OF SAINT-GERMAIN-DES-PRÉS IN 1734

1   Annexe.
2   Guest rooms.
3   Refectory.
4   Chapter-house.
5   Main cloister.
6   Lady Chapel.
7   Abbatial palace.
8   Stables.
9   Prison.

A Bit of History

A powerful abbey – Founded in the 8C, the Benedictine abbey of St-Germain-des-Prés became sovereign ruler of its domain, answerable in spiritual matters to the Pope alone. The monastery was sacked four times in 40 years by the Normans, then rebuilt and enlarged each time. In the 14C, when Charles V enclosed the city, the abbey fortified itself with crenellated walls, towers and a moat linked to the Seine. From 1674 the abbey was used as a State prison, and at the Revolution it was completely destroyed: the library burned, the royal tombs disappeared, the church turned into saltpetre works, and the rest of the buildings demolished. The church and the abbatial palace are all that remain of the famous Benedictine abbey.

Walking Tour

①An afternoon in St-Germain-des-Prés

Place du Québec
Charles Daudelin's fountain reproduces the effect of the snow-melt breaking up great layers of ice, reminiscent of Canadian winters. Famous jewellers (Cartier) and fashion houses (Armani) replaced older book shops and boutiques in 1998.

Église St-Germain-des-Prés★★
The 11C Romanesque church, the oldest in Paris, has altered considerably in appearance. The chancel flying buttresses are contemporary with Notre-Dame; of the three original bell-towers only one remains; it was restored in the 19C when it was crowned with its

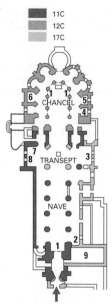

11C
12C
17C

Place St-Germain des Prés

Rue de l'Abbaye

A Picasso sculpture, *Homage to Apollinaire,* has been placed in a small square on the corner of place St-Germain-des-Prés. The impressive brick and stone former **Abbatial Palace** at no 5 was built in 1586 by the Cardinal-Abbot Charles of Bourbon. The palace was remodelled in 1699 by Abbé de Fürstenberg and sold in 1797 as State property. The angle pavilion and the Renaissance façade have been restored to their original appearance.

Rue de Furstemberg★

This old-fashioned street with its charming square shaded by paulownia and white-globed street lights was built by the cardinal of the same name, through the former monastery stableyard. Nos **6** and **8** are the remains of the outbuildings.

Rue Cardinale

Twisting and turning, it was created in 1700 by Fürstenberg through the long monastery tennis court. Still partially lined by old houses (nos **3-9**) it extends to a picturesque crossroads with rue de l'Échaudé (1388) and rue Bourbon-le-Château.

▶ *Take rue de l'Échaudé to reach boulevard St-Germain then turn right.*

Boulevard St-Germain

Just off place St-Germain-des-Prés are the **Café des Deux-Magots** and the Café de Flore, the famous meeting spots for Left Bank intellectuals and artists in the 1950s and 1960s. Opposite, the Brasserie Lipp (no 151) is a popular venue with politicians, writers and celebrities. Further on, two 18C mansions survive (nos **159** and **173**).

▶ *Take the rue de Seine towards the Odéon to the rue Toustain, turn right.*

The old St-Germain Fair

Rue de Montfaucon at one time gave access to the St-Germain fairground. The fair, founded in 1482 by Louis XI for the benefit of the abbey, had until the Revolution (1790) a considerable

present pitched roof. The original porch is hidden by an outer doorway added in 1607.

The church's small dimensions are explained by the fact that it was built as a monastery chapel and not as a parish church. Grand scale restoration work in the 19C left vaults, walls and capitals painted in garish colours. Off to the right of the cradle vaulted porch, is the Merovingian sanctuary with the tomb of St Germanus, known as **St Symphorian's Chapel** (*Tue, Thu 2pm–5pm. ☎01 55 42 81 18).*

1) Modern wrought-iron grille by Raymond Subes.
2) Our Lady of Consolation (1340).
3) Tomb by Girardon (17C).
4) Mausoleum of James Douglas, a 17C Scottish nobleman attached to the court of Louis XIII.
5) **Descartes'** and the learned Benedictines, Mabillon's and Montfaucon's tombstones.
6) Boileau, the poet and critic's tombstone.
7) Statue of St Francis Xavier by N Coustou.
8) Tomb of John Casimir, King of Poland, who died in 1672, Abbot of St-Germain-des-Prés.
9) St Symphorian Chapel.

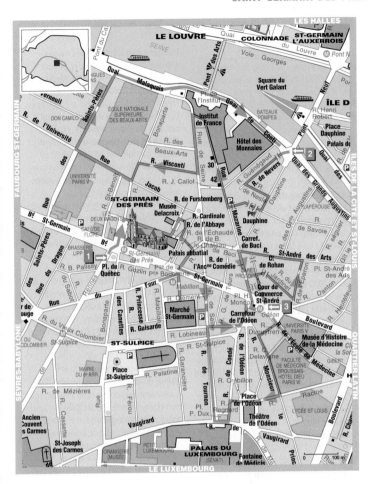

effect on Paris' economy: a forerunner of International Exhibitions and world-trade fairs today. In 1818 the covered **St-Germain market** was built on part of the site.

2 Around the Institut de France

&*see INSTITUT de France.*

3 The Odéon district

&*see ODÉON.*

Museum

Musée Eugène-Delacroix

6 place de Furstemberg. ◔*Wed–Mon 9.30am–5pm.* ◔*1 Jan, 1 May, 25 Dec.* ✆*5€, no charge 1st Sun in the month.* ☎*01 44 41 86 50. www.musee-delacroix.fr* A museum dedicated to Delacroix, leader of the Romantic painters, has been made of the colourist's last studio-home where he lived from 1858 to 1863. Works by Delacroix and his friends, with changing exhibitions.

René Descartes (1596-1630)

Often referred to as "the father of modern philosophy", Descartes was also a prominent mathematician and scientist. Most well known for his statement 'I think, therefore I am', his tomb can be found in the Church of Saint-Germain-des-Prés.

Address Book

NIGHTLIFE

Café de Flore – *172 blvd St-Germain, 6th arr.* ☎*01 45 48 55 26. www.cafe-de-flore.com. Daily.* Opened during the Second Empire, the Café de Flore has become one of the capital's most prestigious establishments, primarily due to the renown of some of its former literary regulars, including Apollinaire, Breton, Sartre and Simone de Beauvoir, and Camus.

Les Deux Magots – *6 pl. St-Germain-des-Prés, 6th arr.* ☎*01 45 48 55 25. www. lesdeuxmagots.com. Daily. Closed one week in early Jan.* Like its neighbour, the Café de Flore, this establishment was frequented by the capital's intellectual elite from the end of the 19C onwards. Since 1933 a literary prize, named after it, is awarded every year in January.

Brasserie Lipp – *151 blvd Saint-Germain, 6th arr.* ☎*01 45 48 53 91. www. brasserie-lipp.fr. Daily.* Opened in 1880, it has always been a meeting place for men and women of letters and politics: Verlaine, Proust, Gide and Malraux used to meet here and Hemingway wrote *A Farewell to Arms* here. This superb 1900 and 1925 establishment is now a listed monument.

Café Mabillon – *164 blvd St-Germain, 6th arr.* ☎*01 43 26 62 93. Daily.* This old Saint-Germain-des-Prés café has recently been renovated and is now in vogue with the neighbourhood's trendy clan.

La Rhumerie – *166 blvd St-Germain, 6th arr.* ☎*01 43 54 28 94. www.la rhumerie.com. Daily.* Founded in 1932, this establishment specialises in rums from all over the world.

SHOPPING

Emporio Armani – *149 blvd St-Germain, 6th arr. Other shop: 25 pl. Vendôme 1st arr -* ☎*01 45 48 62 15. Closed Sun and public holidays.* The sober, sophisticated style of this designer appeals to the young and the not so young. The shop, in line with the designs, is a tasteful blend of luxury and modernism. It also boasts an Italian tea shop which is very popular with its well-heeled clientele.

La Hune and L'Écume des Pages – *170 and 174 blvd St-Germain, 6th arr.* ☎*01 45 48 35 85/45 48 54 48. Daily. Closed public holidays.* These two book-shops both close late and are also keen contributors to the neighbourhood's cultural life (book signings, etc.).

Marché Saint-Germain – *rue Clément, 6th arr.* Ⓜ*Mabillon.* ☎*01 43 29 80 59. Closed Sun.* This pleasant covered mar-ket houses a number of fashion shops and a large food hall.

Rue de Furstemberg – *rue de Furstem-berg, 6th arr.* Ⓜ*Mabillon.* Jac Dey, Pierre Frey, Verel de Belval, Taco and Manuel Canovas – this discreet little street is almost entirely devoted to home decoration.

Sonia Rykiel – *194 blvd St-Germain, 6th arr,* ☎*01 49 54 60 60. www.soniarykiel. com. Closed Sun and public holidays.* The designs of this legendary, extremely talented designer are often inspired by her other passions: literature, cinema or food.

Le Carré Rive Gauche – *7th arr.* Ⓜ*Rue-du-Bac or St-Germain-des-Prés. www.carrerivegauche.com.* This associa-tion houses some 120 art galleries and antique dealers spread out through rue des Saints-Pères, rue de l'Université, rue du Bac and along quai Voltaire. Each one has a brochure in which their various specialities and addresses are indicated.

Debauve et Gallais – *30 rue des Sts-Pères.* ☎*01 45 48 54 67. www. debauve-et-gallais.com. Closed Sun and public holidays.* This chocolate-maker, established in 1800, counted the kings of France among his customers. The shop is officially listed as a historic monument.

WHERE TO STAY AND EAT

Turn to the back of the guide for selected hotels, restaurants, bistros and cafés listed by *arrondissement*. This district is in the 6th arrondissement.

FAUBOURG SAINT-HONORÉ ★

This old faubourg imparts a leisured elegance with its luxury shops, art galleries, antique shops and haute couture boutiques particularly around Rue Royale and Rue de l'Élysée, where the French president lives in the Palais de l'Elysée.

Nearby neighbourhoods: **PALAIS-ROYAL, TUILERIES, PLACE DE LA CONCORDE, MADELEINE, CHAMPS-ÉLYSÉES, ST-LAZARE.**

- ▯ **Information:** Pyramides welcome centre, 25 rue des Pyramides.
  ☏08 92 68 30 00 (0.34€ per min). http://en.parisinfo.com.
- ▶ **Orient Yourself:** This quarter lies directly to the north of the Champs-Elysées.
- ℗ **Parking:** Underground parking off the place Beauvau.
- ⊘ **Don't Miss:** The Galerie Royale shopping passage off rue Boissy d'Anglas.
- ◷ **Organizing Your Time:** Allow an hour or two for leisurely window shopping.
- ⦿ **Also See:** CHAMPS-ELYSÉES, PLACE DE LA CONCORDE, MADELEINE.

Sights

Rue du Faubourg-St-Honoré ★

Starting from the rue Royale, this street of luxury boutiques and art galleries is bordered by elegant mansions. Empress Eugénie was certainly superstitious: the street bears no number 13. Her sister-in-law Pauline lived at the **Hôtel de Charost** *(no 39)*, today home to the British Embassy. At no 41, the Hôtel Edmond de Rothschild was built in 1835 by the architect Visconti.

Palais de l'Élysée

55 rue du Faubourg-St-Honoré.
⚯*Closed to the public.*
The mansion was constructed in 1718 for the Count of Évreux. It was acquired for a short time by the Marquise de Pompadour and then by the financier Beaujon who enlarged it. During the Revolution it became a dance hall. It was home to Caroline Murat, Napoléon's sister, then Empress Josephine who redecorated it; Napoléon signed his second abdication here after his defeat at Waterloo, on 22 June 1815, and it's also where the future **Napoléon III** lived and planned his successful *coup d'état* of 1851. Since 1873 the Élysée Palace has been the Paris residence of France's president.

Place Beauvau

A fine wrought-iron gate (1836) marks the entrance to the 18C mansion built for the Prince of Beauvau-Craon, occupied by the Ministry of Home Affairs since 1861.

Avenue de Marigny

On the right, at no 23, is the former Hôtel de Rothschild and its park, now used by the Elysée Palace for visiting dignitaries. Just before the Champs-Elysées is the **Théâtre Marigny**, built by Charles Garnier in 1883.

Palais de l'Élysée

Address Book

NIGHTLIFE

Bar de l'Hôtel Bristol – *112 rue du Fg-St-Honoré, 8th arr.* ☎*01 53 43 43 42. www.hotel-bristol.com. Daily. www.hotel-bristol.com.* The muted, sophisticated ambience of this bar has all the charm of a grand palace frequented by celebrities from the worlds of fashion, the media, politics or business. Both rooms are decorated with paintings and fine tapestries. The inner courtyard has a delightful flowered terrace.

SHOPPING

Hermès – *24 rue du Fg-St-Honoré, 8th arr.* Ⓜ*Concorde.* ☎*01 40 17 47 17. www.hermes.com. Closed Sun and public holidays.* Since it first began as a harness-maker when Thierry Hermès opened the first shop in 1837, this family business has never ceased to grow, while retaining its original founding spirit. The equestrian influence remains strong in this establishment dedicated to quality before all else.

Les Caves Taillevent – *199 rue du Fg-St-Honoré, 8th arr.* Ⓜ*Ch.-de-Gaule-Étoile, Ternes or St-Philippe-du-Roule.* ☎*01 45 61 14 09. www.taillevent.com. Closed Sun, Mon, public holidays and 3 weeks in Aug.* Whether on the shelves or hung on the walls, all the bottles on display are dummies, the real ones are kept in a ventilated cellar. In addition to the best vintage wines, they also stock a fine selection of regional wines. Friendly and efficient staff.

Rue du Faubourg-Saint-Honoré – *rue du Fg-St-Honoré, 8th arr.* Ⓜ*Concorde or Madeleine.* From rue Royale to place Beauvau, rue du Faubourg-Saint-Honoré is entirely devoted to fashion and luxury goods. All the leading brand names are there: Lolita Lempika, Lanvin, Hermès, Cartier, Guy Givenchy, Versace, Laroche, Dior, Louis Ferraud etc.

WHERE TO STAY AND EAT

Turn to the back of the guide for selected hotels, restaurants, bistros and cafés listed by *arrondissement*. This district is in the 8th arrondissement.

▶ *Continue along the Faubourg St-Honoré.*

Avenue Matignon

This street is lined with art galleries dedicated to contemporary Fine Art: Maurice Garnier, Taménaga, Daniel Malingue, Bernheim-Jeune. The auction house Christie's is located in a 1913 mansion designed by René Sergent.

Rue du Colisée

Named after a Roman-style 40 000-seat theatre built in 1770 by Le Camus, this street is home since 1941 to the mythical Art Deco establishment, *Boeuf sur le Toit* (no 34).

▶ *Continue along the Faubourg St-Honoré.*

Église St-Philippe-du-Roule

154 rue du Faubourg-St-Honoré. Guided tours available by appointment. ☎*01 43 49 24 56.* The church designed by **Chalgrin** in imitation of a Roman basilica was erected between 1774 and 1784. The ambulatory was added around the apse in 1845. A fresco over the chancel of *The Deposition* is by Chassérieu.

Maison Paul Poiret once occupied no 107. This couturier (1879-1944) was one of the first modern clothes designers, banning the whale-bone corset and launching a taste for strong theatrical styles and colours. He integrated exotic features into dress design (harem-inspired *jupes-culottes*, Japanese-style kimono sleeves and long, ankle-clinging hobble skirts) and may have been responsible for the revival of huge plumed hats. After World War I he employed **Raoul Dufy** to paint his fabrics; his fashion house was the first to launch its own perfume.

SAINT-LAZARE

Ⓜ ST-LAZARE (LINES 3, 12 AND 13)

BUSES: 20, 21, 24, 26, 27, 28, 29, 32, 43, 53, 66, 80, 84, 94, 95

Those who dislike crowds should avoid this district! Every morning and evening, thousands of commuters pass through the Gare St-Lazare on their way to and from the suburbs. The major department stores in the area attract yet more people, and the café terraces are a good place to sit and watch the world go by.

Nearby neighbourhoods: **OPÉRA, MONCEAU, GRANDS BOULEVARDS, MADELEINE.**

- **Information:** Pyramides welcome centre, 25 rue des Pyramides. ☎08 92 68 30 00 (0.34€ per min). http://en.parisinfo.com.
- **Orient Yourself:** St-Lazare is behind the Opéra Garnier and Grands Magasins.
- **Parking:** Underground parking on the rue du Havre and place de Budapest.
- **Don't Miss:** The panoramic views from the 9th floor of Printemps Maison.
- **Organizing Your Time:** Allow a half hour to visit this district, longer to shop.
- **Also See:** OPÉRA, MADELEINE, GRANDS-BOULEVARDS, PARC MONCEAU.

Quartier Saint-Lazare

The neighbourhood – The St-Lazare main-line **railway station** links northwest France (Dieppe, Caen, Le Havre) with Paris, shuttling people from the suburbs to town or out to the coast and seaside. The exciting development of the railway was especially well captured by the Impressionist painter **Claude Monet**. The area around was developed in the 19C to accommodate a middle-class society in standardised, comfortable apartment blocks served by convenient large department stores.

Place de l'Europe – The major intersection of six important roads straddles the railway lines north of St-Lazare. It also marks the boundary between the bourgeois neighbourhood to the west and a more working-class quarter to the east, as defined at the time of the Restoration and the Second Empire.

Sights

Église St-Augustin★
Place St-Augustin. The church was designed by Baltard between 1860 and 1871 and was the first ecclesiastical building to consist of a metal infrastructure clad in stone. The innovative means of construction meant that the traditional Gothic design could be retained without any need for external buttressing.

▸ *From place St-Augustin, turn left on boulevard Haussmann to square Louis-XVI.*

Chapelle Expiatoire
Square Louis-XVI (entrance 29 rue Pasquier). ⏱*Thu–Sat 1pm–5pm.* ⏱*Some public holidays.* ⏿*5€.* ☎*01 44 32 18 00.* The cemetery, opened in 1722, was used for the Swiss Guards killed at the Tuileries on 10 August 1792, and the victims of **the guillotine** at place de la Concorde. These last numbered 1 343 and included Louis XVI and Marie-Antoinette, whose remains were disinterred and transported to the royal necropolis at St-Denis in 1815. The tombs of Charlotte Corday (who assassinated Marat) and Philippe-Égalité are on either side of the chapel leading into the chapel.

Boulevard Haussmann
Printemps department store was founded in 1865 and owed its immediate success to its proximity to the station. It was the first to install lifts, and boasts fine window displays for children at Christmas. **Galeries Lafayette** was originally a tiny haberdasher's founded

Address Book

SHOPPING

Augé – 116 blvd Haussmann, 8th arr. Ⓜ St-Augustin. ☎ 01 45 22 16 97 . Closed Sun and public holidays. Founded in 1850, this family enterprise has the oldest cellar in Paris. Venture into its authentic surroundings and discover the best of what France's vineyards have to offer. Foreign wines also available. Reasonable prices.

Galeries Lafayette – 40 blvd Haussmann, 9th arr. Ⓜ Chaussée-d'Antin or Havre-Caumartin. ☎ 01 42 82 34 56. www.galerieslafayette.com.

Closed Sun and public holidays. It would be impossible to go on a shopping spree in Paris without envisaging a trip to this major department store, where all the brand names have an outlet.

Printemps – 64 blvd Haussmann, 9th arr. Ⓜ Havre-Caumartin RER Auber. ☎ 01 42 82 50 00. www.printemps.fr. Closed Sun. This temple to fashion features the work of all the world's leading design houses. Divided into three buildings which are linked by passageways. A large panorama terrace tops the Printemps de la Maison.

---

in 1895 by Alphonse Khan. Its dome and balustrades were designed by Ferdinand Chanut in 1910. On 19 January 1919, the aviator Védrines landed his Caudron G3 on the shop's roof terrace.

Museum

Musée Gustave-Moreau★

14 rue de La Rochefoucauld. Ⓒ Wed–Mon 10am–12.45pm, 2pm–5.15pm. Ⓒ 1 Jan, 1 May, 25 Dec. ☜ 5€. ☎ 01 48 74 38 50. www.musee-moreau.fr.

Gustave Moreau (1826-98) bequeathed his house and collection from a life's work to the French nation with specific instructions that it should remain intact: 850 paintings, 7 000 drawings, 350 watercolours and wax sculptures. Moreau was greatly influenced by the Colourist techniques of Delacroix and the neo-Mannerist Chassériau; he delighted in the fantastical, biblical and mythological subjects, reworking such figures as Sappho, Salome, Orpheus and Leda throughout his life.

An especially designed cabinet with wings holds many of his drawings. The cramped and cluttered living quarters were situated on the first floor: note a working sketch by Poussin and a rare portrait of the artist by Degas.

Marcel Proust (1871-1922), spent 12 years at 102 boulevard Haussmann. The second-floor bedroom is open to the public by appointment.

The author of À la recherche du temps perdu (Remembrance of Things Past) chose to live in his aunt's flat for the macabre reason that he had witnessed his uncle die there, and this memory might provide inspiration for his writing.

Being very susceptible to noise, Proust tended to work at night and struggled to sleep by day through the noise of the boulevard below; to this end he had the bedroom muffled with cork tiles and heavy curtains. There he would spend days on end shut-up in bed, brewing various vapours to help his chronic asthma.

His main distraction, other than occasionally venturing out to socialise with the upper classes at the **Ritz**, was the théâtrephone which relayed live performances of opera down an early version of the telephone, at some exorbitant expense.

When Du côté de chez Swann, the first volume of the collection, was submitted to the Gallimard publishers, it was turned down by André Gide who subsequently admitted that his decision had been the "gravest mistake ever made".

ÎLE SAINT-LOUIS★★

Ⓜ PONT MARIE (LINE 7) – BUSES: 24, 63, 67, 86, 87, 89

Peaceful quays and unpretentious Classical architecture make Île St-Louis an attractive residential districts right in the heart of Paris. Its central street is lined with tiny art galleries, quirky gift boutiques and gourmet food shops.

Nearby neighbourhoods: ÎLE DE LA CITÉ, CONCIERGERIE, SAINTE-CHAPELLE, NOTRE-DAME, MAUBERT, JARDIN DES PLANTES, LE MARAIS, BASTILLE.

- **Information:** Carrousel du Louvre welcome centre, Place de la Pyramide Inversée, 99 rue de Rivoli. ☎08 92 68 30 00 (0.34€ per min). http://en.parisinfo.com.
- **Orient Yourself:** This island is in central Paris to the east of Île-de-la-Cité.
- **Parking:** Underground parking on the Right Bank at rue de l'Hôtel de Ville.
- **Don't Miss:** The famous ice cream at Maison Berthillon.
- **Organizing Your Time:** Allow an hour to explore this tiny island.
- **Also See:** ÎLE-DE-LA-CITÉ, NOTRE-DAME, ST-PAUL, QUARTIER LATIN.

A Bit of History

Île aux Vaches and Île Notre-Dame

– Originally there were two islands where in the Middle Ages judicial duels, known as the Judgements of God, were held. Early in the reign of Louis XIII, the contractor Christophe Marie joined the islets, constructed two stone bridges, and developed the land for resale in lots with a regular layout of intersecting streets and a homogenous Classical style of architecture. What makes Île St-Louis unique is its atmosphere of old world charm and provincial calm. Bankers, lawyers and nobles accounted for the first residents, now replaced by writers, artists and those who love old Paris. Behind massive panelled doors, studded with bosses and nails, lie secluded courtyards that have hardly changed since the 17C.

Walking Tour

②Tour of the island

See map ÎLE DE LA CITÉ.

Pont St-Louis

This modern metal arched bridge (which replaced the original Pont St-Landry in 1970) links the two Parisian islands. Closed to traffic, it's a peaceful place to

Quai de Bourbon at night

© Erick Nguyen/Dreamstime.com

Address Book

NIGHTLIFE

Berthillon – *31 rue Saint-Louis-en-l'Île, 4th arr.* ☎*01 43 54 31 61. www.berthillon-glacier.fr. Closed Mon, Tue and during school holidays.* Headquarters of Paris' most famous ice-cream maker, renowned for their delicious sorbets.
Le Flore en l'Île – *42 quai d'Orléans, 4th arr.* ☎*01 43 29 88 27. Daily.*
This tearoom has a superb view of the apse of Notre-Dame.

WHERE TO STAY AND EAT

Turn to the back of the guide for selected hotels, restaurants, bistros and cafés listed by *arrondissement*. This district is in the 4th arrondissement.

appreciate the views of Notre-Dame, le Panthéon and the Hôtel de Ville.

Quai de Bourbon
From the picturesque tip of the island with chain linked stone posts and canted 18C medallions, there is an altogether delightful **view**★ of the church of St-Gervais-St-Protais. A little further on are two magnificent town houses (nos **19** and **15**) which once belonged to parliamentarians. At no **19** the sculptress **Camille Claudel** had her studio (ground floor) between 1899 and 1913.

Pont Marie★
Constructed by Christophe Marie in 1635 and rebuilt in 1670.

Quai d'Anjou
At no **29**, in a former wine cellar, Ford Madox Ford established his journal *The Transatlantic Review* in collaboration with John Quinn, Ezra Pound and **James Joyce**. The Marquise de Lambert, hostess of a famous literary salon, lived at no **27** (Hôtel de Nevers). The famous painter, sculptor, caricaturist and politi-

cal satirist **Honoré Daumier** lived at no **9** between 1846 and 1863.

Hôtel de Lauzun
No 17 (⊶Closed to the public).
The mansion was erected in 1657 by Le Vau for Gruyn, a military supplier who was imprisoned shortly afterwards for corruption. It belonged for only three years to the Duke of Lauzun, who nevertheless left it his name. The poet, Théophile Gautier, lived there during the 1840s when he founded his Club des Hachischins, experimenting first with Baudelaire and later with Rilke, Sickert and Wagner. The house now belongs to the City of Paris.

Square Barye
This small garden at the tip of the island is the last trace of the terraced estate of a house that once belonged to the financier, Bretonvilliers.

Pont de Sully
This bridge (1876) on the tip of Île St-Louis has a good **view**★ of Notre-Dame, the Cité and Île St-Louis. In the

St Louis (1214-1270)

Île Saint-Louis was named after King Louis IX the only French King to be made a saint. A member of the House of Capet, Louis ascended the throne in 1226 aged 12.

At that time France was the foremost Christian country in Europe. It had the largest army and had, in Louis, the model Christian King, benevolent, devout and brave. He put an end to the Albigensian Crusade in 1229 and took part in two further crusades to the Middle East, the Seventh in 1248 and the Eighth in 1270. After some initial success, both ended in failure but this did not damage his reputation. He died in Tunis during the Eighth Crusade, probably from dysentery, and by this time his reputation was such that Pope Boniface VIII canonised him in 1297.

17C there was a bathing beach here that was popular with the Court and the aristocracy.

▶ *Follow quai de Béthune then turn right onto rue de Bretonvilliers which leads to rue St-Louis-en-l'Île.*

Hôtel Lambert★
No 2.
The mansion of President Lambert de Thorigny, known as Lambert the Rich, was built in 1640 by Le Vau and decorated by Le Sueur *(sketches now at the Louvre)* and Le Brun.

Église St-Louis-en-l'Île★
No 19 bis. ⏰*Tue–Sun 9am–noon, 3pm–7pm.* ☎*01 46 34 11 60.*
The church is marked outside by an unusual iron clock and its original pierced spire. Designed by Le Vau, who lived on the island, building began in 1664, but was completed only in 1726. The ornate interior, in the Jesuit style, is highly decorated: woodwork, gilding and marble of the Grand Siècle (17C), statuettes and enamels.

Hôtel de Chenizot
No 51.
A very fine doorway surmounted by a faun mask and a majestic balcony mark

this house which, in the middle of the 19C, accommodated the archbishop.

Quai d'Orléans
There is a splendid **view**★★ of the east end of Notre-Dame and the Left Bank.

Museum

Bibliothèque Polonaise de Paris★
6 quai d'Orléans.
☎*01 43 54 35 61.* *Guided tours on request Sept–Jul, Wed 2pm, 3pm,4pm and 5pm, Sat 9am,10am, 11am and noon.* ⏰*Public holidays.* *5€.*
A 17C building houses three museums, including the **Adam-Mickiewicz Museum**, a small museum with portraits, mementoes, manuscripts, documents relating to the poet (1798-1855) and his family. Note the busts by Bourdelle and David d'Angers. The **Salle Chopin** is a permanent exhibition devoted to Chopin, featuring the original manuscripts of his Polonaises and other compositions as well as portraits of his close friends and family. The collection includes sculptures of Berlioz and Beethoven by **Boleslas Biegas** (1877-1954), whose work is the subject of the third museum, along with other Polish artists.

CANAL SAINT-MARTIN★

Ⓜ RÉPUBLIQUE (LINES 3, 5, 8, 9 AND 11), JACQUES BONSERGENT (LINE 5), GONCOURT (LINE 11), JAURÈS (LINES 2, 5 AND 7B)

This peaceful, old-fashioned canal, dug at the time of the Restoration to link the Ourcq Canal at La Villette with the Seine via the Arsenal, is still navigated by numerous barges. The raised level of the watercourse straddled with iron footbridges, its nine locks and rows of trees, make for a serene Paris landscape.

Nearby neighbourhoods: **RÉPUBLIQUE, LA VILLETTE, BUTTES-CHAUMONT.**

- 🚹 **Information:** Pyramides welcome centre, 25 rue des Pyramides. ☎08 92 68 30 00 (0.34€ per min). http://en.parisinfo.com.
- ▶ **Orient Yourself:** The canal is in the northeast end of Paris, above République.
- 🅿 **Parking:** Underground parking on the rue du Faubourg du Temple.
- �️ **Don't Miss:** The historic architecture of the Hôpital St-Louis's inner courtyard.
- ⏰ **Organizing Your Time:** Allow an hour to visit the Canal St-Martin district.
- 🧒 **Especially for Kids:** Kids of all ages enjoy the canal cruises to La Villette.
- 🚶 **Also See:** RÉPUBLIQUE, LA VILLETTE, BELLEVILLE.

A Bit of History

Napoléon ordered the construction of the Canal in 1802 to provide much needed fresh water from the Canal de l'Ourq. It was not actually completed till 1825 and during the nineteenth century the district was occupied by labourers. Subsequently allowed to deteriorate, it received a boost in 1938 when the area was refurbished for the Marcel Carné film *Hôtel du Nord,* starring the popular Parisian actress Arletty. However, during the 1960s the Canal began to fall into disuse and nowadays it is very popular with strolling tourists who like to watch the barges navigate the locks and middle class professionals who snap up the canal side apartments.

Walking Tour

Along St-Martin Canal

▶ *Starting from place de la République, take rue du Faubourg-du-Temple as far as boulevard Jules-Ferry. Turn left onto square Frédéric-Lemaître.*

Square Frédéric-Lemaître

From here there is an attractive view of one of the canal's locks. The canal disappears into an underpass, resurfacing beyond place de la Bastille as the Arsenal Basin (*see BASTILLE) Follow the canal, climbing with it as it passes through its

Canal Saint-Martin

P. Gajic/MICHELIN

nine locks. The tiny squares give way to metal footbridges. When a barge gliding along the still waters has to negotiate a lock, the canal suddenly comes to life.

▶ *Take avenue Richerand to visit the Hôpital St-Louis via rue Bichat.*

St-Louis Hospital

One of the oldest Parisian hospitals, **St-Louis** pioneered the science of dermatology. The brick and stone buildings of the **central courtyard**★ are reminiscent of place des Vosges and place Dauphine. The buildings of steeply pitched roofs and dormer windows are separated by flower-decked courtyards.

▶ *Retrace your steps to St-Martin Canal.*

Square des Récollets

A **swing bridge** crosses the canal, connecting rue de Lancry and rue de la Grange-aux-Belles. Between two smaller footbridges nestles the square named after a Franciscan convent which stood nearby, at 150 rue des Récollets.

Montfaucon Gallows

This area was once dominated by gallows that could hang up to 60 condemned people at a time. After the assassination (1572) of Admiral Coligny, his body was displayed here. Although already in disuse during the 17C, it was 1760 before the gallows were dismantled.

Hôtel du Nord

102 quai de Jemmapes.
This building lent its name to the film by Marcel Carné (*see A Bit of History, above*), who reconstructed the canalside setting in his studio. Today it is a café-restaurant with live shows.

▶ *Continue along the canal to place Stalingrad.*

Rotonde de la Villette

Place de la Bataille-de-Stalingrad.
The rotunda, one of the ring of tollhouses designed by Ledoux serves as a storehouse for archaeological finds.

▶ *Follow the left-hand quay of the Bassin de la Villette.*

Address Book

NIGHTLIFE

Chez Prune – *36 rue Beaurepaire, 10th arr.* ☎*01 42 41 30 47. Daily. Closed 25 Dec and New Year's Day.* Situated on the edge of the Saint-Martin Canal, the retro bistro Chez Prune is a popular hangout with the local youth who come here for snacks or a drink. A selection of unusual paintings hangs on the walls, giving the place a trendy feel.

Opus Jazz & Soul Club – *167 quai de Valmy, 10th arr.* ☎*01 40 34 70 00. http://opusclub.free.fr. Closed Mon, Tue.* Under the beams and lofty ceiling of this former British Officers' mess, music is the key word: funk, soul, groove, theme evenings and concerts (jazz, gospel, etc.).

WHERE TO STAY AND EAT

Turn to the back of the guide for selected hotels, restaurants, bistros and cafés listed by *arrondissement*. This district is in the 10th arrondissement.

The walk finishes with the impressive sight of the **transporter bridge** in rue de Crimée, which opens to let boats pass from the Bassin de la Villette to the Canal de l'Ourcq.

▶ *The Crimée metro station is a few steps away to the left. It is also possible to walk back along the other side of the Bassin as far as the Jean-Jaurès metro station.*

Boat Trips★

For details about various boat trips along the canal, see Planning Your Trip.
Boat trips pass through the nine locks and take the tunnel built by Baron Haussmann in 1860, which is 1 854m/6 082ft long, lit and ventilated by openings at street level. Underneath place de la Bastille, it is possible to see the grilles of the crypt where those killed in the uprisings of 1830 and 1848 are buried.

SAINT-SULPICE★

Ⓜ ST-SULPICE (LINE 4), MABILLON (LINE 10) – BUSES: 48, 63, 70, 84, 95, 96

The district has long been famous for selling religious trinkets, which became known as St-Sulpice art and often reached heights of kitsch. It has come under the influence of neighbouring St-Germain-des-Prés and its shops now include bookstores and upscale fashion boutiques.

🛈 **Information:** Carrousel du Louvre welcome centre, Place de la Pyramide Inversée, 99 rue de Rivoli. ☎08 92 68 30 00 (0.34€ per min). http://en.parisinfo.com.
▶ **Orient Yourself:** A Left Bank district between Luxembourg and St-Germain.
🅿 **Parking:** Underground parking at place St-Sulpice.
🖼 **Don't Miss:** The Delacroix mural paintings in the Eglise St-Sulpice.
🕓 **Organizing Your Time:** Allow two hours to explore this neighbourhood.
👁 **Also See:** LE LUXEMBOURG, ST-GERMAIN-DES-PRÉS, ODÉON, MONTPARNASSE.

Sights

Place St-Sulpice

Initiated in 1754, the square was designed as a semicircular space defined by uniform façades of the type at no **6** (at the corner of rue des Canettes), designed by Servandoni. But this did not materialise. The central fountain was erected by Visconti in 1844 and is known as the Fontaine des Quatre Points Cardinaux after the sculpted portraits of

©yam/Fotolia.com

Église Saint-Sulpice

Bossuet, Fénelon, Massillon and Fléchier, facing the cardinal points of the compass. Shops bearing famous names such as Yves Saint-Laurent and Christian Lacroix are found along the northern side of the square.

Église de St-Sulpice★★

The church, dedicated to the 6C Archbishop of Bourges, St Sulpicius, was founded by the abbey of St-Germain-des-Prés as a parish church for peasants living in its domain. Rebuilding began in 1646 with the chancel. A succession of six architects took charge over a period of 134 years.

Exterior

In 1732 a competition was held for the design of the façade and won by a Florentine, Servandoni, who proposed a fine façade in the style of the Antique, in contrast to the rest of the edifice. The final façade differs considerably from Servandoni's original concept. The colossal pediment has been abandoned; the belfries are crowned not by Renaissance pinnacles but by balustrades; the towers are dissimilar, the left one being taller and more ornate than the other which was never completed.

Interior

The interior is extremely impressive by its size. Of the 20 artists who worked on the internal paintings, Delacroix's genius dominates. His **murals**★, painted between 1849 and 1861, illustrate *St Michael Killing the Demon* (ceiling), *Heliodorus Being Driven from the Temple*, and *Jacob Wrestling with the Angel* (left wall). The **Lady Chapel**★ in the apse was painted under the personal supervision of Servandoni. The Virgin and Child group behind the altar is by **Pigalle**. The **organ loft**★ was designed by **Chalgrin** in 1776. The organ, rebuilt in 1862, is the largest in France and considered one of the finest. Two stoups abutting the second pillars of the nave are made from giant shells given to **François I** by the Venetian Republic and by Louis XV to the church of St-Sulpice in 1745.

In the transept, a copper band inlaid in the floor stretches from a plaque in the southern *(right)* transept to a marble obelisk in the northern *(left)* arm. At noon at the winter solstice, a ray of sunlight, passing through a small hole in the upper window in the south transept, strikes marked points on the obelisk in the far transept. At the spring and autumn equinoxes the ray is caught by the metal plaque at noon.

▶ *Take rue St-Sulpice, then turn left onto rue Mabillon.*

Marché St-Germain

This covered market combines a food hall and commercial clothing boutiques.

Rue Guisarde and rue Princesse

It is pleasant to wander these pedestrianised streets, pretty to look at by day and busy with activity at nightfall.

Rue des Canettes

Duckling Street takes its name from the low relief at no **18**. It is a lively place to go out in the evening with many bars, restaurants and nightclubs.

SAINTE-CHAPELLE★★★

Ⓜ CITÉ (LINE 4) – BUSES: 21, 38, 85, 96

Built in the 13C by St Louis in the centre of Île de la Cité to house holy relics, the Sainte-Chapelle comes as close to perfection as any religious edifice anywhere. The chapel is a Gothic marvel, a symphony of stone and stained glass, and the deep glow of its windows is one of the great joys of a visit to Paris.

Nearby neighbourhoods: ÎLE ST-LOUIS, CHÂTELET-HÔTEL DE VILLE, QUARTIER LATIN.

- 🅸 **Information:** Carrousel du Louvre welcome centre, Place de la Pyramide Inversée, 99 rue de Rivoli. ☎08 92 68 30 00 (0.34€ per min). http://en.parisinfo.com.
- ▶ **Orient Yourself:** The chapel is on Île-de-la-Cité next to the Palais de Justice.
- 🅿 **Parking:** Underground on rue de Lutèce.
- 🚫 **Don't Miss:** The intricate wooden spire, the fifth created over the centuries.
- 🕐 **Organizing Your Time:** Allow a half hour to visit the chapel.
- ♿ **Also See:** CONCIERGERIE, NOTRE-DAME, ÎLE ST-LOUIS, ÎLE DE LA CITÉ.

A Bit of History

A sacred shrine – Baudouin, a French nobleman who had been on the Fourth Crusade before becoming Emperor of Constantinople, was forced to pledge the Crown of Thorns against a loan of money from the Venetians. Unable to meet his debts, he appealed to **St Louis** (Louis IX) who redeemed the payment and retrieved the Crown in 1239. Ultimately, the creation of suitable reliquaries would cost more than twice as much as the construction of the chapel.

This exceptional building, erected in only 33 months, is attributed to **Pierre of Montreuil** (known also as Pierre of Montereau); it was consecrated in 1248. Consisting of two superimposed chambers, the upper level was used by the sovereign and his court, the lower by his household.

During the Revolution the reliquary shrine was melted down; some of the relics were saved and are now in Notre-Dame. Between 1802 and 1837 the building was used to archive judiciary papers that were stacked high against the lancet windows; restoration was undertaken by Duban and Lassus (1841-67).

Visit

4 boulevard du Palais. ♿ 🕐*Mar–Oct, 9.30am–6pm; Nov–Feb, 9.30am–5pm.* 🕐*1 Jan, 1 May, 1 and 25 Dec.* 🚫*7.50€.* ☎*01 53 40 60 97. www.monum.fr.*

Exterior

Completed just 80 years after Notre-Dame cathedral, the Sainte-Chapelle is perhaps the apogee of Gothic architecture. Its innovative great windows

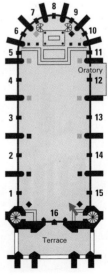

UPPER CHAPEL

Address Book

NIGHTLIFE

Castel – *15 rue Princesse, 6th arr.* ☎*01 40 51 52 80. Tue–Sat 9pm–5am. Closed Aug.* A combination of dance, high fashion and conversation much in vogue with Paris' wealthy and famous. Whether for dinner or just a drink, the elegant, opulent settings are very pleasant, for those who manage to get in. Smart dress only.

Chez Georges – *11 rue des Canettes, 6th arr.* ☎*01 43 26 79 15. Closed Sun, Mon, Aug and between Christmas and New Year.* An old café with a somewhat anarchic look to it. It is probably one of the district's few remaining genuine (and cheap) addresses. Old posters on the walls, a bar, a few benches, stools and the traditional tiles. Regulars gather in the basement cellar to dance and drink red wine.

SHOPPING

Christian-Lacroix – *2–4 pl. St-Sulpice, 6th arr.* Ⓜ*St-Sulpice.* ☎*01 46 33 48 95. www.christian-lacroix.fr. Closed Sun and public holidays.* A designer, known for his flamboyant, flowery, even precious style who seeks to bridge the gap between haute couture and street fashion. Each garment is a celebration.

La Procure – *3 rue de Mézières, 6th arr.* Ⓜ*St-Sulpice.* ☎*01 45 48 20 25. www.laprocure.com. Closed Sun and public holidays.* An institution! 750 sq m/897sq yd, of which 400 sq m/478sq yd are devoted to theology, religious history and biblical exegeses. From the rarest ancient document in Acadian to the latest translation of the gospels, this bookshop is a treasure trove of knowledge.

Village Voice – *6 rue Princesse, 6th arr.* Ⓜ*Mabillon or St-Germain-des-Prés.* ☎*01 46 33 36 47. www.villagevoicebookshop.com. Daily.* Run by an Englishman since 1981, this charming bookshop has a good range of English-language literature and review; readings held regularly.

Yves Saint-Laurent – *6 pl. St-Sulpice, 6th arr.* Ⓜ*St-Sulpice.* ☎*01 43 29 43 00. Closed Sun and public holidays.* A living legend. 40 years of creativity have forged the style of this artist so loved by women and whose inventions have marked the history of fashion. This shop presents four of the Rive Gauche collections.

WHERE TO STAY AND EAT

Turn to the back of the guide for selected hotels, restaurants, bistros and cafés listed by *arrondissement*. This district is in the 6th arrondissement.

Sainte-Chapelle

©Katja Sucker/Fotolia.com

(15m/49ft high) make the walls appear to be built of glass rather than masonry; its vault is not reinforced with great flying buttresses, but rather anchored in place by a sculpted gable and balustrade. This remarkably delicate feat of balance and counter-balance was so perfectly engineered that no crack has appeared in seven centuries. The spire soars to 75m/246ft.

Interior

In the **lower chapel**, forty columns, decorated in the 19C, carry the central vault (only 7m/23ft high and 17m/55.7ft wide), contained by the external buttresses. The floor is paved with tombstones. A spiral staircase to the right leads to the **upper chapel**, a great bejewelled glass-

Upper chapel, Sainte-Chapelle

house. The chamber is encircled by blind arcading, its capitals delicately carved with stylised vegetation; attached to each shaft is a figure of an Apostle holding one of the Church's 12 crosses of consecration – the six original ones *(pink on the plan)* are most expressive (the others are in the Musée Cluny). The painting is modern. Two deep recesses in the third bay were reserved for the king and his family. The oratory was added by Louis XI: a grille enabled him to follow the service unnoticed. The reliquary shrine would have stood at the centre of the apse on a raised platform surmounted by a wooden baldaquin. Of the two twisting staircases enclosed in the open-work turrets, the left one is original.

The **stained glass** is the oldest to survive in Paris. Of the 1 134 scenes represented over a glazed area of 618sq m/6 672sq ft, some 720 are original. The king summoned the best master-craftsmen from work recently completed at Chartres (1240) hence their similar treatments: roundel-scenes, brilliant use of colour eclipsing simplicity of composition. The principal theme is the celebration of the Passion, as foretold by the Prophets and John the Baptist. The windows should be read from left to right and from bottom to top, with the exception of nos **6, 7, 9** and **11** which read lancet by lancet.

1) Genesis – Adam and Eve – Noah – Jacob *(damaged by the storm of December 1999)*.
2) Exodus – Moses and Mount Sinai.
3) Exodus – The Law of Moses.
4) Deuteronomy – Joshua – Ruth and Boaz.
5) Judges – Gideon – Samson.
6) Isaiah – The Tree of Jesse.
7) St John the Evangelist – Life of the Virgin – The Childhood of Christ.
8) Christ's Passion.
9) John the Baptist – Daniel.
10) Ezekiel.
11) Jeremiah – Tobias.
12) Judith – Job.
13) Esther.
14) Kings: Samuel, David, Solomon.
15) St Helena and the True Cross – St Louis and the relics of the Passion.
16) 15C Flamboyant rose window: the Apocalypse.

LE SENTIER

Ⓜ BOURSE (LINE 3), SENTIER (LINE 3), BONNE-NOUVELLE (LINES 8 AND 9)

BUSES: 67, 74, 85

The Sentier quarter is the centre of the rag trade, or textile wholesalers. It's a busy, noisy district devoid of retail shops, but nonetheless there are some interesting corners worth exploring.

🄸 **Information:** Pyramides welcome centre, 25 rue des Pyramides.
☎08 92 68 30 00 (0.34€ per min). http://en.parisinfo.com.

▶ **Orient Yourself:** Bordered by the boulevard Bonne-Nouvelle, rue Réaumur, rue St-Denis and rue Notre-Dame-des-Victoires.

🄿 **Parking:** Underground parking on boulevard Bonne-Nouvelle.

☺ **Don't Miss:** The relief statues carved into the Passage du Caire entrance.

🕐 **Organizing Your Time:** Allow a half hour to explore this district.

🕯 **Also See:** MONTORGUEIL, GRANDS-BOULEVARDS, FAUBOURG POISSONIÈRE.

Walking Tour

▶ *Start from Ⓜ Sentier. Take rue Réamur and turn left onto rue des Petits Carreaux.*

Place du Caire

The former **cour des Miracles** (Courtyard of Miracles): a large courtyard, unpaved, stinking and muddy, lay hidden in a labyrinth of blind alleys, easily defensible passageways and darkened streets. Thousands of rogues, ruled by their own king, occupied the area which remained off-limits to any but their own. Victor Hugo's novel *The Hunchback of Notre-Dame* is a wonderful depiction of this wayward life. The neighbourhood was eventually cleared in 1667.

▶ *From rue du Caire walk through passage du Caire.*

Passage du Caire

🕐*Sun.* A building decorated with Egyptian motifs (sphinx, lotus, hieroglyphs) marks the entrance of the passage intersected by three covered arcades. Napoléon's victorious campaign in Egypt in 1798 aroused great enthusiasm in Paris. A taste for the Egyptian style influenced all the decorative and applied arts, architecture and fashion included. Here street names reflect the craze, borrowed from campaigns against the Turks and the Marmalukes (rue du Nil, rue du Caire, rue d'Aboukir).

▶ *Walk to rue de Cléry via rue d'Alexandrie and rue St-philippe.*

Rue de Cléry

Fronted by clothes shops, this street is the old counterscarp of the Charles V perimeter wall.

▶ *Turn left onto rue des Degrés, where a stairway gives access to the former ramparts and leads to the back of the church of Notre-Dame-de-Bonne-Nouvelle.*

Église Notre-Dame-de-Bonne-Nouvelle

The Classical belfry is all that remains of the church built by Anne of Austria – the rest of the building dates from 1823 to 1829. Note the painting by Mignard above the door in the south aisle of Anne of Austria and Henrietta-Maria, wife of Charles I of England; one at the end of the north aisle showing Henrietta of England and her three children before St Francis of Sales; an Annunciation by Lanfranco *(centre of the chancel, light switch on the right)*, and a painting by Philippe de Champaigne *(to the right)*. In the Lady Chapel there is a fine 18C Virgin and Child attributed to Pigalle.

A small **treasury** contains a 17C alabaster statue of St Jerome, two depictions of the Deposition and an 18C silk garment worn by Abbot Edgeworth of Firmont, who accompanied Louis XVI on his way to the guillotine.

SÈVRES-BABYLONE ★

Curious travellers who wander outside the well-known St-Germain and St-Sulpice districts will find this elegant residential neighbourhood dotted with interesting shops and lively cafés.

Nearby neighbourhoods: **FAUBOURG ST-GERMAIN, ST-SULPICE, INVALIDES, MONTPARNASSE.**

- **Information:** Pyramides welcome centre, 25 rue des Pyramides.
  ☎08 92 68 30 00 (0.34€ per min). http://en.parisinfo.com.
- **Orient Yourself:** Located between Montparnasse and St-Germain-des-Prés.
- **Parking:** Underground parking in front of the Bon Marché department store.
- **Don't Miss:** Fashionable people-watching from the cafés on rue de Sèvres.
- **Organizing Your Time:** Allow two to three hours to visit all of the sights.
- **Especially for Kids:** The Square Boucicault has a large playground.
- **Also See:** ST-GERMAIN-DES-PRÉS, FAUBOURG ST-GERMAIN, ST-SULPICE.

Walking Tour
See map.

- *Start from boulevard du Montparnasse near Metro station Duroc.*

Rue du Cherche-Midi
This long street links Montparnasse with Sèvres-Babylone, and contains several fine townhouses. At no 89 is the **Hôtel de Montmorency**, which today houses the Malian embassy, and at no 85 the **Musée Hébert** (*see Museums and Other Attractions*).

- *Make a short detour along rue Jean-Ferrandi to the right.*

Former artists' studios are nestling in narrow, flowered culs-de-sac. On the corner of rue de l'Abbé-Grégoire is the Maison de Laënnec, once owned by René Laënnec (1781-1826), inventor of the stethoscope. The **Hôtel de Rochambeau** at no 40 was home to Count Rochambeau, who, in 1780, was sent by Louis XVI to lead the French allied army in the American War of Independence against the British.

Carrefour de la Croix-Rouge
Intersection of rue de Sèvres and rue du Cherche-Midi. This crossroads was probably the site of a pagan temple dedicated to Isis pre-dating the abbey of St-Germain. A red cross or calvary would have been installed in the 16C to rid the place of impious associations: hence the name. The present bronze Centaur statue is by the sculptor César.

- *Follow the rue du Dragon left onto boulevard St-Germain then left again onto rue des Saints-Pères.*

Rue des Saints-Pères
The name is a distortion of St-Pierre to whom a chapel (*no 51*) was dedicated in the 17C. It is now the Ukrainian Catholic church of St Vladimir the Great. Among the fashion boutiques are two prestigious institutions: the National Foundation for Political Sciences, and the French Protestant Library at no 54.

- *Turn right onto the rue de Grenelle.*

Rue de Grenelle
This street is lined with old mansions and couture boutiques. On the left, at no 5 rue de la Chaise, is the Hôtel Vaudreuil, given by Napoléon to the Borghese family, in-laws of his sister Pauline. Next door (*no 7*) stood the Abbaye aux Bois where Mme Récamier and her mentor, the novelist Chateaubriand, held salons between 1819 and 1849.

▶ *Return to the rue de Grenelle.*

The beautiful **Fontaine des Quatre-Saisons**★ carved by **Bouchardon** between 1739 and 1745 stands outside nos 59–61. Behind the fountain is the house where **Alfred de Musset**, the Romantic poet, lived from 1824 to 1839.

▶ *Turn left onto rue du Bac.*

Chapelle Notre-Dame-de-la-Médaille-Miraculeuse
140 rue du Bac.
This is the chapel where the Virgin is said to have appeared to the novice Catherine Labouré from the convent of St-Vincent de Paul on 18 July 1830 – she was later beatified by Pius XII.

Le Bon Marché
Corner of rue de Bac and rue de Sèvres.
This department store, founded on the site of three former leprosy clinics, was the venture of Aristide Boucicault and his wife (1852). Success was achieved by several new practices we now take for granted such as undercutting of competitors, permitting an exchange of unwanted goods, and discount sales. A tour of the *Épicerie* is a must.

Boulevard Raspail
Dominating the intersection at rue de Sèvres, the **Hôtel Lutétia** *(no 45)* was built in 1907 by the architects Boileau and Tanzin; the façade was sculpted by Binet and Belmondo. Roughly hewn square blocks of rock at no 52-54 mark the site of the former Prison du Cherche-Midi (1853-1954). Captain Dreyfus

Address Book

NIGHTLIFE

Bar Lutèce – *45 blvd Raspail, 6th arr.* Ⓜ*Sèvres-Babylone.* ☎*01 49 54 46 46. www.lutetia-paris.com. Daily.* Luté-Jazz evenings, Wed–Sat from 10pm and piano-bar daily from 6pm. Two comfortable 1930s lounges welcome, in addition to its regulars, celebrities from the arts and letters. St-Germain-des-Prés is just down the road. In addition to the spacious room (adorned with an Arman sculpture), from 6pm onwards the Ernest Bar, a more intimate lounge, with its sculpture-cigar box signed by Hiquily, opens.

SHOPPING

Poilâne – *8 rue du Cherche-Midi, 6th arr.* Ⓜ*Sèvres-Babylone or St-Sulpice.* ☎*01 45 48 42 59. www.poilane.fr. Closed Sun.* Not so long ago, penniless artists could be found here exchanging paintings for bread with this remarkable craftsman. The decoration has not changed since 1932, neither has the manufacturing method (6hr of preparation) of the bread which remains the best-known in Paris.

La Grande Épicerie de Paris – *38 rue de Sèvres, 7th arr.* Ⓜ*Sèvres-Babylone.* ☎*01 44 39 81 00. www.lagrandeepicerie. fr. Closed Sun.* The handsome art deco façade of this branch of the Bon Marché houses one of the capital's largest gourmet food halls. Equally excellent wine cellar.

Le Bon Marché – *24 rue de Sèvres, 7th arr.* Ⓜ*Sèvres-Babylone.* ☎*01 44 39 80 00. www.lebonmarche.fr. Closed Sun.* This place was founded in 1852 by a highly inventive shopkeeper. His old French style and policy of selecting only the best products and fashion designers has led to the success of this large yet exclusive department store.

Rue du Bac – *rue du Bac, 7th arr.* Ⓜ*Rue-du-Bac.* A multitude of home-decorators have grouped themselves in the streets between rue de Grenelle and rue de Sèvres: L'Occitane, MD Contemporain, Dîners en ville, Le Cèdre Rouge, the Conran Shop, etc. A pleasant walk which can be finished off with a sorbet from the Bac à glace ice cream shop!

WHERE TO STAY AND EAT

Turn to the back of the guide for selected hotels, restaurants, bistros and cafés listed by *arrondissement*. This district is in the 6th arrondissement.

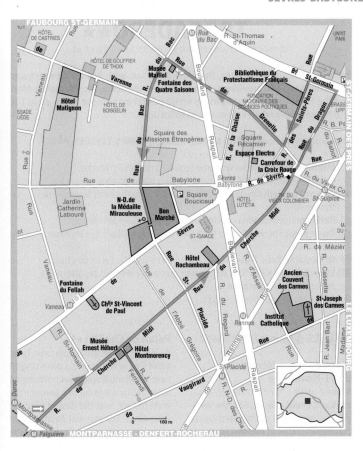

was imprisoned here in 1894. Later, the prison served as a World War II interrogation centre.

Museums and other Attractions

Ancien couvent des Carmes★

70 rue de Vaugirard. ○*Mon–Sat 7am–7pm, Sun 9.15am–7pm.* ☎*01 44 39 52 00.*
The 17C Carmelite order cultivated the balm for making their Eau des Carmes (a kind of herbal cordial drink) in the gardens. During the troubled years of the Revolution 116 priests were killed here. The **Église St-Joseph-des-Carmes**, built between 1613 and 1620, is the first example of the Jesuit style in Paris. Note the **Bernini Virgin**★ in the transept.

Musée Maillol★ (Foundation Dina Vierny)

61 rue de Grenelle. ⚪○*Wed–Mon 11am–6pm.* ○*Public holidays.*⊜*8€.* ☎*01 42 22 59 58. www.museemaillol.com.*
This museum draws from the private collection of Dina Vierny, once model of Maillol and eminent art dealer. It comprises not only the paintings and sculptures of her Catalan mentor, **Aristide Maillol** (1861-1944), but those of several of his contemporaries: Bonnard, Cézanne, Degas, Duchamp, Dufy, Gauguin, Kandinski, Renoir, Rousseau, Poliakoff.

TROCADÉRO★★

Ⓜ TROCADÉRO (LINES 6 AND 9) – BUSES: 22, 30, 32, 63, 82

Set in the Trocadéro Gardens, the Chaillot Palace, with its broad terrace and powerful fountains, provides a raised view over the Seine, the Champ-de-Mars and the Eiffel Tower. This imposing architectural monument of the early 20C also houses rich and diverse museum collections.

Nearby neighbourhoods: **TOUR EIFFEL, ALMA, CHAMPS-ELYSÉES, PASSY.**

- **Information:** Pyramides welcome centre, 25 rue des Pyramides. ☎08 92 68 30 00 (0.34€ per min). http://en.parisinfo.com.
- **Orient Yourself:** On the Right Bank overlooking the Eiffel Tower across the Seine.
- **Parking:** Underground parking on the avenue Georges Mandel.
- **Don't Miss:** The views from the Palais de Chaillot's Café de l'Homme restaurant.
- **Organizing Your Time:** Allow two hours to visit the Palais de Chaillot.
- **Especially for Kids:** Special programmes every Wednesday afternoon at the Musée de la Marine.
- **Also See:** EIFFEL TOWER, PASSY.

Sights ⓒ*See map EIFFEL TOWER.*

Place du Trocadéro et du 11-Novembre

Named after a fort the French army captured near Cadiz in 1823, the semi-circular square is dominated by an equestrian statue of Marshal Foch. it is a café-lined central point from which major roads radiate to the Alma Bridge, the Étoile, the Bois de Boulogne and the Passy quarter.

Palais de Chaillot★★

Built in 1939, the spectacular, low-lying palace of white stone, consisting of twin pavilions linked by a portico and extended by wings curving to frame the wide terrace, was the design of architects Carlu, Boileau and Azéma. Eight gilded figures line the terrace along the wings – *Flora* by Marcel Gimont being the most famous. Before the left pavilion stands a monumental bronze of Apollo by **H Bouchard** balanced on the Passy

Palais de Chaillot viewed from the Tour Eiffel

P. Galic/MICHELIN

side, with *America* by Jacques Zwoboda. From the **terrace** you get a wonderful **view**★★★ of the Seine and the Eiffel Tower; at the end of the Champ de Mars is the handsome 18C École Militaire. The **gardens**★★★ were designed for the 1937 Exhibition. A long rectangular pool on an axis with the Iéna Bridge follows the slope down the Chaillot Hill to the banks of the Seine. The pool, bordered by stone statues (*Youth* by Pierre Loison and *Joie de Vivre* by Léon Divier), is at its most spectacular at night when the powerful fountains are floodlit.

Théâtre national de Chaillot

Beneath the palace terrace is one of the capital's largest theatres *(access through the hall in the left pavilion)*. Firmin Génier created the TNP (Théâtre National Populaire) in 1920 In 1988, Jérôme Savary, of Grand Magic Circus fame, became the prolific and sometimes provocative director of the newly baptised Théâtre National de Chaillot.

Museums and other Attractions

Musée nationale de la Marine★★ [Kids]

Palais de Chaillot, 1, place du Trocadéro et du 11 Novembre. ♿🕐*Wed–Mon 10am–6pm.* 🕐*1 Jan, 1 May, 25 Dec.* ⊚*6.50€; under-18s no charge.* ☎*01 53 65 69 69. www.musee-marine.fr.*

The Maritime Museum was founded in 1827 by order of Charles X. Scale models and important artefacts from the naval dockyards trace maritime history. The models of galleys and sailing ships date from the 17C. The **Ports of France**★ is a series of canvases by the 18C artist, Joseph Vernet. The *Royal Louis* is a rare model from the Louis XV period. From the Revolution and the First Empire, there is the *Emperor's Barge* (1811). The history of merchant shipping, steam ships and the navy is accompanied by film shows. The visit ends with two modern French warships: the nuclear submarine Le Triomphant (1996) and the Charles-de-Gaulle (1999).

Art Deco statue, Palais de Chaillot

R. Besse/MICHELIN

Musée des Monuments français★★

Palais de Chaillot, 1, place du Trocadéro et du 11 Novembre. 🕐*Mon, Wed, Fri–Sun 11am–7pm, Thu 11am–9pm.* ⊚*7€.* ☎*01 44 05 39 10.*

This museum of France's monumental art and mural painting, comprising casts and replicas, was the brainchild of the Gothic Revival architect and restorer of medieval monuments Viollet-le-Duc. First opened in 1879, it was recently restored and reopened in Sept 2007.

Musée de l'Homme★★ [Kids]

Palais de Chaillot, 1, place du Trocadéro et du 11 Novembre. 🕐*Mon–Fri 10am–5pm, Sat–Sun 10am–6pm.* 🕐*Public holidays.* ⊚*7€, under-18s 5€* ☎*01 44 05 72 72. www.mnhn.fr.*

This museum, part of the National Natural History Museums, houses prehistorical anthropology and palaeontology galleries, with a focus on temporary expositions. Its collections are arranged mainly according to geographical region and include the brain of scientist, mathematician, physicist, and philosopher Rene Descartes as well as the Inca mummy which inspired Edvard Munch's painting 'The Scream'.

JARDIN DES TUILERIES ★

Ⓜ CONCORDE (LINES 1, 8 AND 12), TUILERIES (LINES 1 AND 7)
BUSES: 42, 68, 72, 73, 84, 94

Stretching between the Louvre and place de la Concorde, the elegant statues and fountains of the Tuileries Gardens make it easy for weary museum-goers and shoppers to forget that this haven witnessed some of the most turbulent events in Paris' history.

Nearby neighbourhoods: **LE GRAND LOUVRE, PLACE DE LA CONCORDE, CHAMPS-ÉLYSÉES, PALAIS-ROYAL, FAUBOURG ST-HONORÉ.**

- 🛈 **Information:** Carrousel du Louvre welcome centre, Place de la Pyramide Inversée, 99 rue de Rivoli. ☎08 92 68 30 00 (0.34€ per min). http://en.parisinfo.com.
- ▶ **Orient Yourself:** The gardens stretch along the Right Bank of the Seine.
- 🅿 **Parking:** Parking is possible at outside the east and west ends of the gardens.
- 👁 **Don't Miss:** The view of the Arc de Triomphe from the western terrace.
- 🕐 **Organizing Your Time:** Allow two hours for the museums and gardens.
- 🧒 **Especially for Kids:** A playground and toy boat rentals are popular with kids.
- 👣 **Also See:** LE GRAND LOUVRE, PALAIS-ROYAL, CHAMPS-ELYSÉES.

A Bit of History

The lost château – Named for the clay dug here for making tiles – or *tuiles* – the land was purchased in 1563 by Catherine de' Medici for a château adjoining the Louvre, a project she entrusted to **Philibert Delorme**. Work was abruptly halted when the Queen Mother learnt that her horoscope predicted that she would die near St-Germain (the Tuileries was in parish St-Germain-l'Auxerrois). In 1594 Henri IV ordered work to proceed

and the Pavillon de Flore was built with a riverside gallery linked to the Louvre. Louis XIV spent three winters at the Tuileries In 1664, Le Vau revamped the exterior and constructed the Pavillon de Marsan for Louis XIV, who spent three winters at the Tuileries while building progressed on the Louvre.

The 18C – In 1715, on the death of the Sun King, the Regency installed the young Louis XV in the Tuileries. In 1722, he moved the court back to Versailles,

Jardin des Tuileries

Address Book

WALKS

The Garden covers some 25ha/62 acres from the two sphinxes which mount guard opposite the Pavillon de Flore (brought back from Sebastopol after the city was seized in 1855) to the national gallery of the Jeu de Paume, opposite the Hôtel Talleyrand on rue de Rivoli.

FAIR

Kids Every year a fair is held in the gardens from June 21 to Aug 25. The Ferris wheel and other attractions can be seen from afar.

CHILDREN

Kids Along rue de Rivoli, the Tuileries Garden has a wide range of activities for children with swings, merry-go-rounds, go-karts, roller-skating areas, horse and donkey riding and play areas. There is also a pond in the middle where small toy sailing boats can be rented (in the summer).

NIGHTLIFE

Café Véry – *Tuileries gardens, 1st arr.* ☎*01 47 03 94 84. Daily.* What better place to stop for a drink than under the leafy chestnut trees of the Tuileries Garden. Snacks and refreshments also available: salads, sandwiches and classic French dishes are served in the glass and blond-wood pavilion. In the evening, the entrance is via the gate from place de la Concorde.

SHOPPING

Galignani – *224 r. de Rivoli, 1st arr.* ⓜ*Tuileries.* ☎*01 42 60 76 07. Closed Sun and public holidays.* Founded in 1801, the bookshop is still run by the Galignani family. This prestigious firm is proud to have been the first English bookshop established on the continent. Excellent history, art and cooking sections.

WHERE TO STAY AND EAT

Turn to the back of the guide for selected hotels, restaurants, bistros and cafés listed by *arrondissement*. This district is in the 1st arrondissement.

---

and the palace was abandoned as a residence and Paris' first public concert-hall was set up in the Salle des Suisses in 1725. It drew many major composers and musicians, including **Mozart** (1778). The Comédie Française moved here in 1770, staging **Beaumarchais**' *Barber of Seville* and Voltaire's *Irène* before 1782.

Troubled times – On 17 October 1789 the royal family were forced back to Paris by the angry mob. On 20 June 1792 the palace was invaded by rioters and two months later, on 10 August, the palace was attacked: 600 of the defending 900 Swiss guards were slaughtered and the palace was ransacked while the king

---

Rue de Rivoli

Rue de Rivoli crosses the site of the former Tuileries **Riding School**. In 1789 the school was hastily converted into a meeting place for the Constituent Assembly. Sessions were subsequently held there by the Legislative Assembly and the Convention. On 21 September 1792, the day following the French victory over the Prussians at Valmy (commemorative tablet on a pillar in the Tuileries railings opposite no **230**), it became the setting for the proclamation of the Republic and the trial of Louis XVI.

In 1944 the German General von Choltitz, Commandant of Paris, who had his headquarters at the **Hôtel Meurice** (no **228**), took a momentous decision in the capital's own history by refusing to follow Hitler's orders to blow up the capital's bridges and principal buildings when the tanks of General Leclerc's division and the Resistance were known to be approaching. He surrendered on 25 August and Paris was liberated intact. At the far end by place de la Concorde several commemorative plaques record the heroism of those who fell during the Liberation.

took refuge in the Legislative Assembly. During the Convention, the buildings served as ministry offices.

Final decline – **Napoléon III** (Bonaparte) took up residence on 20 February 1800, and under him, the architects **Visconti** and Lefuel completed the Galerie Rivoli, thereby completing the union of the Tuileries and the Louvre. During the Commune uprisings (1871), the Tuileries Palace was burnt down. In 1883, the stone ruins were purchased by a Corsican family who used the stones to build a replica palace in Ajaccio (this too was burnt down in 1978).

The gardens – Catherine de' Medici envisaged an Italian-style park, complete with fountains, a maze, a grotto, populated with terracotta figures by **Bernard Palissy**, and a menagerie for her palace next to the Louvre. Henri IV later added an orangery and a silkworm farm. In 1664 Le Nôtre raised two terraces lengthways and of unequal height to level the sloping ground, creating the magnificent central axis; he created the pools and designed formal flower beds, quincunxes and slopes. Colbert was so delighted that he intended the gardens to be kept for the royal family, but was subsequently persuaded by the author, Charles Perrault, to allow access to the public. In the 18C chairs were made available for hire and toilets installed. Louis-Philippe reserved a part of the gardens for the royal family.

Visit

The Tuileries Today

The gardens have recently undergone a substantial restoration programme. Parts designed by Le Nôtre remain unaltered, although some sculptures have been moved and others added, including the fine collection of **nudes**★ by **Maillol**, Rodin's *The Kiss*, and works by Dubuffet, Ernst, Calder, Giacometti, Arp and Picasso. Steps and ramps afford access at several points to the terraces (the **Feuillants** on the north side, the **Bord de l'Eau** on the south) which run the length of the gardens

and culminate in the Jeu de Paume and Orangery pavilions.

From the riverside terrace there is a splendid **view**★★ over the gardens, the Seine and, in the background, the Louvre. This was the playground of the royal princes including the sons of Napoléon I and III. Below, an underground passage running the length of the terrace to place de la Concorde enabled Louis-Philippe to escape from the palace in 1848. The **central alley** affords a magnificent **vista**★★★.

The octagonal pool

Around the huge octagonal basin are arranged statues, terraces, slopes and stairways in one single architectural whole. Works are listed starting from the eastern side of the basin, going counter-clockwise.

- *The Seasons* (N Coustou and Van Clève)
- Arcade from the Tuileries Palace
- Bust of Le Nôtre (Coysevox) – the original is in St-Roch (🕭 see *PALAIS-ROYAL*).
- *The Tiber* copied from the Antique
- *The Seine* and *The Marne* (G Coustou)
- *The Loire* and *The Loiret* (Van Clève)
- *The Nile* copied from the Antique
- *Fame* on a winged horse after Coysevox *(on the left of the main gate)*
- *Mercury* on a winged horse after Coysevox *(on the right of the main gate)* – originals in the Louvre.

Arc de Triomphe du Carrousel★
– 🕭 see *LE GRAND LOUVRE*.

Museums and Other Attractions

The two pavilions, the **Orangerie** and the **Jeu de Paume** were built during the Second Empire and have served as art galleries since the beginning of the 20C.

Musée de l'Orangerie★★

♿🕘*Wed–Mon 9am–12.30pm (by reservation only), 12.30pm–7pm (Fri 9pm).* 🕘*1 May, 25 Dec.* ✆*7.50€.* ☎*01 44 77 80 07. www.musee-orangerie.fr.*

The Massacre of the Swiss Guards

Louis XVI and his family were expelled from Versailles following the fall of the Bastille in 1789 and went to live at the Tuileries Palace. Sensing the danger they were in, the king and his family tried to escape in June 1791, but were arrested after being discovered at Varennes near the border with Germany.

They were brought under escort back to the Tuileries where they were confined and protected only by the king's faithful Swiss Guard. There they remained for the next year but by the summer of 1792 there was no longer a desire to retain the monarchy. On 10th August the Tuileries Palace was stormed by the people of Paris led by Danton and others. The Royal Family had already escaped to the General Assembly Hall, but the Swiss Guards set about defending the Palace unaware of this. At first they threw cartridges out of the windows as a gesture of peace but fighting soon broke out. A note arrived from the king ordering the Swiss Guard not to fire on the insurgents but they were heavily outnumbered and had no choice.

The result was a massacre in which 600 of the 900 Swiss Guards died in the fighting. A further 60 were killed after being taken prisoner and many died in prison. It is estimated that only about 100 survived.

Reopened in 2006 after extensive renovations, the two oval rooms on the ground floor are hung with panels from the water-lily series painted by **Monet** of his garden at Giverny, in Normandy known as the **Nymphéas**★★★. The lower-level galleries accommodate the Walter-Guillaume Collection (Impressionists to 1930). This famous collection presents the work of many artists including Soutine, Picasso, Modigliani, Cézanne, Renoir, Derain, Matisse and Rousseau.

Galerie nationale du Jeu de Paume

♿ ◷ Wed–Fri noon–7pm, Tue noon–9pm, Sat–Sun 10am–7pm. ◷ 1 Jan, 1 May, 25 Dec. ⊛6€. ☎01 47 03 12 50. www.jeu depaume.org.

Since 2004 this converted "old tennis court" is home to the Galerie Nationale du Jeu de paume, the Centre national de la photographie, and the Patrimoine Photographique. It includes collections of photography, film, video, and installations.

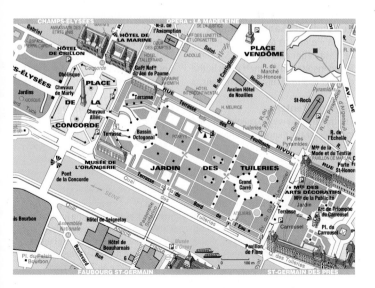

VAUGIRARD

Ⓜ VAUGIRARD (LINE 12) – BUSES: 39, 70, 80, 88, 89

The old village of Vaugirard was a small rural dependency of the St-Germain-des-Prés abbey until it became a district of Paris in 1860. Today it's a quiet residential area, with a popular book market in Parc Georges-Brassens. The southern border is at the Porte de Versailles, where major trade fairs are held year-round.

Nearby neighbourhood: **MONTPARNASSE.**

- **Information:** Pyramides welcome centre, 25 rue des Pyramides. ☎08 92 68 30 00 (0.34€ per min). http://en.parisinfo.com.
- **Orient Yourself:** Located in the southwest corner of the Left Bank.
- **Parking:** Street parking possible around the parc Georges-Brassens.
- **Don't Miss:** The old artist ateliers of the passage de Dantzig.
- **Organizing Your Time:** Allow at least an hour for this large district.
- **Especially for Kids:** Playground in the parc Georges-Brassens.
- **Also See:** TOUR MONTPARNASSE.

Sights

Parc Georges-Brassens★ [Kids]
Rue des Morillons. This park was created in the 19C on the site of the old Vaugirard abattoirs. A few vestiges survive: the horse hall, two bronze bulls by the animal sculptor Cain at the main entrance, and the auction belfry reflected in the central basin. A wooded hill dominates the park with its children's play areas, a belvedere, a climbing rock and a vineyard harvested in early October with great fanfare.

Rue and villa Santos-Dumont
Access via rue des Morillons. Zadkine, Fernard Léger and Georges Brassens found inspiration for their work in the discreet charm of this corner of Paris.

Passage Dantzig
The three-storey wine pavilion designed by Eiffel for the Exposition Universelle,

of 1900 was salvaged from scrap by the sculptor Boucher, and adapted for use as artists' lodgings and studios. Known as **La Ruche**★, among its most famous lodgers were Fernand Leger (1905), Chagall (1910), Soutine, **Modigliani** and the Swiss novelist Blaise Cendras. The second generation included the sculptors **Zadkine**, **Brancusi** and Kisling.

Rue de Vaugirard
This is Paris' longest street, running between the Latin Quarter and the Porte de Versailles. Shops tend to cluster around intersections of rue de la Convention and rue de Vaugirard, rue Lecourbe, rue du Commerce and rue St-Charles.

Louis Pasteur

Louis Pasteur (1822-95) is hailed as one of the greatest scientists ever to have lived. At 25, in his laboratory at the École Normale Supérieure, he established the principle of molecular dissymmetry; at 35, that of fermentation; at 40, he laid the foundations for asepsis thus refuting preconceived ideas about spontaneous generations, and he studied the ruinous diseases affecting beer and wine production and of the silkworm; at 58, he studied viruses and vaccines. He isolated the rabies virus, researching its prevention and delivered an antidote for the first time on 7 July 1885.

PLACE DES VICTOIRES★

Ⓜ ÉTIENNE-MARCEL (LINE 4) – BUSES: 29, 67, 74, 85

Unusual shops, picturesque arcades and passageways – this is an elegant district for a pleasant stroll to discover old Paris or, just simply, window-shop.

Nearby neighbourhoods: **PALAIS-ROYAL, LES HALLES, GRANDS BOULEVARDS.**

- **Information:** Pyramides welcome centre, 25 rue des Pyramides. ☎08 92 68 30 00 (0.34€ per min). http://en.parisinfo.com.
- **Orient Yourself:** Located to the north of the Palais-Royal.
- **Parking:** Underground at La Bourse.
- **Don't Miss:** Galerie Vivienne Arcades.
- **Organizing Your Time:** Allow an hour for this district.
- **Also See:** PALAIS-ROYAL, MONTORGUEIL, OPÉRA.

Walking Tour
See map PALAIS-ROYAL.

Place des Victoires★

In 1685 Marshal de la Feuillade commissioned a statue of the king from the sculptor **Desjardins**. The statue, unveiled in 1686, showed the king, crowned with the laurels of victory, standing on a pedestal adorned with six low-relief sculptures and four captives representing the vanquished Spain, Holland, Prussia and Austria.

The statue was melted down in 1792 and the present equestrian statue of the Sun King was sculpted by Bosio in 1822.

> ▶ *Take rue Vide-Gousset, from the north side of the square, which leads to place des Petits-Pères. Make a brief detour up rue du Mail.*

Rue du Mail

Note the faun's mask and cornucopias adorning the doorway at no 5 and the capitals with interlaced snakes at no 7: these two 17C mansions make up the Hôtel Colbert, formerly owned by Louis XIV's minister (the grass snake is Colbert's emblem).

Basilique de Notre-Dame-des-Victoires

The basilica (built 1629-1740) served as the Petits-Pères monastery chapel, dedicated in honour of the king's victories. It served as the Stock Exchange from 1795 to 1809.

> ▶ *Take passage des Petits-Pères to reach the Vivienne and Colbert galleries.*

The Arcades

Built in 1823, the **Galerie Vivienne** is one of the prettiest arcades in Paris. Light floods through the glass roof. Notice the half-moon windows on the mezzanine, and the mosaics designed by the Italian artist Facchina. There are old bookshops clothing boutiques and a tearoom.

Rue des Petits-Champs

Look through the grille at no **8** for a glimpse of the courtyard and stone façade of the **Tubeuf** mansion (1648-55). Opposite stands **Colbert's** mansion (1665). On the right is the **Passage Choiseul**, immortalised by the writer **Louis-Ferdinand Céline**, who lived at

Place des Victoires

P. Gajic/MICHELIN

nos 64 and 67 as a child and gave a cutting description of it in his work *Mort à Crédit (Death on the Instalment Plan)*.

▸ *Turn right at rue de Richelieu.*

Square Louvois
The square accommodates a fine fountain by Visconti (1884), whose four allegorical sculptures represent France's major four rivers: the Seine, the Rhône, the Loire and the Garonne.

Bibliothèque nationale de France: site Richelieu
58 rue de Richelieu.

The Collections
The present national collection was founded upon François I's library from Fontainebleau, endowed with a copy of every book subsequently printed in France. As of 1998, when printed works and periodicals were transferred to the new buildings at the François Mitterand site (*see BERCY*), this part of the library has kept the specialised collections from antiquity.

A home fit for a royal library
In the 17C the Hôtel Tubeuf was enlarged by Mansart and named after Cardinal Mazarin art collection it housed. On the first floor is the magnificent **Mazarin Gallery**★ by Mansart (*access during temporary exhibitions*). The great staircase leads to the **Medals and Antiques Museum**★ (Mezzanine level; ◷*Mon–Sat 1pm–5.45pm, Sat 1pm–4.45pm, Sun noon–6pm; ◷1 Jan, 15 Aug and 25 Dec; ≈3.30€; ☎01 53 79 83 30*).

▸ *Continue up rue de Richelieu.*

The former **Hôtel de Nevers**, on the corner of rue Colbert, was designed by Mansart and has served to accommodate in turn Mazarin's personal library, Mme de Lambert's literary salon (18C), and the royal medal collection.

▸ *Turn right at rue Colbert and left at rue Vivienne.*

La Bourse (Stock Exchange)
Paris' first exchange was John Law's bank. When it went bankrupt a public exchange was founded (1724). It was located in the Palais Mazarin (now part of the Bibliothèque Nationale), before being transferred to the church of Notre-Dame des Victoires. Napoléon commissioned Brongniart's building in 1808, and it was inaugurated in 1826.

Address Book

SHOPPING
Kenzo – *3 & 6 pl. des Victoires, 1st arr.* Ⓜ*Sentier.* ☎*01 40 39 72 03. Closed Sun.* These spacious, ready-to-wear boutiques for men and women. present the collections of this Japanese designer who has combined Eastern and Western influences to create his own sober, elegant style.

Jean-Paul Gaultier – *6 rue Vivienne, 2nd arr.* Ⓜ*Bourse.* ☎*01 42 86 05 05. Closed Sun.* Located in the former stables of the Palais-Royal, Jean-Paul Gaultier's shop is well worth a visit. Its extravagant design is a distinctive hallmark of this designer whose reputation is worldwide.

L. Legrand Filles et Fils – *1 rue de la Banque, 2nd arr.* Ⓜ*Bourse.* ☎*01 42 60 07 12. www.caves-legrand.com. Closed Sun.* This authentic wine cellar and fine grocery shop is the home of a reputed family of wine dealers. From the classical to the unusual, let yourself be guided by the master of the house and don't forget to take a look at their selection of regional goodies.

Ventilo – *27 bis rue du Louvre, 2nd arr.* Ⓜ*Les Halles.* ☎*01 44 76 82 97. www. ventilo.fr. Closed Sun, one week in summer, 1 May and Whitsun.* This highly elegant boutique with its oriental-style décor, also has a tearoom much appreciated by chic Parisians. Three floors of sportswear and classic clothes, but also beauty care products and decorative objects for the home.

LA VILLETTE ★★

Ⓜ PORTE DE LA VILLETTE (NORTH: CITÉ DES SCIENCES ET DE L'INDUSTRIE – LINE 7) AND
PORTE DE PANTIN (SOUTH: CITÉ DE LA MUSIQUE – LINE 5) – BUSES: 75, 139, 150, 152

The city's largest park extends between the Porte de La Villette and the Porte de Pantin, a vast green space that's home to two modern museum complexes, concert venues, cinemas, and play areas specially designed for children.

- **Information:** Pyramides welcome centre, 25 rue des Pyramides. ☏08 92 68 30 00 (0.34€ per min). http://en.parisinfo.com.
- **Orient Yourself:** La Villette is located in the far northeast corner of the city.
- **Parking:** Underground parking at the Porte de Pantin.
- **Don't Miss:** The excellent temporary exhibitions at the Cité des Sciences.
- **Organizing Your Time:** Allow a half day for this vast park complex.
- **Especially for Kids:** The Dragon slide and Cité des Enfants are kid favourites.
- **Also See:** PARC DES BUTTES CHAUMONT.

Cité des Sciences et de l'Industrie ★★★

See map.

♿⏱*Explora: Tue–Sun, 10am–6pm (Sun 7pm); see Address Book for more details. Cité des Enfants: Tue–Sun, 9.45–11.30am, 1.30pm–3.15pm (Sun 10.30am–12.30pm, 2.30pm–4.30pm)*⏱*1 May and 25 Dec.* ⚲*6€–10.50€.* ☏*01 40 05 80 00. www. cite-sciences.fr.*
Designed by architect Adrien Fainsilber and opened in 1986, this interactive complex has three aims: to inform, to teach and to give pleasure. It succeeds in all three, in a contemporary setting interwoven with elements of water, vegetation and light.

Explora ★★   Kids
Levels 1 and 2. Explore today's and tomorrow's world by means of a variety of exhibitions and interactive shows, models and hands-on activities. The permanent exhibits include a huge presentation of Space (*on Level 1, south gallery and level 2, mezzanine*).
On **Level 1's south gallery** are exhibits on the Earth's water, OcΩeans (the most recent French submarine explores the wreck of the Titanic, forecasts earthquakes and studies underwater oases), **Hothouses, the gardens of the future** (how to grow plants without soil, and the dangers of tampering with nature), Cars, Aeronautics, Energy (the Earth's resources transformed by man into

energy), Computer science, Sounds (listen to a multitude of sounds, from a rubbing noise to a buzzing noise, a whistling noise…), and Mathematics.

In **Level 1's north gallery** is an exhibition on **Images** (how to transform what we see: photography, cinema, television, video films, digital images).

Level 2's north mezzanine presents **Rocks and volcanoes** (earthquakes, volcanic eruptions), the immensely popular **Planétarium** (astronomical phenomena are described with projections of actual real-life images, a simulator and triphonic sound), **Man and health**, **Medicine** *(take a trip through the human body and learn that drugs are not the only means of curing people)*, **Biology** and **Light effects**.

Finally, the **Level 2 west mezzanine** houses the **Stars and galaxies** exhibit exploring the solar system, the birth and death of a star, and the instruments used by astronomers and astrophysicists.

Cité des Enfants   Kids
Ground floor. A hands-on interactive section reserved for 3 to 5 and 5 to 12 year-olds. Play, observation and experimentation in the world of science and technology. There is plenty to keep older children intrigued, as they find the answers to scientific and technical

La Géode

questions during sessions lasting 1hr 30min.

Médiathèque

Levels – 1 and – 2 for adults, ground floor for children. This library provides not only books and printed data, but also access to externally held computerised published information in the form of video, CD-ROM and other educational material.

La Géode★★ 〔Kids〕

In the park just outside the museum. The most comfortable viewing is from the top of the hall. ◔*Tue–Sun 10.30am–8.30pm (hourly sessions).* ☎*01 44 84 44 84 or www.lageode.fr.* ◔*1 May and 25 Dec.*
The shining steel globe, 36m/118ft in diameter, seems to hover over a sheet of water. Inside, the auditorium is equipped with a hemispherical aluminium 1 000m2/11 000sq ft screen, perforated for sound. The wide-angle lens encompasses a 180° field of vision. The multimedia system projects films with scientific and cultural themes.

L'Argonaute

Outside, next to the Géode, ◉*3€.* This submarine was launched on 29 June 1957 at Cherbourg; it has covered 210 000mi,(336,000 km) and was submerged a total of 32 700hr before finally coming to rest beside the Géode.

Le Simulateur (Cinaxe) 〔Kids〕

Outside. ◔*Tue–Sun. 11am–1pm, 2pm–5pm, film every 15min.* ◉*4.80€ at the Cinaxe ticket window. Children under age 4 not allowed, not advisable for pregnant women and heart patients. Reservations* ☎*01 44 84 44 84.*
The Cinaxe simulator enables up to 60 people to physically experience a particular film action – a flight through outer space, or driving round a motor-racing track, during a 4 to 5min ride. This sensation is in part achieved by the capsule's actual hydraulic motion, and partly through wearing 3-D glasses *(provided).*

Cité de la Musique 〔Kids〕

Located at the southern entrance to the park near the Porte de Pantin, Music City, designed by Christian de Portzamparc, houses all the facilities needed to study dance and music in France today. The western part contains the **Conservatoire national supérieur de musique et de danse de Paris** (Paris National Conservatory of Music and Dance), whereas on the eastern side is a concert hall and a music museum.

Address Book

THE MUSEUMS

Cité des Sciences et de l'Industrie – 30 av. Corentin-Cariou. ⓂPorte de La Villette. ☎01 40 05 80 00. www.cite-sciences.fr.

Musée de la Musique – 221 av. Jean-Jaurès. ⓂPorte de Pantin. ☎01 44 84 44 84. www.cite-musique.fr.

PAYING ACTIVITIES

It is possible to purchase a combined ticket to both places.

Explora: ✆8€ (under-25s and adult accompanying an under-16: 6€; under-7s free). Additional charge for the Planetarium: 3€.

Cité des Enfants (3–5 years or 5–12 years): ✆6€ per child for 1hr 30min. Reservations: ☎08 92 69 70 72.

Géode: ✆10.50€ per projection. Reservations: b08 92 68 45 40.

Cinaxe: ✆4.80€ at the Cinaxe. Not suitable for very young children.

FREE ACTIVITIES

Cité des métiers: Mon–Sat (closed public holidays) 10am–6pm, Sat noon–6pm. Level –1.

Médiathèque: Noon–6.45pm (7.45pm on Tue and Fri) Closed Mon. Levels –1 and –2 for adults; ground floor for children.

Salle Louis Braille: Computerised reading room for the blind. Level 1, inside the Médiathèque, by appointment.

Cinéma Jean-Bertin: Documentaries, scientific and technical films. Ground floor; projection times available on location.

Mediterranean aquarium: Level – 2.

SOUVENIRS AND GIFT SHOP

Boutique Explorus – Ground floor. The shop sells games, gifts and other souvenirs, including lots of really fun toys which demonstrate scientific principles. A **bookshop** stocks catalogues of the exhibitions, together with guide books. Post cards and scientific reviews and books.

WHERE TO STAY AND EAT

♨Turn to the back of the guide for selected hotels, restaurants, bistros and cafés listed by arrondissement. The museum and park are in the 19th arrondissement.

Café de la musique – 221 av. Jean-Jaurès, 19th arr. ☎01 48 03 15 91. Daily. Conveniently located next to the Cité de la Musique, this café is modern and elegant, a charming place to sit and enjoy a cup of coffee or a fine meal. Inside, red and green armchairs alternate around little round tables. Outside, the terrace facing the green swathe of the park is a very inviting place to enjoy the late afternoon sun and a drink. The Cité des Sciences et de l'Industrie has several bars, cafés, restaurants, etc., which are located on levels –1, 0 and 1.

Musée de la Musique★

♿ⓉTue–Sun noon–6pm, Sun 10am–6pm. ⏰Public holidays. ✆7€. ☎01 44 84 44 84. www.cite-musique.fr.

The museum contains around 900 **musical instruments** from the 17C to the present time. An audio-visual tour, taking the visitor through the history of Western music, includes Stradivarius and Amati violins, some 50 spinets, harpsichords, and pianos, guitars, recorders, bass viols and lutes. Also on display are and instruments once owned by famous musicians (Berlioz, Chopin and Fauré, Adolphe Sax).

Parc de la Villette★ Kids

The park, which lies between the Cité de Sciences et l'Industrie and the Cité de la Musique, was designed by **Bernard Tschumi** around three principle sets of features: follies, galleries and play areas. It has become a favourite place to spend a summer evening in the park watching films projected on a giant outdoor screen; the ambience is friendly and relaxed. Chairs and mats are available for hire. Check the programme in any events magazine, such as Pariscope.

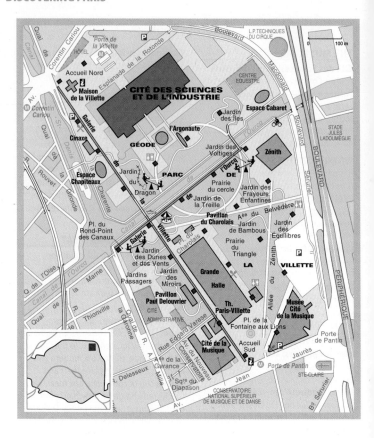

Red pavilions, built of enamelled iron over a concrete frame, punctuate the park every 120m/393.7ft on a grid pattern. **Follies**, more usually denoting 18C fanciful pavilions, are here designed with a particular function be it a slide, weather vane or viewing platform.

La Grande Halle

This former cattle market auction hall has been skilfully converted into a space for a variety of activities: concerts, circuses, theatre and dance productions, trade fairs and other assemblies.

Playing fields

One is triangular, one is circular; both are large, flat grassy spaces, eminently suitable for all kinds of ball games and sun bathing.

Gardens

There are ten gardens in all in the park, with delightful play equipment for children. One favourite area, the Jardin des Dune, is designed around the theme of wind and dunes; parents sit on benches while the children run, climb and swing in the different sections, according to their age group. The vast bamboo garden, has been laid out in a 6m/19.7ft pit to create a micro-climate.

BOIS ET CHÂTEAU DE VINCENNES ★★

Ⓜ CHÂTEAU DE VINCENNES – RER: VINCENNES

Vincennes is known for its vast woodland with its natural attractions, its famous zoo, beautiful flower garden and racecourse, making it one of the capital's most popular recreation areas. It also boasts a mighty fortress, once a royal residence that witnessed some of the most dramatic events in French history.

- **Information:** Pyramides welcome centre, 25 rue des Pyramides. ☎08 92 68 30 00 (0.34€ per min). http://en.parisinfo.com.
- ▶ **Orient Yourself:** The park lies at the southeastern border of Paris.
- 🅿 **Parking:** Street parking possible outside the Parc Floral.
- **Don't Miss:** Sign up for a tour of the recently restored château keep (*donjon*).
- 🕐 **Organizing Your Time:** Allow an entire day to enjoy the Bois de Vincennes.
- **Especially for Kids:** The Parc Floral has train rides, mini golf and jungle gyms.
- **Also See:** BERCY (Le Cinématique Française).

A Bit of History

The Forest – Philippe Auguste enclosed the wood as a royal hunt with a wall 12km/7.4mi long and stocked it with game in the 12C. **Charles V** built a small château within it on a low hill. In 17C the forest became a fashionable place to go walking. A military firing range was opened in 1798, the first of a series of enclaves in the forest made exclusively for military purposes. Napoléon III ceded the estate at Vincennes – excluding the château and military installations – in 1860 to the City of Paris, to be made into an English-style park, after London's Hyde Park.

The Château – This medieval Versailles has two distinct features within its walls: a tall forbidding keep and a majestic group of 17C buildings. Philippe Auguste built the first manor house in the 12C, to which Louis IX added a Holy Chapel. This popular king was known to receive his subjects quite unceremoniously at the foot of an oak. Construction on the fortified castle under Valois Philippe VI, and Charles V completed it in 1396.

The classical pavilions – Mazarin, appointed governor of Vincennes in 1652, had symmetrical royal pavilions designed and built by Le Vau to frame the main courtyard facing south over the forest. In 1660 the young Louis XIV spent his honeymoon in the King's Pavilion.

Other uses – From the beginning of the 16C to 1784, the keep, no longer favoured as a royal residence, was used as a State prison. The disgrace of detention in Vincennes was far less than at the Bastille. Among the most famous were the Great Condé, the Prince de Conti, Fouquet (guarded by d'Artagnan), **Diderot** and Mirabeau. In 1738 part of the château became a porcelain factory, transferred to **Sèvres** in 1756.

The castle keep, Vincennes

P. Gajic/ MICHELIN

Duc d'Enghien

From the bridge over the moat can be seen, at the foot of the Tour de la Reine on the right, the column marking the spot where the Duc d'Enghien, Prince of Condé, was executed by a firing squad on 20 March 1804, accused of plotting against Napoléon (his body was exhumed on the orders of Louis XVIII and reburied in the Royal Chapel).

The military establishment – Under **Louis-Philippe**, Vincennes was incorporated into the Paris defence system: a fort was built beside the château, the ramparts were reinforced with massive casemates, and the complex virtually buried below glacis. Under Napoléon the château had been converted into a formidable arsenal. The towers were reduced to the height of the perimeter wall and mounted with cannon, the rampart crenellations were removed, and the keep reverted to a prison. On 24 August 1944 the Germans, before their departure from the castle, shot 26 resistance fighters, exploded three mines, breaching the ramparts in two places and damaging the King's Pavilion, and set fire to the Queen's Pavilion.

Restoration – The first restoration of Vincennes was entrusted by **Napoléon III** to **Viollet-le-Duc**. Repair work carried out sporadically has lasted over a century and has only recently been completed. The main courtyard looks again much as it did in the 17C, the moat around the keep having been redug, the 19C casemates removed and the pavilions and keep restored.

Château de Vincennes

Sept–Apr, daily 10am–5pm; May–Aug, 10am–6pm. The moat, keep and Sainte-Chapelle can only be visited with a guided tour (information at the Accueil Charles V). 1 Jan, 1 May, 1 and 11 Nov, 25 Dec. Guided tours (45min or 1hr 15min) 7.50€, no charge 1st Sun in the month (Oct–May). 01 48 08 31 20. www.chateau-vincennes.fr.

Outside the Walls

A walk round the outside of the château, following the embankment around the

moat provides a good sense of scale. The **Tour du Village**★, a massive tower 42m/138ft high, which survived the 19C alterations, served as the governor's residence in the Middle Ages, where he could survey the drawbridge entrance. Continue down the **Cours des Maréchaux** along the perimeter wall. It was in the penultimate of the five truncated towers along the east wall, the Tour du Diable, that the porcelain factory was established. The arcades of the Classical Vincennes portico, overlooking the forest and closing the perimeter wall on the south side, come into view as you reach the château esplanade. The **Tour du Bois** in the middle was reduced by Le Vau in the 17C when he transformed the gate into a state entrance (appearing as a triumphal arch from inside).

Cour Royale

The main courtyard is closed to the north by a portico, framed by the two royal pavilions. Anne of Austria and Louis XIV's brother lived in the Pavillon de la Reine, where the governor, Daumesnil, died of cholera in 1832; the last royal occupant was the Duke of Montpensier, Louis Philippe's youngest son. Mazarin died in the Pavillon du Roi in 1661.

Donjon★★

On the western side, the walls are dominated by the impressive **keep** (donjon), erected in 1337, a fine surviving example of medieval military architecture. The 52m/170.6ft-tall tower is enclosed by a fortified wall and a separate moat. The base of the stone wall was reinforced to protect against sapping (breaching defences by undermining a wall), and turrets defended the corners. At sky level, a roofed sentry path, complete with battlements, and machicolations with gun embrasures below, ran right around the inner tower. The ground

Daumesnil's Refusals

In 1814 when the Allies called for the surrender of Vincennes, the then governor, **General Daumesnil**, known as Peg Leg having lost a leg at the Battle of Wagram, retorted "I'll surrender Vincennes when you give me back my leg".

At the end of the Hundred Days, the castle was again called to surrender, and there came a second refusal. Five months later, however, the doors were opened to Louis XVIII.

In 1830 Daumesnil was still governor as insurgents attempted to attack Charles X's ministers imprisoned in the keep. The governor refused them entry, announcing that before surrendering he would blow himself and the castle sky-high.

floor served as the kitchens. The main room on the first floor originally served as a royal reception room hung with tapestries. Mirabeau was imprisoned for three years in one of the towers where he wrote a scathing condemnation of royal warrants. A wide spiral staircase leads to the second floor and the royal bedchamber. Henri V of England, Charles VI's son-in-law, died of dysentery in this room in 1422.

Chapelle Royale★

⚷ *Temporarily closed for restoration.* The Royal Chapel, begun by Charles V in the 14C in place of the one built by **St Louis**, was completed only in the 16C in the reign of Henri II. The building is pure Gothic; the façade with its beautiful stone rose windows is Flamboyant. The windows in the chancel, are filled with unusually coloured mid-16C **stained glass**★ featuring scenes from the Apocalypse. The storm of December 1999 shattered several of the windows, currently under restoration.

The Park

The **Lac Daumesnil**★ *(to the west),* the **Lac des Minimes** *(to the east)* and the **Lac de Gravelle** *(to the south)* are all popular focal points for walkers and boaters alike. The islands are accessible across bridges: Île de Reuilly has a café and Île de la Porte Jaune a restaurant.

Foire du Trône or foire aux Pains d'épice

The thousand-year-old Throne or **Gingerbread Fair** is held each spring *(Palm Sunday–Easter)* on the Reuilly Lawn near Lake Daumesnil. The fair recalls a concession obtained in 957 by the monks of St Antoine's Abbey to sell a piglet-shaped rye, honey and aniseed bread in memory of their saint during Holy Week. Nowadays, the yearly fun fair is better known for its flashy midway and stomach-churning rides.

Centre bouddhique du Bois de Vincennes

40 bis route de ceinture du Lac Daumesnil. ⏰*Apr–Oct: access to the temple on religious feast days. Call for information.* ☎*01 43 41 54 48.*
South of Lake Daumesnil is the Buddhist Temple of Paris, housed in one of the 1931 Colonial Exhibition buildings. The new roof with 180 000 tiles carved with an axe out of a chestnut tree is noteworthy. Inside is a monumental gilded statue of Buddha (9m/29.5ft).

The Zoo and other Attractions

Le parc zoologique de Vincennes★★   Kids

Avenue Daumesnil. Ⓜ *Porte Dorée.* ♿⏰*Mon–Sat 9am–6pm, Sun and public holidays 9am–6.30pm (last admission 30min before closing);* ⏵*5€.* ☎*01 44 75 20 10. www.mnhn.fr.*
To the west of the park, 535 mammals and 600 birds of some 82 different species live in natural surroundings close to their familiar habitat. Around 120 births take place every year. At the centre is an artificial rock 65m/213ft high inhabited by wild mountain sheep.

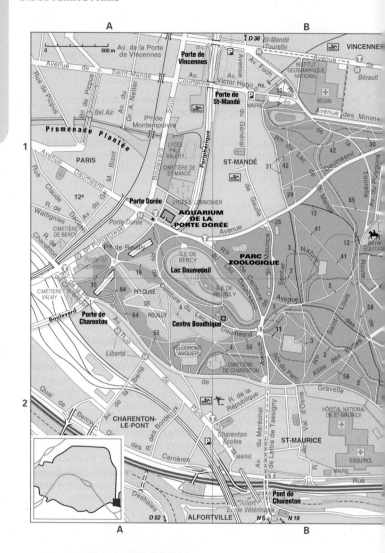

BOIS DE VINCENNES

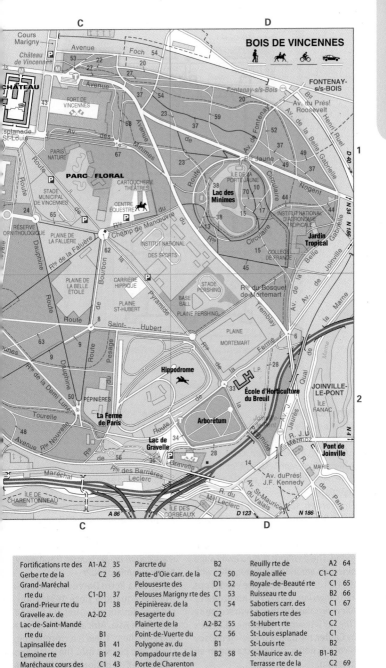

BOIS DE VINCENNES

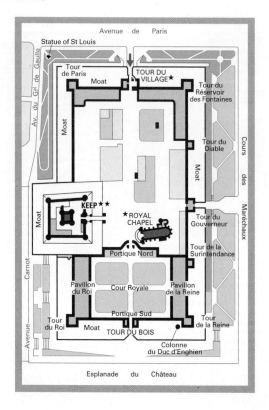

Parc Floral★★

Route de la Pyramide. 🚴♿🕐*Apr–Sept, 9.30am–8pm; Oct–Dec, 9.30am–6.30pm; 1 Jan–2 Feb, 9.30am–5pm, Feb 3–Mar 2, 9.30am–6pm; Mar 3–Mar 30, 9am–7pm.* ✆*5€.* ☎*01 43 28 41 59. www.parcfloral deparis.fr.*

The garden, landscaped by D Collin in 1969, extends over 30ha/75 acres and includes hundreds of species. The **Vallée des Fleurs** is delightful all year round. The pavilions tucked away amid pine trees around the lake, together with the Hall de la Pinède, house exhibitions and shows (art, dance, and horticulture). Alleyways lined with modern sculpture (*The Tall Woman* by **Giacometti**, *Stabile* by **Calder**, the polished-steel *Chronos* by Nicolas Schöffer…) suggest an open-air museum.

The **Dahlia Garden** from Sceaux, south of Paris, has been recreated near the Pyramid *(in flower September-October).* The water garden with its water-lilies and lotus is at its best from July to September. There are also a **Four Seasons Garden**, and gardens growing medicinal plants *(best seen from May–October)*, irises *(May)* and bamboo. Flower shows are held throughout the year: orchids *(early March)*, tulips *(from April)*, rhododendrons and azaleas *(from May)*.

Palais de la Porte Dorée★★ 🧒

293 avenue Daumesnil. Ⓜ*Porte Dorée.* 🕐*Tue–Fri 10am–5.30pm, Sat–Sun 10am–7pm.* ✆*4.50€.* ☎*01 53 59 58 60. www.aquarium-portedoree.fr and www. histoire-immigration.fr.*

Palais de la Porte Dorée has housed a tropical aquarium since 1931. Thousands of aquatic creatures are housed here, from Asia, Africa, South America and elsewhere. There is a crocodile pit, sharks and piranha fish. The Palais also houses the **Cité nationale de l'histoire de l'immigration** – a museum on the history and culture of immigration.

Arboretum de l'École du Breuil

Route de la Ferme. RER: Joinville-le-Pont. 🕐*Year-round Mon–Fri 8am–4pm; from*

King Charles the Wise (1337-1380)

Although kings Philippe Auguste and St Louis of the House of Capet were the first to have a manor house on the site of Vincennes, it was not till the next century that King Charles V of the Valois dynasty actually had a Château built there.

Born at Vincennes in 1337, Charles became Dauphin of France in 1350 on the accession to the throne of his father King Jean II the Good. He was, in fact, the first heir to the French throne to use the title, derived from the Dauphiné region which had belonged to his grandfather. He was Regent from 1356 till 1360, (and again in 1364) during the captivity of his father in England following the end of the disastrous (for the French) first phase of the Hundred Years' War, in which a large part of Western France was ceded to the English by the Treaty of Brétigny.

On becoming King in 1364, he set about recovering the lost territories and had the good sense to recognise the military talents of the minor Breton nobleman du Guesclin. A great part of the lands conceded under the Treaty were eventually regained under the generalship of du Guesclin, with the added bonus that he was able to rid France of the Tard-Venus or mercenary soldiers who had terrorised the South West following the end of the hostilities. He simply hired them and took them to Spain where they became engaged in the civil war then raging.

Not all of Charles' policies were quite so successful. For example, towards the end of reign his support for the anti-Pope Clement VII over the legitimately elected Urban VI, brought about the Papal Schism which was to split Europe for forty years. However, the sobriquet 'Wise' remained with him due to his many astute decisions, amongst which he managed to stabilise the currency, create a standing army and a powerful navy. Also, he was a patron of the arts and amassed a large library of books, having many classic texts translated into French to enable his advisers to read them.

10am weekends and public holidays. ⊘*0.75€.* ☎*01 40 71 74 00/01 53 66 14 00.* This school specialises in horticulture and landscape design; it has beautiful gardens. The arboretum extends over 12ha/29.6 acres and includes 2 000 trees of 80 different species.

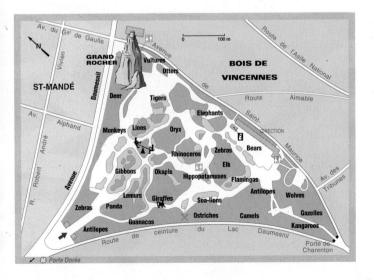

The Orangery, Château de Versailles
©Cosmo Condina/Tips Images

DISNEYLAND RESORT PARIS★★★

Opened in 1992 under the name EuroDisney, **Disneyland Paris** is an enormous holiday resort outside Paris with hotels, a 27-hole golf course, Disney Village entertainment and shopping complex, and campsite. The Disney Studios opened in 2002, and other new developments are planned through to 2017.

Information: *See Address Book.*

▶ **Orient Yourself:** The resort is located 30km/18mi east of Paris in Chessy.

Parking: Parking on-site, 8€/car, 5€/motorcycle, 20€/campingcars.

Don't Miss: The Disney Parade of characters down Main Street daily at 4pm.

Organizing Your Time: Allow two days to visit the entire resort.

Especially for Kids: "Meet & Greet" Disney characters at specific restaurants.

Also See: CHÂTEAU DE VINCENNES.

A Bit of History

A magician called Walt Disney

Born in Chicago in 1901, Walt showed great ability in drawing. After World War I, in which he served as an ambulance driver in France, he returned to the United States where he met a young Dutchman called Ub Iwerks, who was also passionate about drawing. In 1923 the pair produced in Hollywood a series of short films called **Alice Comedies** and in 1928 Mickey Mouse was created. There next followed the era of the Oscar-winning, full-length animated cartoon films: The **Three Little Pigs** (1933), **Snow White and the Seven Dwarfs** (1937), **Dumbo** (1941). Disney productions also developed to include films starring real people, such as **Treasure Island** (1950) and some mixing of the two, for instance **Mary Poppins** (1964) which won six Oscars.

Disneyland Park★★★

Disneyland: Mid-Jul to end Aug: 9am–11pm; Sept to mid-Apr: 10am–8pm, Sat-Sun and public holidays 10am–8pm; mid-Apr to mid-Jul: 10am–8pm, Sat 9am–8pm. Disney Studios: high season and weekends 9am–6pm, low season 10am–6pm. ☎01 60 30 60 30. For guided tours, contact the City Hall (Disneyland Park) on Town Square in Main Street, USA: 8€ (children 5€). Disneyland Passport

in high season: 1 day/1 park: 49€ (children 3–11 years: 41€); Park Hopper (Passepartout) 1 day 59€, (children 3–11 years: 51€); 2 days 108€ (children 92€); 3 days 134€ (children 114€); 4 days 157€ (children 134€); 5 days 167€ (children 142€) Tickets allow total freedom of movement between both Parks. Ticket usually valid for one year. www.dlrpmagic.com

This theme park, like those in the United States and Japan, is a realisation of Walt Disney's dream of creating a small, enchanted park where children and adults can enjoy themselves together. The large Disneyland Paris site (over 55ha/135 acres) is surrounded by trees and comprises five territories or lands, each with a different theme.

Every day there's a **Disney Parade★★**, a procession of floats carrying all the favourite Disney cartoon characters. On some evenings and throughout the summer the **Main Street Electrical Parade★★** adds extra illuminations to the fairytale setting.

Main Street USA

Enter the park onto the main street of an American town at the turn of the 20C, bordered by shops with Victorian-style fronts. Horse-drawn street cars, double-decker buses, fire engines and Black Marias transport visitors from Town Square to Central Plaza while colourful musicians play favourite ragtime, jazz and Dixieland tunes. From Main Street station a small steam train, the **Euro Dis-**

Address Book

🪙 *For coin ranges, see the Legend on the cover flap.*

GETTING THERE

RER: (line A) Marne-la-Vallée-Chessy; by TGV from Lille, Lyon, Avignon, Marseille, Bordeaux, Nantes and Toulouse, by shuttle from Orly and Roissy-Charles-de-Gaulle airports; by car via motorway A4 direction Metz; exit at junction 14 and follow signs to Disneyland.

GENERAL INFORMATION

Hotel reservations – ☎ 01 60 30 60 30.
Internet – www.disneylandparis.com.
Booking a show – Entertainment programmes and booking facilities are available from City Hall, located in Town Square, just inside Disneyland Park.
Currency exchange – Facilities are available at the parks' main entrance.
Disabled guests – A guide detailing special services available can be obtained from City Hall (Disneyland Park) or from the information desk inside Walt Disney Studios Park.
Lockers and storage – Near the main entrance and beneath Main Street Station.
Rental – Guests can rent cameras and video cameras from Town Square Photography, pushchairs and wheelchairs in Town Square Terrace (Disneyland Park) and in Front Lot (Walt Disney Studios Park).
Animals – They are not allowed in the theme parks, in Disney Village or in the hotels. The Animal Care Center is located near the visitors' car park.
Baby Care Center, Meeting Place for Lost Children, First Aid – Near the Plaza Gardens Restaurant (Disneyland Park) or in Front Lot (Walt Disney Studios Park).

MAKING THE MOST OF THE THEME PARKS

Tips – To avoid long queues at popular attractions, it is best to visit these attractions during the parade, at the end of the day or better still to get a **Fast Pass** issued by distributors outside the most popular attractions in both parks; this ticket bears a time slot of 1hr

during which time you may have access to the attraction without waiting in line.
Disneyland Park: Indiana Jones (Adventureland); Space Mountain (Discoveryland); Peter Pan's Flight (Fantasyland); Big Thunder Mountain (Frontierland); Star Tours (Discoveryland).
Walt Disney Studios Park: Rock'n Roller Coaster (Backlot); Flying Carpets (Animation Courtyard); Studio Tram Tour (Production Courtyard).
Where to eat – Park maps include a list of eating places and their location within the parks, with symbols indicating those offering table service and vegetarian meals. For a quick meal go to the **Bella Notte, Colonel Hathi's** or the **Plaza Gardens** in Disneyland Park, or to the **Backlot Express Restaurant** in Walt Disney Studios Park.
Take time and go to one of the following table service restaurants to enjoy a fine meal enhanced by an original décor (booking recommended, ☎ 01 64 74 28 82 or call at City Hall): **Silver Spur Steakhouse, Blue Lagoon Restaurant, Walt's Restaurant** and **Auberge de Cendrillon** in Disneyland Park or **Café des Cascadeurs** in Walt Disney Studios Park.

EATING OUTSIDE THE THEME PARKS

🪙 *For coin ranges, see the Legend on the cover flap.*

DISNEY VILLAGE

Enjoy a culinary trip to the New World.
🍽 **Annette's Diner**, ☎ 01 60 45 70 37.
🍽🍽 **Rainforest Café**, ☎ 01 60 43 65 65.
🍽🍽🍽 **The Steakhouse**, ☎ 01 60 45 70 45.

A FEW MILES AWAY

🍽🍽🍽 **L'Ermitage**, *Allée Jean-de-La-Fontaine, écluse de Chalifert, 77144 Chalifert; 6km/3.7mi N of Disneyland Resort Paris along N 34 then D 45.* ☎ 01 60 43 41 43. www.notrermitage.com. *Booking essential*. Founded in 1860, this riverside restaurant continues to offer its guests a convivial atmosphere, particularly at weekends (disco Fri, cabaret on Sat and old-time dancing on Sun).

neyland Railroad★, travels across the park and through the **Grand Canyon Diorama.**

Frontierland

The conquest of the West, the gold trail and the Far West with its legends and folklore are brought together in Thunder Mesa, a typical western town. The waters here are plied by two handsome **steamboats**★, the *Mark Twain* and the *Molly Brown*. In the bowels of **Big Thunder Mountain**★★★ lies an old gold mine which is visited via the mine train: this turns out to be a runaway train which hurtles out of control to provide a thrilling ride. A tour of the dilapidated **Phantom Manor**★★★ overlooking the rivers of the Far West is a spine-chilling house of hundreds of mischievous ghosts. The horseshoe-shaped **Lucky Nugget Saloon**★ saloon – every western town had its saloon – presents the dinner show **Lilly's Follies.**

Adventureland

Access this land of exotic adventure from Central Plaza, through Adventureland Bazaar. In the tropical Caribbean seas, marauding pirates attack and loot a coastal fort and village in the famous action-packed encounter, **Pirates of the Caribbean**★★★. Courageous archaeologists brave the ruined temple deep in the jungle in **Indiana Jones et le Temple du Péril… à l'envers**★★★, while the giant tree, **La Cabane des Robinson**★★ (27m/89ft high) offers panoramic views from the ingeniously furnished home of the shipwrecked Swiss family Robinson from J D Wyss' novel.

Fantasyland

Based around Walt Disney's familiar trademark, Sleeping Beauty's castle, this land recalls favourite fairy tales by authors such as Charles Perrault, Lewis Carroll and the Brothers Grimm. **Le Château de la Belle au bois dormant**★★, with its blue and gold turrets crowned with pennants is at the very heart of Disneyland. Inside, Aubusson tapestries recount episodes from this famous story. Below, in the depths of the castle, a huge scaly dragon appears to be sleeping. **It's a Small World**★★ is a delightful musical cruise in celebration of the innocence and joy of children throughout the world, while **Alice's Curious Labyrinth**★ is a maze lading to the Queen of Hearts' castle. Fly in a boat through the skies above London and in Never-Never Land on **Peter Pan's Flight**★★ or visit the lovable puppet Pinocchio and his friends on **Les Voyages de Pinocchio**★.

Enjoyable tours lead through the mysterious forest in mining cars from the dwarfs' mine with **Blanche-Neige et les Sept Nains**★.

Discoveryland

This is the world of past discoveries and dreams of the future with great visionaries such as Leonardo da Vinci, Jules Verne and HG Wells and their wonderful inventions. **Space Mountain**★★★ – **De la Terre à la Lune** is a fantastic journey through space, based on Jules Verne's novel *From the Earth to the Moon* (1873), while **Star Tours**★★★ presents a breathtaking inter-planetary experience full of special effects inspired by the film *Star Wars*. In the Imagination Institute, Professor Wayne Szalinski demonstrates his famous shrinking machine in **Honey I Shrunk the Audience**★★, and **Le Visionarium**★★ 360° screen reveals the wonders of Europe.

Walt Disney Studios Park

Inaugurated on 16 March 2002, this park is entirely dedicated to the wonders of the cinema. It offers guests a chance to take a trip backstage and discover some of the secrets of filming, of animation techniques and of television.

Front Lot

The park entrance is overlooked by a 33m/108ft-high water tower, a traditional landmark in film studios. In the centre of the Spanish-style courtyard, planted with palm trees, stands a fountain dedicated to Mickey. **Disney Studio 1** is the reconstruction of a famous Hollywood film set, Hollywood Boulevard.

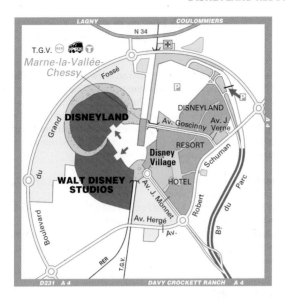

Animation Courtyard

This area offers a tribute to Walt Disney's invaluable contribution to the development of animation. **Animagique**★★★ celebrates Disney's full-length animation films; spectators find themselves at the centre of a 3D cartoon, next to Mickey, Donald Duck, Dumbo's pink elephants, and Pinocchio. The **Art of Disney Animation**★★ is an interactive discovery of the secrets of animation and **Flying Carpets**★★ is a film set where Aladdin's Genie guides guests onto flying carpets!

Production Courtyard

Here spectators are allowed to see what happens in the usually out-of-bounds backstage areas of cinema and television studios. **Cinémagique**★★★ is where fiction meets reality, as spectators literally go through the screen and become the actors and heroes of the film. You can take a **Television Production Tour**★★ of Disney Channel France and the possibility to watch the live filming of *Zapping Zone*.
Sit back and enjoy the **Studio Tram Tour**★★ through amazing film sets until you reach **Catastrophe Canyon!**★★★

Back Lot

Action, thrills and special effects! Set on a meteorite-threatened space station, **Armageddon**★★ is a thrilling (and particularly loud) experience! At a similar decibel level, the **Rock'n Roller Coaster**★★★ is a unique musical experience inside a recording studio; be prepared to be propelled at full speed on a breathtaking journey… (not for the faint-hearted!).

Disney Village★

Situated just beside the theme parks and Disney Lake, the tall polished steel columns of Disney Village can be seen from afar. In the main street of this American town it's always party time, with a happy, childlike atmosphere. On summer evenings, after the park closes, there is plenty going on here, and shops, restaurants and bars are always busy. Night-birds can round off the evening in the **Hurricanes** disco.
The famous adventures of pioneer William Frederick Cody (1846-1917), alias Buffalo Bill, are the inspiration for **La Légende de Buffalo Bill**★★, a cabaret dinner which evokes the story of the Wild West, complete with horses, bison, cowboys and Indians.

SAINT-DENIS★★

Ⓜ ST-DENIS-BASILIQUE (LINE 13) – RER: ST-DENIS (LINE D)

In 1840 the village of Saint-Denis numbered a few thousand inhabitants; the industrial revolution brought this number to 100 000 and made the town one of the main manufacturing centres of the northern suburbs. Most of the town was razed and rebuilt in the 1970s. The inauguration of the Stade de France in 1998, gave this densely populated town new hopes for future prosperity. For visitors however, the most interesting sight in Saint-Denis remains its basilica, which houses the mausoleum of the kings of France.

Information: 1 r. de la République, 93200 St-Denis. ☎01 55 87 08 70. www.saint-denis-tourisme.com.

▶ **Orient Yourself:** Located north of Paris on the way to Roissy-CDG Airport.

🅿 **Parking:** Underground parking at place Jean-Jaurès near the Basilica.

Don't Miss: The chapel in the Basilica displaying Louis XVIII's funeral robes.

🕐 **Organizing Your Time:** Allow at least two hours for this excursion.

Also See: CHANTILLY.

A Bit of History

Monsieur St-Denis – Legend has it that after his beheading in Montmartre, the Evangelist St Denis, first bishop of Lutetia, got to his feet, picked up his severed head and walked north out of the city, and is said to have been buried where he was found. The place soon attracted pilgrims from near and far. In AD475 a large village church was erected on the site. Dagobert I had it rebuilt and offered it to a Benedictine community who took charge of the pilgrimage. This abbey

Basilique St-Denis

was to become the most wealthy and the most celebrated in France. Towards AD750 the church was dismantled a second time and rebuilt by Pepin the Short, who set up a shrine under the chancel to receive the sacred remains of saints.

Basilique St-Denis★★★

Mausoleum for the kings of France

Over a remarkable span of 12 centuries, all but three of the kings of France, from Dagobert I to Louis XVIII, were buried at St-Denis. In 1793 Barrère asked the Convention for permission to destroy the tombs. They were opened and the remains thrown into unmarked graves. Alexandre Lenoir salvaged the most precious tombs and moved them to Paris, entrusted to the Petits-Augustins, later to become the Museum of French Monuments. In 1816 Louis XVIII returned the tombs to the basilica.

Construction of St-Denis

This basilica marks a turning point in the development of French architecture: it was the first large church to feature a unity of design in plan and style. This, combined with its significance as a centre of pilgrimage, proved to be the springboard for subsequent late 12C cathedrals and the evolution towards the Gothic style (Chartres, Senlis and Meaux). Suger supervised construction from 1136-1147 on the west front, the first two bays of the nave, the chancel, crypt and the Carolingian nave. The amazing rapidity of the whole operation was due to his dedication and help from parishoners in transporting the stone from the Pontoise quarries. In the early 13C the north tower was crowned by a magnificent stone spire. In 1247 **Pierre de Montreuil** was appointed master mason by St Louis and remained in charge of the work until his death in 1267.

Decline and Restoration

The basilica subsequently fell into disrepair. The French Revolution caused further ravages and in his *Genius of Christianity,* Chateaubriand lamented the sorry state of the church. Napoléon gave orders to repair the damage and reinstated public worship in 1806. The architect Debret aroused a wave of public indignation on account of his poor knowledge of medieval methods. He was succeeded by **Viollet-le-Duc,** who studied a number of original documents which guided him in his work. From 1858 up to his death (1879), he toiled relentlessly and produced the basilica that stands today. The choir and west front (although much restored) provide some idea of the original.

Exterior

The absence of the north tower mars the harmony of the west front. In the Middle Ages the building would have been fortified, from which some crenellation survives at the base of the towers. All three doorways have been restored. The columnar figures of the doorways feature the Wise and Foolish Virgins *(centre),* the labours of the months *(right)* and the signs of the Zodiac *(left).* On the north side of the basilica, the nave is supported by double flying buttresses.

Interior

🕐*Apr–Sept, daily 10am–6.15pm, Sun and public holidays noon–6.15pm (Oct–Mar, 10am–5pm, Sun noon–5.15pm).* ☞*Guided tours daily at 10.30am and 3pm. Last admission 30mins before closing.* 🕐*1 Jan, 1 May and 25 Dec.* ◔6.50€. ☎ *01 48 09 83 54. http://saint-denis. monuments-nationaux.fr*

The basilica is marginally smaller than Notre-Dame: 108m/354ft long, 38m/125ft wide in the transept and 29m/95ft high. The elegant nave is attributed to Pierre de Montreuil.

Tombs★★★

St-Denis Basilica houses the remains of kings, queens and royal children, as well as those of leading personalities who served the French court, such as Bertrand du Guesclin (**1**). It is possible to date most monuments simply from their appearance, thus they serve as a chronological chart of French funeral art through the Middle Ages and into the Renaissance. Up to the Renaissance, the only sculpture to adorn tombs was in the form of **recumbent figures**. Note the 12C funeral slab of Clovis (**2**) and Fredegonde (**3**), worked in mosaic and copper, from the abbey of St-Germain-des-Prés.

Around 1260 St Louis commissioned a series of effigies of all the rulers who had preceded him since the 7C. The figures were mere allegories but they provide a telling example of how royalty was portrayed towards the mid-13C. They include the imposing tomb of Dagobert (**4**), with its lively, spirited scenes, the recumbent statues of Charles Martel (**5**) and Pepin the Short (**6**), and the female effigy carved in Tournai marble (**7**).

The tomb of Isabella of Aragon and Philippe III the Bold (**8**), who died in 1285, shows an early concern for accurate portraiture imbued with a strong sense of personality. Towards the middle of the 14C, the wealthy oversaw the building of their tomb in their own lifetime. The effigies of Charles V by Beauneveu (**9**), Charles VI and Isabella of Bavaria (**10**) are therefore extremely lifelike.

During the Renaissance, **mausoleums** took on monumental proportions and were lavishly decorated. They had two tiers, representing life and death, each contrasting sharply with the other. On the upper level the king and his wife are featured kneeling in full regalia; on the lower level, the deceased were pictured lying down as naked cadavers. Admire

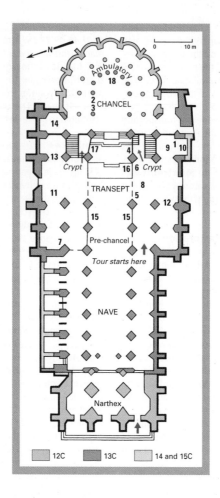

the twin monument built for Louis XII and Anne of Brittany (**11**), and that of François I and Claude de France (**12**). After commissioning the royal tomb, **Catherine de' Medici,** who survived her husband Henri II by 30 years, actually fainted in horror on seeing herself portrayed dead according to the standard convention; she therefore ordered a new effigy to be made showing her asleep. Both, by Primaticcio (**13**), and Germain Pilon (**14**), are here displayed.

Chancel

The beautiful pre-Renaissance stalls (**15**), in the pre-chancel were taken from the Norman Château at Gaillon. The splendid Romanesque **Virgin**★ in painted wood (**16**) was brought from St-Martin-des-Champs. The episcopal throne opposite (**17**) is a replica of Dagobert's royal seat (the original lies in the Medals and Antiquities Gallery at the Bibliothèque Nationale in Paris – ⓒsee PLACE DES VICTOIRES). At the far end, the modern reliquary of saints Denis, Rusticus and Eleutherius (**18**) stands at the edge of Suger's **ambulatory**★, with its wide arches and slim columns.

Crypt★★

The lower ambulatory was built in the Romanesque style by Suger (12C) and restored by Viollet-le-Duc. In the centre stands a vaulted chapel known as Hilduin's Chapel. Beneath its marble slab lies the burial vault of the Bourbon family, including the remains, among

Tomb of Louis XII and Anne of Brittany

others, of Louis XVI, Marie-Antoinette and Louis XVIII. The communal grave in the north transept received in 1817 the bones of around 800 kings and queens, royal highnesses, and princes of the blood.

Museums and other Attractions

Musée d'Art et d'Histoire

22 bis rue Gabriel-Péri. ◷*Wed–Mon 10am–5.30pm, Thu 10am–8pm, Sat–Sun 2–6.30pm.* ⦸*Public holidays.* ₰*4€, no charge 1st Sun in the month.* ☎*01 42 43 05 10. www.musee-saint-denis.fr.*

The museum is set up in the former Carmelite convent, founded by Cardinal de Bérulle in 1625 and occupied by Louis XV's daughter Madame Louise de France between 1770 and 1787. The refectory and kitchen contain archaeological finds. from St-Denis or from the old hospital. On the second floor are drawings, paintings and documents relating to the Paris Commune of 1871.

Stade de France★

◷*One-hour guided tours daily from Visits 1 hour long, Sept–Mar, Mon–Fri 10.30am, noon, 2.30pm, 4.30pm. Sat, Sun and public holidays 10.30am, noon, 2.30pm, 3.30pm, 4.30pm, French school holidays, every hour between 10am and 5pm, Tours in English at 10.30am and 2.30pm. Apr 1 –Aug 31 every hour between 10am and 5pm, in English 10.30 and 2.30pm.* ₰*10€ (family pass for 2 adults, 2 children under 12: 29€).* ☎*08 92 700 900. www.stade france.com*

This huge yet elegant structure was designed by four architects: Zublena, Macary, Regembal and Costantini. It was the last major construction project of the 20C, built in a record 31 months, and inaugurated with great ceremony on 28 January 1998. It was the setting for the 1998 World Cup, which the French team won for the first time. The elliptical structure can be adapted to accommodate all kinds of events; thanks to a system of moveable seats, the number of spectators can be increased from 80 000 for matches to 100 000 for concerts.

CHÂTEAU DE VERSAILLES★★★

Symbol of absolute monarchy and the apogee of the arts in France during the reign of the Sun King, Versailles became the residence of the court and seat of government from May 1682 until the Revolution.

🛈 **Information:** 2 bis av. de Paris, 78000 Versailles. ☎01 39 24 88 88. www.versailles-tourisme.com.

▶ **Orient Yourself:** The town of Versailles is 22km/13.6mi southwest of Paris.

🅿 **Parking:** Street parking at the château; underground on avenue de l'Europe.

👁 **Don't Miss:** The restored Domaine de Marie Antoinette in the château park.

🕘 **Organizing Your Time:** Allow two days to fully appreciate Versailles.

Kids **Especially for Kids:** Boats and bicycles can be rented in the château park.

👜 **Also See:** CHARTRES, FONTAINEBLEAU.

A Bit of History

The birth of the Sun King's palace – The original château was a small hunting lodge around the present Marble Court, built in 1624 for **Louis XIII**, who had Philibert le Roy reconstruct it in brick and stone in 1631. The young **Louis XIV** saw Versailles as the perfect place to build his own château far from the mobs of Paris, a magnificent palace of immense proportions and opulence never seen before. He wanted to demonstrate the glory of the French arts as well as establish the absolute power of the Sun King. He commissioned a renowned team to realize his dream: the architect **Louis Le Vau**, the landscape architect **Le Nôtre**, and the decorator **Le Brun**.

Construction began — and continued to some extent for almost a century — in 1661 with the gardens, embellished for Louis XIV's splendid festivals. In 1668 Le Vau constructed stone façades around the original château, creating an "envelope" which concealed the old façades.

The height of the French Monarchy – **Jules Hardouin-Mansart** succeeded Le Vau, adding the Galerie des Glaces (Hall of Mirrors) and two wings in the south (1682) and the north (1689). Under Colbert and Le Brun, the Gobelins factory and the artists of the Académie Royale designed the main furniture and decoration with the remarkable stylistic unity which defines Versailles Classicism. Court life at Versailles revolved around a complex system of etiquette and magnificent feasts.

Revolution and Restoration – Under **Louis XV** changes to the interior included the creation of the Petits Cabinets. He added the Petit Trianon and gardens in the château park next to the Grand Trianon, which was eventually given to **Louis XVI**'s queen Marie-Antoinette, who would expand and embellish it with a private theatre and hamlet. When the **Revolution** drove Louis XVI from Versailles, a century of royal occupation came to a close. In the 19C, **Louis-Philippe** transformed part of the palace into a museum dedicated to French history. Since 1914 the State, supported by private patronage (including that of John D Rockefeller), has carried out important restoration work and refurbished the palace which is listed as one of UNESCO's World Heritage Monuments.

Le Château★★★

👁 *see Floor Plan*

🕘*Tue–Sun 9am–6.30pm (9am–5.30pm 20 Nov–9 Mar),* 🕘*Some public holidays. Regular entrance* 👛*13.50€–15€. Includes access to the King's and Queen's State Apartments, the Chapel and Opera House, the History of France Galleries, the Dauphin's Apartments and at weekends the Mesdames' Apartments and the Coach Museum (high season only); free for children under 18 (audio guide 6€).*

The Versailles Pass High Season, public holidays and days of the Grandes Eaux Musicales (Apr–Sept), 20€ weekdays, 25€ weekends, Low Season Pass (Nov–Mar) 16€ includes all of the above plus access to the Grand Trianon, Marie-Antoinette's Estate in high season, and the Château Gardens Passport. ☎01 30 83 76 20. www.chateauversailles.fr.

A complete tour of the palace, gardens, park and the Marie-Antoinette's Estate takes two days. If you have only one day it is recommended that you begin with the interior of the château, where the most magnificent apartments are to be found. The park and gardens are best enjoyed at leisure. For an unforgettable experience, visit them on one of the Jours des Grands Eaux Musicales, when all the fountains are turned on, to a musical accompaniment.

Entrance

Beyond the palace's wrought-iron railings, created under Louis XVIII, lie three courtyards. In the centre of the forecourt, the **Cour des Ministres** (Ministers' Court) is a statue of Louis XIV commissioned by Louis-Philippe. Next is the **Cour royale** (Royal Court)

which only persons of high rank were permitted to cross in horse-drawn carriages. The two bordering wings were furnished with a colonnade under Louis XV. Finally there is the **Cour de Marbre**★★ (Marble Court) with its black and white marble pavement, the heart of Louis XIII's château.

Across from the château entrance is the semi-circular **Place d'Armes**★★, framed by **La Grande Ecurie**★ (Royal Stables) by Jules Hardouin-Mansart. The north wing now houses the **Academy ofEquestrian Arts** (☎08 92 68 18 91.www.acadequestre.fr) and the **Coach Museum** (🕐weekends Apr–Oct, 9am–6.30pm; ⊜2€, free access with Pass), which presents a collection of magnificent coaches used at Versailles, including Lo-uis XVIII's funeral hearse and Charles X's Coronation coach.

State Apartments, Chapel, and Opera

▶ *From the visitors' entrance (A), (B2) for Pass holders, go though the vestibule to the Chapel Room (a) on the ground floor.*

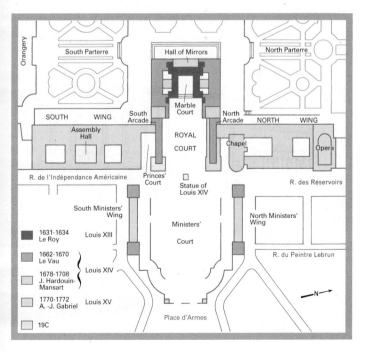

Chapelle royale★★★

The two-storey palatine chapel with a royal gallery is dedicated to St Louis. It was constructed by Jules Hardouin-Mansart, and finished in 1710 by his brother-in-law Robert de Cotte. The ceiling is the work of the painters Jouvent, Coypel and La Fosse. The marble altar sculpted by Van Clève is decorated in front with a gilded bronze low relief representing a Pietà by Vassé.

▶ *Proceed through the Galerie de Pierre to the Royal Opera.*

Opéra Royal★★

The opera house begun by Gabriel in 1768 was inaugurated in 1770 for the marriage celebrations of the dauphin, the future Louis XVI, and Marie-Antoinette. The first oval hall in France, it received other exceptional technical touches from the engineer Arnoult: for festivals the floor of the stalls and circle could be raised to the level of the stage. The balconies' low-relief sculptures, executed by **Pajou**, represent the gods of Olympus and the children and their signs of the zodiac.

Initially reserved for the court, the opera hosted sumptuous receptions on the occasion of visits from the King of Sweden in 1784, of Emperor Joseph II in 1777 and 1781, and of **Queen Victoria** in 1855. The National Assembly held session here from 1871 until 1875. On 30 January 1875 the adoption of the Wallon Amendment here laid the foundation of the Third Republic. A reception for **Queen Elizabeth II of England** in 1957 coincided with completion of the final restoration.

▶ *The tour continues upstairs, back through the galerie to the State Apartments.*

Château de Versailles

Grands Appartements★★★

The six-room suite with decoration by Le Brun was the king's apartment from 1673 to 1682. Then Louis XIV took up residence definitively at Versailles and had a new apartment designed around the Marble Court. Three times a week on Mondays, Wednesdays and Thursdays from 6pm to 10pm the king held court in the Grand Apartment.

Salon d'Hercule★★

Known as Hercules' Salon, this room, begun in 1712 and completed in 1736, owes its name to the ceiling painted by Lemoyne. The artist needed three arduous years to cover the 480sq m/5 167sq ft ceiling with a painting of Hercules entering the Kingdom of the Gods. The artist committed suicide in 1737 shortly after finishing it. Two Veronese canvases occupy their original places: **Christ at the House of Simon the Pharisee**★, and *Eliezer and Rebecca*.

Salon de l'Abondance (b)

When the king held court during the time of Louis XIV there were three buffets, one for hot drinks and two for cold. The ceiling painted by Houasse portrays all the royal magnificence and the gold ware collections of Louis XIV in *trompe-l'œil*.

Salon de Vénus (c)

The ceiling was painted by Houasse and like the ceilings of the following rooms it features decorated panels with gilt stucco borders. This was originally where courtiers entered the rooms through the Royal Court by the Ambassadors' Staircase, sumptuously designed to impress visitors. It was torn down by Louis XV in 1752.

Salon de Diane (d)

Billiard room under Louis XIV. Notice the bust of Louis XIV by Bernini (1665), a stunning example of Baroque work-

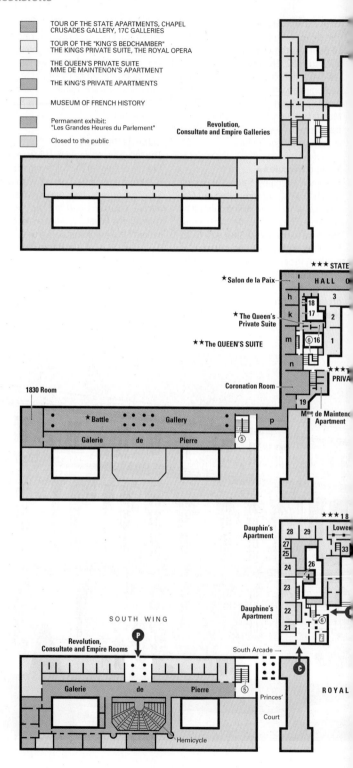

TOUR OF THE STATE APARTMENTS, CHAPEL
CRUSADES GALLERY, 17C GALLERIES

TOUR OF THE "KING'S BEDCHAMBER"
THE KINGS PRIVATE SUITE, THE ROYAL OPERA

THE QUEEN'S PRIVATE SUITE
MME DE MAINTENON'S APARTMENT

THE KING'S PRIVATE APARTMENTS

MUSEUM OF FRENCH HISTORY

Permanent exhibit:
"Les Grandes Heures du Parlement"

Closed to the public

Revolution,
Consultate and Empire Galleries

★★★ STATE

HALL O

★ Salon de la Paix

h   18   3

k   17   2

★ The Queen's
Private Suite

m   6 16   1

★★ The QUEEN'S SUITE

n

1830 Room

Coronation Room

★★★
PRIVA

19

Mᵐᵉ de Maintenon
Apartment

★ Battle   • • •   Gallery   •

Galerie   de   Pierre   ⑤   p

★★★ 18

Dauphin's
Apartment   28   29   Lower

27
25   33
24   26
23
22
Dauphine's
Apartment   21   6

SOUTH WING

Revolution,
Consultate and Empire Rooms   P

South Arcade

Galerie   de   Pierre   ⑤

Princes'   C

Court   ROYAL

Hemicycle

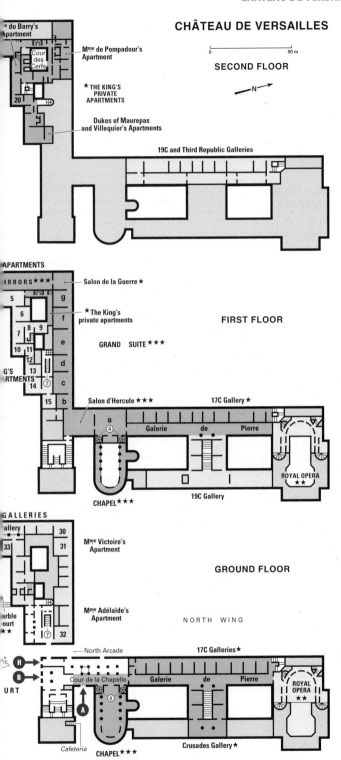

CHÂTEAU DE VERSAILLES

0   50 m

SECOND FLOOR

N →

e du Barry's Apartment

Cour des Cerfs

Mme de Pompadour's Apartment

20

★ THE KING'S PRIVATE APARTMENTS

Dukes of Maurepas and Villequier's Apartments

19C and Third Republic Galleries

APARTMENTS

IRRORS ★★★ — Salon de la Guerre ★

5

6

g

f

7   8   9

10   11

12

13

14

d

c

15   b

★ The King's private apartments

GRAND SUITE ★★★

G'S ARTMENTS

⑦

FIRST FLOOR

Salon d'Hercule ★★★

17C Gallery ★

a

④

Galerie   de   Pierre

ROYAL OPERA ★★

19C Gallery

CHAPEL ★★★

GALLERIES

allery

30

33

31

Mme Victoire's Apartment

GROUND FLOOR

arble ourt ★★

⑦

32

Mme Adélaïde's Apartment

NORTH WING

— North Arcade

17C Galleries ★

H →

B →

Cour de la Chapelle

URT

Galerie   de   Pierre

ROYAL OPERA ★★

④

A

Cafeteria

CHAPEL ★★★

Crusades Gallery ★

359

Address Book

GETTING THERE

RER: (line C) Versailles Rive-Gauche – Château de Versailles; by commuter trains from St-Lazare (Versailles Rive-Droite) and Montparnasse (Versailles-Chantiers) rail stations; by car from the Porte de St-Cloud, take Motorway A13 to exit 1 and follow signs to Versailles-Château (16km/10mi). Average travel time: 30-45min.

MAKING THE MOST OF VERSAILLES

CHÂTEAU

Entrances – The various tours of the château start from different entrances: Entrance **A**: State apartments (except groups, use entrance **B**) Entrance **B2**: State apartments (Pass holders) Entrance **C2**: The Dauphin's and Mesdames' apartments Entrance **D**: Guided tours (same-day bookings) Entrance **H**: Access reserved for handicapped visitors Entrance **P**: The milestones of the French Parliament history

Music – Concerts of works by 17C and 18C French composers given by the Baroque Music Centre (October to December) in various venues: the Opéra Royal, the Chapelle Royale, the Salon d'Hercule, the Galerie Basse. Information and reservations, ☎01 39 20 78 00, www.cmbv.com.

PARK

Fêtes de Nuit – These shows take place seven times during the summer around the Bassin de Neptune; they end with a fireworks display.

Grandes Eaux Musicales – Water displays reminiscent of those which took place during the reign of Louis XIV. Spectators are given an itinerary starting from the Bassin de Latone and ending at the Bassin de Neptune and Bassin du Dragon where a breathtaking finale takes place.

For more information on the shows call ☎1 30 83 78 89. www.chateauversailles.fr

PARK AND GARDENS

Tourist train – Tour of the grounds (45min) with stops at the Trianons and Grand Canal. Departure from the Terrasse Sud of the château. High Season: 10am–6.15pm, low season 11.30am–5pm. ⊜6€ (children 11–18 years: 4.50€). ☎01 39 54 22 00. www.train-versailles.com.

Bicycle hire – There are two rental points in the grounds (Feb–end Nov): near the Grand Canal and Grille de la Reine, daily (except rainy weather) Apr–Aug 10am–6.30pm, Feb–Mar,Sept–Oct until 5.30pm, Nov until 4.30pm. ⊜5€ per hour. ☎01 39 66 97 66.

Boat hire – Mar, Sept–Oct 11am–5.30pm, Apr–Aug 10.30am–6.30pm, Nov noon–4.30pm. ⊜11€ (1hr, boat for 4 people). ☎01 39 66 97 66.

Calèches – Horse-drawn carriage rides in the Gardens, North Terrace departure point . ☎01 30 97 04 40. www.parisinfo.com.

WHERE TO EAT

🖾 For coin ranges, see the cover flap.

IN TOWN

⊜⊜**Au Chapeau Gris** – 7 rue Hoche. ☎01 39 50 10 81. www.auchapeaugris. com. Closed mid-July to mid-Aug, Tue evening and Wed - booking essential. Au Chapeau Gris is literally an institution, said to date back to the Age of Enlightenment. A grand ambience and décor fit for Versailles are the setting for traditional French cuisine which never goes out of fashion. One of Versailles' most sought-after restaurants.

⊜⊜⊜**Le Bœuf à la Mode** – 4 r. au Pain (place du Marché-Notre-Dame). ☎01 39 50 31 99. Open daily.Closed Christmas weekend. Guests will appreciate the convivial atmosphere of this 1930s style bistro serving traditional cuisine, specializing in meat dishes.

⊜⊜**Le Baladin** – 2 r. de l'Occident (St-Louis district). ☎01 39 50 06 57. Closed Sun and Mon in winter, Sun and Mon evening in summer - booking recommended. This pleasant restaurant in the old St-Louis district is appreciated for its refined cuisine; the terrace is sought after in fine weather.

🍴🍴🍴**Valmont** – *20 r. au Pain.*
☎*01 39 51 39 00. www.levalmont.com.*
Closed Sun evening and Mon.
This prettily restored old house on place des Halles will undoubtedly catch your eye. Venture inside and you will soon be conquered by the excellent service, charming decoration, a clever blend of tradition and modernity, elegantly laid tables and succulent traditional French meat and fish dishes.

IN THE PARK
🍴🍴**La Flotille** – *Parc du Château, Grand Canal.* ☎*01 39 51 41 58. www. laflottille.fr. Closed evenings. Booking essential Sun.* On the edge of the Grand Canal, in the château park, this small late 19C pavilion and its glass surround resembles an open-air café. It proposes two formulas, restaurant and brasserie, depending on your mood. The food is decent but the terrace makes all the difference in summer!

---

manship. Paintings by La Fosse and Blanchard.

Salon de Mars (e)
Guard-room before 1682, this room was later used by Louis XIV for balls, games and music. Two paintings have been restored to their 18C places: *Darius' Tent* by Le Brun and *The Pilgrims of Emmaüs after Veronese*. On the side walls, *Louis XV* by Rigaud and *Maria Leczczynska* by Van Loo occupy their original places. The ceiling with its martial scenes is by Audran, Jouvenet and Houasse. Above the fireplace hangs one of Louis XIV's favourite paintings, *King David* by Domenichino in which he is pictured playing the harp. It originally hung in the King's Bedchamber.

Salon de Mercure (f)
Formerly the antechamber, it served as a place where kings were laid in state. In 1715 Louis XIV was kept here a whole week in his coffin, with 72 ecclesiastics keeping vigil to ensure that four masses could be said simultaneously every day from five in the morning until noon without interruption. The ceiling is by JB de Champaigne.

Salon d'Apollon or Salle du Trône (g)
The throne stood on a central platform beneath a large canopy. The three hooks would have supported a canopy. It was here that ambassadors were received, and that dances and concerts were put on when the king held court. The ceiling features *Apollo in a Sun Chariot* by La Fosse.

Galerie des Glaces★★★
Crossing the **Salon de la Guerre**★ (War Salon), which links the Grand Apartment and the Hall of Mirrors, notice the large oval low relief by Coysevox representing Louis XIV triumphing over his enemies. Designed by Jules Hardouin-Mansart in 1687, the **Hall of Mirrors** was the show-piece under Louis XIV where court celebrations and elaborate receptions for foreign potentates took place. The hall is 75m/246ft long, 10m/33ft wide, and 12m/40ft high, and it is illuminated by 17 large windows echoing 17 glass panels on the opposite wall. The 578 mirrors of glass which compose these panels are the largest that could be manufactured at that time. The hall enjoys the last rays of the setting sun.

On the ceiling **Le Brun** executed the most important cycle of his career as the king's chief painter. The cycle illustrates the life of Louis XIV and his military victories until the Treaty of Nijmegen in 1678. The Hall of Mirrors was abundantly decorated with solid-silver furniture cast under Louis XIV. The German Empire was proclaimed in this room on 18 January 1871 and the **Treaty of Versailles** was signed on 28 June 1919. From the central windows one has a good **view**★★★ of the Grand Perspective.

▶ *Detour from the Hall of Mirrors into the King's Apartments.*

Appartement du Roi or Appartement de Louis XIV★★★
The king's suite stretches around the Marble Court. Designed between 1682 and 1701 by Mansart in Louis XIII's

château, the decoration marks a clear break in the evolution of the Louis XIV style. The ceilings are not coffered but painted white; the white and gold panelling replaces the marble tiling; large mirrors adorn the fireplaces. After the guard-room (**1**), an antechamber (**2**) leads to the Salon de l'Œil de bœuf (**3**). Here gentlemen attended the ceremonious king's rising *(le lever)* and retiring *(le coucher)*. The decoration marks the first flowering of the Louis XV style.

Chambre du Roi (4)

This was the bedroom of Louis XIV from 1701 and it was here that he died. Above the bed, the alcove decoration represents France watching over the sleeping King and was sculpted by Coustou. The wall hangings are faithful reproductions of the summer furnishings of 1705. The paintings belonged to the King's personal collection.

Salle du Conseil (5)

Characteristic of Rococo, the Council Chamber was created under Louis XV by uniting two rooms. In this room decisions were made that involved the destiny of France, among them the decision to participate in the American War of Independence.

▷ *Return to the Hall of Mirrors and continue to the Queen's Apartments.*

Appartement de la Reine★★

Entrance to the Queen's Suite is through the **Salon de la Paix**★ which is decorated with a canvas by Lemoyne of Louis XV presenting peace to Europe. The Queen's suite was constructed for Louis XIV's wife Queen Marie-Thérèse who died here in 1683.

Chambre de la Reine (h)

Le Brun's original decoration for Marie-Thérèse was redone for Queen Maria Leczczynska between 1729 and 1735. The white and gold woodwork, the greyish tones of the ceiling by Boucher, and the doors decorated by Natoire and De Troy demonstrate the inclination towards the Rococo under Louis XV. Marie-Antoinette had other renovations

made in 1770; the two-headed eagle and the portraits of the house of Austria recall the Queen's origins. The floral wall hangings were rewoven to the original pattern in Lyon, matching exactly the original hanging of the Queen's summer furnishings of 1786.

In France, royal births were public events: in this room 19 children of France were born, among them Louis XV and Philip V of Spain.

Salon des Nobles de la Reine (Peers' Salon) (k)

In this one-time antechamber presentations to the queen took place. This room was also where queens and dauphins of France lay in state. The room has been restored to the way it looked in 1789. In the **antechamber (m)** note the painting by Madame Vigée-Lebrun of *Marie-Antoinette and her children* (1787).

Salle de gardes de la Reine (Queen's Guards-room) (n)

This room protected her against intrusions such as that which occurred on the morning of 6 October 1789, when a rioting mob tried to invade the Queen's Suite and had to be fought off by the royal guard in a prolonged and bloody scuffle.

Salle du Sacre

The Coronation room was initially used as a chapel from 1676 to 1682; otherwise this large guard-room housed the sessions of Parliament, which passed laws here. Louis-Philippe had the room altered to accommodate three enormous paintings: *Murat at the Battle of Aboukir* by Gros, *Champ de Mars Eagles* and *The Consecration of Napoléon* by **David**.

Salle de 1792 (p)

The walls of this large unfurnished room, situated at the angle of the central part of the palace and the south wing, are covered with portraits of warriors and battle scenes. Note Coignet's *The Paris National Guard Departs to Join the Army*, in which Louis-Philippe appears in the uniform of a lieutenant-general.

Galerie des Batailles ★ (Battle Gallery)

🕐 *Tue–Sun. Call to confirm hours.*
☎ *01 30 83 76 20.*

Designed in the south wing in 1836 under Louis-Philippe, the History of France Galleries created a sensation. The 33 vast pictures evoke France's greatest military victories and include works by **Horace Vernet, Eugène Delacroix** and **Baron Gérard.** At the end of the gallery is the **Salle de 1830,** devoted to Louis-Philippe's accession to the throne.

Dauphine's and Mesdames' Apartments

▶ *Start from Entrance (C2), on the ground floor.*

Dauphin's Apartments – Heir to the Throne

These are the private rooms of the Dauphin Louis, son of Louis XV, restored in the 20th century by Pierre de Nolhac. After his first wife, Marie-Therese Raphaelle of Spain, died, he moved here with his second wife, Marie Josèph of Saxony, who gave him seven children, including the future Louis XVI.

The apartments consisted of a first anteroom and a second anteroom with windows overlooking the Parterre d'Eau. The bedchamber **(29)** has the original wainscotting by Verberckt, and a brown marble fireplace decorated with bronzes by Caffieri representing *Flora* and *Zephyr*. The corner salon **(28)**, with four windows overlooking the gardens to the south and east, is decorated by paintings by Jean-Baptiste Oudry. The large writing desk was made for the room by Bernard Van Riesen, a Dutch cabinet maker who signed his furnishings with B.V.R.B. Louis' library **(27)** has decorations over the doors by Vernet.

Dauphine's Apartments

The Dauphine's apartments were connected to her husband's, with a small office **(25)** separating her bedchamber **(26)** from the library. The last three kings of France – Louis XVI, Louis XVIII, and Charles X – were born in the bedchamber. The original wainscotting has disappeared in the large salon **(23)** , but

there are two paintings of Louis XV by **Riguad** and **Van Loo** in the Dauphine's two antichambers **(21, 22)**.

Mesdames' Apartments

🕐 *Weekends only.* Of Louis XV's ten children with Marie Leszczyska, eight were girls. The three eldest grew up at Versailles in the south wing's apartments known as the Enfants de France, while the others were educated at the Abbey of Fontevrault. As adults, the princesses finally settled into the the ground floor apartments across the Marble Courtyard from their brother, the Dauphin.

The apartments of Madame Victoire **(30-31)** and Madame Adélaïde **(32)** have been restored to look the way they did before Louis-Philippe, including the bedrooms, antechambers, and salons; however most of the furnishings were lost during the Revolution. A few personal effects have been recovered, including the intricately designed organ that belonged to Adélaïde.

King's Private Apartments

🌿 *Guided tour. Entrance included in Passeport.*

Appartement intérieur du Roi ★★★

The King's Private Suite served as private apartments to Louis XV, reserved for those closest to him. Here the king removed himself from the constraints of the Court. The rooms were designed by Gabriel and are decorated with carvings by Verberckt: shells, foliated scrolls and Rococo flower motifs are scattered everywhere.

Chambre à coucher (6)

Louis XV, and then Louis XVI, retired to this bedroom after they had performed the rising and retiring ceremonies which took place in the Grand Apartment. It was here that Louis XV died of smallpox on 10 May 1774.

Cabinet de la Pendule (7)

The Clock Room served as a gaming room when the king held court. Until 1769 it owed its name to the astronomi-

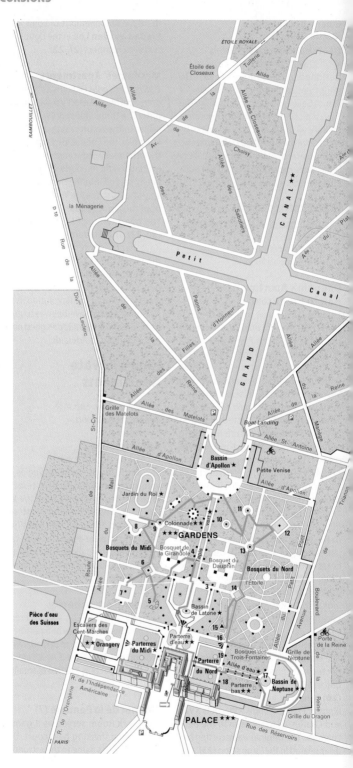

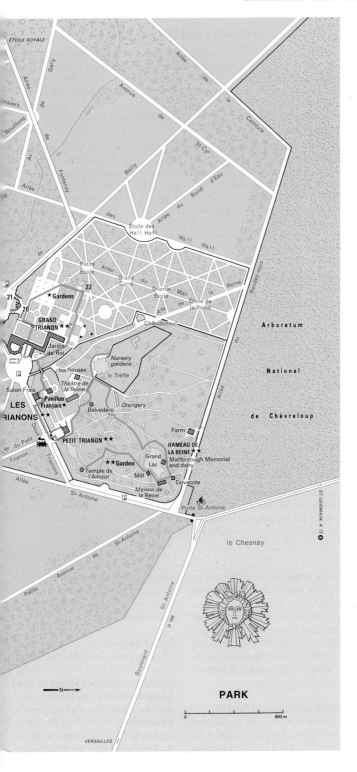

ÉTOILE ROYALE

Allée

de

la

Ceinture

Avenue

de

St-Cyr

Allée

de

Gally

Av.

Fontenay

Bailly

Allées

de

Travers

Bouillons

de

de Ice

Allée

du Rond d'Eau

des

Étoile des
Hall Hall

Ha!! Ha!!

de

Petite
Étoile

Allée

du

Grand
Carré

Grande
Étoile

Mail

la

Reine

Rendez-vous

★ Gardens

Grand
Étoile

de

Étoile de
la Reine

22

21

20

GRAND
TRIANON ★★

Jardin
du Roi

Châteauneuf

Allée

du

Arboretum

National

de Chèvreloup

Ice-houses

Théâtre de
la Reine

Nursery
gardens

le Trèfle

Salon Frais

Pavillon
Français ★

LES
TRIANONS ★★★

Belvedere

Orangery

Farm

Allée

PETIT TRIANON ★★

HAMEAU DE
LA REINE ★★

Allée

se du Petit

Trianon

Deux Trianons

★ Garden

Grand
Lac

Marlborough Memorial
and dairy

Temple de
l'Amour

Mill

Dovecote

Maison de
la Reine

Allée

St-Antoine

Porte St-Antoine

ST GERMAIN A 13

le Chesnay

St-Antoine

Avenue

de

Petite

St-Antoine

D 186

Boulevard

N

PARK

0   400 m

VERSAILLES

Versailles and the Sun King

Born in 1638 Louis XIV succeeded to the throne of France in 1643 and reigned until 1715, the longest reign of any European sovereign. Although Louis was not the only monarch to live at the Palace of Versailles, he will forever be the one most associated with it. The building was begun in 1624 during the reign of Louis XIII, his father, although at first it was a simple hunting lodge. Whilst still the Dauphin, Louis took possession of the building in 1632 and began a programme of minor improvements.

It was not until well into his reign, however, that Louis began to develop Versailles into the building we know today. He became increasingly convinced that the way to avoid the unrest, which had troubled his father's reign, was to move the Court away from Paris to Versailles. He was determined to centralise the Government and reduce the power of the nobility and, following the death of his First Minister Mazarin in 1661, Louis assumed absolute power and began to rule without resort to advice from anyone. Although he probably did not utter the phrase 'L'État, c'est moi', ('the State, it is me') he certainly embodied the sentiment and it was no coincidence that he became known as 'the Sun King', because everything had to revolve around him.

Louis employed the services of the most well known architects and landscape designers of his day. There began a programme of works that was to transform the old hunting lodge into a palace that would eventually become the largest in Europe. The idea was to build a palace so large that he could keep all his potential opponents in one place and thus stifle any rebellious rumblings – in fact, he believed that they would be so consumed by their personal rivalries that they would not have the time or the inclination to trouble the monarch.

Although some building works had taken place between 1664 and 1668, these were mainly to prepare the Palace for a party known as the Plaisirs de l'Île enchantée, which Louis held to celebrate the two Queens, Anne of Austria, the Queen Mother, and Marie-Thérèse, his wife. Much more extensive work took place during the period 1669-72 with the construction of the Grand Appartement du Roi and the Grand Appartement de la Reine. In 1682 Louis officially installed the Court at Versailles, finally accomplishing what he had set out to achieve – the creation of a small town consisting of government buildings which allowed him to exercise the absolute power he craved.

The Bourbon monarchy was to remain at Versailles until they were compelled to leave during the Revolution, ironically a state of affairs brought about, in part at least, by the absolute power which the Sun King had insisted upon having one hundred years before and which now was leading to the downfall of his heirs.

cal clock whose works were built by Passemant and Dauthiau with bronze embellishments by Caffiéri.

When crossing the **Antichambre des Chiens** (Dogs' Antechamber) (**8**) note the Louis XIV panelling. In the dining room called **Retours de chasse** (Hunters' Dining Hall) (**9**) Louis XV gave private dinners on hunting days.

Cabinet intérieur du Roi (10)

The Corner Room became a workroom in 1753. As an example of Verberckt's Rococo style, the furniture is remarkable; the medal cabinet is by Gaudreaux (1739), corner cupboards by Joubert (1755) and a roll-top **desk**★ by Oeben and Riesener (1769).

Salles neuves

The new rooms were designed under Louis XV in the place of the Ambassadors' Staircase. In the **Cabinet de Mme Adélaïde** (**12**), the child **Mozart** played the harpsichord. The medal cabinet by Benneman is a masterpiece. The following rooms, Louis XVI's **Library** (13) and the **Porcelain Salon** (**14**) show the evolution of Versailles style towards sober Neoclassicism. The most notable is the **Salon des Jeux** (Louis XVI's Gaming Room) (**15**) as it appeared in 1775; corner cupboards by Riesener (1774), chairs by Boulard and gouache landscapes by Van Blarenberghe.

Other tours include **The Queen's Private Suite, The milestones of the French Parliament's history, and Madame de Maintenon's Apartments.**

Grand Park and Gardens★★★

See map.

Apr–Oct, daily 7am–8.30pm, Nov–Mar, 8am–6pm. Free access to the gardens Nov–Mar and weekdays (3€). Apr–Oct; 7€ on weekends (for the Musical Fountains event, 5€ after 5pm; free entrance with Pass). Free acces daily to the Grand Park; 01 30 83 77 80).

Laid out principally by **Le Nôtre** during the years 1660 to 1670, the park and gardens are masterpieces of the art of French landscape gardening, in which nature is ordered geometrically according to the principles of Classicism. The basins, fountains and statues are perfectly integrated with nature.

There's a magnificent view from the **Parterre du Midi**★ (**1**), overlooking the **Orangery**★★ and **Pièce d'Eau des Suisses**. On each side of the Orangery descend the **Escaliers des Cent-Marches** (100-step Staircases). Louis XIV's favourite view was from the **Parterre d'Eau**★★ (**2**), where the grand perspective or east-west axis symbolically retraces the path of the sun, from the **Latona Basin**★ and fountain to the **Apollo Basin**★, continuing along the **Grand Canal**★★.

3) Bosquet du Dauphin

4) Bosquet de la Girandole

5) Bosquet des Rocailles

6) Bassin de Bacchus

7) Bosquet de la Reine

8) Bassin du Miroir, overlooking the **Jardin du Roi**★

9) Bassin de Saturne, leads to the **Colonnade**★★

10) Bosquet des Dômes

11) Bosquet de l'Encelade

12) Bosquet de l'Obélisque

13) Bassin de Flore

14) Bassin de Cérès

15) Basquet des Bains d'Apollon

16) The top of the **Parterre du Nord** has a good view of the château.

17) The **Bassin du Dragon** overlooks the **Bassin de Neptune**★★ and **Parterre Bas**★★.

18) Allée d'Eau★

19) Bosquet des Trois Fontaines

Domaine de Marie-Antoinette★★

Apr–Oct, daily noon–6pm (7.30pm for the gardens); Nov–Mar, Grand Trianon and gardens of the Petit Trianon noon–5.30pm. Entrance Apr–Oct: 9€ (5€ after 5pm); Nov–Mar 5€; annual ticket 20€; free entry with Paris Pass. 01 30 83 76 20. www.chateauversailles.fr.

No trip to Versailles would be complete without visiting the newly renovated **Marie-Antoinette's Estate** located on the northern edge of the Grand Park. It started with the **Grand Trianon**★★, built as a personal retreat for Louis XIV in 1687, with its own **gardens**★ overlooking the **Petit Canal** (**21**) and romantic **groves** (**22**). Next door is the **Petit Trianon**★★ (1768), where Marie-Antoinette spent much of her time with her children. She had a private theatre, an English-style **garden**★ with lakes and folies, and the replica of a village, **le Hameau de la Reine**★★, complete with thatched-roof houses, farm animals and mill.

CHÂTEAU DE CHANTILLY★★★

MICHELIN LOCAL MAP 305: F-5 OR MAP 106 FOLD 8

The name Chantilly brings to mind a château, a forest, a racecourse and the world of horse racing in general. Because of its remarkable setting, its park and the treasures in its museum, the Château de Chantilly is considered one of the major sights in France. Chantilly is also rapidly becoming an important cultural centre, thanks to the activities of the Centre des Fontaines, with its library boasting 600 000 titles (philosophy, art, religion etc).

- 🛈 **Information:** Office de tourisme de Chantilly, 60 av. du Mar. Joffre, 60631 Chantilly. ☎03 44 67 37 37. www.chantilly-tourisme.com.
- ▶ **Orient Yourself:** Chantilly is about one hours drive north of Paris. Take junction 7 from the Autoroute du Nord.
- 🅿 **Parking:** At the Château.
- 👁 **Don't Miss:** The facsimile of '*Les Très Riches Heures du duc de Berry*'.
- 🕐 **Organizing Your Time:** Allow half a day to see the Château and Park.
- 👣 **Also See:** ST-DENIS.

A Bit of History

From Cantilius to the Montmorency – Over the past 2 000 years, five castles have occupied this part of the Nonette Valley. Above the ponds and marshes of the area rose a rocky island where **Cantilius**, a native of Roman Gaul, built the first fortified dwelling. His name and achievement gave birth to Chantilly. In the Middle Ages the building became a fortress belonging to the Bouteiller de France, named after the hereditary duties he carried out at the court of the Capetians; originally in charge of the royal cellars, the Bouteiller was one of the king's close advisers.

In 1386 the land was bought by the chancellor, d'Orgemont, who had the castle rebuilt. The feudal foundations bore the three subsequent constructions. In 1450 the last descendant of the Orgemont married one of the Barons of Montmorency and Chantilly became the property of this illustrious family. It remained in their possession for 200 years.

Constable Anne, Duc de Montmorency – Anne de Montmorency was a devoted servant to a succession of six French kings from Louis XII to Charles IX. This formidable character gained a reputation as warrior, statesman, diplomat and patron of the arts. For 40 years, apart from a few brief periods, he remained

Château de Chantilly

D. Pazery/ MICHELIN

the leading noble of the land, second to the king. Childhood friend and companion-in-arms to François I, close adviser to Henri II, he even had some influence over Catherine de' Medici, who looked favourably upon the man who had advised her on cures for her infertility.

Constable Anne owned 600 fiefs, over 130 castles and estates, four mansions in Paris and numerous posts and offices. He was immensely wealthy. When he went to court he was escorted by 300 guards on horseback. Through his five sons and the husbands of his seven daughters, he controlled most of the country's highest positions and had connections with Henri II, as well as with all the other most distinguished French families.

In 1528 the feudal castle of the Orgemont was demolished and the architect Pierre Chambiges replaced it with a palace built in the French Renaissance style. On a nearby island Jean Bullant erected the charming château which still stands today; the Petit Château. It was separated from the Grand Château by a moat – now filled in – which was spanned by two superimposed bridges. An aviary was set up in the tiny garden on the island. Constable Anne ordered great loads of earth and built the terrace which bears his statue.

The last love of Henri IV – Henri IV often stayed at Chantilly, with his companion-in-arms Henri I de Montmorency, the son of Constable Anne. At the age of 54 the king fell in love with his host's ravishing daughter Charlotte, aged only 15. He arranged for her to marry Henri II de Bourbon-Condé, a shy and gauche young man, whom the king hoped would prove an accommodating husband. The day after the wedding, however, Condé left the capital with his wife. Henri IV ordered them to return to Paris. The young couple fled to Brussels, where they stayed under the protection of the king of Spain. Henri IV raged, implored, threatened and even went as far as to ask the Pope to intervene. Only when he was murdered by Ravaillac did the two fugitives return to France.

Henri de Montmorency – Encouraged by Louis XIII's brother, the scheming Gaston d'Orléans, the schemer Henri II de Montmorency plotted against Richelieu. He was

Statue of Henri IV

S. Sauvignier/ MICHELIN

defeated at Castelnaudary near Toulouse and made a prisoner after receiving 18 wounds, including five by bullets. By way of an apology, he bequeathed to Cardinal Richelieu the two *Slave* statues by Michelangelo, now in the Louvre; those at Chantilly and Écouen are replicas.

The Great Condé – Charlotte de Montmorency and her husband the Prince of Condé – the couple persecuted by Henri IV – inherited Chantilly in 1643 and the château remained family property until 1830. Descendants of Charles de Bourbon, like Henri IV, the Princes of Condé were of royal blood and the heir apparent to the title was called the Duke of Enghien.

The Great Condé was the son of Charlotte and Henri II. He applied himself to renovating the Château de Chantilly with the same energy and efficiency he had shown in military operations. In 1662 he commissioned Le Nôtre to redesign the park and the forest. The fountains at Chantilly were considered the most elegant in France and Louis XIV made a point of outclassing them at Versailles. The work lasted 20 years and the result was a splendid achievement, part of which still stands today.

The Last of the Condés – The Prince of Condé died at Fontainebleau (*see FONTAINEBLEAU*) in 1686, to the king's great dismay. During the religious ceremony preceding the burial, Bossuet delivered a funeral oration which became famous.

The great-grandson of the Great Condé, Louis-Henri de Bourbon, alias "Monsieur le Duc", was an artist with a taste for

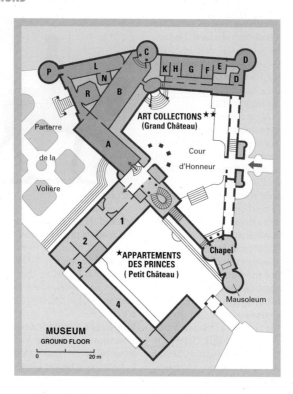

ART COLLECTIONS ★★
(Grand Château)

Parterre

de la

Volière

Cour
d'Honneur

★APPARTEMENTS
DES PRINCES
(Petit Château)

Chapel

Mausoleum

MUSEUM
GROUND FLOOR
0   20 m

splendour, who gave Chantilly a new lease on life. He asked Jean Aubert to build the Grandes Écuries, a masterpiece of the 18C, and set up a porcelain factory which closed down in 1870.

The Château d'Enghien was built on the estate by Louis-Joseph de Condé in 1769. His grandson the Duke of Enghien, who had just been born, was its first occupant. The father of the newly born baby was 16, his grandfather 36. The young prince died tragically in 1804; he was seized by the French police in the margravate of Baden and shot outside the fortress of Vincennes on the orders of Bonaparte.

During the French Revolution the main building was razed to the ground, though the smaller château was spared. Louis-Joseph was 78 when he returned from exile. His son accompanied him back to Chantilly and the two of them were dismayed: their beloved château was in ruins and the park in a shambles. They decided to renovate the estate. They bought back the plots of their former land, restored the Petit Château, redesigned and refurbished the grounds. The prince died in

1818, but the duke continued the work. He was an enthusiastic hunter and at the age of 70 he still hunted daily. Thanks to his efforts, Chantilly became the lively, fashionable place it had been in the years preceding the Revolution. As in former times, the receptions and hunting parties attracted crowds of elegant visitors. The renovation and restoration work was a source of income for the local population.

The duke was worried by the Revolution of 1830, which raised his cousin Louis-Philippe to the throne, and considered returning to England. A few days later, he was found hanging from a window at his castle in St-Leu. He was the last descendant of the Condé.

The Duke of Aumale – The Duke of Bourbon had left Chantilly to his great-nephew and godson the Duke of Aumale, the fourth son of Louis-Philippe. This prince gained recognition in Africa when he captured Abdel-Kader and his numerous relations. The Revolution of 1848 forced him to go into exile and he returned only in 1870; in 1873

Address Book

For coin ranges, see the Legend on the cover flap.

WHERE TO STAY

Pavillon St-Hubert – *In Toutevoie, on the banks of the Oise. 60270 Gouvieux. 3.5km/2mi W of Chantilly via D 909. ☎03 44 57 07 04. www.pavillon-saint-hubert. com. 18 rooms. Restaurant.*
A former hunting lodge and its lovely garden by the Oise offering small rooms reminiscent of the inns of yore. The dining room, furnished in the Louis XIII style, is adorned with hunting trophies. Terrace in the shade of sycamore trees, with the Oise River in the background.

Château de la Tour
– *Chemin de la Chaussée, 60270 Gouvieux. 3.5km/2mi W of Chantilly via D909. ☎03 44 62 38 38. www.lechateaudelatour. fr. Closed Christmas period. 41 rooms. Restaurant.* This early 20C domain, formerly belonging to a famous banker, overlooks a spacious park that can be contemplated from the terrace. There are modern and old-fashioned bedrooms available for the asking; elegant dining rooms with a Louis XIII flair.

WHERE TO EAT

La Capitainerie "Les Cuisines de Vatel" *In the château. 60500 Chantilly.*
☎03 44 57 15 89. www.restaurantfp-chantilly.com. Closed Tue and evenings – Reservations advisable. One would be hard put to find a more prestigious setting for a restaurant than this one, located under the ancestral arches of kitchens once governed by the illustrious chef Vatel. The inviting décor features copper ware, porcelain, old ovens, the original brick fireplace and leather chairs. The menu changes with the seasons.

Auberge le Vertugadin – *44 r. du Connétable, 60500 Chantilly. ☎03 44 57 03 19. Closed Sun evening.* Follow the road to the Château de Chantilly to find this 19C manor with green window frames and shutters. There are two dining rooms to choose from, countrified or gentrified, plus a gravel terrace. The fixed-price and à la carte menus evolve with the seasons.

La Belle Bio – *22 r. du Connétable, 60500 Chantilly. 0.5km/0.3mi from the Château. ☎03 44 57 02 25. Closed Sun evening and Mon.* No, you're not entering a grocer's shop, but rather a '100% organic' restaurant. The colourful décor is charming, and the menu is chock full of tasty, imaginative dishes (fish, meat, vegetables). Highly recommended.

---

he presided over the court martial that sentenced Marshal Bazaine.

From 1875 to 1881 the duke commissioned Daumet to build the Grand Château in the Renaissance style. This castle, the fifth, still stands today. Back in exile between 1883 and 1889, he died in 1897 and the Institute of France inherited his estate at Chantilly, together with the superb collections that constitute the Condé Museum.

Visit

The Château★★★

Guided visits (30min): 22 Mar–Oct, Wed–Mon 10.30am–6pm; 5 Nov–21 Mar, 10.30am–5pm (last admission 45min before closing). Château and park 10€ (under-18s no charge when with adult). ☎03 44 27 31 80. www.chateau dechantilly.com.

From Chapelle-en-Serval, crossing Chantilly Forest, the château suddenly rises into view from the carrefour des Lions; it appears to be floating on the water in a superb setting of rocks, ponds, lawns and stately trees.

From Paris, take N 16; do not drive through the town but turn right after the lower road and into the shady Route de l'Aigle which skirts the racecourse.

The road from Senlis through Vineuil offers a good view of the château and its park; leaving Vineuil, turn left at each junction.

Try to picture the Château de Chantilly at the time of the Condé when the two main buildings were still divided by an arm of water: the 16C Petit Château (or

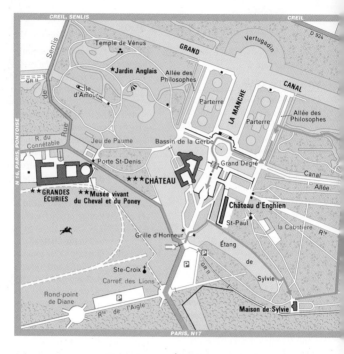

The following labels appear on the map:

CREIL, SENLIS — CREIL — CREIL
D 924
Senlis
Temple de Vénus
GRAND
Vertugadin
★Jardin Anglais
Allée des Philosophes
CANAL
GR II
Île d'Amour
LA MANCHE
Parterre
Allée des Philosophes
R. du Connétable
Rue
N 16, PARIS PONTOISE
de Senlis
Jeu de Paume
Parterre
Porte St-Denis
Bassin de la Gerbe
★★★CHÂTEAU
Grand Degré
Canal
Allée
★★GRANDES ÉCURIES
★★Musée vivant du Cheval et du Poney
Château d'Enghien
St-Paul
la Cabotière
R'e
Grille d'Honneur
Étang
Ste-Croix
Carref. des Lions
de
Rond-point de Diane
Sylvie
R'e de l'Aigle
Maison de Sylvie
PARIS, N17

barbican) and the Grand Château, for which Daumet used the foundations of the former stronghold.

Cross the constable's terrace, which bears the equestrian statue of Anne de Montmorency, and enter the main courtyard through the main gateway (Grille d'Honneur), flanked by the two copies of Michelangelo's *Slaves*.

Cabinet des Livres

D. Pazery/MICHELIN

The Duke of Aumale did not intend to establish a **museum**★★ for educational purposes; he merely wanted to build up a fine art collection. He therefore hung the works in chronological order of purchase though favourite ones were sometimes placed in a separate room. The curators have respected his layout.

According to the terms of the duke's legacy, the Institute must agree "to make no changes to the interior and exterior architecture of the château." Moreover, it is not allowed to lend any of the exhibits.

The reception hall is the starting point for guided tours of the chapel and the various apartments as well as for unaccompanied tours of the collections. if a group has already formed, it is best to join it . It is advisable to interrupt a visit to the collections if the custodians announce a guided tour of the apartments.

Appartements des Princes★

Situated in the **Petit Château**, this suite, occupied by the Great Condé and his descendants, was embellished with Regency and Rococo **wainscoting**★★, especially in the 18C thanks to the Duke of Bourbon. It was not occupied by the

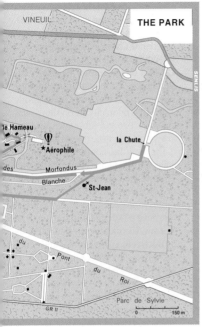

XVI commode was designed by Riesener and made by Hervieu.

Salon des Singes (3)
A collection of monkey scenes (*singeries*) dating from the early 18C is a masterpiece by an anonymous draughtsman; note the fire screen depicting the monkeys' reading lesson.

Galerie de Monsieur le Prince (4)
The Great Condé had ordered his own battle gallery, which he never saw completed (1692). The sequence was interrupted from 1652 to 1659 during his years of rebellion. A painting conceived by the hero's son portrays him stopping a Fame from publishing a list of his treacherous deeds and asking another Fame to issue a formal apology.

Chapelle
An **altar**★ attributed to Jean Goujon and some 16C wainscoting and stained-glass windows from the chapel at Écouen were brought here by the Duke of Aumale. The apse contains the **mausoleum** of Henri II de Condé (*see above*) (bronze statues by J Sarrazin taken from the Jesuit Church of St-Paul-St-Louis in Paris) and the stone urn which received the hearts of the Condé princes. Up to the Revolution, the Condé necropolis was at Vallery in Burgundy, where another sepulchral monument celebrating Henri II still stands.

The Collections★★ (Grand Château)

▶ Cross the Galerie des Cerfs **(A)** with its hunting theme; note the 17C Gobelins tapestries.

Galerie de Peinture (B) – The variety of paintings here reflects the eclectic tastes of the Duke of Aumale. Military events are illustrated on huge canvases (*Battle on the Railway Line* by Neuville, Meissonnier's *The Cuirassiers of 1805*). Orientalism is well represented with Gros' work, *The Plague Victims* of Jaffa, H Vernet's *Arab Sheikhs holding Council*, and *The Falcon Hunt* by Fromentin. Note,

Duke of Aumale who had taken up residence on the ground floor.
The antechamber and part of the library, the work of the Duke of Aumale, are located on the site of the old moat.

Cabinet des Livres★ (Library) (1)
This contains a splendid collection of manuscripts, including **The Rich Hours of the Duke of Berry** (*Les Très Riches Heures du duc de Berry*) with 15C illuminations by the Limbourg brothers. This extremely fragile document is not permanently exhibited but visitors may see a facsimile by Faksimile Verlag of Luzern.
Another interesting reproduction is the psalter of Queen Ingeburge of Denmark. Among the ornamental motifs feature the monogram of the Duke of Aumale (H O for Henri d'Orléans) and the Condé coat of arms (France's "broken" coat of arms with a diagonal line symbolising the younger branch of the family).

Chambre de Monsieur le Prince (2)
This title referred to the reigning Condé Prince, in this instance the Duke of Bourbon (1692-1740), who installed a wainscot at the far end of the room, into which were embedded panels painted by C Huet in 1735. The famous Louis

too, the famous portrait of *Gabrielle d'Estrées in her Bath* (16C French school), the portraits of Cardinals Richelieu and Mazarin by Philippe de Champaigne, and *The Massacre of the Holy Innocents* by Poussin.

Rotonde (**C**) – The *Loreto Madonna* by **Raphael**, **Piero di Cosimo's** portrait of the ravishing Simonetta Vespucci, who is believed to have been Botticelli's model for his *Birth of Venus*, and Chapu's kneeling statue of Joan of Arc listening to voices are exhibited here.

Salle de la Smalah et Rotonde de la Minerve (**D**) – Family portraits of the Orléans (17C, 18C and 19C) and of Louis-Philippe's relations in particular: Bonnat's picture of the Duke of Aumale at the age of 68.

Cabinet de Giotto (**E**) – A room devoted to Italian Primitives: *Angels Dancing in the Sun* (Italian School, 15C).

Salle Isabelle (**F**) – Numerous 19C paintings including *Moroccan Guards* by Delacroix, *Horse Leaving the Stables* by Géricault, and *Françoise de Rimini* by Ingres.

Salle d'Orléans (**G**) – The glass cabinets contain **soft-paste Chantilly porcelain** manufactured in the workshops founded in 1725 by the Duke de Bourbon (armorial service bearing the Condé coat of arms or the Duke of Orléans' monogram).

Salle Caroline (**H**) – 18C painting has pride of place here, with portraits by Largillière and Greuze, *Young Woman Playing with Children* by Van Loo, *The Worried Lover* and *The Serenade Player* by Watteau, or *Snowstorm* by Everdingen.

Cabinet des Clouet (**K**) – A precious collection of small and extremely rare **paintings**★★ executed by the **Clouets**, Corneille de Lyon etc portraying François I, Marguerite of Navarre (stroking a little dog) and Henri II as a child etc.

Galerie de Psyché (**L**) – The 44 **stained-glass windows** (16C) that tell the story of the loves of Psyche and Cupid came from Constable Anne's other family home, Château d'Écouen.

Santuario★★★ (**N**) – This houses the museum's most precious exhibits: Raphael's *Orléans Madonna*, *The Three Ages of Womanhood*, also known as *The Three Graces*, by the same artist; *Esther and Ahasuerus*, the panel of a wedding chest painted by Filippino Lippi and 40 miniature works by Jean Fouquet, cut out of Estienne Chevalier's book of hours, a splendid example of French 15C art.

Cabinet des Gemmes (**P**) – This contains jewels of stunning beauty. The Pink Diamond, alias the Great Condé (a copy of which is permanently on show), was stolen in 1926 and subsequently found in an apple where the thieves had hidden it. The room also boasts an outstanding collection of enamels and miniatures.

Tribune (**R**) – Above the cornice of this polygonal room are painted panels representing episodes from the life of the Duke of Aumale and the house of Orléans. The paintings include *Autumn* by **Botticelli**, *Love Disarmed* and *Pastoral Pleasures* by **Watteau**, a portrait of Molière by **Mignard**, and on the "Ecouen Wall", three superb works by **Ingres**: a self-portrait, *Madame Devaucay* and *Venus*.

Petits Appartements★ Access by the stairway off the reception hall. The Duke of Aumale had these private apartments designed and decorated by painter Eugène Lami specially for his marriage in 1844.

Park★★

&. ⓒ*22 Mar–Oct: 10am–8pm (last entry 6pm); 5 Nov–21 Mar, 10.30am–6pm (last entry 5pm).* ⊛*5€ (under-18s no charge when with an adult).* ☎*03 44 27 31 80.*

Jardin anglais –The landscaped English-style garden was laid out on the surviving relics of Le Nôtre's park in 1820. Its charm derives from the pleasant groves (plane trees, swamp cypresses, weeping willows) rather than from the symbolic monuments: remains of a Temple of Venus and of Love (Île d'Amour).

Chapelle St-Jean – The chapel was erected on the estate by Constable Anne in 1538, with six other chapels, in memory of the seven churches of Rome he had visited in order to gain the indulgences granted to those who undertook this pilgrimage. He obtained from the Pope the same privileges for the chapels at Chantilly. Two other chapels still stand on the estate: St Paul's, located behind the Château d'Enghien, and Ste-Croix, on the lawns of the racecourse.

▶ *Take allée Blanche along the banks of the Canal des Morfondus.*

La Chute – These tiered waterfalls mark the start of the Grand Canal.

▶ *Return along allée Blanche; cross the Canal des Morfondus at the footbridge.*

Le Hameau – Dating from 1775, this was built before the more famous Trianon at Versailles. Under the influence of Jean-Jacques Rousseau, French princes used to seek new horizons by creating miniature villages.

The mill and a few half-timbered buildings used to accommodate a kitchen, a dining room and a billiard room. The barn provided a drawing room that was restored by the Duke of Aumale. All the big parties included supper in this charming spot in the park.

▶ *Skirt the brook by the small village.*

Parterres – The parterres are framed by two avenues of young lime trees, called "The Philosophers' Path" because the great writers who visited Chantilly used to pace up and down the shaded avenue, exchanging their views and ideas.

The circular Vertugadin lawns lie along the line of La Manche, flanked by delightful stretches of water. Between La Manche and the round basin (Bassin de la Gerbe) stands Coysevox's statue of the Great Condé, framed by the effigies of La Bruyère and Bossuet (statues of Molière and Le Nôtre, seated, may be seen in the near distance). A monumental stairway (Grand Degré) leads from the parterres up to the terrace; on either side of these imposing steps are grottoes, their carved decoration representing rivers.

Le Potager des Princes

17 r. de la Faisanderie. ⏰*From 22 Mar, Mon, Wed–Fri 2pm–5.30pm (Sat–Sun 6pm); by reservation Mon.* ⬨*7.50€.* ☎*03 44 57 39 66. www.potagerdesprinces.com.* Originally designed by André Le Nôtre and Jean-Baptiste de la Quintinie, this garden includes an area reserved for farmyard animals, an orchard, a rose garden and a vegetable garden where

Park in Château de Chantilly

©Simo Nannu/Bigstockphoto.com

medicinal and culinary herbs grow next to traditional vegetables.

Grandes écuries★★ (Stables)

Jean Aubert's masterpiece constitutes the most stunning piece of 18C architecture in Chantilly. The St-Denis Gateway – built astride the road leading to town – marks the site of an uncompleted pavilion. The most attractive façade of the stables overlooks the racecourse.

Musée Vivant du Cheval et du Poney★★

♿⏰*Wed–Mon 10am–6pm; shorter hours in winter; contact for precise details.* ⬨*9€ (4–17yrs 7€).* ☎*03 44 27 31 80. www.musee vivantducheval.fr.*

This museum is brought to life by the 28 saddle and draught animals – 18 horses and ten ponies, bred in France or in the Iberian Peninsula – which occupy the stalls and boxes built in the days of the Duke of Aumale.

Forêt de Chantilly

The vast wooded area has been reshaped by hunting enthusiasts over 500 years. The network of paths through the forest is suitable for country walks, and the light soil favours riding activities; training sessions take place at carrefour du Petit Couvert every morning. The forests of Coye, Orry and Pontarmé are reserved for walkers.

CHARTRES★★★

POPULATION 40 361

MICHELIN LOCAL MAP 311: E-5 OR MAP 106 FOLDS 37 AND 38

Chartres is the capital of Beauce, France's famous corn belt, but for tourists the town is known mainly for the Cathedral of Our Lady, a magnificent edifice, now a UNESCO World Heritage Site, which reigns supreme over a picturesque setting of monuments and old streets.

- **Information:** Pl. de la Cathédrale, 28000 Chartres. ☎02 37 18 26 26. www.chartres-tourisme.com.
- ▶ **Orient Yourself:** Chartres lies off the A 11. The town is situated on a knoll on the left bank of the River Eure, in the heart of the Beauce. The cathedral dominates the Old Town, known as the Quartier St-André.
- **Parking:** There is a large underground car park at Le Bouef Couronne, and street parking (paid) along the blvd de la Résistance and the blvd Maurice Violette.
- **Don't Miss:** For a bird's-eye view of the cathedral, stand behind the Monument aux Aviateurs Militaires, a memorial to the French Air Force high above the east bank of the river. The view★ is impressive.
- **Organizing Your Time:** Allow 90min to 2hr to visit the cathedral and at least 4hr to visit the Additional Sights (the tour of the agricultural museum, which is west of town, requires a minimum 2hr alone).

A Bit of History

A Town with a Destiny

Since ancient times Chartres has always had a strong influence over religious matters. It is believed that a Gallo-Roman well on the Chartres plateau was the object of a pagan cult and that in the 4C this was transformed into a Christian cult by the first evangelists. Adventius, the first known bishop of Chartres, lived during the middle of the 4C. A document from the 7C mentions a bishop Béthaire kneeling in front of Notre-Dame, which points to the existence of a Marian cult.

In 876 the chemise said to belong to the Virgin Mary was given to the cathedral by Charles the Bald, confirming that Chartres was already a place of pilgrimage. Up to the 14C the town of Chartres continued to flourish.

The Pilgrimage

Chartres Cathedral was consecrated to the Assumption of the Virgin Mary in 1260; in the Middle Ages it attracted many pilgrims.

In 1912 and 1913 the writer and poet **Charles Péguy** (1873-1914) made the pilgrimage to Chartres. The strong influence it had on his work inspired a small group of enthusiasts after World War I to follow suit and led, in 1935, to the establishment of the "Students' Pilgrimage" (*during Whitsun*).

An exceptional man

In the **Église St-Jean-Baptiste** in the Rechèvres district to the north of the town lies the body of the abbot **Franz Stock**, whose tomb is still a place of pilgrimage.

This German priest, chaplain to the prisons of Paris from 1940 to 1944, refused to retreat with the Wehrmacht and was taken prisoner. At the Morancez prison camp near Chartres he founded a seminary for prisoners of war and was the Superior there for two years. He died in February 1948 at the age of 43.

Visit

Cathedral★★★

Allow 1hr 30min. The 4 000 carved figures and the 5 000 characters portrayed by the stained-glass windows demanded a lifelong commitment from the specialists who studied them.

Chartres Cathedral

A Swift Construction

The building rests upon the Romanesque cathedral erected by Bishop Fulbert in the 11C and 12C: there remain the crypt, the towers and the foundations of the west front, including the Royal Doorway, and fragments of the Notre-Dame-de-la-Belle-Verrière stained-glass window. The remaining sections of the cathedral were built in the wake of the Great Fire of 1194; princes and dignitaries contributed generously to the work, while the poor offered their labour.

These efforts made it possible to complete the cathedral in 25 years, and to add on the north and south porches 20 years later, with the result that the architecture and decoration of Notre-Dame form a harmonious composition almost unparalleled in the history of Gothic art. By some miracle, the Wars of Religion, the French Revolution and the two World Wars spared the famous basilica, which Rodin referred to as "the Acropolis of France" on account of its aesthetic and spiritual value. Only the cathedral's "forest" – the superb roof timbers – were destroyed by flames in 1836, and subsequently replaced by a metal framework.

Beneath the cathedral close, where it is planned to build an international medieval centre, archaeological excavations covering an area of some 1 200sq m/ 12 912sq ft are currently in progress. The remains of two 13C houses have been uncovered.

Exterior

West front

The two tall spires and the Royals Doorway form one of the most perfect compositions encountered in French religious art. The New Bell-Tower on the left was built first; the lower part dates back to 1134. Its present name dates from the 16C, when Jehan de Beauce erected a stone spire (115m /377ft high) to replace the wooden steeple which had burned down in 1506. The Old Bell-Tower (c. 1145-64), rising 106m/384ft, is a masterpiece of Romanesque art, forming a stark contrast to the ornate Gothic construction. The Royal Doorway and the three large windows above date from the 12C. Everything above this ensemble was built at a later date: the rose-window (13C), the 14C gable and the king's gallery featuring the kings of Judah, the ancestors of the Virgin Mary. On the gable, the Virgin Mary is depicted presenting her son to the Beauce area. The **Royal Doorway**★★★ (Portail Royal), a splendid example of Late Romanesque architecture (1145-70), represents the life and triumph of the Saviour. The Christ in Majesty on the central tympanum and the statue-columns are famous throughout the world. The elongated features of

The Royal Doorway

the biblical kings and queens, prophets, priests and patriarchs study the visitors from the embrasures. While the faces are animated, the bodies remain rigid, in deliberate contrast to the figures adorning the arches and the capitals. The statues were primarily designed to be columns, not human beings.

North porch and doorway

Leave the west front on your left and walk round the cathedral, stepping back to get a clear view of its lines. The nave is extremely high and unusually wide. The problem of how to support it was brilliantly resolved with the construction of three-tiered flying buttresses; the lower two arcs were joined together by colonnettes. The elegant Pavillon de l'Horloge near the New Bell-Tower is the work of Jehan de Beauce (1520).

The ornamentation of the north porch is similar to that of the doorway, executed at an earlier date. Treated more freely than those on the Royal Doorway, the characters are elegant and extremely lively, illustrating a new, more realistic approach to religious art. The statue of St Modesta, a local martyr who is pictured gazing up at the New Bell-Tower, is extremely graceful.

Once again, the decoration of the three doors refers to the Old Testament. The right door pays tribute to the biblical heroes who exercised the virtues rec-

ommended in the teachings of Christ. The central panel shows the Virgin Mary and the Prophets who foretold the coming of the Messiah. The door on the left presents the Annunciation, Visitation and Nativity, together with the Vices and Virtues.

In the bishop's garden, the raised terrace commands a view of the town below lying on the banks of the lower River Eure. Before reaching the garden gate, look left and note the archway straddling a narrow street. It used to open into the Notre-Dame cloisters.

East end

The complexity of the double-course flying buttresses – reinforced here with an intermediate pier as they cross over the chapels – and the succession of radiating chapels, chancel and arms of the transept are stunning. The 14C St Piat Chapel, originally separate, was joined to Notre-Dame by a stately staircase.

South porch and doorway

Here, the upper stonework is concealed by a constellation of colonnettes. The perspective of these planes, stretching from the arches of the porch to the gables, confers to this arm of the transept a sense of unity that is lacking in the north transept.

The theme is the Church of Christ and the Last Judgment. In the Middle Ages, these scenes would usually be reserved for the west portal, but in this case the Royal Doorway already featured ornamentation. Consequently, the scenes portraying the Coming of a New World, prepared by the martyrs, were destined for the left-door embrasures, while those of the Confessors (witnesses of Christ who have not yet been made martyrs) adorn the right door.

Christ reigns supreme on the central tympanum. He is also present on the pier, framed by the double row of the 12 Apostles with their lean, ascetic faces, draped in long, gently folded robes.

Among the martyrs, note the statues standing in the foreground: St George and St Theodore, both admirable 13C representations of knights in armour. These figures are quite separate from the columns – the feet are flat and no longer slanted – and are there for purely decorative purposes.

The most delightful feature of the sculpted porch is the display of medallions, grouped in sets of six and placed on the recessed arches of the three doorways: the lives of the martyrs, the Vices and Virtues etc.

Returning to the west front, note the Old Bell-Tower and its ironical statue of a donkey playing the fiddle, symbolising man's desire to share in celestial music. At the corner of the building, stop to admire the tall figure of the sundial Angel.

Access to the Bell-Tower★

May–Aug, Mon–Sat 9.30am–12.30pm, 2pm–6pm, Sun 2pm–6pm; Sept–Apr, Mon–Sat 9.30am–12.30pm, 2pm–5pm, Sun 2pm–5pm – last ascent 30min before closure. 1 Jan, 1 May and Mon, Whitsun (afternoons), 25 Dec. 6.50€. 02 37 21 22 07. www.monuments-nationaux.fr

The tour (195 steps) leads round the north side and up to the lower platform of the New Bell-Tower. Seen from a height of 70m/230ft, the buttresses, flying buttresses, statues, gargoyles and Old Bell-Tower are most impressive. It is still possible to recognise the former Notre-Dame cloisters thanks to the old pointed roof. Enclosed by a wall right up to the 19C, this area was frequented by clerics, especially canons.

Interior

The nave (16m/52ft) is wider than any other in France (Notre-Dame in Paris 40ft; Notre-Dame in Amiens 46ft), though it has single aisles. The vaulting reaches a height of 37m/121ft and the interior is 130m/427ft long. This nave is 13C, built in the style known as early or lancet Gothic. There is no gallery; instead, there is a blind triforium.

In a place of pilgrimage of this importance, the chancel and the transept had to accommodate large-scale ceremonies; they were therefore wider than the nave. In Chartres, the chancel, its double ambulatory and the transept form an ensemble 64m/210ft wide between the north and south doorways.

Note the gentle slope of the floor, rising slightly towards the chancel; this made it easier to wash down the church when the pilgrims had stayed overnight.

Stained-glass windows★★★

The 12C and 13C stained-glass windows of Notre-Dame constitute, together with those of Bourges, the largest collection in France. The Virgin and Child and the Annunciation and Visitation scenes in the clerestory at the far end of the chancel produce a striking impression.

West front

These three 12C windows used to throw light on Fulbert's Romanesque cathedral and the dark, low nave that stood behind, which explains why they are so long.

The scenes (bottom to top) illustrate the fulfilment of the prophecies: (right) the Tree of Jesse, (centre) the childhood and life of Our Lord (Incarnation cycle) and (left) Passion and Resurrection (Redemption cycle).

You can feast your eyes on the famous 12C "Chartres blue", with its clear, deep tones enhanced by reddish tinges, especially radiant in the rays of the setting sun. For many years, people believed that this particular shade of blue was a long-lost trade secret. Modern laboratories have now established that the

Detail of the Redemption cycle,
central window of the west front

H. Champollion/ MICHELIN

sodium compounds and silica in the glass made it more resistant to dirt and corrosion than the panes made with other materials and in other times. The large 13C rose-window on the west front depicts the Last Judgment.

Transept

This ensemble consists of two 13C rose-windows, to which were added a number of lancet windows featuring tall figures. The themes are the same as those on the corresponding carved doorway: Old Testament (north), the End of the World (south).

The north rose (*rose de France*) was a present from Blanche of Castille, mother of St Louis and Regent of France, and portrays a Virgin and Child. It is characterised by the fleur-de-lis motif on the shield under the central lancet and by the alternating Castile towers and fleurs-de-lis pictured on the small corner lancets. The larger lancets depict St Anne holding the infant Virgin Mary, framed by four kings or high priests: Melchizedek and David stand on the left, Solomon and Aaron on the right.

The centre roundel of the south rose shows the risen Christ, surrounded by the Old Men of the Apocalypse, forming two rings of 12 medallions. The yellow and blue chequered quatrefoils represent the coat of arms of the benefactors,

the Comte de Dreux Pierre Mauclerc and his wife, who are also featured at the bottom of the lancets.

The lancets on either side of the Virgin and Child depict four striking figures – the Great Prophets Isaiah, Jeremiah, Ezekiel and Daniel – with the four Evangelists seated on their shoulders.

The morality of the scene is simple: although they are weak and lacking dignity, the Evangelists can see further than the giants of the Old Testament thanks to the Holy Spirit.

Notre-Dame-de-la-Belle-Verrière★ (1)

This is a very famous stained-glass window. The Virgin and Child, a fragment of the window spared by the fire of 1194, has been mounted in 13C stained glass. The range of blues is quite superb.

Other stained-glass windows – The aisles of the nave and the chapels around the ambulatory are lit by a number of celebrated stained-glass windows from the 13C verging on the sombre side. On the east side, the arms of the transept have received two works of recent making, in perfect harmony with the early fenestration: St Fulbert's window *(south transept)* (2), donated by the American Association of Architects (from the François Lorin workshop, 1954), and the window of Peace *(north transept)* (3), a present from a group of German admirers (1971).

The Vendôme Chapel (4) features a particularly radiant 15C stained-glass window. It illustrates the development of this art, which eventually led to the lighter panes of the 17C and 18C.

Parclose★★

The screen was started by Jehan de Beauce in 1514 and finished in the 18C. This fine work consists of 41 sculpted compositions depicting the lives of Christ and the Virgin Mary. These Renaissance medallions, evoking biblical history, local history and mythology, contrast sharply with the Gothic statues of the doorways.

Chancel

The marble facing, the Assumption group above the high altar and the low-relief carvings separating the columns were added in the 18C.

Organ (5)
The case dates from the 16C.

Vierge du Pilier (6)
This wooden statue (c. 1510) stood against the rood screen, now sadly disappeared. The richly clothed Virgin is the object of a procession celebrated annually.

Treasury
🕐May–Aug 9.30am–12.30pm, 2–6pm (Sun, 2–6pm). Sept-Apr, 9.30am–12.30pm, 2–5pm (Sun 2pm–5pm). Last entry 30min before closure. 🕐1 Jan, 1 May and Mon, Whitsun (afternoons), 25 Dec. ☞6.50€. ☎02 37 21 22 07. www.monuments-nationaux.fr
Chapelle St-Piat has been built to house the cathedral treasury. It is linked to the east end of the cathedral by a Renaissance staircase. Inside are some superb items of church plate.

Chapelle des Martyrs
This chapel has been refurbished and now contains the **Virgin Mary's Veil**,

laid out in a beautiful glass-fronted reliquary. Pilgrims used to pray to this veil, calling it a tunic or "Holy Chemise."

Crypt★
☞Guided tours (30min) Apr–Oct, Mon–Sat 11am, 2.15pm, 3.30pm and 4.30pm (end Jun to mid-Sept: additional tour at 5.15pm). Nov–Mar, Mon–Sat at 11am and 4.15pm. 🕐1 Jan, 21 Jun, 25 Dec and public holidays. ☞2.70€. ☎02 37 21 56 33.
The entrance is outside the cathedral, on the south side (see plan above). This is France's longest crypt (220m/722ft long). It dates largely from the 11C and features Romanesque groined vaulting. It is a curious shape; the two long galleries joined by the ambulatory pass under the chancel and the aisles and give onto seven chapels. Of the seven radiating chapels, only three are Romanesque. The other four were added by the master architect of the Gothic cathedral to serve as foundations for the chancel and the apse of the future building.

St Martin's Chapel (7)
Located by the south gallery, this chapel houses the originals of the stat-

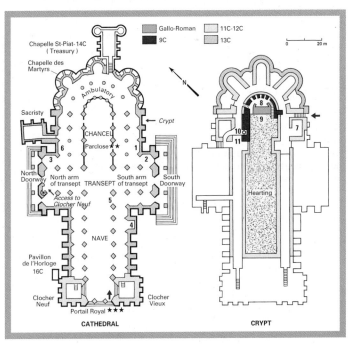

Address Book

For coin ranges, see the Legend on the cover flap.

WHERE TO STAY

La Ferme du Château (Bed and Breakfast) – *in Levesville, 28300 Bailleau-l'Évêque. 8km/5mi NW of Chartres via N 154 and D 134. ☎02 37 22 97 02. 3 rooms: meals*. This elegant Beauce farm offers pretty, comfortable rooms that have been decorated with a light hand. Neighbouring a small châteu, the farm is very quiet and its kind, hospitable owners are very discreet – a quality we appreciate!

Hôtel Le Grand Monarque – *22 pl. des Épars. ☎ 02 37 18 15 15. www.bw-grand-monarque.com. 50 rooms. Restaurant*. A 16C coaching inn at the heart of the city. The comfortable rooms have a personal touch; some are embellished with cheerfully flowered patterns and canopies while others are more sober. Snug dining room with ornamental wood carvings and works of art.

WHERE TO EAT

Le Pichet – *19 r. du Cheval-Blanc. ☎02 37 21 08 35. http://le-pichet.com.* Just down the street from the cathedral, a very friendly little bistro that suits our tastes. Inside, there is a pleasant jumble of bric-a-brac: wooden chairs, a collection of coffeepots, pitchers, old street signs and other good stuff. The food is traditional French cuisine and you will be served by waiters dressed in Renaissance style!

Le Café Serpente – *2 r. du Cloître Notre-Dame. ☎02 37 21 68 81. Closed evenings of 24 and 31 Dec. Reservations requested in winter.* A bicycle on the ceiling, posters on the walls and enamelled plaques in the stairwell comprise the décor of this thoroughly genial old café opposite the cathedral. On your plates: appetising salads, brasserie fare and authentic cuisine at all hours.

Le Tripot – *11 pl. Jean-Moulin. ☎02 37 36 60 11. Closed 3 weeks of Aug, Sun–Mon.* This house built in 1553 used to accommodate a real tennis court called 'Le Tripot'. Well-preserved rustic interior and contemporary cuisine.

SHOPPING

Galerie de Chartres – *10, rue Claude Bernard ZA du Coudray. ☎02 37 88 28 28. Showings: Wed, 9am–noon, 2–6pm.* This establishment organises auctions for an inter-national clientele every weekend in the 16C Eglise Sainte-Foy (ceramics, weapons, stamps, silverware, cameras, radios etc.). Specialises in the sale of collectable dolls and toys.

Marché aux légumes et volailles – *Pl. Billard.* Each Saturday morning, the covered Vegetable and Poultry Market displays colourful stands featuring authentic Beauce produce. This carrousel of sights, tastes and fragrances is one of the most popular markets in the area.

Galerie du Vitrail – *17 Cloître Notre-Dame, 28000 Chartres ☎02 37 36 10 03. www.galerie-du-vitrail.com. Mid-Oct–mid-Apr Tue–Fri 10.30am–1pm, 2–6.30pm, Sat 10.30am–6.30; mid-Apr–mid-Oct Tue–Sat 10am–7pm, Sun, Mon and holidays 11am–1pm, 2–7pm.* This atelier was founded in 1946 by Gabriel Loire, and is continued today by his grandchildren. The art and technique of making stained glass are carefully explained, beginning with artists' models (as designed by Adami, Miro or Fernand Léger, for example) and ending with the finished product created by master glass crafters. Many unique pieces can be obtained in the boutique and a specialised library can be visited.

ON THE TOWN

Brûlerie les Rois Mages – *6 r. des Changes. ☎02 37 36 30 52. Tue–Sat 9.15am–12.15pm, 1.45–7.15pm, Sun 9.15–12.15.* Enter this "retro" coffee-roasting shop and choose among the wide variety of coffees roasted on site and the dozens of teas to enjoy in the brûlerie or take home.

La Chocolaterie – *14 pl. Marceau. ☎02 37 21 86 92. Tue–Sat, 8am–7.30pm; Sun–Mon 10am–7.30pm.* A highly useful address for stocking up on gourmet treats to take home as souvenirs, such as macaroons or Mentchikoffs, a local chocolate speciality. The very cosy tearoom offers sofas and a fireplace; there's a pleasant terrace in summer.

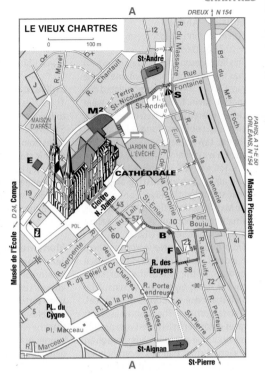

ues on the Royal Doorway: the sundial Angel etc.

▶ *A staircase, starting from the ambulatory, leads down to a lower crypt.*

Crypt St-Lubin (8)

This crypt served as the foundations of the 9C church. A thick, circular column with a visible base backs onto a Gallo-Roman wall (**9**), its bond easily recognisable by the alternating bricks and mortar. The crypt was a safe place that protected the cathedral treasures in times of social unrest or natural disaster. Thus, the chemise of the Virgin Mary survived the Great Fire of 1194.

Puits des Saints-Forts (10)

The lower part of this 33m/108ft deep shaft has a square section characteristic of Gallo-Roman wells. The coping is contemporary. The name dates back to 858; it is believed that several Christian martyrs from Chartres were murdered during a Norman attack, and their bodies thrown down the well.

Chapelle Notre-Dame-de-Sous-Terre (11)

A sacred retreat where pilgrims indulge in fervent praying. Since the 17C the chapel, together with the north gallery of the crypt, has played the part of a miniature church. It originally consisted of a small alcove where the faithful came to venerate the Virgin Mary. The interior of the chapel and its decoration were refurbished in 1976.

Additional Sights

Old Town★ (Quartier St-André and Banks of the Eure)

Follow the route indicated on the plan below.

This pleasant walk leads past the picturesque hilly site, the banks of the River Eure, an ancient district recently restored and the cathedral which is visible from every street corner. In the summer season, a small **tourist train** tours the old town.

Église St-André

🕐*Temporarily closed for restoration.*
☎*02 37 21 03 69.*

This Romanesque church (*deconsecrated*) was the place of worship of one of the most active and densely populated districts in town. Most of the trades were closely related to the river: millers, dyers, curriers, cobblers, tanners, drapers, fullers, tawers, serge makers etc. The church was enlarged in the 13C, and in the 16C and 17C it received a chancel and an axial chapel resting on arches that straddled the River Eure and rue du Massacre. Unfortunately, both these structures disappeared in 1827 leaving a much less picturesque church.

Cross the Eure by a metal footbridge. There is a good **view**★ of the old humpback bridges. At the foot of the shortened nave of St Andrew's lie the remains of the arch that once supported the chancel. *Wander upstream.* The wash-houses and races of former mills have been prettily restored. Rue aux Juifs leads through an ancient district that has recently been renovated, featuring cobbled streets bordered by gable-ended houses and old-fashioned street lamps.

Rue des Écuyers – This is one of the most successful restoration schemes of the old town. At nos 17 and 19 the houses have 17C doorways with rusticated surrounds, surmounted by a bull's-eye window. Stroll along the street to rue aux Cois. The corner building is a delightful half-timbered villa, with an overhang in the shape of a prow. Opposite stands Queen Bertha's stair turret, a 16C structure, also half-timbered.

Central District

Place du Cygne

The street has been widened into a little square planted with trees and shrubs (*flower market on Tuesdays, Thursdays and Saturdays*) and is at present an oasis of calm in this lively shopping district in the town centre.

At the end of rue du Cygne, on place Marceau, a monument celebrates the memory of the young local general who died at Altenkirchen (1796) at the age of 27. His ashes have been shared among Chartres (funeral urn under the statue on place des Épars), the Panthéon and the Dome Church of the Invalides in Paris.

Église St-Pierre★

This 12C and 13C Gothic church used to belong to the Benedictine abbey of St-Père-en-Vallée. The belfry-porch dates from pre-Romanesque times. The **Gothic stained-glass windows**★ can be traced back to the late 13C and early 14C, before the widespread introduction of yellow staining.

The oldest stained glass is that in the south bays of the chancel.

Monument de Jean Moulin

Jean Moulin was *préfet* (chief administrator) of Chartres during the German invasion; on 8 June 1940, despite having been tortured, he resisted the enemy and refused to sign a document claiming that the French troops had committed a series of atrocities. As he was afraid of being unable to withstand further torture, he attempted to commit suicide.

Moulin was dismissed by the Vichy government in November 1940 and, from then on, he planned and coordinated underground resistance, working in close collaboration with General de Gaulle.

Arrested in Lyon on 21 June 1943, he did not survive the harsh treatment he received from the Gestapo.

Grenier de Loëns

From the 12C onwards, this half-timbered barn with treble gables in the courtyard of the old chapter house was used to store the wine and cereals offered to the clergy as a tithe. Renovated to house the **Centre international du Vitrail** (♿🕐*9.30am–12.30pm, 1.30pm–6pm, Sat 10am–12.30pm, 2.30pm–6pm, Sun and public holidays 2.30pm–6pm.* 🕐*1 Jan, 25 Dec.* ✆*4€.* ☎*02 37 21 65 72. www.centre-vitrail.org*) which organises stained-glass exhibitions, the building now features a large hall with beautifully restored roof timbering and a magnificent 12C cellar with three aisles.

FONTAINEBLEAU★★★

POPULATION 15 942

MICHELIN LOCAL MAP 312: F-5 OR MAP 106 FOLDS 45, 46

It was not until the 19C that Fontainebleau started to develop, owing to the growing popularity of country residences and the general appreciation of its unspoilt forest. The area owes its name to a spring at the heart of a forest abounding in game, which was known as the "Fontaine de Bliaut" or "Blaut", probably after a former owner. However, Fontainebleau essentially owes its fame to the castle and the park named on UNESCO's World Heritage list. In addition, the town is the ideal starting point for excursions to Vaux-le-Vicomte, Barbizon or Courances.

- **Information:** Office du tourisme du pays de Fontainebleau-Avon, 4 rue Royale, 77300 Fontainebleau. ☎01 60 74 99 99. www.fontainebleau-tourisme.com.
- **Orient Yourself:** Fontainebleau is 60km from Paris, via the A 6, and then the N 37.
- **Don't Miss:** The Renaissance features of the castle, especially its famous horseshoe staircase.
- **Organizing Your Time:** You can easily spend a whole day here.

A Bit of History

The Palais de Fontainebleau owes its origins to royalty's passion for hunting; it owes its development and decoration to the kings' delight in amassing works of art and displaying them in their "family home." This palace has an extremely distinguished past; from the last of the Capetians up to Napoléon III, it was designed for and occupied by French rulers.

A hunting lodge
A spring – called Bliaut or Blaut fountain in the middle of a forest abounding in game – prompted the kings of France to build a mansion here. The exact date is not known but it was probably before 1137 as a charter exists issued under Louis VII from Fontainebleau, dating from that year. Philip Augustus celebrated the return of the Third Crusade here during the Christmas festivities of 1191 and St Louis founded a Trinitarian convent, whose members were called Mathurins; Philip the Fair was born here in 1268: unfortunately he also died here following a serious riding accident.

The Renaissance
Under François I almost all the medieval buildings were pulled down and replaced by two main edifices, erected under the supervision of Gilles Le Breton.

The oval-shaped east pavilion – built on the former foundations – was linked to the west block by a long gallery. To decorate the palace, François I hired many artists; he dreamed of creating a "New Rome" furnished with replicas of Classical statues.

The actual building consisted of rubble-work as the sandstone taken from the forest was too difficult to work into regular freestones. The harled façades are enlivened by string-courses of brick or massive sandstone blocks.

Henri II's château
Henri II pursued the efforts undertaken by his father. He gave orders to complete and decorate the ballroom, which remains one of the splendours of Fontainebleau Palace. The monograms – consisting of the royal H and the two intertwined Cs of Catherine de' Medici – were legion. In a form of ambiguity that was generally accepted in its day, the two C's placed immediately beside the H form a double D, the monogram of the King's mistress Diane de Poitiers.

When Henri II was killed in a tournament, his widow Catherine de' Medici sent her rival to Chaumont-sur-Loire (*see The Green Guide Châteaux of the Loire*) and dismissed the architect in charge of the building work, Philibert Delorme, who was Diane's protégé. He was replaced by the Italian Primaticcio;

Château de Fontainebleau

those working under him, including Niccolo dell'Abbate, favoured light, cheerful colours.

Henri IV's palace – 17C

Henri IV, who adored Fontainebleau, had the palace enlarged quite significantly. The irregular contours of the Oval Court were corrected and he gave orders to build the Kitchen Court and the Real Tennis Court (*Jeu de Paume*). These he had decorated by a new group of artists of largely Flemish, and not Italian, inspiration: frescoes were replaced by oil paintings on plaster or canvas. In the same way, the plain wood panelling highlighted with gilding gave way to painted wainscot. This was the Second Fontainebleau School, whose representatives moved in Parisian circles.

The House of Eternity

Louis XIV, XV and XVI undertook numerous renovations aimed at embellishing their apartments. The Revolution spared the château but emptied it of its precious furniture. Napoléon, who became consul, then emperor, thoroughly enjoyed staying at the palace. He preferred Fontainebleau to Versailles, where he felt haunted by a phantom rival. He called the palace "The House of Eternity" and left his mark by commissioning further refurbishments. The last rulers of France also took up residence in this historic palace. It was eventually turned into a museum under the Republic.

Military and Equestrian Tradition

Throughout French history, whether under monarchic or republican rule, independent units have been posted to Fontainebleau. Tradition, it seems, favoured the cavalry, present in the 17C with the king's bodyguard. A number of racecourses and riding schools were created under Napoléon III; the Centre National des Sports Équestres perpetuates this tradition, while the forest caters to riding enthusiasts.

The history of the town has been marked by several military organisations, notably the École Spéciale Militaire (1803 to 1808, before St-Cyr), the polygon-shaped École d'Application d'Artillerie et du Génie (1871 to 1914) and the SHAPE (Supreme Headquarters, Allied Powers, Europe) headquarters of NATO, which gave the town a cosmopolitan touch from 1947 to 1967.

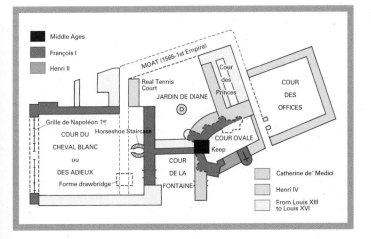

Legend:
- Middle Ages
- François I
- Henri II
- Catherine de' Medici
- Henri IV
- From Louis XIII to Louis XVI

MOAT (1565-1st Empire)

Real Tennis Court
JARDIN DE DIANE
Cour des Princes
COUR DES OFFICES
COUR OVALE
Grille de Napoléon 1er
COUR DU CHEVAL BLANC ou DES ADIEUX
Horseshoe Staircase
Keep
Forme drawbridge
COUR DE LA FONTAINE

The Palace★★★

Exterior *1hr*

Cour du Cheval Blanc or des Adieux★★ – This former bailey was used only by domestics, but its generous size soon earmarked it for official parades and tournaments. It was sometimes called the White Horse Court after the day Charles IX set up a plaster cast of the equestrian statue of Marcus Aurelius in Rome; a small slab in the central alley marks its former location.

The golden eagles seemingly hovering above the pillars of the main gate remind visitors that the Emperor had this made into his main courtyard. He gave orders to raze the Renaissance buildings that lay to the west of the court, but kept the end pavilions. It is clear, walking between the two long wings, that only the one on the left

with its brick courses has retained the elegance that characterised the work of Gilles Le Breton, François I's favourite architect. The right wing – which boasted the Ulysses Gallery decorated under the supervision of Primaticcio – was dismantled by Louis XV and rebuilt by Jacques-Ange Gabriel.

At the far end of the court the main block, fronted by a balustrade marking the site of the former moat, was completed in several stages from the reign of François I to that of Louis XV. Nonetheless the façades show a certain unity of style. The large horizontal planes of the blue slating are broken by the white façades, the trapezoidal roofs and the tall chimneys of the five pavilions. The celebrated horseshoe staircase executed by Jean du Cerceau during the reign of Louis XIII is a harmoniously curved,

The Farewell

On 20 April 1814 **Emperor Napoléon Bonaparte** appeared at the top of the horseshoe staircase; it was 1pm. The foreign army commissioners in charge of escorting him away were waiting in their carriages at the foot of the steps. Napoléon started to walk down the staircase with great dignity, his hand resting on the stone balustrade, his face white with contained emotion. He stopped for a moment while contemplating his guards standing to attention, then moved forward to the group of officers surrounding the Eagle, led by General Petit. His farewell speech, deeply moving, was both an appeal to the spirit of patriotism and a parting tribute to those who had followed him throughout his career. After embracing the general, Bonaparte kissed the flag, threw himself into one of the carriages and was whisked away amid the tearful shouts of his soldiers.

extravagant composition showing clearly royalty's taste for splendour.

Cour de la Fontaine★ – The fountain at the edge of the pond (*Étang des Carpes*) used to yield remarkably clear water. This was kept exclusively for the king's use and to that end the spring was guarded by two sentinels night and day.

The present fountain dates back to 1812 and is crowned by a statue of Ulysses. The surrounding buildings feature stone masonry and the whole ensemble forms a pleasant courtyard. At the far end, the Galerie François I is fronted by a terrace; it rests on a row of arches which once opened onto the king's bathroom suite. The **Aile de la Belle cheminée** on the right was built by Primaticcio around 1565. The name originated from the fireplace that adorned the vast first-floor hall until the 18C. At that point in history Louis XV – who had turned the room into a theatre and rechristened it Aile de l'Ancienne Comédie – dismantled the fireplace, and the low-relief carvings were scattered. The monumental external steps consist of a dog-legged staircase with two straight flights in the Italian style.

On the left the Queen Mothers' and Pope's wing ends in the Grand Pavilion built by Gabriel.

Étang des Carpes★ **(Carp Pond)** – In the centre of the pond – alive with carp – stands a small pavilion built under Henri IV, renovated under Louis XIV and restored by Napoléon. It was used for refreshments and light meals.

Porte Dorée★ – Dated 1528, this gatehouse is part of an imposing pavilion. It was the official entrance to the palace until Henri IV built the Porte du Baptistère. The paintings by Primaticcio have all been restored and the tympanum sports a stylised salamander, François I's emblem. On the two upper levels are Italian-style loggias. The first floor – its loggia sealed off by large bay windows – used to house Mme de Maintenon's suite.

The ballroom is flanked by an avenue of lime trees. The view from the bay windows is splendid and it is regrettable that the initial plans to build an open-air loggia were changed on account of the climate. The east end of the two-storeyed chapel dedicated to St Saturnin can be seen in the distance.

Porte du Baptistère★ – The gateway opens onto the Oval Court. The base of the gateway is the rustic entrance with decorative sandstone that once held the drawbridge across the old moat. It opened onto the Cour du Cheval-Blanc and was designed by Primaticcio. It is crowned by a wide arch surmounted by a dome. The gateway is named after the christening of Louis XIII and his two

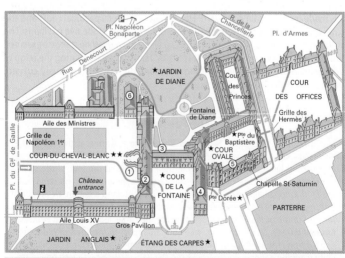

① Horseshoe staircase
② Aile des Reines-Mères et du Pape
③ Galerie François 1er
④ Aile de la Belle Cheminée
⑤ Ballroom
⑥ Real Tennis Court

sisters, Élisabeth and Chrétienne, celebrated with great pomp on a dais on 14 September 1606.

Cour Ovale★ – This is by far the most ancient and the most interesting courtyard of Fontainebleau Palace. The site was the bailey of the original stronghold; of the latter there remains only the keep, named after St Louis, although it was probably built prior to his reign. François I incorporated it into the structure he had erected on the foundations of the old castle, shaped like an oval or rather a polygon with rounded corners. Under Henri IV, the courtyard lost its shape, although not its name; the east side was enlarged, and the wings were aligned and squared by two new pavilions framing the new Porte du Baptistère. The general layout of the palace was preserved.

Cour des Offices – The entrance faces the Porte du Baptistère and is guarded by two arresting sandstone heads depicting Hermes, sculpted by Gilles Guérin in 1640. The Cour des Offices was built by Henri IV in 1609; it is a huge oblong, sealed off on three sides by austere buildings alternating with low pavilions. With its imposing porch executed in the style of city gates, it bears a strong resemblance to a square. Walk through the gate and admire its architecture from place d'Armes; the sandstone front presents rusticated work and has a large niche as its centrepiece.

Continue the tour of the palace exterior. The east and north wings of the Cour des Princes are two functional buildings designed or redesigned under Louis XV to provide further accommodation for members of the court.

Jardin de Diane★ – The queen's formal garden created by Catherine de' Medici was designed by Henri IV and bordered by an orangery on its northern side. In the 19C the orangery was torn down and the park turned into a landscape garden. Diana's fountain, an elegant display of stonework dated 1603, has survived in the middle of the grounds. It has now resumed its original appearance; the four bronze dogs formerly exhibited in the Louvre Museum sit obediently at the feet of their mistress, the hunting goddess.

Grands Appartements★★★

♿🕐 Apr–Sept, Wed–Mon 9.30am–6pm; Oct–Mar, Wed–Mon 9.30am–5pm; last admission 45min before closing. 🕐1 Jan, 1 May, 25 Dec. ✆12.50€ (under-18s no charge), no charge 1st Sun in the month. ☎01 60 71 50 70. www.musee-chateau-fontainebleau.fr.

The main apartments are reached by the stucco staircase (a), the Galerie des Fastes (b) and the Galerie des Assiettes (c) which features 128 beautifully decorated pieces of Sèvres porcelain.

Chapelle de la Trinité★ – The chapel takes its name from the Trinitarian church set up on the premises by St Louis. Henri IV had the sanctuary reinforced by vaulting and then decorated. Martin Fréminet (1567-1619), one of the lesser-known followers of Michelangelo, painted the arches with strong, vigorous scenes characterised by perspective and a daring use of foreshortening. The scenes represent the mystery of the Redemption and a number of figures from the Old Testament.

It was in this chapel that Louis XV was wedded to Marie Leszczynska in 1725 and that Louis Napoléon, later to be Napoléon III, was christened in 1810.

Galerie de François I★★★ – This gallery was built from 1528 to 1530 and was originally open on both sides, resembling a covered passageway. When Louis XVI enlarged it in 1786, he filled in the windows looking onto Diana's garden. A set of false French windows was fitted for reasons of symmetry. The greater part of the decoration – closely combining fresco and stucco work – was supervised by Rosso, while the wood panelling was entrusted to an Italian master carpenter. François I's monogram and his emblem the salamander were widely represented.

The scenes are difficult to interpret (there are no explanatory documents), though they seem to split into two groups, one on either side of the central bay which is adorned with an oval painting depicting two figures: Danaë by Primaticcio and *The Nymph of Fontainebleau* (1860) after Rosso.

The east side, near a bust of François I, features mostly violent scenes, perhaps referring to the recent misfortunes of

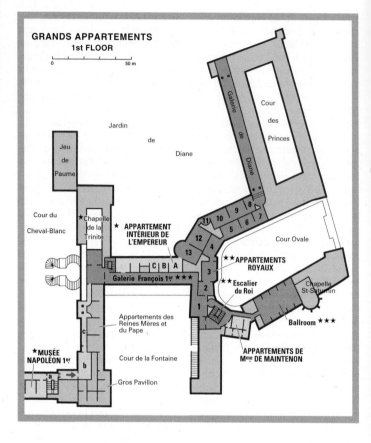

GRANDS APPARTEMENTS
1st FLOOR

the French king (the defeat of Pavia, the king's captivity in Madrid), the inescapable nature of war and death (the battle between the Centaurs and the Lapiths, Youth and Old Age, the Destruction of the Greek fleet). Beneath the vignette depicting Venus and Love at the edge of a pond, note the miniature picture set in a tablet, representing the château around 1540 with both the gallery and the Porte Dorée clearly visible.

On the west side, near the entrance, the décor exemplifies the sacred qualities of the royal function – Sacrifice, the Unity of the State – and the concept of filial piety in the old-fashioned sense of the word (the twins Cleobis and Biton): the king, his mother Louise of Savoy and his sister Marguerite d'Angoulême were devoted to one another.

The most striking scene is the portrait of an elephant whose caparison bears the royal monogram; the pachyderm

no doubt symbolises the perennity of the monarchy.

Escalier du Roi★★ – The staircase was built in 1749, under Louis XV, in what was once the bedchamber of the Duchess of Étampes, François I's favourite. The murals – the history of Alexander the Great – are by Primaticcio (note Alexander taming Bucephalus above the door) and dell'Abbate (Alexander placing Homer's books in a chest, on the far wall). Primaticcio's stucco work is highly original; the upper frieze is punctuated by caryatids with elongated bodies.

Salle de Bal★★★ (Ballroom) – This room (30m/100ft long and 10m/33ft wide) was traditionally reserved for banquets and formal receptions. It was begun under François I and completed by Philibert Delorme under Henri II. A thorough restoration programme has revived the dazzling frescoes and paintings by Primaticcio and his pupil

Salle de Bal

dell'Abbate. The marquetry of the parquet floor, completed under Louis-Philippe, echoes the splendid coffered ceiling, richly highlighted with silver and gold. The monumental fireplace features two telamones, cast after Antique statues in the Capitol Museum in Rome.

Appartements de Mme de Maintenon – Note the delicate wainscoting in the Grand Salon, most of which was executed in the 17C.

Appartements royaux★★ – At the time of François I, Fontainebleau featured a single suite of apartments laid out around the Oval Court. Towards 1565, the regent Catherine de' Medici gave orders to double the curved building between the Oval Court and Diana's Garden. Subsequently, the royal bedrooms, closets and private salons overlooked Diana's Garden. The original suite now houses antechambers, guard-rooms and reception rooms where the king used to entertain his guests.

Salle des Gardes (1) – Late 16C ceiling and frieze.

A wide arch leads from the **Salle du Buffet (2)** to a chamber in the oldest tower of the castle.

Salle du Donjon (3) – Until the reign of Henri IV this sombre room was occupied by French kings who used it as a bedroom, hence its other name, the St Louis Bedroom. The equestrian low-relief sculpture (c. 1600) portraying Henri IV

on the fireplace came from the "Belle Cheminée." It was carved by Mathieu Jacquet.

Salon Louis XIII (4) – It was here that Louis XIII was born on 27 September 1601. His birth is evoked by the coffered ceiling which depicts Cupid riding a dolphin (the word dauphin means both dolphin and heir to the throne). The panel with painted wainscoting is crowned by a set of 11 pictures by Ambroise Dubois; the Romance between Theagenes and Chariclea, works dating from c 1610.

Salon François I (5) – Of Primaticcio's work there remains only the fireplace.

Salon des Tapisseries (6) – This room, having been the queen's chamber, the guard-room and the queen's first antechamber, became the empress's principal drawing room in 1804, the guardroom once more in 1814 and finally the Tapestry Salon in 1837.

The fireplace dates from 1731 and the Renaissance ceiling in pine wood is the work of Poncet (1835). The furniture was made during the Second Empire (mid-19C). The tapestries telling the story of Psyche were manufactured in Paris in the first half of the 17C.

Antichambre de l'Impératrice (7) – Formerly the queen's guard-room, this chamber was built on the site of the old royal staircase; the ceiling and panelling are both dated 1835. The Gobelins tapestries, executed after cartoons by Le Brun, illustrate the four seasons. The Second Empire furniture features a console, a carved-oak writing desk (Fourdinois, 1865) and a set of armchairs of English inspiration. Note the two Indian-style enamel vases produced by the Sèvres factory.

Galerie de Diane – This long gilt passageway (80m/263ft) was decorated during the Restoration and turned into a library under the Second Empire.

Salon blanc- Petit salon de la Reine (8) – In 1835 the room was decorated with furnishings from an earlier period: Louis XV wainscoting, Louis XVI fireplace inlaid with bronze etc. The furniture is Empire: chairs in gilt wood by Jacob Frères, settee, armchairs and chairs from St-Cloud, mahogany console and heads of fantastic animals in bronzed, gilt wood (Jacob Desmalter).

Grand Salon de l'Impératrice (9) – This drawing room, formerly the queen's gaming room, features a ceiling painted by Berthélemy; the scene is Minerva crowning the Muses.

The furniture dates from the reign of Louis XVI (chests by Stöckel and Beneman, seats upholstered with painted satin, a carpet made by the Savonnerie works) or from the First Empire (seats and chests by Jacob Desmalter, the so-called "Seasons Table" made of Sèvres porcelain and painted by Georget in 1806-7, and a carpet rewoven to an old design). The two sets of furniture are displayed in turn.

Chambre de l'Impératrice (10) – This used to be the queen's bedroom. The greater part of the ceiling was designed for Anne of Austria in 1644; the wood panelling, the fireplace and the top of the alcove were created for Marie Leszczynska in 1747 and the doors with arabesque motifs were installed for Marie-Antoinette in 1787. The brocaded silk was rewoven according to the original pattern in Lyon at the end of Louis XVI's reign. Among the furniture note Marie-Antoinette's bed, designed in 1787 by Hauré, Sené and Laurent, a set of armchairs attributed to Jacob Frères and several commodes by Stöckel and Beneman (1786). The vases are Sèvres porcelain.

Boudoir de la Reine (11) – This delightful room was designed by Marie-Antoinette. The wainscoting was painted by Bourgois and Touzé after sketches by the architect Rousseau. The ceiling – representing sunrise – is the work of Berthélemy. The roll-top writing desk and the work table were made by Riesener in 1786.

Salle du Trône (12) – This was the king's bedroom from Henri IV to Louis XVI; Napoléon converted it into the throne room. The ornate mural paintings, dating from several periods, were harmonised in the 18C. Above the fireplace is a full-length portrait of Louis XIII, painted in Philippe de Champaigne's studio.

Salle du Trône

Salle du Conseil (13) – This room was given a semicircular extension in 1773. The ceiling and panelling are splendid examples of Louis XV decoration.

Five pictures by Boucher adorn the ceiling, representing the four seasons and Apollo, conqueror of Night. The wainscoting presents an alternation of allegorical figures painted in blue or pink monochrome by Van Loo and Jean-Baptiste Pierre.

Appartement Intérieur de l'Empereur★ – *Visit included in the tour of the Grands Appartements.* **Napoléon** had his suite installed in the wing built by Louis XVI, on the garden side running parallel with the François I Gallery.

Chambre de Napoléon (A) – Most of the decoration – dating from the Louis XVI period – has survived. The furniture is typically Empire.

Petite chambre à coucher (B) – A little private study which Bonaparte furnished with a day bed in gilded iron.

Salon de l'Abdication (C) – According to tradition, this is the room in which the famous abdication document was signed on 6 April 1814. The Empire furniture in this red drawing room dates back to that momentous time.

The François I Gallery leads to the Vestibule du Fer-à-cheval, at the top of the curved steps of the same name. This was the official entrance to the palace from the late 17C onwards. Both the gallery of the chapel and the Appartements des Reines-Mères give onto this hall.

Musée chinois★ – *Intermittently, check the information each day. Apr–Sept, Wed–Mon 9.30am–6pm; Oct–Mar 9.30am–5pm. 1 Jan, 1 May, 25 Dec. Admission included in the ticket for the visit to the Grands Appartements. 01 60 71 50 70.*

This small museum, commissioned by Empress Eugénie on the ground floor of the Gros Pavillon, comes as a surprise because of the contrast between the comfortable, heavy furniture and the slender elegance of the objects on show. The collection was originally the booty captured during the Franco-British conflict with China in 1860, especially as a result of the ransacking of the imperial palace. The following year, a delegation

of Siamese ambassadors completed the collection with a number of opulent presents, an event which was faithfully recorded in a painting by Gérôme.

The tour begins in the **antechamber** decorated with two luxurious Siamese palanquins. The "**nouveaux salons**" beyond are decorated with crimson wall hangings, padded armchairs, ebony furniture and objects from China and Siam. Most of the collection, however, is to be seen in the **cabinet de laque** decorated with 15 panels from an 18C Chinese fan. Note the four large tapestries on the ceiling and the huge glass-fronted cabinet filled to the brim with objects, including a copy of the Siamese royal crown.

Musée Napoléon I★

The **museum** *(1hr 15min guided tours on request: daily (except Tue) Apr–Sept 9.30am–6pm; Oct–Mar 9.30am–5pm. 1 Jan, 1 May and 25 Dec. Telephone in the morning for information. Admission included in the ticket for the visit to the Grands Appartements. 01 60 71 50 70)* is dedicated to the Emperor and his family; it occupies 15 rooms on the ground level and first floor of the Louis XV wing. Exhibits include portraits (paintings and sculptures), silverware, arms, medals, ceramics (Imperial service), clothing (coronation robes, uniforms) and personal memorabilia. Thanks to the numerous works of art and furniture adorning their interior, these apartments have kept their princely character.

The rooms on the first floor evoke the Coronation (paintings by François Gérard), the Emperor's various military campaigns, his daily life (remarkable folding desk by Jacob Desmalter), the Empress Marie-Louise in formal attire or painting the Emperor's portrait (picture by Alexandre Menjaud) and the birth of Napoléon's son, the future King of Rome (cradles).

The ground floor presents the Emperor's close relations. Each of the seven rooms is devoted to a member of the family: Napoléon's mother, his brothers Joseph, Louis and Jérôme and his sisters Elisa, Pauline and Caroline.

Address Book

For coin ranges, see the Legend on the cover flap.

GETTING THERE

To access from Paris take the SNCF rail link from Gare de Lyon.

WHERE TO STAY

Hôtel Victoria – *112 r. de France.* ☎*01 60 74 90 00. resa@hotelvictoria.com* P *20 rooms.* This 19C building is a pleasant, relaxing place to stay. Most of the rooms on its three floors have been redone in shades of yellow and blue; five of them have a marble fireplace. Breakfast is served on the veranda or the terrace looking toward the garden.

Hôtel de la Chancellerie – *1 r. de la Chancellerie.* ☎*01 64 22 21 70. www. hotel-la-chancellerie-fontainebleau. com. 25 rooms .* This small hotel in the heart of the city is located in the former buildings of the chancellery. The small rooms are bright and practical and the reception is amiable. An appealing address for those on a budget.

WHERE TO EAT

L'Île aux Truites – *6 chemin de la Basse-Varenne, 77870 Vulaines-sur-Seine – 7km/4.2mi E of Fontainebleau dir. Samo-reau.* ☎*01 64 23 71 87. Closed 20 Dec to 25 Jan, Thu lunch and Wed – Reservations required.* A pretty thatched-roof country house well-situated on the banks of the Seine. Diners can savour trout and salmon culled from the restaurant's fish tank while enjoying an incomparable view of the river and forest. Summertime, meals are served outdoors.

Croquembouche – *43 r. de France.* ☎*01 64 22 01 57. Closed Aug, Christmas school holidays, Sun evening, Thu lunch and Wed.* A plain and simple restaurant in centre city frequented by regular patrons who appreciate the warm reception, the inviting dining room decorated in soothing colours, and the traditional food prepared from fresh produce.

ON THE TOWN

Le Franklin-Roosevelt – *20 r. Grande.* ☎*01 64 22 28 73. Mon-Sat 10am–1am.* This wine bar aims to please. Note the inviting décor featuring mahogany furniture and red leatherette wall seats, the library dedicated to the period between 1890 and 1920, the intimate ambience with jazz in the background and some fine vintages on the wine menu. Heated terrace.

SHOPPING

La Ferme des Sablons – *19 r. des Sablons.* ☎*01 64 22 67 25. Tue–Fri 8am–1pm, 3.30–7:30pm; Sat 8am–7.30pm; Sun 8am–1pm. Closed Aug.* A third of the 130 varieties of cheese sold by this cheese shop are matured on site, including the house speciality, le Fontainebleau, a soft white cheese with cream. There is also a selection of local products. A pleasant, pastoral setting.

SPORT

Jeu de Paume de Fontainebleau – *Château de Fontainebleau.* ☎*01 64 22 47 67. http://jdpfontainebleau.free. fr. Daily 9am–9pm.* The jeu de paume, a sport whose descendants include tennis and squash, has been played since 1601 in this indoor court of the Château de Fontainebleau. Visitors can watch a match or try a game themselves.

Petits Appartements et Galerie des Cerfs

Guided tours (1hr15) on request daily (except Tue): Apr–Sept 9.30am–6pm; Oct-Mar 9.30am–5pm. *1 Jan, 1 May and 25 Dec. Telephone in the morning for information. Admission included in the ticket for the visit to the Grands Appartements.* ☎*01 60 71 50 60.*

These rooms are located on the ground floor below the François I Gallery and the Royal Suite overlooking the Jardin de Diane.

Petits Appartements de Napoléon I – This suite comprises François I's former bathroom suite (located beneath the gallery and converted into private rooms under Louis XV for the king, Mme de

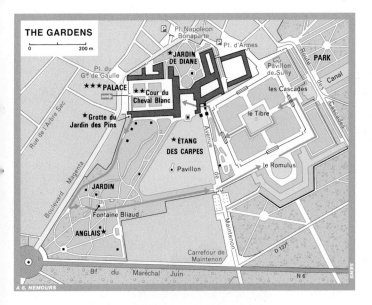

THE GARDENS
0   200 m

P   Pl. Napoléon Bonaparte
P   Pl. d'Armes
★ **JARDIN DE DIANE**
Pl. du Gal de Gaulle
PARK
Pavillon de Sully
★★★ **PALACE**
les Cascades
★★ **Cour du Cheval Blanc**
★ **Grotte du Jardin des Pins**
le Tibre
Rue de l'Arbre Sec
★ **ÉTANG DES CARPES**
le Romulus
Pavillon
Boulevard
Magenta
JARDIN
Fontaine Bliaud
ANGLAIS ★
Avenue de
Maintenon
Carrefour de Maintenon
D 137^c
B^d   du   Maréchal   Juin
N 6
A 6, NEMOURS
SENS
Route des Cascades
Canal

Pompadour and Mme du Barry), and the ground floor of the new Louis XVI wing, situated under the Imperial Suite. The rooms opening onto the garden have been decorated with Louis XV wainscoting and Empire furniture.

Appartements de l'Impératrice Joséphine★ – This suite of rooms adorned with Louis XV panelling was designed for Joséphine in 1808. It lies beneath the grand royal suite.

The study, with its large rotunda, is located beneath the Council Chamber (*first floor*). The Empire furniture here has a feminine touch: Marie-Louise's tambour frame, her easel etc. The Salon Jaune constitutes one of the palace's most perfect examples of Empire decoration. The gold-coloured wall hangings provide an elegant setting for Jacob Desmalter's choice furniture set off by a large Aubusson carpet with a white background.

Galerie des Cerfs★ – The gallery is decorated with deer heads. The mural paintings show palatial residences at the time of Henri IV, seen in perspective. It was in this gallery that Queen Christina of Sweden had her favourite, Monaldeschi, assassinated in 1657.

Gardens★

These consist of the Jardin de Diane, the Landscape Garden, the parterre and the park.

▶ *Follow the route indicated on the map below.*

Grotte du Jardin des Pins★

This rare ornamental composition carved in sandstone reveals the popular taste, copied from the Italians, for ponds, manmade features and bucolic landscapes in vogue toward the end of François I's reign. The rusticated arches are supported by giant telamones. The frescoes have disappeared.

Jardin anglais★

The garden was created in 1812 on the site of former gardens (featuring a pine grove) redesigned under Louis XIV and abandoned during the Revolution. The Bliaut or Blaut fountain, which gave its name to the palace, plays in a small octagonal basin in the middle of the garden.

Park

The park was created by Henri IV, who filled the canal (in 1609) and had the grounds planted with elms, pines and fruit trees.

Pont Alexandre III at dusk
©Paul Reid/Dreamstime.com

WHERE TO STAY

👜 *See Address Book (opposite page) for a list of hotels by neighbourhood.*

👜 *For coin ranges, see the Legend on the cover flap.*

For a further list including prices of hotels and restaurants, look in the red-cover **Michelin Guide Paris and Environs**.

ECONOMY CHAIN HOTELS

These can be useful, as they are inexpensive (from around 27€ to 55€ for a double room) and generally located near main roads. While breakfast is available, there may not be a restaurant; rooms are small, with a television and bathroom.

🛏 **Etap Hôtel**: ☎0 892 688 900 (in France, 0.34€ per min); www.etaphotel.com.
🛏 **Mister Bed**: ☎01 46 14 38 00; www.misterbed.fr.
🛏 **B&B Hôtels**: ☎01 72 36 51 06; www.hotel-bb.com.

Note: Some establishments won't accept pets, while others will put them up for a fee. Remember to enquire when you reserve.

BED AND BREAKFAST

Bed & Breakfast (France)
PO Box 47085, Henley-on-Thames, London SW18 9AB
☎0871 781 0834;
Fax: 0871 781 0835;
www.bedbreak.com.

Alcôve et Agapes
8 bis rue Coysevox, 75018 Paris
☎01 44 85 06 05; www.bed-and-breakfast-in-paris.com.

Une Chambre en Ville
10 rue Fagon, 75013 Paris
☎01 44 06 96 71;
www.chambre-ville.com.

YOUTH HOSTELS

There are two main youth hostel *(auberge de jeunesse)* associations in France.

● **Ligue Française pour les Auberges de Jeunesse,**
67 rue Vergniaud, 75013 Paris,
☎01 44 16 78 78; www.auberges-de-jeunesse.com.

● **Fédération Unie des Auberges de Jeunesse,**
27 rue Pajol, 75018 Paris, ☎01 44 89 87 28; www.fuaj.org. Holders of an International Youth Hostel Federation card should contact the IYHF in their own country for information and membership applications (US ☎202 783 6161; UK ☎01707 324 170).

Selected Hotels by District

For each neighbourhood described in the *Discovering* section, the corresponding *arrondissement* is always mentioned, so that you can choose among the establishments listed geographically. To make your stay in Paris a success, we have included a wide range of establishments. Whether in bustling, lively neighbourhoods or close to the main monuments, from the most sophisticated to the simplest, there is something for every budget, enabling visitors to get a real sense of life in the capital. You may also wish to experience the posh décor and atmosphere of the mythical palace hotels by dropping in for brunch or a cup of tea. But please remember: correct attire is often *de rigueur* in these elegant places. Rooms are rented per night and breakfast is extra unless otherwise noted. It is recommended to reserve ahead – Parisian hotels are often fully booked. Keep in mind that you are expected to reconfirm if you plan to arrive after 5 or 6pm. This is essential in many hotels, where your room may be given away if you fail to call or fax your confirmation and your time of arrival.

Obviously, comfort and quality were essential selection criteria. Each and every establishment was visited and inspected. It is, of course, possible that things have changed since our last stay. Please let us know if it has!

Address Book

1ST ARRONDISSEMENT

CHÂTELET-HÔTEL DE VILLE – CONCORDE – HALLES – LOUVRE – MADELEINE – PALAIS-ROYAL – TUILERIES

◎◎▤█**Hôtel Britannique** – *20 av. Victoria.* ▥*Châtelet.* ☎*01 42 33 74 59. www.hotel-britannique.fr. 40 rooms.* ☑*14€.* How very British! Reminiscent of a scene from an Agatha Christie novel, the English flavour of this hotel located just behind Châtelet is further accentuated by the copies of Turner paintings hanging on the walls. Rooms, though less representative, are nonetheless pleasant and breakfasts are ample.

◎◎▤█**Hôtel Ducs de Bourgogne** – *19 rue du Pont-Neuf.* ▥*Pont-Neuf.* ☎*01 42 33 95 64. www.hotel-paris-bourgogne. com. 50 rooms.* ☑*11€.* This 19C building halfway between the Pont Neuf and the Forum des Halles is set right in the heart of the capital. Antique furniture and a tasteful colour scheme give the lobby a plush feel, while the rooms, of varying sizes, are more sober.

◎◎▤█**Hôtel Place du Louvre** – *21 rue des Prêtres-St-Germain-l'Auxerrois.* ▥*Pont-Neuf or Louvre-Rivoli.* ☎*01 42 33 78 68. www.esprit-de-france. com. 20 rooms.* ☑*11€.* An excellent address for Louvre lovers. At a minute's walk from the museum, one could easily spend the days visiting its every corner from top to bottom and from morning 'til night, if so desired. The hotel's other strong points are its central location, shipshape rooms and 5th floor duplexes.

2ND ARRONDISSEMENT

GRANDS BOULEVARDS – HALLES – PLACE DES VICTOIRES – SENTIER

◎**Hôtel Tiquetonne** – *6 rue Tiquetonne.* ▥ *Étienne-Marcel.* ☎*01 42 36 94 58. Closed Aug and Christmas school holidays. 47 rooms.* ☑*5€.* A modest family hotel in a semi-pedes-

trian street a few steps from Les Halles and Rue Montorgueil. The bright rooms, with their old-fashioned charm, are quite well kept and, above all, very inexpensive.

◎◎**Hôtel Favart Opéra** – *5 rue Marivaux.* ▥*Richelieu-Drouot.* ☎*01 42 97 59 83. www.hotel-favartopera.com. 37 rooms.* ☑*8€.* Goya, the artist, stayed here in 1824 while sketching life *à la Parisienne.* And what better glimpse could one have? Located just opposite the Opéra-Comique, this hotel is set in a very lively neighbourhood. Some rooms have period furniture and exposed beams overhead.

◎◎**Hôtel Vivienne** – *40 rue Vivienne.* ▥*Bourse.* ☎*01 42 33 13 26. www.hotel-vivienne.com. 45 rooms.* ☑*6€.* Two minutes from the stock exchange and the Palais-Royal, this tidy little establishment enables visitors to discover Paris on foot: the Grands Boulevards, department stores and Opéra Garnier are all just a few strides away. Simple rooms and a pleasant welcome.

3RD ARRONDISSEMENT

MARAIS – RÉPUBLIQUE

◎◎**Hôtel de Roubaix** – *6 rue Greneta.* ▥*Réamur-Sebastopol.* ☎*01 42 72 89 91. www.hotel-de-roubaix.com. 53 rooms.* An old-fashioned hotel with a grandmotherly feel near the Centre Pompidou and Les Halles. Tiled bathrooms with walk-in showers and breakfast included. At these rates, book well in advance!

◎◎▤█**Hôtel Pavillon de la Reine** – *28 pl. des Vosges.* ▥*Chemin-Vert.* ☎*01 40 29 19 19. www.pavillon-de-la-reine.com. 31 rooms.* ☑*25€.* Set in a courtyard garden on the Place des Vosges, this is one the most beautiful hotels in the city. Protected from the commotion of the capital, you'll delight in the refined décor where handsome woodwork, old stones, beautiful fabrics and antique furniture all create a posh, cosy atmosphere.

⊜⊜⊜**Meslay République** – *3 rue Meslay.* Ⓜ*République.* ☎*01 42 72 79 79. www.parishotel-meslay.com. 39 rooms.* ⊿*8.50€.* Situated in a quiet street a stone's throw from the Place de la République, this hotel with a listed façade lays Paris at your feet. A few steps from the Marais, not far from the Bastille and close to the business districts, it is perfect for business and pleasure.

4TH ARRONDISSEMENT

BASTILLE – BEAUBOURG – CHÂTELET- HÔTEL DE VILLE – ÎLE SAINT-LOUIS – MARAIS – NOTRE-DAME

⊜⊜**Hôtel Jeanne d'Arc** – *3 rue de Jarente.* Ⓜ*Saint-Paul or Bastille.* ☎*01 48 87 62 11. www.hoteljeannedarc.com. 36 rooms.* This hotel behind the Place du Marché-Ste-Catherine was built in the 17C. The lobby is adorned with a unique mirror framed by mosaics. The prices are reasonable and the degree of comfort very satisfactory, so book ahead. The colourful renovated rooms are the best; the others are more ordinary.

⊜⊜⊜**Acacias – Hôtel-de-Ville** – *20 rue du Temple.* Ⓜ*Hôtel-de-Ville.* ☎*01 48 87 07 70. www.acacias-hotel. com. 33 rooms.* ⊿*9€.* This old building is not particularly attractive, but the location is excellent. The well fitted-out bedrooms are decorated in a simple, modern spirit.

⊜⊜⊜**Andréa Rivoli** – *3 rue St-Bon.* Ⓜ*Châtelet or Hôtel-de-Ville.* ☎*01 42 78 43 93. 32 rooms.* ⊿*9€.* You won't regret having chosen this extremely well located, central hotel: from the reception desk to the bedrooms, while passing through the breakfast room, everything here is spanking new. Up-to-the-minute décor and air conditioning throughout. A sure bet.

⊜⊜⊜**Hôtel du 7e Art** – *20 rue St-Paul.* Ⓜ *Saint-Paul.* ☎*01 44 54 85 00. 23 rooms.* ⊿*8€.* The name says it all: cinema, and more particularly the films of 1940–60, is the underlying theme of this hotel's interior design. Ask for a room with exposed beams on the 3rd or 4th floor. Guest laundry room. The breakfast room has a rustic appeal.

⊜⊜⊜**Hôtel Hospitel** – *1 pl. du Parvis.* Ⓜ*Cité.* ☎*01 44 32 01 00. www.hotel- hospitel.com. 14 rooms.* ⊿*8€.* It would be hard to find a more central location than this hotel next door to Notre-Dame Cathedral. It's actually hidden on the top floor of the Hôtel Dieu Hospital, and although usually reserved by family of hospital guests, its air-conditioned, spotless rooms are open to the public when available. Private bath, TV and telephone, and room service for meals (⊜). A true deal.

⊜⊜⊜**Grand Hôtel Malher** – *5 rue Malher.* Ⓜ*Saint-Paul.* ☎*01 42 72 60 92. www.grandhotelmalher.com. 31 rooms.* ⊿*9€.* Conveniently situated for strolling around the Marais, this hotel has an ancient façade that conceals modern rooms decorated with painted wood furniture and colourful fabrics. Pleasantly quiet on the courtyard side; well-soundproofed on the street side.

⊜⊜⊜**St-Louis Marais** – *1 rue Charles-V.* Ⓜ*Bastille.* ☎*01 48 87 87 04. www. saintlouismarais.com. 19 rooms.* ⊿*10€.* A most charming little establishment, this hotel is housed in a building dating from 1740. The smallish rooms are stylish, with their ceilings crossed by time-worn beams. Rustic, carefully thought-out décor in the reception area.

⊜⊜⊜**Hôtel de la Place des Vosges** – *12 rue de Birague.* Ⓜ*Bastille.* ☎*01 42 72 60 46. www.hotelplacedesvosges.com. 16 rooms.* ⊿*8€.* Here's a hotel with character. Built in the 17C, its reasonably sized rooms are simply furnished, while the reception area blends old stones, exposed beams and tapestries. A sophisticated stopover next to one of the most beautiful squares in Paris.

⊜⊜⊜**Hôtel Bretonnerie** – *22 rue Ste-Croix-de-la-Bretonnerie.* Ⓜ*Hôtel-de-Ville.* ☎*01 48 87 77 63. www.bretonnerie. com. 22 rooms, 7 suites.* ⊿*9.50€.* Treat yourself to a sojourn in this private 17C mansion in the bosom of the Marais. The peaceful environment, beamed ceilings and old-fashioned fabrics all contribute to the warm appeal of its rooms.

5TH ARRONDISSEMENT

JARDIN DES PLANTES – JUSSIEU – LUXEMBOURG – MAUBERT – MOUFFETARD – QUARTIER LATIN

⊜**Hôtel Les Argonautes** – *12 rue de la Huchette.* Ⓜ*Saint-Michel.* ☎*01 43 54 09 82. www.hotel-les-argonautes.*

com. 25 rooms. ⬭5€. Restaurant⬭⬭. African masks, objects, drawings: a rich décor from the colonies greets you as soon as you walk in. The halls are also quite colourful, contrasting with the sobriety of the bare-walled bedrooms. All around the hotel, various and sundry bars and restaurants teem with life.

⬭⬭**Hôtel de L'Espérance** – 15 rue Pascal. ⓂLes Gobelins or Censier-Daubenton. ☏01 47 07 10 99. www.hotelde lesperance.fr. 38 rooms. ⬭8€. Two strides from Rue Mouffetard and its picturesque fruit and vegetable market, this charming little establishment is decked with flowers, both in window boxes and on the patio. The comfortable, relatively peaceful rooms are decorated in cheerful colours.

⬭⬭**Hôtel St-Jacques** – 35 rue des Écoles. ⓂMaubert-Mutualité. ☏01 44 07 45 45. www.hotel-paris-stjacques. com . 35 rooms. ⬭9.50€. Situated in the heart of the Latin Quarter, here's a hospitable stopover in a 19C building that has retained all of its original plaster mouldings. The bedrooms are spacious, decorated with tasteful furniture and well soundproofed. The lobby walls are decorated with pretty murals. Reasonably priced.

⬭⬭**Hôtel Sunny** – 48 blvd du Port-Royal. ⓂLes Gobelins. ☏01 43 31 79 86. www.hotelsunny.com. 37 rooms. ⬭6€. What are the assets of this hotel hidden behind a façade of the Haussmann style? The functional rooms, with their old rose textiles (ask for one on the courtyard side), the impeccable orderliness and the location just ten minutes' walk from the Panthéon and the Luxembourg gardens.

⬭⬭**Familia Hôtel** – 11 rue des Écoles. ⓂCardinal-Lemoine. ☏01 43 54 55 27. www.hotel-paris-familia. com. 30 rooms. ⬭. This charming little hotel is just a stone's throw from the Mouffetard quarter. Despite its rather out-of-date pseudo-Italian interior, complete with frescoes in the corridors and some of the rooms, it remains a practical, unassuming address. Reasonably priced.

⬭⬭**Hôtel des Grandes Écoles** – 75 rue du Cardinal-Lemoine. ⓂCardinal-Lemoine. ☏01 43 26 79 23. www. hotel-grandes-ecoles.com. 51 rooms.

⬭9€. These three houses resembling rural cottages feature a pretty garden that provides a welcome island of quietude. The main building has retained its somewhat archaic charm, while the other two have been tastefully renovated. Very sought after…

⬭⬭**Hôtel du Mont-Blanc** – 28 rue de la Huchette. ⓂSaint-Michel. ☏01 43 54 22 29. 42 rooms. ⬭6€. Restaurant ⬭⬭. Located in a little street lined with bars and Greek restaurants, this hotel opposite the legendary Théâtre de la Huchette is perfect for all those looking to stay in a neighbourhood as lively by night as by day. The rooms are functional and suitably fitted-out; those in back are quieter. Reasonably priced for the capital.

⬭⬭⬭**Grand Hôtel St-Michel** – 19 rue Cujas. ⓂLuxembourg. ☏01 46 33 33 02. www.grand-hotel-st-michel. com. 46 rooms. ⬭15€. Located near the Sorbonne and the Luxembourg Gardens, this entirely renovated hotel is pleasant indeed. The rooms, with their painted furniture and fluffy feather quilts, are cosy; some have a balcony with a view. Vaulted breakfast room.

⬭⬭⬭**Hôtel Select** – 1 pl. de la Sorbonne. ⓂCluny – La Sorbonne. ☏01 46 34 14 80. www.selecthotel. fr. 67 rooms. Situated on the Place de la Sorbonne, this hotel unifies old stones and new tastes. The drawing rooms are laid out in a gallery around a patio-cum-greenhouse, the staircase, lined with tropical plants, leads up to corridors of bare granite and breakfast is served in a room with stone arches.

6TH ARRONDISSEMENT

INSTITUT DE FRANCE – LUXEMBOURG – MONTPARNASSE – ODÉON – QUARTIER LATIN – SAINT-GERMAIN-DES-PRÉS – SAINT-SULPICE – SÈVRES-BABYLONE

⬭**Hôtel Stella** – 41 rue Monsieur le Prince. ⓂOdéon. ☏01 40 51 00 25. www. site.voila.fr/hotel-stella. 24 rooms. It doesn't get any more authentically old Parisian than this hotel. There are no TVs, no elevator, and no breakfast service, but the exposed wooden beams, tiled floors, aged furnishings and wonky staircase give it the kind of atmosphere that Hemingway, Sartre and Henry Miller must have known in their day. Pick your room online.

🛏️ **Hôtel Delhy's** – *22 rue de l'Hirondelle.* Ⓜ*Saint-Michel – Notre-Dame.* ☎*01 43 26 58 25. 21 rooms.* This little gem in the heart of Paris will delight those on mini budgets. Hidden behind a porch on the place St-Michel, this charmingly old-fashioned family hotel provides quiet accommodation for tired travellers. Most rooms have shared shower and WC.

🛏️ **Hôtel de Nesle** – *7 rue de Nesle.* Ⓜ*Odéon.* ☎*01 43 54 62 41. www.hotel denesleparis.com. 20 rooms.* A minor miracle right in the centre of the Latin Quarter. Each room is decorated according to a different theme, including the colonies, the Orient, the countryside, Molière. the result is surprisingly successful. The garden, planted with Tunisian palm trees, soothes the eyes and the soul.

🛏️ **Résidence du Palais** – *78 rue d'Assas.* Ⓜ*Odéon.* ☎*01 43 26 79 32. www.residencedupalais.com. 24 rooms.* 🍽*10€.* Located on a street overlooking the Luxembourg Gardens, this family-run residence offers breakfast and dinner (🍽) daily in a convivial setting. Rooms are basic but spacious, including quadruples and suites for families. Long stays possible for reduced rates.

🛏️ **Grand Hôtel des Balcons** – *3 rue Casimir-Delavigne.* Ⓜ*Odéon.* ☎*01 46 34 78 50. www.balcons.com. 50 rooms* 🍽*12€.* "Paris is planted in my heart," wrote the Hungarian poet André Ady after a stay here. Downstairs, an enchanting art nouveau style; upstairs, more standardised rooms with small balconies overlooking the street. Reasonable prices for the neighbourhood. Plentiful buffet breakfast.

🛏️ **Hôtel Sèvres Azur** – *22 rue de l'Abbé-Grégoire.* Ⓜ*Saint-Placide.* ☎*01 45 48 84 07. www.hotelsevresazur. com. 31 rooms.* 🍽*10€.* Closed Aug 4–22. Located in a quiet street near the Bon Marché department store, this charming hotel with a tiny flower-filled courtyard has sunny yellow rooms and attractive waxed-wood furniture. Perfect for putting oneself in a Parisian's shoes and strolling about St-Germain-des-Prés and Montparnasse.

🛏️ **Millésime Hôtel** – *15 rue Jacob.* Ⓜ*Saint-Germain-des-Prés.* ☎*01 44 07 97 97. www.millesimehotel.com. 21 rooms.* 🍽*16€.* This 17C hotel right in the heart of St-Germain des Près has a spectacular (listed) period staircase. It offers its guests top-quality comfort in a charming setting. The modern bedrooms have sunshine-coloured walls.

7TH ARRONDISSEMENT
TOUR EIFFEL – FAUBOURG SAINT-GERMAIN – INVALIDES – ORSAY

🛏️ **Hôtel L'Empereur** – *2 rue Chevert.* Ⓜ*École-Militaire or La Tour-Maubourg.* ☎*01 45 55 88 02. www. hotelempereur.com. 38 rooms.* 🍽*10€.* The Empire style comes as no surprise in this hotel located just opposite the Invalides: consider it a tip of the hat to Napoléon, who is buried under the Dome… Ask for a refurbished room; they echo the establishment's historic flavour and are more pleasant.

🛏️ **Hôtel Lévêque** – *29 rue Clerc.* Ⓜ*École-Militaire.* ☎*01 47 05 49 15. www. hotel-leveque.com. 50 rooms.* 🍽*9€.* A rare find – jot down the address! This hotel located in a small, lively street in the shadow of the École Militaire offers sober, well-furnished, bright rooms at very affordable prices. Given its solid reputation, advance booking is most recommended.

🛏️ **Hôtel Malar** – *29 rue Malar.* Ⓜ*École-Militaire or La Tour-Maubourg.* ☎*01 45 51 38 46. www.eiffeltower-paris-hotel.com. 22 rooms.* 🍽*11€.* These two buildings constructed under Louis-Philippe have been renovated many times over. The rooms, fitted out with handsome furniture, come with pretty two-toned bathrooms. Summers, breakfasts are served in the small inner courtyard.

🛏️ **Hôtel St-Thomas-d'Aquin** – *3 rue du Pré-aux-Clercs.* Ⓜ*Rue du Bac or Saint-Germain-des-Prés.* ☎*01 42 61 01 22. www.hotel-st-thomas-daquin.com. 20 rooms.* 🍽*9€.* Chic boutiques, antique shops, art galleries and literary cafés: Left Bank Paris is yours for the taking, just a minute's walk from this hotel, which is gradually being renovated. Comfortable, modern bedrooms; bathrooms reminiscent of ships' cabins.

○○◎**Hôtel du Palais-Bourbon** – *49 rue de Bourgogne.* M*Varenne.* ☎*01 44 11 30 70.* *www.hotel-palais-bourbon.com.* *32 rooms.* Built in 1730, this hotel near the Rodin museum and the Invalides is a pleasant surprise. The attractive rooms have parquet floors, wood furniture and air conditioning. Single rooms are small but very good value; doubles are spacious. There are also several family rooms. Breakfast is included in the price.

○○◎**Hôtel Lindbergh** – *5 rue Chomel.* M*Sèvres-Babylone or Saint-Sulpice.* ☎*01 45 48 35 53.* *www.hotellindbergh.com.* *26 rooms.* ▭*8€.* One of the men who designed Lindbergh's famous monoplane, The Spirit of St. Louis, supposedly stayed in this 19C hotel right near the Bon Marché department store. The rooms are decorated in a 1930s-40s style, some with flat-screen TVs. Very hospitable welcome.

○○◎**Hôtel Muguet** – *11 rue Chevert.* M*École-Militaire or La Tour-Maubourg.* ☎*01 47 05 05 93.* *www.paris-hotel-muguet.com.* *48 rooms.* ▭*9.50€.* Small, basic and discreet, this hotel is set in a quiet side street half-way between the École Militaire and the Invalides. The well-maintained rooms are spotless and air-conditioned. Little flower-decked courtyard at the rear where breakfasts are served summers. Reasonable rates for Paris and free WiFi.

○○◎**Hôtel de la Tulipe** – *33 rue Malar.* M*Invalides or La Tour-Maubourg.* ☎*01 45 51 67 21.* *www.hotel-delatulipe.com.* *22 rooms.* ▭*10€.* Built in the 17C, this yellow residence is now home to a small, charming hotel with a Provençal slant. The paved, tree-covered courtyard is pretty and the small bedrooms are tastefully decorated: wicker, stone and beams complement each other
to a tee.

○○◎**Hôtel Verneuil** – *8 rue de Verneuil.* M*Solférino or Musée-d'Orsay.* ☎*01 42 60 82 14.* *www.hotelverneuil.com.* *26 rooms.* ▭*13€.* A delightful stopover just a few steps from St-Germain-des-Prés, this hotel wants for nothing. Although the bedrooms are a bit cramped, their refined, elegant interior decoration gives them an incomparable charm. Over half are air-conditioned.

8TH ARRONDISSEMENT

CHAMPS-ÉLYSÉES – CONCORDE - FAUBOURG-SAINT-HONORÉ – SAINT-LAZARE

○○**Modern Élysée** – *9 rue Washington.* M*George V.* ☎*01 45 63 27 33.* Closed Aug. *26 rooms.* ▭ The name gives the game away: this hotel is situated right near the Champs-Elysées. The reasonably spacious rooms are impeccably maintained; those overlooking the small inner courtyard are quieter. Reasonable prices, given the location.

○○◎**Hôtel Madeleine Opéra** – *12 rue Greffulhe.* M*Madeleine.* ☎*01 47 42 26 26.* *www.hotel-madeleine-opera.com.* *25 rooms.* ▭*7€.* A great bargain hotel on a quiet side street in the Madeleine shopping and theatre district, this is a comfortable, contemporary hotel with a historic Art Nouveau façade. The lobby has a Provençale theme with terracotta floor tiles, wrought-iron furniture and bright fabrics. Rooms have a more classic décor with carpeted floors and pale walls.

○○◎**Hôtel New Orient** – *16 rue de Constantinople.* M*Europe or Villiers.* ☎*01 45 22 21 64.* *www.hotel-paris-orient.com.* *30 rooms.* ▭*11€.* This hotel's inviting façade is in perfect keeping with the smart interior. The wooden staircase and immaculate rooms complement the warm, hospitable ambience. Rooms equipped with free WiFi.

○○◎**Hôtel d'Albion** – *15 rue de Penthièvre.* M*Miromesnil.* ☎*01 42 65 84 15.* *www.hotelalbion.net.* *26 rooms.* ▭*10€.* Midway between the Champs-Élysées and La Madeleine, here's a hotel located in an unexpectedly quiet street. The commodious rooms each have their own pleasant personality; ask for one on the courtyard if possible. Summertime, breakfast is served in a pleasant mini-garden.

○○◎**Champs-Élysées** – *2 rue d'Artois.* M*Saint-Philippe-du-Roule.* ☎*01 43 59 11 42.* *www.champselysees-paris-hotel.com.* *35 rooms.* ▭*9€.* A convivial establishment housed in a late 19C building that has been modernised. The entrance and bedrooms have been revamped in the art deco spirit. Breakfast room under handsome stone arches.

⊜⊜⊜⊟**Hôtel Powers** – *52 rue François-Ier.* 🅼*George-V or Alma-Marceau .* ☎*01 47 23 91 05. www. hotel-powers.com. 55 rooms.* ⊆*16€.* This discreet, agreeable establishment is situated just a stone's throw from the world's most celebrated avenue. The reasonably spacious yellow rooms are cosy, with their antique furniture and elegant ceiling mouldings reminiscent of an English manor. Sauna.

9TH ARRONDISSEMENT

FAUBOURG POISSONNIÈRE – GRANDS BOULEVARDS – OPÉRA – PIGALLE - SAINT-LAZARE

⊜⊟**Hôtel Chopin** – *10 blvd Montmartre, 46 passage Jouffroy.* 🅼*Richelieu-Drouot.* ☎*01 47 70 58 10. www.hotel-chopin.com. 36 rooms.* ⊆*7€.* Located in a covered passage dating from 1846, also home to the Grévin wax museum, this little hotel is surprisingly quiet, considering the effervescent neighbourhood. The colourfully painted rooms must be booked well in advance.

⊜⊜⊟**Hôtel Langlois** – *63 rue St-Lazare.* 🅼*Trinité.* ☎*01 48 74 78 24. www. hotel-langlois.com. 27 rooms.* ⊆*12€.* Located in the up-and-coming Nouvelle Athènes district, this old-fashioned hotel in a 19C building has spacious rooms with renovated bathrooms and antique furnishings that seem to have been here since the post-war era. A popular hotel, it's best to book early.

⊜⊜⊟**Résidence du Pré** – *15 rue Pierre-Sémard.* 🅼*Poissonnière.* ☎*01 48 78 26 72. www.leshotelsdupre.com. 40 rooms.* ⊆*10€.* Two minutes from the Gare du Nord, this modest establishment situated in an old building is well-maintained: the practical rooms are clean and functional, if not wildly original. Free WiFi.

10TH ARRONDISSEMENT

FAUBOURG POISSONNIÈRE – GRANDS BOULEVARDS – CANAL SAINT-MARTIN

⊜⊜**Hôtel Caravelle** – *41 rue des Petites Écuries.* 🅼*Bonne-Nouvelle or Poissonnière.* ☎*01 45 23 08 22. 38 rooms.* ⊆*6€.* Here's a good address for travellers looking to stay in the capital, in the heart of

a lively quarter with a spicy aroma. The small bedrooms are immaculate and rather merry, with their multi-coloured curtains and bedcovers.

⊜⊟**République Hôtel** – *31 rue Albert-Thomas.* 🅼*République.* ☎*01 42 39 19 03. www.republiquehotel.com. 40 rooms.* ⊆*8€.* Situated in a rather quiet street between the Place de la République and the Saint-Martin Canal, this hotel lodges guests in small white rooms. Simple comfort and décor – at these prices, one shouldn't expect too much fuss.

⊜⊜⊟**Hôtel Albert 1er** – *162 rue Lafayette.* 🅼*Le Peletier or Cadet .* ☎*01 40 36 82 40 .www.albert1erhotel.com. 55 rooms.* ⊆*15€.* A few short steps from the Gare du Nord, here's a practical address that puts Sacré-Cœur and the St-Martin Canal almost at your doorstep. The bright rooms are well-maintained, air conditioned and sound-proofed. Marble bathrooms and cane furniture.

⊜⊜⊟**Hôtel França**is – *13 rue du 8-Mai-1945.* 🅼*Gare-de-l'Est.* ☎*01 40 35 94 14. 72 rooms.* ⊆*8.50€.* This hotel, located opposite the Gare de l'Est in a busy area, offers excellent value for money. The rooms, decorated in a 1970s veneered furniture style, are clean, well-fitted out and soundproofed. Turn-of-the-century drawing room and reception area.

11TH ARRONDISSEMENT

BASTILLE – BELLEVILLE – FAUBOURG SAINT-ANTOINE – RÉPUBLIQUE

⊜⊜**Hôtel Grand Prieuré** – *20 rue du Grand-Prieuré.* 🅼*Oberkampf.* ☎*01 47 00 74 14. www.hotelgrandprieure.fr. 32 rooms.* ⊆*6€.* A hotel not far from République offering clean, functional rooms with a bath or shower. Trendy travellers will be interested to learn that it is just a minute from Rue Oberkampf, known for its succession of fashionable restaurants and cafés.

⊜⊜**Hôtel Nord et Est** – *49 rue de Malte.* 🅼*Oberkampf.* ☎*01 47 00 71 70. www. hotel-nord-est.com. 45 rooms.* ⊆*8€.* This small, unassuming hotel is well-situated in a quiet street near République. Run by the same family since 1929, the cheerful welcome makes one feel at home, even if the facilities are rather basic.

⊜⊜⊟**Hôtel Beaumarchais** – *3 rue Oberkampf.* 🅼*Filles-du-Calvaire.* ☎*01 53*

36 86 86. www.hotelbeaumarchais.com.
31 rooms. 🍽10€. This century-old,
flower-decked building has recently
been rejuvenated. The rooms, painted
with vivid colours and endowed with
gracefully curved furniture, are as
charming as can be. The verdant inner
courtyard is a welcome summer refuge.

🍽🛏**Hôtel Campanile** – 9 rue du
Chemin-Vert. Ⓜ Chemin-Vert. ☎01 43
38 58 08. www.campanile.fr. 157 rooms.
🍽7€. A chain hotel housed in a
modern building between Bastille and
République. Its assets: all rooms have
air conditioning, those on the uppermost floor have a terrace and, when the
weather is fine, breakfast is served in
the tiny garden.

🍽🛏**Grand Hôtel Français**
– 223 blvd Voltaire. Ⓜ Nation. ☎01 43
71 27 57. www.grand-hotel-francais.fr.
40 rooms. 🍽10€. Its location a stone's
throw from the Place de la Nation and
the principal Metro and RER lines is
one of the chief advantages of this
handsome, fully restored hotel. The
bedrooms, decorated with colourful
fabrics, have WiFi and soundproofing.
Hospitable welcome.

12TH ARRONDISSEMENT

BASTILLE – BERCY –
FAUBOURG SAINT-ANTOINE

🍽**Lux Hôtel Picpus** – 74 blvd Picpus.
Ⓜ Picpus. ☎01 43 43 08 46. www.paris
luxhotel.com. 38 rooms. 🍽7€.
Close to the Place de la Nation, this
hotel has a cut-stone façade and basic,
modern rooms . A bit on the small side,
but they have the essential amenities
including WiFi.

🍽**Hôtel Amadeus** – 39 rue Claude-
Tillier. Ⓜ Reuilly-Diderot or Nation. ☎01
43 48 53 48. www.amadeushotel.net.
22 rooms 🍽5€. Seen from the outside,
this small hotel is nothing special. But
inside the hotel is bright and modern.
The very quiet bedrooms, furnished in
wicker, change colour with every floor.

🍽**Venise Hôtel** – 4 rue Chaligny.
Ⓜ Reuilly-Diderot. ☎01 43 43 63 45. www.
hoteldevenise.com. 28 rooms. 🍽7.50€.
This family-run establishment is located
near the original Viaduc des Arts and
its landscaped promenade. The rooms,
practical above all, change colours at

each floor; the washrooms all come with
a bathtub. Free WiFi.

🍽**Inter Hôtel Alcyon** – 17 rue de
Prague. Ⓜ Ledru-Rollin. ☎01 43 43 66 35.
🅿 37 rooms. 🍽8€ . Restaurant 🍽.
This hotel's location within reach of
the Bastille is ideal for night owls. The
rooms, some of which are rather narrow,
have been decorated without too much
fuss; the bathrooms are well equipped.

🍽🛏**Hôtel Le Quartier Bercy Square**
– 33 blvd de Reuilly. Ⓜ Daumesnil or
Dugommier. ☎01 44 87 09 09. 61 rooms.
🍽9€. Although it is located in the heart
of Paris, this hotel is a peaceful port
in the city storm. Most of the rooms,
smallish but neat and tidy, give onto
one of the two verdant inner courtyards.
Breakfasts served outdoors in summer,
on the veranda in winter.

13TH ARRONDISSEMENT

GOBELINS

🍽**Résidence Les Gobelins** – 9 rue
des Gobelins. Ⓜ Les Gobelins. ☎01 47 07
26 90. www.hotelgobelins.com. 32 rm.
🍽8€. Situated on a little paved road
just next-door to the Manufacture des
Gobelins, this hotel looks as though it
belongs in a village. The small, basic
rooms are quiet and colourful. A pretty,
flower-decked patio livens up the breakfast room.

🍽**Touring Hôtel Magendie** – 6 rue
Corvisart. Ⓜ Corvisart . ☎01 43 36 13 61.
🅿 112 rooms. 🍽 6.60€. Located in a
small street behind Boulevard Arago,
this contemporary budget hotel has
particularly attractive rates for the many
single rooms. Refurbished, they are
somewhat cramped but quiet; those
overlooking the courtyard are particularly peaceful.

🍽🛏**Hôtel Résidence Vert Galant**
– 43 rue Croulebarbe. Ⓜ Les Gobelins
– ☎01 44 08 83 50. www.vertgalant.com.
15 rooms. 🍽8€. Overlooking a large
park on a quiet street, this modern
residence behind the Manufacture des
Gobelins has its own interior garden and
rooms with kitchenettes. The hotel's
Basque restaurant (🍽🍽)is popular
with locals.

🍽🍽🛏**Hôtel Manufacture** –
8 rue Philippe-de-Champagne.
Ⓜ Place-d'Italie. ☎01 45 35 45 25. www.
hotel-la-manufacture.com. 56 rooms.

⌂*10€.* Very close to the Place d'Italie, the rooms of this recent establishment are practical and well-fitted out. All are sound-proofed and air conditioned; five of the rooms on the top floor are bigger, one with a view of the Eiffel Tower.

14TH ARRONDISSEMENT

DENFERT-ROCHEREAU – MONTPARNASSE – MONTSOURIS

Hôtel Daguerre – *94 rue Daguerre.* Ⓜ*Denfert-Rochereau.* ☎*01 43 22 43 54. 30 rooms.* ⌂*10€.* Although entirely refurbished in 1994, evidence of the hotel's 1920s architecture can still be glimpsed, such as the façade or the amusing fountain at the entrance. Near to Montparnasse, this hotel in a busy shopping street has rooms that are soberly decorated but immaculate, and the prices are reasonable.

Hôtel Delambre – *35 rue Delambre.* Ⓜ*Vavin or Edgar-Quinet.* ☎*01 43 20 66 31. www.delambre-paris-hotel.com. 30 rooms.* ⌂*11€.* This fully refurbished modern establishment is just a few minutes from Montparnasse. The bright, functional rooms and cheerful welcome have already resulted in a regular clientele of guests, happy to have found lodgings for a reasonable price in this neighbourhood.

Hôtel Moulin Vert – *74 rue du Moulin-Vert.* Ⓜ*Pernéty.* ☎*01 45 43 65 38. www.hotel-moulinvert.com. 28 rooms.* ⌂*8€.* This small hotel with the classic Parisian façade is bright and cheerful, and the bedrooms, while a bit compact, are well maintained in either pastel or primary colours.

Hôtel L'Aiglon – *232 blvd Raspail.* Ⓜ*Denfert-Rochereau or Raspail.* ☎*01 43 20 82 42. www.esprit-de-france. com. 47 rooms.* ⌂*11€.* Two minutes from the Cartier foundation and just behind the Montparnasse cemetery, this hotel sports a decidedly Napoleonic personality. Cherry or softwood furniture and appealing fabrics give the rooms their pleasant feel.

Hôtel Istria – *29 rue Campagne Première.* – Ⓜ *Raspail.* ☎*01 43 20 91 82. 30 rooms.* ⌂*10€.* Man Ray stayed here, Elsa Triolet and Aragon loved here and Raymond Radiguet was unfaithful to Cocteau here. This small hotel, popular with many artists of Montparnasse's

golden era, has retained all the charm of its colourful past. Refurbished rooms.

Hôtel Lenox Montparnasse – *15 rue Delambre.* Ⓜ*Vavin or Edgar-Quinet.* ☎*01 43 35 34 50. www.paris-hotel-lenox.com. 52 rooms.* ⌂*12€.* The early 20C façade of this building situated in a popular side-street off Montparnasse is most attractive. Behind it lies a pleasant establishment, particularly the large suites on the 6th floor. All rooms are decorated with handsome antique mirrors.

15TH ARRONDISSEMENT

JAVEL – MONTPARNASSE – TOUR EIFFEL – VAUGIRARD

Hôtel de l'Avre – *21 rue de l'Avre.* Ⓜ*La Motte-Picquet-Grenelle.* ☎*01 45 75 31 03. www.hoteldelavre.com. 26 rooms.* ⌂*8€.* Very colourful indeed. A bright yellow lobby in memory of Provence and a luscious green garden to enjoy at breakfast. The white, yellow or blue bedrooms promise snug, quiet nights in a simple yet cosy ambience.

Hôtel Printania Porte de Versailles – *55 rue Olivier-de-Serres.* Ⓜ*Convention.* ☎*01 45 33 96 77. www. paris-hotel-printania.com. 21 rooms.* ⌂ *8€.* Right next door to the Parc des Expositions, here's a small hotel whose bedrooms, practical and very well looked after, are decorated in soft pastels. The breakfast room, repainted in the shades of southern France, is delightful.

Hôtel Avia – *181 rue de Vaugirard.* Ⓜ*Pasteur.* ☎*01 43 06 43 80. www.saphirhotel.fr. 40 rooms.* ⌂*7.50€.* A modern hotel close to Montparnasse and the Porte de Versailles. Bedrooms are spacious, suitably fitted out and decorated with colourful fabric.

Lutèce Hôtel – *5 rue Langeac.* Ⓜ*Convention or Porte-de-Versailles.* ☎*01 48 28 56 95. www.feel-like-home. com. 37 rooms.* ⌂*8€.* Built between the World Wars, this hotel has sound-proofed rooms with WiFi. Three of them have balconies; those on the 6th and 7th floors offer a view of the roofs of Paris. Summertime, breakfast is served in the inner courtyard.

Saphir Hôtel – *10 rue du Commerce.* Ⓜ *La Motte-Picquet – Grenelle.* ☎*01 45 75 12 23. www.saphirhotel.fr.*

32 rooms. 🖥*7.50€.* You're just a minute's walk from the Eiffel Tower when you stay in this small, very well-kept establishment without airs. Functional, tidy rooms; ask for one overlooking the inner courtyard where breakfasts may be taken in summer.

🛏🛏🍽**Timhotel Tour Eiffel** – *11 rue Juge –* Ⓜ*Dupleix.* ☎*01 45 78 29 29. www.timhotel.com. 39 rooms.* 🖥*€ 8.50.* This spruce-looking hotel has worked hard in order to appeal to younger travellers. The fashionable interior decoration with wood-panelling, comfortable wicker furniture and brightly coloured curtains and convenient metro links to the centre of Paris suit their needs admirably.

16TH ARRONDISSEMENT

AUTEUIL – BOIS DE BOULOGNE – MUETTE-RANELAGH – PASSY – TROCADÉRO

🛏**Camping Le Bois de Boulogne** – *Allée du Bord-de-l'Eau (between the Suresnes Bridge and the Puteaux Bridge).* ☎*01 45 24 30 00. www.campingparis. fr. Reservations recommended. 435 sites. Food service.* Located in the Bois de Boulogne, this campground, which is only for those residing outside of greater Paris, is predictably noisy, but the prices can't be beat. Sites closest to the Seine are the quietest. The price for a tent site for one night and for two people is 16.80€. In summer there's a shuttle service to and from the Porte-Maillot metro station every quarter of an hour. Mobile home rentals.

🛏🛏🍽**Hôtel Ambassade** – *79 rue Lauriston.* Ⓜ*Boissière or Kléber.* ☎*01 45 53 41 15. www.hotelambassade.com. 38 rooms.* 🖥*14€.* This renovated hotel benefits from the quietude of the surrounding residential neighbourhood although it is only a few hundred metres from the Champs-Élysées. Rooms have Art Deco style furnishings, air-conditioning and granite bathrooms.

🛏🛏🍽**Queen's Hôtel** – *4 rue Bastien-Lepage.* Ⓜ*Michel-Ange – Auteuil.* ☎*01 42 88 89 85. www.queens-hotel.fr. 22 rooms.* 🖥*8€.* Tucked away in a quiet street, this small hotel run by an ex-journalist has an eclectic style. Each one has a different style, hung with modern paintings from the owner's private collection. Six rooms have a jacuzzi.

🛏🛏🍽**Hôtel Gavarni** – *5 rue Gavarni.* Ⓜ*Passy.* ☎*01 45 24 52 82. www. gavarni.com. 25 rooms –* 🖥 *15€.* Two minutes from the Rue de Passy, beloved of all fashion and shopping addicts, this hotel with a spruce red brick façade and refurbished interior with elegant touches. The rooms are small, smart and well fitted out. Very hospitable welcome.

🛏🛏🛏🍽**Hôtel Hameau de Passy** – *48 rue de Passy.* Ⓜ*La Muette.* ☎*01 42 88 47 55. www.paris-hotel-hameaudepassy. com. 32 rooms.* A stone's throw from the Trocadéro in a little pedestrian sidestreet, this hotel is a salutary refuge where the commotion of the capital fades away. The small, white, modern rooms all open onto a tree-filled park: true luxury amidst the hustle and bustle of the capital. Breakfast included.

🛏🛏🛏🍽**Régina de Passy** – *6 rue de La Tour.* Ⓜ*Passy.* ☎*01 55 74 75 75. www. hotel-paris-passy.com. 62 rooms.* 🖥*15€.* Interesting architecture at this 1930s residence located in the chic shopping district around Passy. The hotel's regular guests appreciate the warm reception, spacious rooms and, from the fifth floor up, balconies from where one can gaze at the Eiffel Tower. Each one has a different style.

17TH ARRONDISSEMENT

CHAMPS-ÉLYSÉES – MONCEAU

🛏**Hôtel de Paris** – *17 rue Biot.* Ⓜ*Place-de-Clichy.* ☎*01 42 94 02 50. 30 rooms.* 🖥*6€.* In close proximity to the very lively Place de Clichy, this establishment has been overhauled from A to Z. The small rooms all come with well-equipped bathrooms attached. Breakfasts served on the patio in summer.

🛏🛏🍽**Hôtel Prince Albert Wagram** – *28 passage Cardinet, access via 11 rue Jouffroy.* Ⓜ*Villiers-Malesherbes.* ☎*01 47 54 06 00. www.hotelprincealbert.com. 33 rooms.* 🖥*6€.* Hidden in an alley, this recently renovated hotel ten minutes by metro to the Opéra district and the Arc de Triomphe. The highly practical rooms are a bit tight, but very well maintained.

🛏🛏🍽**Résidence Malesherbes** – *129 rue Cardinet.* Ⓜ*Villiers or Malesherbes.* ☎*01 44 15 85 00. 21 rooms.* 🖥*7€.* A small, very pleasant hotel with a family feel. The cosy rooms have warm colours, curtains and bedspreads matching the carpet, and a practical corner kitchenette. Breakfast is served in your room. Reasonable weekly and monthly rates.

🖥🖥🖥 **Hôtel Banville** – *166 blvd Berthier.* Ⓜ*Porte-de-Champerret.* ☎*01 42 67 70 16. www.hotelbanville.fr. 38 rooms.* 🛏*20€.* Terribly romantic, this small hotel with its 1926 façade combines classic and contemporary style. From Amélie's Room, complete with terrace, to Marie's Apartment, adorned with lace and trimmings, four-poster bed and soft lighting, all of the rooms are simply delightful.

🖥🖥 **Hôtel Flaubert** – *19 rue Rennequin.* Ⓜ*Ternes. .* ☎*01 46 22 44 35. www. hotelflaubert.com. 41 rooms.* 🛏*9€.* What a lovely surprise! Behind the very ordinary looking façade of this hotel there's a pocket-sized, verdant courtyard giving onto a few of the rooms. Simple but well maintained, brightly coloured rooms and affordable prices.

18TH ARRONDISSEMENT

MONTMARTRE

🖥🖥 **Ermitage Hôtel** – *24 rue Lamarck.* Ⓜ *Lamarck-Caulaincourt.* ☎*01 42 64 79 22. www.ermitagesacrecoeur.fr.* 🛏 *12 rooms.* This private residence dating from the Second Empire was built by a wealthy gentleman for his mistress. Rooms with a personal touch; four of them overlook the roofs of Paris, while those with a terrace giving onto the garden are the most popular. Breakfast included.

🖥🖥🖥 **Hôtel des Arts** – *5 rue Tholozé.* Ⓜ*Abbesses or Blanche.* ☎*01 46 06 30 52. www.arts-hotel-paris.com. 50 rooms.* 🛏*8€.* A noteworthy address near the Moulin de la Galette and the Place du Tertre. In the lobby, visitors can admire paintings by Roland Dubuc, an artist from Montmartre. All of the rooms have been renovated and are attractive and colourful. Book well in advance.

🖥🖥🖥 **Comfort Hôtel Place du Tertre** – *Sacré-Cœur, 16 rue Tholozé.* Ⓜ*Abbesses or Blanche.* ☎*01 42 55 05 06. www. comfort-placedutertre.com. 46 rooms.* 🛏*8€.* A top-rate location between the Moulin de la Galette and the Rue des Abbesses for this entirely refurbished hotel. The practical rooms, enlivened

by colourful carpets, curtains and bedspreads, benefit from the peaceful surroundings.

🖥🖥🖥 **Hôtel Roma Sacré Cœur** – *101 rue Caulaincourt.* Ⓜ*Lamarck-Caulaincourt.* ☎*01 42 62 02 02. 57 rooms.* 🛏*7.80€.* Two minutes from the Sacré-Cœur in one of Montmartre's livelier streets, this hotel provides accommodation in the heart of the artists' quarter. The clean, functional rooms are well-soundproofed.

19TH ARRONDISSEMENT

BELLEVILLE – CANAL SAINT-MARTIN - LA VILLETTE

🖥 **Balladins** – *219 rue de Crimée.* Ⓜ*Crimée.* ☎*01 40 38 91 00. www.balla dins.com. 40 rooms.* 🛏*7.50€.* Those visiting La Villette and its many attractions will appreciate the proximity of this hotel. The renovated rooms have light wood furniture and bright bedspreads. Agreeable breakfast room.

20TH ARRONDISSEMENT

BELLEVILLE – PÈRE-LACHAISE

🖥🖥 **Hôtel Lilas-Gambetta** – *223 av. Gambetta.* Ⓜ*Porte-des-Lilas.* ☎*01 40 31 85 60. www.lilas-gambetta.com. 34 rooms.* 🛏*9€.* The 1925 façade of brick and cut stone conceals a contemporary interior and furniture from the 1970s and 80s that will charm fans of the genre. The quietest rooms give onto a charming little courtyard where breakfast is served in summer.

🖥🖥 **Hôtel Paris-Gambetta** – *12 av. du Père-Lachaise.* Ⓜ*Gambetta.* ☎*01 47 97 76 57. www.hotelparisgambetta. com. 32 rooms .* 🛏*8€.* This appealing hotel near the Père-Lachaise cemetery is a tranquil stopover in a quiet street shielded from the urban fracas. Well-soundproofed rooms furnished in the 1980s style.

🖥🖥 **Hôtel Palma** – *77 av. Gambetta.* Ⓜ*Gambetta.* ☎*01 46 36 13 65. www. paris-hotel-palma.com. 32 rms.* 🛏*6€.* Situated on a noisy avenue right near the Père-Lachaise, this hotel offers small, soundproofed and air-conditioned rooms in sunny orange, yellow and red tones at very reasonable prices.

WHERE TO EAT

👆*See individual Sights in the Discovering section for additional places to eat.*

👆*For coin ranges, see the Legend on the cover flap.*

Selected Restaurants by District

FOR ALL BUDGETS...

The selected restaurants are listed by neighbourhood and by price range with the nearest metro station listed. In addition, each of the neighbourhood descriptions in the Discovering section tells you which arrondissement to look for in this directory.

The following pages contain listings for establishments where you can get a meal under 16€, and stylish restaurants for budgets up to 50€. Nothing but the best will do? There are also top-rate restaurants listed here, offering Epicurean feasts and magnificent décors. You'll want to remember that correct attire is generally *de rigueur* in these stylish places.

...AND FOR ALL TASTES

In order to provide you with as many choices as possible, we have selected typically Parisian *brasseries* and *bistros*, as well as traditional, exotic or otherwise distinctive establishments. You'll also find simple venues where you can stop in for a salad, a bit of quiche or a sweet snack.

A few fervent defenders of France's regional cuisines are included as well, giving you the opportunity to sample the diversity of the country's culinary heritage. Yearning for something yet further afield? Follow the guide to Italian, Spanish, Argentinian, Japanese, Thai and other cuisines of the world. There's something here for everyone. Many restaurants in Paris serve lunch from 12.30pm to mid-afternoon and dinner from 7.30pm to 10pm. Some *brasseries* are open all day without a break, while other establishments continue serving until midnight and beyond. Remember to reserve your table, especially in the evening.

FOR EVEN MORE CHOICES...

If you have not been able to find exactly what you're looking for among our many hotel and restaurant listings, do consult the red-cover **Michelin Guide Paris**. It offers a varied list of Parisian addresses, including those that have been awarded the famous Michelin stars. The "Bib Gourmand" symbol designates establishments serving fine food at reasonable prices.

Bon appétit!

Restaurant near the Panthéon

©Eric Belisle/iStockphoto.com

Address Book

1ST ARRONDISSEMENT

CHÂTELET-HÔTEL DE VILLE – CONCORDE – HALLES – LOUVRE – MADELEINE – PALAIS-ROYAL – TUILERIES

Le Relais du Pont-Neuf – *18 quai du Louvre.* Ⓜ *Pont-Neuf or Louvre-Rivoli.* ☎*01 42 33 98 17.* Located on the quays along the Seine, here's a little neighbourhood address where you can hang up your hat and relax. The décor, with its pink pastel walls, is agreeable and the menu has original flair.

La Potée des Halles – *3 rue Étienne-Marcel.* Ⓜ *Étienne-Marcel.* ☎*01 40 41 98 15. Closed Aug, Sat lunch, and Sun.* This old Halles bistro serves unpretentious meals and has a very affordable fixed-price menu. Tourists, regulars and the trendy set mingle here, enjoying the handsome art nouveau wall tiles and the cheerful atmosphere. Unfussy service.

Saudade – *34 rue des Bourdonnais.* Ⓜ*Pont-Neuf or Châtelet.* ☎*01 42 36 30 71. Closed Sun.* This small Portuguese restaurant near Les Halles is well appreciated by fans of southern cuisine. Typical dishes cooked in olive oil are served in a simple setting decorated with traditional enamelled wall tiles. The fixed-price lunch menu is tempting; the atmosphere is livelier in the evening. Soirées Fado first Tue of month.

Lescure – *7 rue Mondovi.* Ⓜ*Concorde.* ☎*01 42 60 18 91. Closed Aug, 23 Dec–1 Jan and weekends.* This little neighbourhood bistro has been run by the same family since 1919. Popular among the locals, you'll have to wiggle your way into the tiny dining room with its closely placed tables in order to savour tasty fare served at very reasonable prices.

Chez Clovis – *33 rue Berger.* Ⓜ*Les Halles or Châtelet.* ☎*01 42 33 97 07. Closed Sun and public holidays.* This little bistro set in the Halles Quarter seems to belong to the past, with its handful of tables surrounding the bar and its old photos on the walls. Calf's head, *blanquette* (veal stew in white stock), steak and long-simmered dishes recall the Paris of yesteryear with a sigh of nostalgia. The terrace offers a view of the Saint-Eustache church.

Café de l'Époque – *2 rue du Bouloi, Galerie Véro-Dodat.* Ⓜ*Palais-Royal – Musée-du-Louvre.* ☎*01 42 33 40 70.* Midway between Les Halles and the Louvre, this 1826 café at the entrance to the Véro-Dodat Gallery is now a restaurant. The authentic Parisian bistro décor is elegant and subdued, while the fare is traditional: salads, terrines, *foie gras, andouillette* and homemade pastries.

Le Fumoir – *6 rue de l'Amiral-Coligny.* Ⓜ*Louvre-Rivoli.* ☎*01 42 92 00 24. www.lefumoir.com. Closed 1–21 Aug, 25 Dec–1 Jan.* Opposite the Louvre, this fashionable bar and restaurant with its brown lacquered tones has a retro appeal. Enticed by the city-style fare, martini bar and views of the Louvre, patrons come here to chat, read the paper or borrow a book from the library. Sunday brunch.

Brasserie Le Louvre – *Pl. André-Malraux.* Ⓜ*Palais-Royal – Musée-du-Louvre.* ☎*01 42 96 27 98. www.hoteldulouvre.com.* Between the Louvre and the Palais-Royal, this restaurant is remarkably well situated within the Louvre Hotel. Inaugurated in 1855 by Napoléon III himself, its terrace is set under the arcades of the Place du Palais-Royal when weather permits. Brasserie-style décor and affordable fixed-price menus.

Café Marly – *93 rue de Rivoli*. Ⓜ*Palais-Royal – Musée-du-Louvre.* ☎*01 49 26 06 60.* Opposite the pyramid and under the Louvre's arcades, this hip restaurant serves contemporary cuisine in a setting that successfully melds moulded ceilings, wooden floors and modern furniture. Summertime, have a drink on the terrace – it's one of Paris's prettiest. Serves until 1am.

Palais Royal – *110 Galerie de Valois.* Ⓜ*Palais-Royal – Musée-du-Louvre.* ☎*01 40 20 00 27. Closed 15 Dec–30 Jan, Sat from Oct–May and Sun.* What could be more delightful than taking a seat here in the gardens of the Palais-Royal for lunch, dinner or just an afternoon drink? In winter, the room under the arcades is very pleasant; its art deco theme and the contemporary cuisine are well-matched.

Café Ruc – *159 rue St-Honoré.* Ⓜ*Palais-Royal.* ☎*01 42 60 97 54. Reservations recommended.* Halfway between the Louvre and the Palais-Royal, the atmosphere of this café-restaurant is warm and welcoming. Decorated by Jacques Garcia in a neo-baroque style with green walls and red velvet, it offers an eclectic menu and modern cuisine. During fashion-show season, reporters, designers and mode people fill the place to the brim.

🍴🍴🍷🍺**Le Grand Vefour** – *17 rue de Beaujolais.* Ⓜ*Palais-Royal – Musée-du-Louvre.* ☎*01 42 96 56 27. www.relais chateaux.com. Closed Aug, 23–31 Dec, Fri eve and weekends.* Located beneath the arches of the Palais-Royal, this former 18C café is luxuriously decorated with woodwork, mirrors and frescoes, setting the stage for an exquisite meal. Gourmet diners come here to indulge in the famous *ravioles de foie gras* in truffled cream sauce or any of their other justly celebrated specialities. More moderately priced lunch menu.

2ND ARRONDISSEMENT

GRANDS BOULEVARDS – HALLES – PLACE DES VICTOIRES – SENTIER

🍴**L'Arbre à Cannelle** – *57 passage des Panoramas.* Ⓜ*Grands-Boulevards.* ☎*01 45 08 55 87. Closed eves, Sun and public holidays. Two weeks in Aug, 25 Dec–1 Jan.* This former chocolaterie situated in the Passage des Panoramas has Napoléon III woodwork and a tea room. If tempted by quiches, pies, salads, gourmand platters or the daily special, ask for a table in the room with the beautiful ornamental ceiling.

🍴**La Cocarde** – *7 rue Marie-Stuart.* Ⓜ*Étienne-Marcel.* ☎*01 40 39 05 09. Closed Sat and Sun. Reservations recommended.* What does this little place hidden in a pedestrian street of the Halles district have to recommend it? The warm-toned décor, the young, enthusiastic service, healthy servings of traditional fare and very reasonable prices, no less.

🍴**Domaine de Lintillac** – *10 rue St-Augustin.* Ⓜ*Quatre-Septembre.* ☎*01 40 20 96 27. Closed ten days in Aug, Sat lunch and Sun. Reservations recommended.* Flavours of Southwest France abound in this restaurant located between the Bourse and the Opéra Garnier. The prices are quite low because many ingredients come straight from the

owner's property in Corrèze. The décor is simple and the service pleasant.

🍴**A Priori Thé** – *35-37 galerie Vivienne.* Ⓜ*Bourse.* ☎*01 42 97 48 75. Closed eves. Reservations required for lunch.* Extend your enjoyment of window shopping in the historic Galerie Vivienne with lunch on the terrace of this elegant tea room. Home made pastries and *plat du jour* served at lunch. Non-smoking room.

🍴**À La Grille Montorgueil** – *50 rue Montorgueil.* Ⓜ*Châtelet-les-Halles or Sentier* ☎*01 42 33 21 21.* A butcher's shop during the Halles' golden era, this old house tucked away in Rue Montorgueil is now home to an attractive 1920s-style bistro. A superb bar stands proudly at the entrance and there is a vaulted cellar. Typical bistro cookery.

🍴🍷**Le Gallopin** – *40 rue N.-D.-des-Victoires.* Ⓜ*Bourse.* ☎*01 42 36 45 38. www.brasseriegallopin.com.* Monsieur Gallopin had the Cuban mahogany bar that stands in this brasserie built to seduce his beloved in 1900. Restored with brio, Le Gallopin is still a most pleasurable place to have a meal served by the staff in white aprons, as is only befitting. Service until midnight.

🍴🍷🍺**Le Grand Colbert** – *2 rue Vivienne.* Ⓜ*Bourse.* ☎*01 42 86 87 88. www. legrandcolbert.com.* Daily noon–1am. Worthy of a film-set, with its mosaics, murals, fine high ceiling, long wall seats and vast bar, this 19C brasserie is frequented more for the setting than the food. Attractive fixed-priced menu. Serves until 1am.

🍴🍷🍺**Café Drouant** – *pl. Gaillon.* Ⓜ*Opéra or Quatre-Septembre.* ☎*01 42 65 15 16. www.drouant.com. Closed Aug.* This Parisian institution, home of the Académie Goncourt since 1914, offers two possibilities. The 'Café Drouant' menu is served in a more sober dining room, while the restaurant boasts a characteristic art deco décor. An opportunity to try this mythical citadel without risking bankruptcy.

3RD ARRONDISSEMENT

MARAIS – RÉPUBLIQUE

🍴**L'Apparement** – *18 rue des Coutures, St-Gervais.* Ⓜ*St-Sébastien-Froissart.* ☎*01 48 87 12 22. Closed Sat lunch. Reservations requested eves.* The little rooms of this café just opposite the Picasso Museum garden are appealingly homey, lined in wood and decorated with a varied array of paintings and furniture. Fine selection of salads at lunchtime; cocktails and cold meals in the evening. Sunday brunch.

◎**Chez Janou** – 2 rue Roger-Verlomme. ⓂChemin-Vert. ☎01 42 72 28 41 🖃. This charming 1900s bistro, which has retained its original décor, features a superb ceramic-covered wall. The menu has been replaced with an attractive lunch special and dishes of Provençal inspiration listed on the hallowed slate bill of fare.

◎◎**Ambassade d'Auvergne** – 22 rue du Grenier-St-Lazare. ⓂRambuteau or Étienne-Marcel. ☎01 42 72 31 22. www.ambassade-auvergne.com. Local flavour guaranteed: the rustic ground-floor dining room is sure to transport you to the hilly reaches of this rural region of central France. Hams and sausages hang above the large communal table that reunites fans of typical fare from Auvergne.

◎◎**Chez Jenny** – 39 blvd du Temple. ⓂRépublique. ☎01 44 54 39 00. www.chez-jenny.com. Jean-Charles Spindler, a marquetry craftsman, accomplished a tour de force when he decorated this Alsatian brasserie founded in 1932. The marquetry artwork in different types of wood and the sculptures in the upper floor rooms are well worth a visit. Brasserie-style cuisine.

◎◎**L'Estaminet d'Arômes et Cépages** – 39 rue Bretagne, Marché des Enfants Rouges. ⓂSébastien-Froissard. ☎01 42 72 34 85. www.aromes-et-cepages.com. Closed Sun dinner and Mon. A Provencal bistro atmosphere pervades this convivial restaurant hidden in the corner of one of the city's favourite markets. Stall holders, locals and the curious gather around communal tables for hearty, farm fresh cuisine and excellent wines by the glass.

◎◎◎**Caves St-Gilles** – 4 rue St-Gilles. ⓂChemin-Vert. ☎01 48 87 22 62. Reservations requested. Closed 25 Dec–1 Jan. Wine, beer and sherry flow freely in this lively tapas and wine bar, washing down the hors d'oeuvres and mixed platters sampled at the small bistro tables. Spanish décor, accordingly noisy and friendly atmosphere.

◎◎◎**Chez Omar** – 47 rue de Bretagne. ⓂArts-et-Métiers. ☎01 42 72 36 26. Closed 24 and 31 Dec🖃. The couscous served in this old neighbourhood bistro-style eatery has been delighting fans for over twenty years. With its noisy, casual atmosphere, this has been the 'in' place to dine since its discovery by the capital's top models a few years ago.

4TH ARRONDISSEMENT

BASTILLE – BEAUBOURG – CHÂTELET-HÔTEL DE VILLE – ÎLE SAINT-LOUIS - MARAIS – NOTRE-DAME

◎**L'As du Falafel** – 34 rue des Rosiers. ⓂSt-Paul or Hôtel de VIlle. ☎01 01 48 87 63 60. Closed Fri–Sat. Simply the best falafel in town, located in the heart of the Jewish district. Look for the long lines and pick up a falafel special (with eggplant) to go or get a table in one of the two dining rooms (one air conditioned). Very fresh ingredients and rapid service.

◎**Le Pain Quotidien** – 20 rue des Archives. ⓂHôtel-de-Ville. ☎01 44 54 03 07. www.lepainquotidien.fr. Closed 25 Dec. Located in the heart of Paris's gay district, the terrace of this bakery-grocery-tea room under a canopy of horse-chestnut trees is all the rage. You may also take a seat at one of the large communal tables indoors to enjoy a salad or an open-faced sandwich. Sunday brunch it's at its most lively.

◎◎**Bofinger** – 3 rue de la Bastille. ⓂBastille. ☎01 42 72 87 82. www.bofingerparis.com. Founded in 1864, this restaurant is a Parisian landmark. The venerable seats of its Belle Époque décor have cushioned the bottoms of some of the most famous politicians, writers, artists and musicians of the 20C. The brasserie, with its handsome glass roof, remains as crowded today as ever before. Reservations recommended. Serves until 1am.

◎◎**La Brasserie de l'Isle St-Louis** – 55 quai de Bourbon. ⓂPont-Marie or Cité.☎01 43 54 02 59. Closed Aug, Thu lunch and Wed. No Reservations. After visiting Notre-Dame, cross over the Pont St-Louis and take a seat in this traditional brasserie with its well-worn wooden furniture. Indoors or on the terrace in summer, amidst regulars and tourists, you'll enjoy the street artists and musicians playing in front of the bridge.

⊜⊜**Chez Marianne** – *2 rue des Hospitalières-St-Gervais.* Ⓜ*Saint-Paul.* ☎*01 42 72 18 86. Reservations requested .* This restaurant-cum-delicatessen on the Rue des Rosiers in the Jewish quarter serves a blend of Mediterranean and Central European food. Clients compose their own meals from a selection of victuals on display. Ask for a table in the room opposite the wine racks or, in summer, on the terrace.

⊜⊜**Le Petit Bofinger** – *6 rue de la Bastille.* Ⓜ*Bastille.*☎*01 42 72 05 23.* Opposite the famous Bofinger brasserie, this little bistro run by the same team offers a simpler menu in an amusing 1950s décor with wall frescoes, tube chairs and woodwork. The reasonable fixed-price menus are popular with the regular clientele. Serves until midnight.

⊜⊜**Thanksgiving's Bayou la Seine** – *20 rue St-Paul.* Ⓜ*Saint-Paul.* ☎*01 42 77 68 28. www.thanksgivingparis.com. Closed Sat and Sun eve, Mon, Tue, one week May, first two weeks Aug.* Ever tasted Louisiana cooking? This little restaurant in the Marais provides an opportunity to discover real Cajun dishes in a small, simple dining room. There is also an American grocery just next-door for homesick Yankees.

⊜⊜⊜**Au Bourguignon du Marais** – *52 rue François-Miron.* Ⓜ*Saint-Paul.* ☎*01 48 87 15 40. Closed Jul 19–Aug 28, Sun, Mon and holidays.* This restaurant and wine merchant's gives Burgundy the starring role, both in your wine glass and on your plate with such delectable recipes as the parsleyed house ham or the *andouillette à l'aligoté*. All is served in a pleasant, contemporary setting. Mini-terrace.

⊜⊜**L'Enoteca** – *25 rue Charles-V.* Ⓜ*Sully-Morland or Saint-Paul.* ☎*01 42 78 91 44. Closed 13–21 Aug. Reservations recommended.* This Italian restaurant has acquired a fine reputation thanks to its superior Italian wine list and creative cuisine. Set in a charming 17C house, the decoration is a pleasing combination of old beams, ochre-coloured walls and hand-blown Murano lamps.

⊜⊜**Vins des Pyrénées** – *25 rue Beautreillis.* Ⓜ*Bastille or Sully-Morland.* ☎*01 42 72 64 94. Closed two weeks Aug,*

Sat lunch. How very inviting, this former wine merchant's boutique with its elderly bottle racks, collection of labels from the past, old-fashioned postcards, handsome marble bar and oilskin tablecloths. Bistro fare and very relaxed service.

5TH ARRONDISSEMENT

JARDIN DES PLANTES – JUSSIEU – LUXEMBOURG – MAUBERT – MOUFFETARD – QUARTIER LATIN

⊜**Au Piano Muet** – *48 rue Mouffetard.* Ⓜ*Place-Monge.* ☎*01 43 31 45 15. Closed lunch except weekends.* The perfect place to come in from the cold, here's a nourishing halt that offers traditional dishes as well as the house specialities, raclettes and fondues. The décor – exposed beams and stone walls – is inviting and the atmosphere convivial.

⊜⊜**Les Bouchons de François Clerc** – *12 rue de l'Hôtel-Colbert.* Ⓜ*Maubert-Mutualité.* ☎*01 43 54 15 34. Closed Sat lunch and Sun.* Two minutes from Notre-Dame, this restaurant located in a traditional old Parisian house continues to lure customers back with its list of wines sold at store price. In either the pleasant dining room or the romantic vaulted cellar, choose one of the fixed-priced menus and enjoy your pick of reds, whites and rosés.

⊜⊜**Café Littéraire** – *1 rue des Fossés-St-Bernard, in the Institut du Monde Arabe (ground floor).* Ⓜ*Cardinal-Lemoine or Jussieu.*☎*01 40 51 38 38. www.yara-prestige.com/english. Closed eves and Mon. Reservations recommended.* This small restaurant with Moorish benches proposes salads, a daily special and a buffet of Mid-Eastern pastries. It's basic and inexpensive; there's a (mint) tea room in the afternoons. Those with more ample means can go upstairs to the Ziryab and enjoy a wider choice and an unforgettable view.

⊜⊜**La Fourmi Ailée** – *8 rue de Fouarre.* Ⓜ*Saint-Michel or Maubert-Mutualité.* ☎*01 43 29 40 99. www.parisresto.com.* Just across the river from Notre-Dame, this cosy tea room has a fireplace and old books lining the walls. Quiches, pies, salads and afternoon tea for light budgets. A non-smoking mezzanine and a few terrace tables in the summer.

⊜**Mirama** – *17 rue St-Jacques.* Ⓜ*Maubert-Mutualité, Cluny or Saint-*

Michel. ☎01 43 54 71 77. This little Chinese restaurant in the Latin Quarter is popular with everyone: Asians, tourists and Parisians cluster at its doors for one of the tightly-packed tables upstairs or in the cave-like cellar. Serves generous helpings of well-prepared food at reasonable prices.

Moissonnier – *28 rue des Fossés-St-Bernard.* Ⓜ*Cardinal-Lemoine.* ☎01 43 29 87 65. *Closed Aug, Sun and Mon.* In a somewhat outdated but impeccably managed bistro décor, this little restaurant, a stone's throw from the Institut du Monde Arabe, serves healthy portions of traditionally prepared Lyonnais specialities. Affordable fixed-price lunch and dinner menus.

El Palenque – *5 rue de la Montagne-Ste-Geneviève.* Ⓜ*Maubert-Mutualité* ☎01 43 54 08 99. *Closed 24 Dec–2 Jan and Sun.* Take a trip to faraway Argentina without leaving Paris. Try succulent meat dishes from the pampa accompanied by the fruits of South American vineyards, all served in a *rancho* setting. Quite an adventure!

Le Perraudin – *157 rue St-Jacques.* Ⓜ*Luxembourg.* ☎01 46 33 15 75. *Closed Sun and Aug.* Worthy of a scene from a Maigret detective novel, the feel of this former coal merchant's with its bistro chairs, chequered table-cloths, bar and old mirrors is utterly authentic. Appetising bistro cuisine full of old-fashioned flavours and *Tarte Tatin* for those with a sweet tooth. No reservations.

Le Buisson Ardent – *25 rue Jussieu.* Ⓜ*Jussieu.* ☎01 43 54 93 02. *Closed Aug, Sat lunch and Sun.* This little house opposite Jussieu university with its 1923 frescoes and neighbourhood bistro flair is always crowded. If the lunchtime menu is excellent value, the evening menu is just as good. Relaxed, friendly atmosphere and good food.

Le Reminet – *3 rue des Grands-Degrés.* Ⓜ*Maubert-Mutualité.* ☎01 44 07 04 24. *Closed two weeks in Feb, three weeks in Aug, Tue, Wed.* This terrific address close by Notre-Dame has everything to attract diners and keep them coming back: a young chef at the ovens, toothsome cuisine, a fixed-price lunch menu and a very affordable weekday dinner menu. The wine list is tempting.

6TH ARRONDISSEMENT

INSTITUT DE FRANCE – LUXEMBOURG – MONTPARNASSE – ODÉON – QUARTIER LATIN – SAINT-GERMAIN-DES-PRÉS – SAINT-SULPICE – SÈVRES-BABYLONE

Crêperie St-Germain – *33 rue St-André-des-Arts.* Ⓜ*Saint-Michel.* ☎01 43 54 24 41. Fancy a snack near the Place St-Michel? This crêperie with an original Moorish décor has two sister-restaurants at no 27 of this busy little street: "Les Pêcheurs" for the maritime ambience and "Les Arts" which has little alcoves. Spoilt for choice?

Cuisine de Bar – *8 rue Cherche Midi.* Ⓜ*Sèvres-Babylone or St-Sulpice.* ☎01 45 48 45 69. *Closed Sun and Mon.* This long dining room decorated with a contemporary style specializes in fresh, open-faced sandwiches (*tartines*) on Poilâne bread and scrumptious desserts. Don't miss the *fondant au chocolat*!

À la Duchesse Anne – *5 place du 18 Juin 1940.* Ⓜ*Montparnasse-Bienvenüe.* ☎01 45 48 97 21. *Closed Sun.* A great tea room at the foot of the Montparnasse tower and train station, serving savoury tarts, sandwiches, pastries and dishes to take away or eat in the dining room.

Le Machon d'Henri – *8 rue Guisarde.* Ⓜ*Mabillon.* ☎01 43 29 08 70. This bistro, with its classy dark green façade, is often full at lunch. Seated elbow to elbow, customers enjoy tasty little dishes of Lyonnais inspiration in a décor of exposed beams, painted stones and well-stocked shelves displaying bottles of wine. Lively atmosphere.

Le Bistrot d'Opio – *9 rue Guisarde.* Ⓜ*Mabillon or Saint-Germain-des-Prés.* ☎01 43 29 01 84. www.bistrot-opio.com. Sunny colours, wrought-iron, bistro tables, scents of the south and the song of cicadas in the background: both of the small dining rooms of this pleasant restaurant exude the charm of the south. Mediterranean cuisine prepared with olive oil, *naturellement*.

Bouillon Racine – *3 rue Racine.* Ⓜ*Odéon or Cluny-la-Sorbonne.* ☎01 44 32 15 60. www.bouillon-racine.com. This former workers' canteen with a listed art nouveau décor on two levels serves typical French brasserie fare in an elegant setting. Attentive service, valet parking at night, and a large selection of Belgian beers.

Casa Bini – *36 rue Grégoire-de-Tours.* Ⓜ*Odéon.* ☎*01 46 34 05 60. Closed Aug 10–17, 25 Dec, Jan 31.* Located in a side street off St-Germain-des-Prés, this Italian restaurant serves a fine selection of antipasti, toast with mozzarella, carpaccios and pasta. Decorated with sobriety in the modern bistro style; the upstairs dining room features enormous beams. Attractive lunchtime menu.

7TH ARRONDISSEMENT

TOUR EIFFEL – FAUBOURG SAINT-GERMAIN – INVALIDES – ORSAY

Les Jardins de Varenne in the Musée Rodin – *77 rue de Varenne.* Ⓜ*Varenne.* ☎*01 45 50 42 34. www.horeto.com. Closed eves and Mon.* Visitors and regulars looking for a bite to eat convene under the trees of the delightful terrace belonging to this pavilion hidden in the lovely gardens of the Rodin Museum (☜1€ to enter the garden). Simple salads, mixed platters and sandwiches available from the self-service section.

L'Auvergne Gourmande – *127 rue St-Dominique.* Ⓜ*École-Militaire.* ☎*01 47 05 57 03. Closed Sun, two weeks Aug.* Two guest tables for five and eight diners separated by a bookshelf filled with wine bottles, old porcelain on the walls, slate place settings: what an imaginative décor for this restaurant housed in an old butcher shop. Hearty cuisine from the Auvergne region.

Chez Françoise – *Aerogare des Invalides.* Ⓜ*Invalides.* ☎*01 47 05 49 03. www.chezfrancoise.com.* Founded in 1949, this brasserie has been given a facelift while still respecting its vintage style. Popular with the government representatives from the National Assembly next door, who enjoy the upscale brasserie fare in a lively atmosphere.

Le P'tit Troquet – *28 rue de l'Exposition.* Ⓜ*École-Militaire.* ☎*01 47 05 80 39. Closed 10–23 Jan, 1–23 Aug, Sat lunch, Mon lunch and Sun. Reservations requested.* This little bistro, just a few minutes from the Champ-de-Mars, will delight second-hand treasure hunters: bottles, mirrors, lace, lamps and other odds-and-bobs grace the dining room. Epicureans will savour the market-fresh

fare, chalked up on a slate. Popular among Parisians.

La Poule au Pot – *121 rue de l'Université.* Ⓜ*La Tour-Maubourg.* ☎*01 47 05 16 36. Closed Sat lunch and Sun.* The brown façade, so typical of the old Parisian bistros, sets the tone of this eatery with its 1930s ambience. Pleasant interior with red leather wall seats, a ceiling edged with crown moulding and decorative windows. Traditional cuisine.

Ribe – *15 av. de Suffren.* Ⓜ*Champ-de-Mars, Tour-Eiffel or Bir-Hakeim.* ☎*01 45 66 53 79.* A short distance from the Eiffel Tower, this restaurant's interior is inspired by colonial England. Parisians and tourists alike appreciate the reasonable prices as well as the traditional French fare: onion soup, terrines, and steak in pepper sauce.

Sancerre – *22 av. Rapp.* Ⓜ*Pont-de-l'Alma.* ☎*01 45 51 75 91. Mon–Sat 8am–3pm, 6.30–10.30pm. Closed Sun, Aug, Dec 23–Jan 2.* This countrified restaurant is a genuine ambassador for the village of Sancerre in the Berry region. Opening at 8am, it offers ample snacks such as terrines, omelettes, *andouillette* cooked in Sancerre wine, *crottins de Chavignol* (aged goat's cheese) and home-made pies. All liberally washed down with a glass of the region's best – *à votre santé!*

Thoumieux – *79 rue St-Dominique.* Ⓜ*Solférino.* ☎*01 47 05 49 75. www.thoumieux.com.* Half-way between the Eiffel Tower and the Invalides, this busy, old-fashioned bistro with red velvet seats and art nouveau chairs serves generous helpings at reasonable prices: *cassoulet,* duck *confit,* leeks and lentils in vinaigrette all feature prominently. Non-stop service on Sunday.

Le Vauban – *7 pl. Vauban.* Ⓜ*Saint-François-Xavier.* ☎*01 47 05 52 67.* For a wonderful view of the church of the Dôme des Invalides, take a seat on the very popular terrace of this brasserie or in the stylish dining room featuring trompe l'œil marble work. A well-thought-out menu awaits diners lunch and evening.

Au Bon Accueil – *14 rue de Monttessuy.* Ⓜ*Pont-de-l'Alma.* ☎*01 47 05 46 11. Closed weekends.* Just down the road from the Eiffel Tower, this restaurant lives up to its name: the

Pleasant Welcome. Two small, cheerful dining rooms and friendly service with a smile. The decoration is elegant and refined, the menu is simple, and the cooking is flavoursome and inventive. Add reasonable prices, and you have an unbeatable recipe.

La Maison de l'Amérique Latine – 217 blvd St-Germain. MSolférino or rue-du-Bac. ☎01 49 54 75 10. www.mal217.org. Closed Sat, Sun, Jul 26–Aug 21, 20 Dec–1 Jan, weekends and eves from Oct–Apr. As soon as the weather becomes warm enough, the restaurant's lovely terrace is set up in the garden. A refreshing haven from the summer heat, this private 18C mansion on Boulevard St-Germain is a rare find. French cuisine in the restaurant, or light, Latin-American fare in the bar.

8TH ARRONDISSEMENT

CHAMPS-ÉLYSÉES – CONCORDE – FAUBOURG-SAINT-HONORÉ – SAINT-LAZARE

Bar à Vin Nicolas – 31 pl. de la Madeleine. MMadeleine. ☎01 42 68 00 16. www.nicolas.com. Daily 9.30am–8pm. Closed Sun. The Nicolas wine stores are a familiar Parisian sight; this one also has a restaurant where you can enjoy a fine glass of wine and a light meal of salad, quiche, charcuterie, cheese or a prepared dish. Modern setting and rather impersonal service.

Granterroirs – 30 rue de Miromesnil. MVilliers. ☎01 47 42 18 18. www.granterroirs.com. Closed 5–15 Aug and weekends. Reservations advised. Big oak tables, shelves stocked with local products, baskets garnished with small-label wines and specialities of different regions. The French countryside has come to Paris via this deluxe grocery store-cum-restaurant. Delectable salads, open-faced sandwiches, assorted gourmand platters and house desserts. No smoking.

Gust – 35 blvd Malesherbes. MMadeleine. ☎01 42 65 15 84. Closed Sun and eves. The local office workers have latched onto this upscale sandwich shop where the bread is top quality and the ingredients fresh. Packed full at lunch.

Le Bistrot de Jean-Luc – 41 rue de Penthièvre. MMiromesnil. ☎01 43 59 23 99. Closed 1–20 Aug and weekends. The small dining room with its big mirror is as simple as they come, but never mind. The tempting bistro menu and wide choice of wines by the glass are the main draw of this likeable little neighbourhood restaurant. Easy on the wallet.

La Fermette Marbeuf 1900 – 5 rue Marbeuf. MAlma-Marceau. ☎01 53 23 08 00. www.fermettemarbeuf.com. A minute's walk from Avenue Georges-V, the 1900s décor of this brasserie featuring ceramics and period windows will appeal to fans of classic Parisian restaurants. A period glass roof illuminates the second dining room. Traditional cuisine.

Le Griffonnier – 8 rue des Saussaies. MMiromesnil. ☎01 42 65 17 17. Closed Sat–Sun, three weeks in Aug. A 17C house is the setting for this wine bar serving appetising little dishes of the bistro genre. Rustic and something of a tight squeeze but quite jolly all the same. The cream of the Beaujolais crop is savoured here every year.

Lô Sushi – 8 rue de Berri. MGeorge-V. ☎01 45 62 01 00. www.losushi.com. A simple formula: sushi served in a minimalist setting created by the famous decorator Andrée Putman. Designed for fun, the idea is simple: you take a seat at the bar and take your sushi from a little conveyor belt. Much favoured by the jet-set who flock here every night.

Théâtre du Rond-Point – 2 bis av. Franklin-D.-Roosevelt. MFranklin-D.-Roosevelt. ☎01 44 95 98 21. www.theatredurondpoint.fr. Closed Aug and Sun eve. To reach this red and grey-toned restaurant, adorned with posters and other mementoes from former shows, you have to cross the lobby of the attractive theatre just alongside the Champs-Elysées. The terrace in the shade of horse chestnut trees is popular when the weather is fine.

L'Appart' – 9 rue du Colisée. MFranklin-D.-Roosevelt. ☎01 53 75 42 00. Daily till 2pm, Closed 15 Jul–27 Aug, Sat lunch, Sun. An engaging address right near the Champs-Élysées. Whether in the living room, study or kitchen of this restaurant arranged like a private apartment, you'll sample contemporary cuisine in a relaxed ambience. Service until midnight. A large selection of whiskies at the bar.

◯◯🏛**Brasserie Mollard** – *115 rue St-Lazare.* Ⓜ*Saint-Lazare.* ☎*01 43 87 50 22. www.mollard.fr.* The nothing-special exterior leads to a gem of the art nouveau period in its large, listed dining room designed by Edouard Niermans (Negresco in Nice, Hôtel de Paris in Monaco). Superb mosaics and decorated wall tiles from Sarreguemines. Straightforward brasserie cuisine.

◯◯🏛**Ladurée – Champs-Élysées** – *75 av. des Champs-Élysées.* Ⓜ*George-V* ☎*01 40 75 08 75. www.laduree.fr.* Can one possibly resist such gourmand temptations? In addition to the forty or so house pastries, the menu offers such savoury treats as salads, gourmet sandwiches, sample platters and traditional dishes, all served in a magnificent Napoléon III décor with charming drawing rooms upstairs. *Très chic!* Service until midnight.

9TH ARRONDISSEMENT

FAUBOURG POISSONNIÈRE – GRANDS BOULEVARDS – OPÉRA – PIGALLE – SAINT-LAZARE

◯**Autour d'une Assiette**– *1 r Chaptal.* Ⓜ*Pigalle.*☎*01 42 81 15 01. Closed weekends.* The name says it all: this restaurant proposes complete meals around one dish. Exotic, Baltic, Italian, or Asian, the dishes are copious and well-presented. The home made desserts are worth a second look. Colourful retro décor in the dining room.

◯**Déli-cieux** – *60 blvd Haussmann, Printemps de la Maison store, 9th floor.* Ⓜ*Havre-Caumartin.* ☎*01 42 82 62 76. www.printemps.com. Closed Sun and eves except Thu.* Enjoy panoramic views over Paris from this 9th floor self-service cafeteria at the Printemps Maison department store. When the weather is nice, seating is available on the large wooden deck terrace. Cold and hot dishes, salads, sandwiches.

◯**Tea Follies**– *6 place Gustave Toudouze.* Ⓜ*St-Georges.* ☎*01 42 80 08 44. Reservations recommended.* A tiny tearoom with a cosy décor. When the sun is shining some tables appear on the square outside. Salads, savory tarts, hot dishes and pastries are served daily. Sunday brunch is usually packed.

◯◯**I Golosi** – *6 rue de la Grange-Batelière.* Ⓜ*Grands-Boulevards.* ☎*01 48 24 18 63. www.igolosi.com. Closed 11 Jul–2 Aug, Sat eve and Sun.* At the entrance to the Passage Verdeau, this Venetian bistro serves cuisine with a decidedly Italian accent in a modern, elegant interior graced with Murano lamps, furniture from Trevise and a Venetian tiled floor. The entry has a small wine bar and shop, plus a few tables at lunchtime.

◯◯**Menthe et Basilic** – *6 rue Lamartine.* Ⓜ*Cadet.* ☎*01 48 78 12 20. Closed Sat lunch, Mon eve and Sun. Reservations requested.* The décor and cuisine of this pleasant sienna-walled restaurant conjure up southern France. The clever lighting system creates an intimate ambience and the nicely presented, delectable food is served with a smile.

◯◯**Paprika** – *28 av. Trudaine.* Ⓜ*Anvers.* ☎*01 44 63 02 91. www.le-paprika.com. Closed 1 Jan, 24-25 Dec.* On the same spot as the Âne Rouge, where socialist radicals rallied in the early 20C, this restaurant is now a citadel of Hungarian cooking. Try the cold meats, national dishes and Hungarian wines. Live Gypsy music in the evening.

◯◯**Au Petit Riche** – *25 rue Le Peletier.* Ⓜ*Le Peletier.* ☎*01 47 70 68 68. www.aupetitriche.com. Closed Sun.* An institution in this business district. Since 1858, bankers and stock-brokers have convened in the cosy comfort of this handsome room, plotting the course of the universe. Excellent selection of Loire wines. Serves until 12.15pm and attracts the post-theatre crowd.

◯◯**Le Barramundi** – *3 rue Taitbout.* Ⓜ*Richelieu-Drouot.* ☎*01 47 70 21 21. www.barramundi.fr. Closed Sat lunch, Sun, Aug 5–16.* The bar-lounge on the ground floor plays popular 'world music', whilst downstairs the spacious restaurant, a blend of Indian and African influences, is very popular with the business lunch bunch. Mediterranean cuisine with a spicy tang. Trendy crowd.

10TH ARRONDISSEMENT

FAUBOURG POISSONNIÈRE – GRANDS BOULEVARDS – CANAL SAINT-MARTIN

◯**Hôtel du Nord** – *102 quai de Jemmapes.* Ⓜ*Jacques-Bonsergent* or *République.* ☎*01 40 40 78 78. Closed two* *weeks in Aug, Sun night in winter*. It was in front of this very façade alongside the canal St-Martin that Arletty huskily said the now-famous words *"atmosphère, atmosphère"* to Jean Gabin in Marcel Carné's classic film *Hôtel du Nord*. Now a café-restaurant with a retro feel, it serves classic cuisine and organises live music in the evenings.

Le Sporting – *3 rue de Récollets (corner of quai de Jemmapes)*. Ⓜ *Jacques-Bonsergent*. ☎*01 46 07 02 00*. This old neighbourhood café has been redone with a retro atmosphere for a stylishly scruffy clientele of artsy types in the latest trainers. Traditional bistro fare presented on the slate. Some tables on the terrace facing the Canal St-Martin.

Brasserie Flo – *7 cour des Petites-Écuries*. Ⓜ *Château-d'Eau*. ☎*01 47 70 13 59. www.floparis.com* . Set in a paved cul-de-sac, this turn-of-the-century brasserie takes you back to a Paris of yore. Benches overhung with gleaming copper coat-hooks, old paintings and stained-glass windows: a picturesque setting for the appetising cuisine. Serves until 1.30am. Valet parking evenings Tues-Sat.

11TH ARRONDISSEMENT

BASTILLE – BELLEVILLE – FAUBOURG SAINT-ANTOINE – RÉPUBLIQUE

Chez l'Artiste – *153 rue de la Roquette*. Ⓜ *Philippe-Auguste*. ☎*01 43 79 96 19*. A pretty Italian restaurant that's both modern and cosy, with a fine selection of pastas and salads. The superb terrace under the trees is perfect for a summer meal or an afternoon *aperitif*.

Bistrot Les Sans Culottes – *27 rue de Lappe*. Ⓜ *Bastille or Ledru-Rollin*. ☎*01 48 05 42 92. Closed Mon*. Before venturing into the nocturnal throng of the Rue de Lappe, stop off here and savour the turn-of-the-century flavour of this bistro. Complete with bar, percolator, woodwork and moulded ceiling, menu on a chalk-slate and delicious chocolate cake, it's the perfect lair for party-goers. A few rooms available.

Bodega La Plancha – *34 rue Keller*. Ⓜ *Voltaire*. ☎*01 48 05 20 30. Closed two weeks in Aug, Sun lunch and Mon* ⌐. Be prepared for a lively evening in the 12sq m/129sq ft of this Basque restaurant plastered with posters, old photos

and postcards. Seated elbow-to-elbow, diners cheerfully tuck into Basque specialities: *pimientos, chipirons à l'encre* (squid in ink sauce) and Basque cake.

Chez Paul – *13 rue de Charonne*. Ⓜ *Bastille*. ☎*01 47 00 34 57. Reservations recommended eves*. Chez Paul is truly as old as it feels. A century ago it sold coffee, coal and lemonade; today the regular clientele contributes to the family spirit of the place. Old mirrors, advertising posters and pictures on the walls; well-prepared bistro-style cuisine on the plate.

Mansouria – *11 rue Faidherbe*. Ⓜ *Faidherbe-Chaligny*. ☎*01 43 71 00 16. Closed Mon lunch, Tue lunch and Sun*. Former ethnologist Fatima Hal is a Parisian reference in the field of Moroccan cooking, even publishing a cookbook of her country's recipes. This restaurant serves food cooked by women, in accordance with tradition, and served in a typical Moroccan décor.

Le Souk – *1 rue Keller*. Ⓜ *Ledru-Rollin or Bastille*. ☎*01 49 29 05 08. www.lesoukfr.com. Closed Mon. Reservations recommended eves. www.lesoukfr.com*. Go beyond the spice shop and enter this Moroccan house featuring sculpted woodwork, Oriental-style paintings and North African music to experience a meal from the southern side of the Mediterranean. Enjoy the generous helpings of couscous, a selection of vegetarian dishes, and the subtly spiced *tajines*.

Taco Loco – *116 rue Amelot*. Ⓜ *Filles-du-Calvaire*. ☎*01 43 57 90 24. Closed two weeks in Aug, Mon lunch and Sun*. Aficionados appreciate this simple Mexican restaurant, with its typical décor and authentic, family-style dishes prepared in the cooking space in the middle of the dining room. A convivial meal at affordable prices.

Blue Elephant – *43 rue de la Roquette*. Ⓜ *Bastille or Voltaire*. ☎*01 47 00 42 00. www.blueelephant.com. Closed Sat lunch*. A little corner of Thailand in the shadow of the Bastille. Set in the bustle of a lively street, this restaurant's doors open to reveal an exotic décor of green plants, wicker furniture and typical tablecloths. It's like stepping into another world rich with a thousand flavours. Service until midnight.

Maison Chardenoux – *1 rue Jules-Vallès.* Ⓜ *Charonne.* ☎*01 43 71 49 52.* No, you're not dreaming – you're still in the heart of Paris! With its authentic décor from 1904, venerable furniture and old paintings, this little restaurant is as inviting as can be. Customers gladly squeeze into the narrow dining room to savour the delicious, revitalising cuisine.

12TH ARRONDISSEMENT

BASTILLE – BERCY – FAUBOURG SAINT-ANTOINE

Le Grand Bleu – *blvd de la Bastille, Arsenal yacht harbour.* Ⓜ *Bastille.* ☎*01 43 45 19 99.* No, you're not dreaming – you're still in the heart of Paris! Seated at the terrace overlooking the capital's charming yacht harbour and garden, you're beneath the Bastille, scarcely 50m from its Génie-topped column. Meals are served on the veranda when the sun is playing hard to get. Fish and seafood specialities.

L'Aubergeade – *17 rue Chaligny.* Ⓜ *Reuilly-Diderot.* ☎*01 43 44 33 36.* Keep this address in your note pad. You'll appreciate the pretty varnished wood décor, the tables nearly touching one another, the relaxed atmosphere and the generous portions of traditional dishes that are easy on the wallet.

L'Ébauchoir – *45 rue de Citeaux.* Ⓜ *Reuilly-Diderot.* ☎*01 43 42 49 31.* www.lebauchoir.com. *Closed Sun and lunch Mon. Reservations recommended eves.* Every lunchtime the neighbourhood descends on this eatery for unequivocally traditional fare in a veritable bistro setting. Oak tables, painted walls and a large fresco. Evenings, the atmosphere is more intimate and serene.

Jean-Pierre Frelet – *25 rue Montgallet.* Ⓜ *Montgallet.* ☎*01 43 43 76 65. Closed Feb school holidays, Aug, Sat lunch and Sun.* Although one could almost miss the narrow façade of this restaurant next-door to the busy shops of this little street, it is well worth crossing the threshold to take a seat and savour the luscious cooking. The owner-chef worked for years in the country's best restaurants before opening his own establishment.

Le Vinéa Café – *26-28 cour St-Émilion.* Ⓜ *Cour-Saint-Émilion.* ☎*01 44 74 09 09.* www.vinea-cafe.com. The spirit of wine still haunts Bercy: witness this former warehouse where old beams and stone walls cohabit with a hip menu, a few bistro-style dishes and a revamped décor. A quick drink at the striped bar or on the terrace before heading for the nearby cinemas is also an option. WiFi.

Quincy – *28 av. Ledru-Rollin.* Ⓜ *Ledru-Rollin.* ☎*01 46 28 46 76.* www.lequincy.fr. *Closed 10 Aug–10 Sept, Sat–Mon* ⌐. This establishment's forte is savoury, substantial, provincial fare with no unnecessary fuss. The decoration is reminiscent of a country inn with wood panelled walls, wooden beams, chequered tablecloths and straw chairs. The atmosphere is jovial and the menu enticing.

Le Train Bleu – *At the Gare de Lyon (1st floor).* Ⓜ *Gare-de-Lyon.* ☎*01 43 43 09 06.* www.le-train-bleu.com. A must! This opulent 1900 brasserie with its luxurious frescoes and gold-leaf covered mouldings belongs to Paris's historic heritage. Originally designed for weary train travellers, it's now a gourmet restaurant popular with locals and visitors alike. Their English-style bar is a pleasant place for afternoon tea and light meals.

13TH ARRONDISSEMENT

GOBELINS

Chez Gladines – *30 rue des Cinq-Diamants.* Ⓜ *Corvisart or Place-d'Italie.* ☎*01 45 80 70 10* ⌐. *Closed three weeks in Aug.* This country-style Basque restaurant in the Butte-aux-Cailles is always full. Oversized salads with potatos and bacon are served on rustic wooden tables covered in red-checkered tablecloths. Fill up on just a few euros.

Des Crêpes et des Cailles – *13 rue de la Butte-aux-Cailles.* Ⓜ *Corvisart or Place-d'Italie.* ☎*01 45 81 68 69.* ⌐. A popular crêperie in the heart of the Butte-aux-Cailles, sweet and savoury crêpes to eat in the tiny dining room or to take away. A great selection and friendly service.

L'Avant Goût – *26 rue Bobillot.* Ⓜ *Place-d'Italie.* ☎*01 53 80 24 00.* www.lavantgout.com. *Closed Sun and Mon. Reservations required.* Close to the Place d'Italie, a little bistro specialising in simple, gourmand dishes. Thanks to the solid reputation and very appetising menu, this inviting, cheery establishment is full at lunch and dinner.

Les Cailloux – *58 rue des Clnq-Dia-mants.* ⓜ*Corvisart or Place-d'Italie.* ☎*01 45 80 15 08. www.lescailloux.fr. Closed three weeks in Aug, Sun and Mon. Reservations recommended.* Overlooking the crossroads of the Butte-aux-Cailles neighbourhood, this stylish retro trattoria is decorated with wooden floors, muted milk-chocolate walls, and large windows. Fine Italian cuisine served by friendly staff for an elegant, yet convivial, atmosphere.

◷**Le Jardin des Pâtes** – *33 blvd Arago.* ⓜ*Les Gobelins.* ☎*01 45 35 93 67. Closed 23 Dec–6 Jan and Sun.* A few minutes' walk from the Manufacture des Gobelins, this terrace under the boulevard's horse chestnut trees prolongs the flower-decked façade of a tiny wood-furnished dining room. The menu features original pasta dishes made from organic and freshly milled flours.

◷◷**Nouveau Village Tao-Tao** – *159 blvd Vincent-Auriol.* ⓜ*Nationale or Place-d'Italie.* ☎*01 45 86 40 08.* Just a few strides from Chinatown, here's a stopover for those who wish to continue their Asian adventure. Chinese food, of course, but also Thai dishes are served in the typically orientalist décor; the fixed-price lunch menus are a particularly good value; evening meals are à la carte.

14TH ARRONDISSEMENT

DENFERT-ROCHEREAU – MONTPARNASSE – MONTSOURIS

◷**Crêperie Le Petit Josselin** – *59 rue du Montparnasse.* ⓜ*Edgar-Quinet or Notre-Dame-des-Champs.* ☎*01 43 22 91 81. Closed Aug and Mon.* Crêperies have flourished in the area around the Gare Montparnasse, where Bretons used to arrive in the capital and settle down. In this one – a culinary ambassador of Brittany – crêpes are prepared under the eyes of onlooking diners. Carved wood art and Quimper porcelain on the walls.

◷◷**Au 14 Juillet il y a toujours des lampions** – *99 rue Didot.* ⓜ*Plaisance.* ☎*01 40 44 91 19.* Second-hand bric-a-brac here and there, walls covered with old posters, an aged wood-burning stove, porcelain lights and coloured lamps illuminating the bar make up the décor of this bistro sporting a singular, festive name: 'There are always lanterns on 14 July'. Slate *menu du jour.*

◷◷**Au Moulin Vert** – *34 bis rue des Plantes.* ⓜ*Plaisance or Alésia.* ☎*01 45 39 31 31. www.aumoulinvert.com.* A spot of greenery in the heart of Paris, this historic restaurant opened in 1905. Green furniture, white tablecloths and vigorous house plants on the veranda; imposing deciduous trees and an arborvitae hedge by the terrace. The traditional fare is good value for the money.

◷◷**La Régalade** – *49 av. J.-Moulin.* ⓜ*Alésia.* ☎*01 45 45 68 58. Closed Aug, Mon, Sun. Reservations required.* This Parisian bistro, located on a busy avenue, welcomes guests cheerfully and offers first-rate meals in the crowded dining room. Quite popular with the regulars, the restorative fare spotlights regional flavours based on the daily market offerings.

◷◷◷**La Coupole** – *102 blvd du Montparnasse.* ⓜ*Vavin.* ☎*01 43 20 14 20. www.lacoupoleparis.com.* A temple of Parisian nightlife that needs no introduction. A famous night-club in the early 20C, this 1920s brasserie has retained its splendid original décor featuring frescoes, a superb bar and long bay windows. It continues to cater to late-night patrons in a noisy, lively atmosphere until 1am. Dancing in the adjacent salon.

◷◷◷**Monsieur Lapin** – *11 rue Raymond-Losserand.* ⓜ*Gaité.* ☎*01 43 20 21 39. www.monsieur-lapin.fr. Closed Aug, Mon, Sat lunch. Reservations requested.* Behind the amusing façade evoking a flower-decked country inn, Mister Rabbit has pride of place. He is celebrated both through the décor and on the menu, where he is prepared in every imaginable manner. Pleasant, retro interior. The gourmand menu is easy on the budget.

15TH ARRONDISSEMENT

JAVEL – MONTPARNASSE – TOUR EIFFEL – VAUGIRARD

◷**L'Infinithé** – *8 rue Desnouettes.* ⓜ*Convention.* ☎*01 40 43 14 23. www. infinithe.com. Closed eves, Mon and Sun except the 1st Sun of each month. Reservations recommended.* This tiny *salon de thé* does a fine job of reviving the 1930s. The interior has been carefully chosen – woodwork, dressers, small pedestal tables, embroidered tablecloths and sugar bowls found in second-hand shops contribute to the upbeat atmosphere. Delicious house pastries.

⊜ ⊜ **Le Beau Violet** – *92 rue des Entrepreneurs.* Ⓜ*Commerce.* ☎*01 45 78 93 44. Closed Aug and Sun. Reservations required eves.* The perfect place for taking a culinary trip to Corsica without leaving Paris. The dishes, simmered in the hearth and served in copper ovenware, are heavenly; the décor and music give voice to the Corsican spirit. You can almost smell the ocean!

⊜ ⊜ **Bombay Café**– *19 av. Félix-Faure.* Ⓜ*Félix-Faure.* ☎*01 40 60 91 11.* A pleasant colonial-style décor evokes the spirit of this Indian city with carved wood, old photos from the Raj, and vintage uniforms. The English-inspired cuisine has some spicy touches. Tearoom in the afternoon and brunch on Sundays.

16TH ARRONDISSEMENT

AUTEUIL – BOIS DE BOULOGNE – MUETTE-RANELAGH – PASSY – TROCADÉRO

⊜ **Carette** – *4 place du Trocadéro.* Ⓜ*Trocadéro.* ☎*01 47 27 88 56. www.carette-paris.com.* Founded in 1927, this pretty pink tearoom with the vast covered terrace is a neighbourhood classic. All of the elegant locals come for tea and pastries served in dainty china cups. The macarons are a must, made with the original recipe since the opening.

⊜ ⊜ **Le Bistrot des Vignes** – *1 rue Jean-Bologne.* Ⓜ*La Muette – by rue de l'Annonciation* – ☎*01 45 27 76 64. www.bistrotdesvignes.com. Reservations recommended.* Hurry to this bistro, then relax and settle in for a while. The colourful décor of stained wood is very inviting, and the cuisine – between Provence and Aveyron down south – is absolutely delicious. Warm reception; young, efficient service.

⊜ ⊜ **Brasserie de la Poste** – *54 rue de Longchamp.* Ⓜ*Trocadéro.* ☎*01 47 55 01 31. Closed Sat for lunch.* This neighbourhood brasserie has acquired a regular clientele that appreciates the accessible prices and generous helpings served in the long, narrow dining room. The hospitable atmosphere and 1930s-style décor have undoubtedly contributed to its success.

⊜ ⊜ **La Gare** – *19 Chaussée de la Muette.* Ⓜ*La Muette.* ☎*01 42 15 15 31. www.restaurantlagare.com.* Dinner on the platform or a quick lunch in the waiting room: you're dining in the old Passy-La Muette train station. Built in 1854, it now houses a restaurant frequented by the district's jet set. Surprising décor, lively cuisine and terrace in summer. Serves until midnight.

⊜ ⊜ **Le Petit Rétro** – *5 rue Mesnil.* Ⓜ*Victor-Hugo.* ☎*01 44 05 06 05. www.petitretro.fr. Closed three weeks Aug, Sat lunch and Sun. Reservations recommended eves.* Elegant art nouveau tiles grace this charming little bistro set in an ultra-chic neighbourhood. Try the first room, with its lovely old bar, or discover the new dining room. The lunch *menu du jour* is more affordable than the evening menu. Hearty country specialities, choucroute, home made foie gras, and boudin noir.

⊜ ⊜ ⊜ **Al Mounia** – *16 rue de Magdebourg.* Ⓜ*Trocadéro or Iéna.* ☎*01 47 27 57 28. www.al-mounia.pagesrestos.com. Closed Sun. Reservations required eves.* Carvings and oriental friezes are part of the authentic Moroccan décor of this restaurant which serves *pastillas, couscous* and *tajines* on gigantic copper platters to guests comfortably seated on low sofas. The staff are all in traditional dress. Order ahead for *méchoui* (spit-roasted lamb).

⊜ ⊜ ⊜ ⊜ **Le Pré Catelan** – *rte de Suresnes in the Bois de Boulogne – from Porte Maillot take the Allée de Longchamp, then the Allée de la Reine.* ☎*01 44 14 41 14. www.precatelanparis.com. Closed 1–24 Feb, 27 Oct–5 Nov, Sun except lunch from 6 May–26 Oct and Mon.* Situated in the Bois de Boulogne on the edge of the enchanting Pré-Catelan garden, this Second Empire pavilion is a marvellous site indeed. The luxurious interior, winter garden and beautiful summer terrace beguile the Paris elite who continue to flock here to savour the exceptional (Michelin-starred) cuisine. Attractive lunch menu.

17TH ARRONDISSEMENT

CHAMPS-ÉLYSÉES – MONCEAU

⊜ ⊜ **La Table Oliviers & Co** – *8 rue de Lévis.* Ⓜ*Villiers.* ☎*01 53 42 18 04. www.oliviers-co.com. Closed Aug.* This restaurant-cum-grocer's is an idea whose time has come. Wooden shelves displaying foodstuffs sharing an olive oil theme surround one big, common dining table where original savoury and sweet victuals are served.

⊜⊜**Café d'Angel** – 16 rue Brey. Ⓜ*Charles-de-Gaulle – Étoile or Ternes.* ☎*01 47 54 03 33. Closed Aug, Christmas– New Year and weekends.* An old-fashioned look for the latest cuisine, flavoursome and gourmand, defines this little bistro close to the Étoile. You can view the establishment's young chef working in the kitchen from your table in the dining room where leatherette benches, old tiles and a slate menu set the tone. Quite reasonably priced at lunchtime.

⊜⊜**Grain d'orge** – 15 rue de l'Arc-de-Triomphe. Ⓜ *Charles-de-Gaulle – Étoile.* ☎*01 47 64 33 47. Closed Sat lunch and Sun.* The young chef's native Flanders inspires the menu here. Two minutes from the Arc de Triomphe, the red velvet wall seats, large decorative mirrors and handsome bar define the amusing art deco style. Wine list enhanced by a choice of beers…

⊜⊜**La Table Oliviers & Co** – 8 rue de Lévis. Ⓜ*Villiers.* ☎*01 53 42 18 04. www. oliviers-co.com. Closed Aug.* This new restaurant-cum-grocer's is an idea whose time has come. Wooden shelves displaying foodstuffs sharing an olive oil theme surround one big, common dining table where original savoury and sweet victuals are served.

⊜⊜⊜**Bistrot St Ferdinand** – 275 rue Péreire. Ⓜ*Porte Maillot.* ☎*01 45 74 33 32. Reservations recommended, especially eves.* Located beside the Palais de Congrès in the very lively quarter of Porte Maillot, this equally lively restaurant is frequented by the business community , tourists and even the occasional airline crew. Unusual cinema like décor. Aperitifs are served on the house and the set menu is very good value for money.

⊜⊜⊜**Caves Petrissans** – 30 bis av. Niel. Ⓜ*Pereire or Ternes.* ☎*01 42 27 52 03. Closed end Jul–early Aug and weekends.* Over 100 years old, this establishment is a Parisian institution. The familiar bistro atmosphere, refreshing cuisine and noteworthy wine cellar contribute to its success. The leatherette booth seats and

terrace on the pavement in summer are ever in demand.

18TH ARRONDISSEMENT
MONTMARTRE
⊜**Le Vieux Chalet** – 14 bis rue Norvins. Ⓜ*Abbesses or Anvers.* ☎*01 46 06 21 44. Closed Dec–Mar, Sat, Sun eve and Mon* 🍴. Yes, it is possible to sample simple fare without risking wreck and ruin just 50m from the exclusive Place du Tertre. Venture into this hundred-year old countrified inn and enjoy its heavenly terrace-garden far from the madding crowd, as did Apollinaire and Picasso in their day. Unpretentious home-style cooking.

⊜⊜**L'Été en Pente Douce** – 23 rue Muller. Ⓜ*Anvers.* ☎*01 42 64 02 67. www.parisresto.com. Closed 25 Dec and 1 Jan.* From Sacré-Cœur, walk down a few steps into this side street and take a seat on the charming terrace of this former baker's shop, now a restaurant-cum-tea room. You'll savour salads, pastas, mixed platters and pastries just opposite a pretty public garden.

⊜⊜**La Mère Catherine** – 6 pl. du Tertre. Ⓜ*Abbesses.* ☎*01 46 06 32 69.* One of Montmartre's pride and joys. In addition to its legendary location, this 17C establishment became famous after housing Danton and his disciples. Decidedly rustic interior and a terrace that's assailed by enthusiasts whenever the sun shines.

⊜⊜**Aux Négociants** – 27 rue Lambert Ⓜ*Château-Rouge.* ☎*01 46 06 15 11. Closed Aug, weekends.* Located at the foot of the Butte Montmartre, this establishment dedicated to wine is immediately likeable. Simple décor with a handsome bar and photos by Doisneau immortalising bistro life. Nourishing, traditional fare on the menu.

⊜⊜**Rughetta** – 41 rue Lepic. Ⓜ*Blanche* ☎*01 42 23 41 70. Closed Christmas and New Year. Reservations recommended.* This cheerful, colourful little Italian restaurant in one of Montmartre's lively streets is truly delightful. The closely set tables are generally besieged as the chef skilfully whips up dishes from his native land.

⊜⊜**Le Verger de Montmartre** – 37 rue Lamarck. Ⓜ*Lamarck.* ☎*01 42 62 62 67.* Beyond the discreet façade lies a soothing interior of brown and orange tints, furnished with a mind to originality. Traditional cuisine and very nice welcome. A philosophical dinner-debate (en français) is held the first Thursday of the month.

19TH ARRONDISSEMENT

BELLEVILLE – CANAL SAINT-MARTIN – LA VILLETTE

Le Pacifique – 35 rue de Belleville. MBelleville. ☎01 42 49 66 80. Situated in the centre of Belleville, this Chinese restaurant is a favourite with locals and Asians who come share the steamed specialities and other typical dishes. Local events can be followed without leaving the table thanks to the large picture windows. Open until 2am.

Le Rendez-Vous des Quais – 10 quai de la Seine – Cinémas MK2. MStalingrad ☎01 40 37 02 81. www.mk2.com. A holiday spirit inhabits this restaurant on the banks of the Bassin de la Villette, adjoining the cineplex. Before or after your film, stop here and enjoy the superb terrace, especially delightful during the summer. Much frequented by Parisians. The wine list is put together by Claude Chabrol, the film director.

Le Fleuve Rouge – 1 rue Pradier. MPyrénées. ☎01 42 06 25 04. Closed weekends, Aug. It's no surprise that this little restaurant, as simple as they come, is so popular with the natives: the atmosphere is always convivial and the portions of home-style cookery are ever generous. Vietnamese dishes on demand; unfussy, friendly service.

L'Hermès – 23 rue Mélingue. MPyrénées. ☎01 42 39 94 70. Closed Sun, Mon, Wed lunch, Easter and Aug. Finding the discreet blue façade of this small restaurant near the Buttes-Chaumont takes some doing, but it's worth the effort. The dining rooms have been renovated, the lunch menu is a bargain, and each month a new exhibition is on show.

20TH ARRONDISSEMENT

BELLEVILLE – PÈRE-LACHAISE

Pascaline – 49 rue de Pixérécourt. MTélégraphe. ☎01 44 62 22 80. A small neighbourhood restaurant where wine reigns supreme. The owner has a rare talent for bringing unjustly overlooked vintages to light while the cuisine reveals the flavours of Auvergne. Nice terrace in pleasant weather.

Le Vieux Belleville – 12 rue des Envierges. MPyrénées. ☎01 44 62 92 66. www.le-vieux-belleville.com. Closed Aug 15, Mon, Tue and Wed eves and Sun. This establishment rings with the inimitable Parisian twang of days gone by. The décor, principally black and white photos and vinyl, sings the praises of songsters from the 1940s and 50s. Homey cooking and no-frills service.

Les Allobroges – 71 rue des Grands-Champs. MMaraîchers. ☎01 43 73 40 00 Closed Easter, Aug, public holidays, Sun eve and Mon. Granted, this restaurant is far from the heart of Paris, but it is well worth a visit nonetheless. Behind the handsome light wood façade, you'll savour food from menus devised by the proprietor, a self-taught enthusiast, in an animated, convivial setting. A must if you're in the neighbourhood.

Bistro Chantefable – 93 av. Gambetta. MGambetta. ☎01 46 36 81 76 Closed 24-25 Dec. After paying your respects at the Père-Lachaise cemetery, come and join the living in this bistro situated behind the town hall. The crown moulding, fine bar, old sheen, healthy selection of wines, seafood and palatable dishes are a hit with the local population. Convivial ambience.

Le Rez-de-Chaussée – 10 rue Sorbier MMénilmontant or Gambetta. ☎01 43 58 30 14. Daily. A retro bistro with an agreeable second-hand shop atmosphere. Tables on wrought iron stands, frosted glass wall lights, aged clocks and black and white photos: the imaginative décor tips its hat to the 1930s and 40s. Progressive cuisine.

Zéphyr – 1 rue du Jourdain. MJourdain. ☎01 46 36 65 81. Closed three weeks Aug, Dec 24–2 Jan. Reservations recommended. Rediscover the 1930s Paris in this pretty period bistro. The original art deco interior, featuring frescoes, woodwork and old light fixtures, has been carefully preserved. Reigning good humour, inventive cuisine and an ample choice of wines. Often packed.

ENTERTAINMENT

&See Discovering Paris for additional night spots.

Address Book

THEATRE

Kiosque Théâtre – *Pl. de la Madeleine.* MMadeleine. *Tue–Sat 12.30pm–2pm, Sun 12.30–4pm.* Theatre tickets can be bought here on the day of the performance for half the normal price (for the most expensive shows). You can choose from over 100 shows and 120 plays (more private than state-run theatres). You'll want to go with alternative choices in mind, as you may not get what you want. No credit cards.

Comédie-Française – *Pl. Colette.* ☎01 44 58 15 15. MPalais-Royal. *www. comedie-francaise.fr. Tickets: 11am–1pm Closed end Jul–Sept and 1 May.* Founded in 1860 by Louis XIV, the repertoire consists principally of traditional drama composed by the classical French playwrights. Theatregoers can admire the famous seated figure of Voltaire by Houdon in the public foyer, as well as the chair in which Molière himself fell ill while playing *Le Malade Imaginaire* on 17 February, 1673.

Théâtre National de Chaillot – *1 pl. du Trocadéro.* ☎01 53 65 30 00. MTrocadéro. *www.theatre-chaillot. fr. Tickets: Mon–Sat 11am–7pm, Sun 1pm–5pm.* Inaugurated in 1920, from 1930 to 1972 this stage was home to the Théâtre National Populaire (TNP) under the supervision of some of the world's finest directors, including Jean Vilar and Georges Wilson. Here Gérard Philipe gave unforgettable performances as the lead roles in *El Cid* and *Lorenzaccio.* Certain shows are accessible to those with impaired sight or hearing.

Odéon Théâtre de l'Europe – *Pl. de l'Odéon.* ☎01 44 85 40 40. MOdéon. *www.theatre-odeon.fr. Tickets: Mon–Sat 11am–6.30pm.* Jean-Louis Barrault and Madeleine Renaud made this one of Paris's premier playhouses up until 1968. Productions of Paul Claudel's *Tête d'Or,* Ionesco's *Rhinoceros* and Samuel Beckett's *Waiting for Godot* and *Happy Days* were staged here. Since 1990, Odéon's mission has been to stage European productions. Extensive renovations to the 18C theatre were completed in 2006.

Théâtre National de la Colline – *15 rue Malte-Brun.* ☎01 44 62 52 52. MGambetta. *www.colline.fr. Tickets: Mon–Sat 11am–6.30pm, Sun 1pm–4.30pm. Closed Jul–Aug.* The staging of modern drama is this national theatre's vocation. Alain Françon has been the director since 1997.

Théâtre du Rond-Point – *2 bis av. Franklin-Roosevelt.* ☎01 44 95 98 21. MFranklin-Roosevelt. *www.theatre durondpoint.fr. Tickets: Tue–Sat 2pm–7pm, Sun noon–4pm. Closed summer.* First a panoramic view-point, then a skating rink, Rond-Point has been a playhouse since 1981. Its current director, Marcel Maréchal, alternates repertory theatre and contemporary creations.

Théâtre Marigny – *Av. de Marigny.* ☎01 53 96 70 00. MChamps-Elysées-Clémenceau. *www.theatremarigny.fr. Tickets Mon–Sat 11am–6.30pm, Sun 11am–3pm. Closed Jul–Aug.* Amadeus produced by Roman Polanski, *Cyrano de Bergerac* by Robert Hossein, *Les Variations Enigmatiques* with Alain Delon and *La Dame aux Camélias* starring Isabelle Adjani have been among this theatre's finest moments. Long directed by the Compagnie Renauld-Barrault, followed by Elvire Popesco and Robert Manuel.

Théâtre de la Renaissance – *20 blvd St-Martin.* MStrasbourg-St-Denis. ☎01 42 08 18 50 or 01 42 02 47 35. *Ma sœur est un chic type* and *Un air de famille* (Family Resemblances) by Bacri and Jaoui are two of this theatre's greatest hits to date. Guy Bedos and Fabrice Lucchini have also graced the stage of this playhouse dedicated to quality entertainment. A cut above the usual boulevard fare.

Théâtre Mogador – 25 rue Mogador. ☎01 53 32 32 32. ⓜTrinité. www.mogador.net. Tickets; Mon–Sat 10am–7pm, Sun 10am–4pm. Built in 1914 along the lines of the Palladium in London, this is Paris's largest private theatre (1 805 seats). Over the years, the programme has featured variety shows, operettas, drama (Cyrano de Bergerac, La Femme du Boulanger) and films. Currently dedicated to musicals, Jérôme Savary, Jeanne Moreau and Dee Dee Bridgewater have worked wonders here.

Théâtre des Variétés – 7 blvd Montmartre. ☎01 42 33 09 92 (res) or 01 42 33 11 41(theatre). ⓜGrands-Boulevards. www.theatre-des-varietes.fr. Tickets: Mon–Sat 11am–7pm, Sun 11am–4pm. Closed Jul–Aug. Feydeau's La Puce à l' oreille (Meet me at the Pussycat), Marcel Pagnol's Topaze, Jean Poiret's La Cage aux folles (Birds of a Feather), and, more recently, Le Dîner de cons (The Dinner Game) were all created in this theatre, one of Paris's oldest.

La Cartoucherie – Rte du Champ-de-Manœuvres, Bois de Vincennes. ⓜChateau de Vincennes. ☎01 43 74 88 50 or 01 43 74 24 08. This group of theatres, composed of five independent playhouses (Théâtre du Soleil, Théâtre du Chaudron, Épée de bois, Théâtre de l'Aquarium and Théâtre de la Tempête), was created in the 1970s on land formerly belonging to the army. The woody, peaceful setting and the quality and variety of its shows have contributed greatly to its success.

OPERA AND DANCE

Opéra-Bastille – Pl. de la Bastille. ⓜBastille. ☎01 40 01 17 89/08 92 89 90 90. www.opera-de-paris.fr. Tickets: Mon–Fri 9am–6pm, Sat 9am–1pm. Closed mid-Jul–mid-Sept. Designed by Carlos Ott, this opera house marries technical prowess and public outreach. Inaugurated in 1989 by François Mitterrand, it began its first season in spring, 1990, with a revival of Hector Berlioz' Les Troyens, under the direction of the conductor Myung-Whun Chung.

Opéra-Comique (Salle Favart) – 5 rue Favart. ⓜRichelieu-Drouot. ☎08 25 00 00 58 or 01 42 44 45 46. www.opera-comique.com. Tickets: Mon 9am–2pm, 3.15pm–6pm, Tue–Sat 9am–9pm, Sun 11am–3pm, 4.15pm–7pm. Closed Aug. The Opéra-Comique is also known as the **Salle Favart**, its original name. Operas such as Bizet's Carmen (1875), Léo Delibes's Lakmé (1883), and Pelléas et Mélisande, which dazed the world of opera in 1902, all made their débuts here.

Palais Garnier – 8 rue Scribe. ⓜOpéra, RER Auber. ☎01 40 01 18 11 or 08 36 69 78 68. www.opera-de-paris.fr. Tickets: Mon–Sat 11am–6.30pm. Closed mid-Jul–early Sept. Built from 1862 to 1875 by Garnier, a young architect, this theatre's impressive size and luxurious decoration make it a fine example of Second Empire architecture. It has been the home of the National Academy of Music since 1875. One can admire the magnificence of the stairwell and foyer, along with the splendid hall, embellished in 1964 by a ceiling painted by Chagall.

Théâtre de la Ville – 2 pl. du Châtelet. ⓜChâtelet. ☎01 42 74 22 77. www.theatredelaville-paris.com. Tue–Sat 11am–8pm, Mon 11am–7pm. A multidisciplinary people's theatre, featuring ballet, drama, and popular, traditional and classical music. With an eye to encouraging contemporary creativity, this stage has showcased many fine artists, from Pina Bausch to Nusrat Fateh Ali Kahn.

CLASSICAL AND CONTEMPORARY CONCERTS

Châtelet-Théâtre Musical de Paris (TMP) – Pl. du Châtelet. ⓜChâtelet. ☎01 40 28 28 40. www.chatelet-theatre.com. 10am–7pm by telephone or 11am–7pm at theatre. In 1909, Serge de Diaghilev's Russian Ballet presented Borodin's Prince Igor here; the following year, Gustav Mahler conducted his own Symphony No 2 and Caruso was acclaimed for his performance of Verdi's Aïda.

Cité de la Musique – 221 av. Jean-Jaurès. ⓜPorte-de-Pantin. ☎01 44 84 44 84. www.cite-musique.fr. Tue–Sat noon–6pm, Sun 10am–6pm. Inaugurated in 1995, this musical village complex designed by the architect Christian de Portzamparc includes a modular concert hall that adapts to the pieces given, an amphitheatre, documentation centres, musicians' workshops, a Music Museum, a bookshop and a café.

Maison de Radio-France – *116 av. du Prés. Kennedy.* ☏*01 56 40 15 16.* Ⓜ*Passy. www.concerts.radiofrance.fr.*
The Maison de Radio France holds a wide range of music concerts: jazz, classical, traditional and contemporary (the "Présences" festival in February, for example); performances are inexpensive or free. The Olivier-Messiaen hall also stages concerts by Radio-France's choir and orchestra.

Salle Pleyel – *252 rue du Fg-St-Honoré.* Ⓜ*Ternes.* ☏*08 42 56 13 13. www.salle pleyel.fr. Mon–Sat noon–7pm. Closed Jul–Aug.* Paris's Symphony Orchestra, along with some of the world's most gifted conductors and musicians (Fedor Chaliapine, Arthur Rubinstein, R. Casadesus, Pablo Casals, Yehudi Menuhin, etc.), have given many dazzling performances at this Art Deco theatre, completely renovated in 2006.

Théâtre des Champs-Élysées – *15 av. Montaigne.* Ⓜ*Alma-Marceau.* ☏*01 49 52 07 41. www.theatrechampselysees. fr. Closed Jul–Aug.* Constructed in 1913 and belonging to the historical register since 1953, the Théâtre des Champs-Élysées offers music lovers a choice between the traditional evening programme and Sunday morning concerts. The world's greatest conductors, including Karl Bœhm, Herbert Von Karajan, and many others, have waved their batons here. In addition, some of the planet's finest ballet troupes have also performed here, such as the Russian Bolchoï and Kirov Ballets, Maurice Béjart, Roland Petit's Ballet de Paris and Josephine Baker's famous Revue Nègre.

JAZZ-ROCK

Jazz-Club Lionel Hampton – *81 blvd Gouvion-St-Cyr.* Ⓜ*Porte-Maillot.* ☏*01 40 68 30 42. www.jazzclub-paris.com. Concerts from 10.30pm.* Since 1976, all the greatest names in jazz have played here, including Count Basie and the Modern Jazz Quartet. Traditional jazz (New Orleans, Swing) concerts alternate with rhythm 'n' blues. A modern club that remains true to its jazzy origins.

Le New Morning – *7-9 rue des Petites-Écuries.* Ⓜ*Château-d'Eau.* ☏*01 45 23 51 41. www.newmorning.com. 8pm–1am Closed Aug.* Jazz, world music, salsa, blues: the New Morning is an efferves-

cent, eclectic club that has produced Chet Baker, Dexter Gordon, Art Blakey and James Carter as well as Compay Segundo, The Cranberries and The Fugees…

Le Petit Journal Montparnasse – *13 rue du Cdt-Mouchotte.* Ⓜ*Montparnasse-Bienvenüe or Gaîté.* ☏*01 43 21 56 70. www.petit-journal.com. Open Mon–Sat 7am–2am, concerts: 10pm. Closed mid-Jul–mid-Aug and certain public holidays.* A bastion of classical jazz boasting a lengthy inventory of great names: Baden Powell, Claude Bolling, Didier Lockwood, Eddy Louiss and Richard Galliano, in addition to songsters with a jazz, swing or blues slant, like Claude Nougaro, Manu Di Bango and Bill Deraime who appreciate the club's unique atmosphere.

Élysée-Montmartre – *72 blvd de Rochechouart.* Ⓜ*Anvers.* ☏*01 44 92 45 47. www.elyseemontmartre.com. Concerts 7.30pm–10.30pm.* The Élysée-Montmartre is as popular with artists as the public. Tricky, Metallica, Bjork, Burning Spear, David Bowie and Iggy Pop have played here, enjoying the close contact with fans and the charm of the hall. Enthusiasts are also keen on the theme evenings, especially the traditional ball held the 1st and 3rd Saturdays of each month.

VARIETY

Olympia – *28 blvd des Capucines.* Ⓜ*Opéra .*☏*01 47 42 25 49 or 08 92 68 33 68 (reservations by tel). www.olympia hall.com. Shows: 8.30pm, Sun 5pm. Closed Aug.* The most popular music-hall performers have given shows in this concert hall formerly managed by Bruno Coquatrix, the outstanding talent scout. Demolished in 1997, the Olympia was entirely rebuilt just a few dozen metres from the original site.

Zénith – *211 av. Jean-Jaurès. Porte-de-Pantin.* ☏*01 42 08 60 00. www.le-zenith. com.* The Parc de la Villette's vast grey and red hall (6 335 seats) is appropriately named: many artists at the zenith of their careers play here, including the greatest names in rock and pop.

Palais Omnisports de Paris-Bercy (POPB) – *8 blvd de Bercy.* Ⓜ*Bercy.* ☏*08 25 03 00 31. www.bercy.com.* The POPB hosts the capital's biggest music and sports events. Rock and pop's greatest stars – Elton John, Bruce Springsteen, Sting and Madonna, to name but a few – fill the stadium. As for sports, tournaments include figure skating (the Lalique Trophy), go-karting, rollerblading, indoor cycling (Open des Nations), and equestrian competitions.

Casino de Paris – *16 rue de Clichy*. [M]*Trinité*. ☎*01 49 95 22 22* . *www. casinodeparis.fr*. Maurice Chevalier and Josephine Baker made their names in this century-old theatre that now produces contemporary stars like Jacques Higelin, Sylvie Vartan, Eddy Mitchell and the hit musical *Starmania*.

La Cigale – *120 blvd Rochechouart*. [M]*Anvers or Pigalle*. ☎*01 49 25 81 75*. *www.lacigale.fr*. Born in 1887, La Cigale (The Cicada) has vibrated to the tune of the great Mistinguett, Maurice Chevalier and Arletty. Redecorated in 1987 by Philippe Starck, the stage of its handsome Italian-style theatre now welcomes variety artists, together with international rock and pop musicians.

Le Bataclan – *50 blvd Voltaire*. [M]*Oberkampf*. ☎*01 43 14 00 30*. *www. le-bataclan.com*. Built in 1864, the Bataclan was named after an Offenbach operetta. Successively a café-concert hall, a revue theatre and a cinema, it has hosted stars as dissimilar as Buffalo Bill and Edith Piaf. Today it is a well-established member of the rock and clubbing circuit: The Cure, LL Cool J, Massive Attack, Elvis Costello have played here.

CABARETS, REVUES

Moulin-Rouge – *82 blvd de Clichy*. [M]*Blanche*. ☎*01 53 09 82 82*. *www. moulin-rouge.com*.Tickets: 9am–1am. Since 1889, the Moulin Rouge has enthralled spectators from all over the world with its sumptuous productions: from the French Cancan – immortalised by Toulouse-Lautrec – to Maurice Chevalier, from Colette to Mistinguett, and from Ella Fitzgerald to Elton John. "Féerie", the Moulin Rouge's new revue, carries on the tradition with dancers who are as gorgeous as ever…

Crazy Horse – *12 av. George-V*. [M]*George V*. ☎*01 47 23 32 32*. *www. lecrazyhorseparis.com*. One of the capital's most beautiful revues. Magnificent dancers burn up this stage night after

night performing original choreographed works.

Folies-Bergère – *32 rue Richer*. [M]*Cadet or Grands-Boulevards*. ☎*01 44 79 98 98*. *www.foliesbergere.com*. Tickets 10am–6pm. Loïe Fuller and Yvette Guilbert, Maurice Chevalier, Yvonne Printemps and Mistinguett, Josephine Baker and Charles Trenet – the legendary stars of yesteryear whose spirits now haunt this theatre all crossed paths here. Note the art deco façade and the gigantic hall of Hollywoodian proportions.

Le Lido – *116 bis av. des Champs-Élysées*. [M]*George V*. ☎*01 40 76 56 10*. *www.lido. fr*. Without a doubt Paris's most international revue show. The celebrated Bluebell Girls show off their feathers, glitter and stunning anatomy with panache. Over 600 costumes, dozens of decors, fountains and superb lighting effects combine to produce this ever popular show.

Le Paradis Latin – *28 rue du Card.-Lemoine*. [M]*Jussieu or Cardinal-Lemoine*. ☎*01 43 25 28 28*. *www.paradis-latin.com*. This fêted Parisian cabaret was designed by Gustave Eiffel and inaugurated in January 1889 to mark the World Fair. The dancers (male and female), lights, sets and music all participate in upholding the magic of this revue where the French Cancan still kicks up its heels.

CAFÉ-THÉÂTRES

Here is a list of a few of the lively *café-théâtres* which are a speciality of Paris, mixing humour, song and often a bit of late-night carousing. If you don't speak French, you're likely to feel left out, and would be better off taking in a show at one of the cabarets listed above.

Café d' Edgar-Théâtre d' Edgar – *58 blvd Edgar-Quinet*. [M]*Edgar-Quinet*. ☎*01 42 79 97 97*. *www.edgar.fr*. Mon–Sat 2.30pm–7.30pm. The Café d'Edgar is one of Paris's most famous café-théatres with a reputation for comedy and original shows. Its *Babas-cadres* has been a hit for over 15 years and is still going strong.

Café de la Gare – *41 rue du Temple*. [M]*Hôtel-de-Ville*. ☎*01 42 78 52 51*. Shows 8pm and 9.45pm, Sun 8.15pm. Set in the heart of the Marais, this hallowed hall of merriment has been open for three decades. Patrick Dewaere and Coluche both started their careers here. Today, one comical creation after another is staged under the venerable beams of this old carriage inn.

Le Caveau de la République – *1 blvd St-Martin.* Ⓜ*République.* ☎*01 42 78 44 45. www.caveau.fr. Shows Tue–Fri 8.30pm, Sat 4.30pm, Sun 3.30pm. Closed early Apr–mid-Sept.* Open since 1901, this establishment continues to operate along the same lines as when Pierre Dac performed here: 6 comedians follow one another for 2 hours 15 mins of stand-up comedy. Laurent Ruquier, François Morel, Smaïn and Patrick Sébastien are just a few of France's famous comedians whose illustrious careers began here.

Le Lapin Agile – *22 rue des Saules.* Ⓜ*Lamarck-Caulaincourt.* ☎*01 46 06 85 87. www.au-lapin-agile.com. Tue–Sun 9pm–2am.* This cabaret located in a rustic little house looks surprisingly bucolic in the urban environment. It owes its name to the sign painted by André Gill in 1875 – still visible today – of a rabbit *(lapin)* leaping out of a stew-pot. Le Lapin has remained true to its origins, when Apollinaire, Bruant, Modigliani and Picasso used to spend an evenings here: song, satire and like in the old days – *sans* microphone.

Les Blancs-Manteaux – *15 rue des Blancs-Manteaux.* Ⓜ*Rambuteau.* ☎*01 48 87 15 84. www.blancsmanteaux.fr. 7pm–11pm.* A hotbed of talent for the past thirty years, this café-théâtre gave many performers their first taste of fame (Renaud, Jacques Higelin, Bernard Lavilliers, Romain Bouteille, Anne Roumanoff, Michèle Laroque and more). Several different artists share the stage every night: the show must go on!

Les Deux Ânes – *100 blvd de Clichy.* Ⓜ*Blanche.* ☎*01 46 06 10 26. www.2anes. com. Shows Tue–Sat 8.30pm, Sat Matinée 4.30pm. Closed Jul–Aug.* Since 1922, the tradition of French songs and Montmartre humour has been kept alive at the Two Donkeys in the form of biting satire targeting news and politics.

CINEMAS

When consulting a cinema programme, it should be remembered that foreign films shown in France can be divided into two categories: VO or VF. VO *(version originale)* means that the film is shown with its original soundtrack and subtitled in French. VF *(version française)* means that the film has been dubbed. This does not apply to French films which are in French, unless otherwise stated.

Cinéma L' Entrepôt – *9 rue Francis-de-Pressensé.* Ⓜ*Pernety.* ☎*01 45 40 07 50. www.lentrepot.fr.* Film buffs appreciate this movie house's particularly thoughtful programme: films in V.O., experimental feature-length cinema, after-film debates, weekend concerts, etc. A vast bar and a restaurant with a garden terrace are very popular when the weather warms up.

Cinéma Le Grand Rex – *1 blvd Poissonnière.* Ⓜ*Bonne-Nouvelle.* ☎*08 92 68 05 96. www.legrandrex.com.* 7 theatres, including one with 2 750 seats (on 3 levels), and another with 504 places. Two giant screens, one of which is 21m across; Dolby stereo sound. V.F. (dubbed) box-office type films. This cinema, built in 1932, is famous for its starry night-sky ceiling which rises 24m above the oriental/art deco interior.

Cinéma Mac-Mahon – *5 av. Mac-Mahon.* Ⓜ*Charles-de-Gulle-Etoile.* ☎*01 43 80 24 81. www.cinemamacmahon.com. Closed Aug.* This cinema was a giant shrine to the Hollywood film goddess during the 1950s and 60s. Today the Mac-Mahon continues to present movies in their original format and context (with news reels of the period). One screen. Dolby stereo sound. Classic films, V.O. only. Cocktail bar.

Cinéma UGC Ciné Cité Bercy – *2 Cour St Emilion.* Ⓜ*Cour St-Emillion.* ☎*01 36 68 68 58/08 92 70 00 00. www.ugc.fr.* 18 theatres with giant screens, 4 500 seats, Dolby AS/R and DTS numeric sound. Films in V.O. Primarily box-office type films. Café and snacks. This large cinema complex is built on the site of Bercy's former wine warehouses.

La Pagode – *57 bis rue de Babylone.* Ⓜ*Saint-François-Xavier.* ☎*09 62 23 05 33.* The excellent programme of the 7th *arrondissement's* only movie theatre puts the accent on artistic and independent films, while the oriental atmosphere transports one to a universe made of mystery and splendours of the past. This superb Japanese pagoda was a gift that the then director of the Bon Marché store gave his wife in 1896. The home of oriental galas for over 20 years, it became a cinema in the 1930s.

La Cinémathèque Française – *51 rue de Bercy.* ⓂBercy. ☎*01 71 19 33 33. www. cinemathequefrancaise.com. Closed Aug.* Founded in 1936 by Henri Langlois and Paul-Auguste Harlé, the Cinemathèque has been preserving and cataloguing films from all over the world, including the entire works of Marcel L'Herbier and René Clair, as well as a large number of short films and pre-war works. It moved to the contemporary space designed by Frank Gehry in 2005.

Max Linder Panorama – *24 blvd Poissonnière.* ⓂGrands-Boulevards. ☎*01 48 24 00 47/08 92 68 00 31. www.maxlinder panorama.com.* 1 giant screen, 615 seats (on 3 levels). THX Dolby stereo SR, DTS and SRD numeric sound. Excellent acoustics. V.O. films. Box-office programme featuring high-quality films with an accent on culture. Bar. Purchased by Max Linder himself, this cinema is the only one in Paris to bear the name of a film director.

CHILDREN'S ENTERTAINMENT

The main public gardens have marionette shows, usually on Wednesday afternoon, Saturday and Sunday, and during the school holidays. You need to arrive before show time to buy your tickets in advance. Adults should sit in the back rows!

Guignol & Compagnie – *Jardin d' acclimatation, Bois de Boulogne.* ⓂSablons. ☎*01 45 01 53 52. www.guignol.fr. Wed, weekends, public and school holidays at 3pm and 4pm.* ◉*2.70€ (including park entrance fee).*

Guignol Anatole – *Parc des Buttes-Chaumont.* ⓂLaumière. ☎*01 43 98 10 95. Outdoors theatre (mid Mar–end Oct): Wed, weekends and holidays at 3pm and 4.30pm.*

La Vallée des Fleurs – *Parc floral de Paris, Bois de Vincennes.* ⓂChâteau-de-Vincennes. Park admission covers events.

Shows include theatre, mime, clowns and marionettes.

Marionnettes des Champs-Élysées – *Rond-Point des Champs-Élysées.* ⓂChamps-Élysées. ☎*01 42 45 38 30. www.theatreguignol.fr. Wed, weekends and school holidays at 3pm, 4pm and 5pm. 3€. Closed Aug.*

Marionnettes du Champs-de-Mars – *Av. du Gén.-Margueritte.* ⓂÉcole-Militaire. ☎*01 48 56 01 44. Wed and weekends at 3.15pm and 4.15pm.*

Marionnettes du Luxembourg – *Jardin du Luxembourg.* ⓂVavin. ☎*01 43 26 46 47 or 01 43 29 50 97. Wed, weekends, school and public holidays at 3pm, 4pm and 5pm (extra show at 11am weekends).*

Marionnettes du parc Georges-Brassens – *Parc Georges-Brassens, rue Brancion.* ⓂPorte-de-Vanves. ☎*01 48 42 51 80. Summer: Wed, weekends and school holidays at 3pm, 4pm and 5pm; winter: same days at 3.30pm and 4.30pm. Closed mid-Jul–mid-Aug.*

Mélo d' Amélie – *4 rue Marie-Stuart.* ⓂÉtienne-Marcel. ☎*01 40 26 11 11.* 2–8 yrs old: a musical comedy combining magic, reality and fantasy.

Théâtre Astral – *Parc floral de Paris (Bois de Vincennes).* ⓂChâteau-de-Vincennes. ☎*01 43 71 31 10. Reservations required. Shows Wed, weekends, public and school holidays. 3–8 yrs old.*

Métamorphosis – *55 quai de la Tournelle.* ⓂMaubert-Mutualité. ☎*01 43 54 08 08. Tue–Sat at 9.30pm, Sun at 3pm.* Magic and illusion aboard a barge...

Cirque Alexandra Bouglione – *Jardin d' acclimation, Bois de Boulogne.* ⓂSablons. ☎*01 45 00 87 00. Wed at 2.30pm, weekends at 4pm.*

Cirque Diana Moreno Bormann – *1 rue de la haie Coq.* ⓂPorte-de-la-Chapelle ☎*01 64 05 36 25. www.cirque-diana-moreno.com. Wed, weekends, school and public holidays at 3pm.*

Cirque d' hiver Bouglione – *110 rue Amelot.* ⓂFilles-du-Calvaire. ☎*01 47 00 28 81. www.cirquedhiver.com. Nov–late Jan.* The Bouglione family enchants viewers of all ages.

Cirque du Grand-Céleste – *22 Paul Meurice.* ⓂPorte-des-Lilas. ☎*01 53 19 99 13. www.grandceleste.com. Wed and school holidays (except Mon) at 3pm, Sat at 3pm and 8.45pm, Sun at 4pm.*

A

INDEX

INDEX

INDEX

INDEX

INDEX

MAPS AND PLANS

LIST OF MAPS

COMPANION PUBLICATIONS

MICHELIN MAPS AND PLANS

Make the most of your trip to Paris by keeping a good map to hand as you discover the city. Each of the places described in this guide is associated with the references which correspond to Michelin map 10, a fold-out street map.

Other formats are also available for your convenience:

- No **106**, Paris and environs (scale 1:100 000), which covers the road network as far as Fontainebleau to the south and Senlis to the north, provides tourist information.
- No **101**, the **suburbs of Paris** scale (1:53 000).
- No **18**, **north-west suburbs**, no **20 south-west suburbs**, no **22 south-east suburbs**, no **24 south-east suburbs** (scale 1:15 000).

For getting around Paris, you have a choice of:

- **Paris Tourisme**, no **52**, which shows monuments, museums, shopping, shows and practical information. Tourist and metro plans are also included. (scale 1:20 000).

- **Paris Transport**, no **51**, with a plan of the bus, metro and RER routes. Also includes information on taxi station locations, rental cars and railway stations.
- **Paris** no **54** shows one-way streets and car parks; it is very useful if you are driving a car (scale 1:10 000).
- **Paris Atlas** no **56**, with a street index, one-way streets, pedestrian only streets, car parks, and metro – RER – bus routes (scale 1:10 000).
- **Paris** no **55**, which is the same as no **54**, but with an index.
- **Paris Atlas by arrondissements**, no **57**, with street index, one-way streets, car parks, and metro – RER – bus routes (scale 1:10 000).
- **Paris Plan Poche** no **50** gives the major roads.
- And of course, the **map of France** no **721** shows a view of all of the Paris region, and how to travel to and from the city by road. The whole country is mapped on a scale of 1:1 000 000.

LEGEND

★★★ Highly recommended

★★ Recommended

★ Interesting

Tourism

	Sightseeing route with departure point indicated	AZ B	Map co-ordinates locating sights
	Ecclesiastical building		Tourist information
	Synagogue – Mosque		Historic house, castle – Ruins
	Building (with main entrance)		Dam – Factory or power station
	Statue, small building		Fort – Cave
	Wayside cross		Prehistoric site
	Fountain		Viewing table – View
	Fortified walls – Tower – Gate		Miscellaneous sight

Recreation

	Racecourse		Waymarked footpath
	Skating rink		Outdoor leisure park/centre
	Outdoor, indoor swimming pool		Theme/Amusement park
	Marina, moorings		Wildlife/Safari park, zoo
	Mountain refuge hut		Gardens, park, arboretum
	Overhead cable-car		Aviary, bird sanctuary
	Tourist or steam railway		

Additional symbols

	Motorway (unclassified)		Post office – Telephone centre
	Junction: complete, limited		Covered market
	Pedestrian street		Barracks
	Unsuitable for traffic, street subject to restrictions		Swing bridge
	Steps – Footpath		Quarry – Mine
	Railway – Coach station		Ferry (river and lake crossings)
	Funicular – Rack-railway		Ferry services: Passengers and cars
	Tram – Metro, underground		Foot passengers only
Bert (R.)...	Main shopping street	③	Access route number common to MICHELIN maps and town plans

Abbreviations and special symbols

A	Agricultural office (Chambre d'agriculture)	P	Local authority offices (Préfecture, sous-préfecture)
C	Chamber of commerce (Chambre de commerce)	POL.	Police station (Police)
H	Town hall (Hôtel de ville)		Police station (Gendarmerie)
J	Law courts (Palais de justice)	T	Theatre (Théâtre)
M	Museum (Musée)	U	University (Université)
			Hotel
			Park and Ride

Some town plans are extracts from plans used in the Green Guides to the regions of France.

Michelin Apa Publications Ltd

A joint venture between Michelin and Langenscheidt

Suite 6, Tulip House, 70 Borough High Street, London SE1 1XF, United Kingdom

© 2009 Michelin Apa Publications Ltd
ISBN 978-1-906261-37-5
Printed: September 2008
Printed and bound: Himmer, Germany

Walking tours

*For descriptions of these tours,
turn to the Planning Your Trip section following.*

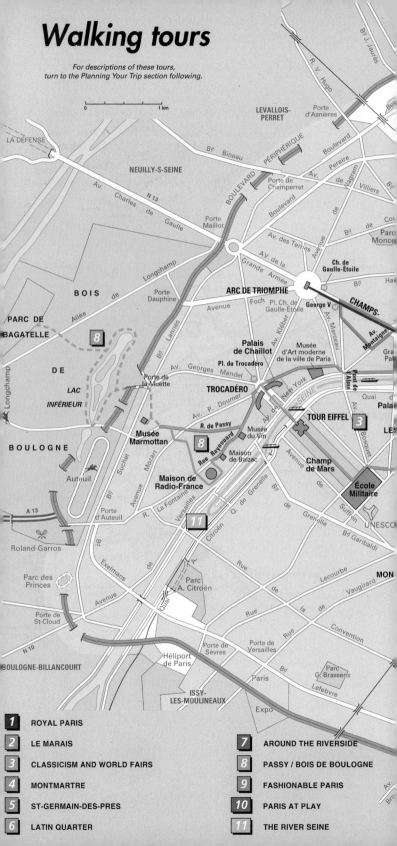

1	ROYAL PARIS	**7**	AROUND THE RIVERSIDE
2	LE MARAIS	**8**	PASSY / BOIS DE BOULOGNE
3	CLASSICISM AND WORLD FAIRS	**9**	FASHIONABLE PARIS
4	MONTMARTRE	**10**	PARIS AT PLAY
5	ST-GERMAIN-DES-PRES	**11**	THE RIVER SEINE
6	LATIN QUARTER		

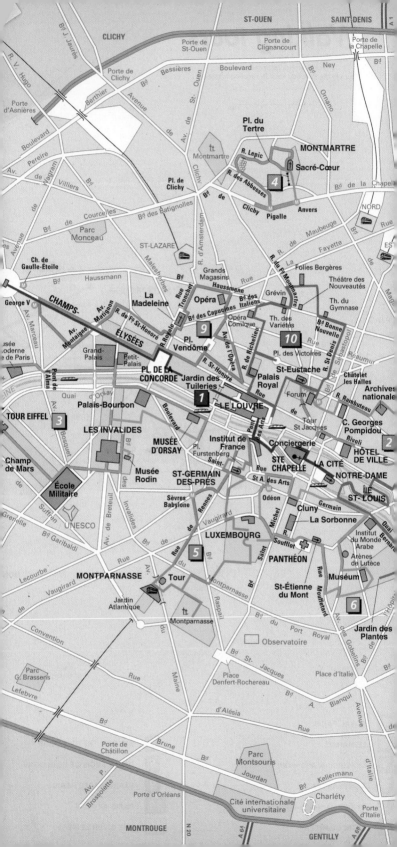

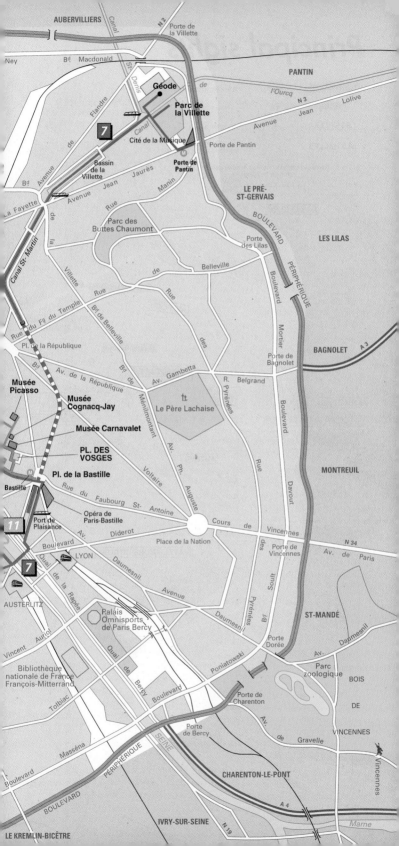

Principal sights

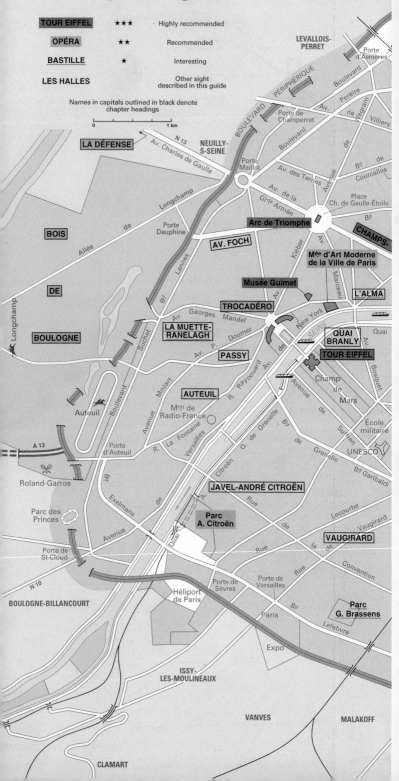

TOUR EIFFEL	★★★	· Highly recommended
OPÉRA	★★	Recommended
BASTILLE	★	Interesting
LES HALLES		Other sight described in this guide

Names in capitals outlined in black denote chapter headings

0 ____ 1 km

LEVALLOIS-PERRET

Porte d'Asnières

BOULEVARD PÉRIPHÉRIQUE

Porte de Champerret

Boulevard

Av. de Wagram

Pereire

Villiers

LA DÉFENSE

Av. Charles de Gaulle

N 13

NEUILLY-S-SEINE

Porte Maillot

Boulevard

Av. des Ternes

Avenue

B⁴ de Courcelles

Place Ch. de Gaulle-Étoile

Longchamp

Av. de la Grde Armée

Porte Dauphine

BOIS

Allée

de

Porte Dauphine

Arc de Triomphe

CHAMPS-

AV. FOCH

Lannes

Mée d'Art Moderne de la Ville de Paris

DE

Longchamp

Av. Georges

Mandel

Musée Guimet

Kléber

L'ALMA

B⁴

Suchet

TROCADÉRO

Av.

New York

Marceau

BOULOGNE

Auteuil

LA MUETTE-RANELAGH

Doumer

PASSY

SEINE

Quai

QUAI BRANLY

TOUR EIFFEL

Bosquet

Mozart

Av.

R. Raynouard

Avenue

Champ de Mars

A 13

AUTEUIL

Mon de Radio-France

de

École militaire

Porte d'Auteuil

R. La Fontaine

Versailles

Q. de Grenelle

B⁴ de Grenelle

Bd Garibaldi

UNESCO

Roland-Garros

Citroën

JAVEL-ANDRÉ CITROËN

Rue

Lecourbe

Parc des Princes

Exelmans

Parc A. Citroën

Vaugirard

Avenue

Quai

Rue

de

la de

VAUGIRARD

Porte de St-Cloud

N 10

Porte de Sèvres

Porte de Versailles

Porte de Versailles

Rue

Rue

Convention

Paris

B⁴

Lefebvre

Parc G. Brassens

BOULOGNE-BILLANCOURT

Héliport de Paris

Expo

ISSY-LES-MOULINEAUX

VANVES

MALAKOFF

CLAMART